VIOLENT
ENVIRONMENTS

VIOLENT ENVIRONMENTS

EDITED BY

Nancy Lee Peluso

and

Michael Watts

Cornell University Press

ITHACA AND LONDON

First published 2001 by Cornell University Press
First printing, Cornell Paperbacks, 2001

Printed in the United States of America

Library of Congress Cataloging-in-Publication Data

Violent environments / edited by Nancy Lee Peluso and Michael Watts.
    p.   cm.
    Includes bibliographical references and index.
    ISBN-13: 978-0-8014-3871-4 (cloth: alk. paper)
    ISBN-10: 0-8014-3871-3 (cloth: alk. paper)
    ISBN-13: 978-0-8014-8711-8 (pbk.: alk. paper)
    ISBN-10: 0-8014-8711-0 (pbk.: alk. paper)
    1. Violence.   2. Environmental protection—Economic aspects.   3.
Economic policy.   4. Natural resources.   I. Peluso, Nancy Lee.   II. Watts,
Michael.   III. Title.
HM1116.V56   2001
333.7—dc21   00-011827

Cornell University Press strives to use environmentally responsible suppliers and materials to the fullest extent possible in the publishing of its books. Such materials include vegetable-based, low-VOC inks and acid-free papers that are recycled, totally chlorine-free, or partly composed of nonwood fibers. For further information, visit our website at www.cornellpress.cornell.edu.

Cloth printing   10 9 8 7 6 5 4 3 2 1
Paperback printing   10 9 8 7 6 5 4 3

Dedication

This book is dedicated to the memory of Ken Saro-Wiwa and eight other Ogoni activists, hanged in November 1995 by the Nigerian military junta of President Sani Abacha. All were the terrible casualties of environmental violence.

It would have been easy to have explained [the popular forest violence on the 1720s in Berkshire] by some gesture toward an (unprovable) demographic crisis, precipitating demands upon the forest's resources. But there is no convincing evidence as to such a crisis, demographic or ecological or agrarian. Farmers and forest officers had rubbed along together, in a state of running conflict, for many decades and they were to do so for many more. What appears as crisis was a conflict in the broadest sense political.

Edward Thompson, *Whigs and Hunters,* 1975

Contents

Acknowledgments

A book of this sort could not have come to fruition without substantial debts to any number of persons, foundations, and institutions. The idea for the volume came from a workshop on "Violence and the Environment" held at the University of California, Berkeley, in September 1998. We planned the workshop in close collaboration with Donald Moore and are indebted to him for his ideas and selfless commitment to the project. The workshop was funded by generous support from the Ford Foundation and the Institute for Global Cooperation and Conflict. It was hosted by the Institute of International Studies, whose staff was critical to the success of the workshop. Only three of the papers presented at that workshop are not presented here, but we thank Jeffrey Paige, Ajanta Subramanian, and Mike Davis for their enthusiastic participation in discussions. James Scott, David Sonnenfeld, Melanie Dupuis, Peter Vandergeest, Dick Walker, Mariane Ferme, and Eric Stover served as commentators on panels at that workshop. Although their remarks are not specifically included, their incisive commentaries have left an indelible mark on the volume. Aaron Bobrow-Strain significantly assisted production of the volume by providing editorial and substantive comments, as well as helping to research the materials reviewed in the introductory chapter. We greatly appreciate his willingness to be available at otherwise busy times. Denise Leto, Letitia Carper, Christina Erickson, and Eowyn Greeno provided clerical and administrative assistance. Eowyn also made all the arrangements for the three-day workshop. Finally, we thank the scholars whose work is included here for a thought-provoking and stimulating series of discussions and exchanges.

N.L.P.
M.W.

I

Violent Environments and Green Security

1

Violent Environments

Nancy Lee Peluso and Michael Watts

> Internal zones of violence and enclaves of protection, both spatial and
> metaphorical, map out geographies of power. (Gilsenan, 1996: 4)

> It is time to understand "the environment" for what it is: *the* national se-
> curity issue of the early twenty-first century. (Kaplan, 1994: 58)

> [Civil wars in Africa] are caused not only by historic conflicts but also
> by . . . deterioration of not only the economy but the environment in
> which people live.
>   President Clinton (cited in Ó Tuathail, Dalby, and Routledge, 1998)

In his enormously influential *Atlantic Monthly* essay, "The Coming
Anarchy: How Scarcity, Crime, Overpopulation, and Disease are Rapidly
Destroying the Social Fabric of Our Planet," journalist Robert Kaplan conjured up a surreal picture of an African continent in the throes of an apocalyptic crisis: overpopulated, undernourished, and driven to barbaric acts
of violence by irrational spirit power. Crushed under the unbearable
weight of "eco-demographic" pressures, Africa was, as Kaplan pointed out,
once again the "Dark Continent." But the coming anarchy was not confined to Africa; it was, in Kaplan's account, endemic to the developing
world, as his brief sojourn in Cambodia, Iran, Russia, and Central Asia
confirmed to him.[1] Foreign policy would be shaped, he claimed, by:
"[s]urging populations, spreading disease, deforestation and soil erosion,
water depletion, air pollution, and possibly rising sea levels . . . —developments that will prompt mass migrations and in turn incite group conflicts"
(1994: 58).

---

1. Kaplan subsequently published *The Ends of the Earth* (1997) and *The Coming Anarchy*
(2000), which further developed his ideas and his political visibility.

3

Within weeks of publication, Under Secretary of State Tim Wirth[2] had faxed a copy of the article to every U.S. embassy in the world; top UN officials were discussing its implications behind closed doors (Richards 1996: xiv). Kaplan subsequently was invited to the White House, and Vice President Al Gore championed "The Coming Anarchy" as a model of the sort of green thinking that he had assiduously sought to promote during the 1990s. President Clinton's June 29, 1994 address to the National Academy of Sciences specifically invoked Kaplan's article and "the more academic" work of Tad Homer-Dixon as "the beacons for a new sensitivity to environmental security" (Simmons 1997).[3] Within a year, James Woolsey, Director of Central Intelligence, and William Perry, Secretary of Defense, were singing the praises of "an aggressive environmental program because it is critical to the defense mission" (Perry, cited in ECSP I 1995: 53). With the establishment of the Senior Director post for Global Environmental Affairs in the State Department, environmental degradation caused by resource scarcity and population growth was enshrined within the National Security Council of the United States government (Simmons 1997: 132; for a review, see Deudney and Matthew 1999).

Notwithstanding the propitious moment at which Kaplan's article appeared, the rapidity with which policy makers and their advisors took up the security diagnosis from "The Coming Anarchy" was astonishing. Particularly since the mid-1980s, neo-Malthusian narratives of the purportedly deleterious consequences of population growth had once more taken pride of place on the international development agenda.[4] This resurgent Malthusianism coincided with the revolutionary events of 1989, the fall of the Berlin Wall and the vertiginous collapse of the Soviet socialist system. In short order, the end of the Cold War was declared by politicians and pundits alike, the much vaunted power of the Soviet Union was shown to be hollow, and the very meaning of national security was thrown into question.[5] The United States' so-called Peace Dividend—the savings on military expenditures generated by the termination of Cold War hostilities—in tan-

2. "Resource scarcities are a root cause of the violent conflicts that have convulsed civil society in Rwanda, Haiti and Chiapas. . . . Professor Tad Homer-Dixon . . . warns that in upcoming decades, resource scarcities 'will probably occur with a speed, complexity and magnitude unprecedented in history.' " Tim Wirth, address to the National Press Club, July 12, 1994.

3. Robert Kaplan's other bestseller, *Balkan Ghosts*, an essentialist and deeply flawed account of "eternal hatreds" and immutable national character in the region, also influenced President Clinton and contributed in no small way to the President's catastrophic decision to not intervene in Yugoslavia.

4. The 1995 Cairo Population Conference and the agenda that was adopted as a result of its deliberations was simply one iteration of this newfound Malthusianism at the highest levels of multilateral governance.

5. State intelligence apparatuses also had vastly exaggerated Russian military might.

dem with the closure of some military bases and renewed debates over the military budget had dramatically re-posed the security question for the 1990s and beyond.[6] In the political space created by the geopolitical interregnum of the 1990s, environmental security (and the prevention of Greenwar) came to fill a historic vacuum.

Violent Environments provides both a critique of the school of environmental security and alternative ways of understanding the connections between environment and violence. We reject automatic, simplistic linkages between "increased environmental scarcity," "decreased economic activity," and "migration" that purportedly "weaken states" and cause "conflicts and violence" (Homer-Dixon 1994: 31). We see violence as a site-specific phenomenon rooted in local histories and social relations yet connected to larger processes of material transformation and power relations. This volume's authors draw on rich bodies of literature not normally included in high-level debates over environment and security—political ecology, agrarian studies, and recent anthropological studies of violence. Our approach is not intended to merely identify the "environmental triggers" of violent conflicts nor does it start from a presumed "scarcity." Rather, *Violent Environments* accounts for ways that specific resource environments (tropical forests or oil reserves) and environmental processes (deforestation, conservation, or resource amelioration) are constituted by, and in part constitute, the political economy of access to and control over resources.

Our starting point is the entitlements by which differentiated individuals, households, and communities possess or gain access to resources within a structured political economy. It grants priority to how these entitlements are distributed, reproduced, and fought over in the course of shaping, and being shaped by, patterns of accumulation. All forms of political economy have as their foundation the transformation of nature in social, historical, and culturally informed ways—what Marx broadly construed as the labor process. We start by seeking to understand the changing contexts of nature transformation, who performs the labor, who bears the burdens, and how its benefits are claimed, distributed, and contested.

Conditions of resource scarcity do not, contrary to the claims of Homer-Dixon and others, have a monopoly on violence. In our view, it is not sim-

6. Some aspects of the Peace Dividend, as reported by Rowan Scarborough (1998) include: the Pentagon budget has dropped 37 percent since 1985—the peak for President Reagan's military budgets—and 30 percent since the dissolution of the Soviet bloc following the destruction of the Berlin Wall; 1999 defense spending authority is $270 billion—down from $429.8 billion in 1985 and $385 billion in 1989, in inflation-adjusted 1999 dollars; in the past nine years, the Pentagon has shed some 700,000 active duty troops; by contrast, in 1962 the Pentagon was consuming roughly half the total U.S. budget—a proportion that has dropped to less than 16 percent in the proposed 1999 budget.

ply *shortage* but also abundance and processes of environmental rehabilitation or amelioration that are most often associated with violence (Peluso 1993; Schroeder 1995). Transformations and instabilities in the conditions and characteristics of nature, environment, or natural resources produce a concomitant shifting of the positions of resource users, whether poor peasants or powerful transnational corporations. The specification of actors—peasants, indigenous peoples, workers, the state, transnational capital—in a particular historical moment of violence is made with respect to their positions within precise systems of accumulation and fields of power.

The forms of violence, who engages them, and their dynamics are accordingly expanded and deepened analytically by conceptualizing violence as a sort of habitus. As Dumont (1992: 277) puts it: "Violence is a habitus. . . . , at once structured and structuring: structured because the idea of violence results from historical events, stored as the memory of past deeds, of past encounters, of past frustrations; and structuring because the idea of violence informs human actions, determines the acceptability, even the banality of violence, if not the ability to erase the scandal of its occurrence."

Different forms of violence emerge, in our view, from particular forms of what Michel Foucault called "governmentality" (Foucault 1982; see also Gordon 1980; Dean 1999). Foucault was concerned to show how the human species and the human body, through scientific categories rather than juridical ones, became the object of systematic and sustained political attention. New sets of operations or "technologies" were brought to bear on the functioning of institutions, the purposes of which were to regulate, normalize, and discipline—to forge docile bodies and subjects. Governmentality embraces the calculated practices by which the state and other institutions and practices direct categories of social agents in specific ways. Governmentality is about the disciplining of forms of life and we wish to extend this Foucauldian notion to the realm of Nature and resources (what he in passing called "territory").

Violence stands awkwardly in respect to environmental concerns. The environment is increasingly present and yet frequently hidden by both the perpetrators and observers of violence alike. Very little work has explored explicitly the ways that environmental violence reflects or masks other forms of social struggle. In general, the ways different forms of violence systematically figure in environmental struggles remain seriously undertheorized.

This oversight is especially curious in the late twentieth century, precisely because John Keane's (1996) "aura of strangeness," invoked as a marker of twentieth century forms of violence, is in some ways an equally apt description of contemporary conservation or strategies of sustainable development. Global trends toward economic and political liberalization have brought an explosion of new property claims and protectionist strategies. In these, some of the resources and environments providing the fuel for capitalist expansion are intentionally kept out of production and exchange while they produce new "natural" landscapes and commodities. Violent forms of surveillance and compliance are used to enforce these naturalized structures of resource control, but they are made stranger by the ways in which they are hidden from particular points of view. Some forms of conservation and resource development are meant to simultaneously structure and conceal violence from their international constituencies. Others are used as new expressions of existing local tensions deriving from religious, ethnic, gender, and class conflicts. Zones of peace and tension, and their manners of representation, seem to provide lessons basic to understanding the changing landscapes of conservation and environmental management.

The Genesis of Green Security

> We [the Clinton Administration] believe that environmental degradation is not simply an irritation but a real threat to our national security. (Madeline Albright, April 21, 1994, cited in ECSR 1995: 81)

Kaplan's polemical and apocalyptic treatise, which recapitulated many of the historical tropes through which the West has sought to represent and enframe Africa[7] and other parts of the colonized world, marked something of a sea change in thinking about security over the period since the oil crisis of the 1970s. More critically, it marked the maturity of the field of "environmental security" (see Deudney and Matthew 1999). What Kaplan and other policy *aficionados* had in common was the presumption of an ineluctable connection between environmental degradation, population growth, alleged resource scarcity, and the proliferation of "small wars" that haunt the post-Cold War planet. This intellectual pedigree is of some antiquity of course. Since the Reverend Thomas Malthus's controversial prediction two centuries ago—that vice, misery, and war would be the inevitable handmaiden of demographically-driven food scarcities—a causal link between environmental scarcity and violence has been something of a Holy Grail. Current iterations of "environmental security" and "Greenwar" suffer, in our view, from both the historic failings of Malthusian thinking and an untenable theory of political economy and political action. Many of these past and present scenarios of scarcity and war are informed by a

---

7. Kaplan's article is replete with imagery of "traditional" family structure, spirit power, sexual urges, "wild zones," and primitive violence (see Dalby 1996 for an excellent critique). The parallels with Conrad's *Heart of Darkness* are striking and unsettling.

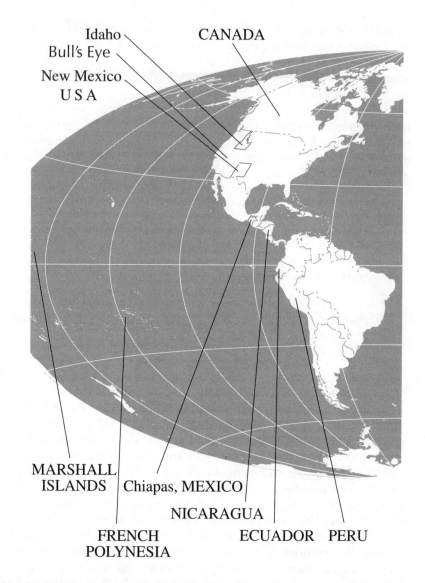

Idaho
Bull's Eye
New Mexico
USA
CANADA

MARSHALL
ISLANDS   Chiapas, MEXICO
NICARAGUA
FRENCH   ECUADOR PERU
POLYNESIA

deep fear of the poor and of their claims to resources, despite radical changes in the world since Malthus's time.

The history of how the environment has become a fundamental security issue is an intriguing, and largely untold, transnational story linking policy and academic communities on both sides of the North Atlantic (Dalby 1998, 1999, n.d.). It begins in a sense with the environmental and biological debates that emerged from World War II. After the dropping of the atomic bomb, a panoply of new studies appeared on the political implica-

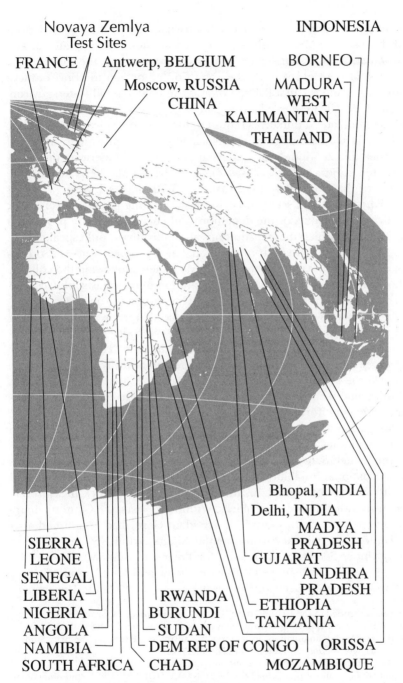

Novaya Zemlya
Test Sites

FRANCE Antwerp, BELGIUM

Moscow, RUSSIA

CHINA

INDONESIA

BORNEO

MADURA
WEST
KALIMANTAN
THAILAND

Bhopal, INDIA
Delhi, INDIA
MADYA
PRADESH
GUJARAT
ANDHRA
PRADESH

SIERRA
LEONE
SENEGAL
LIBERIA
NIGERIA
ANGOLA
NAMIBIA
SOUTH AFRICA

RWANDA
BURUNDI
SUDAN
DEM REP OF CONGO
CHAD

ETHIOPIA
TANZANIA

ORISSA
MOZAMBIQUE

Map 1.1 *Location of Case Studies in Violent Environments*

tions of natural and other disasters. Somewhat later in the 1960s, serious food shortages in Africa and Asia and oil scarcities a decade later placed environmental and subsistence concerns directly onto the geostrategic landscape of the Cold War. By the 1972 Conference on the Environment in Stockholm and the first Palme Commission held a decade later, environment and security were explicitly linked.[8]

These multilateral initiatives required, however, the voices of key public intellectuals like Lester Brown and Norman Myers to provide institutional legitimacy and a window of understanding to the American public. A much-cited 1989 article in *Foreign Affairs* by Jessica Matthews marked the key role of the World Resources Institute (WRI) in the U.S. engagement with environment and security. Fortuitously, growing public concern over global climate change, ozone depletion, and chemical warfare provided a constituency to which these institutions and individuals could speak.

To further legitimate both international and national concerns, the release of new historical and state security documents following the collapse of the Soviet Union provided a new recognition of the catastrophic ecological costs of various forms of socialism (Homer-Dixon 1999). Coincidentally, a number of well-funded research projects were in train, including the Environmental Conflict Project (ENCOP) in Switzerland and the International Peace Research Institute (PRIO) in Oslo. The Woodrow Wilson Center set up its Environmental Change and Security Project in 1994, just down the road from WRI, where, in a sense, it had all begun. Today, environmental security as an institutional project is truly global, with academic centers in Toronto, Zurich, Oslo, Cambridge, New York, and Paris. All have garnered significant foundation support, and many are linked to national militaries.[9]

In the United States, the connections between environmental problems and international instability were first recognized formally in the National Security Strategy of 1991.[10] Institutional footholds in quick measure became institutional foundation blocks. Within two years, the Clinton administration (particularly through Vice President Gore) had established a senior Director for Global Environmental Affairs at the NSC, an office of Deputy Under Secretary of Defense for Environmental Security, and the post of National Intelligence Officer for Global and Multilateral Affairs at the National Intelligence Council. In the 1990s the CIA, the Department

---

8. This was extended in the second (1989) Palme Commission on Disarmament.
9. Key foundations supporting environment and security efforts in the United States include the MacArthur Foundation, in its programs to refocus Peace and Security Studies, and the Carnegie, Mellon, and Alton Jones Foundations.
10. In fact, Sam Nunn and Al Gore established the Strategic Environmental Research and Development Program—which joined the DOD, NOAA, DOI, EPA, USGS, and other agencies—in 1990 to "harness some of the resources of the defense establishment to confront the massive environmental problems facing our nation" (ECSR 1995: 60).

of Defense, and the U.S. Army established environmental strategy and policy centers as part of a larger effort to "green" themselves (Ross 1997).[11] In 1994, a Task Force on State Failure addressed environmental factors in such failures, and the following year the first major interagency conference was held on "Environmental Security and National Security." An important 1996 Memorandum of Understanding among government agencies reflected the extent to which a number of defense and intelligence agencies were now "greening" their security and intelligence work (Goodman 1997). Not least, the Department of Defense (DOD) joined with NATO to launch a pilot study entitled "Environment and Security in the International Context." By the end of the first Clinton administration, a particular sense of environmental security had infiltrated deeply into _Clinton_ state security apparatuses, but it was an infiltration that extended more broadly within NATO powers.

In turn, the military establishment showed remarkable flexibility, seizing upon environmental security as its new lodestar. Within a short period of time, the Pentagon could seriously present itself as an unimpeachable advocate for sustainable development (Butts 1994). The massive toxic legacy of the military in the U.S. West, for example (rendered by Valerie Kuletz in *The Tainted Desert*) where Native American and federal lands have been devastated by nuclear and other testing, now represents the basis for the Department of Defense becoming "the federal leader in agency environmental compliance and protection" (Secretary of Defense Cheney quoted in Butts 1994: 106). Environmental degradation was, in short, good for military business.

Since the early 1970s, then, a substantial industry around environmental security has arisen in the context of a distinctive set of geopolitical conditions: the end of the Cold War, the need of overfunded militaries to legitimize their existence in the face of clamoring for the "Peace Dividend," and the emergence of "new" forms of violence (often articulated as the "clash of civilizations" within putatively weak or rogue states) representing "threats to global peace and security," such as Islamic terrorism or ethnic cleansing (Huntington 1996).

Malthus Resurgent: Contemporary Renderings of Environmental Violence and Conflict

> My key finding is straightforward: . . . scarcity of renewable resources—what
> I call *environmental scarcity*—can contribute to civil violence, including insur-

11. Homer-Dixon was a key voice in promoting environment and conflict within the strategic agenda of the U.S. Department of Defense (Simmons 1997).

gencies and ethnic clashes. . . . [I]n the coming decades the incidence of such violence will increase. . . . (Homer-Dixon 1999: 177)

Political, social, economic, ethnic, religious, or territorial conflicts, or conflicts over resources or national interest, or any other type of conflict, *are seen as the manifestation of deeper environmental conflict.* (Baechler 1998: 24; emphasis added)

√ Environmental security (ES) is a complex field and a contested term. Much of the debate has turned on the concept of *security* itself and how a conservative security constituency has seemingly joined hands with a more radically inclined green activism.[12] As a field of knowledge, ES is transnational, expansive, and embraces a number of fields ranging from the environmental consequences of war to environmental terrorism to the greening of the military to formal international relations.[13] Equally, ES contains a plethora of different approaches and theoretical positions (e.g., neo-Malthusian, neorealist, sociobiological). We have chosen to focus here on the most elaborated and most visible work on the links between environmental processes and forms of conflict.[14]

Without question, the two most influential studies globally[15] have been conducted by two large comparative projects, one Swiss, led by Gunther Baechler, and one Canadian, led by Tad Homer-Dixon.[16] Baechler's Environmental Conflicts Project (ENCOP) includes forty case studies and Homer-Dixon's Environmental Change and Acute Conflict Project (ECACP) contains sixteen. Both researchers are political scientists, respectively based in Berlin and Toronto. These two projects provide the theoretical building blocks for much of the theoretical work on ES and the cornerstone for policy interventions and discussions. Our focus here on this research reflects both its global importance and visibility to the field of ES

12. Much ink has been spilled on whether the environmental security field is, or is not, wedded to standard realist or neorealist regime theory and whether the rendering of environment as a security issue carries with it the danger of "militarizing" green politics (see the journal *Environment and Security* 1995–99).

13. See, for example, the bibliographies published on the Woodrow Wilson website: http://ecsp.si.edu.

14. For reviews of the field see, e.g., Deudney and Matthew 1999; Suliman 1999.

15. We are not dealing here with the work of a third institutional project, namely that of the International Peace Research Institute (PRIO) in Oslo under the direction of Nils Petter Gleditch (see *Conflict and the Environment* 1997). Gleditch argues that both Homer-Dixon and Baechler tend to ignore political variables. He focuses on the relations between democracy and environmental conflict and says that environmental degradation and violent conflict are mediated by "regime type" (1997: 99).

16. ENCOP is funded by the Swiss government via the Swiss Peace Foundation; ECACP is funded jointly by the American Academy of Arts and Sciences and the University of Toronto.

and its striking lack of critical scrutiny by social scientists outside the fields of security studies and international relations.

The massive three-volume ENCOP report published in 1996–97 provides a typology of conflicts (intrastate, interstate, global) including center–periphery conflicts, cross-boundary or migration conflicts, water conflicts, and so on, in so-called crisis areas (for example "drylands"). The two central findings are that environmental degradation triggers conflicts if and when "social fault lines can be manipulated in struggles over social, ethnic, political, and international power" and that violence requires a combination of weak states or poor regulatory apparatuses, environmental discrimination, the possibility for coalition building, and existing histories of conflict (Baechler 1996: 24).

Homer-Dixon's (1999) book, *Environment, Scarcity, and Violence,* along with the volume *Ecoviolence* (1998), written jointly with Jessica Blitt and others, summarizes the findings of almost a decade of research by ECACP. Despite his disclaimers, Homer-Dixon's debt to Malthus is clear and explicit. The entire edifice of his argument rests on a notion of environmental "scarcity." In Homer-Dixon's account, environmental scarcity (by which he means scarcity of renewable resources) has three causal forms, namely degradation (supply induced), increased demand (demand induced), or unequal resource distribution. The presence of any of these "can contribute to civil violence" through "resource capture" (generally by "elites") and/or "ecological marginalization" of vulnerable or disenfranchised people. Ecological marginalization is often a result of resource capture (ibid.: 177). Population growth appears centrally as *the* driving force in all of these causal claims. ECACP's analysis is replete with notions from 1960s systems theory and evokes variables prominent in early models of cultural ecology—interactive effects, adaptability, relative deprivation, triggers, and so on. The entire analysis is based on a simple, causal model of social friction and violence with few theorized intervening processes.

There is an immediate, if unacknowledged, affinity between these models and earlier cultural ecological theories of violence and conflict. A quarter of a century ago, anthropologist Andrew Vayda, summarizing a decade or more of work on so-called "primitive violence" by cultural ecologists and ecological anthropologists, concluded, "Warfare . . . [plays a key role] . . . in the maintenance of man/resource balances" (Vayda 1976: 4). Resource scarcity played a key role in narratives of primitive war just as it represented a central factor in determining human adaptive responses to environments.

The most prominent hypothesis of these theories was the purported function of war in self-regulating social–ecological systems (see, e.g., Rappaport 1967, 1968; Siskind 1973; Sweet 1970; Netting 1973; Divale 1976; cited in Ferguson 1984). War served the same functions as population collapse following a period of excessive biological growth. For scholars examining the short term, war was maladaptive, causing resource damage, loss of work time, mortalities, and losses of male laborers and warriors. For those taking a longer, social evolutionary view, war was seen as part of a grand adaptive process. War or violence was seen, thus, to be a part of human instinctual mechanisms for being the fittest, surviving, and acquiring the valuable spoils that go with it (Lathrap 1968).[17] Suttles (1961), for example, saw violent conflict as a means of population spacing that temporally or spatially situates people in suitable places (a means of creating niches, in effect) as a means of avoiding scarcity. Vayda (1969) explicitly connected warfare with the drive to gain access to preferred locations for agriculture, even in the absence of population pressure.

War in this construction resulted neither from a conscious decision of its participants nor from structural forces but rather constituted instinctual responses to population and resource disequilibria. In this way primitive war was distinguished from modern forms of warfare: those who engaged in primitive warfare were seen to be acting on instinct with no power to determine for themselves how or whether to start or stop. This false consciousness/primitive instinct hypothesis was criticized by the social evolutionists in the mid-1970s who brought back simplistic, deterministic views of the material causes of primitive war: namely, resource (including land) scarcities. Little if any importance was attributed to the means by which societies decided to go to war. Violence was a "natural" outcome of adaptive structure. In other words, war was both naturalized and depoliticized.[18]

Environmental security frames violence by referring to the same kinds of groups and to the same hyperlocal levels of analysis as the early cultural ecologists while simultaneously insisting on making global claims. Where Iban "headhunters" or Yanomamo "fierce people" once were seen to threaten local competitors, violent primitives today threaten all of "us"

17. In the 1970s, facing mounting evidence of minimal pressure on land in many "primitive societies," a contingent of cultural ecologists turned to protein scarcity as an explanation for the "function of violence" (Bennet-Ross 1971; Durham 1979; cf., Chagnon 1974, 1977; Nugent 1981; Rappaport 1968; Vayda 1976). Reflecting protein "fetishism" in Western understandings of nutrition, these theories posited that scarcity of meat drove peoples such as the Yanomamo of Brazil and the Maring of New Guinea to war (see, e.g., Harris 1977; Vayda 1961). The great protein debate, sparked by this contention, demonstrated the extent to which cultural ecologists relied on "pre-emptive theorizing" (Nietschmann 1980).

18. Actor-based cultural ecological studies began to provide some new frames for the social causes of war in the mid-1970s and 1980s (see, especially, Orlove 1980; Chagnon 1983; Ferguson 1984: 36). Ferguson did not abandon the cultural ecological approach to warfare but looked beyond both population variables and the local ecosystem, emphasizing instead the importance of nonmaterial motivations such as prestige, politics, and revenge, as well as material concerns such as labor control and subsistence. Chagnon's life work on the Yaromamo has recently been challenged as false and constructed in unethical ways, causing a major scandal in the anthropological community.

and, according to the Greenwar model, undermine international security. ES typically avoids the "primitive" label (but not always: see Kaplan 1996; Myers 1993b), but the naturalization of violence as an outcome of scarcities due to population pressure and mismanagement by the poor or the underdeveloped world is demonstrably calibrated into its models of conflict. As they analyze the violent politics of the North (e.g., Nazi Germany, the Balkans, or Ireland), ES theorists resort to ethnicity and religion in crude, essentialized ways and avoid the complex empirical realities (Homer-Dixon 1999; Kaplan 1999). Environmental security is in one sense then, cultural ecology writ large—with the obvious caveat that contemporary solutions to security problems necessitate large-scale and systematic state intervention.

Three conspicuous conceptual weaknesses are evident in the ENCOP/ ECACP approaches to environmental violence, some of which are implicit in our remarks on their analytical affinities to cultural ecology. Because a number of other chapters in this volume (Hartmann, Fairhead, Bobrow-Strain, Richards, Watts) provide full critiques of the work of Homer-Dixon and his colleagues in particular, we limit our attention here to a number of fundamental theoretical concerns, what we call *analytic moments* and what Homer-Dixon refers to as "the genesis of scarcity," "social effects," and "violent conflict" (1999: 134). Our critique serves as a counterpoint from which our own political ecology of violence, outlined in the following section, can be understood and assessed.

In Figures 1.1 and 1.2 we have laid out schematically the two "causal" models of environmental violence associated with ENCOP and ECACP. In both cases, Homer-Dixon and Baechler reject any simple association between environment and interstate war, detaching themselves from these early assumptions of ES in the post–World War II years. Both restrict their analyses to "chronic," "diffuse," and "subnational" violence.

There are some obvious differences of emphasis and terminology in the two models. ENCOP includes nonrenewable resources, which are emphatically excluded from the ECACP model. ENCOP also includes a typology of degraded (crisis) ecoregions, ignored in ECACP, and a different, and in some respects more descriptive, synopsis of violent/conflictual forms. ECACP, conversely, attempts to specify both how environmental degradation is transformed into scarcity and how scarcity causes conflicts (via resource capture, ingenuity, and social effects). Yet the broad outlines of each model—excluding the details of the internal architecture—are *fundamentally similar*.[19] Both are elaborations of a simple causal claim:

---

19. Homer-Dixon's concepts of "resource capture" and "ecological marginalization" function similarly to "discrimination" in Baechler's research. In the same way, "key conflict situations" (Baechler), "adaptation/ingenuity," and "social segmentation/weakened institutions" (Homer-Dixon) fulfill almost identical purposes in the analytical structure.

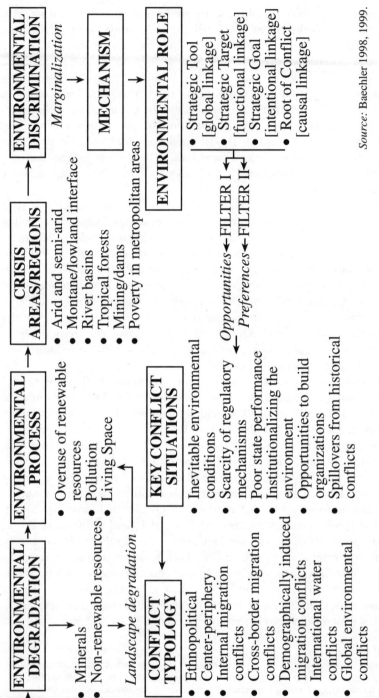

Figure 1.1 The ENCOP Model (after Baechler)

Source: Baechler 1998, 1999.

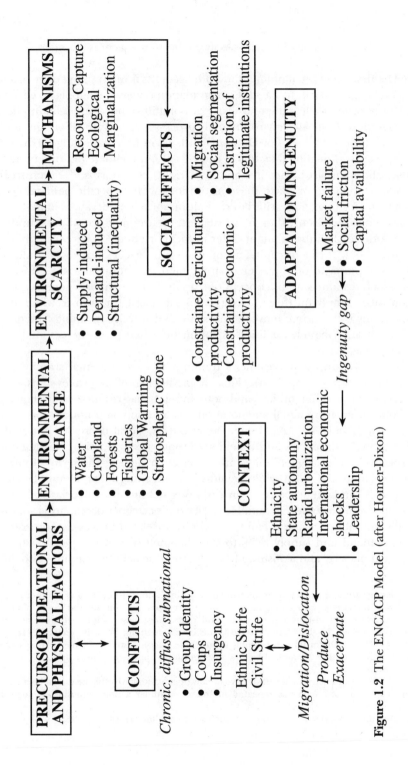

Figure 1.2 The ENCACP Model (after Homer-Dixon)

✳   Environmental Change→Scarcity→Social Consequences→Conflict

The first conceptual moment in both accounts is the framing of environmental change itself. In Baechler, degradation is a *given* (there is no chronicling of processes leading to overuse or pollution), but there is an implicit recognition that all environmental processes generate shortage and scarcity (1998: 31–32). For Homer-Dixon, environmental change is driven by "precursor ideational factors" (1999: 117), an inchoate notion embracing a shopping list of "institutions, laws, rights, and norms."[20] No effort is made to theorize or place these institutions within specific political economic forms (e.g., authoritarian capitalism, social democratic welfare capitalism, postsocialism), thereby to suggest, for example, conditions under which these institutions might differ in form or effect.[21] There is neither a sense of how forms of capital accumulation intersect or ally with specific forms of power to produce "environmental degradation" nor any effort to link such dynamics to his concept of scarcity. Homer-Dixon's genesis question turns simply on three forces: supply, demand (in both of which demography is the prime mover), and structural scarcity, meaning "unequal distribution" (vaguely qualified as "often inherited from the colonial period") (1999: 15).

Homer-Dixon's and Baechler's framings of environmental scarcity are flawed in two obvious ways. First, a privileging of resource shortage/scarcity above other initial conditions implies that resource abundance/surplus or environmental amelioration/restoration could not also be associated with violence.[22] As Homer-Dixon puts it, "local decreases in wealth can cause insurgencies and rebellion" (1999: 133). Scarcity is assumed a priori to be the "trigger" for conflict (Baechler deploys the term; Homer-Dixon shuns the word while retaining its meaning). For Homer-Dixon, *scarcity* is fundamental, just as an orthodox definition of neoclassical economics would assume. Second, Homer-Dixon's category of scarcity is analytically unusable because it embraces wholly unrelated processes. For example, demand and supply refer to the changing size of the pie driven by population size and consumption, although structural scarcity—also in-

---

20. Homer-Dixon includes, in an unexamined fashion, a long list of "factors": corporate liability, contract law, property rights, the state, macroeconomic policies, and so on in a bewildering array of institutions, practices, and rules. How these factors become *causes* is never addressed. In the place of "cause," we have something he calls "context" (1999: 16–17). Homer-Dixon tells us nothing about these "factors" and their interrelationships but simply states that "ideational factors" distinguish his approach from environmental determinism.

21. These unconnected factors thus have no way of explaining why the ideational blame he apportions in Nicaragua was repeated in Indonesia under a polar-opposite ideological framework.

22. Yet, they are indeed, as several case studies in this volume reveal.

cluded in the category of environmental scarcity—is about distribution and to analyze it explicitly requires a theory of class or other social divisions of labor and social power. Understanding structural scarcity requires an effort to theorize how various systems of access to and control over resources emerge and are reproduced. In Homer-Dixon's model, all of this (and more) is folded into what Sayer (1980) would call "incoherent abstraction."

In sum, both models operate from an incoherent (and partial) account of environmental transformation that does not stand on a theory of social transformation or political economy. Nevertheless, both models presume shortage and in fact are *only* concerned with shortage. Their hypotheses are unsystematic and disorganized, despite all the invocation of variables and causation. At best, we are treated to a cursory invocation of "elites," "rents," and "powerful groups."

A second analytic moment speaks to what Homer-Dixon calls "social effects." In both models, these are the mechanisms by which environmental changes are transmitted and given causal efficacy. In both the ENCOP and ECACP models, the mechanisms by which scarcity has some form of social consequence are roughly similar. Homer-Dixon invokes two concepts, both of which rest on population growth[23]: *resource capture* refers to the effects of elite rent-seeking under conditions of inequality; *marginalization*[24] refers to the means by which the poor are forced into particular forms of movement or expulsion (1999: 134). Both processes are slightly different expressions of what Baechler calls "environmental discrimination" (1998: 24–25).[25] Baechler does not explore the specific consequences of discrimination in detail but focuses on *marginalization* of some actors and *poor regulatory performance* (1998: 32) as general effects. Homer-Dixon derives multiple social "effects" from the genesis of conflict; these include constrained agricultural and economic productivity, migration, social segmentation, and the disruption of legitimate institutions. Social effects deriving from scarcity can lead to "grievances" and "opportunities" by contributing to deprivation, by increasing intergroup segmentation, and by weakening institutions such as "the state" (see Homer-Dixon 1999: 147ff).

To avoid the charge of linear causality or determinism, Homer-Dixon then adds what he takes to be the capacity of societies to "adapt" to the so-

23. Despite his claims to the contrary, Homer-Dixon, in all his theoretical work and his case studies, falls back on a standard neo-Malthusian claim about the centrality of population growth. That his forms of scarcity interact reaffirms the centrality of population in his analysis.

24. Both Baechler and Homer-Dixon ignore the large and sophisticated political ecology literature on marginalization, risk, and "discrimination" (see, as one starting point, Blaikie and Brookfield 1987) that predates the environmental security field and draws on a nuanced theory of political economy.

25. "When distinct actors . . . experience inequality through systematically restricted access to natural capital . . . relative to other actors" (Baechler 1998: 24–25).

cial and environmental consequences ("stressors") of degradation, what he calls "social ingenuity." In this adaptability/ingenuity hypothesis, market failures, narrow distributional coalitions, and a lack of capital can increase (or decrease) the prospects for violence: "A persistent and serious ingenuity gap raises grievances and erodes the moral and coercive authority of government, which boosts the probability of serious civil turmoil and violence. The violence further undermines the society's ability to supply ingenuity" (1999: 27).

At another point in his book, Homer-Dixon adds a somewhat different observation on the likelihood of social effects precipitating violence in his note, never developed, that system legitimacy is a critical intervening variable between economic hardship and insurgency or conflict (1999: 144).[26]

The ENCOP and ECACP projects cover an enormous amount of ground in discussing "social effects." Much of this is necessarily relevant to any account of violence. But so much of this work fails dramatically in virtue of its ad hoc character, its tendency to overgeneralize, and a sort of "blender" approach to causality as variable upon variable is thrown into a theoretical stew pot.

We wish to emphasize three fatal weaknesses in both approaches. The first is largely empirical, namely that it must be demonstrated that there are clear and unequivocal connections between "environmental scarcity" and dislocation or hardship, intergroup segmentation, and the weakening of the state. These connections must be *shown*, not simply asserted. The state is often treated as a monolith, and institutions are so briefly sketched that it is impossible to determine how and in what ways institutions are being weakened by "scarcity" (indeed we would argue in many cases that they are not). Homer-Dixon can claim, for example, that "as different ethnic and cultural groups are propelled together under stressful circumstances, we see inter-group hostility" (1999: 142), yet the processes by which this happens (and often does not happen) is left almost wholly unexplained. The second weakness is theoretical underspecificity. Of course "elites" *can* capture resource rents, and of course poor people *may* be dislocated to ecologically marginal areas. However, the contours of the broad political economy (under which complex class and social forces operate) and how the rhythms of environmental change and accumulation shape the processes of exclusion, disenfranchisement, and displacement must be specified. Homer-Dixon's invocation of "structure" (which never moves beyond elites and inequality) is naïve and static as his case study diagrams in *Ecoviolence* reveal (see Figure 1.3, Homer-Dixon and Blitt 1999: 213).

Finally, the ingenuity hypothesis is exceedingly weak and porous. The

---

26. Legitimation processes are indeed key, but this requires exactly the sort of analysis of discursive practices, social power, and hegemony that Homer-Dixon does not offer.

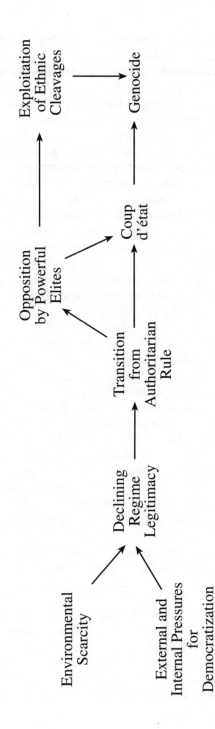

Source: Homer-Dixon and Blitt 1998: 213.

Figure 1.3 Weakened State Legitimacy and State Breakdown in Rwanda

very language employed—adaptation drawn from biological systems theory and ingenuity implying invention—stands in a contradictory relation
to Homer-Dixon's claim that politics can shape whether and how social effects generate conflict. The supply of ingenuity is an astonishingly banal
and inaccurate concept to explain why certain political outcomes occur—
as if all political struggles simply require a nifty invention that the less developed and "transitional" world is too maladapted or pedestrian to ac-
complish. In the way Homer-Dixon deploys it, ingenuity is synonymous
with technological innovation and says nothing about the relations between scarcity and violence as such. His emphasis on market failures reveals a neoclassical theory of both ingenuity and political behavior that is
easy to refute: unrestricted markets with the environmental externalities
they generate are no more models of adaptability than resource or capital
scarcity is an automatic recipe for violence. What Homer-Dixon calls social
friction *is,* of course, an intermediary variable linking environment and violence. Yet this extremely complex field of struggle and the shifting sites of
power must be laid out with much greater specificity and finesse if the idea
of friction is to confer any analytical weight.

The third and final moment in these two models is the genesis of violent
conflict itself. ENCOP and ECACP again have affinities but also different
points of emphasis and terminology. Homer-Dixon focuses on ethnic conflicts (group identity conflicts) and civil strife (insurgency, banditry, coups
d'état), whereas Baechler provides a typology of conflicts focusing on key
actors (migrants, ethnic groups—similar to Homer-Dixon's groups) and
geographical processes (core–periphery, global). The sorts of subnational
conflicts they refer to, however, have similar forms of genesis. For Homer-
Dixon, productivity declines are connected to psychological theories of relative deprivation to explain insurgencies. Social psychological theories of
group cooperation and conflict explain mass migrations that produce
identity conflicts. Some of these conflicts lead to social segmentation and
institutional decline, which in turn lead to both insurgency and coups d'é-
tat. Baechler refers to a number of conflict situations in which poor state
performance, weak regulatory apparatuses, coalition building, and resource dependency are taken to be key. The environment, for both analysts, plays a role as a trigger, target, or catalyst for conflicts of differing
sorts.

In both accounts, the *processes* by which violence occurs are partially explained and often occluded. Homer-Dixon resorts to rather antiquated
theories of social psychology (deprivation) and a state-centric approach to
violence that studiously ignores the dynamics of, for example, intergroup
conflicts not mediated by or through state power. At the same time, he radically underestimates the ways in which the state itself, as a complex and

differentiated entity, exercises extreme violence in a number of arenas. Conflict and violence often are used interchangeably. However, both usages are attached in uncritical ways to simple deprivation or rational actor models of human behavior, outmoded views of culture as shared belief systems and rules of social interaction, and an always monolithic set of unspecified "power relations." The net effect is that the process by which violence occurs is always hidden, and Homer-Dixon and Baechler must fall back on some indeterminate "context" to account for Rwandan genocide, the Ogoni oppression, or Dayak disempowerment. They provide little insight into the lived experiences of actors, rather undifferentiated views of the state and its institutional apparatuses and discursive practices, and nothing of the weight of history and historical memory.

Moreover, both Baechler and Homer-Dixon exclude many behaviors that fall within the rubric of violence. In its classic definition—brutal acts—violence is self-evident. But like much environmental security work, they ignore "its more ineffable nature and the practices and cultural discourses that sometimes put non-physical violence at its center" (Lutz and Nonini 1999: 74). Violence can take a variety of organizational forms (banditry, insurgency, coups, sporadic violence between landlord and tenant, state-sponsored punishment, isolated cases of police brutality) and is both physical and symbolic/cultural (wife-beating, social humiliation). One of the purposes of *Violent Environments* is precisely to expand the horizons of green violence and to see its genesis and practice in terms of something more than brutal physical acts.

In summary, to say that environmental scarcity can contribute to civil violence is to state the obvious. To argue that violence can occur in transitional societies in crisis regions when actors struggle over power (Baechler 1998: 25) or that increased scarcity produces lower productivity that more adversely affects poor people who are displaced and then triggers group identity conflicts or decreases in wealth that spur insurgencies (Homer-Dixon 1999: 133) radically impoverishes our understanding of the formation and phenomenology of violence. Homer-Dixon declares his desire to provide rigor to the study of environmental violence: "If we want to gauge the causal power of environmental scarcity's contribution to specific instances of violence . . . we must gauge its power relative to other factors," yet, oddly, he wants to "try to avoid tangling myself in the metaphysical debate about the relative importance of causes" (1999: 7). Understanding the processes by which some factors become causes is surely central to the social science enterprise. The fact that environmental violence is excluded from the "developed world" is also curious not only because it implies a narrow interpretation of violence (for example, it excludes the violence of cancer alley in Louisiana or of toxic dumping at Love Canal), but also because violence of the sort that Homer-Dixon and Baechler seek to address are very much part of the "zones of peace" of Europe, the Balkans, Japan, or North America.

The critical shortcomings of ES alert us to alternative modes of explanation made possible by political ecology. Political ecologists, as we shall argue, have assiduously sought to include the influences of international political economy and geopolitics in their analyses and to expand the horizon of both what is contended and how. Although Homer-Dixon or Baechler may speak of "triggers" or "context" to animate their theories of action, the origins, extent, and mechanisms for ending or perpetuating violence remain beyond analysis. In our view, places and people must be situated within a theorized political economy to understand the various expressions of power affecting them and the specific circumstances that precipitate violence.

Toward a Political Ecology of Violence

> Dangerous classes, dangerous spaces and representations of danger constantly disrupt the zone of peace, where divisions occur around forms of violence regarded as legitimate or illegitimate, securing citizens' public and private spaces or violating them. . . . The battle . . . is never won. It is continuous. It is vital in mobilizing support, as much symbolic as political and economic. . . . Violence is thus represented and experienced as random and systemic, arbitrary and structured, alien and inherent. (Gilsenan 1996: 4–5)

In the last twenty years, political ecology has attempted to link environment and politics into some sort of unified field.[27] Combining Marxian political economy with cultural studies and the new ecology, political ecology has offered a radical critique of both neo-Malthusian and rigid, structural Marxist formulations of environmental struggles and conflicts (Blaikie and Brookfield 1987; Peet and Watts 1996; Bryant and Bailey 1997). Political

27. A second and complementary approach is "reflexive modernization" associated with the work of Ulrich Beck and Anthony Giddens (1994) and the discursive analysis of so-called ecological modernization associated with Maarten Hajer (1995). Each draws on a concern with modernity as a self-reflexive system and green discourses. Specifically, the focus is on the self-reflexive qualities of modernization and on the ways in which the ecological costs and consequences of capitalist modernity are built reflexively into modernity itself, often through discourses of risk or uncertainty/precaution or through what Rom Harre (1998; with Brockmeier and Mulhauser 1999) calls "greenspeak." These approaches often employ linguistic and discursive analysis rooted in social studies of science and institutional analyses of regulation. Ecological modernization has, not surprisingly, focused on the advanced capitalist states and so-called postmodern societies. See Watts (2000) for a further comparison of political ecology and reflexive modernization.

ecology provides tools for thinking about the conflicts and struggles engendered by the forms of access to and control over resources. Its atten-
tiveness to the power relations inherent in defining, controlling, and managing nature suggests an alternative way of viewing the link between
environment and political action. The environment is an arena of contested entitlements, a theater in which conflicts or claims over property, assets, labor, and the politics of recognition play themselves out (Schroeder
forthcoming; Neumann 1998). One of the strengths of this approach has
been its careful documentation of a panoply of differentiated actors (including households, nongovernmental organizations [NGOs] social movements, communities, capitalist enterprises, and state agents and their institutional networks) and the ways in which they operate in historically and
culturally constituted fields of power.

Contemporary political ecologists take conjunctures or convergences of
culture, power, and political economy as analytical starting points and attempt to integrate discourse (meaning and practice) with the "historical
geography of material practice" (Harvey 1996: 183). In so doing, they recognize that a "dialectic of Nature–Society" relations must seriously address
the causal powers inherent in Nature itself, and not focus solely on the
overwhelming forces unleashed by capital, state, or technology on the environment. Not least, political ecologists recognize that any concern with environmental politics must be sensitive to the expanded repertoire of forms
of political practice (whether mass violence or local discursive struggles),
that is to say, to a deepened sense of the forms of contention themselves.[28]

In *Violent Environments*, we use political ecology to deepen and broaden
the analysis of the theoretical and empirical relationships between violence and the environment. Because both title terms are keywords that
carry their own freight and meanings, our goal is to remap the relative
contours and connections between them. Our approach is not, as the environmental security literature endeavors to do, a search for "environmental
triggers" of violent conflicts. Rather, we provide accounts of the ways in
which specific environments, environmental processes, and webs of social
relations are central parts of the ways violence is expressed and made ex-
pressive: What difference does environmental difference make? This takes
us far afield from the claims of, for example, the Swiss Peace Foundation,
that violence tends to be endemic in regions where there is an environmental crisis coupled to "traditional society–nature relationships [and] . . .
culturally specific approaches to environmental [regulation] . . . that are
acutely at risk" (Baechler 1998: 25).

28. There is, however, no overarching "theory of political ecology" that can be used to explore some set of universal or reductionist truths about the politics of human–environmental relationships (cf., Vayda and Walters 1999).

Contributors to this book specifically explore the production, enactment, and representation of violence against humans in relation to environment—not environmental scarcity per se. This poses sharply the question: What are the parameters and circumference of "environment" and "violence" that permit a sharpening of the analytical connections between the two? We have chosen to focus on environment along four dimensions:

- Environmental degradation associated with nonrenewable resource extraction (including environmental sacrifice associated with the military-industrial complex);
- Environmental change associated with the human transformation of renewable resources;
- Environmental enclosure associated with living space and territory; and
- Forms of environmental rehabilitation, conservation, and preservation.

Typically, the environmental security literature makes efforts to link conflicts and environmental degradation. The latter is understood to mean overuse of renewable resources, overstrain of the environment's sink capacity (pollution), and impoverishment of the space of living (Baechler 1998: 24). However, their exclusion of the most substantial forms of environmental transformation and degradation caused by nonrenewable resource extraction (mining in particular), dam construction, and industrial activity is at once noteworthy and curious.

In *Violent Environments*, we contend that the environments in which violence occurs must be construed broadly to encompass a panoply of environmental uses and forms of extraction, conservation, and rehabilitation. Such an environment is also comprised of the social causes and consequences of environmental degradation, rehabilitation, and preservation. In addition, the particular geophysical and biological characteristics of the resources and environments (and their spatial configurations over which violence occurs) must be construed as environmental and given some sort of causal efficacy. Petroleum, soil depletion, and tropical forests all possess quite different properties and commodity characteristics—aside from their strategic or economic value—that may, and often do, play a role in the dynamics of violence and struggle. Moreover, these environments and resources must not be so overemphasized as to dilute the specific and situated dialectics of environment, social relations, and violence.

For our purposes, we understand violence broadly as practices (brutal acts) that cause direct harm to humans. Those harms have to be understood in physical, symbolic, cultural, and emotional terms. Such a definition encompasses modern war and its concomitant scientific and military activities, sporadic unorganized violence, and the reproduction of memories, rhetorics, and experiences of physical and symbolic violence. We view violence itself and its deployment within the environment or over resources as constitutive of individual, community, and institutional identities, including (perhaps especially) those connected with national states. Thus, state and other institutional forms of coercion, the deployment of terror, and other forms of direct violence against human bodies are all complex social practices that have to be understood in terms of both actual physical harm and the ways and contexts in which such harm is discussed, represented, circulated, coded, and deployed.

political ecology

What sort of "new" political ecology is, then, on offer and how might it be capable of casting a different illumination on environmental violence?[29] Figure 1.4 is a highly schematic depiction that distinguishes a political ecology of violence from the ES approach. The starting point is not a presumed scarcity or precursor ideational factor but the relations between users and nature.[30] This is a reciprocal relationship between nature and humans—humans are naturalized and nature is humanized—in which labor is active, transformative, and social (Watts 1983). The starting point is, then, the appropriation of nature that is necessarily historical (what sort of labor?) and social (the appropriation of Nature is determined by social relations, particularly relations of ownership and control).[31] Nature itself is an important actor in the transformative or metabolic process. The properties of natural resources and environmental processes shape, in complex ways, both the transformation process and the social relations of production. Nature enters in an active way into the production process just as soil degradation demands a human response and reaction to the production process. Forests and minerals and water are, in ways that have to be demonstrated, co-constitutive of the forms of use and disposition of resources.

29. We would argue that the field of political ecology itself is broad and its boundaries porous enough to permit all of these wide-ranging debates and critiques within its circumference. The brilliant work of Soper (1995), Harvey (1996), and the recent collection by Macnaughten (1998) can all legitimately be seen as "political ecological" interventions, if not explicitly in name and terminology. Naturally, in such a complex field, internal tensions within political ecology remain much in evidence. The seemingly ubiquitous mantra that political ecology seeks to link political economy and ecology and that it is in practice a series of perspectives rather than a unified field theory naturally begs some very serious questions: what sort of political economy, what sort of ecology, and what sorts of linkages? (Zimmerer 1996; Watts 1995). To return to the language of Blaikie and Brookfield (1987), how exactly is the thorny nettle of the "dialectics" of Nature–Society to be grasped?

30. In the most general and abstract sense, the study of the human transformation of nature must be "the study of the manifold articulations of history and biology and the cultural mediations through which such articulations are established," which is Escobar's definition of political ecology (Escobar 1999: 3).

31. Political ecology does not *start* with politics as Vayda and Walters (1999) claim, but with the social relations of production as realms of possibility and constraint (Watts 1985). Because this speaks to questions of access to and control over resources (an enormously complex subject that embraces gender, property rights, local forms of governance, cultural institutions, forms of representation, and so on), it must necessarily be about politics.

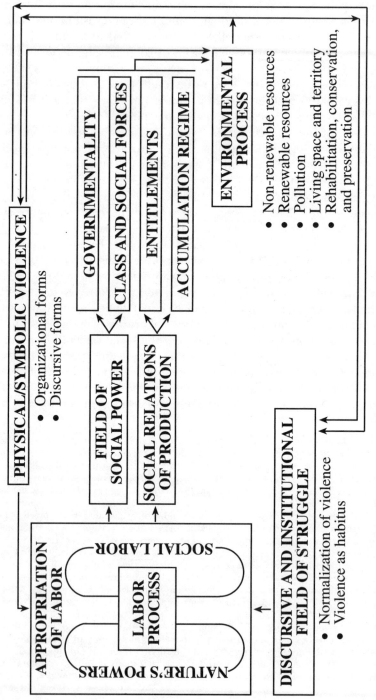

Figure 1.4 A Political Ecology of Environmental Violence

The social relations of production as arenas of opportunity and constraint focus on three broad horizons:

1. *The patterns and regimes of accumulation* (what Perry Anderson called the
   "jagged rhythms and breaks and uneven spatial distributions and displacements of capital accumulation"(1980: 33);
2. *The forms of access to and control over resources* (what we can generally call
   entitlements and modes of enforcement); and
3. *The actors (firms, workers, peasants, state operatives)* that emerge from the social relations of production.

These three vectors frame the key environmental processes we focus on
in our case studies. At the same time, the labor process is the point of incu-
bation of historical and cultural fields of power in which human agency
(organized through differing social forms: firms, the state, households,
and so on) is expressed. In turn these fields of power constitute institutional and discursive fields of struggle. These too shape environmental
processes. From the confluence of these two expressions of political economy—the social relations of production and the social fields of power— *contention*
emerge the forms of contention (always differentiated and varied) that
can encompass both physical and symbolic, organized and disorganized,
state sponsored and "civic," and highly mixed forms of violence.

In our account, there is no single theory of violence as such. Following
Sayer (1980), we examine how causal powers, located in the two spaces of
production and power relations, create forms of social mobilization and
conflict in specific circumstances. It is important to ask, therefore, why violence occurs in some places and not in others, why some factors are more
important than others, and why brutal acts define some conflicts and not
others. The purpose of rich empirical case studies is to reveal how these *cases*
causal forces articulate in specific circumstances.

Violent Environments is, we hope, a testament to a more encompassing, inclusive sense of violence and nonviolence. More encompassing because we
help shift the terrain away from collective brutal acts to "disorganized,"
random, or isolated physical harms, to violence within the nonphysical
realm, and to "the destruction of home and humanity, of hope and future,
of valued traditions and the integrity of community" (Nordstrom 1997:
123). More inclusive because a number of chapters show how communities and groups resist violence and violent threats from the state, not infre-
quently through monumental acts of individual heroism and courage expressed in prosaic and everyday forms.

In keeping with these broad intellectual traditions of political ecology,
the contributors to *Violent Environments* attempt sophisticated analyses of
the relations between violence and the environment. We treat violence as a

site-specific phenomenon deeply rooted in local histories and social relations but also connected to transitional processes of material change, political power relations, and historical conjuncture. Contributors are especially attentive to the simultaneity of symbolic and material struggles over
environmental resources and their articulations with sedimented histories
of violence that shape landscapes and livelihoods. At whatever scales of
analysis their stories are set, the authors provide complex accounts linking
or questioning the connections between violence and the environment.
Their analyses stand in stark opposition to Malthusian causal arguments
based on unqualified notions of population growth or scarcity or both, arguments that ultimately justify violence by states against their own
people.[32]

Organization of the Book

We have arranged the chapters in this volume to illustrate three dynamic
modalities of violent environments: (1) the forms, periodicities, and repertoires of environmental violence, (2) the intersection of violent extraction
with resource and environmental characteristics, and (3) the normalization of environmental violence. Section II examines *the patterns, tactics, or
rhythms of violence* and their associations with particular environmental relationships, particularly those involving land. Section III examines *changing
technologies of extraction and changing loci of resource control in relation to the biophysical characteristics of resources or the environments where they are found.* Section IV examines *the coercive capacity of changing institutions of green governmentality and the normalization of violence.* In addition to these three case
study sections, the chapter by Betsy Hartmann in Section I and this introductory chapter systematically critique the theoretical and policy premises
of conventional environmental security work and focus in particular on
the Homer-Dixon model of environmental scarcity and violence.

32. This volume, for the most part, does not address interstate wars (Iran–Iraq) or some
forms of massive intrastate civil conflict (the Balkans). Both forms of conflict obviously have
enormous environmental consequences—as indeed have Agent Orange in Vietnam, oil despoliation and pollution in Kuwait, and massive deforestation in Central America. Neither
is there significant attention (with the exception of the Garb and Pavolva chapter) to what
one might call the "ecology of the crisis of socialism." Environmental movements (sometimes conflictual) were an integral part of the landscape of the global political events of
1989, and the ecological crisis played a role in the material and economic crisis of many socialist political economies. We recognize that wars, in this age of extremes, are the greatest
source of violence in the world. However, we feel also that it is important to identify environmental connections to so many other forms of violence outside the purview of government agencies that administer and make war. We do not ignore the military question but
look at less explored ways in which it is implicated in violence connected to the environment.

Case studies in Section II focus primarily on the forms and repertoires of spontaneous outbursts, organized actions, and movements related to environmental concerns. Chapter authors ask how environmental violence articulates with wider societal patterns of violence and nonviolent social institutions or cultural practices. We find that environmental violence frequently intersects with other forms of violence emerging from racial and ethnic tensions, state forms of violence, and other social tensions that either come to the surface during transitional periods when social and spatial power relations are rearranged or create those transitional periods. Such an approach builds on earlier work of Taussig (1984, 1987) and Orlove (1994) who weave together political economy and discursive analysis to show how violence enacted around particular forms of resource extraction—rubber collection and wool production—requires cultural processes of coding the "other" as demonic, savage, and the legitimate subject of violence. These cultural processes, in turn, shape the outcomes of violence in ways that would not be predicted by reading directly from class position or economic relations. However, class and political economy remain indispensable to the analysis of violence.

The repertoires of violence here are concerned not only with the reasons for violence but also with the forms and actual practice of violence. The authors move beyond the insurgencies, rebellions, and coups d'état of Homer-Dixon and the trivial typology of Baechler (migration-based conflict or center–periphery conflicts) toward multiple forms of violence (everyday resistance, sporadic clashes, altered recurrences of violence) and violence as performance or spectacle. Theatricality and violent spectacle convey people's dissatisfaction to governments, to prospective international allies, and to their local opponents. Our contributions echo Feldman's ethnography of political violence in Northern Ireland, which rejects the one-to-one correspondence between "the conditions of political antagonism and the relational practices of antagonism" (Feldman 1991: 4). His argument affirms the importance of commonly held material explanations for sectarian violence in Northern Ireland, economic inequality, and ethnic division but does not reduce the conflict to a "symptom" of these structures. Employing a horrifying cascade of ethnographic narrative, Feldman shows how violence comes unhinged from its ideological justifications, is sedimented with its own histories, takes on "its own symbolic and performative autonomy" (ibid.: 21), and resculpts the social relations from which it arose.

In this volume, theatricality is tied into the ways rights are articulated through both the environment and various forms of expressing or experiencing collective identities. Captain Chromosome, who appears in Boal's chapter, is a not-so-imaginary superhero of the gene wars in Northeastern England. Bobrow-Strain's Chiapas performance is a replay with different actors: Maya land claimants violently targeting their violators of an earlier period, similarly allied with the Mexican state. The choices of targets, and the manipulation of the media to garner attention, constitute common themes of opposing sides' violent public performances in both McCarthy's and Boal's contributions.

The strategic deployment of identities (including violent aspects of these identities), the mining of alternative ideologies of rights and laws, and the uses of violence to defend these are themes in each of the chapters in this section. All engage in some way with the cultural politics of violence—how particular groups experience and represent right and wrong in political activity. The pursuit of human rights or rights to resources frequently constitute the terms of these conflicts, although such globally defined categories of rights take on locally mediated meanings. Peluso and Harwell see contemporary communal violence that reinterprets and reconstructs cultural memories of violence performed in earlier periods under quite difference conditions. Violent identities from a distant past are deployed, in this case, to demonstrate indigenous peoples' losses of the power formally connected with resource rights to land and forest that colonial authorities had once given them.

The cases presented here involve strongly divisive, or more properly exclusive, terms of resource allocation—terms based on identities enframed within notions of citizenship—in which excluded groups use violence to gain access to and control of those resources or to redefine those resources and thus transform the terms of access. Throughout this collection, we see these ideas reflected in cases that illustrate the links between the construction of ethnic difference; the ways notions of citizenship, ethnicity, or other forms of belonging overlap with mechanisms for territorial control of valuable resources; and the power underlying the creation of primordial place-based identities. This mechanism may seem like Homer-Dixon's structural violence "B" (where excluded groups seize political opportunities to violently appropriate resources), but it differs in a number of profound ways. First, several of the cases we present show that the types and contexts of violence deployed by excluded groups are not only illegal—unsanctioned by the state—but also abhorrent to mainstream groups in the societies from which these groups are demanding recognition.

Such violence is not an "opportunity"—as Homer-Dixon might call it—but almost a last resort. Richards and McCarthy, for example, talk about groups whose violent tactics—and the representation of these tactics by state and nonstate actors—have worked to virtually ensure their permanent exclusion from national political interaction. Moreover, exclusion from local institutions can create an impetus for alliances between resource claimants and violent, antigovernment groups (e.g., diamond diggers and the RUF in Sierra Leone or temporary links between Wise Use activists and antifederal militias in the United States). At the same time, however, state violence may be used to justify the exclusion of resource claimants because of their involvement in violence not sanctioned by the state. A number of chapters in other parts of this book, such as the one by Baviskar, seek to implicate state authorities in their resource distribution politics as well as in their backing of violence by some groups and not others.

Privatization themes and alliances across state agencies create tensions throughout Section II. Both physical enclosure and the reconfiguration of trade, labor, and production policies guiding permitting and other access policies—both of which are forms of resource reallocation—set the stage for violence in the chapters by Boal and Peluso and Harwell. Past violence repaid by violence in the present is a common theme in Richard's and Bobrow-Strain's chapters. These violent strategies can mimic war or guerrilla warfare and may even be learned inadvertently and passed on from one generation to another. Environmental resources—whether they are specifically land, plants, or nonrenewables such as diamonds—are implicated as part and parcel of social relations. This is not just identity politics (or the group identity conflicts that Homer-Dixon invokes) but identity politics that constitute larger political frameworks of resource access and power. Bobrow-Strain's chapter, for example, examines a case, Chiapas, studied by Homer-Dixon and the ECACP project and provides a rather different account of "scarcity" and struggles in that region, one that turns precisely on a more sophisticated political economy of the region.

A fourth theme is how community is created or reinforced by violence, just as certain forms of community and resource claims are being threatened by change. Moreover, each violent group analyzed in this section regards its contemporary national state as an opponent that created resource scarcities for them by changing rules of access and by changing the relevant categories of rights-holders. These groups' alleged recalcitrance "against the state" is used to justify direct or indirect state violence against them once their activities have been criminalized. In some cases, the resisters' violent defense of their resource claims leads to more restricted enclosures of those resources. However, these novel configurations also may open up the space for social movements based on identity and connections to places and their resources and articulate claims through idioms of human rights, citizenship, and ethnicity that challenge state sovereignty over territorial and resource control.

What McCarthy calls "new moral economies" plays an important role in both the acting out and the telling of violence. Imagined Communities play important roles in the ways violent identities of the present are constructed or justified through past or present violence. McCarthy looks at private rights to the federal lands as commodity management schemes that are connected to the political-economic and moral origins of U.S. citizenship. Boal looks at clashes between different groups' claims to moral authority, health, and well-being in the conflicts over genetically modified seeds. Peluso and Harwell examine ethnic territoriality and citizenship as modes of claiming collective rights to land that parallel the construction of violent identities. Bobrow-Strain examines the shifting of state policy to support both the land claims and the violence of two different groups of rural citizens: ranchers versus indigenous peoples. These chapters confront both nostalgic pasts and utopian futures: sixteenth-century England, the nineteenth-century American frontier, and precolonial Mexico and Indonesia are all seen in heroic contrast to the disappointments of postcolonial states. On the other hand, Richards's diamond diggers in Sierra Leone look forward to a utopian future in which they will be treated as equals with those of different social and economic classes who have excluded them, with all conflicting parties using diamond-derived wealth to do so.

Chapters in Section III, like those of Section II, examine the politics of producing violence through exclusionary practices. Enclosure here is also a central metaphor, particularly in its effect on making resources and the production practices invisible. The analytical thrust of this section differs considerably from Homer-Dixon's and others' environmental security models, because it takes environmental and resource characteristics seriously. Chapters also differentiate between types of nonrenewable resources. The characteristics of these resources engender violence either by their strategic or economic value and spatial location—a factor that affects the nature of their extraction—or by the micropolitics of their production and protection. The commodity and biophysical characteristics of these resources combine with local and international social relations to produce violence. Importantly, all but shrimp are nonrenewable resources. Stonich and Vandergeest show, for example, that it is not only shrimp's natural characteristics but also its geographics of production that facilitate theft and its high value that encourage violent protection.

Violent environmental relations involving the character and value of resources have two primary sites of tension: conditions of resource abundance versus of resource scarcity. Homer-Dixon argues for the primacy of the latter, but we contend that more extensive and destructive violence is likely when the resources are either in great *abundance* or have great economic or strategic value (Fairhead, this volume). Garb, Kuletz, and Fairhead all show that strategic value is simply a code for the production of nuclear weapons—either by the states in whose territories the resources lie (Kuletz, Garb) or by powerful international actors to which these states are formally allied or commercially tied (Fairhead). Stonich and Vandergeest, on the other hand, show that strategic resources do not need to be defined only at such high levels of international intercourse; as critical components of household and regional economies, the stakes for their control are violently high. All of these chapters, however, are not so much about scarcity or abundance per se as about the ways in which particular entitlements are shaped by specific regimes of accumulation and by particular social forces.

Authors in Section III explore not only governmentality—a chief concern in Section IV—but also how the cycles and technologies of state power play out in conjunction with resource commodity claims made by visible and invisible partners. The most powerful partners are often the most invisible, whether these are international players that hide behind national state actors or strategic industries—such as the oil industry—with their own capital and powerful political allies for gaining access to particular resources.

A third theme encompasses the transformative power of the resources authors explore. These transformative powers are simultaneously physical, political, and economic. Petro-magic, which Watts invokes, makes people and states fabulously wealthy, seemingly without effort. The qualities of oil in nature necessarily transform the landscapes of production. Like other forms of "resource madness"—those associated in other centuries with gold and silver or in the present with precious gems and even shrimp—the extraction, production, and trade of oil and the strategic resources in Section III appear to be ubiquitously saturated with criminality, corruption, and violence. These complex relations of extraction and marketing are dependent in important ways on their unique commodity and physical characteristics (something that Homer-Dixon invokes but does not explore).

The production of these resources significantly transforms both human bodies and the earth, although paradoxically, in some cases, these transformations are invisible to the casual observer or purposefully made invisible. Garb's case study describes the violence against human bodies, and Kuletz, the production of a violent landscape. Both chapters explore less familiar impacts of government programs to create, store, and use nuclear weapons. Bodily and environmental degradation remain hidden also because of erasures made possible by the environments themselves. In the case of the U.S. weapons testing ground Kuletz describes, the vastness of the desert creates invisibility; in Garb's Soviet Union, degradation occurs through invisible processes of cancer development. As Watts's chapter reveals, the Ogoni also have been erased as claimants to oil and at the same time have been made victims of what Kuletz calls "sacrificial landscapes." In all these cases of nonrenewable or renewable resources, the by-products of resource extraction or production create further environmental dangers—often invisible or violent in their potential environmental effects. Thus, although they all differ in form, nuclear waste, mining tailings, petroleum spills and waste, and the antibiotics poured into coastal shrimp ponds all produce devastating environmental violence.

A fourth theme informing these chapters, conspicuously ignored in Homer-Dixon's model, is the power of specific resource consumers and the ways this power may lead to violence. Whether these are superpower states with massive military-industrial capacities, vast privileged populations in industrialized countries of the North whose everyday existence depends on the lifeblood of oil, or long-distance consumers of shrimp and other luxury foods, few theories have examined the direct and indirect power of these consumers to affect violent behavior in contexts that seem far removed from the contexts in which these resources find their end uses. These cases reach far beyond Homer-Dixon's bland discussion of "demand-driven scarcity," which focuses primarily on poor people scrambling for crumbs after the world's hegemonic powers have escaped with the bullion.

Contributions to Section IV examine the normalization of violence both in government and nongovernment forms. These chapters all specifically consider modes of governmentality—the forms of calculated practice (in and outside government) to direct categories of social agency in a particular manner for particular ends (Dean 1999). In his treatise of modern governmentality, Foucault showed how a centralized state and its apparatuses made the fostering of life and the care of population a part of a new regime of power that he called "biopower." Biopower brought "life and its mechanisms into the realm of explicit calculation" (1978: 143). In exploring the connections between the state (and its legal, administrative, and security apparatuses) and other institutions and domains of practice, Foucault focused particularly on the body. Our invocation of governmentality conversely raises the question of the calculation of other forms of life, namely, Nature (green governmentality) in its panoply of guises.[33] How does violence intersect with—or emerge from—green governmentality and the expansion, entrenchment, and routinization of resource exclusion? Novel forms of surveillance, regulation, self-policing, and resource exclusion imply new techniques through which the relations among sovereignty, discipline, and population are reconfigured. These chapters explore how such changing contexts and mechanisms of power alter patterns of violence or their representation.

Capitalism requires and generates particular configurations of governmentality: universalistic legal codes, certain types of economic relationships and controls, or, as Scott (1998) puts it, certain ways by which the state can "see" and make legible the resources contained within its terri-

---

33. Foucault does in fact include resources and "territory" (including, as he puts it, its "specific qualities") as constitutive of modern governmentality (see Rabinow 1984: 16).

tory. Group identity politics again emerge in Section IV, but what are centrally problematized are not the ways in which and the reasons that groups are excluded—questions that animate the chapters in Sections II and III. Rather, here the authors examine primarily how violence becomes a state-sanctioned part of local strategies for maintaining control of resources. In other words, the empowerment—including the sanctioning of violence—of certain collectivities or "resource communities" benefits the state by relieving it of its unpleasant and unpopular policing role. Violence is displaced from relationships between people and state to relationships between different groups in a locality. Whereas the state is directly implicated in the cases of Sections II and III, the governmentality implicated in these last four chapters is much more localized and diffuse, reflecting the internalization and diffusion of policing practices and ideologies.

The sovereign rights of states to rule both territories and people are translated or deflected to rights of access over resources and to control over bodies. Sundar, for example, shows how forest management in West Bengal, India, was historically conflated with patriotism and loyalty to the state. Forest encroachments and forest-based rebellions were conflated thus with treason and savagery. Joint Forest Management displaced the sites of violent encounter, however, deflecting attention from the state's role in creating tensions within already fraught contexts. Neumann details similar processes in Tanzanian wildlife conservation institutions, parks where community level management institutions are given violent capacities and do more to bolster state power than to eliminate tensions at the village level. Baviskar examines two internationally connected environmental social movements. She argues that divergences in their internal organizations and external representations create opportunities for the state both to exercise unequal violent coercion and to hide behind masks of normalcy. Similarly, Rajan uncovers the ways in which the scientific and industrial communities engage the government in their cloaking of dangerous aspects of chemical production in India. When the famous explosion at Bhopal took place, the factory managers could hide behind their own cloak of secrecy to hide their knowledge of the conditions that led to the accident, killed many people, and left major scars on the environment.

Rajan's chapter, like the others in this section, also explores the selectivity of historical memory and its relation to violence. In the Bhopal case, within a few days of the explosion, many people—except the victims and their families—had forgotten the incident. In Neumann's case study, the massive—and violent—colonial project in Eastern Africa of geographically separating wildlife and people is forgotten, ignored in narratives about community management of resources today. Sundar's discussion of Joint Forest Management reveals how these new programs are constructed as "gifts" or "subsidies" to rural people as though state control of these particular resources or these particular places were a timeless social fact. Indeed, the massive social and political construction of these wildlife parks and forests has all but disappeared from the official histories of these states and their predecessors. And Baviskar illustrates the ways thoroughly corrupt state institutions of law enforcement and resource management create "new" memories out of whole cloth.

Violent Environments has been deliberately constructed so that important continuities, overlaps, and intersections exist among the four sections. In particular, three themes cut across nearly all the chapters in this volume: the direct and indirect roles of state agencies and actors in creating the conditions for and/or mobilizing violence; the complex dialectics between resources and individual or collective identities and the ways such identities are violently defended or contested; and the ways that communities can be created from, maintained, and protected by violence.

There are no automatic innocents in any of the relations and networks discussed in this book, nor is there necessarily a hope that some abstract state or force (e.g., "democracy") can unproblematically provide for a nonviolent future. The twentieth century as an "age of extremes," as Eric Hobsbawm (1994) calls it, has drawn to a close, but it casts a long shadow over the new millennium. We hope that a better understanding of the specific ways in which history, memory, and the practices of people, states, and the forces of capitalism often come together violently might provide for an optimism of both the intellect and the will.

2

Will the Circle Be Unbroken?
A Critique of the Project on
Environment, Population, and
Security

Betsy Hartmann

I was so gripped by many things that were in that article ["The Coming Anarchy"] and by the more academic treatment of the same issue by Professor Homer-Dixon. . . . You have to say, if you look at the numbers, you must reduce the rate of population growth.

(Clinton 1994)

With the end of the Cold War, the environment and security field has become a vast and well-funded academic and policy enterprise. Much of the field's initial impetus came from the work of Canadian political scientist Thomas Homer-Dixon and his Project on Environment, Population and Security, a joint activity of the University of Toronto, the American Association for the Advancement of Science, and the Canadian Centre for Global Security. This project argued that scarcities of renewable resources, such as water, forests, and fertile land, were already contributing to intrastate violent conflict in many parts of the developing world and could potentially disrupt international security as states become more unstable or authoritarian.

With substantial support from the Pew Charitable Trusts and other private foundations, and the political backing of Vice President Al Gore, Homer-Dixon's model of environmental conflict was popularized and propelled into U.S. foreign policy circles with remarkable speed in the mid-1990s. The critical response from the academy was slow to come, with a few exceptions (Levy 1995; Ford 1995).

Today more critical work is emerging (e.g., Hauge and Ellingsen 1998; Peluso and Watts, Fairhead, this volume; Dalby 1999; de Soysa 2000), and

argument

like Friedmans flat world

39

Homer-Dixon himself is more willing to recognize contextual and institutional factors such as "state capacity" in the evolution of intrastate conflict in his latest book, *Environment, Scarcity and Violence* (Homer-Dixon 1999). The environment and security field is becoming more self-reflective, aware that it has to shed the legacy of Robert Kaplan's (1994; 1996) racialized, sexualized, and apocalyptic "coming anarchy" if it is ever going to attract more Third World and women scholars to the table. Challenging the narrow disciplinary boundaries of International Relations, a new generation of projects is drawing more widely from the social sciences and moving away from the national security framework to embrace the notion of environment and "human security" (Lonergan 1999). The Washington, D.C.–based Woodrow Wilson Center's Environmental Change and Security Project, the field's main hub, is in turn trying to cultivate a more pluralist approach toward the issue.

Despite these developments, Homer-Dixon's models continue to exercise influence in policy circles, impacting, for example, two studies on environment and conflict by the Carnegie Commission on Preventing Deadly Conflict (Kennedy 1998) and the NATO Committee on the Challenges of Modern Society (NATO 1999). Many of Homer-Dixon's basic assumptions—about the nature of the state, the role of population growth, and the causes of environmental degradation—remain underchallenged and overstated.

This chapter takes a close look at the assumptions and research underlying Homer-Dixon's models and case studies in an attempt to widen the space for debate in the environment and security field. It begins with a description of the model's basic features, then moves on to examine the project's major flaws.

Pointing the Arrows

In *Ecoviolence,* Homer-Dixon and coauthor Jessica Blitt lay out the central findings of the Project on Environment, Population and Security based on research on fifteen countries (Homer-Dixon and Blitt 1998).[1] They derive a model for the relationship between environmental scarcity and conflict that has these key features:

1. In certain situations, scarcities of renewable resources such as croplands, fresh water, and forests can cause civil conflict and instability, even though on first inspection the scarcities do not appear to be a direct cause. "Environmental scarcity" generates powerful intermediate social effects

---

1. Bangladesh–India, Mexico (Chiapas), Israel–Palestine, Pakistan, Rwanda, Senegal–Mauritania, South Africa, El Salvador–Honduras, Haiti, Peru, and the Philippines.

(e.g., poverty, migrations, ethnic tensions, and weak institutions) "that analysts often interpret as conflict's immediate causes" (223).

2. While environmental scarcity refers specifically to scarcities of renewable resources, the definition is then widened to include three factors: "the degradation and depletion of renewable resources, the increased demand for these resources, and/or their inequitable distribution" (224). The increased demand for resources is mainly linked to population growth, so population growth, in effect, becomes the second factor, as illustrated in Figures 2.1 and 2.2.

3. In conjunction with population growth, the degradation and depletion of renewable resources induce powerful groups to tighten their grip on them in a process called "resource capture." These groups often use this control to generate profits, thereby intensifying scarcity for poorer and weaker groups. (See Figure 2.1.)

4. Combined with population growth, unequal resource access can force the migration of the poorest groups to ecologically vulnerable areas such as steep hillsides, tropical rain forests, areas susceptible to desertification, and low-quality urban land. The pressure of their numbers and their lack of knowledge and capital then cause "severe environmental scarcity and chronic poverty," a process termed "ecological marginalization" (225). (See Figure 2.2.)

5. Environmentally induced conflict can be avoided if societies adapt to scarcities by using resources more sustainably or acquiring them through international markets. The capacity to adapt, however, depends on whether or not there is "an ample supply of the social and technical ingenuity that produces solutions to scarcity" (226). The outlook is grim for many Southern countries underendowed with efficient markets, research institutions and the like; moreover, environmental stress is likely to diminish their ability to create such institutions in the first place. The result is further impoverishment and migration.

6. Environmental scarcity can weaken the state by threatening "the delicate give-and-take relationship between state and society" (10), increasing the demands on public institutions, encouraging predatory elite behavior, and reducing tax revenues. At the same time it can reinforce group identities based on ethnic, religious, or class differences because "individuals identify with one another when they perceive they share similar hardships" (226). Increased competition between groups leads to social segmentation and reduced social trust. Ultimately, the weakening of the state "shifts the social balance of power in favor of challenger groups . . . and increases opportunities for violent collective action by these groups against the state" (227).

7. By contributing to migrations, economic decline, social segmentation, and weakened states, environmental scarcity helps lead to violent

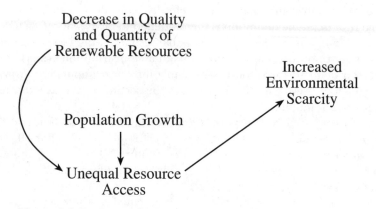

Figure 2.1 Resource Capture

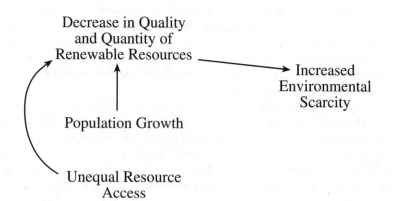

Source: Homer-Dixon and Blitt 1998: 74.

Figure 2.2 Ecological Marginalization

"ethnic conflicts, insurgencies, and coups d'état" (227). These have serious consequences for the security interests of both developed and developing countries, triggering monetary crises, refugee flows, humanitarian disasters, and either the fragmentation or increased authoritarianism of states.

Homer-Dixon's model of environmental conflict thus neatly completes the circle between environment and security. Neat models, however, rarely do justice to complex social realities. There are a number of serious problems with the approach.

Weak Definitional Foundation

First and foremost is the weak definitional foundation upon which the model is built. As Fairhead notes, the concept of environmental scarcity conflates distinct processes—the generation of renewable resource scarcities, environmental degradation, population growth, and the social distribution of resources—into a single, overarching term which is "tantamount to analytical obfuscation" (Fairhead 1997: 18; and in this volume). Environmental degradation is confused with renewable resource scarcity (they are often presented as virtual synonyms) although there is no necessary link between the two. Land shortages, for example, can be an incentive to boost productivity through better agricultural techniques and land improvements (15).

By adding the social distribution of resources into the definition of environmental scarcity, Homer-Dixon creates too automatic a link to conflict because political conflict often revolves around issues of resource control. This is the main tool by which he is able to force very disparate conflictual situations into his universalizing model. The result is a model so inclusive as to be banal (Fairhead 1997: 18). Levy makes a similar critique, arguing that it is difficult to imagine that conflicts in developing countries would not include renewable resource issues: "Developing country elites fight over renewable resources for the same reason that Willy Sutton robbed banks—that's where the money is" (Levy 1995: 57). He also notes that environmental factors interact with such a variety of social processes to generate violence that "there are no interesting mechanisms that are purely and discretely environmental" (58).

Case Study Selection

Levy identifies the central flaw of Homer-Dixon's research program as his choice of cases in which violent conflict and environmental destruction are already occurring, the rationale of which is that these cases can most effectively falsify the null hypothesis that the two factors are not causally related. If, however, as pointed out above, conflict over renewable resources is to be expected in developing countries because these resources are a major source of wealth:

> The more logical research strategy under the circumstances would be to compare societies facing similar environmental problems but exhibiting different levels of violent conflict. That would permit some precision in identifying the conditions under which environmental degradation generates violent conflict and when it does not, and for formulating useful policy advice on how to avoid violent outcomes. By instead taking aim at a null hypothesis that has virtually no advocates, researchers have lost the ability to say anything more than "the environment matters," something not seriously disputed before this work was undertaken. (Levy 1995: 57)

Levy also advises the use of "counterfactuals": The question should be asked how a given case of scarcity might have had different outcomes if the political institutions involved were stronger or more democratic, along the lines of Singapore or Costa Rica, for example. He makes the point, however, that to use counterfactuals effectively, one must have detailed empirical knowledge of those societies, another reason Homer-Dixon should consider places where there is more variation in the operation of the variables he considers important (Homer-Dixon et al. 1996: 59).

Homer-Dixon has vigorously defended his research methods but in so doing has revealed several key biases. He admits his colleagues and he deviate from standard social science inquiry in the way they go about looking at the relationship between the "dependent variable" (conflict) and the "hypothesized independent variable" (environmental scarcity). They are not interested, he writes, "in the whole range of factors that currently cause changes in the value of the dependent variable (conflict)," instead wanting to show the particular impact of one independent variable (environmental scarcity). This is supposed to justify the selection of cases that specifically accentuate the variance of the independent variable (Homer-Dixon 1995b: 2).

This approach easily leads to an overemphasis on scarcity causing conflict because the other independent variables are by definition of secondary importance. The methodological muddle of the term "environmental scarcity" confuses matters even further because, as previously noted, the term conflates distinct social and ecological processes so there really is no "one" variable he is testing.

In his latest book Homer-Dixon shows himself more open to other methodological approaches, though mainly within the bounds of political science. He writes that his methods made sense in the early stages of the investigation, but now, based on this work, researchers can derive "more sophisticated hypotheses" using a broader range of methodologies, such as cross-national statistical analysis and counterfactual analysis (Homer-Dixon 1999: 182). He is particularly interested in cases where violence does not occur even though environmental scarcities are a serious problem.

He continues to stand behind his project's case studies, nevertheless, and they still greatly inform his work, comprising the main body of *Ecoviolence* (Homer-Dixon and Blitt 1998) and serving as supporting evidence in *Environment, Scarcity and Violence* (Homer-Dixon 1999). While it is true that the case studies are more nuanced and attentive to context than the model, there are a number of problems with the way the research is presented and interpreted, as noted in the following sections.

Ghost of Malthus

Homer-Dixon claims he is not a neo-Malthusian in the sense that he does not accept that "finite natural resources place strict limits on the growth of human population and consumption" (Homer-Dixon 1999: 28). He points out how technological and institutional change can boost productivity and induce environmental improvements, and he is critical of the apocalyptic vision of "arch-pessimists" like Paul Ehrlich who believe that humans have already outstripped the earth's resources (28).

Despite these disclaimers, population growth is probably the single largest causal factor of environmental scarcity in both his project's model and case studies, figuring prominently throughout his past and recent writings.

The negative role of population growth is fundamental to the very definition of environmental scarcity. As mentioned previously, it becomes a virtual synonym with the increased demand for resources, which is one of the three components of environmental scarcity. It is central to the processes of "resource capture" and "ecological marginalization."

This automatic equation of population growth with increased resource demand is problematic. It does not necessarily follow that if there are more people, they will consume more—per capita consumption could fall for a variety of reasons. It also may be that increased resource consumption has little to do with demographic factors but instead with increased demand in external markets for a particular product (e.g., teak for Scandinavian style furniture). I will return to this point later.

The relationship of depopulation with environmental degradation does not figure in his model at all. In Brazil, for example, many areas depopulated by poor peasants because of their lack of access to land and agricultural inputs have gone over to ecologically damaging extensive cattle raising, industrial monoculture, and logging (Mello 1997). Similarly, in Mexico the exodus of peasants to urban areas can lead to the loss of valuable micro-habitats and crop genetic diversity previously sustained by their labor (Boyce 1997; Garcia-Barrios and Garcia-Barrios 1990). In Africa low population densities and dispersed settlement patterns have been identified as important factors impeding the development of agriculture (Turner, Hyden, and Kates 1993).

Although in his latest book Homer-Dixon acknowledges the possibility that population growth may in certain cases help spur agricultural innovation and intensification, he is largely pessimistic, remarking, for example, that even under the most favorable conditions, countries in Africa and elsewhere with high population growth rates will not be able to boost yields sufficiently to keep pace with population growth (Homer-Dixon 1999: 34). This contradicts field research that suggests the situation is considerably more complex and context-specific. For example, Tiffen, Mortimore, and Gichuki's study of Machakos District in Kenya found that increasing population densities combined with sound agricultural practices and market access led to boosts in agricultural productivity and environmental improvement (Tiffen, Mortimore, and Gichuki 1994; also see Turner, Hyden, and Kates 1993).

In the end, like many other Northern analysts of Southern countries, Homer-Dixon is prone to blaming population growth disproportionately for environmental degradation, poverty, migration, and ultimately political instability. Thus, he cites population growth as a major cause of the rise of Sandero Luminoso in Peru, violent unrest in Chiapas, and the New People's Army (NPA) insurgency in the Philippines (Homer-Dixon 1999: 18, 23, 78). He also fears the effects of the "youth bulge," the fact that the age structure in most developing countries is heavily weighted toward the young. In language reminiscent of Cold War population and security discourse (Hartmann 1995), he warns that the products of this youth bulge—underemployed, urbanized young men—"are a particularly volatile group that can be easily mobilized for radical political action" (ibid.: 58).

Around the planet, Homer-Dixon claims:

> Population growth and unequal access to good land force huge numbers of rural people onto marginal lands. There, they cause environmental damage and become chronically poor. Eventually, they may be the source of persistent upheaval, or they may migrate yet again, helping to stimulate ethnic conflicts or urban unrest elsewhere. (155)

This description is remarkably similar to what Emery Roe calls the conventional "crisis narrative" for Africa, a stereotypical population/scarcity scenario applied indiscriminately to different countries and designed to justify the intervention of Western development agencies (Roe 1995).[2]

"Crisis narratives" such as Homer-Dixon's not only overstate the role of population growth but also present a simplistic view of environmental degradation.

Barren Slopes and Tropical Tropes

The fact that poor peasants are responsible for most land degradation and deforestation in the Third World is a truism inherited from the colonial era and more recently popularized by *Our Common Future,* the report of the United Nations World Commission on Environment and Development, chaired by Gro Harlem Brundtland, the former Prime Minister of Norway (World Commission on Environment and Development 1987). Fortunately, a new generation of research, primarily focused on Africa, not only challenges these assumptions empirically but also reveals how this "wisdom" originated in the colonial enterprise and, in modified form, continues today to suit the needs of powerful international actors.

Taking a closer look at the critique of conventional environmental understandings of Africa is worthwhile because it helps shed light on some of the key problems in Homer-Dixon's analysis.

In their edited volume *The Lie of the Land,* Leach and Mearns describe the biases in colonial understandings of African environmental change. Chief among these were the ideas of a "climax vegetation community," an ostensible causal link between devegetation and declining rainfall, and the notion of carrying capacity: "that every set of ecological conditions can support a given number of people and/or livestock which, once exceeded, will lead to a spiral of declining productivity" (Leach and Mearns 1996: 10). These ideas were grounded in a conception of ecological equilibrium in which environmental change was a linear deviation from an idealized norm.

The idealized norm in turn was influenced by the perceived "value" of

---

2. Roe describes it thus: "The birth rate of [fill in name of country] is rising; human and animal populations bound forward exponentially; overutilization of the country's scarce resources accelerates; the government tries to create jobs but is less and less able to do so; rural people pour into the cities and the government's rural development policies are helpless in stemming the tide; political unrest becomes explosive, while politicians and civil servants grow ever more venal; and unless something is done to reverse this process [fill in name of country] will become another basketcase. . . ." (Roe 1995: 1065–1066).

the resources in a given environment. Since in Africa professional foresters valued the closed canopy or gallery forest most highly, any conversion of it by local people was seen as "degradation." Yet, as Leach and Mearns point out,

> such conversion may be viewed positively by local inhabitants, for whom the resulting bush fallow vegetation provides a greater range of gathered plant products and more productive agricultural land. Thus the same landscape changes can be perceived and valued in different ways by different groups; what is "degraded and degrading" for some may for others be merely transformed or even improved. (12)

The extent of degradation in Africa was and still is often overstated. This is due not only to value bias but also to faulty scientific methodologies. The exclusion of historical data on landscapes, for example, leads to speculative projections about the past that may romanticize previous environmental conditions. Also, conditions at a particular time may be assumed representative of an abiding state of affairs. For example, the low population densities found in East African savannahs at the beginning of the twentieth century were viewed as the norm by colonial administrators, but in reality they were the result of a severe depopulation of humans and livestock as the result of recent war, famine, and disease (15).

Another critical mistake is taking short-term observations as the evidence for long-term trends. The extent of desertification in Africa thus has been grossly exaggerated through short-term studies of desert expansion, although studies over several decades reveal a fluctuation of desert margins due to climatic cycles. The persistence of alarmist notions of desertification, despite mounting scientific evidence to the contrary, must be viewed in a larger institutional context of who benefits from such beliefs (Swift 1996).

The severity of soil erosion also has been overstated. In Africa this is due to the propensity to extrapolate from small-scale observation plots to entire regions and countries (Leach and Mearns 1996: 15). In the case of Chiapas, Mexico, Howard and Homer-Dixon's estimates are problematic for other reasons. The study emphasizes the role of land degradation, particularly soil erosion, in the creation of environmental scarcity in Chiapas. The authors acknowledge that there has been "no credible long-term study of soil erosion in Chiapas," but nevertheless believe that "by piecing together available data and anecdotal evidence, we can clarify the story of supply-induced scarcities of cropland in the state" (Howard and Homer-Dixon 1998: 32). "Speculate" would be a far better word than "clarify" in this instance (see also Bobrow-Strain, this volume).

They use three sources of data to make their case. First are a set of soil degradation maps, published by The United Nations Environmental Program (UNEP) and the International Soil Reference Center in the Netherlands, in which the data for specific regions are highly aggregated. There is provisional soil degradation information for Chiapas that indicates moderate losses in a number of locations. It is not clear, however, how the data for the maps was generated, especially because there have been no credible long-term studies of soil erosion in the region.

The authors then hypothesize, on the basis of a 1975 study of farming techniques and soil degradation in the Central Highlands, that conditions "have probably worsened" because the population has grown, thereby leading to a shorter fallow period in swidden agriculture (33). They assume that this process also is being replicated in the colonization of land elsewhere. The evidence here is obviously speculative.

Howard and Homer-Dixon then project the extent of soil erosion in Chiapas on the basis of a general model of the economic costs of erosion developed by David Pimentel and colleagues for a temperate ecosystem. They insert indicators for rainfall, soil depth, slope, and so on, for a *tropical* and a more temperate zone in Chiapas into Pimentel's model and come up with estimates of the erosion rate, yield loss, and replacement costs. Given the vast differences between tropical and temperate zones and the variation in temperate zones themselves, this is a dubious exercise.

The use of such models is questionable given their oversimplification of interactive variables. Even soil erosion studies done *in situ* are fraught with errors (Stocking 1996), and Howard and Homer-Dixon's approach is many more steps removed from the actual landscapes they seek to analyze.

In-depth historical, anthropological, and scientific research can do much to challenge the received wisdom on degradation. Through examination of historical data, the comparison of aerial photographs from different time periods, and oral research in local communities, Fairhead and Leach, for example, have shown how areas of forest and savannah vegetation have remained remarkably stable in the northern margins of Guinea's forest zones. This contrasts with the conventional view, carried over from the colonial period, that farmers are encroaching on the forest and using it unsustainably (Fairhead and Leach 1996a).

What, however, about areas that clearly have been degraded? Here, too, historical research can do much to challenge the prevailing belief that the fault mainly rests with the local inhabitants due to their poverty and population growth. A case study of Ukambani, Kenya, reveals how local peoples have been blamed over the course of a century for the degradation of their environment; however, the origins of the problem were largely external, involving, for example, the expropriation of their lands by European settlers and unfavorable integration within the national and global economy (Rocheleau, Steinberg, and Benjamin 1995).

Localizing Blame

One of the principal failings of the environmental scarcity model, in fact, is its neglect of larger economic and political forces that profoundly affect "local" environments and conflicts. In a period of rapid global economic integration, the model is surprisingly insular in scope. Homer-Dixon and his colleagues posit essentially closed systems in which various internal stresses may generate movement outward, mainly through mass migration, but the outside is rarely seen to be pressing in.

In reality no distinct boundary lines can be drawn between the inside and the outside, or between the local, regional, national, and global; they have long been linked through complex patterns of trade, investment, and foreign policy imperatives. Renewable and nonrenewable resources alike have long been the traditional exports of the South. As Fairhead notes, effective demand elsewhere for what a territory has to offer may drive conflict more than environmental decline "on location"; moreover, as argued elsewhere in this volume, conflicts are generated less by resource poverty than resource wealth (Fairhead, Peluso and Watts, Kuletz).

Effective demand elsewhere also may drive environmental degradation much more than local poverty and population growth. Largely missing from Homer-Dixon's model crucial roles of extractive industries—mining, timber, agribusiness, and so on—in the depletion and degradation of local natural resources.

In one instance when Homer-Dixon does refer to them, the conclusion he reaches twists the concept of environmental scarcity and effectively puts the onus back on the local people. He notes how multinational extraction of oil in Nigeria's Ogoniland and copper on the island of Bougainville (Papua, New Guinea) has polluted those regions. This pollution becomes "environmental scarcity," even though it was the abundance of resources that attracted foreign firms to both areas in the first place (Homer-Dixon 1999: 147–148).

He then describes violent insurgencies in Ogoniland and Bougainville as examples of "group-identity and relative deprivation motivations." He writes:

> If the historical identity of a clearly defined social group is strongly linked to
> a particular set of natural resources or a particular pattern of resource use,
> degradation or depletion of that resource can accentuate a feeling of rela-

tive deprivation. Members of the group can come to feel that they are being denied their rightful access to resources that are key to their self-definition as a group. This relative deprivation boosts grievances that may eventually be expressed through aggressive assertion of a group identity. (Homer-Dixon 1999: 147–148)

That local people bonded together to defend their land and livelihoods from absolute, not relative, deprivation hardly seems a special case of group identity. In Ogoniland, in fact, it was the Nigerian military who displayed the most "aggressive assertion of a group identity" in their brutal campaign to protect the interests of Shell Oil. Why, one has to ask, does Homer-Dixon focus on the violence of local acts of resistance and not on the much larger violence of state and corporate enforcers?

Homer-Dixon depicts ecological marginalization as a process by which unequal resource access and population growth force the migration of the poorest groups to ecologically vulnerable areas, such as steep hillsides and tropical rain forests, that they then proceed to degrade. Two problems exist here. First is the assumption that population growth and unequal resource access have equal weight as the "push factors" causing people to migrate to such areas. Second is the failure to articulate the range of actors responsible for "unequal resource access."

An extensive study of deforestation by the United Nations Research Institute for Social Development, for example, notes that while many observers blame deforestation on forest clearing by poor migrants, they ignore the larger forces attracting or pushing these migrants into forest areas, such as the expansion of large-scale commercial farming, ranching, logging, and mining. "To blame poor migrants for destroying the forest is like blaming poor conscripts for the ravages of war" (Barraclough and Ghimire 1990: 130). The study found an absence of any close correspondence between deforestation rates and rates of either total or agricultural population growth.

Homer-Dixon uses deforestation in the Philippines as a classic example of ecological marginalization. Unequal land access and population growth push poor unemployed peasants into ecologically vulnerable uplands where their slash-and burn-farming and small-scale logging destroy the environment. So the story begins and ends, but it is only one small act in a much longer play.

What Homer-Dixon leaves out is that under the Marcos dictatorship fewer than two hundred wealthy individuals controlled a large fraction of the country's forests (Boyce 1993); during that period the country's forest reserves dwindled from 34.6 million acres to only 5.4 million (Jones 1986). The main culprit was not population growth—one study found zero correlation between population growth and rates of deforestation in the country's provinces (Kummer 1992)—but rather the illegal logging concessions Marcos gave to relatives and political friends, as well as his agricultural policies that heightened rural inequalities.

To determine the extent that poor peasants have degraded the upland environment in the Philippines, one needs to look more closely at the dynamics involved. Settlers have moved into the highlands on already existing logging roads. Although they occupy nominally public land, many pay rent to wealthy private landlords who use the money to pay "taxes" to local officials so they can eventually lay claim to the land. As Boyce notes:

> Although upland farmers often do contribute to deforestation, it is misleading to cast them as the main villains . . . what distinguishes upland farmers from other agents of deforestation—loggers, government officials, absentee landlords, and international firms and institutions—is that the upland farmers are among the principal *victims* of the deforestation process. Not coincidentally, they are also the poorest. (Boyce 1993: 238)

Also missing from Homer-Dixon's picture of the Philippines and elsewhere are the consumers of the extracted products. For example, the main cause of deforestation in developing countries is demand for wood and paper, and nearly half that wood and three-quarters of that paper are used in industrialized nations (UNDP 1998). The failure to link the consumption patterns of Northern countries and Southern elites to "local" land uses is a major blind spot in Homer-Dixon's approach. Another is the lack of adequate attention to the role of price fluctuations on the international market in determining resource supply and demand. A detailed rendering of the international political economy of trade and finance is outside the scope of this paper but, as noted in Peluso and Watts, and Fairhead (this volume), that political economy has profound effects on resource use.

For a model that seeks to illuminate the roots of conflict, the lack of reference to the role of the international arms trade also is a major oversight. Missing too is a consideration of the role of militaries in degrading local environments. The German Institute for Peace Policy estimates that one-fifth of all global environmental degradation is due to military and related activities. In modern warfare, the environment has become a militarized target. Even after the cessation of conflict, land mines and the lingering effects of scorched earth practices and chemical warfare obstruct environmental restoration (Seager 1993). Militaries also can directly contribute to the creation of both "social" and "natural" scarcities because they absorb economic resources that could be used for human development and environmental improvements. In developing countries as a whole, for example, military expenditures rose from 91 percent of combined health and education expenditures in 1977 to 169 percent in 1990 (UNDP 1993; see also, Kuletz, and Garb and Komarova, this volume).

The theory of "ecological marginalization" would seem most applicable only to captive populations. Former bantustans, refugee encampments, and urban squatter colonies are what anthropologist Anna Tsing has ironically termed "Malthustans," environmentally degraded areas where population pressure and depleted resources are pushing the environment into a downward spiral (Tsing 1995). But rather than confirm the theory, these "Malthustans" also call it into question because, of course, much larger forces are involved in generating such political and economic captivity.

Exclusion and Enclosure

One of the most fundamental problems with Homer-Dixon's approach is his acceptance of exclusion and enclosure as a given state of affairs, understating the role of the violent processes that lead to them. His case study of South Africa, coauthored with Percival, portrays the bantustans as Malthustans, where overpopulation, depleted resources, and unequal resource access lead to ecological marginalization and then to migration to marginal urban areas where growing black populations in limited areas once more wreak havoc on the environment. The resulting environmental scarcity ostensibly escalates grievances, intensifies group divisions, and weakens institutions, fueling violence that may lock South Africa "into a deadly spiral of conflict" (Percival and Homer-Dixon 1998a: 139).

But why are people made to subsist in limited, marginal areas, whether rural or urban? Why and how are they enclosed? Might the enduring violent legacy of apartheid have more to do with present political unrest than the fact that black people are cutting down trees?

Also important to consider is why people who are excluded and enclosed lack opportunities elsewhere. In their case studies, Homer-Dixon and his coauthors place little emphasis on the possibility of concrete economic and political changes that would provide people with alternative forms of livelihood and/or reduce pressure on the natural resource base. The Chiapas case study does recognize that peasants suffering from acute land scarcity have only limited economic alternatives because of not only structural adjustments in the 1980s that reduced labor absorption in key industries but also the spread of labor-displacing agricultural technologies on large estates (Howard and Homer-Dixon 1998). Yet peasant population growth still figures much more prominently in their analysis than this lack of an economic outlet due to state fiscal and agrarian policies.

Similarly, it is only on the last pages of the South Africa study that Percival and Homer-Dixon briefly sketch alternatives (economic growth, job creation, agricultural extension services, etc.) to the grim scarcity scenario they have laid out. In the case studies generally, the necessity of, and prospects for, market development and industrialization are underplayed. In the absence of these possibilities, the neo-Malthusian scarcity argument appears more convincing.

Wind-Up State

Homer-Dixon's view of the state is oddly old-fashioned. Before the onset of environmental scarcity, the state is essentially presented as a unitary actor, engaged in a "delicate give and take relationship" with society and unlinked from the larger international context of regional and superpower rivalries. Enter environmental scarcity like a *deus ex machina*, and the state becomes the agent of whoever can get their hands first on the turnkey, springing into a flurry of largely destructive activity.

Several points need clarification here. First, whether in times of resource scarcity or abundance, most states always have been arenas of contention between groups making competing claims; the state may be unitary in form but seldom in substance. Second, the "delicate give and take relationship" between state and society may have existed somewhere under a benevolent monarch, or perhaps under an enlightened social democracy, but otherwise state-society relationships have long been fraught with conflict, frequently brutal and violent. Third, the state itself, through state-owned or aided enterprises, parastatal institutions such as marketing boards, contract awards, fiscal policies, and so on, often has played a major role in managing, extracting, and profiting from natural resources.

A pertinent example is the case of development projects. In describing the process of resource capture, Homer-Dixon has noted that agricultural shortfalls due to population pressure and land degradation can induce states to launch large development schemes, such as dams for irrigation (Homer-Dixon and Percival 1996: 35). The benefits of these schemes are then captured by the rich, potentially leading to conflict.

The undertaking of a large development project, however, often has much less to do with agricultural shortfalls than with the links between foreign donors/companies and domestic elites who stand to gain from lucrative procurement and construction contracts awarded to them because of their *prior* cozy relationships with government officials. In this sense, too, the choice of technology—whether environmentally appropriate and conducive to control by small farmers or large, expensive, and even harmful—usually has less to with the actual shortfalls than with who has the power to do the choosing. (See, for example, the case of a World Bank deep tube-well project in Bangladesh in Hartmann and Boyce 1983.)

Homer-Dixon believes that in the absence of adequate adaptation, environmental scarcity weakens states, although a case can be made for the opposite scenario. The client state could use resource scarcities to leverage more foreign assistance and, with this assistance, secure more domestic clients and set up new bureaucracies for aid projects creating yet another avenue of patronage. One could argue that in recent years declining foreign assistance, high levels of debt, unfavorable terms of trade, and financial austerity measures—not shortages of renewable resources—are creating the real "scarcity" that weakens states.

Richards, for example, notes how African patrimonial systems of governance were strengthened in the Cold War period when leaders could use their geopolitical position to bargain for increased aid resources from the West and the Soviet Union. According to him,

> Patrimonialism in the 1990s faces a double crisis. World recession has reduced prices of many raw materials. Countries like Sierra Leone have also seen the exhaustion of some of their best sources of minerals. Meanwhile the ending of the Cold War caused sources of aid money to dry up. There is less money around to maintain the crumbling facade of the "official state." (Richards 1996: 36)

Yet even the weak state finds ways to cope in this new era. Reno describes the key mechanisms by which weak African states have preserved their power. With the end of Cold War superpower support, weak states are re-working their foreign ties, especially clandestine commercial ones. In some cases, they are using foreign firms, such as the South Africa-based Executive Outcomes, to perform important functions of state security (see also Fairhead, this volume). States also sell off national resources to foreign firms since "from a weak state ruler's perspective, it is better to have important state assets fall into the hands of reliable foreigners than to see them removed from his control entirely" (Reno 1997: 172). This suits creditors as well because it meets their demands for revenue generation, and international development agencies are pleased with the resulting "stability." A far more interesting question to ask than "Is environmental scarcity weakening the state?" would be how these post-Cold War relations affect the reconfiguration of the state, patterns of resource exploitation, and the nature of conflict and security.

Homer-Dixon maintains that environmental scarcity also can lead to a kind of localized ethnic and identity politics that causes social fragmentation and more opportunity for powerful groups to seize control of the state. Several observations are warranted here. First, as Fairhead (1997: 16) notes, segmentation and narrow identity affiliations often arise in the context of insecure economic, legal, and political rights, whether the environment is depleted or not. As conflict develops, "the politics of identity" can become "the politics of resource access" particularly when personal property is at stake. This does not mean the property (e.g., land) is always "scarce." Even if it is scarce, this is not necessarily the determining factor.

Second, ethnic violence occurs in many different types of settings—in weak states and strong states, poor states and rich states. Even in the resource-abundant United States, a number of contemporary black riots in urban ghettos have arisen. The precise nature of ethnic conflict is highly cultural and context-specific, not easily forced into any kind of model, especially one that naturalizes the process by linking it to the environment rather than to complex social, economic, and cultural systems.

Third, research on the nature of contemporary civil wars points to the primacy of the economic interests of its perpetrators. "To paraphrase Carl von Clausewitz," David Keen writes, "war has increasingly become the continuation of economics by other means. War is not simply a breakdown in a particular system, but a way of creating an alternative system of profit, power and even protection" (Keen 1998: 11). A recent study of civil wars by Paul Collier corroborates this point. He found that the presence (not scarcity) of primary commodity exports that are easily lootable substantially increases the risks of civil conflict and, interestingly, that ethnic and religious fractionalization substantially *reduces* the risk because it is harder to mobilize a large enough force for a successful rebellion (Collier 1999).

Another problem with Homer-Dixon's conception of the state is the generally negative characterization of oppositional forces. In his latest book he is careful to note that "social conflict—even violent conflict—is not always a bad thing" (Homer-Dixon 1999: 5). Yet he rarely takes a look at social movements other than those that he directly links to environmental scarcity. National and transnational movements for women's rights, economic justice, environment, and peace not only offer alternative scenarios to the insidious social segmentation he portrays, but also are rich sources of alternative research and analysis of the issues he raises. Because of his concern with security, his model is oriented toward the status quo—what is in place is stable, and whatever upsets it is destabilizing, leaving little room for the possibility of *positive* political transformation.

Rwanda Exception

Interestingly, Homer-Dixon and Percival's case study of Rwanda finds that "environmental and population pressures had at most a limited, aggravating role" in causing the genocide there and criticizes commentary that focuses on these pressures as being "too simplistic" (Percival and Homer-Dixon 1998b: 201). In a departure from the norm, they purposefully set about to refute hypotheses that posit a strong causal relationship between environmental scarcity and high levels of grievances, political instability, and the manipulation of ethnic identity. Instead, they identify regime and elite insecurity caused by the civil war and the Arusha accords as the central cause of the conflict and highlight the role of structural adjustment, the fall in coffee prices, and declining food production in creating general economic malaise.

Unlike other case studies, this one makes a strong distinction between the regime and the state:

> The regime is the set of individuals that has gained control of the state's internal relations. In developing societies, the regime usually lacks the support of a large share of the population: it represents the interests of a specific ethnic, economic or military group. The distinction between the internal and external aspects of the state is crucial to our understanding of the Rwandan case: it was the Habyarimana regime, not the Rwandan state, that faced threats to its security. The regime did all it could to maintain its grip on power. (215)

This conception is problematic for several reasons. The separation between the internal and external aspects of the state is overstated because the same actors often are involved in both, and policies overlap. The characterization of developing countries as ruled by a small group ignores the great diversity of political formations. It is useful, however, because it allows Homer-Dixon to deviate from his own previous conceptions of the state to pinpoint specific political actors in the generation of violence in Rwanda. These actors are largely missing from the other case studies or cast as "powerful groups" that gain control of the state because of environmental scarcity.

In Rwanda, it seems, more explicit political human agency exists that is not environmentally determined. The study concludes: "If researchers are to understand complex conflicts like the Rwandan genocide, they must be acutely aware of the issues motivating the conflict's actors. They must not only examine what people do and what physical environment they do it in, but why they do it" (217–218).

It is worth speculating why Rwanda is the exception. Any of the other cases studies also could have found that environmental scarcity played "at most a limited, aggravating role" in generating conflict if political and economic factors were given the same weight that they were in the Rwandan study. One suspects that the Rwanda exception was made for more pragmatic reasons: Homer-Dixon's project did not want to be tarred with the same brush as Robert Kaplan. By 1995 "The Coming Anarchy" (Kaplan 1994), in which Homer-Dixon's work was prominently featured, was coming under critical scrutiny in academic quarters (e.g., Ford 1995 and Olin 1995), and it became prudent to differentiate oneself from its environmental determinism and racial stereotyping of Africans. Homer-Dixon himself describes much of the attention his work received after Kaplan's article as "self-reinforcing media hype" (Homer-Dixon et al. 1996: 50).

Ingenuity Gaps

Homer-Dixon's
Solution ✓

Homer-Dixon's main solution to the problems generated by environmental scarcity is a technocratic one represented by the concept of "ingenuity," by which he means "ideas applied to solve practical social and technical problems" (Homer-Dixon 1999: 109). Both social and technical ingenuity are required, with the former being a precursor of the latter. According to him:

> Social ingenuity is key to the creation, reform, and maintenance of public and semipublic goods such as markets, funding agencies, educational and research organizations, and effective government. If operating well, this system of institutions provides psychological and material incentives to technological entrepreneurs and innovators; it aids regular contact and communication among experts; and it channels resources preferentially to those endeavors with the greatest prospect of success. (110)

Scarcities of resources, especially renewable ones, will demand ever-greater supplies of ingenuity. The need to run resource systems more efficiently will require "tightly coupled and highly complex horizontal and vertical management" (113). Even this may not suffice because "fundamental physical, biological and social constraints may make it difficult to fully compensate for the effects of scarcity" (114).

Homer-Dixon believes one of the strongest barriers to creating the ingenuity to cope with scarcity is scarcity itself because of the "social friction" it generates. In line with his weakening of the state argument, he maintains that scarcity can lead to the formation of small coalitions with narrow interests that prevent the institution building necessary for social and technical ingenuity to flourish.

In the end he falls back on cultural stereotypes to explain whether a country can break out of this vicious cycle or not. In a "culture of selfishness" people resort to narrow coalitions more rapidly than in a "culture of good will" (120). He cites the Philippines as an example of the former: "Filipino culture encourages cooperation within groups rather than among groups; the resulting isolation of groups from each other—the oft-remarked clannishness of the society—undermines the concept of national welfare" (120). Yet the Philippines has one of the most highly so- ✓ phisticated and integrated democratic social movements in Asia, as witnessed in the anti-Marcos struggle.

Similarly, states already penetrated by narrow coalitions are deemed less able to handle scarcity. The example given here is India, which supposedly does not have strong political parties that can mediate between narrow coalitions and the state (121). Yet, India not only has strong political par- ✓ ties but also a well-developed, publicly-funded scientific establishment, an essential ingredient in Homer-Dixon's recipe for ingenuity. Unfortunately, that "ingenuity" also has demonstrated itself in a destructive manner with the development and testing of nuclear weaponry.

Homer-Dixon also takes a narrow, Western view of science, neglecting the role of local knowledge, or what James Scott (1998) calls mētis or practical knowledge, in helping to mitigate scarcity and bring about environmental improvements. "Many of the scarcities facing poor countries demand advanced science like molecular biology that they cannot afford," Homer-Dixon notes (124). Perceiving poor peasants as largely degraders of their environment rather than possible agents of its restoration, he fails to acknowledge the tremendous ingenuity of small cultivators around the world, whose agricultural knowledge is based on close and astute observation. As Scott writes, these cultivators have a vital stake in the results of their own experimentation. Unlike research scientists or extension agents, they live all year in the field of observation and will directly benefit or suffer economically from the impact of their decisions. Moreover, contrary to Homer-Dixon's formula, Scott maintains that the poverty or marginal economic status of these cultivators can itself be "a powerful impetus to careful observation and experimentation" (Scott 1998: 324).

Homer-Dixon claims his theory of ingenuity gaps integrates the neo-Malthusian approach (that focuses on the physical causes of scarcity and poverty) with the neoclassical economics and distributionist approaches (that emphasize social factors such as unequal resource allocation, ineffective markets, and public policies). "Social improvements such as better markets and less unbalanced wealth distribution often alleviate the negative effects of scarcity," he writes. "But a society's capacity to make these improvements—to deliver the required social ingenuity—will be partly determined by scarcity itself, which is powerfully influenced by the society's physical context" (43).

When it comes to poor countries, however, his neo-Malthusian predilections generally win out. He strikes an apocalyptic note, warning that poor societies may lose the race to outrun scarcity, sinking into widespread violence, crisis, and decay. He predicts a world increasingly bifurcated into countries that have an adequate supply of ingenuity to face rising scarcities and those that do not (44).

The concept of ingenuity thus becomes a way to rationalize persistent social and economic inequalities between and within countries and to place the onus on population-related environmental depletion. Through the concept of ingenuity, ideas also become disembodied; the understanding of human agency is largely limited to mechanistic interactions between ideas, institutions, and scarcity.

Underspecification, Overspecification

Emerging as it does from an international relations/security framework, it is perhaps not surprising that the Homer-Dixon model takes too little notice of other social science research in anthropology, geography, and development studies that looks more closely at the dynamics of resource use and distribution from the community level on up. When it comes to identifying actors, the models, and even many of the case studies, are underspecified. The local is not adequately differentiated, nor the global articulated. The poor, when they are differentiated at all, are done so mainly on the basis of ethnicity and religion.

Gender, for example, is not used as a category of analysis. Yet certain views of gender are implicit in the model, particularly given the central and negative role it ascribes to population growth. Subsumed into the analytic frame of population pressure, women, through their fertility, become the breeders of environmental destruction, poverty, and violence. They are the invisible heart of environmental scarcity, made visible only when policies to ease "population growth-induced scarcity," such as "family planning and literacy campaigns" (Homer-Dixon 1994: 16) are put forward.

Important questions about gender are not asked or answered. What are women's property rights, labor obligations, and roles in the management of environmental resources? Is there differential access to resources within the household? How have structural adjustment and other economic policies affected women's health, workloads, and status relative to male family members? Where are investments being made: in basic food production, where rural women most often work, or in export agriculture? If men are forced to migrate to earn cash or to join militaries, how do women cope with the labor requirements needed to sustain food production and maintain infrastructure? And how do all these issues relate to women—and men's—reproductive strategies?

Case studies in Africa, for example, have shown how gender dynamics can have an important effect on agricultural growth. "Increasingly, day-to-day decisions about all facets of agriculture are being made by females, in most cases under conditions in which access to land is invested in males," write Hyden, Kates, and Turner. "This contradiction is one that must be resolved adequately . . . if agriculture is not to stagnate" (Turner, Hyden, and Kates 1993: 418).

Gender analysis also opens a window to view potential *solutions* to the problems of resource degradation, maldistribution, and constraints on agricultural growth. Unfortunately, many current land redistribution and community-based natural resource management schemes have widened the gender gap rather than narrowed it because they have ignored power differences within the household, community, and larger political structures. According to Indian economist Bina Agarwal, rethinking communities from a gender perspective would have a number of advantages:

> Conventionally treated as aggregates of households (at best with class/race/caste differences), communities, if recognized as gendered networks of individuals, could become spaces for creating institutions based on identities derived not only (or even) from household membership, but from socioeconomic need and gender. The examples of communal management of land by women are cases in point. In fact, a gendered perspective on institutions for the collective management of local resources—land, water, forests—would provide a promising new focus for development analysis and policy. (Agarwal 1997: 1379)

Similarly, the "environmental entitlements" framework offers a much more complex, historical, and pluralist approach to understanding both the dynamics of local ecologies and the diverse institutions and differentiated social actors that affect and are affected by them (Leach, Mearns, and Scoones 1997).

As this volume argues, the environment and security field would do well to move beyond its disciplinary boundaries to consider other approaches that are grounded in a more specified political economy and political ecology. Ironically, the main trend is toward greater specification, but of a different nature. Researchers in the intelligence, defense, and environmental fields are struggling to find data and variables they can fit into models that will predict and map the hot spots of the future, where resource scarcities combined with weak state capacity may generate conflict. Increasingly, land use data from intelligence assets, notably remote sensing satellites, are being harnessed for this enterprise. The earth is being studied inch by inch, and social systems broken up into discrete clusters of variables (see, for example, Esty et al. 1999). But the dynamic interface between environmental resources and different sets of actors, with differential access to power, remains largely obscured.

These latest modeling exercises are not Homer-Dixon's approach but may be one of his legacies. He helped misdirect the official gaze, and now it seeks ever-greater resolution and magnification to see what it can see. But like the bear who went over the mountain, all that it can see may be the other side of that mountain, despite all the sophisticated technological tools at its disposal.

II

Forms, Tactics, and Repertoires of Environmental Violence

3

Are "Forest" Wars in Africa Resource Conflicts? The Case of Sierra Leone

Paul Richards

Until Rhodesia became Zimbabwe, African wars were wars of independence. During the 1980s the continent's conflicts mainly were determined by the Cold War or apartheid in South Africa. The 1990s saw a rise in African conflicts escaping earlier categorizations (Chabal and Daloz 1999; Goulding 1999). Seeking to account for these recent conflicts, authors have opted for either the idea of reversion to a long-suppressed African barbarity (Kaplan 1994, 1996) or the notion of a "criminalization of the African state" (Bayart, Ellis, and Hibou 1997).

Duffield (1998) shrewdly notes, however, that current or recent African wars fall, more or less, into two regional groupings: wars from the Horn of Africa to Mozambique that are in effect "old" proxy conflicts, perhaps prolonged by humanitarian interventions, and conflicts in the western half of the continent (from Zaire to Liberia) sustained by abundant local natural resources (oil, gemstones, gold, and timber). Stretching a point, we might label these two groupings "desert" and "forest" wars, respectively.

Some recent literature treats African "forest" wars as predominantly economic phenomena, directed by "war-lord" business elites (Berdal and Keen 1997; Chabal and Daloz 1999; Duffield 1998); the opportunist Charles Taylor in Liberia is seen as the paradigmatic protagonist (Reno 1997; Ellis 1999). All conflicts need resources, but we should be careful to distinguish the plausible idea that war has economic dimensions from the more contentious notion that resource endowments, and in particular resource shortages, "cause" violence (Homer-Dixon 1991, 1994; Kaplan 1994, 1996).

Violence is a social project—it has to be organized or opposed, accepted or rejected, by groups of human agents. Whether or not war achieves specific ends is influenced by environmental factors (including resource endowments). Environments select among social projects, like they select for genes, but they no more cause social life than they cause genes. A resource endowment is a circumstance, and not a social project.

Although agreeing that wars—all wars—necessarily involve resource mobilization, this chapter argues against the notion of "resource wars," a special category of conflict in which a certain configuration of resources, or lack of resources, determines a turn toward violence. "Forest" wars in western Africa or elsewhere, it is suggested, will be understandable only through closer examination of the social projects involved.

If wars in western Africa have a common distinctive feature, it is that the resources in question (e.g., diamonds, uranium, oil) are of strategic significance in industrial countries but of less immediate local utility. In these circumstances, the element of external intrigue, and hence external obfuscation, tends to be rather high. Reporting rarely penetrates beyond the oil or diamonds. The world has limited time for the intricacies of African politics and little capacity to assess grass-roots social change in remote mining landscapes. Anthropologists are not much attracted to such fields, except perhaps by accident (my situation, cf. Richards 1996, 1998). Mining interests, protecting their assets through private security, add to the confusion. As we shall see, advisers to governments, sympathetic to (or implicated in) private security options, are wont to misrepresent the social projects feeding "forest" war as criminal banditry. Insurgents are "rebels without cause" (cf. Bradbury 1995). The sociology of "forest" conflict is buried by default. Here I try to exhume it.

"Forest" War

The "forest" war in Sierra Leone was begun on March 23, 1991, by a group of one hundred or so guerrillas calling itself the Revolutionary United Front of Sierra Leone (RUF), led by a cashiered army corporal Foday Saybana Sankoh. The RUF launched itself from Liberia, with the support of faction leader Charles Taylor, to overthrow the All Peoples Congress (APC), the one-party state regime of (retired) General Joseph Saidu Momoh. The rebels rounded up young diamond diggers and schoolchildren in the heavily forested border zone and inducted them into a "people's army" but failed to win wider civilian support (Abdullah and Muana 1998; Richards 1996, 1998).

The failure of a northern-dominated government army to defend the south and the east of the country against the RUF led to a coup that ushered in a populist military regime, the National Provisional Ruling Council (NPRC), in April 1992. The NPRC realized that the RUF was aiming to provide a focus for the country's unemployed and footloose youth. The NPRC set out to control the same constituency, drafting large numbers of unemployed youth to fight the RUF.

The army was increased from 3,000 to about 15,000, but training was perfunctory and discipline poor. Young irregulars recruited in the border region proved effective in defending their own communities and put the RUF on the defensive, but the urban underclass element in the government army resorted to criminal activities. Looting was rife, and NPRC officers used recruits for private diamond-mining ventures.

With the RUF sequestered in isolated forest reserves on the Liberian border, public confidence in the army plummeted. The popular view among civilians was that the RUF had ceased to exist and that the war was an excuse by the NPRC regime to dig diamonds. In places that were vulnerable to raiding by the RUF, rural civilians turned increasingly to civil defense. A number of militia bands were formed, drawing on initiates to local hunting guilds (Muana 1997).

But the RUF survived and, by selling diamonds to rogue soldiers in return for arms and uniforms, revived. It used these resources to carry out numerous pinprick raids, undermining civilian morale and seizing hostages right across the country. By 1995, these raids were coming sufficiently close to Freetown to threaten panic in the capital.

The NPRC was then forced to seek help from a South African–based security firm, Executive Outcomes (EO). EO also contracted to provide security for a mining company (Branch Energy, a subsidiary of DiamondWorks) planning to exploit kimberlite diamond pipes in Kono, a district heavily destabilized by RUF raids. EO trained and ran military support operations for units of the NPRC forces (Peters and Richards 1998; Shearer 1997). Details of the EO contract were never made public, but it is presumed that diamond-mining opportunities were among the modes of "payment."

Internal and international pressure forced the NPRC to concede elections in early 1996. The outgoing regime had launched a peace process with the RUF, and this was continued by the new democratic government of Ahmad Tejan Kabba and the Sierra Leone People's Party (SLPP). Kabba also reconfirmed the security contract with EO.

Under scrutiny from the Mandela government in South Africa, EO phased out in Sierra Leone in 1997 (and disbanded in 1998) to be replaced by a British-based security company, Sandline International. This group also took over the task of providing security for the mining company Branch Energy. Sandline provided training inputs and specialized support for irregular forces loyal to the Kabba government (the expanded civil defence militia, now known as the Civil Defence Force [CDF]). Branch Energy was granted a kimberlite mining concession reportedly worth $1 billion by the Kabba regime.

Enclaved in camps in forest reserves in the east of the country, the RUF had become an increasingly intransigent and introverted movement. Opposing the elections in 1996, it carried out bizarre attacks, including the random amputation of limbs of women and children, in outlying village communities, revenging itself—so it claimed—on those who supported civil defense (Richards 1998). Despite a peace agreement signed in Abidjan in November 1996, the irregular forces loyal to the Kabba government never suspended their military operations against the RUF, sacking several of the most important rebel forest bases shortly before the signing of the peace accords.

Then in May 1997, fearing the democratic government was planning to disband the army and shift its entire military effort against the RUF to civil defense, a group of army officers and other ranks mounted a coup against the Kabba regime, driving the president into exile in neighboring Guinea and attempting to bring peace to Sierra Leone by inviting the RUF to join a power-sharing regime. The resulting unstable junta was ostracized internationally. With its kimberlite concessions resting on the restoration of the Kabba regime, the mineral-cum-security nexus engaged in the war in Sierra Leone was active in arguing that private security for Kabba was tantamount to support for democracy and good governance (Spicer 1998).

A scandal then enveloped the Blair government in Great Britain about whether Sandline International was assisting the military restoration of the Kabba regime with or without official encouragement. It transpired that Peter Penfold, the British ambassador to Sierra Leone, had been giving President Kabba advice on the Sandline option in a private capacity and that a principal agent of Branch Energy was a recently retired officer of British overseas military intelligence (MI6). The lack of clarity about the boundaries between democracy, private security, and strategic mineral interests was complete. The junta was deposed and the Kabba regime restored (February 1998), largely through the military efforts of the mainly Nigerian troops of the Economic Community of West African States Military Monitoring Group (ECOMOG), assisted by Kabba-loyalist irregulars of the CDF.

RUF elements in the junta withdrew into the forest. Supposedly, they were only a remnant awaiting final mopping up. But RUF intransigence was attracting new support. Perhaps raising the possibility of a renegotiation of kimberlite contracts, new backers appear to have been instrumental in securing Eastern European arms supply and military and training assistance for the RUF, to match the assistance to government forces from EO and Sandline (Richards and Fithen 2001).

Sensing that political changes in Nigeria had weakened the resolve of the Nigerian peace-keeping troops, the rearmed RUF, assisted by Ukrainian mercenaries according to some reports, launched an all-out attack on ECOMOG forces late in 1998, driving the Nigerian peace keepers in disarray toward Freetown. Large parts of the capital were destroyed in an attack launched on January 6, 1999. Bereft of military options, the Kabba government had little choice but to resume the aborted peace process with

the RUF, while the country was left to cope with the widespread devastation and population displacement caused by the fighting (450,000 Sierra
Leoneans are refugees, and perhaps up to one million people have been
internally displaced).

Throughout the war, all factions—RUF, NPRC, CDF, international mercenaries, and ECOMOG—have alternated combat with periods of alluvial
diamond mining. At first sight, warfare in Sierra Leone is nothing other
than alluvial diamond mining by other means. True enough, outsiders
have little interest in Sierra Leone beyond its diamonds. But for Sierra
Leoneans, diamond mining is a means through which social and political
projects are articulated. It will be argued that the war cannot be understood unless we pay attention to these projects.

Alluvial Diamonds

Diamonds were first proved in Sierra Leone in the 1930s. Mining became
important after World War II. The main deposits are found in the south
and east of the country, in the high forest zone, in alluvium and river ter-
races. The percentage of gemstone diamonds is among the highest in the
world (Fithen 1999). The richest concessions were allocated to a De Beers
subsidiary in and around Yengema in Kono District, but the profitability of
industrial extraction was threatened by illegal diggers creaming off some
of the best stones. A tributor scheme regularized the activities of illegal
diggers, but eventually (in the 1980s) formal operations ceased and, with
the best deposits approaching exhaustion, the field was left clear to small-
scale producers.

The APC regime of Siaka Stevens (1968–1985) built its power through a
combination of strong-arm methods and the politics of patronage, applied
to the control of small-scale diamond mining in Kono (Reno 1995; Zack-
Williams 1995). Capital was supplied mainly by a Lebanese trading dias-
pora. Maronite and Shia groups were at one stage equally prominent in
mining and marketing Sierra Leone diamonds, but the Maronites shifted
their resources to other projects during the 1970s and 1980s leaving the
field clear for the Shia groups (Fithen 1999).

A typical small-scale alluvial diamond mining operation is likely to involve a Lebanese "supporter" in partnership with a local landowner or a
political protector from the national elite (a policeman, civil servant, or
army officer, for example). A trusted mine manager will supervise a team
of diggers in the bush. Laborers are generally known as "sand-sand boys."
Many are footloose youngsters from Freetown or the northern part of the
country, drifting through the diamond districts in search of excitement or

laboring because they have run out of resources or patronage to complete their education.

Operators in more accessible parts of the alluvial belt generally have mining licenses and are well-supplied and regularly supervised by mining "supporters" (Zack-Williams 1995). Elsewhere—and especially toward the Liberian border, an area of thick forest reserves—operations tend toward greater informality or outright illegality (all mining in the reserves is illegal, so there is no point in seeking a license). Perhaps especially where illegal, any mining venture requires good contacts, both in the national arena and with local landowners and other power brokers, or it will be subject to claim jumping and sabotage.

As the more accessible claims have been worked out, the border districts have assumed greater importance. Experts claim eight years of uncontrolled digging under wartime conditions in Kono have more or less exhausted the Kono alluvials (Fithen 1999). The lesser field at Tongo, on the edge of the Panguma forest concession northwest of Kenema, remains viable and has been hotly contested by all the main armed factions throughout the war. The best alluvial deposits are now reckoned to be in the southeastern border zone, in an arc below the Gola Forest complex of reserves centred on Zimmi in Soro Gbeima Chiefdom, Southern Province, adjacent to the Liberian border. This area was once strongly dominated by the RUF, but more recently, control of the deposits has been wrested by the CDF. Kono's importance is now especially in terms of kimberlite pipes. Kimberlite requires underground mining, sophisticated skills, and equipment available only from international companies.

Diamonds and Politics

Politics in Sierra Leone is strongly patrimonial (Reno 1995; Richards 1996, 1998; Zack-Williams 1995). Most politicians depend to some degree on having links to the mining industry to secure the resources needed to service networks of clients and followers. The central figures in Siaka Steven's APC system had well-established stakes in Kono diamonds. Emergent politicians have to look to the less well-known deposits, including those along the Liberian border, where the war was first incubated. Some of the confusion in the war is traceable to the fact that this is a region where social and political projects are still taking shape, carefully hidden from rivals in transborder obscurity. An ethnography of the domain around the Gola Forest is very revealing of contested projects and the mixed loyalties on which the war has thrived (Richards 1996).

More has been at stake, however, than simply chasing the lesser worked deposits. Changes in the pattern of diamond mining are altering the mold of patrimonial politics in Sierra Leone (Fithen 1999).

As part of plans to control Kono diamonds, Siaka Stevens uprooted the old colonial government railway line that was the axis of power for the rival Sierra Leone People's Party through the South and East (the axis on which many of the main provincial secondary schools lay, for example). Instead, Stevens built a main road leading directly to Kono through the northern provincial centers of Makeni and Magburaka. This helped secure APC political elites more direct control over the Kono alluvials. With the working out of the Kono deposits, however, the pendulum has swung back to the South and East.

The new alluvial field around Zimmi is more readily accessible from Monrovia in Liberia than from Freetown. Halting cross-border incursions for clandestine mining purposes has been a preoccupation of a Mende ethnic elite centered around retired army captain Samuel Hinga Norman, the Kabba government's Deputy Minister of Defence and chief patron of the CDF. Norman bases his activities on the Southern Province headquarters, Bo. CDF units grew from village civil defense (Muana 1997; Peters and Richards 1998) but are now centered on Bo and the other main diamond town in the Southeast, Kenema. The CDF, as developed by Norman and colleagues, is a well-armed modern militia with an offensive capacity (Richards and Fithen 1999). With assistance from EO and Sandline, it has the motivation and capacity to pursue the RUF into its forest lairs.

The CDF is more than defense of villages against RUF raids. It is a clearly articulated political project by Norman, other SLPP politicians, and some of the paramount chiefs of the region to stablize the relationship between diamond mining and society (Fithen 1999). Under the Stevens system in Kono, much of the finance for mining came from Lebanese merchants and much of the digging was done by itinerant northerners. Neither group has a long-term stake in local social systems in alluvial mining areas. This encouraged a degree of recklessness in pursuit of diamonds. Lack of local social responsibility is, in the opinion of the Norman group, one of the factors causing the war. In the emergent "Zimmi System," as described by Fithen (1999), security and digging are the responsibility of local recruits to the CDF, and the marketing chain (as far as Antwerp and New York) is controlled by an elite of Mende chiefs. Ethnic loyalty and discipline are the intended antidote to the mentality of lawless and violent cut-and-run mining that fed the RUF's cross-border incursion from Liberia during the 1990s.

The shift in balance of alluvial mining toward Zimmi (and Tongo, an area controlled by CDF units loyal to Kenema-based SLPP political figures) has in effect allowed the resurgence of a regionalism drawing on Mende ethnic identity. Although there are questions about the longer-term viability of such a strongly ethnic project in a small and highly intermarried nation, it is clear nevertheless that the Norman/CDF project to control diamond mining in the south is a means to reach social and political ends.

A second change in the diamond landscape pulls in a different direction. This is the shift in balance of resources from alluvials to the recently discovered kimberlite. As noted, kimberlite pipes require investment by international mining companies. Alluvial mining requires complex local brokerage, but kimberlite mining focuses attention on the national level. The key issue is not so much the degree of control or influence exercised over local politics but the sovereignty of the national government. The president and cabinet control the all-important central negotiations with concessionaires. To some extent, kimberlite resources have already revitalized national politics, as reflected in the modernist language of figures such as James Jonah, the Kabba government's Minister of Finance, and Charles Margai, Minister of the Interior. Margai rejects civil defense in favor of establishing a rural police force under the control of a centralized Ministry of the Interior. Kimberlite also helps account for the recent rebirth of the RUF, apparently under the aegis of (Eastern European?) mining-cum-security interests, offering the kind of military assistance provided to the government side by British-linked mining interests.

Evidence for this interpretation will be determined by whether the peace agreement with the Kabba government signed by the RUF in mid-1999 leads to longer-term renegotiation of kimberlite options. It was striking that the Kabba government reconfirmed the Branch Energy concession in early 1999, even as it contemplated a revived peace process with the RUF and ECOMOG was struggling to restore control in the capital. Under the 1999 Lome accords, RUF leader Foday Sankoh assumed a position as head of a national minerals commission, with protocol status of vice-president (making him directly accountable only to the president). Sankoh soon used his position to announce the revocation of all existing mineral agreements.

"Diamonds Are a Curse"

The RUF is supposedly a movement without politics or reason to exist. This is the view of those who have other projects to defend. It will be argued that the RUF is plausibly characterized as a social movement of the "masterless classes" (cf. Rebel 1986)—especially young men excluded from the wider society by the exigencies of diamond mining.

ECOMOG troops were welcomed to Kono in 1998 with a graffito, "Diamonds are a curse." Gemstone diamonds, however, are lumps of carbon of no practical use. What makes for trouble is not the diamond itself but what happens to social cooperation and trust in communities dependent on such a high-value but easily concealed item. "Forest" war in Sierra Leone is shaped by diamonds being extracted far from the beaten track by young migrants (in conditions of chronic suspicion and summary violence) lacking local attachments but "supported" by prominent figures in the country's business and political elite.

Diggings spring up overnight at news of a find. One such camp mushroomed in the heart of the unlogged Gola North Forest in 1988. Several hundred diggers descended on the catchment of the Mobai stream, an area earmarked for strict nature reserve protection (Davies 1987). Tools, supplies, and guns (to hunt for the cooking pot) were all rapidly dragged to the site over the rough forest trails. No women are allowed in an instant camp of lean-to shacks and sleeping platforms for fear of spoiling the diggers' luck. Each gang dug and sifted its piles of gravel in forest seclusion for weeks at a time. When raided by forest guards, the camp disappeared as quickly as it had arisen, leaving a devastated site.

I once asked a young digger what would prevent his absconding with any large stone he found. He told me that diggers always keep their companions under close observation. A digger choking on his chewing gum risked having his stomach slit open on the suspicion that he had swallowed a large stone. Then again, he told me, the police operated with speed and surprising efficiency in diamond cases. The sponsors paid well. To his mind, no diamond was worth the beatings the police were liable to administer to extract the truth.

Diamond mining resembles a lottery. Those who, week by week, fail to draw a winning ticket find themselves more and more abandoned and yet addicted to the harsh, asocial way of life of the pits, hoping that yet one more week might result in that big find. It is not in the interests of an elite, living off diamonds, to draw attention to the way in which its wealth is created. Diamond digging groups are a key to the country's economy, but they constitute a cryptic labor force, carefully screened from outside attention. Social conditions in diamond camps and villages are among the worst in the country, especially in the clandestine diggings scattered along the Liberian border. Yet, politicians invested in diamonds are less than keen to agree to open up such areas with roads or to provide social or educational facilities for the families of diggers, for fear of drawing undue attention to their own sources of wealth.

Contesting this carefully maintained lack of visibility, the RUF political program is a populist call to account for the country's misappropriated mineral wealth. The rebel movement first recruited among the most thoroughly marginalized diggers working the "border-zone limbo-lands." Intimate with the processes through which the magic money sustaining national politics is made and angered by social marginalization, this secret army of gravel sifters was quick to heed the call.

From Insurgency to Violent Enclave

Those who first planned the RUF rebellion were drawn mainly from the ranks of the urban unemployed inspired by student radical debate (Abdullah 1997; Abdullah and Muana 1998). Along with Sankoh, an older and embittered survivor from anti-Stevens struggles in the army of the 1970s, the founders of the movement trained in Libya and then acquired field experience as fighters with the Taylor faction in the Liberian civil war. Taylor later reciprocated by helping the RUF guerrilla launch its campaign in Sierra Leone, accompanied by Liberian and Burkinabe "special forces."

These special forces were responsible for some of the worst atrocities against civilians. Fleeing civilians reported a populist violence—the hacking off of the heads of village merchants, for example—in the name of revolutionary justice by young people who spoke in thick Liberian accents, or even in French. Many of the early guerrillas were Sierra Leoneans but residents for long periods in Liberia or Cote d'Ivoire, whence several had fled from diamond-related trouble at home. Samuel Bockarie, de facto senior field commander of the RUF 1997–1999, is typical of this group.

Adopted son of a Kissi from Kailahun on the Liberia-Guinea-Liberia border, Bockarie is a one-time sand-sand boy who claims not to know his father. Quitting the diamond town of Njaiama in Kono, he drifted through Liberia, working in bars, as a disco dancer and eventually learning a trade as a women's hair stylist. He ended up in Abidjan just as the Ivoirian economic miracle was coming to an end. Encountering a party of Sierra Leonean recruits to the RUF en route to a training camp (in Burkina Faso), he claims (according to his own account) to have jumped aboard their truck on a whim. Diamond diggers are ever gamblers, even to the extent of gambling with their lives.

The RUF was at first a conventional insurgency, moving heavy weapons along roads and seeking to hold terrain and towns. Driven back into the forest, mainly by Sierra Leone army irregulars, it then developed a guerrilla strategy suited to its forest-enclaved circumstances.

This second phase was initiated, according to members of the movement's own account, after two years of war. Driven out of the small towns of Kailahun District, the leadership found itself in late 1993 sequestered behind the Gola North forest reserve in Nomo Chiefdom on the border with Liberia contemplating ignominious withdrawal into Liberia (RUF/SL 1995). The path was blocked, however, by a decline in Charles Taylor's military fortunes in the Liberian war. There seemed little option but to try and survive in the forests.

The new strategy involved abandoning heavy weapons and vehicles in favor of infiltration and widely scattered pinprick raids mounted from secure forest camps via the numerous bush trails crisscrossing the country. Along these trails, the small RUF bands were unopposed by vehicle-bound and at times mapless government forces. A wedge was driven between civilians and the NPRC army through a campaign of dirty tricks. RUF cadres carried out many attacks dressed in the uniforms of NPRC troops or left behind forged army-style identity passes to convey the impression that attacks were the work of rogue government troops.

Isolation in the forest of a movement made up largely of diamond diggers and captive primary schoolchildren, with few elders other than Sankoh, now the RUF's unchallenged leader, seems to have selected rather strongly for values associated with so-called enclave social formations. The enclave—Mary Douglas's preferred term for a formation more often described as a "sect" (Douglas 1993; Douglas and Ney 1998; Sivan 1995)—is a group that was organized on the basis of strong internal mutuality and low levels of hierarchy and "walled off" from (an often-hostile) wider society. Enclave entry and exit costs tend to be high, typically involving harsh initiation procedures and sanctions against, or ostracism of, would-be deserters.

Once an enclave has formed (perhaps as much a response to external attempts to disorganize the group as through any internal ideological commitment), distinctive procedures for maintaining adherence (including information-handling procedures to protect the group against desertion) tend to give it life and values of its own.

The RUF appears genuinely proud of its internal egalitarianism—rotation of command among young fighters, model accommodation, redistribution of looted items such as medicines, strong stand against ethnic or religious divisions, and adaptation to high risks associated with combat as a "lottery of life and death" (RUF/SL 1995). But the enclave also held in place the realization among the leadership group that their own safety—especially after increasingly effective, mercenary-supported raids by civil defense forces under cover of cease-fire agreements—depended on draconian attempts to wall off the group from wider society. Desertion was nearly impossible. Runaways were amputated or killed. Any successful escapees, some crudely scarred with the letters "RUF," risked summary execution by government, civil defense, or peace-keeping forces, as apparent from film footage compiled by Sorious Samura, a Freetown-based filmmaker, broadcast on CNN, January 2000, (cf. Amnesty 1991; Peters and Richards 1998; Richards 1998; Richards and Fithen 1999).

Douglas (1993) and Sivan (1995) suggest that enclave leaders are vulnerable to leadership challenges and hands-on managerial mistakes ("Who made you leader over us?" is a typical enclave cry). One option is to cultivate a distanced, charismatic authority. Foday Sankoh, as the movement's one clear elder, seems to have quickly realized the potential of this approach with the de facto distancing from executive control of his movement thus implied. Many cadres saw Sankoh only after occasional hazardous expeditions to reach his Gola Forest base camp (the Zogoda) or knew him only through field radio broadcasts (Peters and Richards 1998). These radio messages became especially intermittent after EO began to track rebel concentrations through monitoring and triangulation of transmissions.

British advice to the Kabba government appears to have been that after the signing of the 1996 Abidjan peace accords, Sankoh was irrelevant. Others thought it important to break his "sinister" hold over his young followers.

The Kabba government made attempts to split the RUF by encouraging Philip Palmer, a southern member of the RUF team sent to Freetown to implement the Abidjan peace agreement, to step up and replace Sankoh. The plan backfired (RUF/SL 1999), and Palmer was seized by the RUF on a visit to Samuel Bockarie's Kailahun stronghold to encourage disarmament in early 1997.

Perhaps in some desperation (the move might seem reckless in the light of enclave theory), the Kabba regime asked the Nigerian authorities to detain Sankoh, on a visit to Nigeria, and hold him under house arrest. As the theory predicts, this served only to strengthen the distant leader's authority in the eyes of his followers. Despite Sankoh being separated from a supposedly apolitical and fragmented movement for more than two years, it was his release from jail in Freetown, where he was awaiting execution for treason, that spurred the well-coordinated attack on Freetown in January 1999. This event humiliated the largely Nigerian peacekeeping troops responsible for Kabba's restoration to power after an army mutiny in May 1997. A reluctant Kabba government, lacking any real military options, released Sankoh on license to play a major part in resumed peace negotiations in mid-1999, resulting in the Lome Accord.

Rain Forest Casuals

In building secure fortresses in the forest, the RUF touched on a more general problem of social identity and social security within the transborder region. I first became aware of the issue when writing up an ethnographic study of villages adjacent to the Gola Forest (reserved forest making up the middle third of the border between Sierra Leone and Liberia). Working on data collected on the eve of the RUF rebellion, it became ap-

parent I was grappling with two fundamentally distinct kinds of rural communities (Richards 1996, 1998).

Type 1 villages (the majority) were still basically agrarian, with political
leadership exercised through a loose hierarchy of "traditional" chiefs.
These chiefs were linked by a Paramount Chief to a national political system shaped by parliamentarians and certain key figures in bureaucracy
and security services. These figures were well connected to the State House
and the president. These national-level "patrons" would pass benefits
downward through the chiefly hierarchy and expect chiefs to maintain local order and, in a variety of ways, to mobilize local political support when
required. Agrarian villages might have quite high numbers of resident
"strangers" (persons born outside the community), but all such persons
would be "tied in" to the social system either through marriage or formal
ties of clientage. Chiefs always were keenly sensitive to new issues that enhanced traditional authority. For example, I found local chiefs closely
monitored the international "conservation" debate (via BBC World Service) because this gave them an enhanced role in land matters, universally
recognized as belonging to their domain. Young people in such villages
were still remarkably "deferential," respecting local bylaws and in awe of
the mystical forces thought to underpin such laws.

Type 2 villages were radically different. For a start, they were hard to visit
and easily might have been missed. A visit not prearranged caused the
population of some of the smaller and least formal settlements to scatter,
leaving nothing but a cloud of marijuana smoke on the breeze or (in one
case) an abandoned but still spinning "ghetto blaster" humming to itself
on a veranda wall. Some such settlements were no more than temporary
and illegal camps of diamond diggers in reserved forest and unmarked on
the map. Others still sometimes enfolded Type 1 village elements—a small
"traditional" population of farmers might sit alongside a larger population
of predominantly male, part-educated diamond diggers hailing from all
parts of the country. There might still be some vestige of "traditional" authority in such cases, but typically the "town chief" would be closely chap-
eroned by a quick-witted and sharply dressed young man who, it would
transpire, was the agent of the principal mining sponsor in the area (perhaps a senior civil servant or military officer). In the villages closest to the
Liberian border in remote and underpopulated Nomo Chiefdom, at least
some of the sponsorship for diamond mining came from Monrovia. On
one of the few occasions that I was able to engage one of these normally
tight-lipped chiefs' minders in conversation, I was treated to a surprisingly
well-informed lecture about British perfidy in delimiting the border to
Liberian disadvantage. These were off-limits communities, known to and
entered only by those under the protection of the political agents of diamond mining in the region. Not even an official authorization from the

government's district officer could prise open the door to one of the largest of these Type 2 settlements given over to diamond mining on the Liberian border and secluded from prying eyes by a 30-kilometer-thick curtain of high forest. In the end, I risked an uninvited and unannounced visit.

Type 2 communities around the Gola Forest were among the first places to succumb to the RUF in 1991, and it was in such villages that the movement, when close to military disaster in 1993, gathered to reconstitute itself as a forest-camped "environmental" movement. All Type 2 settlements are de facto "camps" lacking public facilities such as roads or schools. Manifestly, they are not places where anyone, given the choice, would seek to make a long-term life by founding a family. Yet some indeed were large, remote, and permanent enough to contain entire families.

I narrowly escaped being thrown out of one Type 2 settlement I visited without prior arrangement in 1989. But because it was clear that I was physically incapable of wending my way the twenty miles or so back over the forested Gendema Hills without a night's rest, I was allowed to stay. Hospitality and curiosity then took over, and conversation flowed—about political corruption, about the World Bank (then visiting Freetown to announce a new packet of reforms), about the prospects of those trapped by diamond digging for half a generation without favorable outcome. The result was that I was asked by the diggers to stay for a day or two to carry out a census of households so that the organizers of the community could appeal to the government for assistance with a road and, above all, a school. It was on the minds of the young residents that they wanted their place to become a home, although none could so regard it without a primary school. (What school teacher would ever agree to stay in a settlement eight hours by forest track from even the roughest road?) Conversation played on a recurrent thought that far from being "forever," diamonds are a gambler's ruin and no basis for making communities that work.

Homelessness and Enclave Culture

The young people of the settlement just noted were swept into the RUF during the invasion from Liberia eighteen months later. It became an RUF stronghold and was later obliterated in fighting. Because the RUF picked up so much of its initial following in Type 2 settlements along the border, where camping in the forest was a long-established reality, it is perhaps not surprising to find evidence within the movement, as it became more and more forest enclaved, of the strong desire to make a home, however fluid and dangerous the circumstances.

These concerns are evident in *Footpaths to Democracy*, a document "ghost-written" by Ghanaian (ex-student radical) consultants to the conciliation agency International Alert as preparation for the Abidjan peace process. It accurately reflects some of the movement's circumstances and beliefs (RUF/SL 1995). The descriptions of life in the forest offer an almost cargo-cultlike attention to idealized detail. *Footpaths* claims, and film footage and interviews with cadres confirm, model "planned" camps based around neat lines of sleeping huts, complete with mosque and church, inside a defensive ring in the forest. Daily life is organized to reflect Libyan *Green Book*–inspired redistribution according to young people's basic needs.

The organized way the RUF set about running its camps, and the draconian discipline asserted therein may have been a factor in the apparent rapid conversion of some captives from Type 2 settlements to the cause. Camp life also gave a certain temporary tangibility to the RUF's stated ambition for Sierra Leone of a road, a school, and a health center in every village.

A shared legacy of "homelessness" thus seems to be a central factor in whether the RUF made sense to its conscripts. Those with families and villages report they longed always to escape. Others lacking any such secure home (however poor it might be) were determined to create a place for themselves and to achieve some kind of social recognition, by whatever violent means it took (Peters and Richards 1998). A stop-at-nothing violence appears to be the special province of the most rootless of the elements making up the RUF—the Liberian-born or Liberian-based "special forces" of Sierra Leonean extraction remaining with the RUF after Liberian (and Burkinabe) fighters supplied by Taylor were withdrawn in 1992.

Even with the collapse of the Abidjan peace accords, many of the local captives still hoped to find their old homes. But the longer-term homeless in the RUF—diamond-digging drifters like Bockarie—had only the option to press on, in the hope they might one day claim recognition from the nation and not the village. This would help explain the anti-ethnic stance of the RUF and why villagers supporting civil defense eventually became the target for a violence more reckless and apparently indiscriminate than the populist antitrader, antigovernment worker violence characteristic of the first phase of the RUF struggle (1991–1993). It was ethnically mobilized villagers who, increasingly, stood between the RUF and this claim to national recognition. Where earlier villagers had simply rejected the RUF revolutionary call, what was now clear to the RUF diehards was that rural society was no home at all but merely an expedient to shed some of the costs associated with the social reproduction of the casual worker in alluvial pits. "Who needs that kind of home?" seems to be have been the conclusion. Wipe out all traces, and begin again.

Camp Burkinabe

One of the persistent popular assumptions about the war in Sierra Leone is that Burkinabe fighters take a leading role in RUF attacks. Evidence of Burkinabe involvement is sketchy. Even so, popular perception may hint at an underlying truth.

The greatest historical example of the "homelessness" of youth in West Africa is that of Burkina Faso, fount of a major coastward migration of youth under French colonialism. Migration to Cote d'Ivoire or Ghana was supposed to equip Burkinabe youth with the resources to return home and take a recognized place in village society.

But labor migration in West Africa no longer works as it once did. In particular, the overexpanded cash crop economy of Cote d'Ivoire ran into extreme economic difficulty in the late 1980s. Burkinabe youths were among its prominent casualties.

Here we should understand that "Burkinabe" stands for impoverished young castoffs, from a wide range of backgrounds, dumped along the migration trails leading into Cote d'Ivoire and unable to fund or face a return home. To survive, a number of "Burkinabes" of this description have drifted into the clandestine activities possible in the dense forest block that stretches from southwestern Cote d'Ivoire, through Liberia, into eastern Sierra Leone. Fearing being trapped into hustling indefinitely and locked out of urban work and rural home, some were quick to jump aboard the militia recruiter's bus, as Taylor's and Sankoh's violent projects to transmute circular migration into "forest" war took shape in the late 1980s.

For many of these "Burkinabes" (and not just young people born in Burkina Faso) in spirit the radical Thomas Sankara, the military ruler of Burkina Faso in the mid-1980s, was a hero. They credit Sankara with trying to address the problem of securing stable futures for footloose youth. His political intervention, however, was a challenge to a business element already threatened by imminent loss of subsidies from France, Africa's last great colonial power, and he was overthrown in a coup in 1987. NPRC Vice-Chairman Solomon Musa (later an RUF ally) and Sankoh are among those in the region who aspired to fill the gap, seeing themselves as revolutionary Pied Pipers to homeless youth.

When from the wreckage of Sankoh's aborted youth revolution in Sierra Leone the RUF invented the world of the forest camps, it opened a chasm in social values between enclaved cadres and deferential villagers whose poverty reproaches their loyalty to diamond-mining chiefs. The RUF tried to rub out the reproach by force. Civil defense emerged in reaction as an attempt to find a better link between "new" (diamond) money and "old" social values. The battle still rages between camp dwellers and neotraditional civil defense, with dire consequences for the civilians caught in between.

Meanwhile, RUF diehard Sam Bockarie's redoubt on the border between Kono and Kailahun—halfway between diamond workplace and agrarian birthplace—is somehow fittingly named for a citadel in which violent egalitarian social values break so sharply with both the individualism of (capitalist) work and the hierarchy of (deferential) home. It is Camp Burkina.

Home at Last?

The cadres at the heart of the RUF suffer a sense of injustice at their social exclusion from a country where the political classes build their power and authority on money made from diamonds in dubious cross-border social terrain. Encouraged by Libyan radicalism, RUF organizers sought common cause with border-zone diggers experiencing the contradictions of an economy in which the beneficiaries of diamond wealth move toward international respectability, while unlucky diggers find themselves driven by rough justice out of the nation and into "limbo-land."

Latent egalitarian tendencies fostered by life in diamond pits were intensified by forest sequestration, where young inductees had little option but to cooperate in elaborating an enclave social world, beset, as they were, by outside attempts to provoke desertion and by threat of summary execution. RUF leaders originally envisaged an end game in terms of triumphant entry to the capital and their acceptance as saviors of the nation. Instead the RUF became a sect by default (Richards 1998). It knows how to survive in diamond-rich forest indefinitely, but no one yet has had the wit to devise a scheme to bring it out of the forest and calm its sectarian anger.

Homelessness is still the movement's bugbear. The RUF anthem insists "Sierra Leone is our home" but then warns parents that their abducted children are "fighting in the battlefield for ever." Indeed, the leading cadres hardly have homes to which to return, yet they retain a strong sense of the nation as their home. This is surely the residual around which peace will have to be constructed.

Conclusion

Insisting that "forest" wars in Africa are economic phenomena narrows the range of options in favor of private security but not in a way—as events suggest—that deals successfully or permanently with the radical homelessness of groups like the RUF. Ignoring, or denying, the social projects of the perpetrators of "forest" war in Africa risks also disabling peaceful social solutions. The cost of such asocial dogmatism will be high. Even though an African refugee costs the United Nations refugee agency only one-fifteenth the average per diem costs of a Kosovo refugee, the agency spends 40–50 percent of its total budget in Africa. The profitability of international mineral extraction is without reference to such high "transaction costs," in part the result of the spread of "forest" war (in Angola, the two Congos, Liberia, Sierra Leone, and the Niger Delta). This is why, more than ever before, it is essential to understand the sociology of resource-linked violence in Africa. British Prime Minister Tony Blair, challenged about support from Sandline International for the restoration of President Kabba, dismissed doubters with the remark, "The good guys won." By implication, the "bad guys" were the RUF. Given Mr. Blair's strong concern to reverse the social exclusion of the young in his own country, following a period of devil-take-the-hindmost capitalism, it is highly ironic if the RUF, as argued here, is best to be understood as a violent attempt to reverse homelessness and social exclusion caused by rampant alluvial diamond extraction in Sierra Leone. The stubborn survivalism of Sierra Leone's "rebels without cause" hints that the violence of "forest" war enfolds within it a social project after all.

4

Territory, Custom, and the Cultural Politics of Ethnic War in West Kalimantan, Indonesia[1]

Nancy Lee Peluso and Emily Harwell

We let them come and settle here and farm. We let them bring their
cows. But they didn't realize that our hospitality had limits. If you visit
someone's house and try to kill your host, there has to be some retaliation (*balas*).

> Dayak villager's comment during a 1991 interview

They [other Dayaks] would come [from all over Borneo] if we asked
them. But the truth is, we don't need them. We are a race of warriors.
Just a few Dayaks are enough to wipe out all the Madurese.

> Statement by a young Dayak in Pontianak, 1997

The state is continually formed and reformed in terms of those included
or excluded as citizens and by what is thinkable and unthinkable.

> (Vickers 1998: 778)

In January and February of 1997, violence exploded in the Borneo province of West Kalimantan, Indonesia, rivaling the region's bloody
political turmoil of the late 1960s. As in the 1960s, the violence began in
the district of Sambas and spread to adjoining districts. Mobs and gangs of

1. The materials presented in this chapter are drawn primarily from Harwell's fieldwork before, during, and after the conflict, Peluso's fieldwork before and after the conflict, local
chronologies of the conflict, and the Human Rights Watch (1997) report. We should note at
the outset that this has been a difficult chapter to write. Many, if not most, of our friends and
colleagues who work in Indonesia advised against it, and we have both considered abandoning the project many times. Ultimately, we felt compelled to write this paper by our desires to
make sense of these events. In no way is this paper meant to be an apology for the horrible
acts committed by individuals. Rather, it is an attempt to contribute to a better understanding of why events occurred in the manner and at the moments that they did. If knowledge is

both Dayaks and Madurese burned houses, destroyed crops, and forced people from their homes; some Madurese were airlifted out by the military. Most normal aspects of daily life were abandoned for more than two months. At least five hundred people[2] were killed in this communal war between these two ethnic groups—Dayaks and Madurese.[3] While many Dayaks lost their lives and property, victims of these battles were primarily Madurese. Some twenty-five thousand Madurese were displaced from the homes they had occupied over the last thirty years. After they left, some local people purchased or appropriated the fields, gardens, and house sites Madurese had formerly occupied. In some locales, Madurese families returned within a few months and began rebuilding their destroyed property with housing grants provided by the national government. Further violence two years later, however, eliminated many of the remaining Madurese from the province's countryside.[4]

Observers have described the violence in 1996–1997 in various ways: as the probable outcome of political manipulation by Indonesian authorities (Human Rights Watch 1997), "a complex cultural clash" (IDRD 1998), and a "classic example of economic tensions manifested as ethnic tensions" (Dove 1997). Davidson (1998) comes closest to our argument by examining macro-structural factors that have set the stage historically for violence. Although each of these analyses contributes to our understanding of the situation, we argue that the violence between the Dayaks and the Madurese was a West Kalimantan–specific experience of Suharto's New Order territorial politics, and especially the politics surrounding property, resources, and ethnicity, the region's long history of violence, and the cultural politics of violent identity production affecting the two groups that clashed.

Both sensationalist and serious media accounts, and other analyses, have attributed this violence to the reenactment of headhunting practices that they claim or imply have characterized "Dayak" cultural practice from time immemorial. In most Dayak accounts, however, long-gone headhunting practices did not motivate the 1997 killings. Such violent ethnic identities, with forms specific to Madurese as well as Dayaks, have been produced and

power, then perhaps this kind of understanding can help in future efforts to prevent the recurrence of massive violence in West Kalimantan and elsewhere. Though we take full responsibility for the material presented here, we appreciate comments on early drafts of this paper from Christine Padoch, Peter Zinoman, Aaron Bobrow-Strain, Michael Watts, Paul and Jennifer Alexander, Robert Hefner, Jack Putz, Michael Leigh, and Jayl Langab.

2. This figure is taken from the final report by Human Rights Watch (HRW), published in December 1997, but the exact toll is impossible to document.

3. The Dayaks are indigenous to the island of Borneo, while Madurese have migrated there over the past two generations, primarily in search of labor opportunities, from the island of Madura off the northern coast of Java, and from Eastern Java.

4. Violent events that occurred after 1997 are beyond the scope of this paper. In explaining the 1999 violence, which involved Malays allied with Dayaks against Madurese, observers describe it as the most ferocious (*ganas*) of any to date (interviews 1999). Parsudi Suparlan (2000) has prepared one preliminary report on this violence.

strategically deployed for decades—not only by state actors and institutions, but also by researchers, journalists, novelists, nongovernment institutions, and local people themselves. Fascinated commentators and actors have simultaneously reinvented, demonized, glorified, and downplayed this legendary form of Dayak violence.

We argue here that the events of 1997 cannot be explained as some primordial return to "headhunting." Headhunting occurred under very specific conditions, was much more prominent in other parts of Borneo, and was documented predominantly (but not only) among other people lumped as "Dayaks," but with different histories and customary practices from those who lived in the regions of the 1997 rural violence in Sambas, Pontianak, and Sanggau districts. Moreover, taking heads is not the same as "headhunting" (*ngayau*). The former is what happens during war, the latter was motivated by the need to fulfill ritual obligations. More clearly, however, the violence strategically associated with these constructions of Dayaks as headhunters can be seen to be part of larger battles to control territory, natural resources, and the activities and claims of the human populations using them.

We believe an analysis of the 1997 violence requires an understanding of earlier patterns of "Dayak" violence, particularly the political violence of the Indonesian military and the Dayaks they incited against rural Chinese in 1967–68.[5] Both 1967–68 and 1996–97 were moments in periods of major global political economic change and of national and local social upheaval and uncertainty. At both times, the legal and everyday terms of governance, resource control, and collective identity were radically transforming. The denouement of the Chinese "Demonstration" in 1968 was the violent displacement from rural areas of some 117,000 ethnic Chinese during the late 1960s and early 1970s[6] from primarily the western sections of West Kalimantan—the same rural districts where the violence against Madurese took place.[7] That conflict—and to a lesser extent the smaller violent incidents between Dayaks and Madurese in the intervening three decades—had some crucial parallels with the events of 1997. In future writings, these two periods will be compared more closely.[8] In this chapter,

5. J. Davidson (1998) also examines the structural similarities of national-level government intervention in various local conflicts in West Kalimantan, going back to the *kongsi* wars of 1850.
6. This figure is from the calculations of Douglas Kammen, personal communication, 1/23/2000. Contemporary accounts from the immediate aftermath of the Demonstrasi—such as Feith (1968)—estimated around 58,000 displaced. Coppel (1984) estimated some 55,000 evicted; this same number is cited in the Human Rights Watch Report on the Davak-Madurese events (1997).
7. Chinese were evicted from all over northwestern West Kalimantan, but the focus of this chapter is primarily on Sambas district and parts of Sanggau and Pontianak districts.
8. N. Peluso is writing a book on violent and nonviolent aspects of the agrarian/forest landscapes of West Kalimantan. See also, "Weapons of the Wild: Strategic Deployment of Wildness and Violence in West Kalimantan, Indonesia." In Candace Slater, ed., *In Search of the Rainforest*. University of California Press, forthcoming.

we show that at the historical moment it occurred in 1997, the "Madurese war,"[9] as local Dayaks and others call it, was intended at least partially to signal a reclamation of the Dayaks' historically occupied spaces, resources, and identities, and to demonstrate the protection of their collective honor. The notion of *kawasan*, or territory, is a crucial part of their collective concerns.

The conjuncture of certain social and geographical relationships have made West Kalimantan unique among the Borneo provinces,[10] for it is the only one that has experienced the kinds of extensive and repeated ethnic violence we describe here. These relationships include the nature of colonial and national rule in the region and, in particular, the value and relative inaccessibility of its natural resources. Until the 1960s, these resources were almost entirely controlled by local people over whom both colonial and early national state hegemony were truly incomplete. West Kalimantan also has a very specific experience with militarization under Indonesian governance. Moreover, the region has a unique social history that shaped the ways ethnicity and citizenship have constituted contested discourses of access to resources through law, custom, and practice. In the thirty years since the establishment of New Order and its bloody arrival in West Kalimantan, the Dayak community's dissatisfaction with agencies of the national state—the military as well as various departments of forest and land management—has only grown. We argue that this dissatisfaction was caused by three longer-term trends that accelerated under Suharto: (1) the state's direct role in the alteration of the spatial and social distribution of resource production activities, which included changing the loci of the territorial authority determining resource access; (2) many, if not most, Dayaks feel excluded from the political and economic benefits flowing from development efforts based on their region's resources; (3) state-sponsored violence and terror that originated in the 1960s continued in full force through 1974 and remained as a threat until the mid-1990s. In other words, Indonesian rule by practical disenfranchisement and violence generated a great deal of resentment in the local people.

These arguments, however, do not explain why violence took place in 1996–97 or why only Madurese were targeted. For this, it is necessary to explore the specifics of Dayak–Madurese social relationships and the rea-

---

9. *Perang Madura.*
10. The island of Borneo is currently divided between Indonesia, Malaysia, and Brunei. The Sultanate of Brunei is an independent nation-state. Sabah and Sarawak are states in the Federation of Malaysia (also collectively known as "East Malaysia," and there are four provinces in the Republic of Indonesia: West, Central, East, and South Kalimantan. References to "the Bornean provinces" in this chapter refer to all these political units, regardless of their national affiliation. References to "Kalimantan" or "Dutch Borneo" refer only to the Indonesian and Netherlands' East Indies territories, respectively.

sons why their respective cultural politics of violence pitted the two groups against each other. While a full exploration of the production of violent identities goes beyond the scope of this chapter, it is critical to understand what makes these violent events different from the increasing violence across Indonesia. We concentrate here on the ways the Indonesian government's discourses of development, ethnicity, and nationality have clashed with alternative discourses of territorial authority and identity production in contexts of extreme tension.

The 1996–1997 Dayak–Madurese War

Two Dayak youths were stabbed at a pop music concert in Sanggau Ledo, Sambas, on December 29, 1996, by a group of Madurese seeking revenge for friends humiliated at a previous concert for "bothering" a Dayak girl. Rumors spread that the two Dayaks had been killed, although they were treated and released from the hospital that night. The police denied having made arrests, although they had in fact arrested two Madurese.[11] A crowd of Dayaks demanding legal and ritual retribution stormed into town and burned houses. Over the next month, thousands of Dayaks rioted through the western districts of West Kalimantan,[12] burning hundreds of Madurese houses and market stalls and destroying Madurese crops. Official reports on damages at the point of origin only—Sanggau Ledo— amounted to some RP. 13.56 billion, then worth approximately U.S. $6 million (HRW 1997). Mosques were left undamaged, even those in Madurese neighborhoods, in a pointed effort not to damage places of religious significance to other ethnic groups, and thus to demonstrate, as some people said, that this particular clash was not about the usual scapegoat of religious differences.

Within a week of the initial riots, some six thousand Madurese from Sanggau Ledo had been evacuated to police and military posts in the city of Singkawang; others continued to engage in violence in other parts of the affected region. Madurese retaliated in organized fashion within the same month. Large gangs of them burned Dayak houses in communities in and around Singkawang and assaulted Dayak women in and around the city of Pontianak (the provincial capital) and elsewhere. On January 28, 1997, a throng of Madurese attempted to burn down a Catholic Non-

---

11. This refusal to reveal information about the arrests was reportedly out of fear that the accused would be victims of the crowd's vigilante justice (HRW 1997).
12. The main areas affected were the Districts (*Kabupaten*) of Sambas, Pontianak, and Sanggau, and the "Dayak groups" most involved in rural violence speak Salako and Kenayatn languages. They self-identify as "Dayak," some call themselves Salako or Kenayatn, respectively.

Governmental Organization (NGO) office in Pontianak, stabbing two young Dayak women in the process[13]. As the Human Rights Watch report observed, "No target could have been designed to cause greater outrage in the Dayak community"—attacking at once icons of Christianity and female vulnerability (attacking young women rather than young men/warriors), and an organization established by Dayaks for self-development (HRW 1997). The vulnerability of other victims of Madurese violence also enraged the Dayak community, including a mentally challenged Dayak man chopped to pieces in a Singkawang market. Madurese youths also set up roadblocks and tried to intercept and kill all passing Dayaks, pulling them from cars and buses and stabbing, shooting, drowning, or dismembering them. One of the victims in this case was a Dayak village leader who was returning home from his daughter's college graduation; ironically, he had earlier forbidden Dayaks under his jurisdiction from joining the violence against Madurese.

By February 2, enraged by the government's inaction to stop the violence, Dayaks passed the "red bowl,"[14] the ritual symbol carried from village to village and used in the past to call other Dayaks to war.[15] By February 5, rituals to awaken the ancestral war spirits were performed on Dayak war parties in villages throughout the area. Hundreds of Dayaks went to the hills for those rituals and descended into the streets in mobs, some walking, some riding in vans or trucks. Many claimed or were believed to be in "the killing trance," their bodies possessed by ancestral warrior spirits who controlled their actions. Others carried amulets and traditional protective objects to protect them from harm, hide them when they were hunting Madurese, and give them the courage to do things most (particularly the massive numbers of them under age 30) had only heard about in stories. The crowds marched, sang, and demanded justice; some burned and smashed Madurese houses; some killed Madurese people and their livestock.

Information, rumors, and misinformation circulated like the red bowl—no one claimed to know where they came from or where they would go next. Once the bowl was sent around and the state of war declared, village residents—the women, children, and the physically challenged—literally took to the hills, hiding as far from the main valley roads as possible. An atmosphere of great fear prevailed, punctuated occasionally by the sounds of village warning gongs, the shrieking of close or distant war cries, the rushing up and down the roads of vans and trucks full of young and old Dayak men and a few women, or of gangs of Madurese on motorcycles or in their

---

13. This NGO, called *Pancur Kasih,* houses a Dayak credit union and a community-mapping project for negotiating for local land rights.
14. *Mangkok merah:* a bowl filled with chicken blood, feathers, and other ritual items carried from one village to another as a call to war against a common enemy.
15. It remains unclear who exactly initiated the red bowl in this conflict.

own vans, and of course the constant rumors of imminent Madurese attacks. Some Dayaks, already victims or anticipating Madurese attacks, took refuge in police barracks; in some barracks they lived side by side with frightened Malays, Chinese, and Madurese. From places of refuge in the village, many women and girls participated in the fight by making bullets out of gunpowder and copper, cooking food for the men guarding village entrances, and listening to or retelling the stories of those returning from forays elsewhere. Groups of Dayaks guarded the entry roads into their villages, took over whole intersections in the interior, and checked the occupants of passing cars and trucks—even military vehicles—watching for the entry of Madurese. Not even the government troops stationed in the province were willing to confront them in the early days of the conflict. The troops claimed the violence was beyond their control.

The media and other storytellers were fascinated with particular forms of the violence. They interviewed people who admitted to having seen members of their war parties consume the livers, blood, or cooked flesh of their victims. Eyewitnesses reported heads paraded on sticks and hundreds of rotting, sometimes headless, corpses stinking up the sides of the highways far into the interior. The eventual fate of most of these missing heads is not clear.[16]

No Chinese were targeted.[17] Chinese shopkeepers closed their shops, and some placed cases of water, dried noodles, and other supplies outside their doors for the Dayak "troops" encamped along the roads at points of entry into villages. They also allowed their trucks and other transport vehicles to be used to carry groups of Dayaks around the region. This is not surprising given that the Indonesian stereotype of tensions between Chinese and *pribumi* (the term for "native" Indonesians) is a poor fit in Sambas historically (see, e.g., Jackson 1970). In addition, Chinese at lower ends of the economic strata, small shopkeepers or people in the transport business, were to some degree actively competing with Madurese entrepreneurs moving into these lower sectors of the business community. This competition, plus the frequently expressed conviction that Madurese were "by nature" thieves who were, more often than not, hot-tempered and quick to draw a knife, partially explains why local Chinese who chose sides chose to ally with the Dayaks.[18]

Nor did angry Dayaks collectively target groups of possible "others."

16. Many heads apparently were sent to two villages where local experts apparently still knew how to ritually treat them, as was customary under the "traditional" practice of headhunting (interviews October 1998). Others remained in the forests among plantation trees or were tossed into gutters alongside the roads.

17. At least one Chinese was reported killed by accident; he had been cutting fodder in a field at the time of one of the first armed confrontations between the military and Dayak villagers in Sambas (authors' interviews 1998).

18. A more important explanation is the long-term relationships between Dayaks and Chinese in this region.

Malays stayed out of the way and would not join up with either side.[19] Javanese and other government-sponsored transmigrants,[20] much more numerous than Madurese in the region, were similarly ignored: none of their houses, shops, livestock, or persons were purposely attacked. This unfolding of violent events eliminated the usual reasons put forward to explain the violence as one of "indigenous people" of Borneo toward any and all migrants: Javanese constitute by far the largest group of immigrants. The actual events also refute the "religious" explanation, since all Malays and many Javanese are Muslim like the Madurese. Finally, the standard explanation for ethnic violence—jealously about the economy—and the usual target of such jealousy—the Chinese—also could not be used. Something else was going on.

Government efforts to step in and "cool" things with makeshift ritual ceremonies at various points only inflamed the situation. Many Dayaks viewed these efforts as purposeful manipulation and misunderstandings of their customary practices, or *adat*. Human Rights Watch investigators reported Dayaks' resentment of the government's perceived interference:

> . . . Dayaks were angry with the army, because it was not the army they were at war with, it was the Madurese, and they did not understand the army's behavior. (HRW 1997)

One aspect of the army's behavior that they clearly did not understand was their use of violence against Dayaks, both when Dayaks were about to attack Madurese communities and after Dayaks had surrendered.[21] A Dayak NGO's response to the HRW report writes the local scorn of the state's role as mediators:

> Recommendations [of the HRW report] that call for the greater intervention of the State to stop attacks and to arrest the organizers of the attacks,

19. At least one Malay who openly sided with the Madurese was reported by informants to have been killed. The reason given by the Dayak narrator of this story was that he was guarding an arsenal of Madurese guns, knives, and other weapons and would not abandon his post. Much later, in additional violence in the Sambas region in March 1999, Malays became involved in similar violent episodes against remaining Madurese. See Suparlan 2000.
20. Note that the Madurese were by and large spontaneous migrants, not part of government-sponsored transmigration programs. Indonesians frequently refer to these spontaneous migrants as "spontaneous transmigrants" to the area. The use of "transmigrants" for these two very different forms of sponsored and unsponsored movement often confuses the interpretation of the situation.
21. This also is one reason that the Dayaks were angry with the army but rarely expressed anger at the police. The police, it seems, did not kill Dayaks outright as the army did, nor did they kick them and torture them in the back rooms of their police stations as did soldiers who in some instances (illegally) took captured Dayaks to their posts for "interrogation."

both Dayak and Madurese, only interferes with the *adat* process and involves the state in a conflict to which it is not party, despite its role in setting up the situation where Dayak land was taken by the Madurese. It is the State's interference in the life of the Dayak that has led to the experience of so much hardship, the taking of land, and threats to culture. (IDRD 1998: 6)

Despite the state's claim to the mediator role, government actors never explained why military and police authorities neither tried very hard to contain the initial rioting in Sanggau Ledo in December 1996 nor stopped Madurese or Dayak rioters from moving elsewhere in the region from the starting point in Sanggau Ledo, to Singkawang, Bengkayang, Samalantan, and Montrado during the first weeks of the conflict. The government neither empowered Dayak leaders with the authority to try and calm their local people nor invited them to work with the police, military, and regional government authorities to come up with an immediate strategy to contain the violence. After the red bowl was passed, the task of stopping things became much more complex. Peacemaking was further complicated by the military's more active involvement in February, the second month of the violence. Groups of soldiers set traps for Dayak groups en route to Madurese neighborhoods and fired directly on approaching, armed Dayak youths in trucks, vans, or on foot. Moreover, once the arrested Dayaks put down their arms, stripped, and put their hands behind their heads, the soldiers fired on them again. The soldiers also went to the roadside rice fields where people were hiding and sprayed their semiautomatic and automatic weapons across the landscape. Many, if not most, of the Dayaks killed in the course of this war were killed by soldiers, often after surrendering.[22] The military was henceforth narrated as the enemy of the Dayaks. However, the military was not targeted subsequently for retaliatory violence because, according to many people we interviewed, the military represented the Indonesian state. This war, they explained, was between Dayaks and Madurese.

Resources and the Politics of Coercion

We need to step back from the specifics of this conflict to study the larger context within which it took place. West Kalimantan province is one of Borneo's richest in terms of easily accessible and valuable resources. Its good ports and strategic coastal location along the sea routes between China and India or the Middle East made it more easily accessible to early traders and settlers from other parts of the wider region, many of whom

22. HRW report; videos made by IDRD; authors' interviews.

traded forest and sea products off this coast for centuries. The Sambas and Mempawa mines produced more gold than any other site on the planet in the late eighteenth century, and these mines were largely controlled by the Chinese miners who had migrated there. They formed political-economic organizations called *Kongsi* to organize extraction, trade, and access to gold. In the mid-nineteenth century, the Dutch launched a major military action against these Chinese to gain control of those lucrative resources and to bolster their weak political power in the region (Irwin 1955). Dutch actions drove many Chinese out—back to China or over the border into Sarawak—and forced others into agriculture. The Dutch also bolstered Malay sultanates as governing institutions, in familiar regional patterns of indirect rule.

It can also be said that for the last one hundred fifty years, West Kalimantan has been the most militarized area of all Borneo, both because of Dutch designs on West Borneo gold and due to British and Dutch colonial politics during the nineteenth century (Irwin 1955). The international border area was a site of violent contention between British and Dutch-claimed parts of Borneo during the Japanese occupation of World War II. Moreover, the province was the key site from which the Indonesian national government operationalized two violent nationalist dramas in the 1960s: the low-intensity conflict against the Federation of Malaysia, called "Confrontation"[23] and the eight-year internal search for communist guerrillas in its aftermath.[24] These "counter-insurgency operations" were meant to secure national unity by determining the color of national and regional politics, permitting no red (communist), only light green (moderate Islam), and shades of gray (central government support). Thus, the first Indonesian troops landed in West Kalimantan to neutralize an "external" enemy and direct violence outward; later the enemy was perceived to be on the "inside," and military violence was directed inward. This pattern would be repeated in subsequent years in Indonesia.

In addition to the thousands of troops stationed in West Kalimantan

23. Sukarno argued that the formation of Malaysia was a neocolonial strategy intended to maintain British hegemony in the region. He also argued that Sarawak was a "natural" geographical part of Indonesia and should become part of the relatively new Indonesian Republic instead of the pending Federation of Malaysia. Thus the name Sukarno used for Sarawak, "*Kalimantan Utara*" or Northern Kalimantan.

24. Confrontation took place between 1963 and 1966 when Sukarno opposed the formation of the Federation of Malaysia—which included both the peninsular states of Malaya and the Borneo states—both the post-World War II British Crown Colonies of Sarawak and Sabah, and the Sultanate of Brunei. The post-Confrontation counterinsurgency effort was equally, if not more, traumatic in the region: it involved massive relocations, enormous military maneuvers, and extensive guerrilla warfare directed inward against the local population of Chinese and involving the creation of a terror-filled atmosphere for everyone. I am grateful to Doug Kammen for reminding me of the extent of these latter operations.

during Confrontation, units of the elite KKO (*Komando Kujan Operasi*), the police Mobile Brigade, and RPKAD took part in operations in Borneo, as did units of the Siliwangi, Diponegoro, and Brawijaya divisions of the army in 1966–1968 (Dennis and Gray 1996: 212). A battalion of special forces troops *(Regimen Pasukan Khusus Angkatan Darat,* RPKAD, the Army Para-commando Regiment) and the Mobile Brigade, a 20,000-man-strong military division, were brought in just after the "Chinese Demonstration" (Coppel 1983: 146). The character of the military presence in the 1960s and 1970s was aggressive: open, actively violent, and a dominant force in the everyday social, political, and cultural experiences of almost everyone in West Kalimantan. The presence of so many troops and their frequent interactions with local people made violence and the fear of it a fact of everyday life.

Very different geopolitics—and a different general mood—prevailed throughout the next thirty years of the New Order. In 1967, the year after General Suharto took over the presidency from President Sukarno, Foreign Investment Act No. 1 and Forest Law No. 5 were passed, enabling the large-scale exploitation of forest resources. Begun simply as a trickle under the Dutch before the war,[25] the demarcation of permanent state forest lands in West Kalimantan had been held up because of World War II, the Japanese Occupation, and the Indonesian Revolution. After Independence, only minimal efforts at forestry were accomplished. The regional uprisings, Sukarno's refusal of the terms of most foreign investment, and the relatively unfavorable world markets for Indonesian forest products deterred extensive forest investment outside of Java. Development and modernization were based on classic models of development economics and the psychological notions of achievement motivation contained within these.

The New Order government systematically excluded Dayaks from positions of political power and, many say, national respect. During fieldwork, people frequently complained to us that after Suharto took power, there were no more Dayak governors and only one or two Dayak District Officers (Bupati). Dayaks rarely occupied positions of authority in municipal or regional government. As discussed in the next section, after the establishment of the Independent Indonesian republic, colonial legal pluralism designating types of land rights or territorial authority by ethnic or "racial" characteristics was abolished and replaced by a claim to "Unity in Diversity" and what was called cultural pluralism. In government terms, however, this "cultural" sector was very limited and did not include, for exam-

---

25. There were only twelve foresters in all of Borneo in 1927. Forest demarcation as state forest only began in 1932, and before the war only a few thousand hectares were actually designated state forests (Peluso and Vandergeest n.d.).

ple, cultures of land and resource ownership. The government represented "Dayak culture" as involving headhunting, powerful magic, "animist" religious beliefs not recognized by the state, and a broad, pejoratively interpreted form of agriculture, shifting cultivation. All these practices were antithetical to the government's ideal attributes of the modern Indonesian citizen. The disorderly, primitive, and violent identities ascribed to Dayaks in general were used to marginalize them nationally: socially, economically, and politically. Even in their own schools, "students are taught not to appreciate their own cultural and social heritage" (Djuweng 1997).

Independence brought new forms of state territorial control over land, resources, and people and enabled both new forms of capitalist and state enterprise in West Kalimantan and the organized and spontaneous resettlement of people from other parts of Indonesia. Most of these changes in the structures of access to land and resources, however, were only realized after Suharto took power in 1960. With the financial and technical assistance of international agencies such as the Food and Agriculture Organization (FAO) and the World Bank, the government mapped, demarcated, and allocated the management of areas they now called production and protection forests to corporate timber concessions and international conservation NGOs. Zoning was the new mechanism by which space was to be organized and people controlled: within particular land use zones, certain people—usually *not* the local people—could conduct specific activities.

The New Order government established boundaries around villages, redesigned whole working landscapes, and ultimately transformed the lifestyles of thousands of people. By 1997, the national policy of development built on resource extraction had rearranged both the physical landscapes of West Kalimantan and the mechanisms of resource access. Spatial reorganization was particularly important to the political economy of this province of Kalimantan, because, unlike East Kalimantan, it did not have the oil and natural gas reserves. Forest and agricultural products were most important in West Kalimantan, with wood products alone providing some 68 percent of the province's total export value in the late 1980s (Cleary and Eaton 1992: 157).

Both organized and spontaneous transmigration, the provision of land to former soldiers for their service to the state[26] (*TransAD*), and road building projects provided opportunities for Indonesian citizens from other regions to come to Kalimantan. These developments occupied huge tracts of land, much of it previously forested. Much of this land was already claimed by local people but their claims were no longer recognized by the new legal system.

26. Called *Transmigrasi Angkatan Darat,* or TransAD, Army Resettlement.

Though the losses of land and resources experienced by local people are difficult to quantify, the zoning categories provide some indication. From 1979–1989, for example, the two five-year plans covering this period allocated a total of 94,290,000 hectares of "Forest Area" for the transmigration program. This area was divided among five land-use zones, defined by the government as parts of State Forest: Limited Production Forest, Regular Production Forest, Conversion Forest, Unclassified Forest, and Conservation/Protection Forest (Potter 1996: 30). According to both agrarian and forest laws, State Forest consisted of all lands not alienated by title or for which continuous use could not be proven; agricultural lands in fallow, therefore, were considered de facto part of State Forest. Although in some cases the assignment of a tract of forest to one of these categories was arbitrary, the most widely disputed areas were often in the tracts called Conversion Forest and Unclassified Forest. In these areas, the commercial "quality" of the forest was often questioned, in many cases because parts of it had been managed locally for field agriculture or the production of perennials such as rubber, fruit, oil seeds, ironwood, and other locally managed species. These two categories alone made up nearly 75 percent of the forest given away to the transmigration program for industrial production and smallholder occupation by people from outside of Kalimantan.

Roads facilitated internal migration as well as transmigration, resource extraction, and the commoditization of land and resources. These in turn brought more people spontaneously from other islands, including many from Madura, seeking land and work. The plantation production of oil palm, rubber, and pulp, as well as the extraction of renewable forest resources and minerals and the secondary processing of many of these products all played specific parts in this territorialization of Bornean resource space. West Kalimantan was a key provider of resource-based revenues for "national" development, but is still the third poorest province in Indonesia. Local residents, especially the Dayak community, see themselves as recipients of only a small proportion of the direct benefits while suffering the greatest losses of territory to resource extraction and production projects and migration. Between 1980 and 1985, for example, although sponsored transmigrants accounted for only six percent of the provincial population, they represented 46 percent of provincial population increase (Potter 1996: 31). These numbers do not account for spontaneous migrants, a much more difficult number to estimate. HRW (1997) says that approximately 2 percent of the West Kalimantan Province population is of Madurese descent.

The military presence in the New Order government of West Kalimantan also changed form over time; it became bureaucratized, a key player in regional government. The other half (non-military) of its "dual function"—as a political player in the development of Indonesia—was put into the foreground. Smaller numbers of troops were stationed there in its later years. The upper echelons of the civil service, most notably the governors and some of the district heads (*Bupati*), were high-ranking military officers. As Kammen (personal communication, 2000) points out, because these provinces were already run as virtual military appanages, they needed the facade of civilian rule and normalcy.[27]

Other Bupati, like most of the region's civil service, were drawn largely, though not only, from local communities of Malays and migrants from Java. Few Dayaks occupied these critical political positions, though a few served as subdistrict officers (*camat*).

However great, these changes alone were not enough to motivate people to attempt the violent eviction of Madurese from the province. The next section shows how New Order policies altered the positioning of Dayak groups under Indonesian rule, as compared to their general political-legal positions with ethnically defined territories of *relative* autonomy (in this part of Borneo) under Dutch rule. Even more ironic was their loss of identity as politically active national citizens in Indonesia's first independent incarnation under President Sukarno. The territorialization of identity as well as rights to land and resources within the broader political entity of Indonesia and the particular forms these have taken historically in West Kalimantan have been powerful forces in the production of local subjectivities and notions of rights.

Producing New Versions of Collective Identities and Tying Access to Resources

The association of ethnicity and citizenship in national legal systems can affect the arrangement of people across landscapes and the means by which people claim rights to resources. While space does not permit an in-depth discussion of the identity politics of Kalimantan, the production and re-production of collective subjectivities is certainly integral to the roots of these conflicts. Territorialization of identity by both states and their subjects is intended to provide people in certain groups preferred access to land, resources, and power.

For example, a central element in current debates about indigenous rights is that indigenous identities are inherently defined by their ties to specific territories (e.g., Kingsbury 1995; Gray 1995; Li 1996). These arguments echo those of some academics and colonial officials, from the turn

---

27. This was also true in Aceh, Kalimantan Barat, and East Timor. Again, I am indebted to Douglas Kammen for this point.

of the century until the present, who have self-consciously identified "tribes" and "tribal" or "native" lands with specific, culturally and geographically bounded peoples (Li, 1996; Eder 1987; Vail 1989). Not surprisingly, such discursive projects as these operate and address audiences at different scales—the river basin, the region, the nation, and the globe—articulating at different historical moments with different political–economic and social moments (Hall 1996; Li 1996). They also have a great deal to do with the nature of territorial authority. Whether one's identity is localized—along a single branch of a river—or regionalized—throughout a province or the whole island of Borneo—has important political implications. "Natives" or "citizens" versus "foreigners" or "aliens" are ways of distinguishing insiders and outsiders and of tacitly or openly justifying all sorts of behavior toward people labeled as such. Labeling people as outsiders is a means of defining their relations to the institutions of state power and their access to benefit flows from its resources. These territorial categories, however, do not deal effectively with so-called indigenous people (in this case, Dayaks) who have moved to cities or intermarried, perhaps frequently through many generations. We look a bit at changing categories and scales of inclusion and exclusion in the next section.

State Constructions of "Natives" and "Native Lands"

In the nineteenth century, when Europeans arrived in Borneo, they found that both Muslim[28] and non-Muslim rural people identified themselves by the names of local rivers or other place names (King 1993; Rousseau 1990). Place-based self-identification helped distinguish between one's immediate neighbors and enemies. The practice was neither intended to identify local groups with "similar" but unfamiliar groups in distant parts of the island nor meant to create an inherent religious component in its etiology.[29]

In the Netherlands East Indies, colonial officers, travelers, and anthropologists constructed these various groupings of people they called collectively "Malays" and "Dayaks" as "natives." This classification was a legal one, meant to differentiate "natives" from what eventually became census categories of "Chinese," "Arabs," or "Indians." Subsequently clumped as "Foreign Orientals," from the 1880s to the early 1940s, these ethnic labels and native or foreign status strictly limited the forms of ownership for rights in Dutch Borneo. Foreigners, especially these foreigners, could not own land.

The Chinese-ascribed characteristic of "industriousness," for example, was simultaneously desired by colonial officials for its potential to build lo-

---

28. Later these people were called collectively "Malay" (Reid 1988; Chew 1990: 11).
29. For example, Malay=Muslim and Dayak=animist or, later, Dayak=Christian.

cal economies and deplored as "rapaciousness" and "craftiness" by those who feared their industry would far outpace the "poor, ignorant natives." These ethnic categories and their essentialized qualities would be tragically echoed in the post-colonial period. Whatever the labels, or intended status, before the arrival of the colonials, locals did not use these kinds of broad names to refer to themselves.

Under Dutch colonialism, the invention of legal pluralism, or multiple legal systems applied to different groups according to ethnicity or race, created a category of "Customary Law" that further fixed and territorialized identity. Although based in part on local practices and customs, the practice of selecting certain ones, writing these down, and litigating disputes through colonial–government-sanctioned "Native Courts" was new. The invention of these legal categories privileged certain local practices as "Native Customary Rights" and certain lands as "Native Lands."[30] As part of this process, colonial governments made their first efforts to separate "native space" from the spaces of "nature" and "waste" (represented as abandoned or underutilized lands) in order to control certain desirable resources and people's resource-related activities. The enclosure of territories—even in the most general sense, as maps were almost never made—for the exclusive use of the current occupants framed local resource practices in new legal terms. This separation of nature and customary land, perhaps more than any other practice, radically affected both the ideas and practices of colonial officials and the formation of local people's collective colonial subjectivities (Lefebvre 1979; Foucault 1979; Sack 1986; Vandergeest and Peluso 1995; Sivaramakrishnan 1997; Harwell 2000; Scott 1998).

Perhaps most important, the category "Native Lands" assumed that particular longhouses or villages exercised some authority over "village territories" (authority which the Dutch called *beshikkingsrecht)* that in some cases extended beyond the permanently farmed parts of the land. Disputes over these lands and their allocation for short- or long-term use were under the jurisdiction of village leaders and were adjudicated, if necessary, through the Native Courts. This creation of a form of formal village jurisdiction over land, resources, and people constituted a state-sanctioned authority between the colonial state and the local populace that was subsequently eliminated by the post-colonial Indonesian state (Peluso and Vandergeest 2001). Yet this state-sanctioned territorial authority was of critical importance to local people's imaginings of the indigenous, including their common identities as "Dayaks."

Legal pluralism's often forgotten fiction was, of course, that both the so-

30. These legal categories grew out of forest and land laws as the colonial state territorialized control of resources and people (Peluso and Vandergeest n.d.).

cial boundaries of ethnic "groups" and the territorial bounds of the "native lands" they occupied had been, as often as not, sites of change, contention, and conflict for centuries. Frequently, a "tribe" attached to a particular place had originated elsewhere: migrating, marrying, or battling their way into new territories that colonial authorities nevertheless assigned to them as theirs "from time immemorial." In addition, these territories also may have been long shared with seasonal or more permanent migrants whose rights were overlooked or de-legitimized as "encroachment" during processes of codification or legal claim. Nevertheless, it is also true that the people ascribed to particular territories frequently had extensive histories of control over the lands constructed as "native." Many of their memories were inscribed in rituals and other practices within the landscape itself (Sather 1990; Brosius 1997; Peluso 1996b).

The homogenous, region-wide categories of "Dayaks" and their "subgroups," the notions of bounded ethnicity and territorialized identities inscribed in legal pluralism were important tools in the colonial authorities' discursive and institutional arsenals of power. In practice, a great deal of ethnic fluidity existed/exists through people's mobility, intermarriage, and religious conversion. These were generally rendered invisible through legal formulas to identify individuals as parts of a group or to facilitate both rule over people and the administration of benefits from resources, especially land (Harwell 2000). Although local people did not always accept this "invisibility," the categories provided a cloak beneath which different aspects of essentialized identities could be constructed, mobilized, or experienced.

Under Sukarno, a political Pan-Dayak movement began to emerge. Dayaks lobbied (unsuccessfully) for the formerly Dutch provinces of West Borneo and South-and-East Borneo to be combined in a single Pan-Dayak province (the Great Dayak)[31] to be integrated as part of the Republic of Indonesia. They did form, however, a Pan-Dayak party, *Partai Dayak,* that had a very strong base in West Kalimantan. Dayak political authority was recognized in some regional and national political appointments, including that of Oevang Oerai, the province's first governor, who Feith described as "a shrewd, dynamic and authoritative figure, who is to the Dayaks what Sukarno was once for the Indonesians"(Feith 1968: 134).[32] However, in the late 1950s, in an effort to promote the nationalist agenda and reduce regionalism, Sukarno eliminated parties that did not have a national constituency, including the Partai Dayak. Dayak politicians joined other par-

---

31. The Great Dayak Province had been a recommendation of the Dutch. To some nationalist leaders it represented the allegedly "misplaced loyalties" of some in Kalimantan during and after the Indonesian Revolution.
32. Oevang Oerai was also the only Dayak to ever serve as a governor of *any* Indonesian Borneo province.

ties across the political spectrum, but most went to the Catholic Party and PARTINDO.

Beginning in the late 1960s, under Suharto's New Order government, economic development imperatives also brought a new set of labels to subjugate Dayak and other rural people. The terms *terasing* (isolated), *tertinggal* (left behind), and *terbelakang* (backward) became keywords for describing "primitive" communities in need of development (Li 1998; Tsing 1996; Ellen 1999). Dayaks were still insiders in the sense of being citizens and *pribumi*,[33] but were poor cousins. Their fervent participation in the politics of the 1950s and 1960s was ignored; so were the relatively high educational achievements of some Dayaks due to opportunities afforded them by the Catholic missions.

Political and economic motives underlay the Indonesian government's construction of Dayaks as primitive, undeveloped, and predisposed to violence. Once the "development deficit" was established through the use of these labels, the "solution" easily followed—"efficient" forest exploitation of their "under-utilized" lands, large-scale export production, forced resettlement from longhouses to villages, and the development of wet-rice agriculture (even though the environment was not always conducive to it) and perennial plantations of oil palm and rubber. These terms were not only a government discourse but also became "common knowledge." As one reporter who spent a month in West Kalimantan during the 1960s violence wrote at the end of an article outlining Dayak "traditions" but speaking only of practices such as the red bowl, drinking blood, hunting heads, and so on:

> That is the outline of Dayak *adat, what we really need to understand if we want to understand them* and find ways to advance our brothers in the interior of Kalimantan. (Kompas Dec. 20, 1997, emphasis added)[34]

The Indonesian state's claim to both the monopoly of violence and also the acceptable forms and means of development, deny the very elements of Dayak identity that are most remembered and yearned for by contemporary Dayaks: local authority over territory, individual and collective strength, self-sufficiency, loyalty to kin, and an intergenerational network enabling the enlistment of help of ancestral spirits when the bounds of honor or local sovereignty were overstepped. The bitterly experienced consequences of the "primitive" and "backward" labels—losses of land, re-

---

33. *Pribumi* is the official word for differentiating "sons of the soil" (the meaning of Pribumi) from Chinese; or "indigenous" Indonesians from citizens of "foreign" origin.

34. Original reads: *Itulah garis besar latar belakang adat suku Daya, jang perlu sekali kita ketahui, bila kita hendak mengerti mereka itu, dan mau mencari djalan2 jang bisa memadjukan saudara2 kita dipedalaman Kalimantan itu.*

sources, and autonomy—contributed to local unity as part of a Pan-Dayak cause.

Moreover, it is important to recognize the Indonesian government's strategic mobilization of the most violent aspects of the Pan-Dayak identities just after Suharto took power and Confrontation ended. After the military was purged of its purportedly communist and other left-leaning members, they sought to purge alleged communists and sympathizers remaining in the forest, including those who had been trained in guerrilla tactics at the military bases in Singkawang and Bengkayang during Sukarno's anti-Malaysia activities (Coppel 1983: 146–47; see also Peluso n.d.).

During this period (1967–68), all rural Chinese of the region were "typed" collectively as communist or "the water in which the communist fish would swim" (Feith 1968: 134) and targeted by the military for expulsion. To do so required the assistance of local Dayaks; it was too difficult for the military to differentiate rural Chinese from rural Dayaks after such a long, relatively peaceful history. One means of accomplishing this involved the military mobilizing local people collectively as "Dayaks"—whatever their linguistic or cultural background—and encouraging them to use ritual "Dayak" practices such as the red bowl in their collective efforts to expel Chinese.[35] The red bowl was of course also an important ritual element in the mobilization against the Madurese in 1997 as well as in several earlier incidents in which violence against Madurese took on a communal character.

The expulsion of the Chinese in 1968 transformed the ethnic composition of the Sambas district landscape. As mentioned earlier, tens of thousands of rural Chinese—some with roots in the region going back two hundred years—were violently evicted and forced to move to the urban areas or leave Kalimantan. This conflict had other territorial dimensions as well—not only in the eviction of people from the very areas the Madurese occupied and were evicted from thirty years later but also in linking violence to the claiming and reallocation of territory. Dayak residents were collectively allocated thousands of hectares of the irrigated rice fields and rubber and fruit gardens converted from swamp or hill forests by the ancestors of evicted Chinese. Not long after the conflict, incoming Madurese migrants also acquired some of these wet rice fields—buying, borrowing, or using this land that Dayaks had acquired.

Once the expulsion of the Chinese was accomplished, the central government acted to suppress the territorialized identities it had helped to construct through violence. As one woman said, "They moved the Chinese out and moved their own people in," referring not only to spontaneous

---

35. The red bowl, however, was only a symbol of Salako/Kenayat'n groups, not all Dayaks.

and sponsored migrants, but also to the huge territorial projects of forestry and rubber or oil palm plantation development, both of which brought new people—now "insiders" as citizens of Indonesia—into the region to seek a living and prosper. But the violent identities and the longing for a Pan-Dayak territorialization were not lost in the wake of the government's neglect. This early episode of New Order violence against Chinese glossed collectively as communists became crucial in Dayaks' reassertion of their own collective identities. It shaped their violent retaking in the late 1990s of territories occupied by Madurese.[36]

From the early 1990s, a new force in forging a Pan-Dayak identity emerged. NGO advocates, and some academics from European, Australian, North American, and Indonesian capitals, have merged agendas for democracy and nature conservation into an internationally powerful movement to promote empowerment/protection of "indigenous peoples," including the Dayaks. As part of this movement, indigenous "cultures" are often constructed as homogeneous and harmonious with their physical environments (Lynch and Talbott 1995; Moniaga 1993). Drawing on colonial discourses, "tribal" identities are revived (in most cases ignoring the individual, social, and environmental changes of the past half-century), linked to "traditional" (or colonial) tribal territories, and reconstituted as part of the indigenous discourse (Li 1996; Zerner 1994). Rather than try to reconstruct some aspect of the recent precolonial past, in which the customary lands of the Dayaks were permeable and dynamic spaces—fought over, lost, abandoned, divided, seasonally used, shared, and conquered—colonially-defined ethnic-territorial spaces are put squarely in the center of some NGO representations of ethnicity and rights. The many years of violence, struggle, and negotiation among and between "Dayaks," "Malays," "Chinese," and "Europeans," during which contemporary territories were constituted, are erased from such depictions, as are urbanization, Christianization, and Indonesianization in their many forms and effects. Yet, when international conservation and development interests construct the indigenous along lines of environmentalism and talk about reclaiming customary lands, it is not surprising in its appeal. Many, if not most, local people embrace the communal aspect of their collective identities.

Madurese in West Kalimantan

Over the thirty years since rural Chinese were evicted in the 1960s, many Madurese have taken their places in the working landscape, migrating from Madura and East Java. They were similar to the Chinese and different from most Javanese and Sundanese in that they tended to come as sponta-

36. See Peluso n.d.

neous migrants and only rarely as part of organized resettlement schemes. A few arrived in West Kalimantan as early as the turn of the century. Many were entrepreneurial and eventually came to compete with urban Chinese, particularly in the transport sector. Madurese are famous as the predominant *becak* or pedicab drivers of Pontianak; they also owned many trucking and passenger transport vehicles. Others came poor and worked as contract laborers building roads or taking part in large-scale plantation schemes, also associated with transmigration.[37] They were also known for raising and trading cattle. Many bought irrigated rice land with the money they saved in these occupations, often the very land that had been converted from swamp forest by Chinese farmers. Others came to dominate many of the interior marketplaces that had once been sites of Chinese stalls along the Singkawang–Bengkayang road: in Pakucing, Samalantan, Montrado.

Madurese living in the rural areas of Sambas, Pontianak, and Sanggau tended to settle in specific hamlets, sometimes mixing with other Muslims: Malays, Javanese, and Sundanese. These hamlets came to be known as *kampung Madura* (Madurese hamlets).[38] Their devout Islam generally (but not always) prevented Madurese from intermarrying with Dayaks. Many *kampung Madura* had their own small mosques or prayer houses. Profound cultural differences—constructed and stereotyped—often precluded extensive intimate interaction between Dayaks and Madurese, or even easy living together—at least for Madurese who could not live comfortably with pigs and dogs in the same living spaces, and those Dayaks who resented these differences. Much more than the Chinese of an earlier era, Madurese were spatially segregated largely by choice.[39] Because they were recent migrants, many of whom in rural areas largely kept to their own customs and ways of life, and because many of them expressed disdain for the Dayaks' ways of life and customs, many Dayaks regarded them as outsiders or foreigners.

---

37. Resettlement schemes have to include a certain percentage of "slots" for local residents. As citizens, "local residents" could be interpreted as Madurese who had lived for a while in West Kalimantan.

38. *Kampung* means village or hamlet or neighborhood.

39. There are conflicting opinions on whether the rural Chinese of West Kalimantan can be said to have been spatially segregated or not. It is likely that different waves of migrants from China had mixed experiences. These waves started in the mid–late eighteenth century (mostly for gold mining), occurred again in the late nineteenth century (mostly for pepper and other sorts of farming), and continued in the early twentieth centuries (for trade and farming). Many miners eventually returned to China, many others married locally and settled down; later migrants often came with wives or families from China. In any case, many rural Chinese only spoke Chinese dialects; others spoke Malay-Indonesian or the local Dayak language in addition to a Chinese dialect. To this day, both Chinese (in Singkawong and the few who have returned to rural areas) and local Dayaks frequently speak multiple languages, with the primary ones being Salako or Kendayat'n (Dayak), Hakka or Tcochieu (Chinese), and Indonesian.

Under colonialism, Madurese had been treated as "natives" in both their "native" island of Madura and, at least in a de facto manner, in eastern Java where many had migrated during and before the colonial period. The Dutch had constructed Madurese as "fierce and ruthless" people and put them to work as soldiers—often constituting elite troops for the Dutch. Many in effect paid their colonial taxes in blood—as conscripts to the colonial military. Glenn Smith has suggested that the forced conscription on Madura was so high that it became the major cause of out-migration in the nineteenth century, so much so that more Madurese lived in East Java than all of the island of Madura by the mid-nineteenth century (Smith 1996).[40] As "evidence" of the contemporary currency of this cultural trait, some people cite their dominance of the criminal rolls: local police records indicate that Madurese are arrested for four out of five crimes in the city of Singkawang. Madurese were viewed by the Dutch and most Indonesians as violent in nature, hence their conscription into the service of the state as elite troops as early as the eighteenth century and their simultaneous branding as criminal types (Smith 1996).

Wherever they went in Indonesia, the Madurese—particularly men— have been stereotyped as dishonest, crime-prone, and violent. They are often blamed for the deterioration of local conditions, creating atmospheres of insecurity and distrust. Because the men typically carry small knives, and some individuals are quick to pull these out in disputes over honor, all Madurese are typed as inherently violent. That these knives were used in a series of violent acts against Dayak men and women over the twenty-plus years since the Chinese were evicted is used as "proof" of this violent nature. They are Indonesian citizens and legally entitled to the same rights as other citizens. Yet this widespread and historically deep stereotype of the "violent Madurese," plus their tendencies to keep to their own communities and customs in much of West Kalimantan, imparts them with a certain mystique among locals. In other words, they continue to construct Madurese as "outsiders."

Indonesian Citizens

As indicated previously, with the end of European colonialism, identities were territorialized in many new ways: through new or more heavily enforced forms of state land enclosure, by states acting in the interests of both international corporations and international conservation groups, by local people, and by new legal techniques applied by the state (Boal 1998;

40. It is not clear whether any Madurese troops were taken to Borneo as part of the *kongsi* wars in 1855. Note also that Madurese did not make up a very large percentage of the colonial army (Kammen personal communication 2000).

Li 1996). Foremost among these have been the attempts of new nation-states to eliminate historical differences in legal status between ethnic groups and those deriving from preferred access to or control over certain territories. This has generally resulted in the invention of a new legal category within Indonesia and elsewhere: the citizen.

In Indonesia, the creation of the national citizen and the attempt to eliminate both the territorialized local ethnic group and the colonial institution of legal pluralism created new problems in the establishment of land control and resource access. So-called ethnic or "cultural" identities—of which there were hundreds across the three-thousand-mile-long archipelago—were officially de-territorialized. The national government emphasizes people's collective identities as Indonesian citizens rather than as territorially based "ethnic groups." That is, not only were local modes of authority eliminated, but also adat or custom was no longer "law," and racially based territorial claims were virtually erased as parts of nationally sanctioned "local culture." The Indonesian government defined cultural practices as language, dress, and artistic expression (music, dance, art)—practices and cultural objects that could be "museumized" and more easily frozen in time (Pemberton 1994).

Of course, these new identities did not emerge smoothly in practice. Local people frequently contested the claims of the state on "state forest lands," the appropriation of land for plantation projects, and the transformation of customary land cultivated as fields, managed forests, and fallows into plantations. These and other state-sponsored projects represented and asserted state control of land and resources. The forms of local contestation varied from tree planting, claiming permanent cultivation rights, open opposition to corporate bulldozers, and to vilifying the formal village leaders who signed away community claims without permission. Nevertheless, in the national courts, old forms of property claims were superceded by uses of the land geared to "development." These national claims were in some ways bolstered by global aspirations on the region's forests, whether by investors for production or environmentalists for conservation.

While nationalist forces under Sukarno had begun the transformation of the political–economic landscapes with the formal elimination of legal pluralism, Suharto's New Order government replaced Sukarno's notions of "self-sufficiency" and his search for a specifically Indonesian style of governance with a self-consciously capitalist reorganization of space and power relations. The state's preferred legal relationship with people was now with individuals, not collectivities in the form of villages, longhouses, kinship groups, or other local territorial entities (Foucault 1979; Peluso and Vandergeest n.d.). Many of the resource claims and property rights of local people to local resources and so-called customary or native land were obviated by the new means of claiming resources as individual citizens within the capitalist state. Of course, because these new discourses of territorial rule were not completely accepted, people and the state engaged in sometimes common fictions. The village leader, for example, was an often-fictionalized power figure, believed for convenience to speak for the people of his village or longhouse. The national government used this notion of a village representative to enable the formal transfer of village land in the name of the people, even against the vehement objections of those very people.

The contemporary Indonesian government constructs all ethnic groups as citizens of Indonesia, equal under the law. All but the Chinese are constructed as "the indigenous people of Indonesia." Local claims to territorial rights are thus diffused by the Indonesian government's declaration of the *national* territory as the boundary marker of national indigeneity or Indonesian-ness (Anderson 1983). In other words, "indigenous Indonesian" is a category now conflated with citizenship—except where the Chinese are concerned. In an odd sort of way, this maintains an "otherness" to the Indonesian citizen of Chinese descent, while enabling the appropriation of local resources (including land) for an increasingly wider group of citizen-claimants, however nonlocal they may be. Citizens who move through organized transmigration programs or spontaneous migration are imagined as rightful occupants and users of nationally-constructed space, even more so when they occupy "state" land that was once considered "unowned" forest.

Madurese, like other migrants, claimed their rights to live in West Kalimantan by appealing to the nationalist discourse of citizenship and the government's encouragement of entrepreneurialism. In various ways, the Madurese are playing out an Indonesian government fantasy of spontaneous development as indigenous entrepreneurs in Kalimantan.[41]

Identity, Resource Access, and Space in the New Order

As mentioned above, Dayaks lost territory and authority after the elimination of ethnicity-based institutions of governance over native customary land. Although ethnic identity was not criminalized, it was replaced in large part by citizenship claims as a means of claiming rights to territory, resources, and power. Meanwhile, capitalist development made land and resources more critical to their efforts to become modern Indonesian citizens and respected political participants. More and more land and re-

41. As such, migrants became idealized individualized subjects of a Foucauldian modern territorial and would-be totalitarian state (Foucault 1979: 216).

sources were taken from rural Dayaks and allocated by the Indonesian state actors and agencies to big capital, big conservation, or resettlement. The options for local people's participation—largely as coolies on their own or others' land or as laborers in the forests appropriated by the state—were unattractive to many Dayaks. New people were brought in who were grateful for access to resources and jobs and glossed as entrepreneurial citizens working to ensure Indonesian development. These circumstances changed both the patterns of economic activity and resource ownership, the patterns of human settlement and movement, and the very composition of the region's working landscape.

Following the most recent Dayak-Madurese war, the ethnic landscape of West Kalimantan underwent another, more radical, transformation, with many Madurese fleeing the countryside for Pontianak or returning to Madura. Additional flare-ups of violence led to most of the remaining rural Madurese—many of them women and children—to board boats and leave, many too uncomfortable to contemplate ever returning.[42] At the time of this writing (mid-2000), refugee camps in Pontianak reportedly are still packed with Madurese with nowhere to go and living in the same kinds of squalid conditions that characterized the Chinese camps of the late 1960s (*Kompas* 1968; *Straits Times* 1998). At least temporarily, Madurese are segregated from the province's rural landscape.

Unlike the Chinese victims of violence thirty years before, the Madurese who left the countryside could legally sell their land.[43] As Indonesian citizens, they had either bought or acquired land from previous owners; the land was already of "private" status. A few Madurese acquired land when they came to work on various government or privately run estates—the rubber and oil palm plantations of the region. Again, this land, though perhaps still mortgaged, had a private or semiprivate status. Indonesian law unambiguously backed Madurese claims to land they had purchased. In the immediate aftermath of the violence, some never had the chance to sell. In one district, anti-Madurese feelings were so strong that local people erected small houses and planted corn on the abandoned properties to claim them.

Ethnocentric attitudes and violence on both sides in this incident can be seen to stem from a clashing of discourses of territorial control and the

42. Violence flared up in 1998–99, but the specifics of this violence, some of which involved Malay youths rather than Dayaks, are beyond the scope of this chapter. See Parsudi 2000 for one report on this violence.

43. Chinese could not own land under Dutch colonial law, so they leased land for long term use. In many places, given the extensive improvements they made, this land was treated as their "own." The land Chinese leased was technically state land and the leasing system called *Huur Overencompst* or *tanah H.O.* State land cannot normally be privatized. It was exceptional, therefore, that land abandoned by the Chinese in 1968 was allocated by the state to local Dayaks. It was ironic that this land was later transferred to Madurese.

specific relations of territory to political/cultural identities. Every interview we have engaged in or written account we have read that tries to explain why the incidents took place has made some reference to territory or the territoriality associated with customary practice and Dayak identity. Many Dayaks have insisted the problem is not with development per se, nor with the influx of people of other ethnic backgrounds into the area—the problem is in *how* development takes place, *who* benefits, and *whether* preexisting Dayak rights, practices, rules—*adat*—are respected within the territories long occupied by Dayaks.

The notion that local practices and Dayak territorial and resource claims, formerly recognized by the Dutch, have not been respected by either the Indonesian government or certain other ethnic groups is one issue that unites even those Dayak groups who were at odds with each other under colonialism. It also starkly illustrates the incomplete hegemony of New Order and other post-colonial ideologies of property rights and national identity. In the analysis of "why the conflict was so widespread and why it included Dayaks from so many different areas and linguistic groups," a major Dayak NGO argues:

> The oppression of the Dayak, the threats from development, the political marginalization and lack of respect for Dayak culture has [*sic*] united Dayaks in West Kalimantan across what were former boundaries. . . . The transgression of *adat* is now more than a localized transgression. (IDRD 1998: 4)

The coalescence of Dayak unity around offenses that are felt locally but perpetrated remotely is the consequence of protracted territorial struggle against translocal (state) interests. In fact, the prerogative to expel the Madurese from the province for their offensive behavior rests fundamentally on a notion of indigenous territorial rights. "This is our home," one Dayak argued. "Where would we run to? They are the newcomers here." As mentioned above, these particular incidents resonated with another recent geopolitical activity, the global "indigenous people's movement," and also can be related to the Dayaks' emerging sense of collective identity. A key feature of this movement is its explicit mobilization of disenfranchised groups by emphasizing discrete, collective identities and linking them to specific "ancestral" territorial entitlements (Harwell 2000). This section has shown the colonial origins of these notions of entitlement.

A Cultural Politics of Violence

The changes in territoriality and resource-related sociopolitical identities still do not explain why only the Madurese and not other groups were the targets of the 1997 violence. In this section, we show that acts of violence, as well as their narration within stories about collective identities, polarized these divisions and helped bind exclusive communities more tightly through the perceived threat of imagined violent "others." In clashing, these images and identities helped ignite and maintain the 1997 violence at such a high level.

Violent identities—both Dayak and Madurese—have been produced and reproduced over time, constituted and strengthened by participation in violence. War techniques involving headhunting rituals and magic for invulnerability—resurrected cultural symbols of "Dayak-ness"—were mobilized by individuals who proudly claimed them, formal and informal leaders calling people to action, and people in government, the military, and outside observers. In related ways, the comments of individual Dayaks, representatives of the Catholic Church, and leaders of Dayak organizations naturalized violent retribution as "part of ancient Dayak culture." Selective uses of historical materials and the generalizing of cultural practices to unify previously disparate and sometimes antagonistic groups supported these constructions.[44]

As mentioned above, however, headhunting and warfare played very different roles for various Dayak groups.[45] The fascination of nineteenth and early twentieth century observers with headhunting obscured the more frequent and more everyday activities of most Iban and Kayans (Padoch 1983; Rousseau 1990). At the same time, the descendants of Salako, Lara, Kenayat'n, and other "Land Dayaks,"[46] who had been frequent targets of Kayan and Iban raids, often claim that their ancestors hunted heads only in retaliation for others' depredations.[47] Despite these protestations—and whether or not they are accurate—storytellers among them claim their ancestors' historical prowess in headhunting as a positive collective memory of their cultural heritage: a sign of collective strength to defend their own territories, authority, and honor.[48]

The historical "facts" and the "evidence" of much headhunting lore may

---

44. The representation of violence and warfare practices assumed to be "inherent" within Dayak culture have been central to state building projects in both colonial and post colonial Indonesia (Harwell 2000). Dayaks themselves have manipulated the construction of their capacities for particular forms of violence and invulnerability under ritual protection (Peluso n.d.).

45. Iban and Kayan were represented throughout the nineteenth century as fierce headhunters who actively engaged in violence to acquire and control forest resources and territory (Freeman 1955; Vayda 1961). See also Maxwell 1996. Salako and Kenayat'n were viewed as less proactively aggressive.

46. The colonial category "Land Dayaks" actually referred to a variety of groups who spoke at least four mutually unintelligible languages.

47. See IDRD 1998; Geddes 1954; the authors' interviews with members of Salako and other "Land Dayak" groups independently confirmed these findings.

48. A few historical pieces mention the viciousness of the headhunters of Sambas, the Salakau river, Mempawah, and other areas occupied by Land Dayaks (esp. Roth 1912), but most focused on other groups as major headhunters (Maxwell 1996).

be unclear, but what matters is how these notions of violent identity meld with contemporary notions of honor and lost authority. These memories, however, have been deployed at times of great political–economic stress and perceived cultural and political threat. As explored elsewhere, however, the violent events of 1967 and 1997 call into question the idea that violence played a minor role in the pre-colonial existence of the Land Dayaks in whose general "territories" the violence took place (Peluso n.d.).

Journalistic sound bites about Dayak culture and violence defined the characterizations that reporters from even respected news organizations made in reporting these events.[49] Some are clearly after the image of the exotic savage. Richard Parry, in a series of articles imbued with the Orientalist fears of an interloper who can neither speak Indonesian nor escape his own imaginings of these "savages," labels all Dayaks "cannibals" and "headhunters."[50] In *The New York Times Magazine*, he lumps the pre-crisis violence in West Kalimantan with all other violence in Indonesia between 1997 and 1999 in a dismissive statement about "headhunting and cannibalism." If anyone could be characterized as putting all Dayaks into "the savage slot" of contemporary Orientalist writing (Trouillot 1991), Parry would be first-named, though he would not be alone (ISAI and IDRD 1999).

Our aversion to this type of account is not meant to defend the violence in West Kalimantan. Rather, such simplistic, racist, and ahistorical accounts reduce the possibilities for understanding how violence erupts and the underlying conditions that make it possible. They also oversimplify extremely complex situations. For example, in contrast to the narratives about a Dayak "culture of violence," numerous accounts of islands of resistance to the violence are never reported. The stories of Dayaks protecting or hiding Chinese and Madurese during violent incidents tend to be excluded from both official reports and many public versions of the stories. In our interviews, accounts of saving friends, working associates, and family members were frequently part of the Dayak narratives. At the same time, many

---

49. For the most complete compilation of news accounts on the 1996–97 incidents, see ISAI and IDRD's *Sisi Gelap Kalimantan Barat: Persetueruan Etnis Dayak-Madura 1997*.

50. In one piece, he refers to someone he gives a ride to as "my cannibal" (*London Times* May 1999). In this piece, Parry conflates everything he ever heard or worried about "the headhunters of Borneo" with those thoroughly "modern" Malays who don't exactly fit his model but are for some reason fighting and cutting off heads more than a year after the Dayak–Madurese war. The analysis of this incident is not actually within the purview of this paper, but the reporter's analysis is indicative of how these stereotypes get constituted. In a longer journalistic account of the 1997 incidents described here, he attributes the cause of violence to "what young men do" when they are coming of age (Parry 1998), simultaneously comparing young Dayak men to men who people the armies and militias around the world and singling them out as horrific examples of ancient violence inflicted within contexts of modernity. (See Peluso n.d. for a more in-depth construction of violent identities.)

people avoid talking about the parts individuals played in inflicting violence, claiming community responsibility for the outcomes.[51]

The production of a violent collective identity for the Madurese victims of Dayak ire was used by many Dayaks to somehow justify or explain the violence they used against Madurese. Beyond these cultural productions of violent identities are the ways in which these imaginaries are mixed with people's personal experiences. This was particularly important to the interpretations given by most Dayak narrators of three aspects of the violence: the violent acts by Madurese against Dayaks that set off the 1997 violence; their culturalist explanations of Madurese incompatibility with Dayaks; and Dayak claims that government involvement in the conflict was inappropriate.

We start with the genesis of the conflict. Dayak narrators inevitably told the origins of the war as a historical litany of violent acts by Madurese against Dayaks. Each of these acts, murders and some rapes, were interpreted by Dayak storytellers as aggressions against the entire Dayak community. The violent acts start either in 1968 or 1974, depending on what the teller includes, and culminate in the 1996 stabbing in Sanggau Ledo that set off the 1996–97 violence. Some of the stabbings were from behind, unacknowledged, and considered by Dayaks to be dishonorable.[52] Seven of the ten incidents were taken care of relatively quickly by police, the perpetrators whisked away and sent to jail for a short time. Three incidents led at the time to violent retaliation either locally or beyond. Madurese perpetrators never atoned for these acts in accordance with Dayak adat, except in 1979 when the government forced the issue.

When the 1996 stabbing was not resolved to local satisfaction, one informal Dayak leader explained that the incidents and people's involvement could be tracked by a series of events that, "according to Dayak culture," justified the engagement of more and more people from farther afield. The events he referred to included both the failure of Madurese leaders to "claim" the aggressors as one of their own and atone for their crimes as a community as well as the repeated violence by other Madurese against Dayak victims.

> First, the families of the boys stabbed in Sanggau Ledo demanded justice and retribution. When this was not accomplished, members of the communities where they or their relatives lived became involved. And when the Madurese began to commit random acts of violence against any Dayak on

---

51. As Arendt (1969: 65) noted long ago, "Where all are guilty, no one is; confessions of collective guilt are the best possible safeguard against the discovery of culprits, and the very magnitude of the crime the best excuse for doing nothing."

52. See Human Rights Watch Asia report (1997); also a document in the author's possession, "Fakta-fakta dari kerusuhan antara etnis madura dan Dayak Kalimantan Barat."

the street, including women, children, and old men, we had to use the red bowl to call all Dayaks to war. (interview October 1998)

While this story uses cultural idioms, it is ultimately a political analysis that authorizes local community violence. The story pointedly does not lead to "so the government should have gone in and captured the Madurese perpetrators and made their community leaders responsible for retribution." Dayaks demanded that the Madurese take community responsibility for individual Madurese who killed Dayaks. Madurese—not central government "representatives"—were deemed responsible to carry out the rituals of retribution and "cooling" of the spaces upset by violence. To these ends, Dayaks were willing to accept Madurese religious leaders—even a national figure from Java—as representatives of the "Madurese community."

On one hand this can be seen as the recalling of ancient rituals and religious beliefs. On the other, these demands constituted a request for recognition of Dayak rights and local customs as they were remembered under previous political forms. These practices were still important in the present, as Dayak demands for Madurese "community" responsibility indicated a disillusionment with the governance of the national state. As the violence escalated on both sides, virtually unstoppable by the police and army for several weeks, its meanings also changed; thus an unresolved and increasingly violent set of interethnic relations became a statement about the ethnic community's lost authority. Violence was used to fill the void in legitimate authority. By using the most famous and threatening symbols of "Dayakness"—headhunting, war rituals, and the assertion of communal responsibility for it all—the violence also came to represent a reconstituted and reinvented Pan-Dayak community.

Paradoxically, however, as community authority was thwarted, national sources of justice and authority also failed. While the biggest previous Dayak–Madurese war, in 1979, also had been sparked by the murder of a Dayak by a Madurese and a mass violence response by Dayaks, the military and police stopped that war. Various accounts attribute this to the rapid and forceful intervention of the armed forces, containing the violence to the victim's village. Also important, as Dayak leaders explained in 1998 interviews, the military in 1979 worked more closely with local Dayak leaders to calm the gathering angry crowds. In other words, the authority and jurisdiction of local Dayak leaders was recognized—albeit temporarily and informally—by the military agents of national state authority. Even so, an estimated thirty or so people died, quite a high number for that time—the height of New Order military strength and capacity to suppress political action.

Violence may also have been easier to stop in 1979, a time of relative prosperity—national oil revenues were so high that Indonesia did not need to take any foreign aid on terms that did not suit the leaders. By 1997, although the national economic crisis and the forest fires had not yet occurred when violence broke out, major speculation about political transition from Suharto had begun. Even the future role of the military was unclear.

In contrast to political economic conditions in 1997, the 1979 military was strong, assertive, and eager to construct symbols that illustrated its unique and powerful role in the government. After the 1979 violence, the military erected a monument—to remember the dead, to symbolize national peace, and to its own role in the peace—at a spot outside the entrance to the town of Montrado. The monument is the same (phallic) shape as the Indonesian national monument in Jakarta. Its base is engraved with "the youth oath" (*sumpah pemuda*)[53] and figures of young Madurese and Dayak men and women dressed in ethnic attire.[54] Early nationalist identity markers are thus jumbled up with selected symbols of "diversity" or ethnic identity—"traditional" clothes. When interviewed in the early 1990s about previous Madurese wars, some Dayak informants referred to the monument as "something the military erected for itself."

Nevertheless, in 1998 other informants referred to the nation-state's adopted symbol of "unity in diversity" in claiming that "the Madurese broke their promise" (interviews 1998). Thus, violence and its local analysis often were used to address a vaguer and more distant entity—the Indonesian government—by contrasting the government's own rhetoric of national citizenship, development, and "unity in diversity" against its actual practices. These comments, among other acts, indicate that most Dayaks were trying to assert their identities as Indonesian citizens at the same time they wanted their Dayak cultural histories recognized. They were not seeking secession from Indonesia.

Although they organized against the Dayaks to burn houses and attack groups and individuals, in seeking justice Madurese actors generally refused to take community responsibility for the criminal acts of individuals that initiated this virulent series of attacks and counterattacks. Rather, they viewed the stabbings, murders, burnings, and raids as individual acts, punishable by the state only; no adat or ethnic group responsibility was considered necessary. The view expressed most frequently was that they were In-

---

53. The Sumpah Pemuda derives from the period in "Indonesian" history, 1928, known as the period of "the awakening of national consciousness." Anti-colonial youth pledged to support the idea of a single people, a single Indonesian language ("one people, one language").

54. Dayaks are dressed in "traditional" costume with feather headdresses; Madurese are in more "modern" clothing complete with the Islamic *peji*, the same type of headdress worn by Indonesia's first two presidents, Sukarno and Suharto.

donesian citizens, subject to the laws and protections of the Indonesian state; they referred to national discourses of citizenship to justify their actions.

Cultural politics do not play out only in the realms of identity, public opinion, and human rights, but also in the nature and form of state power. Differences in the degree of violence directly sponsored or enabled by the army were a consequence, in part, of the political contexts in which events took place, including the terms by which soldiers understood their relations with the citizens and subjects they were shooting (or, as in 1967–68, inciting to violence). In the Dayak–Madurese skirmishes and "wars" of the 1970s, 1980s, and early 1990s, the military cast itself in the roles of mediators and peacekeepers. These roles were possible, however, only because through the 1970s and 1980s New Order coercive politics were at a zenith, bolstered by the terror inspired by early government violence and military action in West Kalimantan. By 1995–96, public dissatisfaction with the Suharto regime and its openly corrupt beneficiaries had peaked and violent signs of its breakdown were appearing in many parts of the country. In 1996–97, the army played a role that was both conflicted and ambiguous; they initially maintained a very low profile, but midway through the conflict came violently crashing in, and were directly responsible for a large percentage of the Dayaks casualties.

Ultimately, although most Dayaks likely did not view the Madurese as a primary driving force in the changing political ecological landscape of West Kalimantan, they were viewed as being among the beneficiaries of these changes. Other migrants to West Kalimantan, such as Javanese, Sundanese, Chinese, and the "local" Malays, all also benefited from the New Order's changes. Yet these latter groups were not seen as perpetrators of the disrespectful and dishonorable treatment of Dayak culture and identity associated with the Indonesian government (as an abstract entity) and the Madurese (as a local community). As one man said during an interview, even van drivers who kill pedestrians by accident must, and do, pay ritual retribution for the taking of a person's life. Moreover, neither the Indonesian government nor the Madurese recognized any kind of Dayak territorial or political jurisdiction by virtue of their ethnicity. Indeed, Madurese presence in West Kalimantan was arguably a product of the previous thirty years of the Suharto regime's efforts to dissociate territoriality and ethnic identity. Ultimately, though, the most important explanation for "why the Madurese?" and not Chinese, Javanese, or Malays, is that Madurese were the only ones who committed purposeful violent acts against Dayaks: first over a period of twenty years in which the earlier offenses were not forgotten (in fact grew in importance as they were narrated as part of a long-term "pattern") and then in rapid succession over a month.

The cultural politics of silence also must be understood as critical influences on modalities of violence. Until 1996–1997, the repressive capacity of the Indonesian government precluded speaking out publicly, taking united action against the acts of individuals, or stating dissatisfaction with development. The weakening of the New Order's legitimacy—evident even before Suharto was forced to step down—enabled people first to act out their frustrations and later to reconstruct a part of their very experience of community through violence. The losses of collective local authority experienced since the end of legal pluralism and the failure of national authority were thus reshaped by local actors into a form unintended by the national policies that led to them: the collective self-authorization of one community to inflict violence against another.

Conclusion

It is both ironic and intended that the state's erasure of territorial ethnic boundaries came at the same time that it was territorializing control over people and resources in West Kalimantan. This chapter has shown how discourses of development, citizenship, and identity are directly linked to changes in access to both natural and state resources and to modes of territorial control that were meant to change the primary loci of collective identities and the sanctioning of property rights. The failure of these new forms of national territorialization explains the underlying conditions for violence, while the cultural politics around violent identity construction and practice explain the specific direction of violence against Madurese. The 1996–97 conflict came to be a representation of the struggle over territory and the means of constituting a stronger Dayak identity through territorial control, social/political positioning, and violence as means of expressing honor and power. Connecting different notions of territorialized identities with violence in this study required an understanding of the history of social relations between Dayaks and Madurese and their positioning vis-à-vis the state and its varied political-economic interests. Conflicts over the rapid changes in the nature and expression of territorial authority, the multiple processes of identity construction and expression, and the radical rearrangement of people and space combined to produce violence. In this way, the violence around identity and territory may be seen as an early symptom of the death throes of Suharto's New Order, not only in West Kalimantan, but also in the many other parts of Indonesia where · ethnicity, nationality, and territory have been violently interconnected.

Through policy, law, and new land use practices, the Indonesian government tried to erase the territorial boundaries of ethnicity constructed through the discourses of Dutch colonial legal pluralism. The Indonesians used both more coercive and insidious technologies of power. These include the establishment of a national land code and the abolishment of legal pluralism in land, and the constitution of a widely defined citizenry. These traveling citizens can make new kinds of claims on territorial resources in West Kalimantan through a number of national programs, entrepreneurial opportunities, and legal mechanisms. At strategic historical moments, however, government and nongovernment actors have mobilized the violent (and "primitive") aspects of Dayak identities for political purposes. Many Dayak participants have willingly wrapped themselves in these identities, reaching for the raw physical and psychological power of violence and terror. Both imagined and experienced social histories have come together, thus, in contemporary forms of violent, territorialized, Pan-Dayak identities as a partial and significant result of the government's territorial strategies.

Many "Kaplanesque" images have been involved in the case we have presented here: notions of "spirit war" (through headhunting imagery), ethnic unrest, and the ever-present Malthusian specter of increasing population in this province in Indonesian Borneo. What we have shown, in contrast to the cookie-cutter models preferred by both Kaplan (1994) and Homer-Dixon (1999), is why such ethnic violence has occurred in this province and how the violence was connected to clashing territorialization strategies of the colonial and postcolonial states. The forms of violence derived from both cultural images of an exotic Borneo past and from more recent historical memories of the political violence of the 1960s and 1970s. Such simultaneous material and symbolic dimensions of violence, and their connections to resource access and control, are ignored by environmental security analysts of political violence. We have shown here that cultural politics can engender violent interactions. To understand these requires much deeper and more nuanced examinations of the many dimensions of social and environmental interactions.

5

States of Nature and Environmental Enclosures in the American West

James McCarthy

And if the wilderness is our true home, and if it is threatened . . . then we have the right to defend that home, as we would our private rooms, by whatever means are necessary.

> Environmentalist Edward Abbey (in Foreman and Haywood 1985: 8)

If you ever come down to Catron County again, we'll blow your fucking head off.

> A New Mexico rancher to a United States Fish & Wildlife biologist, regarding possible endangered species habitat protections on federal land in Catron County (quoted in McCoy 1995)

The same mentality that would level a redwood forest and destroy its ability to regenerate, this is the same mentality that would place this bomb in my car and would do this kind of violence to me. I think that the problem isn't just the economic system, isn't just the social relations, I think that part of the problem is the violence in the society. Violence against humans and violence against the Earth. That's the lesson that this has really taught me.

> Earth First! activist Judi Bari, on being the target of a car bomb
> (Bari 1994: 51)

This chapter looks at actual and threatened violence deployed by two groups in the western United States in the 1980s and 1990s. The first was a subset of the "Wise Use" movement, a coalition of established commodity producers who had long had privileged access to the federally owned land that make up roughly half of the American West:[1] ranchers,

1. Between 1803 and 1850, the United States more than doubled the size of its territory through conquests, purchases, and treaties: the Louisiana Purchase, the acquisition of Florida, the annexation of the northern half of Mexico (including Texas), the Gadsden Purchase, and settlements with Great Britain that gave the United States the Oregon Territory

loggers, and miners in the rural West (see McCarthy 1999). The second was a subset of the radical environmental movement.[2] Both groups used violence in connection with struggles over the federal lands.

Representatives of Wise Use and radical environmental groups, as well as most commentators, portrayed the two groups as holding diametrically opposed views of, and agendas for, the federal lands: commercial use versus ecological preservation. I argue here, however, that Wise Use activists and radical environmentalists who turned to violence in fact had much in common. Both turned to violence out of frustration with the federal land management agencies. Having lost or failed to gain sufficient influence over these agencies and their procedures, they rejected these agencies as the legitimate managers of the federal lands. More broadly, they rejected the legitimacy of government control over these lands, and developed subcultures defined by perceived exclusion from the land management process. From there, it was a relatively short step to seeing the use of violence to achieve their land management agendas as legitimate. Moreover, both groups' collective public identities, views of the federal lands, and uses of violence relied heavily upon appeals to a brief, pivotal, and largely imaginary moment in the nineteenth century history of federal lands in the West: the caesura between the forcible removal of the land's existing inhabitants and large-scale settlement by white Europeans.[3] Americans have long projected onto that moment and landscape the potential of a new Eden—whether for the development of a capitalist agrarian democracy (for Wise Use activists) or for reconnection with a primal Nature (for radical environmentalists) (Cronon 1996; White 1996). Because both groups examined here conceived of the federal lands as a landscape where relations between society and nature could be reconstituted in their ideal form, they viewed them as an exceptional case of both property relations and the use of state authority. In short, they saw them as existing, in a sense, in a "state of nature," in which the use of violence by nonstate actors was legitimate.[4]

(most of what is now Oregon, Washington, and Idaho). By 1853, the contiguous United States had assumed its current configuration. Most of this new territory was in what is now called the West, and most of it remained in federal ownership.

2. Of course only a tiny fraction of the members of each movement threatened to engage in violence, and a smaller fraction yet actually did. Nonetheless, this was how both the participants themselves and various commentators generally identified the two groups.

3. This vision has pervaded European and United States visions of the West, and North America in general, for most of the their intertwined histories. Forcible removal and mass settlement were of course not imaginary; what was imagined was a landscape devoid of human agency or presence. Moreover, even accounts that acknowledge conquest too often present a neatly periodized history—before and after conquest—rather than centuries of interaction and mutual influence (see Limerick 1987; White 1991).

4. That is, the state is not recognized as holding a monopoly on the legitimate use of force.

Violence is far less prevalent in contemporary struggles over federal lands in the American West than in many cases considered in the evolving literature on coercive conservation (Peluso 1996a; Neumann and Schroeder 1995). The contemporary American state has a relatively great capacity to govern its resources, and most citizens accept its authority to do so. It is thus the norm for conflicts over land and resources in the United States to be handled in formal, juridical spheres. In fact, this is an important precondition of the violence examined in this chapter, which derived much of its power not from its magnitude, but from the mere shock of its disruption of the norm.

Yet, while direct violence is less common in environmental disputes in the United States than in many other locales, it is far more common than most people recognize. The history of the federal lands in the American West contains a great deal of violence, some explicit and some subtle. They were appropriated by conquest and their original inhabitants dispossessed; miners, homesteaders, and cattle and sheep ranchers killed each other over them; and the designation of forest reserves from them at the turn of the century prompted arson and assaults on federal employees. In the twentieth century these lands have been a vital component of United States military supremacy (see Kuletz 1998, and this volume).

The chapter proceeds as follows. First I give a brief background of the federally-owned lands in the western United States, primarily those administered by the Forest Service and the Bureau of Land Management (BLM).[5] I then compare violence by the two groups along a number of empirical and theoretical axes, emphasizing their similarities but also attempting to account for crucial differences between them. I summarize each group's origins, its participants, and the contexts and uses of its violence. I posit causes for the violence—both immediate, empirical causes, and broader, structural patterns such as processes of enclosure and territorialization. Then, I explore the performative and narrative aspects of each group's violence: its objects, severity, organizational form, and locations. I next examine each group's attempts to justify its own violence. Finally, I explore the state's very different responses to the violence by the two groups.

Scarcity, Abundance, and the Federal Lands

Who and what many of the federal lands are *for* has never been completely settled. In the rural communities that participated in Wise Use, federal

5. For the purposes of this chapter, the "West" refers to the states of Arizona, California, Colorado, Idaho, Montana, Nevada, New Mexico, Oregon, Utah, Washington, and Wyoming.

ownership of roughly half of the American West had been accepted—for the most part—throughout the twentieth century. But that did not foreclose substantive struggles over these lands. Federal ownership itself has been challenged occasionally by states, counties, and private users. It also is complicated in various ways by easements, life estates, and other property rights (Fairfax et al. 1999). More important, the basic fact of federal ownership leaves unanswered many questions regarding use, access, and control on the federal lands, which have all remained subjects of ongoing contestation: the fact that these lands are "public" leaves their purpose and status continually open to rapid and radical reinterpretation, as definitions of the "public" and the "public good" shift over time. It is not coincidental that the conflicts examined in this chapter were over precisely the federal lands that have had the most multiple and ambiguous purposes: what are now Forest Service and Bureau of Land Management lands.[6]

In a longer historical view, current struggles over the federal lands possess a strikingly direct lineage from struggles over access to and control over land and resources that originated in the enclosure and privatization of common lands in early capitalist England (Marx 1967). The process of enclosure and the debates occurring in England at the time over the relationships between land, resources, and population, directly influenced American land acquisition and policy at a pivotal moment in the nation's history. The United States' drive to acquire vast new territories was driven in part by a fear of reproducing the pattern of "overpopulated" European nations, a pattern that many at the time insisted was rooted in environmental scarcity. When deciding to make the Louisiana Purchase in 1803 and double the territory of the United States, Jefferson was aware of the seminal work of Malthus just five years earlier (see White 1991: 61–63). American land policy from 1785 to 1891 was built substantially around Locke's vision of privatization of "wilderness" land through private labor. The United States thus did not reject England's property institutions and theory but rather set out to acquire so much territory that it could—unlike England—continually satisfy Locke's own, usually forgotten, condition: his theories of property applied only so long as there was unclaimed land of equal quality still available for the taking.

While American zeal for land acquisition was influenced by fears of scarcity, it quickly became dominated by perceptions of abundance as further conquest and purchase swelled the continental United States in the first half of the nineteenth century, mainly through the addition of what is now "the West." Seeking to solidify U.S. territorial claims, settle the region,

6. Rather than those controlled by, for example, the National Park Service or the various branches of military, whose agendas are less ambiguous.

and domesticate its vast but problematic natural resources, the federal government gave land and resources to corporations and individuals on an extraordinary scale. In the second half of the nineteenth century, it transferred approximately half of the West into private ownership, through massive land transfers to railroads and new states and a variety of homesteading and other resource-specific acts (White 1991).

The policy of privatizing the wilderness began to weaken in the last decade of the nineteenth century, though, as new and more specific fears of resource scarcity, anti-monopolist sentiment, and a fundamental national shift towards an industrial, urban development trajectory resulted in the Progressive-era conservation movement, which lasted until roughly 1920. The federal government began to retain ownership of many of its vast landholdings in the West, and justified this with claims that it would manage them for the long-term "public good."[7] Yet, although these lands were retained in federal ownership, most were still explicitly designated as sites of commodity production, for the benefit of both adjacent rural communities and the nation as a whole (Pinchot 1910). Federal ownership was conceived of as a way to ensure sustainable commodity production by private, capitalist actors, *not* as a way to eliminate it in favor of environmental protection. Commodity production on the federal lands increased throughout most of the twentieth century, particularly in the economic boom in the decades after World War II. Alongside the formal administrative governance of these lands evolved a set of informal customs and uses—use beyond permitted levels, trespassing, poaching, and so forth—that was tacitly sanctioned by the Forest Service and the BLM.

Since the 1970s, however, commodity production on the federal lands has been gradually superseded by goals best categorized as "environmental"—certain kinds of low-impact recreation and the protection of endangered species, habitats, and ecological services.[8] While such goals have figured in debates over the purposes of the federal lands for well over a century, only in recent decades has their political support come to equal or surpass that behind commodity production (see Davis 1997; Klyza 1996; Steen 1992; Wilkinson 1992). This pivotal shift was signaled by the 1964 report of the Public Land Law Commission. The Commission concluded that a decisive corner had been turned in federal land management, away from the idea of disposal to private interests and commodity

---

7. For background and overviews, see Pinchot 1910; Steen 1992; Klyza 1996; and White 1991.
8. Certain recreational uses are politically closely aligned with environmental goals because both are advanced by the same environmental organizations, for the most part, and because they are seen as compatible with ecological restoration (e.g., backpacking, kayaking, etc.).

production, and that it was time to make a permanent commitment to federal ownership and a wider range of goals in public land use.[9] This trend has accelerated since then, mainly via the wave of modern environmental legislation passed between the mid-1960s and mid-1970s,[10] much of which did not result in large-scale changes in on-the-ground management practices until the 1980s and 1990s. This legislation changed both the _goals_ and _processes_ of federal land management. Ecological and recreational goals were elevated in status to be either equal or superior to commodity production, and the federal land management processes were greatly opened to citizen participation and lawsuits—openings that environmental nongovernmental organizations (NGOs) have exploited vigorously.[11] These developments have caused drastic shifts in who is allowed to do what on the federal lands. Primary production on the federal lands has declined: grazing fees have risen, formerly grazed areas have been placed off-limits to ranchers, timber sales have shrunk, large areas of federal lands have been set aside as protected endangered species habitat, and so forth.

Wise Use and Radical Environmental Violence Compared

There will be a hundred people with guns waiting for them.
>   Wise Use rancher Kit Laney (quoted in Helvarg 1996)

No compromise in defense of Mother Earth!
>   Earth First! motto

Wise Use Violence Summarized

The highly politicized nature of the federal lands in the West and the growing conflicts over them have led to a proliferation of overtly political groups focused on these lands. These groups cover a wide spectrum, both in what they see as the "highest and best" uses of the federal lands, and in how they attempt to secure those uses. The Wise Use and radical environ-

9. A strengthened commitment to federal ownership did not necessarily equal a greater commitment to environmental goals, of course. But in U.S. politics at the time, the two were closely linked. Privatization of the public lands had always been closely associated with commodity production while during the 1960s, a period of growing environmental regulation at the federal level and rapid growth of various social entitlements (termed at the time the "new property"), permanent federal control clearly pointed towards more environmentally-oriented management of these lands.
10. The Multiple Use and Sustained Yield Act, the Federal Lands Policy and Management Act, the Endangered Species Act, the National Environmental Policy Act, and so on.
11. The literature on these developments is enormous. See Davis 1997, and Coggins and Wilkinson 1987 on federal lands and legislation in particular, and Hays 1987 and Gottlieb 1993 for surveys of the rise of the modern environmental movement.

mental movements represented the opposite ends of that spectrum in terms of preferred land uses, but in terms of tactics, they had more in common with each other than with many of the groups in between them.

The "Wise Use" movement in the American West was essentially a coalition of commodity producers dedicated to maintaining the privileged access to the federal lands that their industries have enjoyed since the mid-nineteenth century.[12] It included more than a thousand national, state, and local groups, with members ranging from multinational corporations to marginal, family-level producers. It first coalesced at a 1988 conference of nearly two hundred organizations, mainly Western-based, including natural resource industry corporations and trade associations, law firms specializing in combating environmental regulations, and recreational groups. During the early 1990s, its grassroots base grew substantially, and local Wise Use organizations proliferated. Many of the key activists were rural Westerners whose families had been engaged in natural resource industries—ranching, logging, mining—on and around the federal lands for generations (McCarthy 1999). Its overall goals, in its own words, were to "destroy environmentalism" and promote the "wise use" of natural resources (Gottlieb 1989). It strategically appropriated the term wise use from the early conservation movement in the United States: "wise use" was Gifford Pinchot's mandate for the first federal forest reserves at the end of the nineteenth century, and he made clear that conservation meant judicious use, not preservation: "The first principle of conservation is development" (Pinchot 1910: 43).[13] Wise Use activists in the 1990s thus attempted to position their agenda of increasing private access to public resources as one of restoring an historic balance that had become skewed in favor of preservation.[14] Wise Use groups in the West employed tactics ranging from grassroots activism to sophisticated media campaigns, and from legal and regulatory strategies to outright physical intimidation and violence (see McCarthy 1999). I focus here on the last of these.

---

12. I refer to the Wise Use movement in the past tense in part to make clear that I am talking about events during the years specified. I also refer to Earth First! in the past tense for the same reason. More broadly, Wise Use has become too dissipated of late to refer to as some sort of cohesive movement. Many Wise Use organizations and activists are still in existence; however, much of what was original and significant about Wise Use was the degree to which these varied interests agreed on a core agenda around which they acted cooperatively for a while. That aspect of Wise Use has fallen apart in the past two years.

13. Pinchot was the first head of the U.S. Forest Service and arguably the single most influential architect of the current system of federal land tenure in the American West.

14. This tension between preservation and use was not new in U.S. environmental politics, of course: nearly every summary of American environmentalism begins with the well-worn tale of the split between Gifford Pinchot and John Muir over the fate of Hetch Hetchy. What was new was that a fairly established equilibrium had been disturbed in favor of preservation, and Forest Service and BLM lands had moved to center stage in these struggles.

Violence associated with the Wise Use movement began in the late 1980s and reached its peak in the mid-1990s. Some was direct and life-threatening: there were at least three bombings of Forest Service and BLM offices, and a Forest Service ranger's home was bombed while his family was there (*New York Times* 12/22/95; *Clear View* 2(2), 1995; Helvarg 1996). Federal employees were physically assaulted and ejected from Wise Use meetings. In March 1996, Wise Use theorist Karen Budd-Falen gave a public talk to a group of ranchers in Eagar, Arizona, who had been told that their grazing permits might be reduced as much as 80 percent. A local Forest Service ranger attended. At the end of the meeting, the ranchers identified the ranger in the crowd and physically ejected him from the building, insisting that it was a private meeting for ranchers. The local police said that the ranger was assaulted and "hauled out" of the building (Associated Press 3/23/96; *Clear View* 3(9), 1996).

Similar incidents of environmentalists and federal lands management agency employees being directly attacked or threatened with severe injury or death were common during the first half of the 1990s. All of these incidents took place in communities where ranchers or timber producers felt that they were being squeezed off of federal lands by increasingly strict environmental regulations. Employees of the Forest Service, BLM, and U.S. Fish and Wildlife Service were most directly responsible for creating or enforcing these restrictions, and so were most often the targets of actual or threatened violence. Environmentalists were also targets when they ventured into some of the rural communities active in the Wise Use movement. There were also direct assaults on property: Forest Service and BLM buildings were burned, and tires on federal and environmentalists' vehicles were slashed (*Clear View* 3(2), 1996; *New York Times* 12/22/95). Over one hundred such instances of apparently Wise Use-related violence were documented between 1989 and 1997 (Helvarg 1996; Arnold 1997: 145). All of the incidents referred to here occurred in places and at times of peak Wise Use activity and were directed against targets of documented Wise Use complaints.

Importantly, however, most Wise Use violence was only threatened. This included both specific threats against individuals and general threats of reprisals if land uses continued to be restricted. For example, in Catron County, New Mexico, one of the centers of Wise Use activity, County Commissioner and rancher Hugh McKeen said in 1993 that ". . . there are a bunch of people here who are slowly buying ammunition. You have very independent people. They want to be left alone. The government oppresses them, and the environmentalists come in here and want to oppress their life" (McKeen 1993). Two much-quoted exchanges occurred at a meeting in the county seat of Reserve held by the U.S. Fish and Wildlife Service to discuss potential protections for the endangered willow flycatcher on federal grazing allotments in the county. In the first, rancher Skip Price drew an enthusiastic response from the crowd when he suggested that any federal attempts to fence off streams on his allotment would "be met with bullets." In the second, a rancher opened the door of a car carrying four Fish and Wildlife employees as they left the meeting and told one of them, biologist Tim Tibbitts, "If you ever come back to Catron County, I'll blow your fucking heads off" (McCoy 1995). In March of 1994, Clyde and Nancy Brown, residents of the town of Reserve, New Mexico, sent the U.S. Fish and Wildlife Service a letter reading, in part, ". . . you bureaucrats had better back off before someone gets seriously hurt. Who among you would want to lose your life for a bird, even if he can sing, or a nearly microscopic size minnow?" (Dowie 1995). Throughout the West, many other federal employees and environmentalists received anonymous death threats, and some received them face-to-face from ranchers and loggers (McCarthy 1999;[15] *Clear View,* Helvarg 1997; Rowell 1996). At other Wise Use meetings, prominent environmentalists were hanged in effigy (*Clear View* 3(1), 1996). In one incident, a Wise Use activist allegedly waved a noose in the face of an environmentalist at a public meeting and told her "This is for you" (Helvarg 1996). Perhaps most frightening was the practice of some Wise Use groups of distributing to their members the names, home addresses, and telephone numbers of environmentalists or federal employees with whom they disagreed (McCarthy 1999; Helvarg 1997).

Wise Use violence and activism had substantial effects on federal land management. Forest Service and BLM land managers admitted that Wise Use activity caused them to relax their enforcement of regulations governing some private uses of federal lands, and made them hesitate to limit those uses in new ways (McCarthy 1999). In Catron County, for example, the Forest Service avoided many potential cuts in grazing permits and enforced existing terms and regulations less strictly for at least several years, while some U.S. Fish and Wildlife Service personnel simply stopped coming to the county when their duties would normally have required them to do so (McCarthy 1999). At a larger scale, Wise Use activism was a crucial factor in Interior Secretary Bruce Babbitt's retreat from a proposed increase in federal land grazing fees early in the first Clinton administration. Wise Use groups also were instrumental in U.S. decisions not to sign on to

15. Between May and December of 1997, I conducted dissertation fieldwork in two counties that were centers of Wise Use activism: Catron County, New Mexico, and Boundary County, Idaho. Due to the sensitive nature of the topic, nearly all of my interviewees chose to remain anonymous. Whenever I cite McCarthy 1999 in this paper, I am referring to the results of this research, much of it from interviews. *Clear View* citations refer to periodic electronic publications produced by the Environmental Working Group in Washington, D.C., an organization established by the Environmental Grantmakers Association to monitor Wise Use activity.

some international environmental treaties, which they saw as having major implications for federal land management and for regulation of private property (Sims 1993: 57; *Clear View* 3(1), 1996). Such changes were critical goals of Wise Use activism.

Wise Use's critics, mainly writers employed by national environmental organizations or their foundation funders, portrayed the entire Wise Use movement as violent. They also tried to link all Wise Use activity to the "militia" or "patriot" movement in the United States, casting both as violent reactions to downward economic mobility by socially and economically marginal white men—thus ascribing to Wise Use both a racial and a class position (e.g., Helvarg 1994, 1995; see Cockburn 1995; Arnold 1997). Thus, in the wake of the 1995 bombing of a federal building in Oklahoma City, environmentalist critics of Wise Use suggested that the movement was somehow implicated in the bombing (e.g., Helvarg 1995). It is true that militia and Wise Use groups had common members and materials in some cases (McCarthy 1999; Helvarg 1996). Some rural counties with lots of Wise Use activity also were sites of very active militias. For example, the formation of a large militia in Catron County, New Mexico, coincided with the peak of Wise Use activity there, and some residents were active in both: armed militia members in camouflage uniforms were conducting pseudo-military exercises on the very Forest Service lands in Catron County contested by the Wise Use movement (McCarthy 1999).

Yet, while there were connections between Wise Use and the militia movement, they were exaggerated for political effect. In Catron County, many residents active in Wise Use had no involvement with the militia and in fact opposed it, contending that it was composed mainly of recent arrivals to the county (McCarthy 1999). Whatever the actual extent and nature of the connections between Wise Use and militia groups, the former backed off from their inflammatory rhetoric after the Oklahoma City bombing. All of the major Wise Use leaders publicly disavowed violence, and most claimed that they had no connections to militia groups (McCarthy 1999).

Radical Environmentalist Violence Summarized

Radical environmentalists turned to violence, broadly defined, starting in the late 1970s and early 1980s.[16] Major events in this turn were the publication of Edward Abbey's novel *The Monkey Wrench Gang* in 1975 and the

---

16. Destruction of property by radical environmentalists has occurred on very small scales on federal lands in the West since at least the 1950s, but only in the period examined here did it became a significant regional phenomenon. See Arnold (1997) for background on earlier events.

formation of Earth First!, the best known of the radical environmental groups, in 1980.[17] Both advocated what they termed "ecotage" and critics have labeled "eco-terrorism": the direct, covert sabotage of development projects that would affect currently undeveloped land. Tactics included spiking trees (to make it dangerous and costly to put them through a sawmill), cutting livestock fences that restricted the movement of wildlife, removing road survey stakes, and sabotaging construction equipment such as bulldozers. Such actions were to be taken covertly—usually at night by individuals or small groups. No centralized organization existed, and the intention was certainly not to be caught and arrested, as in classic civil disobedience tactics. Many radical environmentalists saw each act as an end in itself, but to the extent that there was an overall strategic goal, it was to drive up the costs of such development, making it uneconomic: "Many of the projects that will destroy roadless areas are economically marginal. . . . The cost of repairs, the hassle, the delay, the down-time may just be too much for bureaucrats and exploiters to accept if there is a widely-dispersed, unorganized, *strategic* movement of resistance across the land" (Foreman and Haywood 1985: 12; emphasis in original).

Radical environmentalists originally focused their activities on federal lands in the West, and many in Earth First! believed that these lands should remain their focus (Foreman and Haywood 1985; Bari 1994: 104; Arnold 1997: 255). Earth First! was formed largely as a result of dissatisfaction with wilderness designations on Forest Service and BLM lands, which environmentalists felt were insufficient. A number of radical environmentalists decided that they could not wait for such cumbersome and unsatisfactory federal processes and decided to take matters into their own hands. Earth First! grew rapidly during the 1980s: by 1989 it claimed twelve thousand members and chapters in many states (Nash 1990: 299). Forest Service studies estimated that "monkeywrenching" activities caused millions of dollars of damage to federal and private property on the federal lands (Arnold 1997: 121). Earth Firsters often cast themselves as the vanguard of much broader trends towards "environmentalization" of federal priorities for these lands: many believed that public opinion and federal bureaucracies would eventually embrace their currently extreme agenda for wilderness preservation but feared that the consensus would arrive too late unless they saved nature in the meantime. The fact that their actions were currently illegal was thus, for them, merely an indicator of how far ahead of society in general they were.

17. "Radical environmentalists" is an even more permeable organizational category than the "Wise Use movement." I take Earth First! to be the best proxy for radical environmentalists here, although I have included other individuals and instances where it seems appropriate.

Radical environmentalists insisted that their actions targeted objects and property, not people, and were thus nonviolent. Most of their actions did fit this description. However, this commitment to nonviolence was always rendered suspect by many activists' confrontational rhetoric. More important, some actions by radical environmentalists did cause direct injury to humans. The best-known example was the 1987 case of a sawmill worker in northern California who was severely injured and nearly decapitated when the blade of a machine he was operating hit a spike buried in a log and broke apart. Many Earth First! groups, particularly those in northern California, renounced tree spiking after this widely publicized incident. Others continued the practice, however, making clear that the danger to human life was low on their list of priorities. Earth First! founder Dave Foreman commented: "I think it's unfortunate that somebody got hurt, but you know I quite honestly am more concerned about old-growth forests, spotted owls and wolverines and salmon—and nobody is forcing those people to cut those trees" (cited in Bari 1994: 268). Other incidents in which radical environmentalists were involved resulted in direct physical conflicts with opponents, although none were more than fist fights (Arnold 1997).

Radical environmentalists also were blamed for incidents of life-threatening violence against federal employees. In 1996, a United States Forest Service station was burned to the ground, and a bomb was found on the roof of another in the vicinity of Oakridge in western Oregon. Oakridge was the site of many anti-logging protests in the mid-1990s: in addition to blocking roads to potential logging areas, radical environmental activists had painted anti-logging slogans on Forest Service buildings (Portland *Oregonian* 10/31/96; *Land Rights Advocate* January 1997). In other cases, bombs were wired to gates on Forest Service roads used by commodity producers (*Clear View* 2(3) 1995). Radical environmentalists denied responsibility for the bombs, though, suggesting that their opponents had set them in order to discredit environmentalists.

Most notoriously, Theodore Kaczinsky, the accused Unabomber, turned out to have Earth First! connections of a sort. His journals showed that he had attended Earth First! events and engaged in decades of by-the-book "monkeywrenching" tactics around his Montana cabin. He sent letter bombs to some anti-environmental activists, including Gil Murray, the head of the California Forestry Association, a nonprofit organization affiliated with the Wise Use movement. After Kaczinsky's arrest, Wise Use writers combed through his writings to find substantive overlaps with the radical environmentalist critique of modern society and had considerable success in planting this supposed connection in the national media coverage (Arnold 1997; Rowell 1996; Helvarg 1997; Cockburn and St. Clair 1996). Kaczinsky himself explicitly disavowed any connection to radical environmentalists however, while no Earth Firster! ever advocated his tactics.

Since 1990 or so, Earth First! and other radical environmental groups have shifted steadily toward classic civil disobedience tactics, engaging in mass, public demonstrations in which the arrests of large numbers of activists are central to the group's long-term strategy (see, e.g., *The High Country News* 2/8/93; London 1998). Favored tactics now include blocking roads with human chains, activists chaining themselves to trees or equipment, and "tree-sitting," in which activists build and remain in platforms high in trees scheduled to be cut. Groups in California in particular have focused increasingly on old-growth forests on private land. None of these are covert activities, and none involve damage to property. In fact, this strategy hinges on activists' willingness to expose their bodies to violence by others. However, "monkeywrenching" on federal lands has continued, albeit with less publicity for the most part (e.g., Brooke 1998). One of few incidents in recent years to receive widespread media attention was the arson of several buildings at Colorado's Vail ski resort, which had been planning on expanding into an area of national forest valued as habitat for the endangered lynx.[18]

Causes: Linking Structural and Physical Violence

For both Wise Use and radical environmentalist activists, the use of violence arose out of a combination of structural and proximate factors. In each case, structural circumstances had made many members of each group likely to consider violent tactics and proximate causes triggered the actual use of violence. Let us look first at circumstances and triggers common to both groups, followed by those specific to each.

Wise Use and radical environmentalist activists had much in common at a structural level. Members of both groups resorted to violence not just because of individual events but because they viewed these events as parts of larger processes that pointed to a future that they found unacceptable. Both groups held an agenda for the federal lands that was extreme and uncompromising and would have precluded many other uses. Their agendas thus did not fit into models of "multiple use," consensus, or "win–win" scenarios currently popular with federal land managers, and the activists knew it. In fact, both groups represented fairly marginal positions and constituencies within U.S. society. In consequence, each developed a subculture that rejected much of the rest of U.S. society, was suspicious of outsiders, and placed great value on solidarity within the group and resisting compromises with other actors, including the federal land agencies.

Their most important commonality was that both felt that they lacked

18. This was not done by Earth First! activists but by members of a similar group calling itself the Earth Liberation Front.

influence with the federal land management agencies and, indeed, that those agencies actively opposed them and sided with their opponents. Neither anticipated gaining significantly greater influence in the foreseeable future. Wise Use activists experienced this largely as a loss of what they felt was their former, rightful influence, while radical environmentalists simply had never had much, but both perceived their current situations in quite similar ways. Being unlikely to ever achieve satisfaction through the federal land management agencies and related legal processes, both groups came to reject the legitimacy of those agencies. They justified their rejection, however, on different grounds: Wise Use activists rejected the agencies' authority through appeals to history, constitutional design, and alleged property rights, while radical environmentalists questioned the very institutions of property, modern states, and human authority over nature. Frustration with state arenas and rejection of the legitimacy of those arenas opened the door to their seeing violence as the only hope of influencing the uses of federal lands. None of these conditions automatically created violence, but taken together, they created small groups and individuals ready to turn to violence in response to specific inflammatory events.

This brings us to proximate causes of violence, which also were sometimes the same for the two groups. The following types of events often triggered outbreaks of violence. Leaders of the two subcultures could often incite followers to violence through inflammatory language, threats of what they portrayed as catastrophic developments in federal land management, and so on. Legal losses after drawn-out cases involving federal lands management often left activists feeling that they had exhausted their options in the legal realm and that they had to either give up or take matters into their own hands. Specific regulatory events, whether instituting further environmental protections or permitting further commodity production, could provoke the same reaction. Rapid changes in natural resource industries—a sudden downturn in timber prices and production that forced a mill closure or a rise in gold prices that led to the opening of new mines, for example—also were triggers. Both Wise Use and radical environmentalist groups became adroit practitioners of "guerrilla theater," which often involved violent incidents or rhetoric, as a tactic to quickly focus national media attention on the place or issue most important to a movement at the time. These specific events or goals, however, would *not* have been likely to trigger violence in the absence of the structural conditions discussed previously: it is not the case that losing a legal decision automatically means violence on the federal lands.

Such were the causes common to each group. Let us now look in more detail at causes specific to Wise Use and radical environmentalist violence. The overarching cause of Wise Use violence was reduced access to the federal lands for primary commodity producers who had long had privileged access to them. This reduced access most often was directly traceable to increased environmental priorities and safeguards on these lands, in what might be termed the territorialization of ascendant environmental goals— what I call here a process of "environmental enclosure." Wise Use participants believed they and their communities were in imminent danger of losing their livelihoods. They saw both new environmental regulations and activities by radical environmentalists as aspects of the same process, and as harbingers of a West in which natural resource industries would be forbidden, the federal lands managed as playgrounds for urban elites, and rural communities and their inhabitants relegated to service industry positions low in status, wages, and security. Maintaining access to the federal lands was critical to avoiding this fate. Wise Use participants saw these lands as a still-rich source of natural wealth that could be transformed into a solid basis for regional and community economies. Prohibiting productive uses while resource-dependent economies withered appeared to them like dying of thirst next to a locked reservoir. They of course exaggerated this abundance and had little to say about the substantial evidence that a century of grazing had severely damaged the range; that logging on the national forests was diminishing in part because most of the good, readily available timber had been cut; and that it had been a very long time since natural resource industries were the main pillars of the regional economy (on ecological effects, see Magilligan and McDowell 1997; Riebsame and Woodmansee 1995; on economic significance see following). Nor was this a purely "economic" issue: it had as much to do with individual an collective identities and values as with per capita income (McCarthy 1999).

Wise Use groups realized that changing regulatory and economic priorities on federal lands in the West were inseparable from larger changes in the region's political economy and from contemporary globalization. Although natural resource industries had occupied a major role in the West's economy for over a century and had utterly dominated many rural areas in the region, they had declined sharply in the West since the early 1980s, at least in terms of employment and relative significance to the region's economy.[19] Automation, deindustrialization, and more robust international competition had hit parts of the West hard (Scott 1988; Rodwin and Sazanami 1989). The West's exchange relations with other regions and nations had changed drastically (Gottlieb 1998). Some extraction had shifted toward private land in the region or elsewhere in the United States, while some had relocated outside the country altogether.[20] Western

19. See McCarthy 1999; Albert et al. 1989; Maughan and Nilson 1995; Rasker 1992; Power 1996; Nelson 1997; Snow 1994; White 1991.
20. To list just a few specific examples: much raw timber and pulp were exported to Japan and other Pacific Rim countries during the 1980s and early 1990s; many pulp and paper jobs and new investment went to the southeastern United States; new supplies of timber

natural resource industries facing increased competition, resource exhaustion, and increasing environmental regulations also had seen their federal subsidies decline at the same time (Buttel 1992; Flora 1990). It came as no surprise, then, that resistance to increased international economic and regulatory integration rose steadily on the Wise Use agenda during the 1990s, becoming the national movement's primary issue by the late 1990s (McCarthy 1999).

Alongside these shifting geographies of production were emerging new geographies of conservation. As environmental goals became more important in the management of Forest Service and BLM lands, it became increasingly necessary to resolve or reduce the ambiguities in the agencies' multiple mandates. More and more often, they were resolved in favor of environmental goals at the expense of productive uses. In the language of contemporary conservation, many United States federal lands that had long been "extractive reserves" (e.g., national forests and Bureau of Land Management land) were being managed increasingly as ostensibly pristine "nature preserves"—a shift that ran exactly counter to trends in the management of protected areas worldwide.[21] Long-standing patterns of resource use and access were being rapidly criminalized (see also Thompson 1975).

Viewed in this light, the environmentalization of federal lands policy was, in one of its major effects, quite analogous to the original enclosures in England: sweeping reorganizations of land use and property rights and criminalization of established uses were justified through appeals to the overall social good. The trajectory of property relations involved, though, was precisely opposite in the two cases: in the archetypal English enclosures, widespread use rights on communal lands were extinguished in the process of making those lands private; on the federal lands of the U.S. West, the use rights of a relatively small number of private individuals on these lands were extinguished in the process of seeking supposedly much broader public goods. The first created private property for the few at the expense of larger groups of users; the second overrode the property rights and claims of a few for the sake of much broadly defined social goods.

The turn to violence by many elements within Wise Use was hardly sur-

---

and pulp opened up outside the United States; much mining moved to South America; the cattle industry in the West was hurt not so much by reductions in grazing allotments as by a worldwide plunge in beef prices due to oversupply (Gouveia in Bonanno 1994); and farmers in the West (not to mention electronics manufacturers) had a great deal to lose from the Asian financial crises of 1997 (Glasmeier et al. 1997).

21. The term "extractive reserves" was coined to refer to low-impact uses of forests such as tapping rubber and other latexes from forests in Brazil. As used here, it refers to a timber reserve that the U.S. government set aside for itself.

prising given that they interpreted changing federal land management
practices in precisely these terms. Ron Arnold, the leading Wise Use
spokesman, explicitly referred to the English enclosures and stated: "It's
happening right now. And environmental regulations written by the rich
and powerful are the crowbar prying them [rural commodity producers]
from the land" (Arnold 1997: 187). Jim Catron, an attorney who drafted
Wise Use ordinances in New Mexico's Catron County, wrote that recent urban migrants to the "New West":

> . . . have attempted to destroy [rural] Westerners and their values by de-
> stroying their economic base. [They] advocate that the environment must
> be protected from traditional uses. No economic activity will be left for the
> recalcitrant. The power of the federal government will be harnessed to
> starve out the resistance. Rural Westerners are too independent, too self-re-
> liant, too free. They must be outlawed. (Catron 1995a)

Catron also drew an explicit parallel between environmentalists' criticisms of public land commodity producers and the discursive dehumaniza-
tion of the Irish by the English in the seventeenth century, casting both as
attempts to legitimate the expropriation of resources (Catron 1995e).
Many other Wise Use leaders denied that environmental goods were the
real goals of environmentalists at all, stating, "They are not out to save the
trees; they are out to control the people . . . and their land" (Voight 1996).
Grassroots members repeatedly argued that environmental regulations
were not about protecting the environment at all but were part of a larger
plan to drive people off of the land and into cities, where the government
could control them more easily (McCarthy 1999).[22] The fact that Wise Use
activists saw specific environmental regulations as central tools of this mod-
ern-day "enclosure" process is evidenced by the fact that many of the federal employees targeted by Wise Use violence and threats were those most
effective in shifting the management of the federal lands away from commodity production and towards environmental goals (McCarthy 1999;
Helvarg 1997).

Whether environmental priorities on the federal lands can be considered a form of enclosure is debatable. What is not is that the statements of

---

22. For example, a Wise Use organization in the Pacific Northwest calling itself the Committee for Environmental Justice insisted that U.S. plans to cooperate with Canada in the
designation of new trans-boundary international parks in the region were part of a plan to
remove the government of the United States and institute a single global government, under the control of the United Nations. Existing residents of the area would be forcibly removed, and the world's elite would occupy it, living in a privileged reserve, the borders of
which would be protected by the CIA using "electronic fortifications" (Kehoe, quoted in
Pryne 1994).

Catron, Arnold, and other Wise Use participants reflect fears of rural commodity producers being squeezed off of the land. This raises the question: at what point do unintended consequences of complex processes qualify as structural violence? Although the distinction between direct physical violence and economic displacement is important, at some point the structural undermining of livelihoods must be understood as violence. This is a central point of Marx's discussion of primitive accumulation, in which capitalism comes into the world "dripping from head to foot, from every pore, with blood and dirt" from the enclosures (Marx 1967: 712). Such connections are supported by the pronouncements of some environmentalists that the displacement of workers in natural resource industries in the West is merely a form of "collateral damage" (Kerr, quoted in Arnold 1997: 188).

Radical environmentalists' use of violence also was wrapped up with processes of territorialization and enclosure for environmental ends. But where Wise Use participants saw these processes as rapid and threatening, radical environmentalists saw them as desirable, but too slow and accompanied by insufficient permanent protections. They saw themselves as fighting a battle against relentless capitalist development in which every victory was small and temporary, and defeats more common and permanent. Many felt that their agenda for the federal lands was so far outside the bounds of legal and regulatory debates about nature that there would be no point to their participating in the latter: while the Forest Service still deliberated just how many millions of board feet of timber to cut, radical environmentalists advocated turning half of western North America back into wilderness. Many also felt urgent moral imperatives: they insisted that it was an absolute wrong to permit the cutting of any more trees. They compared their efforts to extend rights to nature to the civil rights movement, which they used more and more as their model of a social movement. This moral framework meant that they were unwilling to grant the state—in any of its guises—the final say on what was right or acceptable; therefore, court rulings, administrative decisions, and such were never the last word for them.

Radical environmentalists in the contemporary West saw rampant development and environmental exploitation all around them and foresaw a future in which Los Angeles and Las Vegas—sprawling, water-hungry metropolises—would typify the region, at nature's expense. The federal lands, to them, offered the most likely enclaves of hope in such a future: they could be islands of biodiversity and ecologically healthy systems in a ruined landscape. Thus, to preserve their remaining natural abundance was only to save the last fragments of something irreplaceable that was already nearly gone. Indeed, activists wanted to go beyond preservation of these islands of nature to restoration, reintroducing species that have disappeared

[handwritten margin notes: "structural violence — undermining of livelihoods", "built on unsustainable practices", "morality of West"]

from their former ranges: wolves, grizzly bears, lynx, and more. The Wildlands Project—the organizational incarnation of an early Earth First! slogan, "Back to the Pleistocene!"—sought to set aside approximately fifty percent of the North American continent as "wild land."

Radical environmentalists often failed to recognize that in many cases the natural abundance they wanted to protect was long gone and, in many others, would take massive, ongoing human interventions and management to construct and maintain. They fully realized, however, that their hopes of recreating the Pleistocene on the federal lands were incompatible with commodity production on those lands. Thus, they too wanted to clarify rights on federal lands, but mainly to ensure that those of commodity producers were extinguished. Radical environmentalists never recognized commodity producers' claims as rights. Thus, they derided public lands ranchers as "welfare cowboys" and called for the complete elimination of all grazing, logging, and mining on the federal lands. Although both groups used the language of clarification in the legal arena, in fact they each expected different outcomes. These outcomes would, in effect, either create or destroy property rights, rather than "clarify" them.

Objects, Strategy, and Forms of Violence: Violence as Theater and Narrative

We have looked at the causes of violence by Wise Use and radical environmental activists. Let us now look more closely at that violence itself: its forms, severity, organization, and locations. Once again, we find important similarities and differences between the ways the two groups used violence and attempted to legitimate that use.

Wise Use violence was directed mainly against human beings: federal employees who enforced reductions of access and use, and environmentalists seen as behind those reductions. Some federal infrastructure and equipment also were targeted. Wise Use violence was often personal. To a much greater degree than radical environmentalists, Wise Use participants would identity specific federal employees or environmentalists in their area as particular "problems." Most Wise Use violence seems to have been undertaken alone and by men. Many incidents occurred in public, with no attempt at anonymity. There seemed to be both considerable knowledge in rural communities of who local perpetrators were and a commitment to protecting them when necessary, including drastically downplaying incidents of real or threatened violence (see McCarthy 1999). I characterize Wise Use violence as "frontier violence" because it often seemed to be modeled on perpetrators' conceptions of how conflict would have been handled in the "Old West." For example, Jim Catron referred nostalgically to a time when ". . . someone causing pain to a community was simply shot" (quoted in Dowie 1995). Perhaps oddly, this sort of frontier violence is actually about becoming modern in a particular way.

Radical environmentalists, by contrast, directed their violence mainly against what they characterized as the machines of industrial capitalism, including both private equipment and federal infrastructure. It was, for the most part, covert: undertaken at night by individuals or small groups and by both men and women. Its perpetrators usually had few or no ties to the permanent residents of communities where their actions took place. If they were residents, their actions were closely guarded secrets. They did have tightly knit communities, however, often built around their participation in Earth First! These communities socially rewarded militancy, direct action, and a rhetorical callousness towards human beings as a species (McCarthy 1999). Earth First! violence must be understood in large part as a product of this group culture. For these reasons and because of the focus on attacking the machinery of development, I label it "anti-modern violence."

Despite these clear differences in the objects and social organization of their violence, the two groups again had much in common. They shared a focus on Forest Service and BLM lands, and used violence mainly in struggles over those lands. They recognized that the claims and rights recognized on federal lands were in a period of intense flux and that who and what they would be used for in the next century was a very open and contested question. Both appealed to a heavily mythologized period of rugged frontier individualism that contributed to a shared preference for direct individual action, macho rhetoric, and eagerness for confrontation.[23] Critically, most of the violence from Wise Use and radical environmentalist activists was *threatened* rather than actual. Both groups took advantage of the fact that the creation of fear of violence is itself a potent tactic. Wise Use violence was clearly designed to intimidate its opponents and so to have effects beyond the sites where force was actually used. Radical environmental violence was intended to raise costs not just for the development projects it attacked but for all such projects. Of course, in neither case were these threats empty; in both cases they were backed up by real acts of violence, thus increasing the power of the threats. Each group also took advantage of the fact that the use of violence by non-state actors remains outside the

---

23. Substantial scholarship has called into question ideas of frontier individualism, suggesting that the lesson of the frontier was, rather, the need for cooperation and massive state developmental initiatives (e.g., White 1991). Others have compiled statistics showing that the Western frontier was no more violent than the United States as a whole and was less violent than East Coast cities at the time. Also, much frontier violence had its roots not in the absence of state personnel or conflicts over land per se, but in the sudden presence of tens of thousands of discharged Civil War veterans, many of whom moved West and brought their guns with them—the first mass infusion of personal firearms into American society.

norm for environmental conflicts in the United States. Violent incidents were, therefore, almost certain to attract extensive media coverage and increase attention to what were in fact marginal political positions. In this respect, both groups used violence for theatrical purposes.

Normalization and Legitimation

Having examined the causes and actual operations of Wise Use and radical environmental violence, let us turn to the issue of their legitimacy. I approach this by asking about the normalization of each group's violence: its place in, or exclusion from, accepted tactical repertoires in a given society. Normalization generally proceeds mainly through the definition of the abnormal or deviant; that is, uses or users of violence that are deemed unacceptable or illegitimate. It is quite difficult for nongovernment groups in the United States to claim the right to use violence and to have their use accepted as a normal part of certain conflicts. Even *threatening* violence was an important discursive tactic in this sense: in such threats, each group implicitly claimed the *right* to deploy violence should it so choose, and so attempted to position itself as a *legitimate* user of force. Both groups went to great lengths to legitimate their own use of violence and to label the other's as deviant. I examine their efforts in three areas: their basic justification for violence; their particular understandings of the federal lands that help to authorize their violence; and finally their construction of closely interwoven conceptions of community, the public good, and their own group identities.

I believe that some Wise Use participants felt justified in using violence because the processes of enclosure and re-territorialization of federal lands for new environmental goals amounted to a violation of what they viewed as a "moral economy" of the rural West (McCarthy 1999).[24] That is, they had a broad, coherent vision of the historical rights and roles of natural resource commodity producers on the federal lands as central to the political economy of the rural West. This moral economy was based on the region's nineteenth-century political economy and implicit and explicit social contracts between the federal government and rural western communities.

Defenders of this view could marshal a substantial array of historical support. Primary commodity producers were clearly privileged as the dominant users of federal lands at formative periods in the history of the West. Productive uses predated contemporary federal land agencies and envi-

24. "Moral economy" is E. P. Thompson's term, which (paraphrasing) he defined as the regulation of ostensibly economic relations according to nonmonetary norms, including customs and usages (1991). Moral economies are consciously articulated mainly when they are threatened by the rationalizations of capitalist markets. It is of course an analytical term; such norms are not necessarily good (Watts 1983).

ronmental legislation. Private ranches and adjacent public grazing lands developed together as an integrated system. Informal, community-recognized property arrangements (most having to do with grazing) existed on many western public lands prior to intensive federal administration. The federal agencies regulating these lands, including the Forest Service, were for decades classic examples of "captured" agencies, largely controlled by resource users with extensive local autonomy (West 1982). Grazing permits for federal lands possessed many of the standard characteristics of a commodity, bolstering arguments that they were a kind of private property. Many families, particularly ranchers, had, as they claim, been working the same land for generations (although they are a very small minority of federal land users, the power of their example in rural Western communities was enormous).[25] The rules governing these producers and their relations to other claimants on the federal lands had unquestionably changed drastically and rapidly in recent decades (see McCarthy 1999).

Such evidence, of course, justified claims regarding land use and access, not the use of violence per se. However, the duration and solidity of these precedents, combined with recent state refusals to honor them, certainly helped to legitimize the defense of these precedents by illegal means. More broadly, Wise Use activists also challenged the federal right to manage these lands at all. Environmentalist critics of Wise Use, as we have seen, sought to undermine these claims as a form of welfare and to link all Wise Use activity to militias and other groups almost universally regarded in popular U.S. culture as deviant and dangerous.

Radical environmentalists, by contrast, justified their direct actions by appeals to urgent ecological goals. They insisted that irreversible ecological harm would occur unless they took action immediately and that, therefore, both morality and nature were on their side. Since they usually espoused a biocentric ethic, they claimed that their concerns trumped merely "human" politics. Their critics, particularly those affiliated with the Wise Use movement, sought to undermine this portrayal and to present radical environmentalists as deviant in almost all respects: anti-human, self-hating, anti-American, opposed to all technological progress, and responsible for extreme violence, including the actions of the Unabomber.

I argue that members of each group felt justified in turning to violence specifically in struggles over Forest Service and BLM lands because they believed at some level that these lands still existed—or _ought_ still to have existed—in a "state of nature." This belief justified both the denial of the state's authority over these lands—and by extension all of the various legal avenues for struggle over them—and the use of violence by non-state ac-

25. For further discussion of these historical precedents see, for example, Hess 1992; Hirt 1994; Klyza 1996; Wilkinson 1992.

tors.[26] The two groups understood the state of nature very differently, however.

For Wise Use activists, the federal lands were in a fundamentally Lockean state of nature: and "waste" land that cried out for improvement ought to be available for the taking. People who put such land to productive use performed a service for society as well as for themselves (Locke 1978). Those who appropriated and cultivated land, lifting it from the wasteful "state of nature," thus deserved both proprietary rights and respect from society. Many public lands ranchers thus saw themselves as contributing more to society than most people by being productive stewards of the public domain—a far cry from the environmentalist view of precisely the same material relations as a form of "cowboy welfare." Wise Use activists did not appeal to Locke explicitly, but they did cite Thomas Jefferson—whose vision for the construction of an agrarian democracy in the United States via privatization of the vast public domain was largely an attempt to instantiate Locke's theory of property (McCarthy 1999; White 1991).

The Wise Use invocation of a Lockean state of nature with respect to the public lands was, however, incomplete and inconsistent. They adopted Locke's positions regarding the desirability of private appropriation of the wilderness and the social utility of strong private property rights, including the potential for private property to act as a check on the power of the state. But they ignored his corollary points: that the state is needed to uphold those property rights, that property is a fundamentally social institution, and that his theories regarding appropriation of the wilderness are only fair if enough land remains for everyone to appropriate as much as they could work (see Bromley 1998; Last 1998).

Radical environmentalists also seemed to view the public lands as being in a state of nature. But their state of nature was quite unlike Locke's: theirs derived from Rousseau and the Romantic tradition that shapes so much of modern Western environmentalism. They constructed the proper state of the federal lands as one of natural harmony, undisturbed by industrialized society or any significant human alteration. To the extent that the actual lands did not live up to this ideal, they wanted to move them towards it, to restore them to a state of pristine wilderness (Cronon 1996). As Foreman wrote, "Monkeywrenching is aimed at keeping industrial 'civilization' out of natural areas and causing its retreat from areas that *should* be wild (1985: 14, emphasis added). Most often, this played out in constructions of these lands as teeming with natural abundance of wildlife and

---

26. It also turned a blind eye to other claims on these lands that have deeper roots in history and tradition, such as those originating with Mexican land grants or the forced removal of Native Americans.

resources, but historically devoid of human actors (e.g., Foreman and Haywood 1985: 10).

Environmentalists' state of nature also invoked ideologies of the American frontier. In the words of Gila Watch, an environmental organization in New Mexico, "Public lands also represent the final American frontier . . . ." (1996). This interpretation of the Western "frontier" follows from a long tradition of Europeans' projections of an idealized, Edenic state of nature onto the geographic edges of their old empires. In this light, the enduring fascination among many radical environmentalists with romanticized visions of "hunter-gatherer" societies is disturbingly reminiscent of the fact that the first proposals for natural parks included provisions for Native Americans inhabiting them in their "primitive" state (Catlin, quoted in Nash, 1990: 35; see also Lewis 1992).

> For many of us, perhaps for most of us, the wilderness is as much our home, or a lot more so, than the wretched little stucco boxes, plywood apartments, and wallboard condominiums in which we are mostly confined by the insatiable demands of an overcrowded and ever-expanding industrial culture. . . . An Englishman's home is his castle; an American's home is his favorite fishing stream, his favorite mountain range, his favorite desert canyon, his favorite swamp or patch of woods or God-created lake. (Abbey, in Foreman and Haywood 1985: 8)

While Abbey speaks here of "wilderness" in the generic sense, the life history and other writings of this prophet of the radical environmental movement all focus on the "undiscovered" federal lands of the West: the Forest Service and BLM lands that offered escape from civilization precisely because they had not been granted park status and so lacked roads, signs, and so forth. This passage also reveals a deep inconsistency in the radical environmentalist view of the federal lands as existing in the state of nature: the very claiming of this wilderness as the spiritual "home" of (white, male) Americans, explicitly making it analogous to freehold property in England, reveals an essentially Lockean relationship to North America hidden within the heart of the Romantic vision.

Radical environmentalists saw their activism as occurring in a "state of nature" in other respects as well. First, they claimed to reject the authority of the state at a fundamental level (while nevertheless constantly appealing to it to enforce environmental laws).[27] Edward Abbey, the movement's foremost spokesman, wrote in the foreword to an Earth First! guide to "monkeywrenching" tactics that: "Representative government in the

---

27. The absence of the state is what defines the "state of nature" in modern Western political theory.

United States has broken down . . . [it] represents money not people and therefore has forfeited our allegiance and moral support. We owe it nothing. . . ." (Foreman and Haywood 1985: 7). Second, having rejected the authority of the state, it is not surprising that many radical environmentalists proceeded to reject the institution of private property. Although public lands were the original focus of Earth First! activism, most of their actions targeted private property on these lands, and later participants argued that land tenure was irrelevant in the defense of nature—unconsciously echoing Rousseau's dictum that all property is theft (Bari 1994: 104–105).

State Responses

The use of violence by both radical environmentalist and Wise Use activists constituted a challenge to federal authority to manage resources and to the state's desired monopoly on the use of force. In fact, both groups' actions arguably met the legal definition of "terrorism" in the United States (which treats attacks on property as equivalent to attacks on humans).[28] Yet, the federal government responded to the two movements' turns to violence in strikingly different ways.

The federal response to Wise Use violence was generally subdued and nonconfrontational. Despite their challenges to state authority, Wise Use participants were still often treated as if they were what they claimed to be: the backbone of the American economy and civil society. On many occasions the federal government failed to take legal action against Wise Use participants even after direct, documented incidents of violence or threats against federal employees (McCarthy 1999, *Clear View* 3(9); Rowell 1996; Helvarg 1997).[29] The explicit strategy of the Justice Department, which had responsibility for most of these decisions, was to avoid adding fuel to the fire. Even though it recognized the danger to federal employees and the illegality of Wise Use actions, it focused on avoiding further conflict with Wise Use participants (McCarthy 1999; Helvarg 1997).

In 1995, at the height of Wise Use activism, the Justice Department convened a meeting of officials from the federal land management agencies for the express purpose of steering these agencies toward less confronta-

28. "[T]he unlawful use of force or violence, committed by a group(s) or two or more individuals, against persons or property to intimidate or coerce a government, the civilian population, or any segment thereof, in furtherance of political or social objectives" (FBI 1995: 162).

29. Important exceptions to this overall response were efforts—largely ignored—by Congressmen George Miller (D-CA) and Charles Schumer (D-NY) to investigate threats to federal employees and environmental activists (*Clear View* 2(2), 1995). But these efforts attracted neither wider congressional support nor follow-up from the Justice Department.

tional tactics in handling disputes with loggers, ranchers, and off-road vehicle users on federal lands in the West (Arnold 1997: 108–109). This explicit decision to minimize or soft-pedal enforcement of environmental laws and regulations, conflicted with the duties of land management agency employees who were the direct targets of Wise Use anger. Thus, the Forest Service and BLM at times sent rangers in dangerous areas out in pairs and had them maintain radio contact. The Forest Service gave employees instructions on what to do if arrested by local sheriffs, as had been threatened in some local Wise Use legislation (McCarthy 1999). The Justice Department ultimately took legal action against some of the county governments most active in the Wise Use movement, but only by legally reaffirming its ownership of the land in question—not by filing criminal charges against people who had threatened federal employees (*Clear View* 3(5), 1996). More recently, the New Mexico State Police issued a report on potentially violent right-wing groups that included the Wise Use movement in that category. Wise Use activists immediately protested this characterization, and the report was amended to exclude most Wise Use groups. Moreover, the same police agreed to prepare a parallel report on radical left groups—not because they saw a need, but in response to Wise Use criticisms that the original report only looked at right-wing groups (Romo, 1998).

In stark contrast, federal responses to radical environmentalists were rapid and severe. Earth First! and similar groups were treated as socially marginal and as genuine dangers to national security. Congress passed a law in 1988 specifically making tree-spiking a felony, with potential penalties far more severe than those for trespass and damage to property—laws that already made the activity clearly criminal (Arnold 1997: 159). In June of 1998, the Crime Subcommittee of the United States House of Representatives held hearings on "eco-terrorism," receiving testimony from major Wise Use leaders (*Clear View* 8/7/98). Both Maine and Oregon introduced laws prohibiting "eco-terrorism" in 1999, defining it in extremely broad and probably unconstitutional terms (*Clear View* 1999).

The FBI took the lead in the federal response to radical environmentalist violence. It formed an environmental crimes task force and mounted elaborate sting operations in the Southwest. Agents infiltrated Earth First! groups and provoked them into taking larger and larger actions, for which they were then arrested (Bari 1994: 54; Rowell 1996). The FBI has long maintained lists of known or suspected radical environmentalists attending public gatherings, and it interrogated suspected activists with little evidence (Cockburn and St. Clair, *The Nation*, 5/6/96). When California Earth First! activist Judi Bari, noted for establishing alliances with timber industry workers, was the victim of a car bomb in 1990, the FBI accused her of planting the bomb herself. The agency eventually dropped the charges due to a complete lack of evidence, but it has since essentially ig-nored abundant evidence pointing to anti-environmentalist sources for the bomb (Bari 1994; Rowell 1996; Helvarg 1997). In sum, Earth First!, which consciously moved toward modeling itself on the civil rights and peace movements, seems to have succeeded at least in provoking similar federal responses: infiltration, provocation, and abuse of basic constitu-tional rights of privacy and due process (Bari 1994; Rowell 1996).

Similar responses to radical environmental activism have occurred at the local level, with local law enforcement officials refusing to investigate as-saults and threats against radical environmentalists and sometimes con-tributing to such violence themselves (Rowell 1996). For example, in 1998 police officers from California's Humboldt County were acquitted of charges of the use of excessive force against environmental activists in a nonviolent demonstration. The environmentalists had chained themselves together in the headquarters of a timber company and in the office of a legislator supportive of logging. When they refused to leave, police care-fully swabbed pepper spray into their eyes. Police claimed that this was the safest and most effective means to get the protesters to leave; critics argued that it represented the gratuitous infliction of pain and that mechanical means of removal had been readily available (Egelko 1998).

In sum, the state vigorously asserted its capacity to use violence and other enforcement techniques against radical environmentalists but largely refrained from doing so against Wise Use activists. Moreover, it quickly dubbed direct actions by radical environmentalists "eco-terrorism," attaching all of the connotations of terrorism to their activities, and suc-ceeded in making this the accepted term for such activities—as seen in the word's inclusion in the latest English-language dictionaries.[30] Such a dis-cursive move marked the direct actions of radical environmentalists as de-viant, while the state's relative silence regarding Wise Use violence went a long way toward normalizing it.

Why this difference? I believe that law enforcement officials saw ardent Wise Use activists as both *more* and *less* of a threat than radical environmen-talists. They were *more* of a threat because their claims to use rights on fed-eral lands were in some cases quite strong, resting on an array of historical precedent, reasonable expectations, and institutional and community sup-port. I argue that the federal land management agencies were reluctant to challenge them directly in part out of fear that they could not be sure of winning easily and quickly. Any sort of protracted contest, in which the agencies had to genuinely struggle or invoke federal military force to as-

---

30. "Ecoterrorism: (function: noun. Date: 1987.) 1: sabotage intended to hinder activities that are considered damaging to the environment 2: political terrorism intended to dam-age an enemy's natural environment." Merriam Webster Dictionary.

sert their control over these lands, would have actually weakened the state by illuminating its ultimate dependence on force. At a more institutional level, Wise Use participants represented important constituencies of the federal land agencies with whom the agencies were reluctant to break ranks entirely.

Wise Use activists also were more of a threat because many of them were far more willing and able to deploy severe violence than were radical environmentalists: many federal land management employees in areas of intense Wise Use activism genuinely feared for their bodily safety (McCarthy 1999). The federal government's understated response to Wise Use violence also was influenced by its experiences in the 1992 siege of white separatist Randy Weaver and his family in northern Idaho, and in the 1993 raid on a militant religious group in Waco, Texas. In each case, armed federal responses arguably worsened volatile situations and were heavily criticized afterwards. Moreover, the social base of Wise Use probably would have expanded significantly in the wake of more federal violence, a circumstance that was not the same for the radical environmentalists. Last, Wise Use activism was *less* threatening insofar as its conceptions of property rights and the transformation of nature for economic purposes sat squarely within the mainstream of social norms in the rural West and U.S. society at large. Indeed, many local law enforcement officials were actively involved in Wise Use: county sheriffs and attorneys were among its prime movers and strongest backers in many counties (McCarthy 1999).

Conversely, I suggest that the state responded so severely to radical environmentalists because they were both *less* and *more* of a threat than Wise Use activists. They were *less* of a threat in two ways. First, their claims to control over federal lands were nowhere near as strong; they had little community support or long history of institutionalized land uses behind them on the Forest Service and BLM lands in the rural West. Similarly, their tactical use of violence could not be legitimated by the strong "moral economy" kinds of historical precedents that Wise Use invoked. Second, they were in fact far less likely to deploy physical violence against law enforcement personnel. Rejecting their claims and tactics outright thus posed no significant risks to the state or its personnel. They were *more* of a threat than Wise Use activists, though, in that their attitudes toward land use and property rights conflicted sharply with social norms in the rural West and capitalist society in general. These norms privilege property rights, property owners, and the imperative to transform nature in the service of capital accumulation. It is at this level that radical environmentalists parted company with most of the mainstream environmental community, which, therefore, did not support them. Radical environmentalists were, therefore, far more readily perceived as genuinely deviant by law enforcement officials than were ranchers and loggers.

Conclusion

Both the Wise Use movement and radical environmentalism rejected or attacked major elements of capitalist modernity. This took the form of appeals to a stable moral economy for Wise Use activists and of a rejection of "industrial society" for radical environmentalists. As part of this anti-modern impulse, both rejected the authority of the state over the federal lands, which they then saw as existing in a "state of nature" and, therefore, an appropriate arena in which to use violence to strengthen claims. The state ultimately helped to mark radical environmental violence as deviant and to normalize Wise Use violence as an accepted part of conflicts in the rural West.

6

Damaging Crops: Sabotage, Social Memory, and the New Genetic Enclosures

Iain A. Boal

> This is a fragile part of the country: nowhere here can be found inde-
> structible gneiss or enduring rocks tried through time and indurated
> through depth of burial. . . . It is a place to feel the ephemeral grasp we
> have on the past.
>
> (Fortey 1993)

> In 1549 A.D. Robert Kett, yeoman farmer, of Wymondham was executed
> by hanging in this castle after the defeat of the Norfolk rebellion of
> which he was leader. In 1949 A.D., four hundred years later, this memo-
> rial was placed here by the citizens of Norwich in reparation and honour
> to a notable and courageous leader in the long struggle of the common
> people of England to escape from a servile life into the freedom of just
> conditions.
>
> Plaque on the wall of Norwich Castle

The harvest of 1997 saw the beginnings of widespread sabotage, both open and clandestine, of genetically engineered plants undergoing field trials in the British Isles. The contested plots have been not only experimental but also rhetorical. Both the contending camps—the agrifood industry (with its associated scientists) and the broad resistance movement—are mobilizing history, social memory, and popular culture to frame their activities. What is on offer from both wings are mostly variations on organicism: the talk is of pollution, purity, monstrosity, and risks to the natural and human order. It has made for some strange bedfellows—Prince Charles and pagan anarcha-pacifists, for example. But one group (operating in East Anglia under the sign of Captain Chromosome) refuses the strategically and epistemologically fatal "nature/artifice" fork. By implicitly claiming Captain Swing and the agricultural Luddites as ancestors, it intuitively grasps the nub of the new developments down on the

146

farm and their historical continuity: genetically engineered crops and patents represent a further seizure of the commons and will bring a new round of enclosures and global proletarianization.

This chapter speculates on the special nature and history of East Anglia that produced this particular manifestation of "Luddism" and its implications for an emancipatory science and technics. Among the fruits of the radical science movement is an explanation of the failure of what might be termed the positivist project and the recognition that all facts underdetermine, and are forged within, some organizing frame, whether acknowledged or tacit. The struggle over the future of plant-genetic technologies discloses this truth at the level of praxis. The current debate has been joined under the twin signs of ancient and modern mythology, Prometheus and Frankenstein. It is, from a political–ecological viewpoint, another mock epic, like the Cold War. If so, then what countermyths and practices might be adequate to the occasion? In other words, who will mobilize, under what banner, to frame the question: "What shall nature be?"

Trouble's Afoot

For the third season rural Britain and Ireland have witnessed extensive Luddite activity directed at the new products of plant-genetic engineering. During the fall of 1997, for example, the Gaelic Earth Liberation Front trampled Monsanto's test field of modified maize in County Carlow and later staged a "Digging the Beet" action; in West Sussex a genetically engineered (GE) oilseed rape field trial was uprooted; GE apple trees were "ringbarked" at Broomfield Agricultural College. Significant sabotage also has occurred in France and Germany. In January 1998 a band of more than a hundred farmers, apparently trained in moral economy, converged on the Novartis drying plant in Nerac, France, and, in a kind of reverse "food riot," destroyed the store of GE maize seeds.[1]

Well over three hundred field trial sites for GE crops in the British Isles have been identified from official sources. Monsanto is the largest firm testing genetically modified crops (120 of the sites). Other organizations include Novartis, Pioneer Genetique, Plant Genetic Systems, Scottish Crop

---

1. The British state attempted to chill the reporting of news of such direct action by mounting "Operation Washington." At the resulting trial in November 1997 at Portsmouth Crown Court, the presiding judge, Major-General Selwood, sentenced three editors of *Green Anarchist* to a draconian three years in prison for distributing issues of the magazine carrying news of eco-sabotage by, among others, the Poultry Liberation Organization (PLO). In the same court the previous month, an identical sentence was passed on a man who had strangled his wife and buried her under the patio.

Research Institute, Sharpes International Seeds, National Institute of Agricultural Botany (NIAB), Leeds University Centre for Plant Biochemistry and Biotechnology, and AgrEvoUK Crop Protection. At least thirty-six test fields were "paid a visit" in the 1998 growing season. The figure was undoubtedly much larger because some firms did not report the sabotage for fear of providing "oxygen" to other direct activists (Vidal 1999). Precise location of the test sites is hampered by inaccurate or misleading coordinates in the public register. The GE crop typically is either surrounded by a barrier crop of a conventional variety and separated by a meter or so or else a central strip is flanked by two conventional ones, in either case placed so as to catch pollen.

Cloak and Digger

The crop saboteurs come in both diurnal and nocturnal varieties. The widest media coverage has gone to an outfit called GenetiX Snowball, based in Manchester, who are organizing openly. It sports an office, mobile phones, a press liaison person, and information packs. Its modus operandi is an amalgam of Gandhian nonviolence and Catholic witness in the Ploughshares tradition. The organizers alert farmers and police of their plans in advance—insisting that those who volunteer for the actions acknowledge "accountability" and show willingness to be grist for the legal mills. Monsanto is seeking to win damages in the High Court against five women from GenetiX Snowball and to enjoin them from "encouraging others" (ibid.). The Snowball is advertised through a clearinghouse called Genetic Engineering Network, which clinically describes the art of "decontamination." Oilseed rape (canola) plants, for instance, are best dealt with by means of a broom handle held horizontally. "People just hold the sticks out in front of them and fall into the plants. They snap very easily this way and instead of just breaking the area around their bodies, each time they fall forwards they take a whole meter square with them."[2]

The Snowballers, though engaged in acts that are being criminalized, have the broad sympathy of "middle England" and organizations such as the Women's Institute, the Townswomen's Guild, The Consumers Association, and the Country Landowners, all of whom have called for a moratorium of between two and five years on commercial GE crops.[3] In this respect it has become a form of guerrilla warfare in classic style with the saboteurs swimming in the sea of a tacitly approving populace. A group

2. Posting on GEN website <www.dmac.co.uk/gen.html> as at 9/22/98.
3. Currently in Britain, the only genetically modified foods available commercially are tomato paste, vegetarian cheese, maize, and soya.

calling themselves the "Kenilworth Croppers" scythed down a display of GE wheat at the Royal Agricultural Show in the summer of 1998, even while it was under heavy guard.

Some of the clandestine groups (with names like the "Lincolnshire Loppers" and "Superheroes against Genetics") have affinities with the mothballed antinuclear movement, and there is cross-membership with veterans of the antiroad movement, which goes some way to account for the style and sheer feistiness of the movement. The direct action campaign against what Thatcher's Minister of Transport called "the biggest road building programme since the Romans" ended in a notable reversal of policy after Thatcher herself had declared, "Nothing can stop the great car economy." In 1992 the roads budget stood at a gigantic £23 billion sterling, at which point two travelers—half punk, half pagan—pitched camp on the ancient and much-loved landscape of Twyford Down, overlooking the watermeadows where Keats wrote "Season of mists and mellow fruitfulness" and placed their bodies in the way of the proposed Winchester bypass. Soon there were thousands joining the direct action ("We shall fight them in the beeches"; "Yurts are definitely the way forward—the Mongols had it sussed"), and within months road protests had sprung up at threatened sites all over the country. Thousands of private security goons were drafted in to try, with brutal tactics, to stop the protests, and in 1994 the road resisters were targeted by the notorious Criminal Justice Act. Still, by 1996 the roads program was essentially scrapped, overwhelmed by a surging public sentiment in favor of limits to the culture of automobilism. George Monbiot, an environmental journalist, described it as "one of the very few genuine triumphs that people power has ever enjoyed. The roads protests have already taken their place in the folklore of these islands" (Evans 1998). And in the language: "bender," "twigloo," "lock-on," "blat," and "digger-diving" have entered the vernacular. The memory of this recent victory for direct action in the countryside is helping to swell the ranks and to constitute the self-understanding of the new agricultural Luddites.

The Rhetorical Turf

When Harry Collins, the sociologist of laboratory life—in a study of research programs, the culture of the "core set" of scientists working in such projects, and their relation to the wider society—concluded that the "degree of certainty which is ascribed to knowledge increases catastrophically as it crosses the core set boundary in both space and time," he wasn't reckoning with the plant geneticists of Norfolk (Collins 1985). Writing in London's *Independent* in the summer of 1998 under the headline "Why I'm happy to 'play God' with your food," Jonathan Jones, a senior genetic engineer in Norwich, replied to a speech by the Prince of Wales on the question of transgenic crop plants, in which the Prince had spoken up for "God's rights" and warned of "living pollution that cannot be recalled" (Jones 1998). Jones, a student of molecular biology and plant genetics at Cambridge in the 1970s, had been in the orbit of the *marxisant* Agricapital group, then joined the gene-splicing firm Advanced Genetic Sciences in Emeryville, California, and in the early 90s was headhunted back to East Anglia to the Sainsbury-funded plant genetics laboratory in Norwich.

Jones's discursive strategy as a genetic engineer changed from previous assertions, of a decade and a half earlier, that modern gene-shifting techniques were smoothly continuous with traditional husbandry. In the face of the new regimes of intellectual property and plant breeders' rights, and perhaps to rationalize patent claims to living forms, Jones puts it thus: "Is this technology significantly different from traditional plant breeding? Yes. Is it worryingly different? No. In fact it's better. It's more precise, it's easier to control, it enables one to take the properties of a plant more directly towards a specific goal" (ibid.). Precision, control, and goal-specificity are the stock-in-trade of technocratic rationality. What is striking on further examination is the way in which Jones stands, in this respect, full square within the same ideological frame as his opponents.

The anathemas, then, have an interesting symmetry: the geneticists as offspring of Victor Frankenstein, producing monstrous creatures in violation of the natural order that are likely to turn on their creators; the Luddites as a violent many-headed hydra trashing science's promise of cornucopia. Neither camp seems to notice that they are both committed to versions of organicism, deploying within that frame the tropes of monstrosity, unnaturalness, and transgression. The bulletins of the GenetiX Snowball talk routinely of "decontaminating" fields of GE crops; Jones says the solution is "an agriculture based in genetics rather than chemistry. Delivering crop protection inside the plant is less polluting than spraying chemicals" (ibid.). A politics of purity lurks within all talk of contamination and pollution. The key difference between the versions of organicism on offer in this debate is that the (green) Promethean scientist is not disturbed by the imputation of "artifice"; indeed, it is not an accusation at all but a reminder of the craftiness necessary to the task as scientist.

In the light of the dominant rhetoric of organicism, it is worth exploring the significance of East Anglia as the location of Luddites operating under the banner of Captain Chromosome, Luddites who sabotage GE crops not because such crops do violence to nature but because they constitute an assault on the commons (Gibbs 1998).[4] Captain Chromosome echoes the

---

4. In Devon, the failure of a legal challenge by a large-scale organic farmer named Guy Watson to Monsanto's GM-maize neighboring field trials (on the grounds of cross-pollination compromising his "organic" status) produced direct action against the trial crops by

rural Luddites of post-Napoleonic War East Anglia and evokes the incendi-arism and machine-breaking of "Captain Swing." An anonymous bulletin on damaging crops is circulating under the rubric "A Little Commotion in Norfolk," a phrase with deep historical resonance in the county, invoking as it does "the Great Commotion" of 1549, when Kett led the uprising against the enclosing landlords.[5]

Genius Loci

Let us then pose the question: What kind of account would be needed for an adequate explanation of the appearance of Captain Chromosome in Norfolk? Any interesting answer would belong, in the phrase of Patrick Geddes, to the "literature of locality" and would address at least the follow-ing: (1) the long history of East Anglian uprisings and resistance to the en-closures, in its regional specificity, from Robert Kett in the sixteenth cen-tury through Captain Swing in the nineteenth, to the Felixstowe animal rights blockade at the close of the twentieth; (2) the histories of field inva-sions, in particular of the institution of "the camping close." The game of camping was an ancient, officially illegal, East Anglian ballgame, "disor-derly and violent"("camp" = Anglo-Saxon "fight"). Under the cover of camp-ball, commoners would range over enclosed fields to protest what they perceived as the infringement of common rights. It was a time of fes-tivity and violence. For generations Kett's uprising was known as "the campyng tyme" (Dymond 1990); (3) the agro-geology of East Anglia and the relation of its postglacial upland (just a few feet above sea level) fertil-ity to its role as a region of agricultural innovation (the Norfolk system, and so on), and later site of plant breeding institutions. The Morley Re-search Centre, now a major site of field experiments for NIAB, lies at ground zero of Kett's uprising; (4) Norfolk and northern Suffolk as coun-tercultural refuges in the fallout of the sixties, and the evolution of the "Peace Convoy" and its relation to the road resistance and crop sabotage; (5) the dichotomization of nature versus artifice undergirds virtually all the discourse of resistance to genetic engineering and the way the land and its productions are conceived. If there is a place in Britain where the nature/artifice opposition qua landscape is least plausible, it is East Anglia.

---

the Genetic Engineering Network. Interestingly, Watson invoked in justification the histori-cal precedent of the Tolpuddle Martyrs. See the report by Geoffrey Gibbs in the *Guardian*, August 5, 1998.

5. Andrew Wood of the University of East Anglia is researching a "history from below" of the Kett uprising. A number of pamphlets were published to coincide with the four hun-dred and fiftieth anniversary of the uprising in July 1999, but all were more or less deriva-tive of the standard historical accounts, fundamentally hostile to Kett.

It holds a special place, scenically, in the national imagination, due in part to Constable and to the painters of the so-called Norwich school.

Ecologically, the broads of Norfolk and the Suffolk border are the most important surviving wetland habitat in lowland Britain. It is now clear that far from being a "natural" landscape, the broadland habitats are relics of opencast peat-mines. J. M. Lambert and her colleagues, paleo-ecologists working in East Anglia in the late 1940s and early 1950s, were inspired by A. G. Tansey and his Cambridge Botany School Ecology Club. They "became incredulously aware of the possibility that these serene stretches of water were not natural, but lay in hollows excavated by long-forgotten generations of turf-cutters" (Godwin 1960). These opencast peat-workings were inundated in the late Middle Ages by a series of marine transgressions from the North Sea, in particular the great flood of 1287 A.D.

So East Anglia is a landscape whose "naturalness" has depended historically on constant human intervention, which reveals the fundamental incoherence of any dichotomy between the natural and the artificial. The reedbeds, to take another example, that are viewed romantically by holidaymakers messing about in boats, are in fact agricultural fields to the commercial sedgecutters, who harvest them for thatch. The restoration of the broads cannot be carried through in terms of some organic pristine nature, but as a worked landscape. The seeds now being modified and patented are the result of the labors of "long-forgotten generations" of farmers and gardeners—no more or less "natural" than the broads with which they are mostly incompatible.

Unnatural Properties

On March 3, 1998 the United States Department of Agriculture (USDA) and the Delta and Pine Land Company in Scott, Mississippi, were granted U.S. patent no. 5723765, a method of producing sterile seeds in the second generation by means of the transfection of a lethal gene: encoding (e.g., catalytic proteins such as diphtheria toxin and ribosomal inhibitor) that renders the seeds produced by the plant incapable of germination. The patent description dissembles the intended purpose of the technique—it speaks of preventing "post-harvest germination, the escape of a plant through natural seed dispersal into a location where it is not desired, or accidental reseeding."[6] Melvin Oliver, the inventor of the USDA labs in Lubbock, Texas, was more candid: "Our system is a way of self-policing the unauthorized use of American technology. It's similar to copyright protection" (*New Scientist* 1998: 22). He said that the seed companies regard the replanting of seeds as theft of their intellectual property and that they have

6. U.S. Patent no. 5723765; detailed description, column 6.

been searching for years for ways to prevent farmers from recycling seeds from their crops. Willard Phelps of the USDA predicted that soon farmers will only be able to buy seeds with the "terminator gene." The U.S. government's aim, he said, is merely to ensure the profits that are made from its introduction are not excessive (ibid.).

Reaction from the Global South to the terminator patent was swift. Camila Montecinos of the Center for Education and Technology in Santiago, Chile, called for the outlawing of the new technology as "an immoral technique that robs farming communities of their age-old right to save seed." Hope Shand of the Rural Advancement Foundation International described it as "terribly dangerous . . . . Half the world's farmers are poor and can't afford to buy seed every growing season. Yet they grow 15 to 20 percent of the world's food" (ibid.).

What could reveal the logic of capital more starkly than patent no. 5723765? It gives the lie to the rhetoric of a green revolution redux and to Jonathan Jones's pieties about feeding the world. This patent is about designing scarcity, a commodity that capitalism has been producing from its inception, and about capital's grappling greater control over agricultural production. It will permit greater appropriation of agricultural surplus and will go some way to redressing the relative failure of capitalist concentration down on the farm by forcing growers back to market every year and making self-produced viable seeds impossible. Hitherto the seed companies have been partially successful in cornering seed input with the "inbred/hybrid" method of germ production (possible for a only few organisms). Yields are compromised because the second-generation plants are not true hybrids, so forcing farmers to buy seeds externally, rather than using the "free goods" of F2 (Lewontin 1998).

Fundamental questions concerning the genetic engineering of organisms require us to be clear on the essential differences between the traditional arts of plant breeding and the new techniques. If there is a revolution technically, it lies in the synergy of two novelties: (1) an exponential expansion of the taxonomic range available for gene transfer (that is to say, traditionally there was no possibility of a fish gene in tomatoes) and (2) the ability to target specific processes in plants. Genetic engineers tend to work with one transgene and a single "objective," exemplifying what Jonathan Jones calls "goal-specificity." By contrast, traditional husbandry (this is still true for organic farming) tends to favor "old-fashioned" varieties that both are acceptable in quality (while perhaps falling short of the ideotype) and have "durable" rather than "race-specific" resistance. But because this implies multiply favorable alleles, durable resistance is harder to test for.

It is not merely a matter of techniques, however. The larger question hinges on the subtle effects of the division of labor necessary for such technical work, parallel to the affective changes under technical reorganization of the labor process involved in animal husbandry with production regimes that operationalize, deskill, fragment, and favor episodic contacts and routines rather than long-term relationships (Benton 1993). Similarly, to return to the question of the fish-antifreeze-gene-in-the-tomato, it might appear that to balk at such a genetically modified organism would be tantamount to collapsing into a "violation of nature" position. There is another principle, however, under which extreme "transgenic distance" might be queried. This is not an organic criterion but rather a full-dress political one, articulated in the name of a Kropotkinian science: the minimizing where possible of gradience and hierarchy, though one could readily imagine such a principle conflicting with other desirable criteria. By the same principle, for example, all fusion research should cease. Although in one sense a "solar" technology, it anticipates the construction on earth (for example, at Culham, Oxford) of an apparatus—a magnetic torus—that has an unacceptably extreme temperature gradient between the magma (as hot as the sun's interior and, a few inches away, the dank Oxfordshire countryside).

Harvests of Violence

The nexus of nature and artifice and the social relations embedded there invite further exploration, particularly of the antinomies of violence and its theaters together with their connections to the Promethean mythos of science and technics. At the dawn of industrial capitalism in factory and field at the nodal points of enclosure, the historic weapons of General Ludd and Captain Swing—hammer and sickle—were refunctioned for the creative destruction of the means of domination. It was remarked then that the abolition of private property should not be daunting to the people because it had already been done away with for nine-tenths of the population, and its existence for the few is solely due to its nonexistence for all the rest.

One hundred and fifty years later, the question on the "campyng close" is this: Under what cover shall we "camp," and who indeed is this "we," to forge of a world in which nine out of ten will be born no longer as trespassers, to usher in a season in which seeds will bear, not corporate copyrights, but the harvest of just conditions.

7

Between a Ranch and a Hard Place: Violence, Scarcity, and Meaning in Chiapas, Mexico

Aaron Bobrow-Strain

Julio Muñoz Rojas spilled coffee down his shirt at Restaurant La Lupita when he heard the news. A caravan of Tzeltal Indians from the nearby *ejido* San Sebastián de Bachajón had entered his 250-hectare ranch just outside Chilón, Chiapas. Wielding machetes and hoes, the peasants quickly erected wooden shelters and began to sow corn in Rojas' pastures. That night, around fires that burned until dawn, they feasted on beef.[1]

Less than two months earlier, shortly after midnight on New Year's Day 1994, several hundred ski-masked Mayan guerrillas launched Chiapas and the plight of the state's indigenous peasants into the international spotlight. With charismatic and media-savvy Subcomandante Marcos as their spokesperson, the Zapatistas quickly shifted from military tactics to a multi-arena "war of position" against the Mexican state that catalyzed an international struggle for democratization and indigenous autonomy in Mexico.[2]

By early February, when emboldened peasants seized dozens of ranches in Chilón, it was clear that the Zapatista uprising had not only initiated a battle between leftist opposition groups and the state but had also opened

1. Rancher names used in this paper are pseudonyms except for those drawn from public press reports. Unless noted otherwise, all quotes are from interviews I conducted with ranchers in the Chiapan municipalities of Chilón, Palenque, Salto de Agua, Yajalón, and Ocosingo during the summer of 1998. I am grateful for the generous support of Hubert Carton de Grammont and Sara Lara Flores of the Instituto de Investigaciones Sociales (IIS-UNAM) in Mexico City during my preliminary fieldwork. Ongoing fieldwork has been made possible by grants from the National Science Foundation and Social Science Research Council.
2. For Gramsci (1971: 239), "war of position" is a multi-arena strategy of political and cultural struggle aimed at the slow "siege warfare" of social transformation rather than a decisive seizing of the state apparatus.

space for the emergence of dozens of geographically specific conflicts between groups spanning the Mexican political spectrum. This chapter examines one set of conflicts that grew in the fissures of the state's wildly destabilized order—a massive resurgence of land invasions and agrarian conflict that pitted land-poor, mostly indigenous, peasants against *mestizo* landowners across the state. During the long spring and summer that followed the Zapatista uprising, peasants occupied tens of thousands of hectares of privately-owned agricultural land.

Throughout Chiapas's long history of agrarian conflict, land invasions have been a key site of violence—violence employed during the seizure of land as well as violence carried out by landowners and state security forces to dislodge or intimidate invaders. While most of the hundreds of land invasions that punctuated the spring of 1994 were resolved with minimal bloodshed,[3] the threat of violence was ever present. This chapter examines the dynamics that led to this post-uprising conjuncture charged with the possibility of violence.[4] In doing so, I hope to exorcise the specter of environmental scarcity that drives—either explicitly or implicitly—many explanations of agrarian conflict in Chiapas (e.g., Renner 1996; Howard and Homer-Dixon 1995).

Unlike analysts who speak of "the Chiapas conflict" as a unitary phenomenon, I argue that the "Chiapas conflict" is, in fact, a constellation of temporally and spatially differentiated conflicts. Chiapas is truly a "warscape" (Nordstrom 1997: 78)—something that can only be understood by examining the ways conflict unfolds, changes, and takes multiple forms across time and space. I analyze the dynamics of conflict in a particular place and a particular historical moment: invasions of privately owned coffee farms and cattle ranches on the northwestern edge of the Lacandon rain forest carried out in the spring of 1994 by peasants affiliated with a diverse set of organizations. I draw primarily on the case of Chilón but incorporate material from the municipalities of Ocosingo, Palenque, and Salto de Agua. The conclusions I draw in this chapter do not necessarily apply to the dynamics of conflict in indigenous villages of Chiapas's central highlands (e.g., the Acteal massacre)[5] or ongoing attacks against Zapatista "autonomous communities" by the Mexican army and state security forces. Instead, I have chosen to examine this particular fragment of the Chiapan "warscape" because it provides a unique case for examining the connections between environmental scarcity and violent conflict.

---

3. As discussed later, many of the 1994 invasions were resolved with government promises to purchase and redistribute invaded land.
4. I address the question of the why landed elites in Chiapas used or refrained from using violence to resolve these land disputes in a forthcoming paper.
5. See Aubry (1997) in *La Jornada* for revealing commentary on paramilitary violence in the central highlands.

These invasions provide a compelling window onto the question of scarcity. Even more than the Zapatista uprising itself, they appear on the surface to reflect a situation in which population growth (in a context of unequal land tenure) outstripped available land and pitted ranchers and peasants against each other in a scramble for survival. I argue instead that the focus on environmental scarcity obscures important dynamics that shape the trajectories of violence in Chiapas. Land conflicts between peasants and ranchers arise not as a result of too many people competing for too little land (e.g., Myers 1993b). They arise from the confluence of national economic reforms, changes in international commodity markets, and local histories of violence and insecurity that reduce *both* ranchers and peasants' capacity to use land intensively and effectively. In this sense, the actual scarcity in Chiapas is not tied to the environment or even land distribution but rather to politically charged forces that push producers toward less effective production.

It is essential, at the same time, to recognize that land is not just struggled over as a productive resource. After critically examining pressures on land in Chiapas and arguing for a more nuanced understanding of scarcity, I conclude by discussing two crucial arenas of conflict in which land invasions play a prominent role distinct from the battle for land as a productive resource: (1) the importance of land invasions in struggles over political and constituencies and municipal power and (2) land and land invasions' central places in the ways different actors construct and contest meanings in the Chiapan countryside. Land invasions, I conclude, represent far more than "natural" reactions to environmental scarcity. Since the 1930s, they have become an institution in the Chiapan countryside, central to a broad range of political and cultural struggles.

"Greenwar" in Chiapas?

Resource scarcities are a root cause of the violent conflicts that have convulsed civil society in Rwanda, Haiti, and Chiapas.... In Chiapas ... resource conflicts underlie the insurgency ... unequal distribution of land and rapid population growth has forced poor peasants—mostly indigenous people—to eke out a meager living by farming environmentally fragile uplands.

Subsecretary of State for Global Affairs Timothy Wirth, address to the
National Press Club (Wirth 1994)

Numerous authors have highlighted the strong connections between resource degradation, environmental protection policies, and the Zapatista uprising (Harvey 1998: 8; Villafuerte, Garcia, and Meza 1997: 141; Leyva and Ascencio 1996: 174–181; Collier and Quaretiello 1994: 49–50). State enclosure of more than 300,000 hectares in the Montes Azul Integral Biosphere Preserve, prohibitions against income generation from timber harvesting, and population growth have eclipsed options for settlers on the fragile rain forest soils of the eastern lowlands. Given these conditions and intensive mobilization efforts by the progressive Catholic Diocese of San Cristobal and independent peasant organizations, it is not surprising that the rim of the rain forest—the region of *las cañadas*—became the heartland of the Zapatista movement.[6]

Few authors link environment and conflict in Chiapas as explicitly as Philip Howard and Thomas Homer-Dixon in their 1995 Project on Environment, Population and Security (working paper, "Environmental Scarcity and Violent Conflict: The Case of Chiapas, Mexico"). Howard and Homer-Dixon place environmental scarcity in the eye of *la tormenta de enero*,[7] contending that, "attribut[ing] a range of revolutionary objectives to the Zapatistas, often obscur[es] the insurgents' principal goal: relief from escalating environmental scarcities that have impoverished their communities (1)."[8]

Howard and Homer-Dixon make a valiant effort to manipulate what they acknowledge is a complicated array of political, economic, historical, and social factors into a straightforward linear model of escalating environmental scarcities. They argue that three factors converged to spark the 1994 uprising: rising grievances caused by escalating "environmental scarcities," the erosion of the corporatist state's ability to resolve these grievances and co-opt dissenters, and the construction of a critical consciousness by church and Zapatista organizers. That the authors can place "environmental scarcity" at the center of this web rests largely on Homer-Dixon's conflation of multiple sources of land pressures under the banner of "environmental scarcity" (Peluso and Watts; Fairhead; Hartmann; all in this volume). In this familiar Homer-Dixon argument, environmental scarcity includes one or all of the following: demand-induced pressures resulting from increasing population, supply-induced pressures stemming from the degradation of remaining resources, and structural scarcity (the product of socioeconomic inequality and "resource capture" by elites).

By questioning the use of "environmental scarcity," even when broadly defined in Howard and Homer-Dixon's terms, I seek to re-politicize struggles that have been de-politicized by being relegated to the realm of

---

6. This chapter focuses on the 1994 land invasions rather than the Zapatista uprising. For reviews of the complicated conjuncture of economic restructuring, political reforms, and indigenous mobilization that led to the Zapatista uprising, see works by Harvey (1994, 1998), Collier and Quaratiello (1994), and Hernandez (1994).
7. "The January Storm," in reference to the Zapatista uprising.
8. In a later article, written without Homer-Dixon, Howard appears to pull back from these strong claims about the environmental roots of the Zapatista uprising (1998: 372).

"natural" processes. Furthermore, I suggest that analyses of peasant –rancher conflicts based on land concentration alone also are flawed. They are flawed because, as I demonstrate later, they paint a compelling historical picture of landed elite[9] power in Chiapas, but fail to account for the steady erosion of large landholding due to peasant mobilization over the past several decades.

The 1994 Invasions

If we tried to do this a year ago, the police would have been here to dislodge us because the government always protects the ranch owners.
> Samuel Diaz Guzman, Institutional Revolution Party (PRI)-aligned peasant leader from Chilón, quoted in Scott (1994a)

[Private property owners] have reached their limit. We continue to maintain control, they keep asking us to keep calm, and that the institutions will act, but we see that that is not the way it is.
> Gonzalo Lopez Camacho, president of the Central Region Cattleman's Union, quoted in *La Jornada* June 21, 1994: 16)

The indigenous protagonists of the 1994–1995 land occupations spanned the spectrum of Mexican politics. Although each group of peasant land claimants stepped into an opening created by the Zapatista uprising, by no means were all of them Zapatista, or even anti-government. Groups ranged from the staunchly independent and pro-Zapatista State Council of Indigenous Organizations (CEOIC) to the government-aligned Teacher-Peasant Solidarity movement (SOCAMA) whose leader Samuel Sanchez Sanchez also founded the right-wing paramilitary organization *Paz y Justicia*. Other groups aligned with opposition political parties like the Party of the Democratic Revolution (PRD) or arose out of organizing efforts by the progressive Catholic diocese of San Cristobal. Some groups split into opposing factions or shifted affiliations in the course of the year. A few groups sprang into existence solely to take advantage of the opportunities afforded by post-uprising chaos and government willingness to buy off invaders, but most groups had histories dating to conflicts in the 1970s and 1980s.

Ejidatarios from the San Gerónimo de Bachajón and San Sebastián de Bachajón *ejidos*[10] carried out the majority of the land invasions in Chilón,

---

9. I use "landed elites" and "ranchers" interchangeably. The former derives from agrarian studies literature, although the latter is the term "ranchers" employ when referring to themselves (both coffee and cattle producers).
10. *Ejidos* represent the basic unit of agrarian reform land redistribution. Barry (1995) succinctly defines *ejido* as "a community-based system of land tenure in which the government

tracing their land claims back to acts of the Spanish crown and strategically wielding eighteenth-century maps and land titles in their demands. By mid-February, some sixteen hundred people had staked claims to more than 4,000 hectares in Chilón and neighboring Sitalá and Pantelhó (Servicios Informativos Procesados 1994: 43). By 1998, the municipalities in my study (Chilón, Yajalón, Sitalá, and Salto de Agua) had experienced two hundred three invasions of more than 16,000 hectares (CESMECA 1998). Local newspaper reports and records kept by the Secretariat of Agrarian Reform concerning these two ejidos speak to more than thirty years of bloody feuds and intracommunity battles that frequently expressed themselves in invasions of agricultural land worked by rival peasants. For many years, rivalries in the two Bachajón ejidos have revolved around political and economic competition between government-aligned peasants and those organized around liberation theology and the progressive Jesuit mission in Bachajón (CDHFBC and CDIAC 1996). On occasion, these rivalries also expressed themselves in the form of invasions of private property outside the ejidos. Thus, by 1994, land invasions were already a familiar political tool used by peasant leaders to acquire land, win constituencies, and make political statements. Often, as in the 1994 case of Francisco Leon's ranch, several groups representing different political affiliations claimed the same property.

News reports of these events painted a picture of a stereotypical landowner laughing all the way to bank in the wake of the 1994 invasions, but the actual experience was far more diverse. While some ranchers I spoke with fell comfortably back on investments in commerce—owning hotels and restaurants, trading cattle purchased from ejidos, or controlling soft drink concessions for entire regions—others now work as waiters, truck drivers, and construction workers.

Days after indigenous peasants occupied Julio Muñoz Rojas' ranch in February 1994, a different faction of ejidatarios staked a claim to a 40-hectare cattle ranch just across the municipal border in Sitalá owned by Aurelio Cosío. Another rancher Francisco Leon remembers heated meetings about self-defense at the local cattlemen's association but never expected that his ranch would be invaded. "Every rancher thought that his relations with the indigenous were excellent." Nevertheless, Leon's land was one of more than twenty ranches invaded in Chilón during the second week of February 1994. On February 14, a few days after the invasion, members of Chilón's local cattlemen's association met with a subsecretary of the state-level Ministry of the Interior (*Gobernación*), the department re-

---

protected privately held parcels and communal lands within the community from the market (12)." Individual members could not sell, lease, or mortgage their parcels before changes to Article 27 of the Mexican Constitution effected in 1992.

sponsible for public security in Mexico. Rojas reports: "He told us that everything would be fine. . . . He promised us that they would liquidate the invasion, but nothing happened."

The grandson of German immigrants who had cut forests in Chilón to grow coffee a century ago, Mario Guttenberg's experience was different from his neighbors. Unlike most other ranchers, Mario Guttenberg fought back directly. Guttenberg displays intense, unconcealed racism towards the state's indigenous peoples, and ranchers all over Chiapas speak of him in hushed tones. He guards his home with Rottweilers and Marcos, a bulky mestizo with short cropped hair and a .45 tucked into his camouflage pants. Over the years Guttenberg sold chunks of his family's large holdings to avoid mandated agrarian reform, but he resisted the invasions in 1994. His neighbor Jose Maria Monteverde explains, "The indigenous fell on us like locusts, and the only ranch that was saved was Mario's. It was saved because he has the balls to risk his life to protect it." As ranchers in the area note, however, Guttenberg's stance has taken a financial toll on him.

After gunmen showered his home with bullets in October 1997, Guttenberg hired a detachment of state police to live on and protect his property. Now he can afford only Marcos. When Guttenberg's wife shows me the crater made by a bullet that grazed her cheek during an attack by unknown assailants on her house in October 1997, she confesses to remaining at the ranch only because their financial crises forced them to sell their home in the state capital. Guttenberg is in the process of selling off other assets, including a coffee processing plant and warehouse he bought in an effort to vertically integrate his operations. Between the money to retain the state police, the effects of a five-year coffee crisis, deep debt, and cutbacks in government subsidized credit, Guttenberg claims he is nearly bankrupt and ready to give up coffee production. But he has no intention of going down without a fight.

Ranchers fumed ominously during the first half of 1994. "We're giving the government until April 20. If there's no positive solution we'll adopt other means," one told a reporter (quoted by Scott 1994b). In June several hundred landowners filled the plaza in front of the state capitol in Tuxtla Gutierrez. They demanded immediate eviction of invaders, damage payments, public investigation of CEOIC leaders, better interest rates, and restructuring of defaulted debts (*La Jornada* June 25, 1994: 16). Three women began a hunger strike that would last until they received compensation for their invaded properties. After days of meetings with government representatives, state-level officials announced that they would immediately begin evicting squatters. Police and landowners began to carry out the order in some areas, but by August, the Federal Commissioner for Chiapas Jorge Madrazo announced that there would be no more evictions (*La Jornada* July 6 and August 6, 1994). Instead, landowners were encouraged to sell land to indigenous claimants who would use government sub-sidized credit packages to make the purchases.

Evictions and violence against land claimants, particularly those in oppo-sition peasant organizations, continued, but the buyout of landowners also proceeded apace. In all, "eviction by judicial order" was used in less than 29 percent of the 1,188 land invasions resolved between 1994–1998 (Villa-fuerte et al. 1999: 147). Between 1994 and 1996, police, army, municipal authorities, landowners, and paramilitary groups detained more than two thousand peasants, killed at least a dozen, and injured scores more in the course of evictions or attempted evictions of land invasions. Despite these statistics, this wave of agrarian conflict was resolved in a *relatively* nonviolent manner compared to other periods (Reyes 2000; Villafuerte et al. 1999).[11]

Under national and international pressure to peacefully settle the Chia-pas conflict and faced with the critical challenge of balancing landowner interests with the need to maintain electoral support among the Chiapan peasantry, Mexican state and federal authorities quickly devised a series of programs and credit funds to purchase invaded farms for peasant land claimants. Between 1994 and 1998, the Mexican government committed almost one billion pesos (the equivalent of well over one hundred million U.S. dollars after the 1995 devaluation) to this effort (Reyes 2000: 14). All across the state, these funds paid for tens of thousands of hectares of land benefiting members of more than sixty peasant organizations. Although as late as May 2000 much of this land had still not been handed over to peas-ants, and many landowners had not yet received their payments, in 1994 and 1995 alone over 150,000 hectares actually changed hands (Villafuerte et al. 1999: 195–96; Reyes 2000). According to producers' association leader Gustavo Aguilar, ranchers ultimately sold more than two-thirds of the invaded land in Chilón. As a result, many ranchers abandoned produc-tion, moving to other regions or taking up other enterprises. The eighty-five-member local cattlemen's association fell to only six active members between 1994 and 1998, and regional production of milk, meat, and cof-fee plummeted.

Between February and December 1994, according to a Mexican Trea-sury document disclosed in *La Jornada*, the state issued 455 checks totaling $68 million dollars for the purchase of 39,049 hectares (*La Jornada* June 2, 1995). The government buyout of ranchers was a politically charged process that pitted peasant groups against each other as well as the state. Not surprisingly, pro-Zapatista groups like CEOIC struggled with the gov-ernment for resolution of their land claims although government-aligned SOCAMA, Rural Association of Collective Interest (ARIC), and the CNC

11. This and other statements in this paragraph are supported by my analysis of an exten-sive database of agrarian conflict from 1970–2000 that I compiled.

reached more favorable agreements with the state (Harvey 1998: 212–215).

Press reports of the buyout contrasted the speed with which payments were issued with the painfully slow agrarian reform process in which an average claim lingered for more than seven years. The recipients of these early payments represented an elite group of high-ranking government officials, including the State Coordinator of Agrarian Concerns and the relatives of several former governors. Less prominent landowners, such as Aurelio Cosío waited years for compensation because they lacked the money needed to expedite their claims. Owners of a prime 10-hectare property, invaded and urbanized on the outskirts of San Cristobal, reportedly secured the equivalent of more than 20,000 dollars per hectare, but most ranchers I interviewed received between 4,000 and 6,000 pesos per hectare.[12]

Aurelio Cosío wore threadbare jeans and a crisply pressed shirt when we talked in July 1998. He was supporting his large family by hauling loads of produce, people, and construction materials along the road between Ocosingo and Yajalón. Of the four ranchers described thus far, he fared the worst in the wake of the land invasions. Cosío reported his losses to the authorities, but the petition "just sat there" because he "didn't have the money needed to grease the wheels." Four and a half years later, he still hadn't been paid by the government. Julio Muñoz Rojas' story was more typical. After surviving by selling his rescued cattle and using the capital to open a pharmacy in Chilón, he eventually received about U.S. $500 per hectare in 1997.

Two different peasant organizations claimed Francisco Leon's family land, 100 hectares of coffee plants and pasture. When the dust finally settled, a group aligned with the ruling Institutional Revolution Party (PRI) finally possessed title to the land, and Leon had received a sizable check for 800,000 new pesos (almost $250,000 before the 1995 devaluation of the peso). But Leon's family was lucky. With his position in government and his sister's former classmate Ernesto Zedillo poised to become president, their claims were resolved faster than those of many neighboring ranchers.

Rethinking Scarcity

> When two groups come together with their claims, and they are both right, the only thing left to do is to tear each other to pieces.
>
> Carlos Castillo, former Chiapan landowner, now ranching in Tabasco

---

12. When the lands were appraised, this amounted to between U.S. $1,200 and $1,850. However, ranchers claim that the payments were not adjusted to compensate for the December 1994 devaluations that rapidly shrank the dollar value to U.S. $600–$950.

An upper class drawing its income from the land [as opposed to earning it
from capital investments on the land] is associated with a static agricultural
product and therefore creates zero-sum conflict between [peasants] and
[the landed upper class]. . . . There is no way to increase the income of either class except by decreasing the income of the other.

(Paige 1975: 23–24)

With a higher proportion of its population rural and working in agriculture than in any other Mexican state, Chiapas offers peasants few opportunities outside of agriculture. Since the 1960s, the state has experienced
high population growth rates, increasing control over resources by a powerful elite, declining state support for improving the productivity of existing peasant landholdings, and little outmigration. To make matters worse,
most observers agree that Chiapas's vast agrarian frontier, the Lacandon
rain forest, can no longer accommodate additional colonists or agricultural expansion by current settlers.

From this initial set of assumptions, it is not a long journey to the conclusion that violence is inevitable in Chiapas. As Jeffrey Paige (1975)
noted, in a region where expanding production depends on dominating
additional increments of land rather than increasing investment, any move
by one actor—peasant, elite, or state planner—takes away possibilities
from someone else. Rather than passively accepting the smooth movement
from scarcity to violence posited by neo-Malthusian theory, however, I critically examine scarcity, asking questions about what exactly is scarce in Chiapas and how have actors constructed or not constructed a "zero-sum
game" over time.

This reexamination of scarcity begins with the three key components of
Howard and Homer-Dixon's broad conception of environmental scarcity:
population growth, resource degradation, and structural scarcity.

Population Growth

Chiapas has experienced dramatic population growth over the past twenty-
five years. From 1970 to 1995 average annual growth rates topped 5 percent, although this figure dropped significantly in the years preceding the
Zapatista uprising (Table 7.1). Chiapas has the highest long-term population growth of any of Mexico's most rural states. Massive migration into
the Lacandon rain forest from every state in Mexico and from neighboring
Guatemala contributed significantly to this growth (Leyva and Ascencio
1996: 52).

Table 7.1 Population Growth, Mexico's Most Rural States

State	1970–1995	1980–1995	1990–1995
Chiapas	5.14%	4.80%	2.33%
Oaxaca	2.41%	2.42%	1.39%
Hidalgo	3.08%	2.43%	2.37%
Guerrero	3.30%	2.55%	2.26%
Natl. Avg.	3.56%	2.42%	2.44%

Source: Calculated from Banamex (1998: Tables 1, 3, 11, and 13)

The lack of employment options outside agriculture and the high proportion of the population engaged in farming suggest that population growth could strain available land. Howard and Homer-Dixon (1995: 8), however, present little evidence for their assertion that the agricultural landscape of Chiapas is getting crowded. Their paper supplies data only on population density for urban San Cristobal de las Casas and its rural periphery, which indeed have experienced a doubling of density since 1950. As population growth rates slow in Chiapas, it is not clear that its population density is significantly higher than other rural states in Mexico. In fact, population densities in Chiapas have not reached the average levels found in many of Mexico's other highly rural states (Table 7.2). Largely thanks to the availability of colonizable land in the Lacandon rain forest, agarian reform recipients in Chiapas still have access to an average of 16 hectares, according to 1988 statistics reported by Neil Harvey (1998: 174). Reyes Ramos's calculations using more recent data (see following) report an *increase* in this average figure.

Table 7.2 Population Density in Mexico's Ten Most Rural States

State	Population Density People/km²	% Population Rural	% Employment in Agriculture
Puebla	136.34	33.4	34.4
Hidalgo	100.66	52.5	40.4
Veracruz	92.53	41.6	33
Tabasco	70.91	47.9	31.8
Michoacan	64.66	35.5	36.9
Chiapas	48.52	55.9	54.1
Guerrero	45.72	45.3	42.3
Oaxaca	33.86	56.5	50.1
Zacatecas	17.81	49.8	36.9
Campeche	12.40	28.8	32.3
Average (10)	62.34	44.7	39.2
Natl. Avg. (32)	46.22	26.5	22.5

Source: Calculated from Banamex (1998: Tables 1, 11, and 13)

More important, however, appeals to aggregate demographic data obscure the local dynamics that shape violence. Broad claims about the connection between population growth and violence need to be examined in specific contexts. A close look at municipal level data indicates that in particular localities there is almost no correlation between population growth, density, and conflict. Some centers of conflict, like the municipality of Tila, have relatively high population densities (128 people/km^2), while others like Las Margaritas and Angel Albino Corzo were sparsely populated (15 and 12 people/km^2, respectively). The five municipalities that accounted for just under half the land invaded in Chiapas had an average population density of fewer than 28 people/km^2. Similarly, some centers of agrarian conflict like Salto de Agua experienced population growth rates well below the replacement rate in the years leading up to 1994, although others like Venustiano Carranza have above average rates (1.59% and 3.19%, respectively) (Instituto Nacional de Estadística, Gesgrafía, e Informática [INEGI] 1997: 71). What matters in this case is, as I argue later, not the number of people in need of land but the ability of people to produce on existing arable land. Evidence will show that, for reasons intimately connected to political and economic developments in Mexico and the world, both peasants and larger landowners have witnessed declining ability to produce on their existing lands in recent decades.

Resource Degradation

Howard and Homer-Dixon base their analysis of resource degradation on conjecture, admitting to the lack of solid research on topics such as soil erosion (1995: 11). What evidence they do present points to a relatively minor role for resource degradation in creating scarcity in this case. Although they predict severe agricultural yield losses in the *future*, they report that currently in the Lacandon rain forest, "soil erosion . . . is only evident on the steepest slopes at the highest elevations (13) and that 20 to 50 percent of the Central Highlands experience only "moderate topsoil loss due to water erosion (13)." Howard and Homer-Dixon attribute a decline in peasant production in the 1980s to the deterioration of soils in the Lacandon rain forest. Reading the source of this observation closely, however, it is clear that degradation is contingent on the withdrawal of government subsidies and supports for farmers, which are central to explaining the decline in production (Harvey 1994: 11). In Chiapas, the significant degradation appears to be the politically contingent ability of producers to cultivate land. Although I do not wish to gloss over the existence of major environmental problems in Chiapas—indeed many reports (e.g., Leobardo and Monterrosas 1994; O'Brien 1995) are quite alarming—Howard and Homer-Dixon's treatment of natural processes (centering soil erosion models and discussions of satellite photos of deforestation in their argument) detracts from the intensely relative and political nature of those processes. As with population growth, the experience of resource degradation is not an absolute but rather hinges on actors' capacity to make land productive.

Structural Scarcity

Chiapas has an agrarian structure in which the private sector controls the most and best land. Behind this agrarian structure cattlemen stand out as the hegemonic sector because they are the principal actors in agrarian conflicts.

(González Esponda and Pólito Barrios 1995: 112)

Ganadero [cattleman] is synonymous with wealthy in Mexicans' minds. They think of ranchers from the north with 2,000 head, so the government assumes that we are all a band of rich landlords. The government never investigated how many hectares we had before they came up with their plan.

Jose Maria Monteverde, Chilón

Howard and Homer-Dixon ultimately present evidence of land scarcity under the banner of "structural scarcity," pointing to the spread of extensive cattle ranches over much of the state and the historical ability of elites to buttress their land claims with violence and political power. This image of Chiapas fits neatly into enduring narratives of landed inequality and of the powerful elites who have dominated the state (e.g., García de Leon 1998; Fernandez and Tarrío 1983). It also fits the classic depictions of the connection between landed elites, repressive production regimes, and violence (e.g., Moore 1966; Paige 1975, 1997). Yet, careful examination of the history of agrarian reform in Chiapas reveals that this type of story only partially explains the complexity of land conflict in the state.

It is common to hear that "the Mexican Revolution never reached Chiapas." This phrase evokes a monolithic vision of the Mexican Revolution that obscures the variety of forms, timelines, and ways in which the revolution was fought, resisted, imagined, and institutionalized in *every* region of the country. Eighty years of struggles over the meaning of The Mexican Revolution in Chiapas have produced both continuity and remarkable transformations in the nature of power relations in the state. Of critical importance for this chapter, agrarian reform was not swift in Chiapas but has been significant, dramatically altering the state's landscape.

Around the turn of the century, German and Mexican elites owned vast

Table 7.3 Land Tenure in Chiapas, 1930 and 1990 (Has.)

Tenure Form	1930	1990
Private Sector	4,011,298	1,839,006
Social Sector (*Ejidos* and *Comunas*)	104,509	4,110,818

Source: Reyes (1992, 1998a) and *Censo Agrícola Ganadero* (1930, 1990).

estates in Chiapas, producing coffee and rubber for international markets. The 1930 agricultural census, carried out in the wake of the Mexican Revolution, found twenty-two estates larger than 10,000 hectares (mostly abandoned) and 4 percent of landowners controlling 67 percent of the arable land in the state (Secretaría de Economía 1930: Table 42). But peasant mobilization and state-sponsored agrarian reform have steadily and effectively broken down large landholdings over the past six decades. The average size of private landholdings dropped precipitously in the decades following the Mexican Revolution (1910–1920) to less than 50 hectares in 1990, while the amount of land held by the ejido sector soared. As the effects of the most recent wave of land struggles begin to be noted, analysis by Reyes (1998: 1, 2) indicates that the "social sector" (*ejidatarios* and indigenous *comuneros*) controls 4.1 million hectares, 56 percent of the surface area of the state, while private landowners control 1.8 million hectares, or 25 percent of the state. In short, despite massive problems discussed later, land tenure in Chiapas underwent a remarkable reversal over the past sixty years (Table 7.3).

In the wake of the 1994 invasions, Reyes (1998: 2) calculates state averages of 18.4 hectares per ejidatario and 23 hectares per comunero.[13] Data on municipal land tenure from the 1990 agricultural census indicate little relation between inequality and invasions. Some highly conflictive areas such as Venustiano Carranza show wide gaps between the social sector and private property (the social sector represents 78 percent of productive units but holds 12 percent of the land). Others such as Tila or Chilón are less skewed (87 percent of units holding 86 percent of the land, and 89 percent of units holding 86 percent of the land, respectively) (INEGI 1994: 5b).[14]

Successive governments preferred to offer unclaimed national lands to peasants rather than disturb the interests of powerful landowners. As a re-

13. It is important to note, however, that this figure represents the average land held by each head of household rather than per capita land holdings. By comparison, the statewide average size of private property over 5 hectares (to exclude very small peasant holdings) was 54 hectares in 1990 and has probably dropped since then (INEGI 1990).
14. This type of census data is meant to present a general impression of land tenure. It cannot account for widespread irregularities at the local level.

sult, official policies opened hundreds of thousands of previously unexploited hectares in the Lacandon rain forest for colonization. This accounts for much of the land distributed during the forty-year period, but sustained attack by mobilized peasants forced the government to partially abandon landowners more than once in Chiapas's history. The following section traces the key moments in the history of Chiapas and redistribution, linking local dynamics to national and international processes.

Revolution Delayed

Technically, the Mexican Revolution reached Chiapas in 1914 when the Carrancista army entered the state hoping to bring it under the Consitutionalist government. On October 30, 1914, the revolutionary governor General Castro proclaimed the Workers Law, abolishing agrarian workers' outstanding debts and outlawing debt servitude (Reyes 1992: 41). Landowners quickly mounted a counter-revolutionary campaign, and ranchers across the state today still revel in tales of the fight waged against Carranza's forces.

By 1920, with Carranza killed in the course of power struggles far from southeastern Mexico, Chiapan landowners triumphed and the "revolutionary" government of the state became simply a fresh expression of landowner domination.[15] In its own Agrarian Reform Law sponsored in 1921 by landowner-governor Tiburcio Fernandez Ruiz, Chiapas established one of the highest allowances for landholdings in the country—subjecting only landholdings greater than 8,000 hectares to expropriation (Benjamin 1996; Reyes 1992: 47).

In 1934, however, Lazaro Cardenas was elected president, and agrarian reform began to take on new meaning throughout Mexico. Cardenas placed land redistribution and the newly formed ejidos at the center of his plans for the nation. During Cardenas' six-year term, 17.9 million hectares were redistributed to almost one million peasants throughout Mexico, transforming hundreds of thousands of agricultural laborers into ejidatarios and dismantling the country's *latifundio* system (North and Raby 1977; Hamilton 1982: 177). These changes came slowly and violently to landowner dominated Chiapas.

As peasant unions, "socialist defense leagues," and communist cells mobilized in the countryside, Chiapas's conservative state government responded by passing legislation to promote the formation of bands of private gunmen, called *guardias blancas* (white guards), retained by landowners to quell unrest. Meanwhile, the federal government shipped arms

---

15. See Benjamin (1996) and García de Leon (1998) for analysis of the survival and triumph of the landed oligarchy during this period.

and young organizers to indigenous communities to help them mount a defense against landowners (Fernandez and Tarrio 1983; Benjamin 1996). The struggle between landowners, peasants, and agricultural workers that raged through the 1930s resulted in a contradictory mixture of continued landowner political–economic dominance and significant land redistribution.[16] Landowners continued to exert strong controls over indigenous populations and deployed an array of creative new mechanisms for avoiding land reform, but this does not change the fact that Chiapas's property landscape had begun to change in significant ways. By 1949, 776,332 hectares had been granted to claimants and some 758,494 hectares actually changed hands (Reyes 1992: 133). The thousands of hectares promised but not delivered represented the beginnings of a snowballing "agrarian backlog" that would soon become a major source of conflict in the state.

Qu'ixin Qu'inal: Colonization of La Selva

In 1946, President Miguel Alemán initiated the colonization of Mexico's "virgin" territory, encouraging peasants to settle in the lowland rain forest of eastern Chiapas. Colonization offered Alemán a convenient way of responding to increased demands for land redistribution in the highlands without having to undertake the unpleasant task of land expropriation (de Vos 1995). Wave after wave of Tzotzil and Tzeltal settlers fleeing poverty in the highlands poured into eastern Chiapas. The settlers followed trails blazed by loggers into the rain forest hoping to establish subsistence farms and build new lives. As was the case in colonization schemes throughout Latin America, poor settlers quickly discovered that, stripped of trees, their soil was virtually worthless. Cattle ranchers, eager to take advantage of booming national demand for beef, followed close behind the settlers, taking over lands that could no longer produce subsistence crops and competing heavily with settlers for access to land. Qu'ixin Qu'inal, "the hot lands" in the language of Tzeltal settlers, ceased to be a promised land and became another outpost of misery.

But the misery elsewhere was worse, and waves of settlers continued to pour into the East. By the 1980s most rain forest land had been claimed (de Vos 1995). What little remained of *la selva* was placed into the Montes Azul Biosphere Preserve in 1972, by a federal act that displaced between 5,000 and 8,000 settlers and further exacerbated tensions (de Vos 1995). Ranchers defended their lands against settlers, often enlisting already established peasants to drive off newcomers (Collier and Quaratiello 1994:

16. See García de Leon (1998: 402–439) and a brilliant article by Rus (1994) for analysis of this period.

41). At the same time, influenced by student radicals from Mexico City and radical Catholic catechists, indigenous colonists formed numerous militant peasant organizations and the inchoate Zapatista army took form in *las cañadas de la selva*.

The Fight for Chiapas: Agrarian Struggle in the 1970s and 1980s

During the 1970s and 1980s Chiapas experienced some of the worst agrarian conflict in its long violent history. By the end of this painful period, a handful of new independent peasant groups had dealt a deathblow to *latifundismo*. While landed elites maintained political and economic power in important ways, their control over vast expanses of Chiapas was crippled. No longer could Chiapas be compared with its neighbor Guatemala where 10 percent of landowners owned 87 percent of the land. Even army general, governor, and rancher Absalom Castellanos Dominguez—who years later would be kidnapped by Zapatista rebels in retaliation for his cruel reign—was forced during the 1980s to preside over the purchase of more than 80,000 hectares after a significant wave of land invasions.

Peasant mobilization in Chiapas paralleled an unprecedented wave of peasant struggles to seize land throughout Mexico. Three key factors spurred this national mobilization: (1) agricultural stagnation resulting from the sector's long subordination to industry under Mexico's Import Substitution Industrialization strategy; (2) a snowballing loss of faith in the possibility of achieving land redistribution through legal means after decades of conservative agrarian reform; and (3) population growth in a context of enclosure and massive agrarian displacement caused by the spread of extensive cattle ranching across the nation (cf. Sanderson 1981; Fox 1993). In Chiapas, widespread dissatisfaction with Secretariat of Agrarian Reform and the "official" corporatist peasant organization's (CNC) inability to resolve thousands of pending agrarian reform claims pushed peasants towards independent movements. At the same time, agricultural crisis was largely felt through the dramatic expansion of extensive cattle ranching across Chiapas that displaced thousands of peasants from the land.

Agrarian Backlog

From 1970–1976 president Luis Echeverría stepped up support of peasant producers and poured money into Chiapas for the construction of massive public works, but this money only seemed to feed the fires of unrest. Led by an emerging vanguard of radical indigenous peasant organizations, newly politicized peasants mounted a militant and sustained challenge to landowner power with marches, protests, and most important, land invasions. Peasants in Chiapas felt countless grievances built up over hundreds of years, but two moved them more than the rest. First, agrarian reform petitions in Chiapas seemed to disappear into a bureaucratic limbo. Claimants often waited generations for action, even after presidential resolutions dictated that the land should be turned over to them. Petitions required a state-wide average of 7.36 years between 1917 and 1984, but even a successful petition rarely meant that peasants would gain title to all the land promised to them. Of 1,880 hectares allocated to a group of peasants in Belasario Dominguez in 1954, for example, only 313 were turned over in 1956, and the children of the original claimants carried the legal battle for the rest of their land into the 1990s (*La Jornada* August 12, 1995; Reyes 1992: 151).

As the backlog mounted, peasants grew dissatisfied with their official corporatist representative, the CNC (Benjamin 1996: 235; Harvey 1990). This frustration provided an opening for independent organizations that catalyzed peasants into taking land reform into their own hands. Often peasants seized land that had been legally declared theirs but had not yet been turned over to them, hoping to accelerate the quiescent agrarian reform bureaucracy.

Cattle Boom

The expansion of extensive cattle ranches provided the second key spark for peasant mobilization. Beginning with the end of World War II and intensifying in the 1960s, several factors combined to launch a national boom in cattle production.[17] Perhaps more than in any other part of the country, this boom transformed agricultural production in Mexico's tropical southern states, where the amount of land dedicated to pasture tripled from 1970–1979 (Villafuerte and Ponitgo Sanchez 1990). By the early 1980s, cattle grazed on more than half of the total surface area of Chiapas (Villafuerte, Garcia, and Meza 1997: 41).

The transition from traditional export agriculture to cattle production turned the world of indigenous peasants still tied to estates through debt bondage and ties of paternalistic affection upside down. While one hectare of coffee plants could require as many as one hundred paid days of labor, the same area used to raise cattle required fewer than two days,

17. Research by Sanderson (1986) and Villafuerte, Garcia, and Meza (1997) describes the process of *ganaderización* (awkwardly translated as "cattle-ification") in northern and southern Mexico, respectively.

according to estimates by Fernandez and Tarrío (1983: 138). Therefore, as landowners responded to rising demand for cattle, colossal state subsidies for livestock production, and falling coffee prices, they evicted thousands of peasants from usufruct plots to make room for pasture. These peasants, whose families had provided labor on estates in return for subsistence plots for generations, were no longer needed by landowners. One researcher (Olivera, personal communication) who spent time near Chilón when this happened in the 1970s remembered: "We literally saw lines of peasants walking on the roads. They would come up to us to say that they were looking for a new *patrón* and ask whether we knew where they could find a new *patrón* to work for." The peasants' feelings of abandonment quickly turned to anger and mobilization. In northern Chiapas, Olivera reports that she and other students organized landless peasants to claim the plots they lost in the transition to cattle ranching, sometimes watching with horror as the peasants' "feelings of sorrow turned into hatred and violence."

Peasant mobilization met with strong resistance. In what Benjamin (1996: 229) calls the "bloody populism" of Luis Echeverría, hundreds of land invaders were violently evicted. In June 1976, for example, the army initiated what it called a "campaign against land invaders," dislodging more than 1,600 families (Reyes 1992: 105). Nevertheless, indigenous persistence commanded results, and in 1983 the government unveiled the "Program for Agrarian Rehabilitation" (PRA). This program attempted to resolve peasant land claims by brokering the purchase of disputed private property from landowners. In the four years of the PRA, the government spent 100 million dollars to purchase more than 80,000 hectares for 9,253 claimants (Benjamin 1996: 248; Reyes 1992: 116). However, the PRA quickly deteriorated into a power struggle over constituencies between independent organizations and the CNC. The weakened CNC, fearing that the PRA would fortify its rivals, promulgated a series of violent "invasions of invasions"—seizures of land occupied by independent peasant organizations in an attempt to maintain its political control over peasant organizing (Harvey 1998: 153). Ultimately, most of the distributed land ended up in the hands of CNC members, generating even more resentment among opposition groups in the countryside. During the same period, Castellanos complemented the PRA with stepped-up protection for private property that had not been invaded.

By the end of the 1980s, decades of struggle had largely dissolved a system of production and exploitation based on the concentration of enormous quantities of land in a few hands. In its place, landed elites began to rebuild relations of domination along new axes—exploiting indigenous communities through monopolies over the commercialization of agricultural produce, for example. Simple explanations, in which ranchers exercise power through the monopolization of land, no longer do justice to this new array of power relations. And (*pace* Paige 1975), as events surrounding the PRA illustrate, land invasions cannot be explained simply as desperate attempts to secure a scarce factor of production (see "Beyond Scarcity," below).

Low-Intensity Conflict: Extensive Agriculture and Land Scarcity

So far, this chapter has tried to insert several empirical wrenches into the gears that grind out stock explanations of agrarian conflict based on the notion of land or "environmental" scarcity. I have shown that land scarcity is a complicated, politically contingent phenomenon. Land scarcity explanations generally fail to account for the effects of peasant mobilization and agrarian reform. After sixty years of peasant mobilization and agrarian reform, land invasions in Chiapas cannot be viewed solely as a clear-cut story in which the lords of vast estates and noble landless peasants fight for survival over scraps of scarce land. Scarcity explanations also rest on a static, absolute understanding of natural carrying capacity, ignoring the fact that the ability of a given landscape to support humans is, within obvious parameters, a social construction.

In this section I argue that, to the extent that peasant–rancher conflict arises from scarcity, the true scarcity in Chiapas is state support for increased production: not a question of scarcity of available land but rather ability to produce on available land. This "scarcity" can only be understood by placing Chiapas in the context of global trends towards liberalization and restructuring of the Mexican economy since the early 1980s.

Although Carlos Salinas was not the first Mexican president to proclaim "the end of agrarian reform," his actions furnished substantial evidence of his sincerity. From 1988 to 1994 Salinas supervised an unprecedented retreat from state involvement in agriculture, privatizing agencies and parastatal corporations charged with supporting producers, gutting programs for subsidized credit, eliminating all but a few guarantee prices, and removing trade protections. Throughout this period Salinas pushed ceaselessly towards his ultimate challenge: privatizing the backbone of Mexico's agrarian reform, the ejido system. Monumental changes to the Mexican Constitution enacted in 1992 finally created the legal framework for this undertaking, opening up to ejidatarios the choice to obtain titles for their individual plots, buy and sell land, and even completely disband the ejido. Nevertheless, few ejidos have pursued privatization beyond the titling of individual plots. Neither the waves of investment and prosperity forecast by free market proponents nor the savage capitalist concentration of land into a few hands prophesied by their opponents have actually occurred.[18]

Most analyses of Chiapas concur, however, that cutbacks of government support for peasant producers of corn and coffee represent one of the key underlying causes of the Zapatista uprising (Harvey 1994, 1996, 1998; Collier 1994; Hernandez 1994). In the late 1980s and early 1990s, peasants were dealt a series of blows connected to neoliberal reforms that most researchers consider the proximate causes of the 1994 uprising. First, in the same year that Mexican Coffee Institute (INMECAFE) was disbanded, exposing coffee producers to market prices, the world price for coffee plummeted from $120–$140 to less than $70 per hundred pounds (Hernandez 1994). This produced massive income loss for the state's 60,000 small coffee producers (*La Jornada* January 16, 1994). Second, as a result of government cutbacks and privatization, neither the credit nor the fertilizer to make poor soils produce were available to peasant basic grain farmers. In 1989, President Salinas dramatically restructured Banrural, the Mexican rural development bank, which up to that point had served as the major source of credit for small farmers (Myhre 1998). By 1989 only 16 percent of ejidatarios had access to credit in the state (Harvey 1996: 190). In one of the most graphic indications of declining state support for production, the total crop area in Chiapas financed by Banrural fell from 285,000 hectares in 1988 to 16,000 hectares in 1996 (Myhre 1998: 54).[19]

Ultimately, this analysis of neoliberal reforms indicates that, beginning in the late 1980s, peasants in Chiapas underwent a widespread decline in their ability to produce on the land already available to them. The demands of insurgent peasants can be viewed in this light as demands for one of two things: either the additional increments of land needed to expand extensive, low-capital production or the political support required to leverage resources to increase production on current landholdings.

This story is fairly well-known. Less well-known is that, while some landed elites have profited from liberalization, many in Chiapas have been devastated. I do not equate the suffering of landed elites forced to sacrifice European vacations with peasant families unable to feed themselves. However, as the next section demonstrates, elite crisis does play a significant

18. The end of agrarian reform has, as many analysts note, had a profound effect on peasant consciousness. Harvey (1994) argues that the changes to Article 27 generated a crisis of expectation in the Chiapan countryside, "cancel[ing] the hopes of many *campesinos* who still aspired to receiving land under the former legislation."

19. Some of this 94 percent decline was compensated by new credit programs as many of *Banrural's* functions were phased out. Nevertheless, most observers agree that overall credit provision to the agricultural sector (especially peasant producers) has fallen dramatically in the past decade (Bartra 1996; Myhre 1998). This is in large part responsible for what de Janvry et al. (1996) call a "crisis of profitability" in the countryside.

role in the social construction of scarcity by significantly foreclosing opportunities for intensification of land use.

Cattle, Coffee, and Elite Crisis

> Ten years ago, 150 hectares meant living in opulence, traveling to Europe, never missing a World Cup. . . . People had a solid line of credit that allowed them to live that way. People were able to work with the banks then. . . . [Now] costs are higher, the price of cattle is the same, and the government doesn't help us out.
>
> Efrain Gonzalez, Palenque rancher

> You take out a loan and spend 300,000 pesos planting coffee, but the interest rate is 20%. Agriculture doesn't return 20%, and then your land is invaded.
>
> Carlos Guttenberg, Yajalón coffee producer

Ranchers have received special treatment from both the state and federal government dating back to the earliest days of the Mexican Revolution, but since the 1980s many traditional legal and economic supports have evaporated (Chauvet 1996, 1997). From the 1950s through the 1970s, the Mexican state provided unparalleled support for cattle ranching, promoting the production of inexpensive beef for the nation's rapidly growing and increasingly prosperous urban middle classes. Successive presidents channeled hundreds of millions of dollars into technical assistance, investment in cattle infrastructure, and, most importantly, highly subsidized credit packages (de la Fuente et al. 1989). During the 1960s and 1970s, the coddled and booming cattle sector contrasted markedly with the rest of Mexican agriculture which was stagnant and abandoned.

Since the early 1980s, ranchers have experienced a marked withdrawal of economic subsidies as a result of restructuring in state support for agriculture. The most significant change in ranchers' relationships with the state stems from the privatization and cutback of credit services. For decades the livestock sector enjoyed privileged access to subsidized loans at interest rates far below the open market rate (*El Economista* June 25, 1997). The 1989 restructuring of *Banrural* changed this, leaving most ranchers ineligible for subsidized credit and forced to seek loans with much higher interest rates from private sector banks. Since then, Mexico's Department of Agriculture and Livestock (SAGAR) reports that the cattle sector has accumulated 881 million dollars in defaulted loans (SAGAR 1997). As expected, ranchers are not happy with these changes. During the 61st National Assembly of the National Confederation of Cattlemen (CNG) held in June of 1997, ranchers accused state and commercial banks of systematically causing the destruction of the livestock industry (*El Economista* June 25, 1997). Ranchers I interviewed in Chiapas during the summer of 1998 consistently echoed this sentiment, complaining that new credit policies made it impossible to earn a living off either coffee or cattle.

At the same time, trade liberalization, undertaken enthusiastically during the Salinas years, undermined the Mexican cattle industry's already precarious position by exposing it to intense competition from the United States (Vazquez 1997). Mexico traditionally exported livestock to the United States, but beginning in the early 1990s the country began to import beef from the United States. Since Mexican tariffs on U.S. beef exports were phased-out with the implementation of the North American Free Trade Agreement (NAFTA) in 1994, imports have steadily grown (except for a brief respite after the 1995 devaluation of the peso) at annual rates of between 47 percent and 82 percent. (National Cattlemen's Beef Association 1997). The total value of U.S. beef exports to Mexico increased 536 percent between 1995 and the first half of 1997 (National Cattlemen's Beef Association 1997). Alarm over this trend prompted the Mexican National Cattle Ranchers Confederation (CNG) to unsuccessfully request an antidumping investigation in 1994 (Tabor 1996). Ranchers in Chiapas, producing almost exclusively for domestic consumption, have watched their traditional markets disappear, saturated by less expensive beef imports.

Ranchers in many parts of Chiapas, particularly in Chilón, who combine cattle and coffee production, have been impacted in similar ways by state restructuring of support for the agricultural sector. After decades of strong support from the state, cutbacks in the late 1980s battered coffee producers of all sizes (Hernandez and Célis 1994). Paired with five years of historic price declines (1989–1994), the restructuring of the coffee sector resulted in a general de-capitalization and technological regression in the industry. Some medium-sized coffee producers have begun to abandon their bean processing equipment, searching for lower-cost production techniques, or have slowly given up on coffee production all together. In Chilón, one coffee producer has fantasies of escaping his current life. "You know, I wouldn't want you to tell [the other ranchers in town], but if someone offered me money right now, I would sell everything in a second. . . . Maybe I could move somewhere up north and raise ostriches, it's the meat of the future you know."

In a context of growing competition from abroad and weakening state support, landed elites are faced with the challenge of intensifying their relatively low-intensity production in order to survive.[20] Subsidy cutbacks and

20. Cattle ranching in the tropics of Mexico, for example, has traditionally taken advantage of easy profits gleaned from extensive, low-capital, and highly subsidized grazing. A study in the 1980s (Payne 1990), for example, found that only 5 percent of producers in southern

sectoral crises have made intensification an almost impossible task. These pressures on producers to use land less intensively are not only economic, however. They are tied up in the experience of a long history of violence, as the next section will show.

Insecurity, Intensity, and Scarcity

> Agriculture has lots of problems and risks. If it rains too much, or not at all. If there are plant diseases. But all that passes. Only land insecurity stays with us forever.
>
> Carlos Guttenberg, Chilón coffee producer

> We're afraid to buy a good bull or cow until we see that a peace agreement is signed and that the government establishes a state of law.
>
> Felipe Martinez, Ocosingo cattle rancher

One final consideration of land scarcity in Chiapas arises from recent contributions to the anthropology of violence. As Feldman (1995: 226) notes, violence is the product of social relations but also "possesses structuring and enframing effects of its own." Violence itself can take on "its own symbolic and performative autonomy" and resculpt the social relations from which it arises (Feldman 1991: 21). Although the final section of this chapter will attend to competing understandings of the meaning of resource struggles, here I observe simply that the history of violent agrarian conflict can shape the contours of scarcity in unexpected ways.

As we turn off the highway into a 90-hectare sorghum field, Paco Jimenez slumps at the wheel of his pickup. In the corner of the field, a handful of indigenous families are cutting down drought-burned plants and erecting small houses from scavenged timber. Paco is young, educated at Mexico's elite Ibero-American University, and brimming with innovative ideas about modernizing his production. His quarter of this sorghum field is part of that plan. Now, as we approach the occupation, he wavers between anger and depression. After a brief discussion with the new arrivals while I wait in the truck, Paco returns. For now his investment is safe, but he is clearly shaken. They have initiated an agrarian reform claim on a section of the field owned by one of Paco's partners who has agreed to sell. Paco's words mirror those of every rancher I spoke with. "No one is going

---

Mexico utilized "modern intensive" practices. On the coast of Chiapas, home to the state's most intensive producers, Vasquez Gomez (1997: 24) reports that only 12 percent of ranchers use fertilized pastures and 19 percent supplemented pasture with other feeds.

to invest in land with all the invasions. If they see your land nicely planted and taken care of, they'll decide to take it."

From special rural police forces sanctioned by state government to "prevent rustling," to close alliances with military and police forces, to legal tricks designed to disguise the existence of large extensions of land by dividing it among family members, history shows that ranchers in Chiapas have refined the art of protecting their investments. Nevertheless, seemingly endless insecurity in the form of land invasions and more prosaic "weapons of the weak" (Scott 1985) has deflated many ranchers' wills to invest in productive investment. In a context of agrarian struggle and the recognition that, in the last instance, property rights may be manipulated by the state for political reasons, a species of "cadastral anxiety"—an underlying ontological awareness of the insecurity of private property—flourishes among ranchers.[21] Many, like Paco and his half-brother, have given up on Chiapas, moving their operations across the border to relatively tranquil Tabasco. Chilón's most modern rancher, whose purebred herd and technified dairy operations won him multiple awards, now milks his cows in Quintana Roo. Most ranchers, however, pine for better times, while diversifying into more stable businesses. In conversation, Mauricio Garza and Carlos Guttenberg discuss the future: "I'm waiting for the next [president] to see what happens. If we don't get support then, I'll turn in my land and do something else."

"We need a dictator, like what happened in Chile with Allende. We need to bring [nineteenth-century dictator] Don Porfirio [Diaz] back to life."

Since the days of David Ricardo, landowners like the Chiapas ranchers have been stereotyped—often accurately— as idle rent-seekers, who reap profits without investment through their control of land.[22] This stereotype certainly hits the mark in Chiapas, and young technically trained ranchers like Paco Jimenez criticize their peers who sit back and don't invest in production. But, with their easy banter about the latest innovation in cattle breeding or tales from recent trips to cattle expositions in Texas, many ranchers display a real desire to intensify. At the same time they are aware that without state support in the form of soft credit, trade regulation, and

---

21. Even after the 1992 reforms to Article 27 of the Mexican Constitution, the state remains the ultimate owner of land within the nation, reserving the right to grant and revoke private property rights according to the dictates of "public interest" (Secretaría de Agricultura y Recursos Hidraulicos [SARH] 1992: 1). Strategic attempts by the state to allay the fears of private property owners through changes in constitutional wording in 1983 (cf. Fox and Gordillo 1989), have not assuaged what I call "cadastral anxiety" among ranchers in Chiapas. Ranchers believe that their property rights have often been sacrificed by the state in order to assure social peace during periods of agrarian upheaval.

22. See Edelman (1992) and Hecht (1985) for sophisticated takes on the "*rentier* logic of *latifundio*."

what is ominously referred to as "a state of law," they might be better off in another profession.

Beyond Scarcity—Other Logics of Resource Struggle

"Greenwar" hypotheses revolve fundamentally around the notion that violent conflicts erupt from competition over scarce material—or "environmental"—resources. Since most analyses concur that land sits at the center of struggles in Chiapas, it is not difficult to understand the conflicts as battles for control over a scarce material resource. This chapter, however, has cast a shadow over these easy explanations of conflict based on land scarcity.

Thus far, I have argued that the primary scarcity in Chiapas is a capacity (and in some cases seen in the previous section, a willingness) to make the most productive use of existing land. This institutional scarcity is rooted in national economic reforms, changes in international commodity markets, and local experiences of violence and insecurity. This final section follows from this starting point and develops the notion that violence in Chiapas is forged, in part, in arenas of power struggles peripheral to the political–economic battle for direct control of productive land. Land and land invasions are central parts of multiple arenas of contestation, not merely in a struggle over productive resources. Numerous authors, including Howard and Homer-Dixon, have pointed to the role ethnic difference plays in generating agrarian conflict in Chiapas. Likewise, an important body of research suggests that it is impossible to separate land conflict in Chiapas from struggles over indigenous autonomy, democracy, and citizenship (Fox 1994; Harvey 1998; Stephen 1997a, 1997b). In this section, I conclude by suggesting two arenas in which land and land invasions play key roles. First, land invasions represent central elements in struggles for political power at the municipal level and among rival peasant organizations. Second, land invasions and agrarian struggle in Chiapas produce a history of violence that itself reshapes trajectories of conflict. By examining the contradictory understandings of land invasions and violence that ranchers narrate, it is clear that this history often disposes ranchers towards violent defense of territory but also can restrain them.

Land and Land Invasions in Local Political Struggles

Since the 1930s when the Cardenista leader Erasto Urbina first began to teach Chiapan peasants the art of carrying out agrarian reform demands, land invasions have played a pivotal part in the state's rural politics. Land invasions stood at the center of efforts to break up large landholdings and light a fire under stagnant bureaucrats in the Secretariat of Agrarian Reform. They also have played an essential role in contests among peasant organizations, particularly between government-affiliated organizations and more radical independent groups. The ability to successfully establish and win land claims enhances these groups' political standing. As Frans Schreyer (1990: 196) observes in his study of agrarian conflict in the Huasteca region of Mexico, successful land invasions represented an important way in which competing peasant organizations demonstrated their relative strength to state agrarian reform bureaucrats.

A case alluded to previously from the early 1980s demonstrates this well. At that time, radical independent peasant organizations had launched a massive wave of land invasions that forced the government to agree to purchase invaded land from its owners (the PRA). The government-affiliated National Peasants Confederation (CNC), already facing declining legitimacy due to its inability to resolve the agrarian backlog, viewed the settlement in favor of independent organizations as a threat. In response, the CNC organized "invasions of the invasions," in which confederation members drove independent groups from their land claims and brokered a deal with the government that channeled redistributed land through the CNC (Harvey 1990, 1998; Reyes 1992). Similar dynamics occurred in 1994 as competing groups often staked claims to the same pieces of land with pro-government organizations often "re-invading" land occupied by opposition groups (or vice versa).

In Chilón, the PRD's sponsorship of land invasions was a critical component of that party's unprecedented victory in municipal elections after the 1994 uprising. The invasion of Aurelio Cosío's land by PRD militants can be seen as a strategic political maneuver, not solely an attempt to obtain land. Triumph in the municipal elections, in turn, provided PRD-affiliated peasants with privileged access to state resources such as credit and public works that they would use to make their land more productive. In numerous occasions, both in Chilón and throughout the state, these politically motivated land invasions didn't last long, with the invaders (typically already owning some property elsewhere) drifting away from the invaded parcel after the initial political statement had been made. Daniel Villafuerte (personal communication May 12, 2000) notes that, in some cases, the original peasant land claimants could not be found once the government agreed to purchase the invaded land.

In 1996, PRI-affiliated indigenous peasants from the San Gerónimo de Bachajón ejido in Chilón began a series of attacks on PRD officials and their peasant supporters. The Chinchulines, as the right-wing paramilitary group called themselves, formed together as early as 1988 as the United Front of Ejidatarios to fight battles for state resources, including concessions to control transportation routes and deposits of sand and gravel. In

April 1996, however, they seized the municipal palace in Chilón, driving the PRD mayor into exile in Tuxtla Gutierrez (*La Jornada* July 12, 1996). The Chinchulines criticized the new administration's channeling of resources to its supporters and demanded the diversion of resources to Chinchulines members.

> From the beginning of his term municipal mayor Manuel Gómez Moreno has acted partially. That is to say, benefiting only the group that helped him assume power and not taking into account the needs of other groups that lack the necessary supports for their subsistence.
>
> Chinchulines declaration, April 22, 1996 (quoted in CDHFBC and CDIAC 1996: 7)

As a result of these and other violent actions, including attacks on land invaders and an assault on a municipal truck carrying peasants to the inauguration of a PRD-sponsored public works program, the Chinchulines won concessions from the state, including a 200,000 peso credit for coffee cultivation, and secured control over transportation concessions (CDHFBC and CDIAC 1996: 6–18, Conpaz 1996: 74–75).

Meanings of Land and Violence

For ranchers responding to land invasions, land embodies a set of meanings that transcend its basic productive utility. Land provides a hedge against currency devaluation. "[It] is the only thing that doesn't devalue. It's a savings account," offered a rancher in Salto de Agua (cf. Edelman 1992). Land also often represents the one legacy, outside of an education, safe from the wild fluctuations of Mexico's economy that ranchers can pass on to their children. For other ranchers land is the foundation of a particular way of life. Many landowners, even those who earn the bulk of their incomes outside of agriculture, "would rather die than give it up." Land provides a tangible link to the heritage of previous generations and the unit through which tradition is passed on to the future. In this sense, particular modes of using land serve as key markers of identity and distinction. To drive home the cultural meanings of land, ranchers frequently dwell in their conversations on the stories of neighbors who died from despair and broken hearts after losing their land to invasions. Given the cultural significance of land for ranchers, it is not surprising to see a disposition towards violent defense of territory even as land's importance to rancher livelihoods declines.

At the same time, other narratives contradict this current. As Michael Taussig (1984) notes, dominant classes often live in unsuspended fear of those they rule (see also Orlove 1994). In Chiapas, even several years after the most severe waves of land conflict, ranchers I interviewed describe life as an ongoing siege lain by semi-savage peasants duped by communist priests. Skittish, tense descriptions of peasants' uses of various forms of everyday resistance betrayed an underlying current of fear behind the veneer of a "no one fucks with me" attitude. "We've seen the killing of cattle, robbing of workers, the theft of pigs and small animals. They set coffee plants on fire. They drive off our workers. I'm up to here with them. They want to drive me off," said Mauricio Garza, vacillating between anger and exasperation.

Rancher's narratives often revolve around rumors of imminent attack. Aurelio Cosío and Gustavo Aguilar recalled anxious hours they spent barricaded in their homes expecting an imminent attack from nearby ejidos during the days of smoke and chaos following the Zapatista uprising. Luis Alvaro Toledo hears whispers from his indigenous ranch hands that members of a neighboring ejido want to ambush him. Ranchers' stories of land invasion sometimes involve, what appear to them to be incidents of unearthly torture inflicted on landowners by peasants. Outside observers, however, note that on these occasions, peasants are often mimicking the punishments inflicted on them by the landowner, or more likely by his father or grandfather.

The palpable sense of siege was particularly sharp in Chilón, where a tiny minority of landowners are in fact surrounded by hundreds of indigenous communities, and racially charged violence extends far back in local histories. Combined with a strong perception of weakening state support, fear of other racial groups exerts a significant influence on ranchers' response to land invasions. On one hand, it propels ranchers to prepare for "self defense" and justifies acts of violence against land claimants. The constant stress of insecurity has prompted most ranchers to arm themselves and few visit their property without a pistol tucked in the glove compartment of their pickup.

At the same time, rancher narratives evoke the hopelessness of struggle against an inevitable tide of defeat. Their stories emphasize fear of indigenous takeover, the vast difference in indigenous and mestizo populations, and what they view as overwhelming government support for the ejido sector. Stories that allege powerful international forces behind indigenous uprisings buttress this sense of resignation. Often drawn from the pages of LaRouchite literature, these stories paint the Zapatista uprising as the product of "British banking interests," the U.S. state department, large foreign corporations, and international intrigue played out by an unlikely coven of characters including Fidel Castro, the European Union, Luis Echeverría, Bishop Samuel Ruiz, and Carlos Salinas. These narratives provide a critical absolution for ranchers. The uprising did not occur because of mestizo exploitation of indigenous people but rather because of mysterious secret plots, typically hatched to win access to Chiapas's rich deposits of uranium. But the stories also construct the conflict as something far bigger than previous land struggles in Chiapas. The belief that shadowy outside forces lurk behind Chiapas's problems serves to relieve ranchers of responsibility for the uprising and agrarian conflict. At the same time, its emphasis on the tremendous, almost magical, power wielded by these uncontrollable outside forces also cultivates a profound sense of powerlessness and pessimism among many ranchers.

Conclusion

Given the complicated and sometimes contradictory nature of ranchers' narratives about land and land invasion, it is difficult to portray their responses to agrarian conflict as mechanical reactions to material scarcity. The movement from the conditions that underlie violence to its actual manifestation is vast. It is a movement, across a space densely populated with memories, symbols, and stories, that teems with the possibility of unexpected outcomes. At the same time, it is important not to assume that the underlying economic or natural conditions of violence are themselves transparent. This chapter demonstrates the importance of critically examining stock interpretations of these underlying conditions based on simple scarcity models. Easy recourse to explanations based on environmental scarcity and unequal land tenure obscure complex dynamics that shape the trajectories of agrarian conflict.

I have shown that, "the Chiapas conflict" cannot be explained using a simple linear model in which underlying scarcities combine with a set of "triggers" to mechanically produce violence (e.g., Howard and Homer-Dixon 1995). The Chiapan "warscape" must be desegregated, and each piece of it must be considered in context. The massive wave of land occupations carried out in the wake of the Zapatista uprising, which on the surface appear as uncomplicated "land grabs" in a struggle for scarce productive resources, are, in fact, far more complex. I have suggested that, after more than a decade of economic restructuring, land scarcity is not only a question of "given" natural attributes or land tenure regimes but also the product of a set of political and economic policies that reduce both peasants' and ranchers' abilities to produce effectively on available arable land.

At the same time, I have shown that land occupations and often violent responses to them are not just struggles over scarce land for production. The events surrounding land invasions are also sites of struggle over control of municipal government and state resources channeled through municipalities, the political influence of different peasant organizations, and the relationship between land and identity in the Chiapan countryside.

Even this is not a complete picture of these multi-arena skirmishes but rather a way of demonstrating that they represent far more than is implied by proponents of environmental explanations.

Finally, by highlighting the ways in which landed elites' control over vast expanses of the state has been steadily and effectively broken down by decades of peasant mobilization and agrarian reform, I am not suggesting, as many ranchers do, that landed elites are innocent bystanders in Chiapas's recent history of exploitation and violence. On the contrary, landed elites continue to exploit indigenous people in multiple ways, particularly through control over transportation and commercialization of farm produce. Control over the few state resources that are channeled into the countryside is also deeply shaped by unequal power relations between mestizo and indigenous elites and indigenous peasants. A more complete picture of the changing forms, channels, and workings of landed elite power in Chiapas awaits further research. In this chapter, I have simply spotlighted the fact that it can no longer be seen as revolving primarily around control over land as a productive resource.

III

Extraction, the Nature of Natural Resources, and Violence

8

Petro-Violence: Community, Extraction, and Political Ecology of a Mythic Commodity

Michael Watts

> Oil, more than any other commodity, illustrates both the importance
> and the mystification of natural resources in the modern world.
>
> (Coronil 1997: 49)

I want to offer some thoughts on the violence that so often attends particular sorts of resource extraction and, quite specifically, the extraction of petroleum—arguably the most important resource of the twentieth century. In exploring what I shall call *petro-violence*, my purpose is not to offer a sort of commodity determinism—petroleum is more violent than coal, or oil extraction breeds Muslim radicalism (Iran) but copper breeds evangelical cronyism (Zambia). I take seriously the idea that the biophysical properties of nature, of a natural resource, matter in both material and analytical ways. It is both difficult and artificial to distill out the narrowly defined biological and geophysical properties of "crude" or "raw" petroleum from the social relations (institutional practices, ideological associations and meanings, forms of extraction, production and use) of petroleum. Petroleum is a commodity not only saturated in the mythos of the rise of the industrial West but also indisputably one of *the* most fundamental building blocks of twentieth century hydrocarbon capitalism. I do believe, however, that a commodity-focus (particularly on a part of nature that has the ideological and practical significance of "black gold") offers a way of thinking about the intersection of environment and violence. I want to consider both *ecological* violence perpetrated upon the biophysical world and *social* violence—criminality and degeneracy associated with the genesis of petro-wealth.

As Daniel Yergin (1991) details in his encyclopedic account of the industry *The Prize*, the entire history of petroleum is replete with criminality,

189

corruption, fabulous wealth, and the worst of rapacious frontier capitalism. Power politics, ruthless exploitation, and thuggery have always been
oil's defining characteristics, and imperialism is its defining moment. It is
to be expected then that in an age of unprecedented denationalization
and market liberalization, the mad scramble to locate the next petrolic El
Dorado continues unabated. As oil prices climb from the catastrophic collapse of the mid 1980s—when the foundations of the oil-states were
rocked by the spectacle of a barrel of oil costing less than $8—the raven-
ous appetite of the oil majors continues.

Petro-violence is in fact rarely off the front pages of the press. The
Caspian basin, for example, reaching from the borders of Afghanistan to
the Russian Caucuses is a repository of enormous petro-wealth. Turk-
menistan, Kazakstan, Azerbaijan, Georgia, and the southern Russian
provinces (Ossetia, Dagestan, Chechnya), have become, in the wake of the
collapse of the Soviet Union, a zone of extraordinary civil conflict and war
as the *San Francisco Chronicle* puts it (August 11, 1998: A8). Oil companies
jockey for position in an atmosphere of frontier vigilantism, and petroleum
has become central to what the Azerbaijani President calls "armed conflict,
aggressive separatism and nationalism." In Colombia, leftist guerrillas blew
up the Cano Limón pipeline, and Occidental Petroleum, in a long running
battle with indigenous populations, was confronted with the prospect of
five thousand U'wa Amerindians committing mass suicide if their "tribal
lands" became the site of oil extraction (*The Economist* June 6, 1998: 34). It
is surely not too much of a stretch to also see the black and sticky residues
of Middle East petroleum in the wreckage of the bombings in Dar es
Salaam and Nairobi. Mr. bin Laden, a son of a contractor who became fabulously rich overnight from the oil rents generously distributed by the Saudi
monarchy, may or may not have been responsible in some way for the
bombings. The very idea of a *fatwa* against the United States, however, can
only be understood in relation to the geopolitics of oil and the radically
destabilizing consequences of the circulation of petro-dollars within the
Muslim world. After all, what began in Iran in 1973 with the Shah's drive to
modernity ended with massive bloodletting and revolution in 1979.

These instances of petro-violence raise the question of the analytical
boundaries of this chapter and of the reach of oil in examining violence. I
shall concentrate here on the point of production (on extraction narrowly
construed) and its immediate social and environmental consequences in
particular. But this local focus cannot be rigidly demarcated from the crucial consequences of oil rents on the state, on national political discourse,
and on the broad rhythms of accumulation. In fact, it is this broader landscape of petro-politics and petro-accumulation that is crucial to understanding the violence of local production and the centrality of the issue
that concerns me here: How is petroleum as a natural resource constitu-

tive of political violence in which narratives of environmental justice or compensation for the costs of ecological distribution are fused with or attached to debates over citizenship and the nation? (See Guha and Martinez-Alier 1998.)

Two sorts of argument are made in this chapter. One is *comparative*, speaking to oil exploitation in two different locations (Nigeria and Ecuador) and the political outcomes at the level of the community and the national body politic: each case releases different *forms* of violence over ostensibly similar *objects* of struggle (the nation, citizenship, and indigenous identity). The other is *theoretical* and turns on how one might think about the specific qualities and properties of a natural resource. Here it is crucial to distinguish three levels at which the theory is operating. One is that oil speaks to a general set of questions about *extraction* and the sorts of violence that might be typically attached to these sets of activities. There is, then, a class of questions that address extraction and violence in general (of which one case is oil). Another level pertains to *rents* and the rents that come to play a key role in national and local politics. In the oil case, rent is derived from the capitalist extraction of minerals but is obviously not unique to it (i.e., it could be an agricultural rent or a rent derived from other sectors). In other words, a part of the oil story turns on a class of phenomena pertaining to rents and *rentier* activities and how both relate to violence and the environment. Oil concerns me here, but it might easily have been silver and the activities of the Hunt brothers. The final level pertains to the *natural resource* and to the biophysical particularities and political and discursive peculiarities of oil: it is finite; it is a black and sticky fluid that is pumped from the ground and transported from the point of production in pipelines; in much of the South it is invariably a national resource with territorial attributes (state landed property); oil is inseparable from the largest forms of transnational capital; and not least oil has its own mythos rendered through its fantastic wealth, its all-encompassing power, and as the lifeline to hydrocarbon civilization.

My entry point is the much publicized struggle by the Ogoni people (a small ethnic society occupying a Lilliputian territory in the oil-rich Niger delta in southeast Nigeria) against Shell and the staggering ecological devastation wrought by the company since 1958 when pumping began. It is also the story of their onetime leader Ken Saro-Wiwa and his efforts to create a space of autonomy and self-determination enshrined in an Ogoni Bill of Rights and in a mass political movement (the Movement for the Survival of the Ogoni People [MOSOP]). Saro-Wiwa and eight others were hanged following a show trial at the hands of a military tribunal; nineteen other key Ogoni leaders were placed in detention and were only released following the return to civilian rule in 1999. Since 1991 Ogoniland has been the site of mass violence (intra- and intercommunity as well as between the state security forces and the Ogoni), and since 1995 it has been under military occupation. Even the return to civilian politics under President Obasanjo in 1999 has not changed the overwhelming sense of siege under which the entire Niger Delta lives (Human Rights Watch 2000).

My argument is roughly as follows: the Ogoni struggle is a response to the violence perpetrated upon the environment by the slick alliance of state and capital. It is an effort by a Nigerian ethnic minority (an "indigenous people") to simultaneously construct representations of other Nigerians as "ethnic majorities" and of themselves as minorities and indigenous people. The struggle also is about political rights and entitlements on which alternative histories and geographies are constructed. Environment (that is to say the particular biological and geophysical properties of what the Ogoni take to be their territory) is of course central to both of these constructions. In my view the Ogoni struggle for recognition is part of an incomplete decolonization of Africa, an effort to redeem something from the carapace of reformist nationalism and to maintain the imaginative liberation of an African people. The Ogoni struggle to identity themselves and others in relation to themselves turns, in large measure, as I shall argue, on articulations of history and geography, on nature and biology.

This brings me to a second point, namely Poulantzas's (1978) observation that "national unity or modern unity becomes a historicity of a territory and a territorialization of a history." Markers of identity may become themselves commodities in the way that the histories of interrelated peoples become spatialized into bounded territories. "Since these spaces appear as being produced naturally, not historically, they serve to root the histories of connected peoples in separate territories and to sever the links between them" (Coronil 1996: 77). There is sort of double movement at work as histories of space are obscured and as social relations between societies are occluded. It is an affliction which effects the Nigerian state as much as it does the Ogoni themselves.

I wish to explore the case of the Ogoni in a comparative light, however, specifically with regard to the events surrounding oil exploration and production in the Upper Amazon, in the Ecuadorian Oriente in particular. There are both interesting similarities and points of departure in these two examples that I shall try to highlight. The comparison also provides a powerful vehicle for exploring the violence that surrounds oil and delving into what Coronil calls the "mystification" of natural resources in the modern world.

Oil, Nature, and Violence in the Nigerian Delta

If the recent history of Nigeria has been the tale of petroleum (Watts 1994; Khan 1994), then Ogoniland has simultaneously been at its center and at its periphery.[1] The great paradox of Ogoniland is that an accident of geological history—the location of more than ten major oil fields within its historic territory—yielded not petro-modernization but economic underdevelopment and an ecological catastrophe. Ken Saro-Wiwa and the Ogoni detested the modern because *they could not get enough of it.* The Ogoni were angry because they could neither afford the cars nor use the roads that were the icons of petro-success. In this sense, the Ogoni story is deeply Benjaminian. Throughout his Parisian production cycle (Cohen 1993) Walter Benjamin employed two alternative vocabularies as a way of investigating base–superstructure relations through the language of dreams. One was *phantasmagoria,* driven by the phantom capitalist commodity; the other was *shock.* In Ogoniland it was the phantasmagoria of petro-commodification (of wealth without effort) and the shock of modernity that frame the rise of MOSOP and what Benjamin himself, in his concern with utopias, called "the moment of awakening."

The Ogoni are typically seen as a distinct ethnic group consisting of three subgroups and six clans.[2] Their population of roughly 500,000 people is distributed among 111 villages dotted over 404 square miles of creeks, waterways, and tropical forest in the northeast fringes of the Niger Delta. Located administratively in Rivers State, a Louisiana-like territory of some 50,000 square kilometers, Ogoniland of one the most heavily populated zones in all of Africa. Indeed, the most densely settled areas of Ogoniland—over 1,500 persons per square kilometer.—are the sites of the largest wells. Ogoniland's customary productive base was provided by fishing and agricultural pursuits until the discovery of petroleum, including the huge Bomu field, immediately prior to Independence. Part of an enormously complex regional ethnic mosaic, the Ogoni were drawn into internecine conflicts within the delta region—largely as a consequence of the slave trade and its aftermath—in the period prior to arrival of colonial forces at Kono in 1901. The Ogoni resisted the British until 1908 (Naanen 1995) but thereafter were left to stagnate as part of the Opopo Division within Calabar Province.

As Ogoniland was gradually incorporated within the colonial state during the 1930s, the clamor for a separate political division grew at the hands of the first pan-Ogoni organization (the Ogoni Central Union) that bore fruit with the establishment of the Ogoni Native Authority in 1947. In 1951, however, the authority was forcibly integrated into the Ibo-domi-

---

1. For a more detailed account of Ogoniland and its relation to oil, see Watts (1997); for the fullest accounts of oil and Nigerian political economy see Khan (1994); Ikein (1990); Lewis (1996); and Forrest (1995). I have written at length on the relations between the petro-boom in Nigeria and the shock of modernity that it precipitated (see Watts 1994).
2. Ogoniland consists of three local government areas and six clans that speak different dialects of the Ogoni language. MOSOP is, in this sense, a pan-Ogoni organization.

nated Eastern Region. Tremendous neglect and systematic discrimination, raised longstanding fears among the Ogoni of Ibo domination.[3] Politically marginalized and economically neglected, the delta minorities feared the growing secessionist rhetoric of the Ibo and led an ill-fated secession of their own in February 1966. Isaac Boro, Sam Owonaro, and Nottingham Dick declared an illegal Delta Peoples Republic but were crushed and subsequently, in a trial that is uncomfortably reminiscent of the Ogoni tribunal in 1995, condemned to death for treason. Nonetheless, Ogoni antipathy to what they saw as a sort of internal colonialism at the hands of the Ibo continued in their support of the federal forces during the civil war. While President Gowon did finally establish a Rivers State in 1967—which compensated in some measure for enormous Ogoni losses during the war—the new state recapitulated in microcosm the larger "national question." The new Rivers State was multiethnic but presided over by the locally dominant Ijaw, for whom many of the minorities felt little but contempt.[4] In Saro-Wiwa's view (1992), the loss of 10 percent of the Ogoni people in the civil war was rewarded with a betrayal by federal authorities: they provided no postwar relief, seized new on- and offshore oil fields, and subsequently sold out the minorities to dominant Ijaw interests.

Traces of Ogoni "nationalism" long predate the oil boom, but they were deepened as a result of it. Ogoni fears of what Saro-Wiwa called "monstrous domestic colonialism" (1992), were exacerbated further by federal resistance to dealing with minority issues[5] in the wake of the civil war and by the new politics of post-oil boom revenue allocation. Rivers State saw its federal allocation fall dramatically in absolute and relative terms. At the height of the oil boom, 60 percent of oil production came from Rivers

3. As constitutional preparations were made for the transition to home rule, non-Igbo minorities throughout the Eastern Region appealed to the colonial government for a separate Rivers State. Ogoni representatives lobbied the Willink Commission in 1958 to avert the threat of exclusion within an Ibo-dominated regional government that had assumed self-governing status in 1957, but minority claims were ignored (Okpu 1977; Okilo 1980).

4. The Ogoni and other minorities petitioned in 1974 for the creation of a new Port Harcourt State within the Rivers State boundary (Naanen 1995: 63).

5. What Rivers State felt in regard to federal neglect, the Ogoni experienced in regard to Ijaw domination. While several Ogoni were influential federal and state politicians, they were incapable politically of exacting resources for the Ogoni community. In the 1980s only six out of forty-two representatives in the state assembly were Ogoni (Naanen 1995: 77). It needs to be said, however—and it is relevant for an understanding of state violence against the Ogoni—that the Ogoni have fared better than many other minorities in terms of political appointments. In 1993, 30 percent of the Commissioners in the Rivers State cabinet were Ogoni (the Ogoni represent 12 percent of the state population), and every clan has produced at least one federal or state minister (Osaghae 1995: 331) since the civil war. In this sense, it is precisely that the Ogoni had produced since 1967 a cadre of influential and well-placed politicians (including Saro-Wiwa himself) that their decision to move aggressively toward self-determination and minority rights was so threatening to the Abacha regime (Welch 1995).

State, but it received only 5 percent of the statutory allocation (roughly half of that received by Kano, Northeastern States, and the Ibo heartland, East Central State). Between 1970 and 1980, it received in revenues a minuscule one-fiftieth of the value of the oil it produced. In what was seen by the Rivers minorities as a particularly egregious case of ethnic treachery, the civilian Shagari regime reduced the derivation component to only 2 percent of revenues in 1982, after Rivers State had voted overwhelmingly for Shagari's northern-dominated National Party of Nigeria. The subsequent military government of General Buhari cut the derivation component even further at a time when the state accounted for 44.3 percent of Nigeria's oil production.

Standing at the "margin of the margin," Ogoniland appears, like Chiapas in Mexico, as a socioeconomic paradox. Home to six oilfields, half of Nigeria's oil refineries, the country's only fertilizer plant, a large petrochemical plant, Ogoniland is wracked by unthinkable misery and deprivation. During the first oil boom, Ogoniland's fifty-six wells accounted for almost 15 percent of Nigerian oil production,[6] and in the past three decades an estimated $30 billion in petroleum revenues have flowed from this Lilliputian territory. It was, as local opinion had it, Nigeria's Kuwait. Yet according to a government commission, Oloibiri, where the first oil was pumped in 1958, has no single kilometer of all-season road and remains "one of the most backward areas in the country" (Furro 1992: 282). Few Ogoni households have electricity; there is one doctor per 100,000 people; child mortality rates are the highest in the nation; unemployment is 85 percent; 80 percent of the population is illiterate; and close to half of Ogoni youth have left the region in search of work. Life expectancy is barely fifty years, substantially below the national average. In Furro's survey of two minority oil-producing communities, over 80 percent of respondents felt that economic conditions had *deteriorated* since the onset of oil production, and over two-thirds believed that there had been no progress in local development since 1960. No wonder that the systematic reduction of federal allocations and the lack of concern by the Rivers government was, for Ogoniland, part of a long history of "the politics of minority suffocation" (Ikporukpo 1996: 171).

If Ogoniland failed to see the material benefits from oil, what it *did* experience was an ecological disaster—what the European Parliament has called "an environmental nightmare." The heart of the ecological harms stem from oil spills—either from the pipelines that crisscross Ogoniland (often passing directly through villages) or from blowouts at the well-

---

6. According to the Nigerian Government, Ogoniland currently (1995) produces about 2 percent of Nigerian oil output and is the fifth largest oil-producing community in Rivers State. Shell maintains that total Ogoni oil output is valued at $5.2 billion before costs.

heads—and gas flaring. As regards the latter, a staggering 76 percent of natural gas in the oil-producing areas is flared (compared to 6 percent in the United States). As a visiting environmentalist noted in 1993 in the delta, "some children have never known a dark night even though they have no electricity' " (*Village Voice* November 21, 1995: 21). Burning 24 hours per day at temperatures of 13,000–14,000 degrees Celsius, Nigerian natural gas produces 35 million tons of carbon dioxide and 12 million tons of methane, more than the rest of the world (and rendering Nigeria probably the biggest single cause of global warming). The oil spillage record is even worse. According to Claude Ake there are roughly 300 spills per year in the delta, and in the 1970's alone the spillage was four times the much publicized Exxon Valdez spill in Alaska. In one year alone, almost 700,000 barrels were soiled according to a government commission. Ogoniland itself suffered 111 spills between 1985 and 1994 (Hammer 1996: 61). Figures provided by the Nigerian National Petroleum Company (NNPC) document 2,676 spills between 1976 and 1990, 59 percent of which occurred in Rivers State (Ikein 1990: 171), 38 percent of which were due to equipment malfunction.[7] Between 1982 and 1992 Shell alone accounted for 1.6 million gallons of spilled oil, 37 percent of the company's spills worldwide. The consequences of flaring, spillage, and waste for Ogoni fisheries and farming have been devastating.[8] Two independent studies completed in 1997 reveal total petroleum hydrocarbons in Ogoni streams at 360 and 680 times the European Community permissible levls (Rainforest Action Network 1997).

In almost four decades of oil drilling, then, the experience of petro-modernization in Ogoniland has been a tale of terror and tears. It has brought home the worst fears of ethnic marginalization and minority neglect: of northern hegemony, of Ibo neglect, and of Ijaw local dominance. The euphoria of oil wealth after the civil war has been displaced by ecological catastrophe, social deprivation, political marginalization, and a rapacious company capitalism in which unaccountable foreign transnationals are granted a sort of immunity by the state.

7. The oil companies claim that sabotage accounts for a large proportion (60 percent) of the spills because communities gain from corporate compensation. Shell claims that 77 of 111 spills in Ogoniland between 1985 and 1994 were due to sabotage (Hammer 1996). According to the government commission, however, sabotage accounts for 30 percent of the incidents but only 3 percent of the quantity spilled. Furthermore, all oil-producing communities claim that compensation from the companies for spills has been almost nonexistent.
8. A spill in 1993 flowed for forty days without repair contaminating large areas of Ogoni farmland. Petroleum residues appear in the rivers at levels of 60 ppm and in the sediments around the Bonny terminal reach lethal levels of 12,000 ppm. In the ecologically delicate mangrove and estuarine regions of the delta, oil pollution has produced large-scale eutrophication, depletion of aquatic resources, and loss of traditional fishing grounds (Benka-Cocker and Ekundayo 1995) that now threaten customary livelihoods.

The hanging of Ken Saro-Wiwa and the Ogoni nine in November 1995—accused of murdering four prominent Ogoni leaders who professed opposition to MOSOP tactics—and the subsequent arrest of nineteen others on treason charges represented the summit of a process of mass mobilization and radical militancy that had commenced in 1989. The civil war had, as I have previously suggested, hardened the sense of external dominance among Ogonis. A "supreme cultural organization" called Kagote, which consisted largely of traditional rulers and high-ranking functionaries, was established at the war's end and, in turn, gave birth in 1990 to MOSOP. A new strategic phase began in 1989 with a program of mass action and passive resistance on one hand and a renewed effort to focus on the environmental consequences of oil (and Shell's role in particular) and on group rights within the federal structure on the other hand. Animating the entire struggle was, in Leton's words, the "genocide being committed in the dying years of the twentieth century by multinational companies under the supervision of the Government . . . ." (cited in Naanen 1995: 66).

A watershed moment in MOSOP's history was the drafting in 1990 of an Ogoni Bill of Rights (Saro-Wiwa 1992). Documenting a history of neglect and local misery, the Ogoni bill questioned Nigerian federalism and minority rights. Calling for participation in the affairs of the republic as "a distinct and separate entity," the bill outlined a plan for autonomy and self-determination in which there would be guaranteed "political control of Ogoni affairs by Ogoni people . . . the right to control and use a fair proportion of Ogoni economic resources . . . [and] adequate representation as of right in all Nigerian national institutions" (Saro-Wiwa 1990: 11). In short, the Bill of Rights addressed the question of the *unit* to which revenues should be allocated—and derivatively the rights of minorities. Largely under Saro-Wiwa's direction, the bill was employed as part of an international mobilization campaign. Presented at the UN Subcommittee on Human Rights, at the Working Group on Indigenous Populations in Geneva in 1992, and at UNPO in the Hague in 1993, Ogoni became— with the help of Rainforest Action Network and Greenpeace—a *cause célèbre*.

Ken Saro-Wiwa played a central role in the tactical and organizational transformations of MOSOP during the 1990s. Born in Bori as part of a traditional ruling family, Saro-Wiwa was already, prior to 1990, an internationally recognized author, a successful writer of Nigerian soap operas, a well-connected former Rivers State commissioner, and a wealthy businessman. Saro-Wiwa also was President of the Ethnic Minorities Rights organization of Africa (EMIROAF) that called for a restructuring of the Nigerian federation into a confederation of autonomous ethnic states, in which an historically powerful federal center was to be radically decentralized and states were granted property rights over on-shore mineral resources (Os-aghae 1995: 327). Under Saro-Wiwa, MOSOP focused in 1991 on links to pro-democracy groups in Nigeria (the transition to civilian rule had begun under heavy-handed military direction) and on direct action around Shell and Chevron installations. It was precisely because of the absence of state commitment and the deterioration of the environment that local Ogoni communities, perhaps understandably, had great expectations of Shell (the largest producer in the region) and directed their activity against the oil companies after three decades of betrayal. There was a sense that Shell *was* the local government[9] (*Guardian* July 14, 1996: 11), but the company's record had been appalling: it had failed the test as company patron to the region. In 1970, Ogoni representatives had already demanded Rivers State government to approach Shell—what they then called "a Shylock of a com-pany"—for compensation and direct assistance (a plea, incidentally, that elicited a shockingly irresponsible response documented in Saro-Wiwa 1992). Compensation by the companies for land appropriation and spillage has been minimal and are (and remain) constant sources of ten-sion between company and community. Shell, deemed the world's most profitable corporation in 1996 by *Business Week* (July 8, 1996 46) netting roughly $200 million profit from Nigeria each year, by its own admission has provided only $2 million to Ogoniland in forty of pumping. Ogoni his-torian Loolo (1981) points out that Shell has built one road and awarded 96 school scholarships in thirty years. According to the *Wall Street Journal*, Shell employs 88 Ogonis (less than 2 percent) in a workforce of over 5,000 Nigerian employees. Furthermore, the oft-cited community development schemes of the oil companies only began in earnest in the 1980s and have met with minimal success (Ikporukpo 1993). Shell only began community efforts in 1992 after twenty-five years of pumping and then provided a wa-ter project of 5,000 gallons capacity for a constituency of 100,000. (*Newswatch* December 18, 1995: 13).

In an atmosphere of growing violence and insecurity, MOSOP wrote to the three oil companies operating in Ogoniland in December 1992 de-manding $6.2 billion in back rents and royalties, $4 billion for damages, the immediate stoppage of degradation, flaring, and exposed pipelines, and negotiations with Ogonis to establish conditions for further explo-ration (Osaghae 1995: 336; Greenpeace 1994). The companies re-sponded with tightened security while the military government sent in troops to the oil installations, banned all public gatherings, and declared as treasonable any claims for self-determination. Strengthening Ogoni re-solve, these responses prompted MOSOP to organize a massive rally—an

---

9. Before cessation of operations in 1993, Shell was the principal oil company operating in Ogoniland, pumping from five major oilfields at Bomu/Dere, Yorla, Bodo West, Korokoro, and Ebubu.

estimated 300,000 participated—in January 1993. As harassment of MOSOP leadership and Ogoni communities by state forces escalated, the high point of the struggle came with the decision to boycott the Nigerian presidential election on June 12, 1993.

In the wake of the annulment of the presidential elections, the arrest of democratically elected Mashood Abiola and the subsequently military coup by General Abacha, state security forces vastly expanded their activities in Ogoniland. Military units were moved into the area in June 1993 and Saro-Wiwa was charged with, among other things, sedition.[10] More critically interethnic conflicts exploded between Ogoni and other groups in late 1993, amidst accusations of military involvement and ethnic war-mongering by Rivers State leadership. A new and aggressively anti-Ogoni military governor took over Rivers State in 1994, and a ferocious assault by the Rivers State Internal Security Task Force commenced. Saro-Wiwa was placed under house arrest, and subsequently fifteen Ogoni leaders were detained in April 1994. A series of brutal attacks left 750 Ogoni dead and 30,000 homeless; in total, almost 2,000 Ogonis have perished since 1990 at the hands of police and security forces. Ogoniland was in effect sealed off by the military. Amidst growing chaos, Saro-Wiwa was arrested on May 22, 1994, and several months later he and eight others were charged with the deaths of four Ogoni leaders with whom there had been increasingly rancorous and conflicted relations.

In spite of the remarkable history of MOSOP between 1990 and 1996, its ability to represent itself as a unified pan-Ogoni organization remained an open question, particularly for Saro-Wiwa. There is no pan-Ogoni myth of origin (characteristic of many delta minorities), and a number of the Ogoni subgroups engender stronger local loyalties than any affiliation to Ogoni nationalism. The Eleme subgroup has even argued, on occasion, that they are not Ogoni. Furthermore, the MOSOP leaders were actively opposed by elements of the traditional clan leadership, by prominent leaders and civil servants in state government, and by some critics who felt Saro-Wiwa was out to gain "cheap popularity" (Osgahae 1995: 334). The youth wing of MOSOP, which Saro-Wiwa had used, had a radical vigilante constituency that the leaders were incapable of controlling. Saro-Wiwa built on over fifty years of Ogini organizing and on three decades of re-sentment against the oil companies, to provide a mass base and a youth-driven radicalism—and, it must be said, an international visibility—capable of challenging state power.[11]

10. The history of events since June 1993 are detailed in Human Rights Watch (1995), UNPO (1995), and the UN Mission (1996).
11. Following the MOSOP precedent, a number of southeastern minorities pressured local and state authorities for expanded resources and political autonomy: the Movement for the Survival of Izon/Ijaw Ethnic Nationality was established in 1994, the Council for Ekwerre Nationality in 1993, and the Southern Minorities Movement (twenty-eight ethnic groups

Fighting for El Dorado: Ecuador and Nigeria Compared

In November 1993 a Philadelphia law firm filed a $1.5 billion class action suit for forty-six plaintiffs from the oil-producing Oriente region of Ecuador on behalf of 30,000 Ecuadorian citizens against Texaco Inc. The heart of the action was a claim of corporate irresponsibility. Specifically cited were serious illnesses and ecological destruction attributable to the oil company, serious water contamination, and the consequences of twenty years of drilling that "caused widespread destruction of the Amazon rainforest and have endangered the lives of tens of thousands of people" (cited in Hvalkof in press: 31). Oil exploration began in the Oriente with the collapse of the rubber economy during the 1920s.[12] By the 1930s the Ecuadorian state has secured state monopoly over all noncultivated lands, American companies were active across the region, and by 1939 a regional company town had been named "Shell" (still in existence!). The oil frenzy commenced in the 1960s. Texaco began its operations in 1967 and in a short time had established an enormous infrastructure including several hundred miles of pipeline. In the last twenty-five years, 300,000 colonists have entered the region bringing overnight boomtowns. The Oriente, which is home to a complex array of Indian communities, had been converted (like the Nigerian delta) into a geopolitical landscape of "blocks" (i.e., concessions). Close to thirty companies operate concessions in conjunction with the Ecuadorian state and the national petroleum company. By the 1990s Ecuador was an *oil nation*: petroleum accounted for at least half of national export earnings and two-thirds of the state's budget (figure 8.1). Ecuador was a member of the Organization of Petroleum Exporting Countries (OPEC) until the early 1990s when pressures to service its debt and its low quota—a reflection of falling oil prices—compelled the Ecuadorian government to withdraw from the organization. What is indisputable is that the discovery of petroleum in Ecuadorian territory, marked by relative isolation and ethnic complexity, marked sort of a Faustian pact in which oil was traded for progress, wealth, and modernity.

The Oriente has a somewhat sordid and violent history of extraction prior to oil of course. The Upper Amazon is most closely associated with the horrors and barbarism of the Putamayo incident just prior to World War I (see Taussig 1987). The Indians of the Putamayo an area on the

---

from five delta states) has been active since 1992. The Movement for Reparation to Ogbia (MORETO) produced a charter explicitly modeled on the Ogoni Bill of Rights in 1992. These groups directly confronted Shell and Chevron installations (Human Rights Watch 1995; Greenpeace 1994) and in turn have felt the press of military violence over the last four years. The point is simply that MOSOP was a flagship movement for a vast number of oil-producing communities and threatened to ignite a blaze throughout the oil-producing delta.

12. My account of Ecuador is derived from Kane (1996); Sawyer (1997 and in press); Brown and Fernandez (1996); and Kimerling (1991).

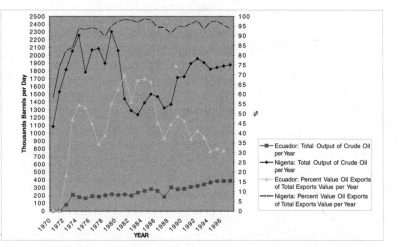

Figure 8.1. Total Crude Oil Output and Percent Oil Exports Value of Total Exports Value (per Year) NIGERIA and ECUADOR: 1970–1997

Peru, Colombia, Ecuador border, were subject to horrifying torture and violence by rubber companies and their subcontractors in search of the original "black gold" (rubber was coined black gold in advance of the 1970s oil boom). The legacy of the rubber barons continues, and local patrons and contractors (now involved in logging, cattle raising, and coca production) deploy debt bondage and labor peonage with Indian workers. The violence of rubber and the conditions of actual or near slavery shaped the production history of the region that the advent of oil did nothing to reduce. The early companies fomented conflicts between Peru, Colombia, and Ecuador, and Shell was involved in a number of violent incidents between Indians and the company as early as the 1940s. During the 1980s, the pressure for debt service coupled with a neoliberal agenda among a series of civilian governments placed new pressures on opening new concessions reflected in the reform of the Ecuadorian hydrocarbon law in 1982. In 1988 ARCO and two other companies were involved in prospecting and drilling in Block 10 in Pastaza Province, which became the site of a long and ongoing struggle. ARCO, working with the state land-titling agency, ran into immediate conflicts with Indian communities whose indigenous claims superseded the concessions. So began a long struggle between Indian organizations, federations and communities, and the oil companies that brought a class action suit five years later.[13]

13. The details of this case, which was rejected in 1994, subsequently appealed, and currently pending, is analyzed in Sawyer (in press).

The parallels to Nigeria are striking, of course.[14] Oil was discovered in the early part of the century in the Niger Delta (ca. 1908), but it was only in the 1950s that commercial deposits were opened up. The vast majority of the on-shore reserves are located in the delta, a region of tropical rain forest and deltaic agro-fishing communities comprising some of the highest population densities in Africa. Like Ecuador, the Nigerian State nationalized the oil industry and has operated historically through complex joint ventures between the Nigerian National Petroleum Company and the oil companies Shell, Elf, Gulf, and Agape in particular and concessional arrangements in which the companies have a substantial autonomy. In Nigeria most oil and the largest concessions are owned by Shell (in sum, 40,000 square kilometers, three times more than their nearest rival), unlike Ecuador, where the major concessions are controlled by ARCO and Texaco. The delta also has a history of earlier colonial (and precolonial) violent "extraction": namely, slavery and rubber between the seventeenth and nineteenth centuries. Violence has fundamentally shaped interethnic relations and has often been played out in the colonial period by claims over local political administrative structures (Native Administrations in the colonial vernacular). A number of the delta communities resisted colonial rule in the early part of the century, and a number harbored secessionist intentions which typically resulted in violent clashes. Oil was a central ingredient, of course, in the civil war in which the Eastern region (Biafra) did secede from the Federation in 1967 (Watts 1996).

Massive waste, corruption, and ecological devastation in oil-producing communities was matched by none of the rewards of petro-development—Ogoniland is, in this regard, Nigeria's Chiapas. The oil bust produced a right and proper resentment among oil-producing communities across the delta. Bristling resentments inevitably were wrapped up with the shift to civilian politics in the early 1990s. Nigeria has been ruled for over thirty of its thirty-eight-year independence by military governments. The Ogoni Bill of Rights and its legal case against Shell came to embody the same explosive tensions as did the Texaco case in Ecuador. Oil had lubricated a struggle over the very nature of citizenship (Watts 1996; Sawyer in press). Nigeria, then, is like Ecuador, only more so.

Nature of Petroleum: Faustian Spectacle of Illusion and Deceit

The spectacle, said Guy Debord in his Lettrist text *The Society of the Spectacle*, "is not a collection of images, but a social relation among people, mediated by images." (Debord 1978: paragraph 4)

14. The history of the Nigerian oil industry is covered in more detail in Watts (1999); Khan (1994); and Ikein (1990).

It is surely incontestable that the social relation of wealth unleashed by the oil booms of the 1970s was a spectacle of Debordian proportions. Images and narratives of unbounded wealth and prosperity conveyed an overwhelming sense that the *élan vital* because modernization had been discovered. A new dawn of modern prosperity and development, and the ambition and drives that were their handmaidens, had arrived for the lucky few. El Dorado had been located and it was an oil well.

But how and why does violence figure into this spectacle of oil and petro-ambition? Why is petroleum extraction such a violent endeavor? What about its physical and social properties? Why does it generate such explosive consequences among the oil-producing communities? In both Ecuador and Nigeria, oil became the basis for important forms of political mobilization—"indigenous" or Indian communities in one case, "ethnic minorities" in another—and for forms of engagement and mobilization that were brimming with violence. In one case, Nigeria, this violence assumed quite extraordinary forms (military occupation, extra-judicial killings, and perhaps a thousand deaths in Ogoniland over a five-year period). In Ecuador (and one might add Peru and Colombia) there has been a long-running struggle marked by popular protests and sporadic violence. In turn, this raises another question: Why did the two cases *differ* in some important ways with respect to petro-violence?

I want to start with the question of oil and its properties, and to use the great Polish journalist Ryszard Kapucinski's account, *The Shah of Shahs*, of the fall of the Shah as a window into the mythos that surrounds "black gold." The Shah's extraordinary drive to modernize Iran during the 1970s was deeply etched into his own insecurities and megalomaniacal character. One cannot fail to recognize, however, the commonalities between the Pahlavi vision and the bristling oil nationalism that saturated the political atmosphere in Caracas or Lagos or Riyyad during the 1970s. Here is Kapuscinski's meditation on oil and its atmospherics:

> Oil creates the illusion of a completely changed life, life without work, life for free. . . . The concept of oil expresses perfectly the eternal human dream of wealth achieved through lucky accident. . . . In this sense oil is a fairy tale and like every fairy tale a bit of a lie.
>
> (Kapuscinski 1982: 35)

> [Oil] is a filthy, foul smelling liquid that squirts obligingly up into the air and falls back to earth as a rustling shower of money.
>
> (Kapuscinski 1982: 34)

> Oil fills us with such arrogance that we begin believing we can easily overcome such unyielding obstacles as time. With oil . . . I [Shah Pahlavi] will create a second America in a generation!
>
> (Kapuscinski 1982: 35)

Oil is a resource that anesthetizes thought, blurs vision, corrupts. . . . Look at the ministers from oil countries, how high they hold their heads, what a sense of power.

(Kapuscinski 1982: 35)

And oil's relation to the Mosque? What vigor, glory and significance this new wealth has given its religion, Islam, which is enjoying a period of accelerated expansion and attracting new crowds of faithful.

(Kapuscinski 1982: 35)

Oil kindles extraordinary emotions and hopes, since oil is above all a great temptation. It is the temptation of ease, wealth, fortune, power. [But] oil, though powerful, has its defects.

(Kapuscinski 1982: 34–35)

Kapuscinski, as a journalist, is acutely sensitive to the political and ideological ether that the oil boom generated in Iran and to the consequences of what seemed, all too briefly, to be the prospect of unimaginable wealth. Running through his observations, however, is a larger theme of how oil as a resource, as a form of extraction and transformation, as a form of wealth, and as a system of meanings are all related. I want to identify eight properties of oil to begin to address, with deliberate provocation, what one might call "the nature of petroleum."[15]

Oil is money ("black gold"). As surely the most global and commercially negotiable of commodities, "Oil *is* money," as the Chair of ARCO once put it (all oil transactions are conducted in dollars). It is instantaneous wealth, despite of the fact that its powers, in a sense, are quite mysterious. Oil as money/value typically creates an ambition and enervation, what one oil commentator called the *élan vital* of growth, appropriate to the magnitude of oil wealth (for example, the Shah's "White Revolution" or "La Gran Venezuela" of President Perez).

Petro-State and Nation: The central idea is taken from Ricardo Hausman (1981) that oil creates specific forms of state landed property. This means, among other things, that nationalized petroleum produces a state (as the owner of the means of production) that (i) mediates the social relations by which oil is exploited (concessions, joint ventures, and so on) and (ii) is simultaneously granted access to the world market.[16] State landed property necessarily converts oil into a theater of struggle in

---

15. I have written about these properties elsewhere (Watts 1997, 1994). I have also pulled upon Terry Karl's book *The Paradox of Plenty: Oil Booms and Petro-States* (1997) and Fernando Coronil's *The Magic State: Nature, Money and Modernity in Venezuela* (1997).

16. As Fine (1984: 284) says, extractive development "depends upon the nature of the ownership of landed property and how it relates to the accumulation process. In other

which its *national* qualities are paramount—an "oil nation," "our oil," and so on.

Petro-Imperialism (The Faustian Pact): Oil is unavoidably an engagement with some of the largest and most powerful forces of transnational capital (who show up on the local doorstep) and with all the contradictions of participating in the world market (boom and bust). Exploitation of oil is, in effect, a pact, a social contract—a Faustian bargain—in which a national project (modernity, development, civilization)—is purchased at the expense of sovereignty, autonomy, independence, tradition, and so on. The realization of oil monies (through the world market) and the localization of oil revenues by the state embody this pact. This is what the founder of OPEC meant when he said that, "Oil can bring trouble."

Evacuative Despoliation (Liquid Mobility): The territorial quality of oil—its enclave character—and the fact that it has limited local linkage effects (oil is labor extensive and typically *evacuated* by pipeline from the source) produces a peculiar sort of double movement. On one hand, wealth literally flows out—it is lost value that flows to the horizon of local territories—and, on the other, it is a sort of subterranean threat to the environment. The pipelines that run through the middle of Ogoni villages are the perfect embodiment of the double movement of evacuation/loss and despoliation/threat.

Hyper-Centralization ("Rentier" States): Oil has a radically centralizing effect. Petro-dollars rush into the exchequer and simultaneously increase the state's dependence on one global commodity. Rents become the basis of politics—this is what Karl (1997) means when she says that public expenditure "displaces" statecraft. Oil rents irrigate the body politic as a way of purchasing some form of state legitimacy or quiescence. Public contracts always massively inflated in a way that cost overruns are politically desirable—the more costly the better—become the metric of political choice. State office degenerates into a prebend, hence the common refrain that petro-states are especially corrupt, "flabby," or fractured.

Petro-Fetishism/Petro-Magic (The El Dorado Effect): Oil creates a world of illusion. People become wealthy without effort creating fabulous waste and fiscal madness (Venezuela's factories with nothing in them, Nigerian iron and steel produced at costs seven times more than the prevailing market price). Money is ephemeral, here today gone tomorrow (boom turns to bust). Wealth that scorches the fingers signifies the loss of the soul. In the popular imagination, oil produces all manner of extraordinary magical events and mythic properties (in Nigeria, the trade in body parts; in

---

words, it concerns the conditions under which capital has access to the land for the purposes of production and accumulation. . . . It potentially depends upon a whole host of factors and conflicts over them, and the balance of economic and political power are related in the form taken by the leases."

Ecuador, new forms of evangelicalism; in Venezuela, fantastic syncretic cults). Among the politicians, bureaucrats, and ruling classes, oil is equally mythic: it "to propels [us] into the twentieth century," as President Carlos Perez put it.

Valorization of Space (Territorial Identities): Because oil has a point of origin and is unavoidably a national commodity (a patrimony), it is to be expected that the transformative potential of oil (how the oil is to be sown in the economy, as Coronil (1997) describes it in Venezuela) invites a debate over who has claims over the resource itself.[17] Here the valorization of territory turns on the contradictions between state-imposed spaces (the concession) and local/indigenous territorial rights (Ogoni land or the Huaorani Ethnic Reserve). The fact that these two territorial claims embody different property claims and rights (national versus customary law) necessarily instigates a debate over how the parts constitute the whole, how the regional and local relate to the national. Oil seems to always invoke the spatial lexicon in which the nation figures prominently. To the extent that oil production is located on lands populated by minorities, territorial disputes are inevitably about identity, rights, and citizenship.

"Monoeconomy/Monopolity" (The Dutch Disease): Oil produces what Karl (1997) calls the "petrolization" of society. The political economy mimics a sort of company town, and oil rents reinforce particular patterns of class power. Access to state petro-dollars underwrites a political class, a *nomenklatura* whose influence is often coupled to regional and ethnic political machines. The boom within the "monoeconomy" produces depressive effects—what economists call the Dutch disease—in other non-oil sectors, such as the collapse of agriculture and of other forms of state revenue generation (i.e., tax collection), which further deepens the "monoeconomic" and monopolitical tendencies.

Petro-Violence

Ideas and deeds only exist in dialectical relationship. So does violence, which is a *habitus* ... , at once structured and structuring: structured because the idea of violence results from historical events, stored as the memory of past deeds, of past encounters, of past frustrations; and structuring

17. One of the few people to explore the spatial and territorial aspects of extraction is Fine (1994) who notes that "unlike agriculture where . . . raw materials can be used extensively without ever larger use of land, in mineral extraction by necessity the absence of a produced raw material as basic to production implies the spatial extension of capital's operations" (285). He is able to show how differing spatial and territorial aspects of differing mining industries shape the distinctive sorts of conflicts in diamond, coal, and oil industries in the United States and the United Kingdom.

because the idea of violence informs human actions, determines the acceptability, even the banality of violence, if not the ability to erase the scandal of
its occurrence.

(Dumont 1995: 277)

How might these eight properties of oil speak to the question of violence? One can plausibly argue that the strategic significance of oil to
North Atlantic industrial capitalism, coupled with the almost unimaginable wealth and power of the oil industry (Shell, after all, has sales in excess of the GNP of at least 127 poor countries), would, in and of themselves, suggest that violence is an expression of the crudest forms of
geopolitical power. This is surely not an unimportant observation. The oil
companies in Ecuador and Nigeria had substantial autonomy and license
to do what they wanted and without recourse; they had the backing of the
military and indeed deployed their own security forces. Their operations
were congruent with a long lineage of local demonic capitalists (whether
rubber barons or slavers) and acted rather like authoritarian local governments. In the space created by a history of prior violence, petro-violence
emerges as a sort of culture of terror and a space of death (Taussig 1987).
I think there is much more to be explained, however, than the might of
petro-capital and the hegemony power of a slick alliance. Here I return to
the properties of oil itself.

Strategic and economic powers of oil actually heighten and amplify the
centrality, or perhaps more accurately the visibility, of the state in public
life (therefore of claims over nation and citizenship) and of transnational
capital in society (therefore of claims of sovereignty and accountability).
As a result, oil sharpens, in a way that few other natural resources and
forms of extraction can, the claims that oil-producing communities in particular have over oil, though the wealth that oil represents animates these
concerns throughout the body-politic. Because oil is state property, the relationship of oil producers (and citizens generally) to the state necessarily
becomes an object of debate. What I, following Stuart Hall (1996), call forms of
articulation often become the basis for exercising these political claims
over national patrimony ("the national oil body"). Articulation is employed here in the double sense endorsed by Hall: as a way of rendering an
identity *(discursive coherence)* and of linking that identity to a political subject and project *(interpolation).* The unity between these two sorts of articulations, in Hall's view, encompasses the process by which an ideology finds
its subject (rather than how a subject locates and articulates an essentialized set of ideas or thoughts. This task always entails the positing of boundaries and edges in an always provisional and contingent way (see Li 1997,
1996). Put differently oil, as a subterranean, *territorial resource* that *is highly
centralized as property around the state,* necessarily channels claims over na-

ture ("our oil") into a sort of "rights talk" (Fraser 1996). The "rights talk" speaks to three questions: (1) local identity, territory and the rights that stem from them, (2) relations between local political and territorial claims and forms of governance (decentralization, participation, autonomy), and (3) links between various identity politics (Indian culture or minority tradition) and notions of citizensip (what we are owed or entitled to). Underlying all three is a notion of a nation-state, on which discussions of community, citizenship, and rights ultimately turn. It is no accident that so much of the rhetoric of oil raises questions of the nation (or the social body) or of national development (the Great Civilization of Iran and La Gran Venezuela, for example). Here is Coronil (1997) on the Venezuelan case:

> [Petro]money throughout this century was the universal equivalent that embodied the promise of universality. In exchange for the nation's money, the state promised to bring modernity to Venezuela. . . . To sow the oil condensed this aspiration, the exchange of the nation's subsoil for international money was justified in terms of the nationalist project. . . . The Faustian trade of money for modernity did not bring the capacity to produce but the illusion of production. (390–391)

Oil, then, simultaneously elevates and expands the centrality of the nation-state as a vehicle for modernity, progress, civilization, and at the same time produces conditions that directly challenge and question those very same, and hallowed, tenets of nationalism and development (the national development project). It is as if oil confers on the state a sort of visibility and a set of expectations associated with all modern states, namely, to respond to the needs and rights of its citizens in the name of development and democracy. And yet the process of accumulation engendered by oil exploitation through the slick alliances in its various iterations—the Faustian pact—reveals the state and the nation to be sham, decrepit, venal, and corrupt notions. At the very same time, oil unleashes through the territorial, economic, and social processes of oil development a set of claims and identity-making that minimally hold the nation-state accountable to its modernist tenets (it promulgates a debate over the shift from subject to citizen), and more radically may challenge the very idea of the nation itself (what is this entity called Nigeria?), posing alternative forms of ethno-nationalism (the Ogoni Bill of Rights) and political relations (Indian confederations).

The question is how these tensions and contradictions are dealt with. In Ecuador one could argue that violence was present but constrained, and these contradictions contributed to a national discussion (still in progress) of a constitutional nature and to the debate over neoliberal reform and agrarian reform in particular (Sawyer 1997). In the case of Nigeria, it produced *mass* violence and a slide into chaos and anarchy because what was at stake in the contradictions was the very existence of a fragile nation itself, a "national symbolic" as Laurent Berlant (1991) calls it that was a "fantasy" (her term). It could easily be understood as such. In comparison to Ecuador, the lack of confederated organizations of minorities and the lack of any constitutional precedent over minority rights made the prospects of talking about this national fantasy in the public sphere almost impossible. Indeed from the vantage point of the state (the military), it was extremely dangerous. In the Nigerian case, this harkened back to the bloody civil war of the 1960s and was read as a call for succession, not a debate over citizenship.

What is striking in reading Sawyer's (1997, in press) detailed account of the ARCO affair in Ecuador or the popular book *Savages* by Joe Kane (1996), is the extent to which the renewed push for oil in the 1980s galvanized the politics of Indian nationalities. The Oriente became a theater, ultimately national in scope, that solidified and deepened the federal quality of oil. The unit of oil exploration and extraction is geographical (the block or concession) that does not correspond with another territorial unit, namely the Indian "tribal" or indigenous lands (*territorio*)—which in the case of Ecuador had a constitutional standing. Property is immediately at issue, then, but property as a social relation is immediately attached to a local identity (the Huaorani case as described by Kane) and ultimately to a larger political project embodied in the Confederation of Indigenous Nationalities (CONAIE) founded in 1980. The story of articulating a variety of Indian identities within the space of Ecuadorian nationalism is complex in two senses: (1) because the likes of ARCO strenuously attempt to divide any notion of an Indian consensus—indeed it assists in the creation of oppositional groups and (2) because local Indian concerns are rapidly transnationalized as they are picked up by a national green movement (*Acción Ecología*) and inserted into the international green networks, hence why we read about their plight in *New Yorker* magazine and why Rainforest Action Network among others take up their cause.

To make a larger claim, then, the Ecuadorian case has the effect of thickening civil society in part because there is a constitutional reference point (in which Indian nationalities could be discussed), a sense of nation and nation-state (robust enough to accommodate the contradictions generated by oil), and a degree of organization (sufficient to give their claims standing in the public arena). All of this is, of course, far from resolved, but the Ecuadorian case reveals something about the structural tensions created by oil and the points at which violence might occur. Intercommunity animosity is manufactured by the oil companies, and guerrillas struggle at the point of production, as increasingly mobilized Indian communities confront recalcitrant and militarized company installations and pipelines often at the periphery of state surveillance and control. It also suggests why in this case state action was mediated by the complex popular alliances (most especially the *indigena-campesinos* alliance formed in 1994 around the *Movilización Por La Vida* demanding that the new *Ley de Desarrollo Agrario* be annulled) that formed around a rethinking of the oil nation and its project.[18]

Here of course Nigeria stands as a striking counterpoint. The centrality of state (and company) violence, however, does not rest solely on the existence of a military junta (the Abacha regime) which was, without question, one of the most brutal in the history of Nigerian post-colonial development. The oil-producing communities had experienced almost forty years of systematic exploitation, marginalization, and neglect. The property and "rights talk" stimulated by the Ogoni case represented precisely the *possibility* of what actually existed as a legitimate entity in Ecuador: namely, some form of confederation of minorities. Saro-Wiwa encouraged this proliferation of minority groups with their own Bill of Rights (for example, MORETO, the Council for Ekwerre Nationality, and MOSIZEN) in communities that contributed much more to the national oil pool than did the Ogoni fields (which ironically by the 1990s were of limited importance). Nigeria's shallow history of nationalist construction (hastily fabricated in 1914 but in effect three regional systems that were nominally integrated as Nigeria in 1960), a brutal civil war against a secessionist oil-producing region (Biafra) in the 1960s, and a much more fragile sense of "nation-state-ness" collaborated to produce a situation in which a seemingly local case of oil-inspired identity politics, cast in large measure as a green movement (compensation for past ecological damages), represented a massive political threat. Saro-Wiwa had simply pointed out that the emperor had no clothes. Nigeria was, as Obafemi Owolawo put it, "a mere geographical expression." What the oil-producing minorities represented, then, not only threatened the slick alliance (compensation from Shell, a share of federal revenues) but also exploded the national fantasy: The very idea of Nigeria and what it might mean to be a Nigerian (as a citizen rather than a subject) (Mamdani 1996).

18. This is a complex story that involved new alliances between regional, local, and national peasant and Indian groups around the agrarian reforms. It also was precipitated by neoliberal reforms that had the effect of vastly increasing oil prices in Ecuador in 1994. This is again an instance of how the link between the nation (*nación*) and the national patrimony (*patria*) embodied in oil is exercised by the fact that citizens now have to pay more for something that is legitimately theirs, and from which they have not benefited. This story is told brilliantly in Sawyer's dissertation, chapter 8–10. She concludes that this struggle by indigenous communities "reconfigured a prevailing law for the first time in Ecuadorian history" (283).

In my rendering, the history of Ogoni tradition and its transfiguration into the Ogoni Bill of Rights was nonetheless very much about resources, geography, and nature. First, in an *empirical sense,* the very idea of Ogoni tradition and culture was explicitly spatial and environmental—an Ogoni territory (Saro-Wiwa 1992: 11) consisting of six territorially rooted claims and three local government areas. Indeed, the term tradition (*doonu kuneke*), as Saro-Wiwa emphasized, meant honoring the land (1992: 12). The fact that the heart of the modern was a land-based resource—petroleum—pumped from within the territory and with immediate consequences for it (environmental contamination) made these empirical geography points all the more compelling. Second, nature was central in an *epistemological* sense; MOSOP argued that rights and entitlements stemmed from this territory and this environment (Saro-Wiwa 1992: 92–93). Land and identity conferred inalienable rights, states of being, in other words. Third, geography was *normatively implicated* in the sense of the autonomy posited in the Ogoni Bill of Rights: autonomy within an ethnically (and hence geographically) reconfigured federation. "In a true federation, each ethnic group no matter how small is entitled to the same treatment," as the Ogoni Bill of Rights put it. Here a particular space confers equality and autonomy, normatively speaking.

Yet it was an unstable and contradictory sort of articulation—to return to Stuart Hall's lexicon. There was no simple Ogoni "we," no unproblematic unity, and no singular form of political subject (despite Saro-Wiwa's claim that 98 percent of Ogonis supported him). MOSOP itself had five independent units—an object of bitter dispute in itself—embracing youth, women, traditional rulers, teachers, and churches. It represented a fractious and increasingly divided "we," as the open splits and conflicts between Saro-Wiwa and other elite Ogoni confirm (Ogoni Crisis, 1996).[19] Saro-Wiwa constantly invoked Ogoni culture and tradition, yet he also argued that war and internecine conflict had virtually destroyed the fabric of Ogoni society by 1900 (Saro-Wiwa 1992: 14). His own utopia then rested on the re-creation of Ogoni culture—because Africa's tribes are "ancient and enduring social organizations" (Saro-Wiwa 1995: 191)—and suffered like all ur-histories from a mythic invocation of the past. Paradoxically, ethnicity was the central problem of post-colonial Nigeria—the corruption of ethnic majorities—and its panacea—the multiplication of ethnic minority power. To invoke the history of exclusion and the need for ethnic minority inclusion in a new federalism, led Saro-Wiwa to totally ignore the histories

---

19. Saro-Wiwa was often chastised by Gokana (he himself was Bane) since most of the Ogoni oil was in fact located below Gokana soil. In other words, on occasion the key territorial unit became the clan rather than the pan-Ogoni territory.

and geographies of conflict and struggle among and between ethnic minorities. The narrative of oil and the slick alliance could not paper over the contradictions within the Ogoni movement and within Saro-Wiwa's vision.

Conclusion

The manner in which the mythic, magical, and biophysical properties of oil enter into these violent struggles—how oil is talked about, framed, and given meaning—is ultimately an empirical question: which is to say, one needs to examine carefully the historical and cultural local context of oil. In Nigeria, and I suspect in Ecuador, too, oil's liquid and subterranean properties and the fact that it is in many respects invisible, flowing through pipelines or being burned as gas, contributes to the popular understanding of petroleum as socially polluting, magical, and all-powerful. Oil is invariably attached to debates over the legitimate sources and use of wealth (a recurrent theme in television soap operas, dime novels, and mobile theater [Watts 1994]) and not surprisingly its power to tarnish and turn everything into shit (oil is "the devil's excrement," as a past president of Venezuela put it). In this sense oil as resource, to take something from Walter Benjamin, becomes a sort of wish image.[20]

Violence in and around the environment is profoundly wrapped up with the properties of that which is exploited. The "green" content of the political mobilization that may be either a cause or a consequence of violence invariably ends up taking on a number of other colors and hues. It is the mythic, magic, and national properties of oil (its wealth, its value, its magical powers to transform) coupled with its subterranean and territorial nature that seem to elevate petro-violence to the point where profound questions of state, nation, and citizen are posed by it and where structural violence is perpetrated in its name.

20. I have explored this idea in Massey and Allen 1998. Susan Buck-Morse refers to the wish image in Benjamin as follows: "In nature the new is mythic because its potential is not yet realized; in consciousness the old is mythic because its powers were never fulfilled. Paradoxically collective imagination mobilizes its powers for a revolutionary break from the recent past by evoking a cultural memory reservoir of myths and utopian symbols from a more distant ur-past. These collective wish images are nothing else but this" (1989: 116).

9

International Dimensions of Conflict over Natural and Environmental Resources

James Fairhead

When linking conflict with environmental issues, there is a temptation to pursue the often-supposed links between poverty and environmental decline (the downward spiral) to more violent conclusions. A narrative linking popular readings of Malthus and Hobbes is pre-formed, merely awaiting expansion and exemplification in the conflict arena—as if conflict were merely the endgame of poverty, and poverty the consequence of environmental decline. Such reasoning exists in the popular press, exemplified not only in the notorious work of Kaplan (1994) to which, fortunately, many critics have since responded (cf. Richards 1996; de Waal 1996; Keen 1997), but also in the tomes of other modern day "catastrophists" like Myers (1996), King (1986), Timberlake and Tinker (1984), and Homer-Dixon (1996).

Twose (1991: 1) terms this loose set of associations the "greenwar" factor, a nomenclature to which I shall adhere. He characterizes it thus:

> The cycle is repetitive and truly vicious. Environmental impoverishment, increasing conflict over resources, marginalization of rural people, social and political unrest, displacement and uncontrolled migration lead to further conflict and the outbreak of wars within and between states. When hostilities grow into organized warfare, the environment inevitably undergoes further degradation. The insidious pattern comes full cycle, as a peacetime population and government struggle to cope with a land left environmentally bankrupt. The seeds are sown for further tension and conflict. (1991: 8)

In this chapter, I critique the way that "environmental degradation" has become incorporated into the international discourse on conflict, particularly the increasing tenor of concern over environment and security. First,

I outline what I see as prima facie reasons for being cautious in examining the causes of conflict in relation to the environment. Then I briefly review some key components of the popular, policy, and academic "greenwar" arguments. Following this, I consider several alternative conceptual frames through which to consider links between environment and conflict and illustrate these in relation to certain cases.

In particular, I shall pursue the argument that conflicts are less generated by resource poverty and bankruptcy than by resource value and wealth. This will permit, I would argue, more refined analysis in several arenas. First, it enables better analysis of the environmental components influencing the dynamics of warfare. It enables more than just an examination of the "causes" of conflict by helping to resolve impacts of environmental issues as conflicts evolve. It thus enables us to consider the conditions in which warfare can lead to displacement, hunger, and disease, rather than looking to these directly from an environmental viewpoint. Second, a resource wealth approach to environment will permit us to consider how the relationship between environmental degradation and conflict is linked to international political economy. Third, in this, it can help resolve differences in environment–conflict dynamics between valuable immobile resources (notably land) and mobile ones (oil, water, diamonds, timber) in this analysis (cf. Väyrynen 1997). Fourth, it shows that conflicts might be about control over valuable resources themselves or over the labor, capital, technology, trade routes, market access, and other factors necessary to make them valuable. Fifth, it may not be environmental decline "on location" that stimulates conflict but the effective demand present elsewhere for the resources that territory has to offer. That demand elsewhere may well be generated through environmental depletion or other causes of supply failures in other historically significant sources. In short, this framework suggests that the environmental causes of conflict, when considered at all, need to be traced in global rather than local frames. This is not the spirit of either the "greenwar" position or "environmental scarcity" analysis. This is important because the major destinations for the resources that have been fueling conflicts in Africa tend to be the industrialized nations.

The chapter therefore attempts to "put environment in its place." The strategy taken is to focus on the many political and economic causes of a few conflicts associated with valuable minerals and then try to see where environmental phenomena fit in. In much of the chapter, I treat environmental components in a decentered way. This approach will provide an alternative perspective from which to assess briefly the "greenwar" concept, which obscures more than it reveals in analyzing the causes of war. In fact, I suggest that even those who promote the idea of "greenwar" and its contemporary relevance do not actually find it useful in their own analysis. Moreover, I shall hint that the concept of "greenwar"—in its ideological circulation or strategic deployment—may itself fuel conflicts rather than assist in defining policies to address them. Like the idea of desertification, the concept is useless yet somehow so "necessary," so repeatedly coined and elaborated, that it must be taken seriously.

Homer-Dixon and colleagues (e.g., 1991, 1994, 1995, 1999) set their analysis of "acute conflict" within the broader nexus of not only environmental change but also population growth and unequal social distribution of resources. Together, these conditions comprise what he terms "environmental scarcity," which his research suggests:

> can contribute to diffuse, persistent, subnational violence, such as ethnic clashes and insurgencies. In coming decades, the incidence of such violence will probably increase as environmental scarcities worsen in some parts of the developing world. This subnational violence will not be as conspicuous or dramatic as interstate resource wars, but it may have serious repercussions for the security interests of both the developed and developing worlds. (Homer-Dixon 1995b)

But Homer-Dixon's concept of environmental scarcity is, I would argue, deeply misleading. It obfuscates environmental degrading components (or lack of them) in conflicts by lumping them together with issues of increased demand and inequality of resource access.[1] Once again, issues that have little, if any, link with environmental degradation come to be glossed over as "environmental," depoliticizing them, and, in Homer-Dixon's case, isolating them from international political economy.

The aim of this chapter is to illustrate a more complex approach through which to examine the ways environmental components (or lack of them) cause conflicts. First, I provide a brief and critical review of works forwarding the "greenwar" and related arguments.

Conflict, Resource Scarcity, and "Greenwar"

In evaluating environmental degradation as a possible cause of conflict, it is important to look beyond environmental change in the vicinity of the conflict, to explore how resource degradation elsewhere alters demand for what any territory has to offer (Blaikie 1985). That is, of course, if "supply failure" can even be traced to absolute resource depletion, as opposed to economic supply failure (e.g., changes in labor costs relating to supply in other producing regions or indeed to warfare in that area of supply).

1. Even though he calls this "stratified environmental degradation" in his most recent book (Homer-Dixon 1999), they all ultimately boil down to the same thing.

Cases abound where supply failure in one region generates increased demand in another. The Allied forces in World War II faced quinine and rubber shortages when Japanese forces invaded Southeast Asia to claim rare and strategic materials (oil, rubber, tin, etc.). Production was stepped up in Allied Africa leading to encroachment by industrial plantations on forest reserves. In the Biafra war, supply problems caused by the Arab–Israel war rendered Nigerian oil reserves more valuable and strategic. Resources also gain value through increased global and regional demand and are not merely problems linked to reduced supply or degraded resources. The central issue when relating water scarcity to conflict is generally extra demand, not aquifer degradation.

Suggesting that the environmental causes of conflict, when considered at all, need to be traced in a global frame has not been the spirit of "greenwar" and "environmental scarcity" analyses. The lack of a global frame is symptomatic in the analytical vocabulary which "environmental scarcity" theorists deploy. It is a vocabulary of "groups" and "societies," arguing, for example, that "societies that adapt to environmental scarcities can avoid undue suffering and social stress," and that if social and ecological adaptation are unsuccessful, environmental scarcity constrains economic development and contributes to migrations and other stressors of conflict (Homer-Dixon 1995). Equally indicative is the focus on "intrastate," and "interstate" dynamics of warfare but not on international political economic concerns that in some cases render such terms simplistic.[2]

As mentioned, the major destinations for the commodities fueling recent conflicts in Africa tend to be the industrialized nations. Intra-African industrial demand hardly features in the world demand for diamonds, gold, oil, high grade timber, niobium, uranium, copper, rutile, bauxite, cobalt, chromium, and other minerals. The cases we examine later illustrate the importance of international capital in modern conflicts in procuring resource contracts during and immediately following conflicts.

The global link seriously challenges the "greenwar" thesis that: "In the complex web of causes leading to social and political instability, bloodshed and war, environmental degradation is playing an increasingly important role" (Twose 1991). Curiously, when read carefully, even those popularizing the "greenwar" concept would agree that few (if any) conflicts can be attributable to environmental degradation. In the book entitled *Greenwar* (Bennett 1991), where one would expect to find evidence of environmental degradation linked to war, the content does not support the general

2. Homer-Dixon argues that environmental scarcity often encourages powerful groups to capture valuable environmental resources and prompts marginal groups to ecologically sensitive areas. These two processes—called "resource capture" and "ecological marginalization"—in turn reinforce environmental scarcity and raise the potential for social instability (Homer-Dixon 1995a, 1999).

thesis. The edited chapters concentrate on: (1) social attachment to and increasing competition for resources, (2) government partiality in resource allocation and official neglect of rights of certain elements in society, including dispossession, and economic marginalization, (3) differential political voice, and (4) availability of arms. These are all political–economic issues, not environmental ones. Only in Chapter 7 of this work is "greenwar" faced more directly. As it is summarized in the introduction:

> Another kind of social breakdown is suffered by people who have been forced to give up their traditional livelihoods because of drought, eroded land, or conflict. They have to move to shanty towns, to camps for the displaced or to new settlements, where their presence can cause more tension and conflict, as they compete with the local population for work and resources, and put further pressure on the surrounding environment. So the vicious circle continues. (Bennett 1991: 7)

Such displacement, within Homer-Dixon's analysis, would create "group identity conflicts" (1994: 20; see also Homer-Dixon 1998). But again, the examples given in Bennett do not substantiate the "greenwar" argument, focusing as they do on the social and economic difficulties faced by displaced women in Sudan and those displaced by the Ethiopian government's resettlement policy.

In the preface to that volume, Twose notes the weakness of the "greenwar" thesis. "The authors do not argue that environmental degradation is ever the sole cause of conflict in the Sahel, or even always the major cause. They do insist that the environment is an increasingly important factor, and that if the implications are not recognized, the prospects for the Sahel's future stability are bleak" (1991: 4; cf. Myers 1996: 81). In short, in a book called "greenwar," the "greenwar" problem is not evidenced.

Homer-Dixon explicitly confuses issues of environmental degradation with issues of natural resource scarcity when forwarding the concept of environmental scarcity. In his analysis, environmental degradation is only one of three main sources of scarcity of renewable resources. The others, in his analysis, are population growth and unequal social distribution of resources. His concept of "environmental scarcity" thus "allows these three distinct sources of scarcity to be incorporated into one analysis" (1994: 8). But why conflate these very distinct issues into one concept? Examining issues of resource scarcity, degradation, and population in one concept is tantamount to analytical obfuscation. For example, water scarcity can be co-extensive with improved water economy and distribution; land scarcity leading to poverty and arguably conflict (André and Platteau 1995) can be co-extensive with land improvement and rehabilitation. Conflating pressure on natural resources with their "degradation" is wrong; the three components of Homer-Dixon's "environmental scarcity" are not facets of the same thing.

Evidence on land scarcity from the central African region indicates just how flawed the "environmental scarcity" concept is. Despite high and increasing population densities, where land shortage clearly undermines the livelihoods of a predominantly (90 percent) rural population, land improvement and improved productivity—not degradation—has often been observed. A relative abundance of labor can lead to more investment in land's productivity such that livelihood decline need not be associated with environmental decline (e.g., Murton 1997; Tiffen, Mortimore, and Gichuki 1994; Lindblane, Carswell, and Tumuhairwe 1997). The balance between investment and dis-investment in land productivity will vary with place, time, technology, tenure conditions,[3] national policies, and individual circumstances, to name but a few factors. These interesting issues, however, are obfuscated within the concept of environmental scarcity. That land values can increase not only due to scarcity but also due to the "land-esque'" capital investments of past users (the term is from Blaikie and Brookfield 1987) is recognized in indigenous economic thought throughout much of Africa (e.g., Pavanello 1995; Fairhead and Leach 1996). In short, one should not automatically confuse scarcity with degradation, a confusion that is written into both Bennett's "greenwar" concept and Homer-Dixon's concept of "environmental scarcity." Environment can improve even while scarcity, poverty, and destitution deepen.

"Greenwar" logic also obscures how land scarcity and land investment contribute to land value and how war may relate less to the impoverishment of land resources than to their value. Several conflicts have occurred in populous countries with few natural or renewable resources, and predominantly rural populations (e.g., Rwanda, Burundi). In these locations, land itself can be immensely valuable. In Rwanda, average farmland was exchanging hands at more than $4,000 per hectare in the late 1980s, and there was a thriving commercial land market despite regulation (Fairhead 1990b; André and Platteau 1995). This was at a time when incomes rarely topped $500 per year. For many small landholders, their land and investments in it represent a massive financial asset, leaving aside how people value the cultural and emotive meanings of land, of particular lands, and of the livelihood security land offers. Moreover, land acquisition is unrepeatable for the majority given their present incomes; only the salaried classes with access to off-farm income and employment related credit schemes are in a position to accumulate land (see, e.g., André and Platteau 1995; Murton 1997). Land is worth fighting for and defending.

3. For example, Rossi (1991); Clay and Lewis (1990).

If by "environmental scarcity" we also mean unequal resource distribution, it becomes banal and causally misleading to suggest, as Homer-Dixon does, that "environmental scarcities are already contributing to violent conflict." Analysts have long been tracing conflicts to issues of the social distribution of resources. One could profitably revert to the more classic concept of resource war, a concept as germane to peace, conflict, and strategic studies as the previous examples probably are. What is the "environmental" issue in this? Why conflate into one concept the very relationships that are interesting to pull apart and explore? A conflict, with its causes in phenomena that Homer-Dixon groups together as "environmental scarcity," need have absolutely nothing to do with the environment. So why call it environmental? It is only by a sleight of hand that these scarcities are so termed and that conclusions can be forwarded that we should focus our attention on "environment" when considering conflict prevention, mitigation, and resolution. It takes attention off more pressing issues.

While one can easily accept that environmental scarcity, as Homer-Dixon defines it, can cause conflict, in no case do Homer-Dixon and colleagues show that resource degradation was a causal component. Take, for example the conflicts in the Senegal river valley. It is argued, with justification, that the conflict relates to powerful classes gaining control over land that had been newly irrigated at public expense. Homer-Dixon's research team renders the conflict environmental by suggesting that the land was itself irrigated by agricultural development programs to offset reduced productivity from desertified lands elsewhere. This connection is both tenuous and forced, and it lacks evidence. It overlooks all of the political–economic reasons why dams get built and overplays "desertification."

To the extent that "greenwar" arguments do maintain that degradation provokes conflict, there is a tendency to exaggerate the extent of ecological deterioration. There are many structural political and economic reasons why perceptions of environmental degradation have been exaggerated by colonial and post-colonial states (Fairhead and Leach 1995, 1996, 1997; Swift 1996; Hellden 1991). Linking violent conflict to environment is adding to this tendency. We are now left deducing that "if there are conflicts, then there must have been degradation."

Norman Myers forges this deduction in a classic example of argument by innuendo and association, not by empirically grounded linkages.

> Sub-Saharan Africa is racked with political turmoil and violence. There have been more than 200 coups or attempted coups since 1950. We have seen how Ethiopia has endured prolonged war; the same goes for several other countries, notably Sudan, Chad, Angola, and Mozambique. Each of these countries also suffers widespread environmental travails in conjunction with wall to wall poverty. Can it be coincidence? (Myers 1996: 71)

In short, "greenwar" and "environmental scarcity" approaches have a tendency to confuse, not clarify the origins of conflict. This is not conducive to creating policies for peace. The crux of the "greenwar" position is that governments are failing to concentrate on conservation as a means of defusing conflict. It puts conservation on the peace agenda and on an equal footing with allocation issues. For example, drawing on the "greenwar" concept, Angela Merkel, Germany's former environment minister, argued that "the greenhouse effect, desertification and increasing scarcity of water are likely to cause violent conflicts and millions of environmental refugees" (cited in Robins and Pye-Smith 1997).[4] Yet the case has, I would argue, never been made convincingly.

The implication is that environmental mitigation is an issue for national security. As Homer-Dixon has argued, if environmental stress is a root cause of conflict, this makes issues of sustainability, environmental protection, and the distribution of wealth and resources central elements of peace building (Homer-Dixon, personal communication to Robins in Robins and Pye-Smith 1997). In the interests of peace, governments should be investing in such things as sustainable forestry and water conservation.

We need to be particularly careful with these kinds of associations because causal ascriptions of conflict (like famine) to local environmental factors often have the effect of depoliticizing the deeper causes of conflict. Considering conflicts to be "environmental–population" in origin might obscure the political origins of what are so definitively political events. A literature criticizing causal ascription of famine to neo-Malthusian and environmental factors has long shown how such analyses not only misrepresent the causes and dynamics of famine (Watts 1983; Devereaux 1993) but also—through their effects on policy—contribute to the problem (de Waal 1989; Keen 1994; Macrae and Zwi 1994).

Similarly, obfuscation of political causes of conflict within depoliticized environmental and neo-Malthusian explanatory frames may impede moves towards resolving conflicts. This obfuscation enables such environmental arguments to be wielded intentionally as a political weapon on behalf of one side or another. Moreover, environmental reductionism not only diverts attention away from actors in the conflict but also implies that mediators should "keep their distance" in what might be an essentially irresoluble set of affairs, or act only indirectly on what are perceived to be the

4. "Inter-state tension, refugees, revolutions, civil wars, urban riots and rural unrest are clearly connected to environmental bankruptcy; to deforestation, overgrazing, to soil erosion, and landlessness, to drought and hunger and migration to cities, as well as to disputed rivers and underground aquifers. The UN, foreign aid agencies and African governments must tackle the environmental causes of violence if they wish to move towards a peaceful continent" (Timberlake 1985: 198).

"root environmental causes." So "greenwar" reasoning might not only de-
politicize conflict but also may do so in a way that strongly orients how outside parties consider their role in conflict resolution—and their role in
contributing to conflict.

Finally, we all need to be cautious in engaging with the conceptual and
methodological reflections suggested by any particular author, including
ourselves. Each will be affected by the specifics of the wars with which they
have the most engaged experience. I am no exception, and my analysis will
surely be inflected by the conflicts in the Democratic Republic of Congo
(DRC) and Rwanda, and in the Sierra Leone and Liberia nexus. Given the
paucity of data of a reliable sort and given the immensity and complexity
of war as political event, the work of comparison is inevitably a rather subjective, interpretative enterprise.[5]

Rethinking the Role of the Environment

I would like to present several hypotheses around which to reframe consideration of environment—conflict linkages. The first of these is that conflicts are less generated by resource poverty than by resource wealth. It is
the very wealth that the environment offers—its potential value—that
drives conflict. Conflicts are environmentally caused, from this perspective,
less from the push of their impoverishment than from the wealth they create. This perspective does not preclude attention to environmental scarcity
but sets its analysis within a rather more political–economic framework, as
is the goal of most chapters within this book.

While it is tempting for environmental theorists to consider environmental depletion as a cause of conflict (with people driven to struggle for
the meager entrails of a slaughtered earth), it is instructive to observe that
major conflicts tend to be in areas of high-value "environmental" (primary) resources (diamonds, gas, timber, oil, metals, nuclear, and space age
elements) or in areas that impinge on their profitable extraction. In Angola, competition over diamonds, uranium, gas, and oil fuel the enduring
conflict; in Sierra Leone and Liberia, it is diamonds, gold, rutile, and timber; in Sudan, it is oil; and in the Democratic Republic of Congo, diamonds, gold, niobium, rubidium, uranium, copper, gas, oil, and timber do
the same. Oil and minerals fueled the older conflicts in Biafra (Nigeria
1967–1970), Ogaden (1977), Chad (c. 1985). Although each of these

5. This paper was first written in 1997. Subsequent events and political realignments in
these conflict regions have made some of the political analysis dated. For this reason, references to "Zaire" have been changed to "DRC." The chapter should be read with this in
mind.

wars has domestic dynamics, it is inconceivable that the causes and courses of these wars—their endurance, their arming, and their impacts on civilian populations—could be understood without considering these broader re-source value issues. Expansion of these examples later in this chapter will drive the analysis home.

If conflicts are linked to resource wealth rather than to their depletion, then we can forward several further secondary hypotheses. Conflicts might be fought for control over resources themselves, but they could equally well concern struggles over the means to exploit resources, such as control over: (1) a labor force ("tied labor" and shackles of assorted physical and economic sorts), and (2) capital, such as access to international capital markets, balanced perhaps by problems in acquiring responsibilities for national debt. Equally, conflicts occur over the means to make resources valuable, such as control over: (1) means of communication and trade routes, and (2) political means to "access" markets, or (3) the markets themselves. Thus it will be instructive to examine certain case studies of conflict dynamics in relation to factors of production other than the pri-mary resource and in relation to market access.

These hypotheses can be used to illustrate that conflicts are not merely over the resources per se but over the means to exploit the resources. In many cases, this translates into control over a labor force. In Liberia and Sierra Leone, warlords are able to profit by using the conflict to recruit la-bor by force: enslavement by creating slaves as "political outlaws," by forc-ing them to commit atrocities or physically branding captured populations with the distinctive mark of those who commit such atrocities). Equally, re-cruits were enticed to join up, offered "ways of life" and a future (job/drugs/videos/educational programs/food security) in an otherwise difficult climate in which to derive a livelihood (see also Richards 1996, and this volume).

In economic conditions that favor gaining control of tied labor, the dis-tinction between war and peace fades. As Keen writes: "War can usefully be seen as a deepening of exploitative processes already existing in 'normal' times, a continuation and exaggeration of long-standing conflicts over re-sources [such as labor . . .] and a means—for certain groups—of maximiz-ing the benefits of economic transactions through the exercise of various kinds of force against groups depicted as "fair game" in the context of civil (or "holy") war (Keen 1997: 2).

It may be not what lands have lost but what they still have that links envi-ronments to conflict. This is shown in the dynamics of warfare itself. Fac-tions frequently fight for the resources that will finance the fight: for the diamond-producing areas, for the timber regions, and so on. Arguably it is such resources, not the lack of them, that enables many conflicts to en-dure.

Several cases will illustrate this. An initial brief reflection on the Biafra conflict in Nigeria will exemplify the way oil wealth contributed to the conflict and how the global geopolitics of oil interlocked with political fault lines in Nigeria. A more detailed look at the contemporary conflict in DRC and in Angola exemplifies this further. It also enables us to consider how political–economic conditions faced by the populations assist recruitment into armed militias and how such conditions are themselves conditioned by international political and economic interests in the resources of DRC.

Biafra

In 1967, the industrially developed Eastern Region of Nigeria seceded as "Biafra" following ethnic violence rooted in Nigerian political, religious, and colonial history. Yet as Arbatov (1986) argues, while these social tensions were necessary for the war, they were not sufficient (Nafziger 1983). The war also was fueled by mineral competition. The eastern region is rich in oil. Nigeria launched an armed counterattack against secessionists in July 1967 "only after Shell (which was extracting oil in the contested region) agreed to pay its royalties to Biafra rather than to Nigeria" (Arbatov 1986: 34). When Arab states imposed an oil embargo on the United States and Europe during the Arab–Israeli war of June 1967, Nigerian oil suddenly had heightened strategic interest and greater value. The Nigerian state prevented exports from Biafra by imposing a sea blockade. The United Kingdom, which had much to profit from Nigerian oil, first withheld support to Biafra, then gave military and other support to Nigeria. France, on the other hand, gave public and military support to Biafra. A French-owned oil company had obtained huge oil rights from Biafra, indeed the House of Rothschild Bank had obtained exclusive rights from Biafra for ten years to all its deposits of niobium, uranium, coal, tin, oil, and gold. Those in the United States lobbying for Biafra were supported by Mobil oil and other U.S. companies (Cervenka 1971: 113–114, 123–124; Arbatov 1986: 35).

Democratic Republic of Congo (formerly Zaire)

In the Democratic Republic of Congo (DRC), the first decades of Laurent Kabila's "liberation struggle" in the 1970s and 1980s were financed by gold mining. His rebel movement was able to gain and maintain control of a gold-rich region in South Kivu. Mined in an artisanal way, much of the gold was then sold to elements of the corrupt national army, which he was allegedly fighting, in exchange for the "capture" of arms that he needed to continue the fight and to guarantee the supply of mining labor (Schatzberg 1988).

More recently, the astonishing speed with which the Alliance of Democratic Forces for the Liberation of Congo-Zaire (AFDL) headed by Laurent Kabila, routed the national army is linked not only to the corrupt inefficiency of the latter and to the unpopularity of the Mobutu regime, but also to the huge mineral wealth that AFDL would control if successful. I shall dwell on this case at some length to illustrate the broader political–economic issues involved in this conflict. The wealth accruing to Kabila was forthcoming not only because the AFDL captured the mineral reserves as it crossed the country from Kivu to Kinshasa but also because multinational mineral firms became confident that the AFDL campaign was likely to be successful on the international stage.

Crucially, the AFDL had the backing of the United States, which it has since thanked. The United States provided political, logistical, surveillance, and, it is rumored, on-the-ground military support to the movement, and used its influence in DRC to limit the capacity of the national army.[6] The cooperative link between the United States and elements of the AFDL movement dates back at least to 1993.[7] U.S. foreign policy in DRC has been backing (or "hitch-hiking" on) a Uganda/Pan Africanist alignment in southern African politics since the days of the Bush administration in the United States, and of Mulroney in Canada. As an indication, Paul Kageme, the army commander who masterminded (1) the Rwandan Patriotic Front invasion of Rwanda (and is now its vice-president), (2) the ADFL campaign in DRC, and (3) aspects of Museveni's campaign taking Uganda in 1986. Kageme was minister for procurement in Uganda and had been studying at the U.S. Army Command and General Staff College at Fort Leavenworth, Kansas, in 1990. He flew from this training to spearhead the October uprising in Rwanda when Rwigema, the first RPF general, was killed.

---

6. The New Congolese Foreign Minister admits that foreign support was essential to the ADFL and that the support from the United States was especially helpful (Marek 1997 at http://www.marekinc.com/ZWNews060797.html). Reports suggest that the CIA was operational in support of Kabila early in the rebellion (Marek at http://www.marekinc.com/ZWIntello5309702.html). According to Thomas Kanza (former Minister of International Cooperation) the rebellion of 1997 was under preparation with U.S. support from 1993 (personal communication April 1997). Many unconfirmed reports of American and British military assistance (lethal and non-lethal) that effectively assisted the RPA/ADFL forces both during the initial campaign to close the refugee camps on the Zaire border and later during Kabila's campaign to take Zaire. Reports exist of special Afro-American units of the U.S. special Delta Force in operation within the rebel lines, of U.S. military transport (flying under other corporate guises) assisting the campaign logistics, and indeed of American casualties linked to these activities. The latter were reported in the Belgian press. Certain journalists (personal communication, names intentionally withheld) are convinced that there was continuous surveillance of satellite-based communications emanating from Zaire, and that this was at the disposal of AFDL forces.

7. Thomas Kanza, personal communication.

Certain multinational corporations were well-poised to know U.S. strategy and its likely impact on the dynamics of the war. Indeed, North American mineral companies that signed mineral agreements with Kabila to the tune of $3 billion during the military campaign had chosen their advisors with care. Barrick Gold corporation, one of the first to sign contracts with Kabila, counts among its International Advisory Board: George Bush (former CIA director and former U.S. President), Brian Mulroney (former President of Canada), Richard Helms (former director of the U.S. CIA), and Karl Otto Pohl (former governor of the German Bundesbank).[8] The influential consultancy firm Cohen & Woods, which lobbied internationally on behalf of AFDL and eventually for the regime of Laurent Kabila (from April 1999) and which is associated both with mineral deal-making and with linking AFDL with Angolan interests (Reno 1997), is run by Herman Cohen (a former Assistant Secretary of State for Foreign Affairs) and James Woods (a former U.S. Assistant Secretary of State).[9] American Mineral Fields, even more successful in gaining mineral contracts during Kabila's campaign, was lending Kabila its executive Lear jet among other things, to assist the rebels' logistics.

It would be disingenuous to ignore that several firms (AMF, Tenke, Iscor) had also recently signed large contracts with the Mobutu regime that Kabila overthrew. As with the U.S. government, they did not risk backing only one side. Such deals also gave legitimacy for concessions desired in the looming post-Mobutu era. Yet earlier contracts did not revive existing mining that had slumped.[10] In April 1997, the AFDL called on all mining companies to enter into negotiations with it or risk losing control of their concessions. They negotiated protection of staff and equipment and began to pay tax and royalties to AFDL. At this time, the AFDL also acquired diamonds, already mined, selling one stockpile they seized to de Beers for $5 million. Mobutu had inside information gleaned from thirty years of experience when he hypocritically, but correctly, noted on April 25, 1997 that "It is because of copper, cobalt, gold and diamonds that they are in the process of arming Kabila. It is not because they like DRC."

Cynically, one must suppose that such commercial–state interests contributed to one of the most disturbing events of modern times. U.S. aerial reconnaissance photogrammetry confirmed the existence of over five hundred thousand displaced people in three major concentrations fleeing before AFDL forces, according to UN and Oxfam observers who saw this data on November 20, 1997. Yet when the figures were released in a press con-

8. *Africa Confidential*, Vol. 37 No. 25, December 13, 1996; Vol. 38, No. 16, August 1, 1997.
9. Ibid.
10. Copper production fell from 500,000 tons per year (c. 1980) to 30,000 tons per year (1996). Cobalt dropped from 17,000 tons per year to 3,000 tons per year, and the world price shot up from $6 per pound to $25 per pound.

ference in Kigali three days later, the U.S. military claimed that they had located only one significant cluster of people and that these were armed forces, not refugees. As Stockton argues, four hundred thousand people were effectively "airbrushed from history" for political reasons linked to U.S. interests (Stockton 1997: 2).

The involvement of foreign interests in this war might seem somewhat far-fetched. Yet those championing the way that contemporary conflicts sweeping central Africa are bringing African solutions to African problems should be cautious not to overlook the commercial and strategic mineral dimensions to the conflicts (see e.g., Reno 1995, 1997). Certain journalists are heralding the military–political shifts, best characterized perhaps as the "Uganda alignment," or the "Pan Africanist" alignment, as a part of a new "Wind of Change" sweeping the continent (Lindsay Hilsum, Channel 4 news, reporting from South Sudanese [Sudan People's Liberation Army (SPLA)] lines only days after Kabila took power in Kinshasa). Yet other journalists such as Sam Kiley in *The Times* (April 22, 1997: 18) dub the same process as "The Second Scramble for Africa," quoting "a mining magnate based in Johannesburg" who suggests that "Cecil Rhodes must be spinning in his grave at the opportunities he is missing." As *The Economist* put it: "Zaire is the biggest prize since the new mining scramble for Africa started some four years ago" (*The Economist*, May 3, 1997: 62). While spokespeople for the pan-Africanist movement suggest that it is they who are using the U.S. and minerals firms, not vice versa, this is not the view held by all. Subsequent events bear this out. While Kabila soon turned against his older pan-Africanist allies, he could continue to count on the support of the North American minerals firms that helped him to power as a second rebellion flared up. How long he can count on this is an open question as we go to press.

Strategic Materials and Conflict in DRC

In Africa, as elsewhere, when considering conflict in relation to environmental wealth, it is useful to distinguish between (1) immobile materials (notably land, which we shall consider later), (2) valuable mobile materials (gold, diamonds, etc.) and (3) strategic materials (i.e., minerals vitally needed for military, political, or economic reasons). The most significant strategic minerals are those for which supply is highly concentrated in a limited number of states from whom major military-industrial powers must import. Only a few elements can claim this status. As Hveem notes, for example, only three countries account for 100 percent of known global platinum reserves, two countries share 98 percent of known chromium reserves (South Africa, Zimbabwe), and three countries control 90 percent of known manganese reserves. Three countries share 90 percent of molyb-denum production, and three countries (DRC and Zambia) share 80 per-cent of cobalt exports (Hveem 1986: 61–4). According to Hveem, all five major capitalist countries (France, Germany, Japan, the United Kingdom, and the United States) are critically[11] dependent on chromium and cobalt. Other critical minerals include the two elements niobium,[12] used in super-conducting alloys, and tantalum,[13] used in electric and aerospace applica-tions, which are often found together.

Changing patterns of international resource demand have led to a de-crease in mineral self-sufficiency and increased import dependence on many minerals, making more minerals strategic, and more of these criti-cally so. This is the trend into the twenty-first century. For example, while the United States was self-sufficient for most of its industrial raw materials in the 1960s, the National Materials Policy Commission suggests that by the turn of the century, it will depend on imports for more than 80 per-cent of materials. This trend preoccupies many military and economic strategists the world over. Demand is rising due to increased industrial and consumer demand and to the development of new technologies that give minor minerals key roles. For example, cobalt in the expanding superal-loys market is important in aerospace, in the battery industry (including new generation vehicle batteries), which is growing at 40 percent per year, and in the electrical and chemical industries.

All analysts aware of struggles for strategic minerals single out the south-ern African region, which "occupies a prominent position in the strategic thinking of several, if not all, of the major powers" (Hveem 1986). The re-gion supplies Western powers and Japan with several of the most critical minerals including chromium and cobalt:

> which are particularly critical to the vulnerability of the USA, Japan, and Western Europe. Manganese should be classed with these also because of its importance in the ferro-alloy industry, as should platinum and vanadium. Southern Africa is the largest source of supply for these minerals. If to this brief list are added gold and uranium, then the strategic importance of southern Africa becomes even more evident. (Hveem 1986: 73)

Such analysis, dating from the last days of the Cold War, should be tem-pered by subsequent events, but how, and how much, the operation of state–commercial strategizing has altered remains debatable, as we shall

11. That is, when supplies come from few suppliers, over long distances, or from a country of different ideology.
12. Otherwise known as colombium or colombite, atomic no. 41.
13. Ta. atomic no. 73.

see. DRC monopolizes southern Africa's cobalt reserves, having 1.36 million tons of proven reserves, reputedly around 60 percent of global reserves.[14] Its competitors are Cuba (with perhaps 1.04 million tons) and Canada. Add to this DRC's uranium reserves and the more recently discovered and reputedly phenomenally rich deposits of niobium, rubidium, and tantalum, which have been mined in Kivu during the last six years (though not registered in official statistics), and one begins to understand the global strategic and commercial interest in this nation (itself as large as Western Europe). Add to this also the huge reserves of noncritical but valuable conventional resources (copper, gold, diamonds, zinc, and timber). Moreover, the copper, cobalt, zinc, and niobium reserves contain reputedly the best quality ores in the world.

Strategic minerals tend to be "price inelastic": if prices rise, the amount demanded does not fall off. Rather, if supply can be assured, the buyer is often willing to pay a very high price. As Hveem (1986) notes, in strategic terms, embargoes are worse than price increases. Such conditions generate a huge potential for monopolistic behavior. Conglomerates controlling strategic elements can make massive profits (in forming cartels and in intrafirm trade, etc.). At several times in recent history, neither chromium, cobalt, niobium, or tantalum have had a traded world price. Prices tend to be set by producers or negotiated in contractual arrangements. Those who control these minerals can exert huge leverage ("rents") over industries dependent upon their minerals—especially if they form cartels. Control over chromium and cobalt is highly concentrated at the corporate level.[15]

In the 1990s, the reduction in then-Zaire's cobalt output (from 10,000 tons per annum in 1992 to c. 2,000–3,000) forced the price up from about $6 per pound to $25–$33 per pound. This very fact makes access to DRC's cobalt reserves worth more to corporations that control the rest of the world's supply (principally American Mineral Fields [AMF] and Tenke, which control much of Canada's reserves). Informed analysts predict that if DRC's cobalt production picks up again, the price of cobalt may drop from $25 per pound to $7 per pound (*The Economist* May 3, 1997: 62), massively reducing, for example, the value and extraction profitability of American Mineral Field's Canadian reserves. It is not surprising, therefore, that the principal firms competing for DRC's cobalt reserves are AMF and Tenke, which control much of the Canadian reserves and could maintain the value of these by limiting DRC's supply. Cuba, the other major cobalt producer, is presently embargoed internationally.

14. Robert Block, Staff Reporter, *Wall Street Journal*. "Mining Firms Want a Piece of Zaire's Vast Mineral Wealth." May 1, 1997. E-mail circular.
15. In 1986, Anglo-American held the key decision-making position in the global chromium industry, and Belgium's Societé Generale, Anglo American, INCO Canada, Falconbridge Nickel Mines Canada held the key to cobalt (Hveem 1986).

Entrepreneurs will go to some length to secure reserves. Those already with reserves remain undaunted by backing both sides of conflict (even brokering peace negotiations, as Anglo-American did in South Africa). On the other hand, nonestablished firms seeking to capture reserves can back one side, perhaps hoping—in the event of victory—to displace competitors. In DRC, the established major mining corporations were largely francophone, but following the conflict, anglophones are taking over. *Africa Confidential* describes "Considerable brawling among foreign investors" and notes that "French and Belgians, Japanese and South Africans suspect that the advance of the Alliance's troops will mainly benefit North American mining corporations" (*Africa Confidential* 1997: 3).

During the Cold War, many states were willing to assist conglomerates to gain access to mineral concessions for state strategic reasons. Equally, supply governments like Zaire were able to use their resources to exert international leverage, making long-term bilateral barter/counterpurchase agreements guaranteeing mineral supply in return for equally significant materials, often military items (Hveem 1986). Access to southern African minerals has been orienting United Kingdom, United States, French, German, Chinese, and Canadian foreign policy interests for many decades. While Mobutu may himself have been corrupt, it was such structures that enabled him to continue his practices over decades. The United States appears to have been preoccupied for several years with the plans for the post-Mobutu era (especially given his cancer), and its support to the Pan-Africanist Alliance in east and southern Africa, out of which Kabila emerged, appears to have been part of this strategy.

Labor Value and Rebel Recruitment in DRC

Mobutu's endurance had disastrous economic effects for Zaire's population. As argued earlier, conflict may not just be over the valuable resources but over access to their profitable extraction or marketing. In Zaire—at least in its Kivu region—conditions emerged in which accessing cheap labor was essential for profitable enterprise. The value of resources increased as the cost of labor to work them went down. Gaining "tied labor" was a central strategy for employers during peacetime, and this influenced recruitment into the rebel army in the early stages of the conflict.

During the 1970s and 1980s, powerful coalitions had emerged between state administrators, traditional administrators, the "freelance" army and police, and large landholders, which made it possible for large landlords to expropriate land from poorer claimants. New landholders were able to extort heavy labor dues from those who had been living on the lands. It was this situation that enabled employers (merchants, plantation owners, and even small landholders) working in increasingly unprofitable circumstances to pass their problems on to their work forces. So as wages slumped[16] and laborers were reluctant to work for real wages that were less than 6 percent of 1960 levels, employers found it necessary either to draw on "tied labor" (forcing those who squatted on their land to work for them for free) or to rely on the labor of the desperate and land destitute. Under such conditions, employers also were able to recruit labor by "giving protection" to employees. Realizing this, employers were not encouraged to reduce levels of violence and insecurity because their protection racketeering assisted their recruitment of cheap labor. In many cases, landlords were behind the deployment of the violence that became endemic. For some, the only alternatives were speculative gold digging, working as "rebels," or settling in regions in the forest. Those taking any of these avenues did not escape Kivu's predatory political economy. They became subordinates to the mine owners, the rebel leaders, or the land chiefs of the forest tracts. For many, joining the rebel army appeared the better option.

Angola: Natural Resources and the Security for Their Extraction

Across the border in Angola, the protracted conflicts have had Cold War dynamics that again have carried over into "modern" times. At the risk of simplification, during the Cold War, the Soviet Bloc, especially Cuba, supported the Popular Movement for the Liberation of Angola (MPLA), while the Western bloc (including the Republic of South Africa) used to give its support to the opponents, the National Front for the Liberation of Angola (FNLA) and National Union for the Total Liberation of Angola (UNITA). Once again, the competition was ideological, but ideological differences had a dialectical interplay with strategic economic concerns, most notably over Angola's own resource reserves (oil, diamonds, and uranium), and those of its neighbors. For example, Cuban-backed MPLA lent support to Southwest African People's Organization (SWAPO) in Namibia, and to the Shaba secessionists in Zaire. In 1978, for example, opponents of the Government of Zaire, backed by Angola and Cuba, attacked mining installations in Shaba province, leading to an interruption of production, Belgium responded, backed by France, by deploying a military force in Shaba. Apart from Zaire, Cuba at that time dominated world cobalt reserves. During the Cold War, it stood to gain massively from depriving the United States access to this strategic mineral.

Reno (1997) documents how the end of the Cold War has influenced

16. By 1977, the index of real salaries was only 16 percent of what it had been in 1960; by 1979 it was only 6 percent, and since then it has declined further.

the dynamics of the Angolan conflict. He documents how South African security firms, principally Executive Outcomes (EO), now assist the Angolan Government in its fight against UNITA (using mercenaries who had, as South African soldiers, been working alongside UNITA during the Cold War). EO has helped transfer from UNITA to government forces "about $1 billion of earnings from gemstone exports," and also guarded the Soyo oil installations, under attack from UNITA in 1993 (Reno 1997: 176–178). EO's business partners came to control huge oil concessions. Oil generates about $0.8 billion annually, and resource sales enabled the Angolan government to purchase the $0.35 billion needed to pursue the war. EO also helped the Angolan leader stop his own generals from going freelance by using diamond revenues to build an independent power base (Reno 1997: 179). Yet as Reno documents, the United States put pressure on the Angolan government to end its contracts with EO, and a U.S. firm, Military Professional Resources (MPRI), stepped in. MPRI's board of directors includes retired U.S. military officers including Soyster, ex-director of the Defense Intelligence Agency, and "presented its bid to the Angolan government through a private firm run by Herman Cohen" (Reno 1997: 179).

It has been argued that following the end of the Cold War, several relationships central to these dynamics have changed. First, it is argued, the relationship between governments and people have changed, as rulers can no longer seek unlimited support from foreign patrons (e.g., de Waal 1996: 8). Second, it is argued that the relationship between states and corporations has altered from a Cold War position in which governments assisted corporations in endeavors of joint strategic–commercial interest (e.g., with oil and other minerals) to a situation in which businesses operate with political connections. Well-connected firms profit from their knowledge of government policy and their influence over it.

But the relevance of these transformations can be exaggerated. First, the ideological conflicts of the Cold War, and superpower policy itself, were fueled not only by strategic resource requirements but also by well-connected commercial interests. Second, the effect of superpower political withdrawal on the national politics of weak states may not be as dramatic as anticipated. In the new climate, as Reno (1997) argues, rulers of weak states are finding ways other than superpower backing to preserve their regimes. As explicit external superpower support dwindles, multinationals, nongovernmental organizations (NGOs), and international development agencies step in. Leaders of weak governments who had perhaps relied on superpower state support to maintain external and internal security against "strongmen inside state boundaries," now turn to more or less clandestine international commercial ties to do the same task. The internationally condoned sale of national assets (generally to foreign interests) raises international funding and also keeps national resources out of the reach of internal opposition,[17] and one can even sell resources controlled by rivals. Asset sales suit creditors, satisfying their demands for revenue generation. Often, therefore, weak states can continue to use state bureaucracy for patronage and co-optation rather than move to serve popular needs in exchange for popular support. These patterns of continued patronage also often suit aid agencies. Better the familiar weak state than the "failed state," overwhelmed by warfare between local strongmen. Crucially, relations with foreign companies and aid agencies enable weak governments to acquire both foreign exchange liquidity and weapons, despite huge debts and their systematic defaults (Reno 1997).

Links between weak states and international corporate (and development) interests are thus strengthening. But the extent to which these interests are themselves independent of external state support (e.g., of United States, South Africa, United Kingdom, France, Japan, China, etc.) is highly questionable. Companies and development organizations (multilateral, NGO, and bilateral) are providing good proxies (even covers) through which strategic state interests can be pursued ruthlessly. Certainly, it would appear from the evidence in DRC and Angola that there are strong links between U.S. state and commercial interests. And as Reno (1997) demonstrates, the new South Africa also is assisting its investors in moving north, satisfying the needs both of its internal policy (sending belligerent, former internal security forces abroad) and its external policy (encouraging South African-based investment in what are very profitable enterprises). As Reno comments, South Africa, far from showing the way toward stability as a strong country might support a weaker one, is profiting hugely from enduring warfare in the region. There has been an expansion in the demand for security contracts for its security firms well-poised to enter this market and for the armaments to fight the wars, as well as for opportunities to gain linked commercial resource concessions. Indeed, South African firms have a competitive advantage in this market (Reno 1997).

It is certain that the demise of the Cold War has been taken as an opportunity for multinationals (with or without dominant state interests) to gain access to prospecting and reserve rights, which they had earlier been denied. This is what is meant by the "second scramble for Africa." As with the first, it is not being conducted independently of the national interests of major world powers.

Modern orthodoxy now holds that the whole concept of strategic re-

17. In Sierra Leone, as Reno (1997) notes, this includes oil refinery, customs, fisheries, banks, and the lottery.

sources is defunct, arguing that critical minerals have been stockpiled in the industrialized nations and that there are no longer any strategic communication lines at stake. Yet is this true? Evidence from the conflicts in Africa suggests that minerals strategizing does not appear to have fallen off the agenda. The Cold War may be over, but many rival commercial superblocs are present or forming, and the United States is certainly not the last remaining superpower. None of this can be lost on its strategists. In short, the "end of the Cold War" may be a nice myth behind which powerful nations can get on with furthering their strategic interests in other ways.

Conflict in Sierra Leone and Liberia: Natural Resources, Capital, Labor and Trade Routes

Events in Sierra Leone and Liberia echo those in the DRC. Diamond wealth and labor are fueling the war, and, as noted earlier, warlords are able to profit from the climate of conflict to recruit the labor to make those resources valuable. Both the causes and course of the conflict—and its dynamics—have been shaped by resource wealth.

The capacity of each of the many factions in Sierra Leone to finance their struggles was largely linked to diamond mining. The Revolutionary United Front (RUF) in Sierra Leone originally captured the diamond region in the east of the country in 1991 and those in the Kono region in 1992. Their fortunes waxed and waned with their success or otherwise in maintaining these resources in the war until the fragile peace settlement in 1996. Many government army units also operated as soldier-rebels, tempted to go freelance when in control of diamond mining zones. The government's eventual counter-strategy against the RUF and its own renegade soldiers was to secure the major diamond and rutile regions by hiring the international security (mercenary) firm Executive Outcomes. Just how Executive Outcomes' operations were financed by linking success to control over future revenue flows from these resources is brilliantly described by Reno (1997: 181).

Yet events here display how conflict can occur over the capital required for investment in natural resource exploitation, a second factor of production other than the primary resource that might be driving resource wars. In Sierra Leone in the mid-1990s, the RUF rebels (among others) sought to occupy government mining areas, thus threatening the government's ability to repay international debt, and indeed, its ability to be supplied further credit at the Paris Club debt negotiations. As Reno (1997) argues, it was partially this that prompted the government to engage Executive Outcomes, which secured not only the resources, as described above, but also the government's credit worthiness. Across the border, it has been argued that the Liberian conflict has been prolonged by the problems that warlords such as Charles Taylor would have if they were to become legitimate state leaders. In so doing, they would acquire the liabilities of state debt, which can cripple the dynamics of financing a war machine that had been flush with money when acting as an autonomous rebel faction. In acquiring state status, rebel movements also succumb not only to the financial but also the political conditions associated with it. In this way, rebels may be hesitant to pursue profitable conflicts to their less profitable termination. Indeed, as Keen puts it, in the Sudan context "Winning the war" was not the sole, or even the most important, objective of many of those engaging in violence. The primary goal for many was to manipulate violence in ways that achieved economic goals" (Keen 1997: 2).

Wars also are fought over the means to make resources valuable, including control over means of communication and trade routes. At a micro-level, this includes conscription of porterage and "headloading," which occurred in Sierra Leone as much during the recent civil war as during the colonial wars one hundred years earlier. In Liberia, Charles Taylor's National Patriotic Front of Liberia (NPFL) fought to gain control over the railway line to the coast, the railway port, and diamond rich regions. For some time, NPFL was able to export timber onto the international timber markets and used revenues from these exports to finance the war. Preventing this export, whether by disrupting the rail network or the port, was a strategy pursued by Taylor's opponents.

At the macro-level, transport and communications have contributed to many protracted conflicts in the "Horn" of northeast Africa during the Cold War. At the junction of Asia and Africa, and commanding the Suez shipping channel, these states control the sea routes linking the oil producing countries to America and Europe through which 70 percent of oil and other raw materials are imported by Western Europe. During the Cold War, superpower rivalry led to the USSR assisting then Somalia with $181 million in military assistance and $154 million in economic assistance, having designs on the port of Bereba. By 1977, they had delivered $1 billion worth of arms to Greater Ethiopia. This situation enabled Ethiopia to build up a formidable defense capability against its enemy Somalia and for its own internal struggles against separatist forces and domestic foes. As Thiam and Mulira (1993) sum up: "The fact is that the massive military aid granted to Ethiopia and Somalia by both Warsaw pact and NATO countries encouraged the two neighboring states to settle their differences on the battlefield."

This again highlights the international dimensions of African resource conflicts. It is, of course, not merely primary wealth and international/corporate interest that drives conflict. The spoils of war—requisitioning and looting of consumer durables (televisions, cars, etc.)— also enables wars to be fought, whether in financing the purchase of armaments or subsidizing the pay and increasing incentives to soldiers.

Conclusion

As I and others have argued in this book, approaches using concepts such as "environmental scarcity" or "greenwar" in linking conflict to environment are, deeply flawed. Given their popularity in quasi-academic circles, it is necessary to examine certain effects linked to the deployment of "greenwar" arguments. This is the meta-issue in which the relationship between environment and conflict needs to be discussed, not focusing on the relationship between environment per se and conflict but on environmental discourse and conflict. It could be argued that the way in which concern with the environment has been framed historically and within present political configurations is not irrelevant for considering present patterns of conflict. Considering conflicts to be "environmental" in origin can obscure the political–economic origins of what we have noted are definitively political events. We are led to see causes of conflict as internal to nations and "groups," which either "adapt" or not to emergent environmental conditions.

Deploying environmental arguments, whether fortuitously or strategically, can play to the advantage of certain protagonists in these conflicts on the international stage because it deflects analysis away from international commercial concerns and national politics toward those who are environmentally marginalized. Environmental arguments can thus be wielded as political weapons on behalf of one side or another.

The importance of using environmental issues as a mobilizing force in the discourse of international assistance further obfuscates the origins of conflict. As Salih (1997) argues, state, commercial, and indeed development ventures have often been "insensitive to peasants and pastoralists' property rights and to the fragility of the ecosystems in which they live. People lose their land, its productivity, and its resources without receiving compensation." To the extent, however, that such policies contribute to resource depletion, poverty and conflict, it would be erroneous to suggest that resource depletion and the poverty it engendered led to conflict.

In other cases, many people are so marginalized from the benefits of resource extraction that their only experience of it is of the "negative externalities" (pollutants) that extraction and resource processing generate. In both these circumstances, and especially given the position of environmental agendas in international and national politics, forms of resistance can be articulated in environmental idioms. Resistance in Ogoni, in southeast Nigeria, and in the Chipko movement in India are cases in point.

As Salih (1997) argues, it is worth asking whether these "environmental movements" represent dissent about mitigating the environmental destruction and externalities of resource use or are actually movements about rights to resource control and revenue streams. If the latter, despite dissent being articulated in the environmental idiom, these should not be treated as environmental movements.

In this chapter I have considered conflict in relation to the political economy of resource wealth. With a focus on wealth, there is a clear need to examine the scarcities that generate it, and a component of scarcity is often environmental degradation. But, I have argued, to conflate scarcity and environmental degradation within the encompassing term "environmental scarcity" or "greenwar" is at best unhelpful. This effect, of course, is the aim, implicit or explicit, of such analysis.

10

Invisible Spaces, Violent Places:
Cold War Nuclear and Militarized Landscapes

Valerie Kuletz

> The greatest irony of our atmospheric nuclear testing program is that the only victims of United States arms since WWII have been our own people.
>
> U.S. congressional investigators of the Atomic Energy Commission[1]

> The radiation has caused Shoshone, Ute, Navajo, Hopi, Paiute, Havasupai, Hualapai and other downwind communities to suffer from cancer, thyroid diseases and birth defects. We are now the most bombed nation in the world.
>
> Chief Raymond Yowell, Western Shoshone[2]

In 1998, at a time when the Western world imagined that it was approaching a sustainable comprehensive ban on the testing of nuclear weapons, it was confronted with the bold and unapologetic governments of India and Pakistan asserting their nuclear capabilities with multiple displays of violence in the form of nuclear bomb tests. As the first world responded with anger and incredulity, only the alternative press reported that Indian villagers showed signs of radiation sickness such as vomiting, nose bleeds, irritation to skin and eyes, as well as other symptoms of contamination (Reuters, 1998).[3] Most international press reports did not re-

---

1. A statement made by congressional investigators, under the Carter administration, of the Atomic Energy Commission's operational records, 1978 (Schneider, foreword to Gallagher 1993). While this is a revealing statement about the U.S. nuclear testing program, it is important to remember that the United States used the Marshall Islands in the South Pacific until the 1950s when it moved its nuclear testing program to the on-continent site of Nevada. Those who were indigenous to the Marshall Islands (and who were removed from their homelands) constitute some of the first post–World War II victims of nuclear weapons.
2. Cited in Taliman 1994.
3. This information was reported by Reuters, May 17, 1998, for New Delhi (although not generally picked up by other media sources). The information was disseminated by nuclear watch activists throughout the world via e-mail. These particular reports were obtained

veal that some Indian villages in the western state of Rajasthan (such as Khetolai) were less than 5 kilometers from the blast sites. These places and their inhabitants were invisible to the world beyond their local boundaries.[4]

The effects, the costs, and the consequences of "nuclearism" are not easily seen if viewed only from the core powers, from the urban centers of power.[5] In the United States, Southern Paiutes and Western Shoshone settlements encircle the Nevada Nuclear Test Site, and Pueblo and Navajo Indians (among others) live in U.S. uranium mining regions. Like the Rajasthan villagers, these are marginalized peoples whose bodies bear witness to "nuclearism."[6] In the shadow of powerful defense and energy programs, which are themselves often violent concerns, exist local, rural, often indigenous people who experience (because they are simply in the way) the very real violence of the state.[7] These are the incidental victims of the power wars between nuclear states. How do we talk about violence when it is neither seen nor acknowledged?

The state-sanctioned violence to the environment and people in the vicinity of nuclear and militarized landscapes is seriously underreported in literature that purports to address environmental and social degradation and crises. This chapter attempts to direct attention to nuclear and non-instrumental military violence, especially in the forms of nuclear testing and the contamination problems inherent in the transport and burial of nu-

---

from Kate Dewes, New Zealand representative for "Women for a Nuclear Free and Independent Pacific, Australia International Peace Bureau, Oceania."

4. Khetolai is in the Pokharan district, 550 kilometers southwest of New Delhi. Residents were ordered to evacuate their homes less than 3 hours before the explosions, which were conducted on May 14, 1998. Villagers and people in the settlements were not told that atomic weapons were being detonated, only that they needed to evacuate because the army was conducting artillery practice. Other villages in the vicinity (15 to 30 kilometers from the test site) included Dholiya, Loharki, Latmi, and Bhadriyo. All together, at least seven villages are in India's "Alpha Firing Range" in the Pokhran district. This desert region is characterized by its strong prevailing winds, which blow surface sands throughout the area. The nuclear explosions forced a large mound of earth to rise into the air, causing a thick blanket of dust that enveloped nearby villages.

5. "Nuclearism" in this chapter refers to various aspects of nuclear activity, particularly production and testing of nuclear weapons, production of nuclear power, and the storage of nuclear waste from both production projects (the making of energy and bombs). "Nuclearism" here does not necessarily refer to the use of radionuclides in medicine because this constitutes only approximately 1 percent of the nuclear waste stream.

6. This chapter emphasizes the U.S. environment, but marginalized peoples who are subject to "nuclearism" are found in many areas of the world: Tahiti, the Marshall Islands, Kazakhstan, Taiwan, Tibet, Africa, Canada, and Australia as well as elsewhere.

7. I make special reference to "indigenous" peoples because they experience "nuclearism" (in the form of production, processing, uranium mining, testing, and waste storage) more than other groups. However, nonindigenous people also are subjected to radioactive contamination of various kinds, as the white residents of Nevada, Utah, and other rural "downwind" states can attest.

clear waste. Because such activities are legitimated as government or state-sanctioned corporate enterprises and because they are utilitarian and rationalized forms of violence, the burial of nuclear waste and the testing of nuclear and "conventional" weapons often go unrecognized as violent acts. However, fallout from nuclear tests, the incineration of chemical weapons materials, radiation released in the environment from nuclear waste, and heavily militarized regions pose profoundly important and sometimes intractable problems. This type of environmental violence, therefore, must assume greater prominence in the literature on sustainability.

This chapter provides a brief discussion of nuclear colonialism, with particular emphasis on the United States, because it is the historical and contemporary context for understanding this form of violence. I then focus on one particular U.S. region in which "nuclearism" is concentrated. This is the case study of "the Bull's Eye"—a Department of Defense proposal to integrate the U.S. Southwest's weapons test and training ranges into one massive testing theater. At the center of the Bull's Eye lie the Nevada Test Site (NTS), Yucca Mountain, Nellis Air Force Base, and China Lake Weapons Center.[8] In my discussion of the Bull's Eye region, I investigate the invisibility of such large-scale environmental violence and the mechanisms by which the violence of sacrificial landscapes continues to affect disempowered populations. In the process I examine those populations and their relationships with the landscapes in question. Finally, I consider the issue of "nuclearism" as a form of development against the backdrop of nuclear colonialism. Here I identify the enterprises that wish to "develop" nuclear waste dumps on land already viewed as contaminated by nuclear testing, processing, or production, by uranium mining, or by nonnuclear military activities.

Nuclear Colonialism

During the second half of the twentieth century throughout the world, Cold War nuclear weapons testing programs, with their requisite plutonium production facilities, brought into being a variety of landscapes sacrificed to "national security." In the United States this occurred, for example, at the Hanford plutonium production plant in rural Washington and the nuclear weapons laboratories across the country. The most prominent U.S. landscape of sacrifice, however, is the NTS where—from 1952 to

---

8. The Nevada Test Site is the testing range for U.S. nuclear weapons. Nellis Air Force base is a military training and testing range; China Lake is a research, development, and testing center for nonnuclear weapons; and Yucca Mountain is the proposed repository site for 70,000 tons of both temporary and permanent high-level nuclear waste.

1992—the U.S. government has officially detonated 928 nuclear bombs (and numerous "secret" nuclear blasts outside its borders).[9] In the Soviet Union (as noted by Garb, this volume) Kazakhstan, Chelyabinsk, and the cities of Tomsk and Krasnoyarsk in Siberia (among other places) served similar purposes. Until 1963 England used western Australian aboriginal land,[10] and until as recently as 1996 France used Moruroa and Fangataufa atolls in the Tuamotu Archipelago (French Polynesia) for their nuclear weapons testing programs.

All the places used for nuclear testing (and some used for plutonium production and manufacture) were originally inhabited or used by indigenous peoples (or, as Garb notes in this book, in the case of the Soviet Union, by minority ethnic groups). Hence, Fourth World peoples recognized nuclear colonialism early on. This new form of colonialism linked indigenous peoples to the brave new world of the *transuranic elements*,[11] which invade not only traditional landscapes but also the bodies of their local inhabitants.

Adding the term "nuclear" to "colonialism" is a way of seeing how colonialism has maintained itself or transmogrified in the late twentieth/early twenty-first centuries—a period supposedly marked by decolonization. For colonized indigenous peoples, whether they be internally or externally colonized,[12] adding the term "nuclear" is a way of signifying late twentieth-century genocide (Kuletz 1998).[13] Radioisotopes can destroy the reproductive capacity of humans who come in contact with them and consequently are seen as a form of intergenerational violence (and thus genocide). As Grace Thorpe, tribal judge and health commissioner for the Sauk and Fox Nation of Oklahoma, put it: "It [radioactive waste] is a form of genocide because of the harm it can do to the genes and the reproduction of our people. It's a very very important issue to us."[14]

---

9. Today some areas of the test site are contaminated by tritium 3,000 times in excess of safe drinking water standards.

10. The British also conducted tests of hydrogen bombs at Christmas and Malden Islands in 1957 and 1958.

11. The transuranic elements are all human-made elements, such as plutonium, that appear on the periodic table of elements after uranium.

12. It is important to recognize that colonization can happen both internally and externally to the colonizing power. Because people often think of colonization in terms of a colonizing state asserting power in faraway places, those who have been internally colonized, such as American Indians, often get ignored in the literature of colonialism.

13. The accusation of genocide by radiation contamination was a persistent theme in many—if not most—of my interviews with Native Americans in the southwest United States. This view also is held by indigenous peoples in other colonized regions used for nuclear testing in other parts of the world such as in Polynesia, Micronesia, Australia, and Kazakhstan.

14. This statement by Grace Thorpe appears in "Wasteland," a video produced by the Nuclear Free Indian Lands Project / National Environmental Coalition of Native Americans.

Nuclear waste dumps and nuclear testing are usually placed in large, sparsely populated open spaces. Scientific and military collaborations for the creation of both weapons and waste in landscapes of vastness, such as oceans and deserts, are an important aspect of a late twentieth-century colonialism that has threads reaching back into earlier periods of colonial empire-building. In the United States, for instance, Native American communities mostly inhabit the uranium mining regions. The lands that surround the NTS, Los Alamos National Laboratory, and Sandia National Laboratory[15] lie within "Indian Country" (parts of the U.S. Southwest), where more land-based Native Americans are concentrated than any other region in North America.[16] Indian Country also encompasses the five great North American deserts: the Great Basin, Mojave, Sonoran, Navajoan, and Chihuahuan deserts. Desert regions, and the people who inhabit them, are often viewed by those who do not live in them (particularly industrial and governmental representatives) as peripheral zones to larger urban centers. These regions (and the people who live in them) also are often perceived as economically unproductive. Consequently, over the past fifty years in the United States, these particular desert regions have been transformed into one of the largest militarized landscapes in the world. The combination of military occupation and nuclear activities superimposed on traditional[17] and contemporary native land renders these regions (unofficial) internal colonial territories.[18]

Of the many forms of environmental violence in the world today, the violence of nuclear and militarized landscapes is one of the most extreme. Yet it is strangely invisible to most people. The hidden centers (the Depart-

15. The NTS, Los Alamos, and Sandia National Laboratories are all part of the U.S. nuclear weapons complex.
16. The term "land-based Native Americans" refers to nonurban native occupation on reservation land but also land owned by native people in the forms of settlements, colonies, allotment areas, *rancherias*, and villages.
17. Traditional native land here refers to lands that are claimed by particular Indian groups to be aboriginal territories in which they lived, hunted, migrated, and so forth prior to those lands being appropriated by Euro-Americans. For the Western Shoshone this is a good portion of the state of Nevada and parts of eastern California. The important point about traditional land for a nomadic group like the Western Shoshone is that this larger territory allows self-sufficient survival. This landscape includes mountain ranges and desert valleys, both of which were essential for survival in an environment like the Great Basin. (They needed the high mountains in the hot summers and then the low deserts in the cold winters.) Much of this particular land has been taken for military war game and weapons testing purposes. The indigenous settlements thus surround the military regions because the Indians used that land prior to appropriation by the United States.
18. The historical construction of the United States as a nation state out of land previously and simultaneously inhabited by native groups obviously produced countless struggles over both Indian territory and identity. Native history and pre-history in the region of the Bull's Eye, for instance, includes relocated tribes as well as tribes that have lived in the area for more than 12,000 years.

ment of Defense and the Department of Energy) that create and sustain these landscapes of violence ensure their power by maintaining a low public profile and a high insider's (government) profile. The operations of power located in the desert are not centralized but form a dispersed web of power. Those caught within this web of power see and experience the violence done to these landscapes. But they are themselves invisible—for different reasons. They are invisible because they lack power. However, when the nuclear landscape is superimposed on such formally or informally enclosed native spaces, the collective native memory of colonization and genocide reemerges with force and conviction, as the statement by Grace Thorpe attests.

Mechanisms of denial used by the nuclear industry and by government scientists and bureaucrats to obscure twentieth-century nuclear colonialism include (1) denying the harm done to the land and its people by downplaying the extent and consequences of lethal pollutions, (2) legitimating the use of particular regions for weapons testing, waste disposal, and war practice by representing the region as unproductive, useless, and a wasteland, (3) both ignoring and denying the existence of indigenous occupation and use of the land, (4) discrediting knowledge of pollution by local inhabitants, and (5) masking as a form of development use of the land for unrehabilitative practices, such as the "containment" of radionuclides in the form of nuclear waste. While such mechanisms of denial are not new, the toxic materials they seek to obscure are themselves so new to this earth as to defy familiar characterization.

The transuranic elements contain unique properties that lead to complex and problematic containment strategies. Transuranic elements are so unlike anything else that they are in a category of matter all their own. First, they do not exist "naturally" of this earth but are produced by the human splitting of the atom. In this sense (and not an essentialist sense), they are wholly "unnatural."[19] Second, this resource/waste (for it is both)[20] is a commodity/problem with the ability to alter the biological genetic structure of all living things, to mutate cells and cellular growth, to pro-

19. An essentialist sense of "the natural" posits a fundamental order to nature such that anything outside this order is "unnatural." A nonessentialist view of nature understands that what we see as "natural" is often socially constructed, which does not make it an abomination to the "natural" order of things. Much of nature is influenced and constructed by humans and can still be characterized as natural. The unnaturalness of the transuranic elements only refers to the fact that they—as elements—could never exist without human intervention.

20. The transuranic elements can be a "resource" because they are necessary for the production of nuclear energy (within a nuclear power plant). Because the transuranic elements (such as plutonium) are not completely "used up" in the production process, they also become waste. In fact they are made more toxic during the production process and therefore end up as an especially problematic waste.

duce energy in ways that it can power or obliterate whole cities. As such the transuranic elements' power is monumental. Their presence has forever changed our relationship with this planet, including our relationship with other humans and species living here. It is modern, or even postmodern, nature at its most spectacular and dangerous, and it is inextricably woven into the shroud of global governance as "security." The transuranic elements constitute the remnants of Cold War state power that, as waste, remain forever hot.

In sum, nuclear colonialism in the United States constitutes a peculiar sort of environmental violence deriving from its manifestation in vast desert areas, its association with the military, its execution in areas primarily occupied and used by indigenous groups and some marginalized non-indigines, and its deployment of transuranic materials, which have complex and unique characteristics.

The "Bull's Eye": A U.S. Case Study of Environmental Violence and Invisibility

The Scale of Operations

The Bull's Eye is an organizational plan first presented to the military establishment in 1993 by General Colin Powell to integrate the Southwest's high-tech weapons testing and evaluation centers into a single, massive, war-game theater for the twenty-first century (Aviation Week and Space Technology [AWST] 1994). General Powell succinctly describes the reason for the Bull's Eye in the following passage:

> An integrated test and evaluation range structure linking existing ranges across six Western states and supersonic areas off the California coast would provide a land, airspace and sea area to accommodate a large portion of our joint training, test and evaluation needs well into the next century. (*Report on the Roles, Missions, and the Armed Forces of the United States*, Chairman of the Joint Chiefs of Staff, February 1993)

Separate but not unrelated to the Bull's Eye is the Department of Energy's plan to reconfigure the U.S. nuclear weapons complex into a new and improved assembly of weapons research. Initially named "Complex 21" (for the twenty-first century), and later—for public relations purposes—renamed "Stockpile Stewardship," the nuclear weapons complex also appears to be reassembling in the U.S. Southwest. Placing these complexes together makes the Southwestern United States one of the

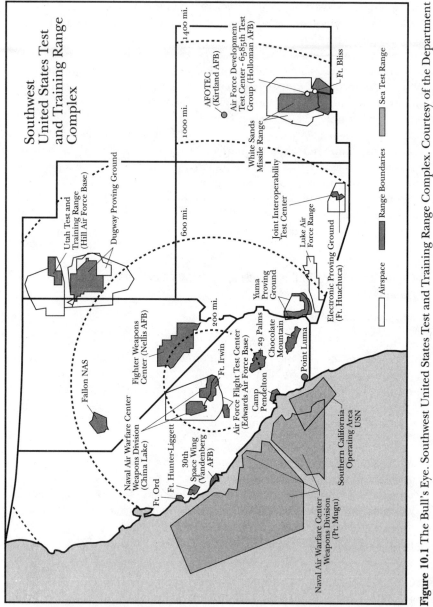

Figure 10.1 The Bull's Eye. Southwest United States Test and Training Range Complex. Courtesy of the Department of Defense.

most militarized and violent landscapes on the earth. This web of power is a stunning show of strength and potential violence. It also is a spectacular reconfiguration of western space. Yet hardly anyone in the general public has taken notice of this momentous transformation except small groups of government watchdogs[21] and the local inhabitants of the West's desert regions, including the many indigenous peoples concentrated in this part of the nation. The invisibility of the landscape to nonlocals and the invisible dangers of the radioactive contaminants in the region are magnified by the profound secrecy surrounding these massive militarized zones.

The *scale* of these secret operations in the desert can only be appreciated by adding up the acreage of ground and air space devoted to weapons and war game activities. Adjacent to the NTS, Nellis Air Force Test and Training Center occupies three million acres; China Lake occupies one million acres; NTS covers one million acres. Airspace above these military reservations and testing ranges is as much as twice the size of their land space. Together, the installations and training and testing arenas constitute a monumental consortium of military and nuclear power in the desert. (See Figure 10.2) This power can be deployed to summon enough force to control and threaten on a global scale. Its power stands in marked contrast to that of the small Indian tribes and relatively powerless communities within its sphere of control. Inextricably intertwined with science and technology, the weapons complex has turned the landscape into a vast weapons laboratory, a "technoscape" of violence. The cloak of scientific legitimacy makes the many violent practices within this landscape invisible, because high-tech science—even deployed for the development of weapons—is represented as objective.

The center of the Bull's Eye comprises three zones of immense violence and power. On its west is China Lake—the site of Gulf War weapons mastery and almost half a century of weapons research and development. This place was the site of the creation of over 75 percent of the "free world's" airborne weapons up to the late 1960s and 40 percent of the entire world's conventional weapons (China Lake Naval Weapons Center 1968). To the south of Death Valley are Edwards Air Force Test Center, Fort Irwin army base, and Twenty-Nine Palms Marine war game theater, as well as Ward Valley, a contested site for multiple state radioactive waste

---

21. In addition to indigenous groups, such as Citizen Alert Native American Project, a variety of persistent watchdog organizations monitor military activity in the desert. Interesting reports have been produced by Citizen Alert, the Rural Alliance for Military Accountability (RAMA) (based in Nevada), and the Progressive Alliance for Community Empowerment, Concerned Citizens for Nuclear Safety (based in New Mexico), among many others.

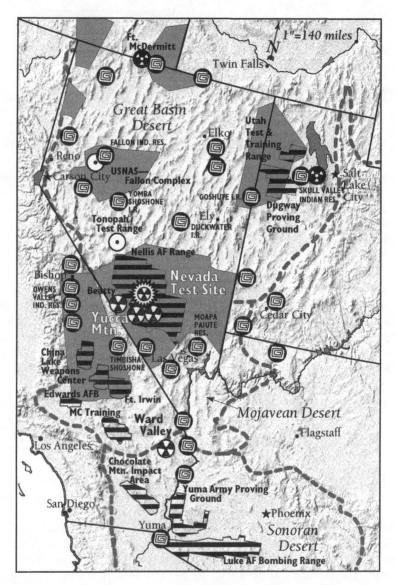

Figure 10.2 Detail of the Bull's Eye. Shaded areas here designate military air space and military operations areas. Such areas extend the zone of military occupation far beyond land holdings. Striped areas are Department of Defense and/or Department of Energy installations. Radiation signs indicate nuclear explosions, radioactive waste dumps, or nuclear research operations. The spirals indicate Native American reservations and colonies within the militarized zone. (Kuletz 1998. Map information compiled by Valerie Kuletz; cartography by Jared Dawson.)

dumping.[22] To the east is the most violently constructed/destructed land-scape in the United States and perhaps the world—Nellis Air Force base's "Fighter Weapons Center," the NTS, as well as Yucca Mountain. The NTS has been used for nearly 1,000 nuclear bomb blasts and numerous radiation dump sites. Yucca Mountain is the proposed home to 70,000 tons of high-level nuclear waste and a national monitored retrievable storage site for high-level nuclear waste.[23] These sites constitute only the center of the Bull's Eye. Concentric circles of violence dilate outward to include more nuclear research centers, weapons testing ranges, toxic waste dumping grounds, uranium mines, war theaters, and electronic and biological weapons warfare stations (Kuletz 1998).

Geography of Invisibility and Its People

The weapons research center called China Lake, near the center of the Bull's Eye, is situated within a vast desert space punctuated by high mountain ranges and low valleys. In the upper Mojave desert at the border of the Great Basin desert, China Lake lies next to the Panamint Valley, the Panamint Mountains, and a place that is not identified on the Bull's Eye but is at its very center, Death Valley National Park. Boundaries here (national, state, county, and institutional) are politically and socially constructed. An invisible line marks off the national sacrifice zone of China Lake from the national treasure of Death Valley. This line is arbitrary, but it works to construct the way most Euro-Americans see these places—one is perceived as desolate and the other as mystically beautiful. Although China Lake's Argus and Coso mountain ranges contain some of the most spectacular "natural wonders" of the Great Basin/Mojave deserts as well as

22. The Ward Valley area is home to three Indian tribes: the Chemehuevi, the Colorado Indian tribes, and the Fort Mojave Indian tribe. After years of struggle to keep their lands from being used as an interstate radioactive waste dump, Indian tribes and their supporters have achieved a hard-won battle to keep the Ward Valley region (at least for the time being) free of radioactive waste.

23. Because many commercial power plants have run out of room to store their high-level nuclear waste (and because they refuse to stop production, which creates high-level nuclear waste), they desperately need interim storage space to contain the wastes until a "permanent" deep geologic repository is built at Yucca Mountain, Nevada. The U.S. government has planned a series of what it calls Monitored Retrievable Storage Sites for this purpose.

Because scientists know that contamination of Yucca Mountain by radiation will occur once the waste is entombed, the Nuclear Regulatory Commission's new proposed (in June 1999) "Repository Licensing Rule" is meant to weaken radiation protection standards for the public and the environment by usurping the Environmental Protection Agency's legally mandated jurisdiction (under the Energy Policy Act of 1992) to set standards for the proposed Yucca Mountain repository. Nevadans in this region have been exposed to radioactivity from two other nearby sources: the NTS and the Beatty "low-level" radioactive waste dump.

important cultural sites for local Indians of the area,[24] to most Californians and out-of-state tourists, China Lake—not to mention its vast testing fields—is a blank spot on the map, a hidden and forbidden zone in the landscape. Neighboring Death Valley is relentlessly displayed as a place to explore and celebrate. The camera's "eye" provides a telling technology here. Having been granted access to the NTS area, the Yucca Mountain Project, and the China Lake testing ranges, I found that government clearance did not mean I could photograph any of it. The camera was forbidden—darkness or visual obscurity prevails. In Death Valley, on the other hand, everyone photographs the desert as they are meant to.

Although it is abundantly displayed, Death Valley also retains hidden worlds. At its center lies a group of invisible people indigenous to the area who call themselves the Timbisha band of the Western Shoshone Indians. Their presence contradicts and disrupts the signifying practices of the Department of Defense and the National Park Service in much the same way that Indian presence in general contradicts and challenges American ideologies of democracy, revealing the hypocrisy of its origin stories.[25]

Other people native to this region (along with local nonnatives) that question the presence of the Department of Defense and the Department of Energy here are the Western Shoshone and the Southern Paiute. Both of these Indian ethnic groups have a unique collective experience and memory of this environment that those for whom it is not a multigenerational homeland of long duration do not have. The Shoshone and Paiutes in particular have been associated with this landscape for at least 12,000 years (as opposed to 150 years for Euro-Americans). While not for all, for many Shoshone and Paiute this desert space and place is part of a complex web of economic, cultural, and spiritual survival as a distinct and identifiable people. Concerning their claim to this land, however, they remain invisible to the military and government forces that have colonized this area. In retaliation, the Western Shoshone actively protest the use of their lands for nuclear and military activities and refuse to assist the Department of

24. I am referring to places such as Coso Hot Springs, an important spiritual site for the Shoshone and Paiute Indians of the region. Also in the Coso range is the largest concentration of petroglyphs (Indian rock art) in the United States. Both Coso Hot Springs and the petroglyph canyons are now situated below the flight paths of test missiles (and missiles can indeed be seen embedded in the rock). The hot springs area is "harnessed" by the Navy for geothermal power production, which has transformed the landscape into an elaborate assembly of pipes and pumping machines.

25. As a Euro-American "origin story," the Manifest Destiny narrative—that God ordained the Euro-American settlers to expand and control the continent of North America from east to west—obfuscates the actual theft of indigenous lands that occurred in the origins of the United States of America. This theft is better explained as an act of what Marx called "original accumulation"—that which provides the means for capitalist investment to come into being as part of a new mode of production (i.e., capitalism).

Defense and the Department of Energy in federally mandated cultural resource studies.

Violent reconstruction of this expansive space into a sacrificial landscape (or an outdoor weapons laboratory, which amounts to the same thing) requires annihilation of the places within it. The little-known history of the NTS/Yucca Mountain region reveals an underlying Indian landscape composed of a web of specific meaningful *places* with paths intersecting and connecting water sites, hunting and gathering grounds, and ceremonial areas, living areas, and other places of Indian activity.[26] Because this history is not well known, the region is seen more as abstract space than as a web of meaningful places. Places are where people live; they are inhabited, nourishing, and they are sometimes sacred. Space, on the other hand, is abstract or "empty" and therefore more easily objectified. Expansive "open" spaces that are sparsely occupied, like deserts and oceans, are used both to hide in and to buffer possible contamination of the world outside the violent forbidden zones. Ironically, the atom—one of the smallest of spaces—requires expansive regions for "containment" when it is split. Unfortunately, there really is no containment. Because of inherent danger and harmfulness, weapons and lethal wastes need empty space. The NTS/Yucca Mountain region was never in recent history some empty space whose "purity" has been violated by the radionuclides in weapons. It was an inhabited landscape.[27]

For the Shoshone and Paiutes in the Bull's Eye, careful resource use patterns within the spaces they inhabited were essential for long-term, sustainable economies of survival. Nomadic desert Indians had to negotiate with, or accommodate themselves to, the land in order to survive. This contrasts to Euro-Americans' practices of forcing the landscape's resources to come to the people who claim them. Water and its large-scale relocation in this region, such as the colossal aqueduct channeling water from the now desiccated Owens Valley to the desert city of Los Angeles, provides a key example of the differences between the two systems of survival.[28] This is not to say that there aren't native peoples engaged in contemporary unsustainable practices. Rather, the existence of alternative knowledge and ecologi-

26. For an in-depth description of indigenous land use in this region, see Kuletz 1998.

27. My interest in seeing the social history of this "nature"/landscape is similar to Boal's accounts of the peat mines that have been mistaken for "pure" nature to the exclusion of the actual human constructions that have been part of that environment. (See Boal in this volume.) In the case of the NTS and native occupation of the region, it must be noted that I am not interested in equating natives with some kind of pure organic nature. The violence here is not one done to "pure" nature but to the integrated human/nature domain.

28. The *scale* of water development is what is at issue here. Some Shoshone and Paiutes also irrigated their crops (for example, the Owen's Valley Paiute-Shoshone group), but the scale of their development did not result in massive regional resource diversion and thus environmental devastation.

cal practices make possible a different relationship between humans and the desert environment, a relationship which many Western Shoshone people have demonstrated over successive generations through a seminomadic existence until the military occupied their lands.

Before the reorganization of desert space under colonial imperatives, in the Great Basin/Mojave desert region, native people historically moved around a great deal to harvest seasonally sown wild plant resources, to hunt game, or to escape oppressive weather patterns (leaving the valleys for the mountains in summer and returning to the warmth of the valleys in winter). Historically, a Western Shoshone man or woman, or a Southern Paiute man or woman, could not survive in the desert without moving about in it. The logic of desert space requires movement. Like many rural societies in other parts of the world, indigenous people in the Great Basin negotiated space with the seasons. Space was thus constructed in time—by the seasons. The large wide-open spaces of the desert were inhabited in cyclical fashion. Cyclical knowledge and experience about the environment helped inform locals of the ebbs and flows of resources that, perhaps, underlie inherently sustainable practices.

When these vast spaces are fenced off, as they have been in the Bull's Eye region, and when the native peoples are therefore fenced in (or fenced out)—when movement is curtailed—it destroys this logic, making another logic necessary for survival. That other logic is to force the desert to "bloom" with massive water schemes to produce food and provide inhabitable, static living spaces. In the Southwest these monumental irrigation projects are doomed, eventually, to failure.[29] Another possibility, another logic is simply to use that space for the radioactive waste of the nuclear era's "metropoli," or to use it as a vast "outdoor laboratory," as testing ranges for the weapons of war. To do this, it is necessary to legitimate its use for these purposes in some way. The U.S. government has legitimated the bombing of this landscape by simply claiming that the land was *already* a wasteland. As one Department of Defense representative put it: "The land was cheap because it really wasn't much good for anything but gunnery practice—you could bomb it into oblivion and never notice the difference" (Skinner 1994: 52). Bolstering this assumption is the environmental science classification of the desert as low on the "productivity" register of ecosystems. When many of the inhabitants also are seen to be part of the "low-use segment of the population," as was noted in one government document in reference to those living downwind from nuclear test-

29. Ground water, one of the most important water sources in the arid West, is not an endless resource. Due to overpopulation, most of the Southwest's large regional aquifers are quickly becoming depleted. The redirecting and damming of the West's great rivers will also prove inadequate with the continued growth of western mega-cities such as Phoenix and Las Vegas.

ing, making the landscape into a sacrifice zone isn't hard to do at all. Such perceptions of the desert and its people are in marked contrast to those of the Shoshone and Paiute.

The U.S. Government began using the desert as a bombing field in the lower Great Basin desert in the 1950s, when, for greater control over its weapons program, the Department of Energy and the Department of Defense code named the NTS region "Nutmeg" and moved its nuclear weapons testing program (until then located in the South Pacific) in to the U.S.'s internal colony known as Nevada.[30] To do this, they had to remove all Western Shoshone and Southern Paiute Indians from the area, an area that is traditional native land and, today, legally Western Shoshone land.[31] As the Nevadans say, the U.S. government simply replaced one peripheral colony (external: the Marshall Islands) in the South Pacific arena with another (internal: Nevada) in its own backyard. As the Western Shoshone say, this is when they became the most bombed nation on the earth.

Invisible Radionuclides

Radiation violence is sometimes visible and immediate, sometimes dramatic and terrifying. Most often it is invisible. The victim of radiation contamination doesn't initially feel it or see it until it is too late. Its violence to the bodies of both humans and non-humans is profound. It invades cells, producing abnormal cellular growth (cancer). It interferes with genetic structure, producing mutations and extreme deformities, and it causes a variety of reproductive failures including miscarriages and sterility. It is relatively easy for institutions responsible for the release of radioactive contaminants to hide it because it often takes time for the effects to reveal themselves. This time gap has been used by the United States and other governments to deny causal links between cancer (occurring ten to twenty years hence) or deformities (which occur in subsequent generations) and radioactive contamination.

Today, however, some accountability has begun to emerge. For example, the 1997 National Cancer Institute statistical report on cancers among "downwinders" (those living downwind from atmospheric nuclear testing on the NTS) has shown that causal links exist (National Cancer Institute [NCI] 1997). The study reveals the mostly (though not exclusively) rural

---

30. Because nearly 90 percent of Nevada is owned by the federal government and because much of that acreage has been used for destructive purposes (weapons testing and waste dumping), many Nevadans see their state as an internal colony to the United States. The period that saw the establishment of the Nevada Test Site also saw the creation of the science city, China Lake, in eastern California, as well other installations of the area.

31. For a description of Shoshone ownership of the Yucca Mountain/NTS area, see the discussion of the Treaty of Ruby Valley in Kuletz 1998: 148–49.

counties where people were contaminated by fallout from the period of aboveground nuclear testing (totaling 120 atmospheric bombs) conducted at the NTS between 1951 and 1963. Underground testing continued until 1992, and 120 secret detonations also occurred in various parts of the Western United States. The NCI study shows that thyroid cancer has been particularly high in the northern Great Plains region (Colorado, Idaho, Montana, South Dakota, and Utah) where wind patterns spread airborne radioactive contaminants to far-flung victims. These people were never told of the danger, although the danger was known. Such secrecy constitutes another violent act. Although the NCI study was completed in 1994, it was kept secret by the government for fear that the public would respond with mass hysteria and because of the report's political and legal implications (in the form of potentially expensive lawsuits). Contamination was highest for people, especially children, who consumed milk from animals with elevated concentrations of radionuclides in their bodies. The animals had consumed contaminated grasses.[32]

Absent from this latest NCI research program were studies of food consumption patterns and living conditions that differed from those of Euro-Americans, such as those found among Native Americans. Contemporary Indian people often have a more direct association with water supplies and consume a greater diversity of wild game. They eat more of the animal and waste less of it than Euro-Americans and thus are more susceptible to higher concentrations of radioactive contaminants. One might think of this as a problem of invisibility within invisibility. Radionuclides are hard to detect because they are already invisible entities and even harder to detect when associated with people whose bodies and habits are invisible to Euro-American policy-makers and scientists. In the case of the Bull's Eye, where Indian colonies are included in the nuclear fallout zone, there have been no adequate epidemiological studies done on native communities, except those attempted by Native people themselves.

Developing Violence: Militarized Economies of the State and Nuclear Waste as a Development Option

Sacrificial Landscapes as Development Options

Today, both indigenous and nonindigenous peoples in these deterritorialized lands (lands that have been used for nuclear and conventional weapons testing, uranium mining, or nuclear weapons production) are

---

32. This concentration down the food chain is known as "magnification."

faced with the possibility of what I call "second-order nuclearism." This is "nuclearism" linked to development options for nuclear or toxic waste containment.[33] Seven regional examples illustrate my claim: (1) U.S. native lands have been targeted for temporary monitored retrievable storage sites (MRS for high-level nuclear waste. Some tribes that are already surrounded by toxic waste and biological weapons stations as well as chemical weapons storage and incineration, are seriously considering the option of storing high-level nuclear waste.[34] (2) The French Polynesian, or Tahitian Island region is now being considered (by some French Parliamentarians) for a nuclear waste dump (specifically the atolls of Moruroa and Fangataufa, which were previously used for nuclear weapons testing). Because the French nuclear testing program significantly bolstered the regional economy, as it pulls out it leaves economic decline in its wake.[35] Taking in nuclear waste thus becomes a tempting development option for a severely depressed economy. Unfortunately, more revenue can be gained from nuclear waste than from traditional development options, such as growing vanilla bean or producing scented oils from Tahitian flowers.[36] (3) The Marshall Islands in Micronesia (specifically Bikini but also other previously irradiated islands used for nuclear testing) have been targeted repeatedly to harbor nuclear and toxic wastes, as well as the incineration of chemical weapons, by nuclear waste industries from the United States and other

33. For purposes of clarity I use the term "second-order nuclearism." However, many of these rural and suburbanized areas support what could be thought of as third- and fourth-order devastation because they also are used as the dumping grounds for chemical weapons, hazardous wastes, as well as for municipal wastes trucked in from afar. (For details on the many abuses to which these regions are made to submit see Kuletz 1998.)

34. Examples of native reservations that are or have been targeted for Monitored Retrievable Storage Site facilities are those of the Mescalero Apache in New Mexico, the Fort McDermitt Paiute-Shoshone tribe at the border of Nevada and Oregon, and the Skull Valley Goshute tribe in Utah. The Skull Valley Goshutes are the tribe surrounded by chemical weapons incineration and other forms of toxic waste. Similarly, the Mescalero Apache reservation is near the Waste Isolation Pilot Plant (WIPP), which is the U.S. military's deep geologic repository for transuranic (plutonium-contaminated) wastes.

35. For instance, in 1995 France was responsible for injecting $1.25 million into the economy. This is more than a third of the entire gross national product. For more on the impact of nuclear testing regimes in the Pacific, see Firth 1997.

"The French tested at Moruroa and Fangataufa from 1966 to 1992, in the atmosphere until 1975, and then underground. Amid intense regional and global opposition, the French conducted a final series of nuclear explosions in 1995 and 1996." (*The Cambridge History of the Pacific Islanders*, p. 324.)

36. There is strong opposition to such possible nuclear dumping future scenarios. Hiti Tau is a Tahitian nongovernmental organization (NGO) that opposes the nuclear tests conducted in the Tahitian region and supporting Maohi (the indigenous name for Tahitians) community development, such as vanilla bean production. The organization has—with the assistance of the Christian World Service—disseminated information about their efforts through a video titled "Hiti Tau: Building a New Nation."

countries. Such proposals have been proffered even as islanders attempt to repopulate the areas from which people had been removed for nuclear testing.[37] In their search for development options, Bikinians (with the help of the U.S. National Park Service) also have initiated plans for a nuclear theme park. (4) The Grants Uranium Belt in the Four Corners area of the American West—home to Pueblo and Navajo Indians—is witnessing a new generation of uranium mining. Native American economies in these areas during the Cold War were altered from pastoral to industrial-extractive to provide uranium for weapons development and commercial nuclear fuel. These native lands are thus scarred by massive uranium mines and tailings. Such toxic extractive industries make it difficult for local communities to attract other forms of development.[38] (5) Similarly, a new wave of uranium development is starting in western Australian Aborigine territory (a region previously used for both uranium mining and nuclear testing).[39] (6) In 1998 the U.S. government asked Australia if it could use the old Australian nuclear testing region (aboriginal territory in which the United States and Great Britain tested their nuclear weapons) as an international dumping ground for nuclear waste. (7) The NTS—homeland of Southern Paiutes and Western Shoshone—is scheduled to store high-level nuclear waste (from commercial and military sources) at the Yucca Mountain deep geo-logic repository (which will harbor 70,000 tons of high-level nuclear waste). Additionally, temporary facilities will be developed in the region for short-term aboveground storage of nuclear waste.

These cases illustrate "development options" (some of which are moving

37. To live on Bikini (where the United States tested twenty-three nuclear weapons) the Bikinians will have to go to great lengths to avoid becoming contaminated by radioactive elements. As a response to living in exile from their homeland, in the 1970s Bikinians attempted to move back to the atoll, but some became contaminated by caesium in the soil (ingestion of high levels of radioactivity occurred from eating and drinking local coconuts), forcing the entire community to evacuate the island. To avoid this in the late 1990s, they have to scrape away all topsoil from around homes and crop regions and replace it with crushed coral to try to filter out radioactive contaminants. They also need to rely on canned and imported foods. Their determination to return to their "homeland" attests to the power of place and its deep connections to identity and cultural survival felt by the Bikinians.

For the time being, the Bikinians have rejected offers to use nuclear waste as a form of development. However, my fieldwork in Micronesia has shown that this position could easily change in the future.

38. During the Cold War period, there were also uranium mining-related accidents that, although not publicized in the national press, were extremely serious. For example, in 1979 the United Nuclear Corporation's tailings dam burst at Church Rock, New Mexico, spilling 100 million gallons of radioactive water into the Rio Puerco on the Navajo reservation. This was only one of many such accidents to contaminate local water supplies.

39. The specific site for this is the mine at Jabiluka (operated by Energy Resources of Australia). Renewed mining is being hotly contested by indigenous people living in the area.

forward, some of which are under consideration) for land that has previously suffered the violence of nuclear and warfare activities of various kinds. These "options" are offered by military weapons programs, international power companies, and radioactive waste containment programs controlled by federal, state government, and independent industries—all of which are significant defense and energy production players in the global arena. What are the options for survival—ask the local, rural, and often indigenous people—once the land has been contaminated? One answer seems to be yet another layer of sacrifice, of violence, now masked as development.

In most of these scenarios, there are those within the affected communities who support such development schemes. Not all indigenous people or local rural groups are against "second-order nuclearism." However, there are just as many, if not more, who do not accept this option. The result is often tremendous conflict within tribal and non-tribal rural communities. Whether these options are supported or opposed is not the point. What must be seen is that a second wave of violence is legitimated upon the first. If the land is contaminated, promoters say, why not make money off it? The problem is that human lives continue to be at stake.

Political Economy of Military Transuranic Violence: Back to the Bull's Eye

The violent construction of a place like the Bull's Eye in the American West (which contains both "conventional" and nuclear testing zones) is certainly part of both the U.S. national and a global political economy. As critical Cold War analysts have shown, weapons research, production, and testing is a self-perpetuating economy. The cost of the nuclear weapons complex alone is so large that it not only constitutes a massive outlay of expenditures for the United States but also acts as a creator of jobs and a market for goods that maintains its own economic force. It is akin to a mountain creating its own weather patterns. For example, as noted in a recent Brookings Institute report: "Since 1940, the United States has spent $5.8 trillion on nuclear weapons programs, more than on any single program except Social Security" (Pincus 1998: A02). As such, nuclear weapons are part of our economic system, our political system, and—because it requires a high level of scientific expertise—our knowledge system as well. In short, they are part of American culture.

Our military and scientific agendas were fused in the symbiotic coupling between post-World War II capitalism and the culture of fear and violence created as a part of the Cold War. Now that the Cold War is "over," we cannot so easily untangle science from militarism and fear. The nuclear power industry and the military establishment are intertwined in various ways, for instance, in the realm of international non-proliferation policy. To maintain control over materials that have the potential to assist in nuclear weapons production, the U.S. government agrees to take back large quantities of the high-level nuclear waste produced by countries that have initiated their nuclear energy programs with U.S. financial and technical support.[40] The toxic waste ends up, at least in part, within the center of the Bull's Eye—in Western Shoshone/Southern Paiute territory at Yucca Mountain.

Contributing to our paralysis within the nuclear web is the disintegration of the comprehensive nuclear test ban treaty, which appears to be dissolving at the same time as it's being formed. It has been destroyed less by India and Pakistan's recent dangerous game of tit-for-tat than by the refusal of the big nuclear powers (particularly the United States) to lay down their arms.[41] In addition, the problem of long-term (read 240,000 years) future storage for this past half-century's nuclear waste stream must be added to the cost of "nuclearism." All together, with links between weapons production, power generation, waste containment, and international policy, the Bull's Eye region is at the heart of a militarized economy at odds with any notion of sustainable economic development that might be proposed by Indians or other people living within its center.

Far from the Western Shoshone vision of a sustainable desert economy within the Bull's Eye is the enterprise known as the Yucca Mountain Project. When the Yucca Mountain Project opens in the next decade,[42] the Department of Energy will be transporting 70,000 tons of high-level nuclear waste from around the country into the Bull's Eye, the center of which is Yucca Mountain. High-level radioactive waste from the nation's nuclear power plants (and some military radioactive waste) will be moved across prairies, through cities, and over mountains to its temporary destination— a holding station on the NTS—to be stored aboveground until the deep geologic repository is ready to accept the waste. Radioactive waste from countries outside the United States will also be sent to Yucca Mountain in accordance with international policies on non-proliferation of nuclear

40. Analyses of the relationship between U.S. commercial policies regarding nuclear technology and power and U.S. nonproliferation policy have been developed by the Western States Legal Foundation, Oakland, California.

41. Although nuclear arsenals have been reduced, it is partly because the major nuclear powers have not accepted total abolition that other previously non-nuclear nations such as Pakistan have rejected treaty requests that they not develop their own nuclear weapons programs.

42. Yucca Mountain is set to open in 2010. There is little doubt that anything will stop this from happening. The U.S. government has been working on the site (studying it and, more recently, constructing it) for the past thirteen years. Billions of dollars have been invested, and no other site is being considered.

weapons. So the Bull's Eye that is Yucca Mountain, which at first glance appears to be a backcountry location far out on the periphery, is in fact a mecca for nuclear waste—pulling the global into the local.

Surrounding the mountain, on the periphery of power, Native Americans watch the activities of the nuclear waste project from their colonies and reservations.[43] Because they have not forgotten what radionuclides can do to human bodies, they hold ceremonial gatherings of protest on the northwestern flank of Yucca Mountain as Yucca Mountain Project engineers scurry about the monumental waste hole they are digging in the mountain's southeastern flank. The global arena of nuclear waste and local Nevada outback collapse into one here at the Bull's Eye of Yucca Mountain—the target of massive amounts of virtually unending violence produced by the transuranic elements. It is important to remember that Yucca Mountain is situated partially within the NTS Site, which makes it a domain of "second-order nuclearism."

Containing the Uncontainable

Waste containment poses as a development solution for the spaces for which we cannot find profitable use. Environmental degradation of the most severe kind, such as that associated with nuclear waste, is a development scheme in this desert domain. The "solutions" that a place like Yucca Mountain promises for the problem of nuclear waste are fantasies of the most dangerous kind.

The question here concerns development or the very idea of development. How do we understand this strange kind of development—one that's about as far from "sustainable" as one can get and masked by vast space, by military secrecy, by scientific cloaks of "objectivity"?[44] How can we understand development as total destruction of the local environment—destruction that is virtually forever in human terms (240,000 years)—with no possibility of rehabilitation (since the dumping grounds can never be decontaminated), and where the development scheme remains flawed from the very beginning? We have no reliable means of keeping radionuclides contained within the earth (Kuletz 1998). The U.S. government persists in a fantasy of control within a context of crisis. It is a crisis because

43. Although not yet open, the Yucca Mountain Project is a massive undertaking of long standing, so there is much to watch and to protest. As noted earlier, Western Shoshone and Southern Paiute tribes live surrounding the affected area.

44. The Yucca Mountain Project is represented by the Department of Energy as a premier science project. It certainly is a scientific endeavor but its "objectivity" is seriously compromised by the urgency of the nuclear waste crisis and the project's location on the Nevada Nuclear Test Site, which is guarded by armed personnel.

there is no more room at existing temporary sites and because the holding casks for nuclear wastes and cooling ponds for hot nuclear rods are leaking. Yet production of the waste continues.

In spite of the reality that nuclear waste cannot be contained, the illusion or simulation of containment remains a form of development because some people will reap economic benefits. It is arguably worse than any other form of harmful development because it is forever. The land used can never be rehabilitated. Like many development schemes, it relies on shortsightedness, which is how some locals get pulled into the state's or the large corporation's agenda to construct a repository. It's a get-rich-quick scheme for some locals and even some tribes, the harms of which promise to affect many future generations. The reasons for this kind of local acceptance go beyond individual greed, although there is that. Many of these tribes are already surrounded by toxic waste, which keeps any other developers from considering their lands for nontoxic development. Other tribes are extremely poor and are promised schools, hospitals, roads, educational programs, and so forth for accepting radioactive waste. Despite this, I have found from my own field experience that most targeted tribes and their individual members are against the use of their reservations for toxic waste. Interestingly, the popular press (along with many academics) finds it more interesting to pay attention to those who accept the waste than to those actively working against it, even though those against it are far greater in number.

The Cold War/post–Cold War military and nuclear power economy produces opportunities for government contractors. Large territories are needed to do business in this economic sector—massive testing ranges for scientists to test and develop new weapons technologies (a form of research that produces its own large-scale waste stream) and large territories for toxic waste enterprises. "Undesirable" land, used previously to support relocated Indian tribes or deemed so unusable that Indians were allowed to inhabit it, has become particularly desirable to toxic waste business concerns. What is desired for the development of waste storage enterprises is sacrificial land, although such land is a commodity that has its limits. If we keep using nuclear power, we will run out of room to store the wastes. As noted by nuclear physicist Arjun Makhijani, "Every four or five years we're making about as much plutonium in the civil sector as we did during the whole Cold War" (Makhijani and Salesks 1992). Although exact numbers vary, the amount of plutonium generated to date is roughly 270 metric tons of military weapons-grade plutonium. Plutonium from the commercial stockpile from nuclear reactors has now reached 930 metric tons. By 2005 it will have increased to 2,130 tons. It takes only 10 micrograms of plutonium to induce cancer in humans, and only several grams of plutonium can kill thousands of people (Schrader-Frashette 1993).[45]

State-Sanctioned Violence Masked as Development

The end result of nuclear waste containment as negative development is the creation of sacrificial land and sacrifice of human and nonhuman lives and well-being because "safe" storage is currently impossible. The environmental violence committed in the name of environmental safety is invisible, like the landscapes in which radioactive waste is interred. Also invisible are the links between weapons, waste, and power generation, which continue because all three aspects are forms of development. By showing their linkages and who is harmed in the process, their inherent contradictions—their violent and dangerous unsustainability—are revealed.

The Cold War may be over, but its economy isn't. The United States may have reduced the size of its armed forces and closed a few military bases, but the military–industrial–scientific complex remains a foundational pillar of its economy. It cannot unravel the knot without, it fears, unraveling its base of survival—not just political survival but economic. All nations— not just the United States or other "northern" powers—continue to expend inordinate portions of their wealth on the development, maintenance, and expansion of their military forces. Certainly those who suffer most are the poor (often women and children) in Third World nations with failing economies—economies that cut social welfare first when succumbing to austerity measures imposed on them by international monetary agents of capitalism, such as the World Bank and the International Monetary Fund. Their military expenditures do not get cut because they feel compelled to secure some place, however small, in the global militarized struggles for power. This, of course, is related to the continuing polarization of the world since the 1960s; differentials between the poorest and the richest countries have increased more than 20 percent. Statistics such as these, as Watts and others have pointed out, undercut a term like "globalization," which implies some kind of unifying order, some kind of equanimity (Johnston, Taylor, and Watts 1995).

But the United States has its own periphery (its own Third World) at its center too—a contradiction at the very heart of its self-construction as a powerful "democratic nation," its first and never-resolved contradiction. The periphery at its center, the contradiction of its own doing that negates

45. The example of how only several grams of plutonium can kill thousands of people comes from Shrader-Frachette's (1991) hypothetical example, which considers the consequences of dispersing plutonium through a ventilation system.

all that it sees itself standing for is the persistence of Indian bodies with Indian identities (however complex those identities might be). Nuclear colonialism is inconceivable (invisible) because if we see it—actually see it— the power relations within American democracy are exposed. Native people, in all their diversity, have never gone away. Those from many different tribes and nations see themselves as internal colonies and, in the American West in particular, as occupied people surrounded by military installations. The Western Shoshone and Southern Paiutes in particular see themselves as now struggling against nuclear colonialism marked by radioactive waste. Like nineteenth-century pioneering and mid-twentieth-century nuclear testing regimes, violence is once again played out on Indian bodies, as well as on any other bodies who also happen to inhabit Indian country.

Two crucial issues concern nuclear waste storage as development. First, this is a state-sanctioned act of violence on the local community immediately and the general population in the long term. Second, this violence results not from some Malthusian necessity but from the self-perpetuating logic of a militarized economy, by those individuals and companies who benefit (in the short term) from it, companies such as General Electric, Du Pont, Westinghouse, and others. To a lesser extent, short-term proponents also include some of those in the local communities whose interests are motivated by profit at the expense of future generations.

Other energy resources could and should be developed. The violence of the nuclear waste dump is not some natural outcome resulting from limited power resources—which is what some might infer as the industrial world recognizes that its oil reserves are limited. Countries like the United States historically chose nuclear power because it was tied to a military economy. This particularly violent turn, however, was of its own making. It could have been avoided had the militarized economy been kept separate from the commercial civilian sector.[46] Those who are paying the price for nuclear power—those now subject to the violence of radionuclides—are the ones Americans need to see if they are to make this immense violence visible to themselves because radiation knows no political or class or ethnic boundaries. In the end, the Bull's Eye becomes the ironic representation of the self-destruction of the centers of Cold War power and violence.

---

46. Because of the nature of nuclear waste, however, this separation between commercial nuclear power and military nuclear weapons can never occur. Although there are easier ways to produce nuclear bomb materials, commercial nuclear power produces some of the key ingredients for nuclear bombs.

11

Violence, Environment, and Industrial Shrimp Farming

Susan C. Stonich and Peter Vandergeest

I say that those who eat shrimp—and only the rich people from the industrialized countries eat shrimp—I say that they are eating at the same time the blood, sweat and livelihood of the poor people of the Third World.

Banka Behary Das, Indian activist, quoted in (Ahmed 1998)[1]

The expansion of industrial shrimp farming has provoked some of the most contentious environmental and social justice debates currently occurring in Asia, Latin America, and Africa. Conflicts among resource users in tropical coastal areas impacted by industrial shrimp farming at times have escalated to violent confrontations—between shrimp farmers and local people, within local communities, and among shrimp farmers themselves. This chapter explores the complex linkages between violence and the environment stemming from the recent expansion of industrial shrimp farming. We begin with two stories, one from Thailand and the other from Honduras, that illustrate how the general association of shrimp farming with violence can take diverse forms depending on the site-specific agrarian context into which the shrimp farming industry moves.

Our argument will be developed in three parts. First, we review examples of violence emanating from shrimp farming and show that the characteristics of industrial shrimp farming create situations of enormous tension and opportunities for violence. Second, we move to a comparison of Thailand and Honduras to show that the specific forms of violence that emerge depend on local agrarian structures and historically based cultures of resis-

---

1. This quote is from a recent report by Faris Ahmed entitled *In Defense of Land and Livelihood: Coastal Communities and the Shrimp Industry in Asia* published by CUSO, the Consumers' Association of Penang, Inter Pares, and the Sierra Club of Canada. Using photographs, stories, and testimonials, Ahmed documents the efforts of fishers and farmers in India, Bangladesh, Thailand, and Malaysia against the spread of industrial shrimp farming.

tance. Shrimp farming in Honduras has provoked open and well-organized resistance, but in Thailand most violence involves either problems
with endemic theft or the repression of unorganized resistance. We finish
the chapter with a few comments on the visibility of different forms of violence in national and international fora and the implications of different
levels of visibility for our analysis of environmental violence.

Stories of Shrimp and Violence

When I (Vandergeest) go to Southern Thailand, I usually visit Jaroon Kanjanapan and his family—I stayed with this family during Ph.D. research ten
years ago, and Jaroon continues to be my primary assistant and informant
on shrimp farming in this area. In October 1998 I arrived just as a family
crisis erupted. Jaroon's younger half-brother had been accused of murder,
and he was hiding from the police. The brother was operating a small
shrimp farm on a former contract-farming scheme with two of his other
half-brothers (not related to Jaroon). Just before their most recent harvest,
a thief had taken some of their shrimp, and, partly as a result, their harvest
was much less than it should have been—just 1,400 kilograms for a 2.5 rai
(6.65 hectares) pond, worth about U.S. $8,000. Given the health of the
shrimp, the harvest should have been closer to 2,500 kilograms. The
brothers believed they knew the identity of the thief—another shrimp
farmer nearby was reputedly stealing shrimp from many farmers in the
area. It is not clear what happened next, but, according to Jaroon, the two
older brothers found the thief at his pond and shot and killed him. The father of the thief immediately reported to the police that all three brothers
had killed his son, initiating the police search.

The usual means of resolving this kind of violence in southern Thailand
would be for the killers to agree, through a mediator, to pay a compensation to the family of the victim. The police, the mediator, and other involved persons would generally receive a portion of the payment. But in
this case the father was asking for a million baht (almost U.S. $30,000),
which was much inflated compared to what was typical in the area prior to
the shrimp farm "rush." The brothers considered the sum unreasonable,
and they were, in any case, unable to pay. Failure to pay, however, could result in a twenty-year jail sentence if the police caught them. When I left,
the brothers were still in hiding, and there was talk of killing the thief's father as a way of dealing with his compensation demands.

During a trip to southern Honduras in 1993, I (Stonich) was taken to a
relatively remote area along the Gulf of Fonseca by the president of the
grassroots, nongovernmental organization by the name of The Committee for Defense and Development of the Flora and Fauna of the Gulf of

Fonseca (CODDEFFAGOLF) to witness the attempted removal of an elderly couple from their home by the owner of a new shrimp farm. For more than forty years, Andina and Fausto had lived in a house built of mangroves and thatched with palm fronds located at the mouth of an estuary that fed the gulf. Like many local families, every day Fausto captured fin fish, shellfish, and mature shrimp for sale in local markets from his small dugout canoe, while Andina collected crabs, mollusks, animals, wood, honey, and other items from the surrounding wetlands. The day before my visit, a member of the Honduran elite with ties to the military had begun construction of a shrimp farm in the area surrounding the elderly couple's home. He had acquired the land through a highly subsidized government concession. Earth-moving equipment had been brought in, and construction of a large shrimp pond that hugged both the estuary and the coastline had begun. By the time of my visit, the elderly couple's home and boat were completely isolated—an islet surrounded by a shrimp pond—completely cutting off access to the sea and the land. By early morning on the day of my visit, at least fifty members of CODDEFFAGOLF had gathered near the site carrying signs and protesting the dislocation of the couple from their long-standing home. The owner of the farm, in return, had brought in his own supporters, including a group of hired thugs and a few soldiers dressed in uniform who surrounded the construction site and attempted to intimidate the protestors. As the protestors yelled, *Basta! Basta!* (Enough! Enough!), the hired guns looked on ominously. It seemed clear to me that if the couple chose not to leave, they would be forcibly evicted. Finally after several hours, he elderly couple decided to leave their home quietly—out of fear and desperation. The members of CODDEFFAGOLF, as best they could, gathered up the couple's belongings and took them away. A few days later, the new farm building constructed by the shrimp farm owner, along with the equipment it enclosed, was mysteriously burnt.

Most observers knowledgeable about the industry are aware that shrimp farming frequently is associated with violence. Often this involves the use of violence by incoming shrimp farmers against local villagers or other opponents of shrimp farming. Sometimes it involves the use of violence by local people affected by shrimp farming against shrimp farms. This is the most visible and politicized type of violence associated with shrimp farming; it is therefore often reported in the media, discussed by scholars, and protested by activists. In contrast, villagers in Southern Thailand agree that the establishment of shrimp farming is associated with an increase in violence, but the kind of violence that they talk about is related to theft or other problems associated with a sudden influx of money, such as gambling. Violence between shrimp farmers and their opponents is important but secondary. This kind of violence is less visible and politicized, but for people living in shrimp farming areas in Thailand, it is of great concern and a key motivation for village-level opposition to the expansion of shrimp farming.

Industrial Shrimp Farming, Environment, and Livelihood Security

Aquaculture frequently is hailed as the "Blue Revolution"—a critical source of high quality animal protein, essential to feed growing human populations as a replacement for stagnating or declining marine stocks (Bardach 1997). According to the doomsday green security scenario discussed in the introduction of this book, environmental violence occurs where population increase leads to resource depletion and thus conflict over increasingly scarce resources. In the optimistic scenario, aquaculture replaces declining marine resources and thus mitigates the potential for violence due to resource scarcity. In this section, we review evidence that links shrimp farming to an increase in violence, leading us to question the simplistic links between population increase, resource depletion, and violence. We will argue that shrimp farming is associated with violence for a set of complex reasons: most obviously, because its externalities degrade coastal resources; but more importantly, because it makes coastal resources more valuable and desirable, and because shrimp is a high-value, portable commodity susceptible to violent appropriation.

During the 1990s, total production of farmed shrimp has grown at a faster rate than any other aquacultural product worldwide. In 1998, world production of cultured shrimp was an estimated 737,200 metric tons, which constituted about 30 percent of the total amount of shrimp produced globally through both capture fisheries and culture (Rosenberry 1998). Approximately 72 percent of cultured shrimp are raised in Asia, and the rest come primarily from Latin America. Cultivated shrimp are the largest consumers of commercial aquacultural feeds and account for the largest number of companies involved in aquaculture (Ratafia 1995). Although 99 percent of cultured shrimp are raised in the Third World, virtually all are exported to industrial countries, principally to the United States, Europe, and Japan.

Industrial aquaculture emphasizes the cultivation of high-value, carnivorous species destined for market in industrial nations, not the nutritional needs of the poor. To produce this high-value commodity, industrial aquaculture both encloses and degrades common pool resources vital for the livelihoods of the rural poor. This is particularly true of shrimp farming—the cultivation of shrimp in brackish water ponds in tropical coastal zones of Asia, Latin America, and Africa. Although shrimp aquaculture proponents in international aid organizations emphasize goals such as broadening the economic bases of coastal areas, generating local employment, and enhancing food security, in practice these rural development goals are subordinated to the overarching objectives of shrimp farming (Bailey 1997), such as profits for producers and input suppliers and export earnings for national treasuries. The optimism prevalent in organizations like the Food and Agriculture Organization of the United Nations (FAO) for the potential of aquaculture in overcoming marine resource degradation has been undermined by social dislocation, ecological change, and environmental destruction.

Shrimp farming usually has located in one of two types of zones: first, in coastal common pool resource zones managed by the state or communally at the local level, and second, near canals or rivers on privately owned agricultural land. In coastal zones, the most serious ecological threats include the destruction of mangrove and other coastal ecosystems associated with the construction of shrimp ponds and related infrastructure, pollution from pond wastes, and disruption of hydrological systems (Barraclough and Stitch 1996). Natural resources from coastal ecosystems traditionally have been critically important to the subsistence and commercial economic strategies of the rural poor—providing food, medicine, shelter, fuel wood, and marketable commodities (Kunstadter, Bird, and Sabhasri 1986). Not surprisingly, the social consequences of shrimp aquaculture have become increasingly contentious. They encompass issues of social equity; loss of goods and services from coastal ecosystems; property and use rights; spiraling land costs; competition for credit, land, and other resources; and the concomitant marginalization of small producers (Bailey and Skladany 1991; Cruz-Torres 1992; Cruz-Torres 1996; Primavera 1991; Primavera 1993; Primavera 1996; Flaherty and Karnjanakesorn 1995; Bailey, Jentoft, and Sinclair 1996).

At the heart of the conflicts stemming from industrial shrimp farming in coastal zones is the enclosure and loss of common pool resources. Coastal zones are frequently claimed as state land but are at the same time claimed and used by local villagers under communal property practices. As long as coastal zones were viewed as relatively worthless, governments allowed coastal peoples to have informal access. Women, children, and men have hunted, fished, and collected wild resources for food, medicine, and construction materials. Small plots of agricultural cultigens (corn, rice, millet, etc.) have provided crops for domestic consumption and for sale in local markets.

The introduction of industrial shrimp farming transforms what had been multiple use/multiple user areas into privately owned, single purpose, high-value resources (Bailey 1988). Although the enclosure and loss of coastal resources are currently the most prominent impacts of industrial shrimp farming, shrimp farming in coastal zones produces a series of other environmental effects that undermine rural livelihoods. Artisanal fishers from Honduras to India report the depletion of catches after the introduction of shrimp farms. Nutrients in shrimp farm effluents have put Songkla Lake, a large lagoon connected to the Gulf of Thailand in Southern Thailand, at the verge of eutrophication, threatening the livelihoods of thousands of small fishers around the lake (Vandergeest, Flaherty, and Miller 1999b). Shrimp farming also may lead to declining human health in coastal communities. Shrimp pond pollution has contaminated local drinking water supplies, forcing women to walk long distances for water (Barraclough and Stitch 1996) or forcing rural people to purchase expensive drinking water delivered by trucks.

The dynamics and impacts of shrimp farming in privately owned agricultural zones are in many respects distinct from those in the coastal zone. In Asia agricultural land is often privately owned by local small landholders, which can block the formation of large farms and lead to more and smaller shrimp farms, many of which may be operated by local villagers. This form of shrimp farming is likely to become increasingly important due to the recent refinement of low-salinity methods in Thailand (Flaherty, Vandergeest, and Miller 1999). These techniques allow shrimp farmers to rely on fresh water from local surface water infrastructures like irrigation canals or rivers for the bulk of their water supply, while trucking in sea or hyper-salinity water from the coast. This technique has permitted the expansion of shrimp farming into irrigated rice zones up to 200 kilometers from the sea in Thailand. Even prior to the rapid expansion of low-salinity farming since 1995, massive numbers of shrimp farms were located in wet rice agricultural areas along the southern Thai coast. The likelihood that low-salinity shrimp farming will spread to other irrigated zones in Asia highlights the need to look at the specific effects of shrimp farming in intensive agricultural as well as coastal zones.

In agricultural areas, shrimp farming competes for or degrades surface water, the key common pool resource associated with wet rice agriculture. In areas near the coast where shrimp farmers pump large volumes of high-salinity sea water directly from the coast, leaching and disposal of sea water into irrigation and drainage canals has led to widespread salinization, destroying rice fields, trees, fresh water fish, and other flora and fauna. Former rice-growing areas along the Southern Thai coast look like they have been hit with defoliants, leaving a devastated landscape including large numbers of dead trees standing amid the litter and messy infrastructure of shrimp farming. Although salinization is not as intense in low-salinity zones, salt leaches into neighboring farms depressing yields, is pumped into the surface water system, or moves down into the groundwater. In these areas, shrimp farmers use large volumes of fresh water, which will likely lead to conflict over water with local farmers as agricultural intensification leads to water shortages (Flaherty, Vandergeest, and Miller 1999).

Chemicals used to control shrimp diseases can pollute both coastal and inland marine resources. The introduction of shrimp farming into agricultural areas often leads to a sudden influx of large quantities of cash, producing inflation and leaving those who do not participate in the industry less able to purchase food and other needs. Small landholders who do not take up shrimp farming themselves often sell or rent land (sometimes because the land has become worthless for agriculture) to absentee shrimp farming entrepreneurs, leading to a loss of local ownership of land. Finally, many researchers report that the adoption of shrimp farming leads to a series of social problems not unlike those we associate with gold rushes—theft, gambling, prostitution, and of course endemic violence (Boonchoo n.d.).

It is important to emphasize that influxes of cash into shrimp farming regions are typically temporary. Self-pollution and disease often undermine shrimp farming in the long run, leaving a legacy of degraded resources, land alienated to urban entrepreneurs or corporations, and/or indebted farmers. The environmental and social effects of shrimp farming forces many rural people to move away both during and after the shrimp rush: for example, an estimated 48,000 people were displaced in the Indian State of Andhra Pradesh in a three-year period (Thamina 1995).

The destructive social and environmental effects of industrial shrimp farming often result from an alliance between the local state and shrimp farming interests. The location of shrimp farming often is preceded by states using land laws to claim coastal lands as state land, which they lease out to shrimp farms. Enclosures often occur through violence, as local police help shrimp companies who hire thugs to force farmers from their land (Barraclough and Stitch 1996; Stonich 1996). When people go to police with their complaints, police often refuse to register their cases. If they do succeed in filing a case, many flee afterwards for fear of police retaliation (Barraclough and Stitch 1996). In India, Bangladesh, and Honduras, well-connected urbanites used links with political leaders and the local administration to lease land for shrimp farms (Gain 1995; Stonich 1991). A duality of interests often pervades the shrimp industry—government officials mandated to oversee the industry also are shrimp farmers, processors, and exporters with personal political and economic interests. Official laws, decrees, and regulations prohibiting the use of coastal areas (mangroves and agricultural lands) for shrimp pond construction often are ignored through lack of sanctions and enforcement.

Crustacean Capitalism

Why has a productive activity that seemed to show such promise to alleviate resource scarcity in fact become so associated with violence and the degradation of livelihood resources? We argue that shrimp farming as an industrial activity is based on a set of processes that creates enormous tensions and potential for violence. These processes are both social and ecological; they involve the specific ways that the biological characteristics of shrimp shape the social processes by which shrimp production is industrialized.

Most important, shrimp farming is based on containment. By containing shrimp in ponds, shrimp farming incorporates the production of shrimp into capitalist production, rather than simply harvesting wild stocks after "natural" growth and maturation. Containment makes possible a dramatic intensification of production, although the degree of intensity as measured by stocking density varies significantly depending on factors such as the availability of land, credit, and labor.[2] Intensification of production leads to concomitant intensification of the ecological externalities of shrimp farming and of risk and instability.

Shrimp farming is designed to contain shrimp but not necessarily the other material flows associated with shrimp farming. Like any other intensive, industrial meat production operation (e.g., cattle, hogs, and chickens), shrimp farming both sucks up large quantities of local resources and requires the disposal of large quantities of polluted water and solids into adjacent areas. In coastal zones, shrimp farmers transform what were relatively "low-value" open access and common property resources into resources with such high value that they will use violence to secure them. In agricultural zones, pollution often makes further agricultural production in adjacent fields impossible, inducing landowners to sell or rent these fields to shrimp farmers, leading to a very high concentration of farms. These tendencies to high concentration increase the demands on local resources for shrimp farming and often lead to an intensifying spiral of expansion, resource degradation, violence, and further expansion. Thus the first way that shrimp farming becomes associated with violence is through its tendency to enclose and degrade the environment on which rural people depend for their livelihoods, producing violent confrontations between shrimp farmers and non-shrimp farmers.

---

2. Shrimp farms vary from extensive through semi-intensive, to super-intensive systems of production. In extensive systems, an enclosure is built close to the sea, often by damming a seasonal lagoon. Tidal flows into and out of the enclosure allow stocking of shrimp, feed, and water exchange. The semi-intensive systems that predominate in much of Latin America and the intensive systems that prevail in much of Asia function more or less as forms of brackish water feedlots for shrimp. Relative intensity of grow-out operations are gauged by stocking densities (the number of seed stock per hectare): extensive farms have low stocking densities (not over 25,000 post-larvae per hectare); semi-intensive operations have medium stocking densities (100,000–300,000 post-larvae per hectare); and intensive farms have high stocking densities (>300,000 post-larvae per hectare). In general, as densities (and intensity) increase, individual farm ponds get smaller, technology gets more sophisticated, capital costs increase, and production per spatial unit (yield) increases significantly.

Containment produces violence not only through the increased demands on local resources but also through the way that it produces a valuable and portable commodity. Wild shrimp harvested from the ocean's
bottom become private property at the moment they enter the net.
Shrimp farming, on the other hand, makes shrimp private property
through its entire life cycle. Whereas the main cost of appropriating wild
shrimp is in the equipment and labor necessary for the act of appropriation (boats, nets, etc.), in shrimp farming the major costs are expended
prior to appropriation (the cost of feed, chemicals, stocking, pond construction, power, and so on), so that shrimp of harvestable size embody significant value added. At the same time, containment facilitates appropriation. Farmers normally harvest shrimp by emptying ponds of water, but
simple throw-nets also can net substantial quantities of shrimp. Even larger
numbers can be taken by dragging nets across a pond. The greater the intensity of the farm operation, the easier and faster it is to appropriate large
quantities of shrimp.

Compared to rice, or even other valuable rural resources such as timber,
the per-kilogram value of shrimp is very high, making transportation easy
for thieves. In 1998, for example, a kilogram of harvested shrimp was
worth U.S. $6 to $10, depending on their size and price fluctuations. The
kilograms of missing shrimp probably obtained by the thief in the story
previously cited were worth approximately U.S. $6,000. In a well-organized
effort thieves can quickly catch and load this quantity of shrimp onto a
pickup truck. This is very attractive compensation for a night's work in a
part of rural Thailand where average annual per capita incomes prior to
the introduction of shrimp were one-third of this amount.

Overall, then, the increased demands of shrimp farming on local resources, together with the high value and portability of shrimp, make violent confrontations between shrimp farmers and non-shrimp farmers and
violence around theft endemic to the industry. However, the link between
shrimp farming and violence does not stop here. A further series of biophysical and social characteristics of shrimp farming heighten its propensity to produce violence.

The most obvious such characteristic is severe ecological and economic
instability, making shrimp farming a very high-risk as well as high-return
activity. Ecological instability follows from the containment of large numbers of shrimp in a small area and the general environmental stress resulting from the siting of large numbers of farms in a narrow coastal zone.
These stresses produce severe problems with disease. Although bacterial
diseases are important, the most unpredictable and difficult to control are
viruses. Viruses are background presences among wild shrimp but break
out frequently under semi-intensive and intensive culture. These outbreaks often bring the spiral of shrimp-farm expansion into agricultural areas to a catastrophic end. Outbreaks are unpredictable and can spread

rapidly from farm to farm, creating tensions between farmers who worry that their neighbors are not taking appropriate shielding measures.

Although disease is the primary source of ecological instability, there are others. For example, flooding induced by heavy rains can quickly wipe out a valuable crop. An extreme example of this was Hurricane Mitch, which struck Honduras and Nicaragua in late 1998. Within a few days, Mitch destroyed virtually all shrimp farms in southern Honduras and in neighboring Nicaragua. Other sources of instability include water scarcity, low salinity problems, and chemical poisoning.

Rapid price fluctuations introduce yet another source of instability. Oversupply and rapid price changes are characteristic of many agricultural commodities that have a substantial time lag between the initial investment and harvest and that are composed of many competitive enterprises, countries, and regions. A period of high prices will induce increased investments by many individual farmers, who then watch prices fall as their crops mature at the same time, creating oversupply. Ecological instability exacerbates price oscillations by heightening supply instability.

Major changes in exchange rates due to global economic instability have further increased price instability since 1997. For example, in Thailand the rapid devaluation of the baht in 1997, from twenty-five baht per U.S. dollar prior to the crisis to fifty baht at its lowest, caused the farm gate price of shrimp in baht to skyrocket. This produced a wave of expansion, with thousands of new farmers establishing shrimp farms based on low-salinity culture techniques in the Central Plains and around Songkla Lake in the South. At the same time, many farms that had stopped operating in the South due to problems with disease in 1995–1996 were brought back into production, and shrimp farming also expanded elsewhere in Thailand. However, a slow appreciation of the baht during the year (to about thirty-six baht per U.S. dollar), a rapid increase in the production of shrimp in Asian countries where currencies had also fallen relative to importing countries, and decreased demand and wholesale prices in recession-ridden Japan caused the farm gate price of shrimp in Thailand to plummet to less than 50 percent of peak prices by November 1998. As a result, many of the new farmers could not recoup their investments, repeating the boom-and-bust cycle of shrimp farming (Court 1998).

The explosive tensions associated with shrimp farming are further exacerbated by the ways different sizes of shrimp are priced. For reasons that have to do with the meaning of shrimp as a prestige consumption good, consumers in North America and elsewhere prefer larger shrimp, so that the unit price of shrimp rises sharply as the size of shrimp increases—the bigger, the more expensive. This means that farmers whose shrimp are nearing harvestable size can obtain a much higher return if they delay harvesting, through the combined effects of increased biomass and increased price per unit mass. However, this makes an already tense situation even more tense. Risk-adverse farmers, or those who have paid off debts, will harvest earlier at smaller sizes and for lower prices, but other farmers who are either more risk tolerant or who desperately need additional income to pay off debts will delay their harvests, thereby risking disease, thieves, and other uncertainties.

A final but crucial reason for the association of shrimp farming with violence is the way that its very high capital intensity, high potential payoffs, and high-risk attracts investment from people who are predisposed to using violence. Some shrimp investors have made money from illegal activities and invest in shrimp as a way of laundering their profits. Although documentation is difficult to find, it has been alleged that shrimp farming has attracted the investments of arms traders in Africa, drug dealers in Latin America, and Bre-X geologists in Indonesia. These people have used violence in other circumstances and have a high propensity to use it against opponents or thieves.

The example of a small landholder rice farmer in Thailand who is considering constructing a one-hectare shrimp farm illustrates the economic advantages and high risks of transforming a rice farm into a shrimp farm. The typical investment for the construction of a one-hectare shrimp farm plus production costs for the first crop is about one million baht (about U.S. $25,000 in late 2000). With luck, this villager can double his profits within several years. These expenditures and incomes exceed the annual incomes of rice farmers many times over—average per capita income in Thailand was only about 77,000 baht in 1997 (U.S. $2,140 at 36 baht per U.S. dollar) (Asian Development Bank 1998), and rural per capita incomes were much lower. If farmers are not so lucky and are struck by disease, plummeting prices, or flooding, they can very quickly accumulate debts many times their previous annual income. Larger farmers in Honduras as well as Thailand invest much larger sums of capital for higher potential incomes but with greater risks. Studies in Thailand in fact show that larger farmers using hired labor, far from being able to protect themselves from disease risks, are more vulnerable than small owner-operated farms (Vandergeest, Flaherty, and Miller 1999a, 1999b; Patmasiriwat 1997).

The convergence of these characteristics helps to explain the outbreaks of violence described in the stories at the beginning of this chapter. The second story illustrates violence between large shrimp farming operations and non-shrimp farmers due to enclosure and the destruction of common pool resources. In situations where large farmers with large quantities of capital invested in shrimp farming believe that they do not receive adequate protection from the state against opposition and sabotage (as is often the case in shrimp producing countries) they will employ private violence to protect their investments and potentially high profits or to remove obstacles to their operations. Local police often help the shrimp companies who hire thugs to force farmers from their land (Barraclough and Stitch 1996; Stonich 1996).

In the first story, the three brothers were operating a shrimp farm on a site of a former contract-farming scheme, which had collapsed due to disease outbreaks and poor management leaving farmers with huge debts. Although we cannot substantiate the accusation, farmers claim that corrupt high-level managers collected millions of dollars from farmers to repay bank debts and fled the country, increasing the financial troubles of both farmers and the company. After British Petroleum, who owned the company during the early 1990s, sold Aquastar, new owners reconstituted the scheme as independent operations that purchased power and water from the company. But the problems with the initial contract scheme had left the three brothers with a debt of more than a million baht. At the same time, they had put most of their land into the shrimp-farming scheme, leaving them no alternative livelihoods in this area other than wage work. Their continued anger over past disasters and their anxiety over their high debts no doubt contributed to their violent response to the theft.

Forms and Repertoires of Violence in Thailand and Honduras

We have described why shrimp farming has great potential for violence. At the same time, the repertoires of violence differ significantly from country to country. In this section we show how agrarian structure and history and the distinction between coastal zone and agricultural zone shrimp farming shape the structure of the industry and explain systematic differences in the trajectories of violence in Thailand and Honduras.

For several years, Thailand has been the world's largest producer and exporter of cultivated shrimp. It currently accounts for about 29 percent of world production. Total production in Honduras is much lower and contributes less than 2 percent of the world's supply of cultivated shrimp. Despite these differences in overall production, cultivated shrimp contribute significantly to export earnings in both countries. Although Thailand has a much larger economy (Gross National Product [GNP] of U.S. $170 billion in 1997) than Honduras (GNP of U.S. $4.4 billion in 1997), the economies of both countries are about equally dependent on the exports of goods and services (37 percent of Gross Domestic Product [GDP] in the Honduras case and 39 percent of GDP in the case of Thailand) (World Bank 1999). In 1996, the value of exports of cultivated shrimp from Thailand was estimated to be U.S. $1.72 billion (Asia Yearbook 1998) and from Honduras, U.S. $164 million (Government of Honduras 1998).

Although the two countries remain economically dependent on the export of cultured shrimp, they differ notably in terms of the average size of farms, land ownership, and intensity of the prevailing farming systems. Farm size is the most obvious difference. The industry in Thailand includes a wide range of sizes, with small, locally owned farms numerically predominant. Rosenberry (1998), a prominent industry analyst, estimates that in 1998, there were 25,000 farms covering 70,000 hectares, giving an average size of just under 3 hectares; he also estimates that 80 percent of the farms are smaller than 1.5 hectares, and less than 2 percent are larger than 10 hectares. Local studies conducted in Thailand suggest similar size distributions (reviewed in Vandergeest et al. 1999a). Most small shrimp farmers were previously wet-rice farmers or small-scale fishers. The integration of small local farmers into the shrimp industry has been enabled by government policies giving farmers access to credit, the presence of preexisting irrigation/drainage systems, and, in a few areas, a tradition and knowledge of aquaculture. At the same time, it is important to note that while large absentee-owned farms (greater than 10 hectares) are small in number, they dominate shrimp farming in certain provinces and contribute significantly to the total shrimp output in Thailand.

The shrimp industry in Honduras is dominated by a few large firms. Altogether there are only about 90 farms in the country, among which a few produce the majority of shrimp. Most of these firms are part of vertically integrated international companies that include feed mills, hatcheries, processing plants, and worldwide marketing (Stonich 1991; Stonich 1995; Stonich, Bort, and Ovares 1997). The two largest firms account for about half the total area in production in the country as well as the majority of exports. The largest enterprise, Grupo Granjas Marinas (Sea Farms Group) is an international company. It ranks among the largest shrimp farming operations in the world, producing from 6,500 hectares, a quantity that accounts for 60 percent of Honduras' cultivated shrimp exports. The second largest integrated shrimp farm in Honduras is Grupo Deli with 700 hectares of ponds that average 20 hectares each. According to the southern Honduras Chamber of Commerce, the shrimp industry provides employment to some 11,900 people through commercial farms, six packing plants, and ice-making operations, although these figures are hotly disputed by local people and other critics of the industry.

Although the case of Thailand shows that small farms can be more efficient than large farms, in Honduras government policies have favored large producers over small independent producers. These include the absence of credit for small farmers and cheap access to state land for large farmers. An additional difference is that small farmers in Honduras do not have a tradition of coastal aquaculture or the Thai's experience with the construction and maintenance of irrigation or other complex water systems.

A second dimension along which shrimp farming in Thailand and Hon-

duras differ is land ownership. Most farms in Thailand are located on titled land in agricultural areas, much of which was under wet rice prior to
shrimp farming. A minority but still significant number of farms have located on untitled land in coastal zones and in mangroves, but these farmers often find ways of securing some kind of land title. In contrast, approximately 70 percent of the 14,000 hectares of shrimp farms in Honduras in
1998 were located on government-leased concessions of national land in
coastal zones, rather than on private property. Relatively easy access to
land in Honduras has facilitated the development of a less intensive industry. Approximately 80 percent of farms in that country use semi-intensive
farming methods, but in Thailand an equally high percentage of farms use
intensive systems of production with extremely high stocking densities—
thirty pieces or more per square meter being typical.

Conflict and Violence Surrounding Shrimp Farming in Honduras

All shrimp farming in Honduras is located in the south along the Gulf of
Fonseca, one of the most environmentally degraded and impoverished regions of the country. Because it is a large, shallow depression, the gulf is
vulnerable to both pollution and siltation. Honduras shares political jurisdiction of the Gulf of Fonseca with Nicaragua and El Salvador, where the
shrimp farming industry also is expanding rapidly. The coastline is dominated by approximately 50,000 hectares of mangrove wetlands that are fed
by five major river systems. The biologically diverse mangrove ecosystems
have many important ecological functions: they provide habitats, especially
nursery areas for aquatic and terrestrial species; they protect coastlines
from inundation and contain sediment to form new land; and they are an
important stopover for an uncounted number of migratory birds. During
the rainy season, the extensive mud flats form temporary shallow lakes that
sustain large populations of fish and shellfish harvested by local inhabitants mostly for domestic consumption.

Today, southern Honduras is a "critically endangered region," designated by the United Nations as an area where basic life support systems, including water and soils, are in jeopardy. Deforestation, erosion, deterioration of watersheds, the indiscriminate use of agricultural pesticides, and
overgrazing have transformed the southern Honduran landscape. The region's Ladino inhabitants, among the poorest in Latin America (according
to most social and economic measures, much poorer than their counter-
parts in Thailand), also are at risk. Recent nutritional assessments conclude that 65 percent of children less than 5 years of age and 37 percent
of first graders suffer from moderate to severe under-nutrition.

Central to the environmental and social transformation of southern
Honduras has been the enclosure and degradation of common pool re-

sources crucial to rural survival strategies since World War II. With the assistance of international donor and lending institutions, the Honduras government has promoted a series of agricultural commodities for the global market—principally cotton, sugarcane, and beef cattle. By the 1960s, growing human impoverishment and environmental destruction provoked extensive migration from the south to urban centers, coastal zones within the region, and to Honduras' last remaining tropical humid forests in the northeastern portion of the country.

Prior to the shrimp boom, coastal areas of mangroves, mud flats, estuaries, and seasonal lagoons were not highly valued by outsiders or violently contested because they were unsuitable for the large-scale cultivation of cotton, sugarcane, pasture, or other commercial crops. Thus the Honduran state, as the legal owner of the coastal wetlands, allowed local people access to much of the zone. The coast was sparsely settled until the 1950s when poor families dislocated first by the expansion of cotton in lowland areas and later by beef cattle (in lowland, foothill, and highland areas) began migrating to these areas. By 1990, some 110,000 people lived in rural areas of the municipalities bordering the Gulf of Fonseca, including an estimated 2,000 artisanal fishers and an additional 5,000 individuals who apportioned their time between fishing and small-scale agriculture.

The settlers survived by exploiting the surrounding common resource area wetlands as well as by clearing adjacent areas to cultivate crops. From the wetlands they collected fuel wood, tannin (from bark), fish, shrimp, turtle eggs, mollusks, crabs, and other animals; some households also produced salt on the wetlands (Stonich 1995). Like peasants everywhere, the livelihood strategies of these households were diversified and flexible. In addition to the exploitation of common property resources in the wetlands and agriculture, they also obtained cash remittances from wage work in the shrimp industry as larvae gatherers and as hired laborers for affluent households.

Unfortunately for these settlers, this region also is considered ideal for shrimp farming. In the context of the chronic economic crises of the 1980s, the Honduran government began promoting "nontraditional" agricultural exports, especially melons and cultured shrimp. By 1987, shrimp became Honduras' third highest source of foreign exchange after bananas and coffee. Investment in the shrimp industry also has been supported by international development organizations, including the World Bank and the United States Agency for International Development (USAID). To facilitate the expansion of the shrimp industry, the state began to assert its legal rights to coastal land through a concession process, thereby supplanting the previous claims of traditional, communal users. Renewable concessions are leased to individuals or corporations for 25 years at a ridiculously low cost of about U.S. $4–5 per year. Over 25,000 hectares have been leased through concessions, although more than half that area remains undeveloped. Small producers or agrarian reform cooperatives have been impeded from participating in shrimp farming by their lack of political power to influence the award of concessions, along with the high costs of farm construction and maintenance, lack of technical assistance, insufficient credit opportunities, and high interest rates. Investors treat their leases much like private property, excluding others by means of armed guards, barbed wire fencing, and "No Trespassing" signs.

Estimates of mangrove loss due directly to the construction of shrimp farms range from about 2,000 to 4,000 hectares. Since World War II, half the Gulf's mangrove areas have been destroyed. Shrimp farming has also degraded marine environments under a largely unregulated open-access system. Much of the seed to stock shrimp ponds comes from captured wild shrimp post-larvae, although the role of hatcheries is increasing. About 1,500 larva gatherers trawl the coastal estuaries in boats or on foot collecting shrimp post-larvae in nets. They work individually or in teams under a variety of contractual arrangements. Although the environmental costs remain poorly understood, artisanal fishers maintain that their catches have fallen since larva gathering began. This may be due to the loss of by-catch: an estimated five other organisms die for each shrimp larva that is captured. In addition, water quality in estuarine areas is declining due to shrimp farm effluent containing high organic loads and low levels of dissolved oxygen.

Enclosures and resource degradation stemming from the explosive growth of industrial shrimp farming has produced significant, sometimes fierce, conflict between powerful shrimp farming interests on one side and artisanal fishers, fisher/farmers, other rural people, and environmentalists on the other. Shrimp farming interests include the national and foreign owners and managers of large farms, powerful bankers and industrialists, government leaders, and military officers. Many are members of the National Association of Shrimp Farmers of Honduras (ANDAH) and stress the economic value of the industry. They claim that environmental destruction is due to factors that are external to the farms: destructive agricultural practices in the highlands that cause erosion, siltation, and ultimately destruction of mangroves; harvesting of mangroves for subsistence use and for sale; and over-fishing by artisanal fishers. These powerful interests were subsidized initially by international development assistance, which is now being replaced by foreign investments channeled through joint ventures. Increasingly, ANDAH is presenting itself as conservationist, even imposing a largely unenforceable moratorium on expansion of farms until environmental assessments are completed.

Important historical, social, economic, and ecological continuities exist between the "Green Revolution," subsequent efforts to affect the internationalization of the agri-food system, and the "Blue Revolution"—exemplified by industrial shrimp farming in Honduras. The intimidation, thuggery, terror, and murder that took place in lowland and foothill areas as part of the expansion of cotton, sugar, beef cattle, and other agricultural commodities are recurring in coastal zones affected by the contemporary expansion of industrial shrimp farming. The "Blue Revolution" includes the same kinds of collusion as did the "Green Revolution" between international and national actors (including financial donors such as the World Bank and the Inter-American Development Bank, development organizations such as the United States Agency for International Development, international agribusiness, national/local elites, and national governments, including the army). There also is continuity in terms of local response. Since the 1950s, Southern Honduras has been a center of well-organized peasant movements resisting the loss of common pool resources associated with the earlier spread of the cotton, sugar, and beef cattle industries. It also was home to a well-established, Jesuit-run radio school movement that emphasized training for both women and men in community organization and mobilization around land and livelihood issues. Not surprisingly, one of the most organized and effective movements against industrial shrimp farming anywhere in the world emerged in that region. Poor people from coastal communities founded a resistance movement in 1988: the grassroots Committee for the Defense and Development of the Flora and Fauna of the Gulf of Fonseca (CODDEFFAGOLF). This organization currently has about 5,000 members. Many of the leaders of CODDEFFAGOLF are children and grandchildren of activists that led those earlier resistance efforts.

Repertoires of resistance have ranged from noncompliance (e.g., poaching within concessions) and protest marches to more violent confrontations, such as physically obstructing earth moving equipment, barricading roads to shrimp farms, destroying canals, and burning farm buildings. To protect themselves, shrimp farmers have turned their farms into sites resembling military posts—farms are surrounded by fences topped by razor wire, lighting systems, lookout towers, and armed guards. In contrast to past peasant movements, CODDEFFAGOLF members have successfully mobilized the backing of an extensive global network that includes the public, the press, and international organizations of environmental and social activists. These groups challenge the transformation of what were multi-use and multi-user coastal resources into private property controlled by national elites and foreigners who have the political connections and power to obtain concessions or title to coastal lands. They contend that shrimp farmers are depriving fishers, farmers, and others of access to mangroves, estuaries, and seasonal lagoons; destroying mangrove ecosystems; altering the hydrology of the region; destroying habitats of other flora and

fauna; precipitating declines in biodiversity; contributing to degraded water quality; and exacerbating the decline in gulf fisheries through the indiscriminate capture of other species caught with the shrimp post-larvae
that are used to stock ponds. As an alternative to current development
practices, CODDEFFAGOLF members have urged the Honduran Congress
to create and enforce protected areas and/or resource extraction reserves
and promote the creation of a tri-national management plan for the gulf.

The state has often sided with the landowning or entrepreneurial
classes in the highly polarized class structure and agrarian struggle. It assists them by providing a legal basis for resource enclosure and by providing military/police support for taking possession of these resources. The
negligible cost at which the state has made extensive areas of coastal land
available to the shrimp farming industry has facilitated the geographic expansion of the industry and the continued domination of semi-intensive
farming systems, requiring large spatial areas and simultaneously using
large amounts of purchased inputs (seed stock, pumping systems, feeds,
chemicals). This semi-intensive system of production, in turn, has exacerbated the loss of common pool resources for the poor rural residents of
Honduras' southern coasts, thereby enhancing resistance, conflicts, and
violence.

Although most violence surrounding shrimp farming has occurred between shrimp farmers and local people, the expansion of the industry also
has generated community conflict—both within and between local communities. These conflicts generally stem from increased competition for
remaining coastal resources (land and water) and also from participation
by local people in the industry—particularly as collectors of post-larvae
used as seed stock for the farms. Basically there is conflict within communities over whether or not local people should take jobs in the industry.
The biggest controversy has been among those who choose to work as
larva gatherers and those who think they should not. Communities along
the coast are among the poorest in the country, and many people will take
any kind of employment—with good reason. This type of conflict also surrounds CODDEFFAGOLF because it cannot represent the interests of all
poor people in the coastal zone.

Conflict and Violence Surrounding Shrimp Farming in Thailand

In the twenty years preceding the economic crisis of 1997, Thailand had
experienced remarkable rates of economic growth, based on the increasingly export-oriented economic policies of the government. Fundamental
to this export-led growth was the enhanced exploitation and destruction
of natural resources, particularly land, forests, water, fish, and mineral resources (Flaherty and Filipacchi 1993). Coastal areas have been subject to

especially heavy development pressure from a wide range of activities, including tourism, offshore and onshore mining activities, industrial development, agriculture, capture fisheries, and shrimp farming. The high cost of private property and the desire of villagers to produce as much as possible from their land facilitated the development of extremely intensive methods of production.

Extensive shrimp farming was practiced since at least the mid-1930s in the upper gulf area near Bangkok. In the 1970s, the Department of Fisheries began to promote the intensification through supplementary feeding and by establishing a shrimp fry hatchery to provide seed stock to small-scale producers. In the mid-1980s, growing demand in Japan, the United States, and Europe, as well as high prices and high profits stimulated many farmers to switch from extensive and semi-extensive farming methods to intensive methods using technologies imported from Taiwan (Flaherty and Karnjanakesorn 1995).

The first wave of expansion was in the upper gulf region. Although previous land uses in this area have not been definitely documented, much of this wave took place at the expense of mangrove forests. The industry in this region collapsed due to disease in the late 1980s, but total production in Thailand continued to rise as the second wave of expansion along the east coast of the southern peninsula compensated for the collapse of the first wave. Although corporate farms were among the first to be established in this area, most land along this coast was under small-landholder wet rice cultivation, and many local farmers soon realized that they could undertake independent operations, leading to the numerical dominance of small owner-operator farms. The industry has also been expanding since the late 1980s along the Andaman and eastern coasts. Along these coasts irrigated rice is less common, and most farms are medium-size operations located either in mangroves or in agricultural land along canals and streams flushed by tidal action. Shrimp farming has continued along all these coasts despite a period of heavy losses due to disease during the mid-1990s. The most recent wave of expansion is in inland rice-growing areas using low-salinity production methods, although a Prime Ministerial order in 1998 banning shrimp farming from land zoned "fresh water" may have forced a decline in inland shrimp farming. Overall, the picture is one of regional diversity in size and ownership, though not in intensity of production.

As in Honduras, shrimp farming in Thailand has been promoted by the government, international development banks, and agri-business as a means of generating foreign exchange and enhancing national income. One corporation Charoen Phakpond (CP) dominates the feed industry and provides powerful political support for the industry. There are also a number of influential shrimp farmers' associations composed mostly of medium and large operators. Shrimp farming has been an astounding success in terms of its ability to generate exports and enhance corporate profits for input suppliers. However, accumulated evidence shows that it has not proven to be economically beneficial to the majority of residents of the coastal and inland communities (Vandergeest, Flaherty, and Miller 1999). Although many thousands of villagers have been able to take up shrimp farming, hundreds of thousands of nearby villagers have not been able to participate due to lack of access to suitable land, water, or credit (Flaherty and Karnjanakesorn 1995). Many of these villagers have seen their groundwater and rice fields salinized and suffered a variety of other negative environmental and social impacts, as discussed previously. Even those villagers who have been able to enter into shrimp farming have found that the promise of riches quickly turned instead to debt and anxiety over the degradation and loss of their land and water resources.

The most common form of shrimp farming violence is not confrontation between shrimp farmers and their opponents but theft of the type described in the first story. Shrimp in ponds nearly ready for harvesting are the most common targets for thieves, but thieves also take expensive equipment, such as pumps and aerators. According to local informants, every shrimp farm has lost at least some shrimp to thieves, and in many cases these losses are major. Where shrimp farming is dominated by larger farms, the area often looks like a series of well-lit armed camps as operators try to defend themselves through bright night lighting, watch towers, barbed wire, and armed guards. The key problem for larger operators is the possibility that guards will collude with thieves. Although smaller owner-operators also build watchtowers, they generally lack lighting and barbed wire. Owner-operators also do not hire guards; instead, they sit in their watchtowers through the night, guns in hand, but in the end they often wisely refrain from challenging well-armed shrimp bandits even when they detect them.

The structure of the shrimp industry facilitates theft as a central form of crustacean violence in Thailand. Most important is that ubiquitous theft would not be possible without highly dispersed ownership. Very large operators, like those in Honduras, can shield themselves by investing in defensive installations, but smaller operators have great difficulty defending their valuable crops. Not only are the smaller Thai shrimp farmers more vulnerable to theft than the large Honduran operations but also the high stocking densities make it easier for thieves to appropriate large quantities of shrimp. The structure of shrimp farming also facilitates theft because corporate processors buy their shrimp not directly from farmers but from many small contractors hired by farmers to harvest and sort shrimp. Thieves have little difficulty selling their catch to these contractors, and processors do not know the difference between legitimately harvested and stolen shrimp.

In some cases, small-scale theft or even sabotage may coalesce everyday resistance to shrimp farms by non-shrimp farmers. Large shrimp farms often are surrounded by a hostile rural population, many of whom would steal shrimp if they could, although these farms are usually well-protected. Since opponents are often poorer and less influential, this kind of violence is clandestine and anonymous. Resistance to shrimp farms also can take the form of sabotage: shrimp are very sensitive to agricultural pesticides and to poisons used to kill rodents. Many stories are circulating around southern Thailand of these kinds of violence, often without specifying the participants. Whether they are true or not, the stories probably help induce shrimp farmers to provide some compensation for lost resources.

At the same time, many shrimp farmers do not hesitate to hire gunmen to eliminate and intimidate individuals opposing their farms or demanding compensation. Local villagers have repeatedly stated to researchers that they are afraid to press for greater compensation for fear of their lives. In at least one district in Central Thailand, residents reported that the cost of eliminating a troublemaker was 30 kilograms of shrimp (between U.S. $100 and $200).[3] Similarly, district-level government officials sometimes are intimidated into not supporting claims for compensation or not enforcing regulations violated by powerful shrimp farmers.

In comparison to everyday forms of violence associated with theft, assassinations, and intimidation, there has been very little of the sort of high-profile violent confrontations between shrimp farmers and peasant organizations that frequently occur in countries like Honduras and India. So far, no militant rural organization linked to global environmental networks has emerged to lead resistance to shrimp farming. Instead, a nongovernmental organization (NGO), the Raindrop Association (Yadfon), represents Thailand in the global movement against industrial shrimp farming. The Bangkok media and middle-class environmental groups have led the opposition to low-salinity farming, although relatively well-to-do orchard and rice farmers from the Central Region have also organized demonstrations and lobby groups to oppose shrimp farming in this region. In the south, rice farmers have staged large-scale demonstrations to press the provincial government to take action against shrimp farmers whose operations were salinizing rice fields (Jaroon Kanjanapan, personal communication). These demonstrations, however, typically do not involve overt violence. Over the past ten years, demonstrations have become very common in Thailand, and they proceed according to a repertoire that is well-known to all participants. The repertoire includes media coverage, often arranged by activists with connections in the print media, and it usually (but not always) avoids violence.

Collective action leading to confrontation and possible violence has oc-

3. Reported by Paul Miller (personal communication).

casionally occurred at the village level. Although active village level resistance to shrimp farming was exceptional until recently, some villagers have collectively mobilized to physically block shrimp farmers from entering their villages with construction equipment. Leaders of villagers engaging in this sort of action take great risks to their own personal safety. Conflicts and disputes also have arisen when public lands (often mangroves and other common pool resources) have been used for farms on the west coast (Ahmed 1998). The situation on this coast is reminiscent of the Honduran experience: land belongs to the state, and ownership is extremely difficult to establish for local villagers but easier for developers who obtain land documents after using the land for several years (Ahmed 1998). Unlike the Honduras case, villagers in these areas have not formed a militant coalition to oppose the expansion of shrimp farming. These types of actions have so far remained sporadic and unreported, so that it is difficult to assess their overall significance.

There are many reasons for the relatively low level of organized opposition to shrimp farming (see Vandergeest et al. 1999a), but in general they follow from the structure of the industry and from agrarian history in Thailand. Most important is that the participation of large numbers of villagers in shrimp farming makes it difficult for rural people to develop local level solidarity against shrimp farming. Even those who do not own shrimp farms themselves become linked to the industry in various ways, for example, as wage laborers or through renting out land. Many villagers who deplore the impacts of shrimp farming are at the same time dependent on the industry. All the cases of village-level collective action against shrimp farming that we know of have occurred where village-level participation in shrimp farming is low (for example, among Muslim villagers on the west coast where most shrimp farming is in the hands of mid-sized Buddhist owners who live in nearby towns and hire labor from Burma or the northeast of Thailand).

The two case studies also reveal the important roles played by history and cultures of resistance in predicting the prevalence of violence. In Honduras, the formation of organized resistance to shrimp farming has drawn on the political experience of previous mobilizations. In Thailand, the expansion of export crops such as rice, cassava, and maize has not been accompanied by resource enclosure; in fact, the government in Thailand has long facilitated the participation of small landholders in the expansion of the agricultural economy. The first major case of resource enclosure in Thailand involved the expansion of national parks and wildlife sanctuaries in inland forests (Vandergeest 1996), not the expansion of export-oriented agriculture. Although there is a history of peasant insurgency in Thailand, it is largely confined to inland forested zones, not the shrimp farming areas. Many of the former leaders of the peasant insurgencies of the 1960s and 1970s, or their children, are the leaders of the current resistance to enclosures of forests for protected areas, a movement that has proven to be extremely sophisticated and effective (Vandergeest 1996). This kind of leadership and culture of resistance is not present, however, in the shrimp farming zones. This may be changing because small-scale fishers have recently formed an effective and militant national organization, which, as we write this chapter, was organizing blockades of a major southern port to press their demands for the end of industrial anchovy harvesting. Although this organization has included shrimp farming as one of its issues, it has so far focused more on the threat of industrial fishing.

In the more complex situation characterizing the shrimp farming industry in Thailand compared to Honduras, the role of the state has been correspondingly more complex. By and large, the state has supported the shrimp industry through technical extension and support, research, and subsidizing the cost of inputs like water. Until recently, the state gave scant legal recognition to collective property rights in resources claimed or degraded by shrimp farms and confirmed landowners' rights to use land as they wished regardless of the consequences for common property resources.

Unlike Honduras, however, where agrarian struggles are more clearly polarized, the state has neither provided shrimp farmers with police and military support in cases of collective confrontation nor have they used violence to put down demonstrations against shrimp farming. Shrimp farmers thus need to rely on the clandestine use of hired gunmen if they want to use violence against opponents. The government also has not openly leased large areas of state-owned coastal land to shrimp farmers. Official policy is that shrimp farming can only take place on titled land. Local land officials, however, have supported shrimp farmers by providing them with land titles to coastal land or by not enforcing land laws. The state's reaction to the violence surrounding theft was described in the first story. Where the perpetrator of violence is not a locally influential person, the police will pursue the case but usually with the goal of mediating a monetary settlement. More recently, the state has reacted to the controversy provoked by the expansion of inland shrimp farming by banning shrimp farms in provinces and coastal areas zoned "fresh water"—an order backed by the threat of coercion from local police.

Visibility

So far we have shown how it is the very high value of shrimp, not some kind of absolute resource scarcity, that leads to the ubiquitous violence surrounding industrial shrimp farming. But we have also shown that the links between industrial shrimp farming and violence are not simple ones. Violence is produced out of a complex set of characteristics common to industrial shrimp farming. Some are related to the impacts of shrimp farming on the value of surrounding land and water resources. Industrial shrimp farming makes coastal resources so valuable that shrimp farmers will use violence to secure them. In addition, intensive shrimp farming produces material flows that degrade surrounding land and water resources important for local livelihoods. Other biophysical, social, and political-economic characteristics of shrimp and shrimp farming that cause violence include shrimp farming's unpredictability and inherent riskiness; the attraction of people to the industry who are prone to using violence; and the portability of shrimp, which can make theft a lucrative enterprise if the shrimp are not protected. Both theft and protection involve violence. The forms of violence that emerge in particular situations differ widely depending on the overall agrarian contexts and political history of the areas where shrimp farming is located, and how these characteristics combine in a variety of ways.

Shrimp production in Thailand and Honduras has, therefore, produced quite different forms and repertoires of violence. Thailand and Honduras constitute a useful comparison because they represent the two general types of agrarian environments into which shrimp farming often moves. In Honduras, most shrimp farms have been built in coastal areas not previously under land title and leased to shrimp farmers by the government. The industry is dominated by a small number of large shrimp farming enterprises, and local participation is relatively low. At the same time, the area has a strong history and culture of organized peasant resistance. As a result, most violence involves conflict between well-organized peasant organizations and large shrimp farming enterprises. Although sabotage is part of the repertoire of resistance, there is much less theft than in Thailand because the large farms are well-protected and because there is no export market for stolen shrimp. In Thailand, most shrimp farms are located in small landholder agricultural zones on titled land, and local participation is often high. The high level of local participation combined with a lack of local history of organized resistance has tended to disable broad-based resistance movements. Instead, the kind of violence most rural people associate with shrimp farming has involved either endemic theft or individual acts of resistance, threats, or assassination.

In this final section, we will add some comments on the implications of these different repertoires of violence for both the visibility of violence and for the ways that conflicts provoked by industrial shrimp farming have been incorporated into transnational networks. Organized resistance to shrimp farming in Honduras has attracted support from a wide range of

U.S. and international environmental groups. CODDEFFAGOLF has attracted this support by framing their resistance as a defense of the integrity of coastal ecosystems on which they depend for their livelihoods. Their success in this regard was marked at the United Nations Conference on Environment and Development (UNCED) in Rio de Janeiro, where they received a Global 500 award for outstanding environmental achievement. CODDEFFAGOLF has been particularly successful in obtaining support from a wide range of U.S. and transnational organizations. For example, Greenpeace recently announced an initiative to promote mangrove conservation in Central America and kicked off the project by sending the Greenpeace vessel *The Moby Dick* in March 1996 to protest the conversion of mangroves to shrimp ponds. CODDEFFAGOLF also has received funds from less confrontational environmental organizations, such as World Wildlife Fund, to undertake conservation efforts. For their efforts to improve local livelihoods, they have received several hundred thousand dollars from the Inter-American Foundation to finance sustainable development projects that integrate agriculture, aquaculture, and salt-making.

It remains to be seen whether this kind of support helps CODDEFFAGOLF achieve their goals, but there is little doubt that this kind of assistance has enhanced peasant organizational capacity. Baviskar (in this volume) argues that peasant groups who are able to create strong linkages to international organizations may find some protection from state-sanctioned violence in those links. The strong links to international organizations has made the violence in Honduras highly visible in international arenas. To some extent, this visibility has protected members from reprisals by powerful supporters of the industry, but members of CODDEFFAGOLF and other community leaders have been harassed by shrimp farm security guards, imprisoned, and received death threats. To date, five artisanal fishers active with CODDEFFAGOLF have been murdered.

Unlike the openly political violence associated with highly organized opposition to shrimp farming, the violence associated with theft and murder in Thailand is relatively invisible outside of the localities where it takes place. Because it is not overtly political, this kind of violence is seldom discussed by scholars and activists. Even where the violence involves acts of local resistance to shrimp farming or the elimination of such resistance through the assassination of the perpetrators, the individualistic and clandestine nature of the violence helps keep it out of national and international forums. Because much of the violence in Thailand is individual and turns around appropriation of the shrimp rather than a defense of the coastal resources, it also is less likely to attract the attention of environmental groups. The exceptions are those areas where mangroves are threatened. For example, Wetlands International, an important environmental group involved in shrimp farming issues in Thailand, pays little attention to shrimp farming in agricultural zones but has documented the loss of mangroves to shrimp farming and initiated collaborative projects with shrimp farming enterprises through which they hope to restore mangroves.

The invisibility of shrimp farming violence in Thailand makes it easy to conclude that there is, in fact, less violence in Thailand than Honduras, India, or other countries with organized resistance movements to shrimp farming whose conflicts are regularly reported in national and international fora. But this impression would dissipate quickly if observers spent time talking to rural people in shrimp farming zones in Thailand. The invisibility of the violence makes it very difficult to count bodies, but there is no reason to believe that it is less than in countries where shrimp farming violence is more organized, political, and visible. Villagers in Southern Thailand who are using new government regulations to block the siting of shrimp farms in their villages (Vandergeest et al., 1999a) cite the increasing levels of violence among villagers, along with the degradation of natural resources, as a key motivation for their opposition to shrimp farming. The murder recalled at the beginning of this chapter was a result of the biophysical, social, and political-economic characteristics of shrimp farming; it was a typical aspect of shrimp farming. At the same time, shrimp farming is a global activity involving multiple transnational actors.

These stories and our analysis of violence and the "Blue Revolution" show the fallacy of simplifying the links between resource degradation, enclosure, and violence. We should cast our nets widely to capture and account for both the highly visible and relatively invisible forms of violence associated with the expansion of resource-intensive activities like industrial shrimp farming.

12

Victims of "Friendly Fire" at Russia's Nuclear Weapons Sites

Paula Garb and Galina Komarova

This chapter examines the consequences of nuclear weapons development as a form of environmental violence. It provides an additional dimension to the understanding of violence that Keane (1996) defines as physical harm, forms of coercion, and the deployment of terror. We stress the need to define environmental violence in a way that includes not only physical but also psychological violence. Valerie Kuletz (1998) and Dalton and colleagues (1999) have described this phenomenon in the United States. Since the beginning of the Cold War, the victims of the accidents in the nuclear weapons industry in Russia have endured this violence. The potential for similar violence exists in the numerous other societies where nuclear weapons are being developed today.

Our focus is on the experiences of the people in Russia who live near the former Soviet Union's primary nuclear weapons production sites at Chelyabinsk, Krasnoyarsk, and Tomsk, where accidents have seriously contaminated the surrounding inhabited areas. The people in these places consider themselves the unknown targets of the nuclear weapons built in their backyards. They bitterly declare that "throughout the Cold War no bomb was ever dropped, except on us." Although the affected population knows that similar accidents have occurred elsewhere, they have reason to believe that the magnitude of the accidents and consequences in their country have been far greater.

The most dramatic of these incidents took place in 1957 at the Mayak Chemical Combine in the closed city of Chelyabinsk-65, now known as Ozyorsk. This is in the Chelyabinsk region of the Urals in Russia, with a population of around 3.7 million. Mayak was the Soviet Union's first weapons-grade plutonium production center. One of these accidents is often referred to as the Kyshtym explosion. Late in the afternoon of September 29, 1957, one of the Mayak facility's 80,000-gallon storage tanks exploded after its cooling system failed. It released over 70 tons and 2.1 million curies of radioactive debris into the atmosphere over a territory about the size of New Jersey. It caused levels of radiation contamination in some parts of the Chelyabinsk region that were twenty times greater than those resulting from the notorious accident at Chernobyl, Ukraine, in 1986. The disaster necessitated the permanent evacuation of approximately 10,700 people (Kellog and Kirk 1997). Over half of these people were evacuated 8 months later, which means that they consumed contaminated food for 3 to 6 months without restriction and continued to eat some contaminated food until their evacuation. The entire population of the region ate the 1957 harvest, which was contaminated with radionuclides (Cochran 1993).

The accidents in Chelyabinsk region were officially acknowledged by the Soviet government after the international outcry over the Chernobyl accident, but the U.S. military establishment and government were aware of the 1957 accident around the time of the explosion. Gary Powers, the U.S. pilot shot down over the Urals on May 5, 1960, was taking photos to assess the impact of the accident. Perhaps none of the nuclear nations wanted to point a finger at the Soviet Union for this horrific environmental and human disaster because similar incidents were occurring in the United States and England (Dalton et al. 1999). If these Western countries had drawn the world's attention to the Soviet accident, they might have opened the door to investigations of their own activities. It appears as though all the nuclear establishments essentially conspired to keep this modern form of violence a secret. Had the Kyshtym explosion become public knowledge, the antinuclear movements might have been launched earlier, and perhaps this public pressure could have prevented many of the subsequent accidents, including the one at Chernobyl.

This chapter highlights the trauma that resulted from the forcible relocation of thousands of people in Chelyabinsk hit by "friendly fire" and on the long-term health and psychological effects suffered by millions of people around all the sites, who inhabit an environment contaminated by the weapons developed during the Cold War. We equate the physical and psychological trauma, as well as the cultural, social, and economic degradation with the violence caused by the direct use of weapons.

In our research in the heart of the Soviet Union's military-industrial complex, we came across hundreds of stories recounting the physical and emotional damage caused by nuclear weapons development. In all the sites where we conducted interviews, comments about people's health were similar to this one we heard in the city of Kyshtym (near the Mayak plant) from a 65-year-old retired worker: "Everyone around me is ill. Young people, from 30 to 40 years old, die of cancer. Cancer is everywhere. All my friends have died. We know it's all because of Mayak." The problems are compounded by the breakdown in the medical system. This same man said, "You come to the hospital and get no attention, no medicine, no treatment. But we all live with radiation. Just recently my younger brother died of throat cancer."

Dr. Gulfarida Galimova, a physician in one of the most contaminated downstream villages Muslyumovo, has been keeping a record of illnesses that she connects to what the people there call the "river disease." She claims that someone in every family in this community of approximately 4,000 has been affected by the radiation in the Techa River, which runs through the village. During its initial stages of operation, in the late 1940s and early 1950s, Mayak dumped untreated radioactive waste into the river. In 1993, Dr. Galimova calculated that the average life span of the women was 47 (72 is the average for the nation), and the average life span of the men was 45 (69 for the nation). She maintains that the death rate and birth mortality rate are significantly greater than for the uncontaminated villages in the same Kunashak region. Dr. Galimova says that sterility has become commonplace among her patients, especially those who went through puberty when Mayak was dumping radioactive waste into the river.

Dr. Galimova's statistics may not hold up under rigorous methodological examination, but they reflect a common perception among the population. According to the results of a 1992 public opinion survey (Dalton et al. 1999), 86 percent of the combined population of two villages near the plant in the Chelyabinsk region felt that their family's health was affected by the activities of the Mayak Chemical Combine. Moreover, approximately half the residents of the cities of Chelyabinsk and Chelyabinsk-70, now known as Snezhinsk (the closed research city nearby Mayak), also said that their families were affected.

The most common opinion about Mayak among Muslyumovo residents was that it was an eternal reality, an inescapable evil that no one knew how to fight. The feeling of doom expressed by all our informants was overwhelming. One woman poignantly summed up the sentiment of her neighbors in Muslyumovo: "We curse Mayak which robbed us of our parents and our health."

These charges, however, have been contested by the nuclear establishment, which maintains that it is nearly impossible to draw a scientific link between nuclear environmental damage and health problems. The government has done rigorous epidemiological testing of these claims almost impossible by falsifying causes of death on death certificates and refusing to release secret data to independent scientists. Although the methods of the Federal Security Services (the successor to the Soviet secret police—KGB) have become far less harsh in the new Russia, they continue to believe that it is unpatriotic and even subversive for citizens to question authorities or to seek independent sources of information and monitoring, particularly in cooperation with independent foreign organizations that are not working officially with the Russian government on such joint projects. Periodically, Chelyabinsk environmentalist activists have been publicly criticized for organizing independent monitoring of the nuclear environment and the health of the population. A typical example of the accusations appeared on September 7, 1994, in the *Rabochaya Gazeta.* The author of the article, "People Don't Investigate Radiation Alone," cited Dr. Alexander Akleev, the director of the Chelyabinsk Branch of the Institute of Biology (now known as the Urals Research Center for Radiation Medicine, URCRM), a high-security research institution that has been keeping records on the contaminated population since the 1950s:

> The director of the Urals research center was very critical of the activities of some nongovernmental organizations, for instance, the Movement for Nuclear Safety. The leaders of this organization tell the population not to trust the research of the center and have organized the illegal collection of blood samples and tried to send them illegally abroad. Why is this necessary if there is an agreement between the Russian and US governments to collaborate in this field? Such actions can only harm the developing contacts between radiologists of our country and foreign experts. . . . Alexander Akleev is convinced that it is not good to stir up the people just to win popularity for a nongovernmental organization.

In another newspaper article on August 18, 1994 (*Chelyabinsk Rabochy,* "This Bears the Stamp of Other Agencies"), Colonel A. Maximov of the Chelyabinsk Federal Security Services implied that the activities of foreign researchers working independently with local environmental activists were initiated by foreign intelligence agencies.

What both sides of this wide divide between officialdom and nongovernmental environmentalists *do* seem to agree on is that psychological trauma is pervasive in these areas. From the victims' point of view, this trauma stems from not having enough information about the environmental damage and the consequences to their health. From the nuclear establishment's perspective, what they refer to as "radiation phobia" is the result of knowing too much. One official put it this way, "The green movement has done more harm to the people by generating 'radiation phobia' than the Chernobyl explosion."

Henry M. Vyner's research (1988) contributes to our understanding about the psychosocial effects of hazardous environmental exposures. According to Vyner, when people learn of their exposure or of subsequent health problems, the invisibility of the contamination creates uncertainty that makes it hard for victims to master their situation. The pressure to make decisions about their lives without adequate information leads

[handwritten margin note: "PTSD"]

people to become fixated on these concerns in a manner similar to that found in post-traumatic stress syndrome. The fixation is related to a belief that one has endured dangerous exposure and needs to take protective actions. Victims can be under stress by what they learn about the exposure as well as by the uncertainties. Institutional denial heightens the trauma.

Concerned citizens in the Chelyabinsk region charge that "radiation phobia" is the result of lies from the officials. A resident of Kashtym (near Mayak) told us, "I've lived here for 50 years and have only heard lies about the accidents. When I spoke up, I was interrogated by the KGB. They tell us now that they're going to start telling us the truth. They're like children who say they won't be bad anymore. I don't believe Mayak officials now, anymore than I did before these revelations. They still haven't really told us the truth."

Kai Erikson's (1972, 1991) research on the psychological trauma suffered by individuals and whole communities as a result of natural and technological disasters shows the important role a sense that the catastrophe has ended plays in victims' recovery. Unlike the natural disasters Erikson describes, the nuclear accidents of the former Soviet Union and Russia have no clear ending. The problems of nuclear contamination will continue far into the future for many generations because of the longevity of chemical and nuclear substances. *[handwritten margin note: "no clear ending"]*

Erikson describes how chronic disaster conditions, such as those existing around nuclear weapons industries, induce deep psychological trauma: "A chronic disaster is one that gathers force slowly and insidiously, creeping around one's defenses rather than smashing through them. The person is unable to mobilize his normal defenses against the threat, sometimes because he has elected consciously or unconsciously to ignore it, sometimes because he has been misinformed about it, and sometimes because he cannot do anything to avoid it in any case" (1972: 255). *[handwritten margin note: "deep psych trauma"]*

In this chapter we argue that it is a form of violence to allow conditions to exist that cause people to fear that physical harm will come to them, not only by causing the environmental damage but also by withholding or manipulating information about the risks. As Mozgovaya (1993: 3) found in her study of the populations in Russia living in areas contaminated by the Chernobyl disaster, 40 percent of teenagers "suffered from fear, a sense of helplessness, and dreaded using food and water for a long time after the disaster. About 16 percent of the teenagers said they suffered from sleeplessness and loss of interest in life. Girls suffered from such feelings twice as frequently than boys." These symptoms were even more widespread among adults. Mozgovaya compared these results with those of people living in noncontaminated areas and found striking differences in self-reporting on mental health. *[handwritten margin note: "form of violence"]*

Mozgovaya explains why there is little hope of addressing these prob-

laws not enforced to combat trauma

lems effectively. She points out that although a law exists to financially compensate the victims of nuclear contamination, the authorities in local governing councils, called soviets, are in charge of implementing the law. Most of the personnel in these councils were trained in the Soviet totalitarian state and tend not to make decisions on their own. They wait, instead, for instructions from their superiors. Thus, even if such officials are sympathetic to the victims and acknowledge their grievances, they avoid taking responsibility.

Psychological trauma in the Russian context derives from people's fear not only of the health effects of contamination but also of reprisals against them if they dared to speak about their concerns or even to ask questions. The plants and the towns where the employees lived were created in a shroud of secrecy. The Mayak complex was built in the late 1940s and early 1950s by political prisoners and German POWs during the reign of terror under Communist party leader Joseph Stalin and head of the secret police, Lavrenty Beria. Officials never told the surrounding communities the nature of these industrial sites. Residents near the Mayak plant remember only rumors that this complex was going to be a soap factory. Eventually they found out that these were defense facilities. Huge fences and armed guards kept outsiders far away. Employees and other residents were sworn to secrecy and had to obey strict rules that guided their movement and that of close relatives in and out of the complex. Even after the Stalin era ended, when citizens were no longer being condemned arbitrarily as "enemies of the people" and sentenced to the notorious gulags by the millions, the repressive system was never fully dismantled. The culture of secrecy and fear remained, preventing citizens from questioning the operation of these facilities, let alone protesting their management and impact on the neighboring communities. Fear, however, was not the only factor. The Stalinist Soviet experience also evoked a strong sense of patriotism and a belief that the nation's defense was of highest priority. Thus, a combination of fear and patriotism has played a role in citizens' acquiescence to the government. These factors still exist in nuclear environmental matters today. Two Russian scientists face criminal charges for having provided the Bellona Foundation with nuclear environmental information. The KGB's successor agency closely watches local environmental activists and their international visitors.

Built during WWII by POW Germans

A brief history of Chelyabinsk's environmental legacy sheds light on the evolution of this tragedy. The first victims of nuclear environmental violence around Chelyabinsk in the early 1950s lived in twenty-two villages along the Techa River. There, researchers at Mayak, in the first years of operation, dumped plutonium into the river assuming that it would be diluted and cause no harm. By 1952 the dumping was stopped because of a dramatic rise in disease and deaths among the inhabitants (Cochran

1993). About 28,000 people along the Techa depended on the river for drinking and irrigation water. Between 1953 and 1956, the government evacuated 6,244 people from villages situated downstream (Kossenko 1997: 55). Officials organized the evacuation of whole populations, leaving ghost towns whose stoic, empty churches still stand along the river as reminders of the plutonium plague. The vast majority of the people were settled in what were to be temporary houses. In time these homes became substandard, but their inhabitants had no choice but to remain living in them. The state-controlled system of housing prevented people from seeking their own housing. They had virtually no choice but to accept what the government issued them.

It is not clear what motivated officials to evacuate people from some of the downstream villages and not to move other villages. For instance, all thirteen villages closest to Mayak were evacuated, but not Muslyumovo, the fourteenth, yet four villages farther downstream were evacuated. The nineteenth village Brodokalmak also was not evacuated.

The next and most disastrous incident was the Kyshtym explosion of 1957. This is how Mikhail Gladyshev (1990: 65–66), former director of Mayak's plutonium facility, recalled the events:

> The day after the explosion it was clear that the radioactive particles thrown high into the air were being carried by the wind to the northeast. The fallout zone included other sectors of the plant, and what was worse, villages, small communities, rivers and reservoirs situated close to our town. The population was evacuated from their villages to other areas. Everyone had to be washed and changed, they all had to be given only new and clean things, new homes had to be found and they had to be taken to them: a massive organizational task! Enormous expenses! What well-chosen and persuasive words had to be said to the people, the vast majority of them Bashkirs. I personally did not take part in this work, but from the accounts of A. N. Zaitsev—it was he who led all the evacuation work—I understood just how difficult this had been. What was surprising was that the evacuation took place relatively quickly and without noise and fuss, in fact so quietly and calmly that fairly soon everyone had got used to their new conditions and new life. It is true that I might not know all the details, since I was not involved myself, but I can say that there was none of the fuss of Chernobyl: people understood the situation and got down to work without unnecessary hysterics.

Evacuees interviewed for this study confirm Gladyshev's observation that the population did not put up any resistance. The people were conditioned by Soviet government to obey orders and to believe that their leaders knew what was best for them. In 1957 the Stalinist reign of terror in the Soviet Union had eased up only a few years before. Each of these communities had seen the secret police take its citizens to the gulags in the middle of the night, never to return, without having committed any apparent crime and without the right to an investigation or trial. People were conditioned not to utter any thoughts critical of the government. Furthermore, government officials forced heads of households to sign papers swearing themselves to secrecy about the circumstances of their evacuation. Keane refers to this sort of conditioning as the "rational-calculating use of violence as a technique of terrorizing and demoralizing whole populations and preventing them from engaging in organized or premeditated resistance" (1996: 31). Bashkirs explain that the harsh military discipline in the pre-Soviet era also helped to mold an obedient population. Between 1798 and 1865, most Bashkir men served as rank-and-file soldiers in the czarist armies guarding Russia's eastern borders.

Even though the 1957 evacuation met with no resistance and went more smoothly than officials expected, both as individuals and as communities, the evacuees suffered deep emotional and cultural trauma from this sudden uprooting from ancestral villages. Men and women informants recalled their resettlement with tears in their eyes as they described how, with only one day's notice and with no explanations offered, Soviet troops ordered them to slaughter their own animals and prepare their homes for burning. They told how they had to part with family heirlooms and cemeteries, how they were loaded onto army trucks that took them to barracks or unheated resort facilities, herded into showers, ordered to give up all their clothing, and issued military attire.

We talked to people in Dal'naya Dacha who worked at one of the health resorts where evacuees were housed from October 1957 to May 1958. They recall caring solely for evacuees from neighboring villages and doing this job without the assistance of Mayak officials or physicians. A woman who worked in the cafeteria of the resort sponsored by Ozyorsk told us that throughout the period during which evacuees were at her resort, no doctors or managers from Mayak even visited the site, "as if," she said, "they were afraid of being contaminated." She recounted her observations of this traumatic experience when, in early October 1957, several hundred Bashkirs and Tatars (a related indigenous ethnic group), whole families with children and elders, were brought to the resort:

> Most of them did not speak any Russian; they chattered to each other in their own language. They lived in buildings that were only used in summer so they weren't heated, and were given free food for only two months. Afterwards they had to find their own food until they left in May, I have no idea where to. All the belongings they brought with them from home were confiscated and burned. The Bashkir women tried to sneak back into the building where they had been forced to leave all their clothing, including their

Signed secrecy papers

1 day's notice

Mayak doctors didn't help treat victims

ethnic attire. As soon as they were seen in these clothes they were made to give them up for burning. Some of them were so desperate they even managed to go back to their villages before they were burned down in order to retrieve food and clothing. The women did all the housekeeping and hunting for food, while the men roamed around town and drank vodka.[1]

One of the evacuees from the 1957 disaster explained that when the soldiers came from Mayak to inform his fellow villagers that they had to leave their homes forever the very next morning, they advised the men to drink up whatever vodka they had in stock to protect themselves from the exposure: "The male villagers did as told. We took all the alcohol out of storage in the village store and homes and drank as much as we could."

After several months the government stopped feeding the evacuees in the barracks and resorts where they had been herded. The people were eventually left on their own to gradually put their lives back together without any government assistance. Some were eventually offered other housing, but many were forced to find shelter and jobs alone. One major obstacle to starting a new life was the commitment they had made when they signed the papers promising not to tell anyone why they had moved. This prevented them from giving a prospective employer a previous work reference. They could not say where they were from and why they left. In fundamental ways they lost control over their lives for a very long time.

The people who wept in front of us reminded one of the authors of the victims of post-traumatic stress that she has interviewed in war zones on another research project in the Caucasus. Informants quite unexpectedly broke into tears as the conversation triggered deep-seated memories. Like other sufferers of post-traumatic stress, they had kept their trauma hidden deep inside. They said that for years they had pushed all thoughts about their past from memory and refrained from talking to anyone about what happened. Some said that we were the first to hear their stories. We felt as though the experiences of these people, who were finally opening up about the past, bordered on the cathartic.

The final Chelyabinsk disaster took place in 1967, during a severe drought in the Urals. Lake Karachai, the repository for Mayak's radioactive wastes since the mid-1950s after dumping into the Techa River ceased, saw its water level decrease dramatically, exposing some of the lake bed where the sediments contained about 120 million curies of radioactive materials. Windstorms carried the radioactive silt into the atmosphere over population centers of up to 40,000 (Feshbach and Friendly 1992).

Before the revelations of the Gorbachev era about the role of Mayak in Chelyabinsk, people were aware of their health problems but did not re-

---

1. Conversation with authors in Dal'naya Dacha, April 1993.

late them to Mayak. In Muslyumovo, for instance, officials told the people since the mid-1950s that their local river was "dirty" but not that Mayak was the source of the "dirt." This industrial site was not allowed to be part of their consciousness because it was a defense plant and completely hidden from view and from any public discourse. People did not talk about these matters and pretended such places did not exist, for fear of saying something that would get them in trouble. It was as if Mayak and the secret cities were invisible.

Of course, it was impossible to keep these disasters and the consequent evacuations a complete secret. Rumors began to circulate throughout the river communities about radiation contamination. Few people knew the term, but even if they did, they understood it simplistically, equating its effects with those of an x-ray. Inhabitants claim that officials never explained to them either the scope of the radiation contamination or the health and environmental consequences.

The people gradually began to understand the effects of radiation on the environment and health as information was released after the 1986 Chernobyl disaster. It was not until 1989, however, under the massive pressure of the environmental movement of the Gorbachev era of openness, that the government officially acknowledged Mayak's extensive contamination.

In April 1991, the Chelyabinsk population became fully aware of the implications of their proximity to the nuclear weapons facility when a public report that Gorbachev commissioned detailed in two volumes the legacy of Mayak. The report is called "Proceedings of the Commission on Studying the Ecological Situation in Chelyabinsk Oblast." The results of this report had the impact of a bombshell on the entire population of Chelyabinsk. The article summed up a study done by a government commission, which revealed that since 1950, the incidence of leukemia among the population exposed to radiation along the Techa River had increased by 41 percent. From 1980 to 1990, all cancers among this population had risen by 21 percent and all diseases of the circulatory system, by 31 percent.

This report is not considered the final word on the tragedy of Chelyabinsk. Doctors in the region say it is impossible to obtain completely dependable health data because officials instructed physicians to limit the number of death certificates they issued with diagnoses of cancer or other radiation-related illnesses. This was part of the general Soviet practice to control health statistics so that rates of certain illnesses would not be embarrassingly high. We learned from a rural physician in Chelyabinsk that once a certain number of illnesses had been reached, no more were to be reported. Another problem is that the Muslim Bashkirs and Tatars, because of religious considerations, would not always permit an autopsy to establish cause of death. When they did allow an autopsy, they were angered to see that a whole team of physicians was at the side of the deceased within hours after death although during the illness the doctors did not appear once to offer the patient aid.

People in Muslyumovo believe that they should have been evacuated away from the contaminated Techa River. They are convinced that all their illnesses are caused by the river, which many of them call the *atomka*, a slang derivative from the Russian word "atomic." They believe that the authorities have kept them there to use them as guinea pigs to study the effects of long-term low-dose radiation. This is why they named their environmental organization "White Mice" after laboratory test mice. Indeed, over the decades they have been summoned periodically to undergo medical examinations and tests at what used to be called the Chelyabinsk Branch of the Institute of Biophysics. In our interviews with Dr. Mira Kossenko, one of the leading physicians there, she openly acknowledged that the institute's doctors were sworn to conceal their true diagnosis from patients and never tell them they were radiation victims. The data they have are still not easily accessible to independent researchers. A promising effort to rescue that information is being conducted by the Joint Coordinating Committee for Radiation Effects Research Program organized and funded by the United States Department of Energy. This program enables U.S. and Russian researchers to analyze existing data and to conduct new research to investigate the possible link between Mayak and the health of the Chelyabinsk population (Kellogg and Kirk 1997). It is still unclear whether other researchers also will gain access.

In the early 1990s, Nina Solovyova (1994), a research physician from Novosibirsk, did an independent study of the people of Muslyumovo. Her work has been criticized by nuclear establishment medical researchers in Russia, including the Urals Research Center for Radiation Medicine, but the people of Chelyabinsk have embraced its results. Solovyova found that 25 percent of Muslyumovo residents exhibited genetic cell deformation. Her control village had evacuees from the twenty-two Techa River villages relocated in the 1950s, as well as people who never lived in contaminated areas. She claimed that when she observed the children in the villages she took samples from, she could tell by looking at them which ones were from the families of evacuees who had been exposed to radiation before being evacuated and which ones were not because of what she felt were obviously exhibited medical symptoms. The sickly look that she saw in these children she referred to as the "Muslyumovo syndrome."

The people of Muslyumovo, who believe that they have this syndrome, feel sure the government is unlikely to finance the relocation of most residents, so some individuals are "evacuating" their own families. One local school teacher, who has three of her own children and is looking for a way to move out, constantly gives her students these three pieces of advice: (1)

(handwritten margin notes:) victims that they weren't evacuated further away so that could be kept as experiments of radiation / named their Environmental organization / "White Mice" / more stats

(handwritten note at bottom:) "atomka" - atomic river (Russian)

don't go near the river, (2) get away from Muslyumovo as soon as possible, and (3) don't marry each other. Simultaneously an opposite trend has been under way. In the economic crisis that has paralyzed Russia in the late 1990s, many villagers have returned to Muslyumovo from the cities where they are unemployed because in the countryside they can at least feed their families off the land. These people seem to cope by taking an attitude of resignation to their plight, choosing between the lesser of two evils—possible health risks or certain hunger. This is the way one man put it: "Of course, everyone understands the extent of the danger and the damage to our health caused by Mayak. At the same time, we've all become used to this, and have given up fighting it." Others cope by simply denying the risks exist.

The populations of the cities of Tomsk and Krasnoyarsk, in Siberia, and nearby villages also have been traumatized by the environmental risks of living near secret plants where uranium and plutonium were processed for nuclear weapons throughout the Cold War, and where similar activities continue today. The plant in the closed city of Tomsk-7 (now known as Seversk) is located 15 kilometers from Tomsk, with a population of over 100,000. The plant in the closed city of Krasnoyarsk-26 (now known as Zheleznogorsk) is 50 kilometers from Krasnoyarsk, an even larger city, which has a population of several hundred thousand more than Tomsk. These plants generated large amounts of highly toxic and radioactive waste that has been disposed of by injecting it, uncontained, a few hundred meters below the surface of the ground near the Tom and Yenisei rivers. These rivers are major sources of drinking water for tens of thousands of people. Almost 40 million cubic meters of liquid radioactive waste, with a total radioactivity of over 1 billion curies, has been injected underground at Tomsk, and at Krasnoyarsk 4 million cubic meters of waste have been injected, with a total radioactivity of 700 million curies (Gusterson 1998).

Until 1989, the populations around these sites had no idea about their activities because the plants were built in the 1950s. Like all the other closed cities of the nuclear weapons industry, it was as though Tomsk-7 and Krasnoyarsk-26 did not exist. Tomsk activists explained that as late as 1989, just before news came out all over the Soviet Union about these closed cities, an industrial bureaucrat at a local party meeting dared to say out loud the name of the Tomsk Siberian Chemical Plant, located in Tomsk-7. For that, he was detained for 2 hours by the KGB. The consequences to this man probably would have been much worse if he had spoken up at such a meeting before the Gorbachev period of openness.

Because of this secrecy, it is still difficult to know the extent of the health impacts of these plants on the local population. As is the case with our research in the Chelyabinsk region, we found that local physicians trying to do independent studies do not have adequate access to information from the nuclear weapons industry. Nevertheless, they have tried on their own to determine links between the environmental problems and the state of the people's health. One such physician is Vladimir Mazharev in Krasnoyarsk.

In his study, physicians examined children and adults in three contaminated areas around Krasnoyarsk. The results showed that more children in the contaminated areas had health problems than did those in the noncontaminated regions. Adults tended to have more psychological problems than did children in the contaminated regions. The study found that the incidence of leukemia in men and women as well as general mortality decreased the farther away the population was from Krasnoyarsk-26.

Tamara Matkovskaya, a pediatrician in Tomsk, examined 213 children in four towns near Tomsk to identify health problems that might be related to an explosion that took place at Tomsk-7 on April 6, 1993. These were the results: 53 percent had ailments of the nervous system; 28 percent, swollen glands; 50 percent, red eyes; 80 percent, anemia; 22 percent were completely healthy. Parents reported that many of these children had vomiting, nausea, and diarrhea right after the explosion. Many of them continued to experience these and other symptoms, such as headaches and drowsiness, throughout the whole summer. Of all these symptoms, according to Matkovskaya, the fatigue and drowsiness continued up to the time when she reported this information to the international conference in September 1994.

These victims regard themselves as the accidental victims of the Cold War, hit by "friendly fire." They assign blame to the Soviet government, which created and managed the sites but which no longer exists and therefore can no longer be made accountable, even though many of the individual administrators are still employed. The anger of the victims also is aimed against local officials and doctors who have withheld information about the consequences. For decades the government sponsored secret medical research based on elaborate tests on thousands of Chelyabinsk residents. Doctors examined and diagnosed these unwitting patients but neither revealed the diagnoses to them nor treated their illnesses. This was a common refrain that we heard from patients who were periodically summoned for testing by the medical center: "If they had only told me how much radiation I had accumulated, I never would have had children."

Patriotic pride in this facility, however, is often expressed by the same people who curse it. Here's a typical statement of this kind:

Mayak is a unique complex, not only in our country, but in the world. Indeed, it has brought our country enormous benefit, and made it among the best in the world. The isotope plant that opened in 1962 produces fiber optics, devices for radiation control, batteries for artificial hearts, new materials and reinforced plastics, and new technology for storing nuclear waste (vitrification). All this brings the state hundreds of millions of dollars in profits. And we should not underestimate the fact that Mayak had Americans worried about the Russian bomb. It's no wonder that Chelyabinsk was one of the main targets for a nuclear weapons attack on our country. But at what price? That's what we must talk about.[2]

Such people are not angry at the government for having this industry but for doing a bad job of protecting the people from the plant's products.

Furthermore, the facilities have no way to compensate the victims for its environmental damage over the course of half a century. In the past they did not want to compensate the victims; today they simply do not have the resources. The lawyers representing these controversial sites do everything possible to throw out of court all the suits that have been filed against them in recent years. They consider that the blame rests with the Soviet system and the state that created these circumstances, not the individual facilities. Of course, the old system and state no longer exist.

The populations of these areas have been responding to this new situation in two ways. The vast majority is passive. They have become more open about their illnesses and sense of victimization but take no action, feeling that nothing will help. Instead they wait for compensation from the government. Their attitude is that of dependence. They tend not to take any precautions anymore against the contaminated land and food or consider the factor of exposure to radiation when choosing a spouse. In recent years the terms "environmental disaster" and "ecocide" have become so common that the people seem to have become numb to the idea of danger and the fear of contamination, especially since the culprit cannot be seen, heard, or touched. They see the problems and dangers posed by the environmental degradation as inevitable evils that are impossible to fight. In Chelyabinsk the religious Muslim Bashkirs and Tatars sometimes say these problems are Allah's way of punishing them for their sins.

The second trend is a more active response, but this is by a small minority. In Tomsk, Konstantin Lebedev, an environmental lawyer, has filed a suit against the closed city of Tomsk-7 to revoke its permit to inject radioactive waste water from cooling nuclear reactors within the complex into water-bearing layers (aquifers) underground. The plant's officials maintain that a water-resistant layer of clay keeps water from the top and bottom layers from mixing. Local environmentalists disagree with this and

2. Gosman Kabirov, presentation made to a conference of the antinuclear groups in the Socio-Ecological Union, Moscow, March 12–14, 1993.

with the extent to which contaminated groundwater migration can affect Tomsk's artesian wells for drinking water. The suit was filed in August 1997 (Whiteley 1999).

In the Chelyabinsk region, those who are fighting the government on nuclear environmental issues are individuals in the small environmental organizations that have developed in the areas considered locally as the most contaminated, such as Muslyumovo. In the early 1990s, local activists organized large rallies. Recently they have organized lawsuits against Mayak to get compensation for radiation victims, pressured the authorities to ensure better housing conditions for the population, and conducted educational campaigns. In the Chelyabinsk region in mid-1997, families seeking compensation for disabilities caused by radiation contamination filed fifty lawsuits against Mayak.[3]

The first case to be successful in court was in July 1997, when the Chelyabinsk regional court upheld the decision of the Ozyorsk city court. A local court fined Mayak 50 million rubles ($8,000) to compensate the Nazhmutdinov family for a disabled son. The 5-year-old Bashkir child was born without his right foot and has a deformed hand. He also has defective digestive and motor systems. The family's lawyers, deploying independent medical expertise, were able to convince the court that there was a link between the child's congenital disabilities and Muslyumovo's radiation contamination. The environmental leaders of Chelyabinsk hope this case will set a precedent for others.

(handwritten margin note: first successful lawsuit 1997 (Mayak))

Another triumph of local activists against the consequences of the Mayak accidents came just before the fortieth anniversary of the 1957 disaster. On July 28, 1997, the governor of the Chelyabinsk region, P. I. Sumin, passed a resolution to move 1,350 families in the Kunashak (669 in Muslyumovo) and Krasnoarmeisk areas to sites farther away from the contaminated areas.

A third victory for the local environmental movement was the election in 1997 of Dr. Gulfarida Galimova, who ran for the job of administrator of Muslyumovo. In the early 1990s, Dr. Galimova was harassed for her environmental activism by her predecessor and other local officials. At one point she lost her job as the village doctor. She continued her efforts on behalf of the population and their health. Voters rewarded her for her consistent and selfless activities by giving her a mandate to defend their interests as the leading official of Muslyumovo.

These victories have not generated more activism, but are sufficient to keep alive the enthusiasm of the small number of activists left in

---

3. *The Moscow Times,* "Plaintiff Wins Nuclear Contamination Suit," Wednesday, July 30, 1997: 3.

no case for *environmental racism*

Chelyabinsk from the much more active era of the late 1980s and early 1990s. Although most activists in areas outside the city of Chelyabinsk are Tatars and Bashkirs, and the majority of radiation victims come from these non-Russian ethnic groups, the activists have not joined forces with Bashkir and Tatar nationalists, nor have they focused on issues of environmental racism. There is no tangible evidence that environmental racism has been a clear factor in this region, nor is there any indication that the local Bashkirs and Tatars regard their situation as the result of policies aimed particularly against their ethnic groups. Most activists in all these contaminated regions insist that the Soviet nuclear policies were nondiscriminatory; they were generally antihuman, and did not target non-Russians. In the cases of Tomsk and Krasnoyarsk, no indigenous groups were affected—these are largely ethnic Russian territories. So there does not seem to be a case for environmental racism.

In contemporary Russia where a fierce struggle for power is under way at all levels of government, the economy hobbles, unemployment persists, and living standards are low, the people of all the areas contaminated by nuclear disasters see no clear solutions to their plight. The dominant reaction is a desperate sense of powerlessness in the face of the formidable problems posed by the nuclear plants and by the economic decline and chaos that have followed the collapse of the Soviet Union.

As Valerie Kuletz points out in her chapter, research and production that was carried out during the Cold War in the name of national defense is being continued in both the United States and Russia in the noble name of development. Chelyabinsk is one of the main sites for reprocessing and storing spent fuel from Soviet style nuclear power plants across the post-Soviet regions. The Tomsk and Krasnoyarsk sites are also being used to process and store enormous amounts of radioactive materials under high-risk conditions. All these sites, both in the United States and Russia, have been made essentially invisible to the public. In Russia this invisibility has been conjured by the silent fear of reprisal and brutally enforced secrecy, to a greater degree under the Soviet state and to a lesser degree in contemporary Russia. The result is a profound sense, among a vast population, of physical and psychological victimization; the people see no end in sight.

IV

Green Government and the Normalization of Violent
Environments

13

Disciplining Peasants in Tanzania: From State Violence to Self-Surveillance in Wildlife Conservation

Roderick P. Neumann

"Game rangers kill 50 villagers in Serengeti park—Tarime MP." So declared the front-page headline of July 23, 1998, in Tanzania's independent English daily, *The Guardian*. The allegation was made by the Member of Parliament (MP) from Tarime in Mara Region, of which approximately one-third falls within the Serengeti National Park boundaries. According to the MP, a group of villagers, suffering from a famine that had gripped Mara Region in 1997, entered the park, armed with bows and arrows, in search of small game. They were discovered by park rangers and disarmed. Rather than turning the suspects over to the local magistrate, however, "the game rangers who arrested them lined up the suspects and shot them," the MP said (*The Guardian* July 23, 1998: 1). The execution allegedly was covered up by disposal of the bodies in the Mara River and transference of the rangers involved to other duty stations. The MP placed responsibility for the murders on a former Minister of Natural Resources and Tourism who had issued a shoot-on-sight directive to rangers in 1997 for "bandits" found in the park. The directive had been issued in response to an increase in violent robberies of foreign tourists, including a murder, in Tanzania's lucrative "northern circuit" of wildlife parks. An investigation of the Serengeti killings, which allegedly occurred on September 24, 1997, is, at this writing, said to be ongoing.[1]

---

1. The government's investigation has so far not resulted in indictments. Independent investigations have been ongoing. In May 2000, the Legal Human Rights Centre in Dar es Salaam said it had gathered enough evidence, including a videotaped eyewitness account, to incriminate the suspect rangers. Efforts to force further government action in the case continue.

This horrific incident, if proved to be true, is unprecedented in the history of state-directed wildlife conservation in Tanzania. This chapter is in part about answering the question, "Why now?" In asking this question, I do not mean to imply that this as an "isolated incident" but rather to argue that it is a symptom of a long-term shift in the nature of the relationship between peasants and the state in the realm of wildlife conservation. It comes, however, at an odd historical moment in African wildlife conservation. For the past decade or more, conservation rhetoric has emphasized the limitations of coercive approaches, and new policies have focused on encouraging local community participation and benefit sharing. The chapter, thus, is also about trying to understand the coincidence of violent coercion with the new "community-friendly" approach to conservation.

In this chapter, I explore several trains of thought related to violence and conservation. I first want to briefly outline why state efforts to control wildlife resources in Africa are inherently violent or at least inherently conducive to violence. A second, lengthier exercise is to categorize the types of violence, to look for historical patterns, and to think about the way political-economic/historical circumstances influence the level of violence. Third, I want to explore, in terms of contemporary social theory, the relationship between the dual conservation policy of paramilitary control of protected areas and community participation and benefit sharing.

To explore these questions, I will rely on examples from the history of national parks and wildlife conservation in Tanzania (though I would argue that similar examples and patterns could be observed in much of sub-Saharan Africa). The information used was obtained during several periods of research between 1989 and 1998. Sources include interviews, archival documents, government and nongovernmental organization (NGO) documents, and a variety of published materials. Many of the examples come from research done in communities near two very different protected areas, Arusha National Park and the Selous Game Reserve. The former is one of the smallest national parks in Africa and is surrounded by some of the highest human population densities in East Africa. The latter is the largest game reserve on the continent and is surrounded by some of the most sparsely populated districts in Tanzania. There are, despite these differences, remarkably similar patterns in the experiences of the surrounding communities with state-directed conservation.

Proclivity of Wildlife Conservation to Violence

I want to begin by positing that violence against people is inherent and perpetually latent in the practice of state-directed wildlife conservation in Africa. Why is this so? First, circumstantial reasons are evident. People involved in hunting or defending crops against wildlife predation are armed with weapons. Indeed, travel on foot in areas of concentrated wildlife populations in Africa practically requires that people bear arms for their own self-preservation. Weapons are, therefore, commonly in the possession of parties involved in disagreements or confrontation over wildlife laws. The ubiquity of weapons allows for situations to easily escalate from angry exchanges of words, to threats, to extreme physical violence.

Second, there are historical reasons. An important part of the process of modern state formation in Africa involved the central government securing control over natural resources, such as wildlife, that were vital to rural livelihoods. This was conducive to violent exchanges, such as assaults and occasionally killings, because the stakes were often high. People had to choose between fighting or going hungry. Furthermore, this shift of control has itself historically been an act of violence against a population because it reduced access to a source of nutrition, usually without providing an alternative.

Another historical reason is that in much of colonial Africa, both European hunting and wildlife conservation efforts were closely associated with military activities. People trained by the state in the use of weapons and the application of violence—former police, prison, or military personnel—have been traditionally the primary source of recruits for game rangers. The result has been, as Tanzania's Minister for Natural Resources recognized four decades ago, that "the Department has tended to be looked on (and behave) like a Special Police Unit rather than . . . technical advisers on game conservation."[2] This history is today reflected in the paramilitary style of organization of most wildlife and park agencies in Africa.

Finally, there are geographical reasons. Almost by definition, areas of wildlife concentration are remote from towns and cities. The implications of this are twofold. First, the possibility of committing an illegal act of violence and escaping prosecution is high. Witnesses are few or nonexistent, evidence can be disposed of with little trace, and discipline among the state's enforcement personnel is more difficult to maintain. Patrols often are conducted in pairs or small groups without the supervision of a senior officer, and accusations of excessive force are difficult to investigate or prove. In a word, violence is made "invisible" by virtue of geographic isolation. Second, the remoteness of wildlife concentrations is a reflection of a geographical pattern of uneven development common to Africa. These are regions with few infrastructural improvements, poor or nonexistent

2. "Report and Recommendations on Game Conservation Policy with Particular Reference to Poaching" by Hugh Elliot, 1958. Tanzania National Archive (TNA) Accession No. 273, MLFW 569: 35.

government social services, and bare subsistence agriculture. These often are places where nutrition from wild is most critical and most habitually relied on and, thus, where people are most tempted to challenge the enforcement of wildlife conservation laws.

Categories and Patterns of Violence in Wildlife Conservation

In this section, I propose three distinguishable categories of violence manifested in the implementation of state-directed wildlife conservation: displacement, increased vulnerability to natural hazards, and person to person. Using examples from throughout Tanzania's colonial and postcolonial periods, I will illustrate each category in turn. In the process I hope to reveal historical patterns and variations in the level and nature of violence and then offer explanations for these.

Displacement

By displacement I mean a population's loss of rights of access to land and natural resources and the removal or destruction of homes, crops, and livestock for the purposes of wildlife conservation. I classify it as a form of violence because African states have rarely provided equivalent livelihood alternatives or adequate compensation for evictees. Hence, the agrarian populations are often less able to sustain themselves and maintain levels of health and nutrition following evictions. A position paper produced by a Tanzanian pastoralist NGO, Korongoro Integrated Peoples Oriented to Conservation (KIPOC), headquartered near Serengeti National Park highlights the violence of this phenomenon.

> Extensive tracks of quality rangelands have been carved into wildlife preserves for exclusive use by wild animals and tourists. . . . In that pursuit African regimes have carried on eviction of indigenous peoples and denied them access to resources vital to the viability of their flexible transhumance system of utilization of their land. These losses of land are accompanied by denial of access to critical sources of water and salt licks as well as sacred sites, of worship and burial. (KIPOC 1992: 14)

Additionally, because people are almost always reluctant to relocate, evictions often have involved either overt acts of violence by agents of the state or coercion by threats of violence and harassment.

Displacement is inherent in the implementation of wildlife conservation policies in Africa for two reasons. First, the maintenance of large expanses of land devoid of human settlement and influence are their cornerstone.

In the case of Tanzania, I have been unable to find an example of protected area establishment that did not require, at the very least, the curtailment of access to livelihood resources (e.g., water, pasture, honey, meat) and, in the extreme, the removal of entire villages.[3] Second, wildlife conservation (in much of Africa) has meant state regulation of the technology, species, season, and location of hunting favorable toward European practices and antagonistic toward African practices (MacKenzie 1988; Neumann 1998). Wildlife policies, thus, often result in decreased access to wild meat protein for a significant portion of the rural population.

As in other tropical regions (e.g., Sundar this volume; Peluso 1992), the model for scientific resource management and conservation was implemented in Tanzania during colonial occupation. The German colonial administration (1894–1916) established the first state hunting laws and game reserves in the territory, then known as German East Africa. Since that time, conflicts between the peasantry and the state over land and natural resources have been endemic in communities bordering protected areas. The British colonial government (1919–1961) based their Game Ordinance of 1921 on that of their German predecessors. The ordinance outlawed certain traditional hunting practices (including the use of nets, traps, snares, and pit-falls) and created game reserves where the governor could prohibit hunting, entry, settlement, cultivation, and the cutting of vegetation. It also required licenses for certain "scheduled" species, such as elephant (*Loxodonta africana*) and rhinoceros (*Diceros bicornis*). The 1940 Game Bill did not significantly alter Tanganyika's game policy, but it did explicitly recognize the importance of wild meat to African livelihoods. It read, "[n]othing in the foregoing provisions of this Part shall make it an offense for a native to hunt . . . for the purpose of supplying himself and his dependents with food."[4] As for game reserves and national parks, certain customary rights also were confirmed in the bill. Any "person whose place of birth or ordinary residence is within the reserve" or "who has any rights over immovable property within the reserve" could enter or reside within. Immovable property, it was ruled, included pasturage for livestock.

Relocations from reserves were deliberated very carefully by the colonial governments who also had to consider the terms of the League of Nations Mandate and, after World War II, were subject to oversight by the United Nations Trusteeship Council. Tanganyika was "mandated" to Britain by the League of Nations following World War I. The territorial mandate was os-

3. For example, dozens of villages and some 40,000 people were resettled outside the boundaries of what eventually became the Selous Game Reserve, mostly during the 1930s and 1940s. In this case, people were relocated into concentrated settlements to facilitate tax collection, disease control, wildlife control, and peasant crop production.
4. Tanganyika Territory, 1940 Game Bill, TNA.

tensibly for Britain to act as the territory's "protector" while interfering as little as possible with existing African land and resource rights.

After World War II, the United Nations Trusteeship Council could and did send delegations to Tanganyika to investigate whether African rights were being respected. Furthermore, any changes in land occupation were to be conducted through the local Native Authorities, part of the Colonial Office's policy of indirect rule. Therefore, overt force was a last resort, and evictions had to follow the rule of law: to appear consensual and to be justified in terms of a greater moral purpose (i.e., other than wildlife protection for European hunting and tourism). A few examples will demonstrate how this was achieved.

The two largest colonial relocations, both in terms of population numbers and geographic extent, were the Selous Game Reserve and Serengeti National Park. The ultimate boundaries of the Selous were, to a large extent, the result of massive resettlements for the control of sleeping sickness in the 1940s (Neumann 1999). The principal justification for the eviction of 40,000 people, therefore, was the improvement of the health and welfare of the residents of the territory, not wildlife conservation. The evacuation of Serengeti was more difficult to justify and complicated by the growth of nationalist resistance to colonial rule. The year that the boundaries were finalized (1951) was the same year the Mau Mau emergency was declared just over the border in Kenya. Officials worried that their eviction of cultivators in Serengeti was "not going to pass unnoticed among local agitators and it is therefore important that it should receive legal sanction."[5] The Provincial Commissioner warned park authorities that the "Government could not tolerate any forced eviction."[6] The political crisis was temporarily solved when officials convinced the Maasai Native Authority to give notice of eviction to the cultivators in exchange for continued pasture and water access.[7] Ultimately, Serengeti was evacuated through a "compromise" agreement whereby the Maasai would remove themselves in exchange for being allowed to occupy the Ngorongoro Crater area, which was excised from the park and gazetted as a "Conservation Area" that accommodated some customary land uses.

A final example demonstrates how various methods of coercion by state agencies can achieve the appearance of consent to relocate. In 1954, colonial authorities convinced 297 families living in five separate communities

5. District Commissioner (DC), Masai/Monduli, to Provincial Commissioner (PC), Northern Province, June 23, 1952, TNA Arusha Regional File T3/2 Accession No. 69.

6. PC, Northern Province, "Memorandum on Serengeti Evictions," January 19, 1955, TNA Arusha Regional File G1/6, Accession No. 69.

7. Molloy, Director, Tanzania National Parks (TANAPA), to PC, Northern Province, "Report on Human Inhabitants, Serengeti National Park," June 8, 1955, TNA Arusha Regional File G1/6, Accession No. 69.

to move outside the proposed Mbeya reserve boundaries.[8] Because the District Officer considered "compulsory eviction politically inexpedient" and the largest community was "extremely averse to moving,"[9] authorities were forced to resort to a combination of negotiation, coercion, and intimidation. As part of its campaign, the government built a road into the area (which had an "important psychological effect on the people"[10] living there), established permanent field stations next to the most resistant communities, and promised them "that if they refused to go, rigid soil conservation rules would be enforced and a *baraza* [local court] erected in the area where swift punishment would be meted out."[11] Realizing "they would have no peace,"[12] the communities surrendered their access rights in exchange for monetary compensation but declined to participate in the government's relocation plan. The villagers had initially resisted the move, in part, because the government's relocation areas were malarial, uncleared bush. Rather than move to these sites after giving in to government pressure, they opted to move in with relatives and friends in already-occupied lands.

Restrictions on African hunting also were politically sensitive and dealt with carefully, despite the constant demands from European hunting and conservation advocates for more restrictions and harsher penalties for Africans. The policy of the government for most of the colonial years was supposedly guided by the idea "that the native should be regarded as having a moral right to kill a piece of game for food."[13] Indeed, many colonial officials were reluctant to further limit African access to wild meat because of the resultant detrimental effects on health and welfare. Conveying the sentiments of the Secretary of State for the Colonies, in 1948 an official informed the provincial commissioners that the government was not interested in creating new restrictions on African hunting. He noted that "a large number of the African population, many of whom suffer from an ill balanced diet, would be deprived of an important source of protein in the form of such game meat."[14] Debating a plan to outlaw the use of poisons for African hunting in 1957, officials in Dar es Salaam anticipated that a ban on use would be unenforceable and very unpopular because of its importance in obtaining meat. As the Secretary for Agriculture and Natural Resources acknowledged, "[i]f we prohibit possession or even manufac-

8. J. G. Cowap, "Report of the History of the Creation of the Mbeya Range Forest Reserve," November 8, 1956, Rhodes House Library, Oxford University, MSS.Afr s.1982.

9. Cowap 1982: 5, 7.

10. Cowap 1982: 9.

11. Cowap 1982: 10.

12. Cowap 1982: 13.

13. Chief Secretary (CS) to PC, Mwanza, May 21, 1929, TNA 13371.

14. MANR to all PCs, October 21, 1948, TNA 37492.

ture that would write the ultimate death warrant of the Bahi tribe which lives solely from the proceeds of the poisoned arrow."[15]

By the time independence came in 1961, laws that prohibited residence in national parks and outlawed most traditional hunting practices were in place, and a great deal of pressure and support from well-organized and highly motivated international conservationists was aimed at African governments to maintain them. At the same time, the new government and international donors saw a comprehensive effort to modernize the economy as the most pressing need for the newly independent but poverty-stricken nation. This justified a range of policies meant to alter rural economies and land use patterns, exemplified by government efforts to consolidate scattered peasant households into village settlements. This policy was eventually enacted on a mass scale in 1974 through "Operation *Vijiji*," a government initiative to resettle eight million peasants into villages.

The drive to modernize also meant that national parks and protected areas were now viewed as key components in economic development. They provided the basis for a tourism industry expected to provide the second greatest source of foreign exchange. A 1962 New York Zoological Society "mission" to Tanzania (led by Royal Little, "an industrialist, deeply interested in the preservation of African wildlife"[16]), crystallized the emphasis on tourism. The point of the mission was to the help the Tanzanian government ask for funds, specifically from the United States Agency for International Development (USAID), for: road development, airfields, accommodations for tourists, wildlife management, and minimization of poaching.[17] Additionally, they hoped the visit would stimulate interest among U.S. corporations for capital investments.[18] Arthur D. Little, Inc., the U.S. business consulting firm, prepared a report, "Tourism: Stimulus for Wildlife Conservation," delivered to the government in 1962. The upshot of the report is that the new tourism industry would largely depend on existing and future national parks. Consequently, Tanganyika National Parks had "to make a determined shift" in their policies "to insure that National Parks play their full part in the economic development of the country" (Tanganyika National Parks 1962: 8–9).

Continued dislocations, especially to establish and manage national parks, were thus supported by a double justification: the creation of new tourist destinations to generate revenue and the concentration of peasant

15. SANR to MANR, April 11, 1957, file notes, TNA Accession No. 273, MLFW 569.
16. Fairfield Osborn, President, NYZS to Clive Mace, Permanent Secretary, Ministry of Lands, Forests, and Wildlife, January 16, 1962, Accession No. 273, MLFW 631.
17. Ibid.
18. J. S. Owen, Director, Tanzania National Parks (TANAPA), to Permanent Secretary, Ministry of Lands, Forests, and Wildlife, March 12, 1962, Accession No. 273, MLFW 631.

populations to facilitate rural development. Former President Julius Nyerere, for example, supported relocations near Serengeti National Park because they coincided with the objectives of the government's "villagization" policy. When touring the area in 1963, the president "instructed the local authorities in the area to work out in collaboration with the National Parks, a scheme to resettle" two hundred households near the park boundary (Tanganyika National Parks 1964: 34).

Although difficult to demonstrate conclusively, there is evidence that the violence of dislocations for wildlife conservation has increased during the postcolonial period. For example, in 1974, the same year that "Operation *Vijiji*" was initiated, Maasai pastoralists, legally resident in Ngorongoro Crater Conservation Area, were summarily evicted by the government's paramilitary Field Force Unit (FFU). "Without explanation and without notice they ordered the immediate eviction of the inhabitants and their cattle. Their possessions were carried out by transport of the Conservation Authority and dumped on the roadside at Lairobi. No explanation was given and no arrangements made for the re-settlement of the evacuees" (Fosbrooke 1990).

The most recent incident of a large-scale forced relocation took place in 1988 in Mkomazi Game Reserve after Maasai and other pastoralists, legally resident when the reserve was created in 1951, refused to obey a government order to evacuate. People resident in the reserve reported that Wildlife Division officials threatened them with guns when they tried to get the eviction decision reversed (Mustafa 1993). They also complained of being beaten by members of the People's Militia and of having their houses burned without warning (Mustafa 1993). After refusing to leave voluntarily, five thousand residents were finally removed in a combined operation of police and Game Department forces in July of 1988. In this and most other cases, the majority of evacuees now reside in villages bordering the protected areas, where they are disproportionately vulnerable to natural hazards (see below).

Final examples come from an unpublished essay written by a Tanzanian lawyer belonging to an organization called Lawyers' Environmental Action Team (Lissu 1999). The essay was written to the Tanzanian press in response to the reported executions in Serengeti (cited above) and provides a litany of recent state violence in the name of conservation. Rangers at Katavi National Park were taken to court in 1998 for shooting three children herding cattle *outside* the boundary in an area designated for park expansion. At Lake Manyara and Tarangire National Parks, Lissu was part of a research team commissioned to investigate the potential for community-oriented conservation. In the process, they uncovered widespread complaints of beatings perpetrated by Tanzania National Parks (TANAPA) wardens against villagers. In the Ngorongoro Crater Conservation Area

(NCCA), recent human rights violations include a 1997 incident in which ten NCCA rangers beat three Maasai herders and slashed their cattle with machetes. Also in the NCCA, seven rangers were involved in the August 1993 shooting death of a Maasai villager accused of poaching. Although they claimed self-defense, eyewitnesses and police investigations suggested an execution, and the government subsequently brought murder charges against the rangers.

Increased Vulnerability to Natural Hazards

For agrarian populations adjacent to protected areas, the implementation of wildlife conservation policies has often resulted in a greater exposure and vulnerability to natural hazards, particularly wild animals, drought, and disease. Death, injury, or reduced levels of health and nutrition can be the result. Greater vulnerability is closely linked to patterns of displacement, either from wildlife conservation or other factors. Kjekshus (1977) has argued that an initial effect of European colonialism on Africans in Tanzania was loss of control over their environment and, subsequently, greater vulnerability to natural hazards, resulting in a decline in population. In the early colonial era, the creation of game reserves combined with human depopulation as a result of both disease and European military conquest, resulted in the spread of tsetse fly and the invasion of wildlife into previously cultivated areas (Iliffe 1979: 201–202). Administrators of the period also blamed hunting restrictions. A district officer in the Central Province in the 1920s and 1930s documented the retreat of cultivation as tsetse flies spread, attributing it to the "drastic steps" by the Game Department to stop the people there from hunting.[19] As exemplified by the history of the Selous Game Reserve, therefore, conquest, disease, settlement, and depopulation were related to wildlife conservation in complex ways.

British colonial officials were aware of some of these relationships and knew that some species, notably elephants, were increasing in population to the detriment of African peasant production. Game species were observed to behave "more like rabbits than large animals" around cultivated fields, and increasing wildlife populations meant that the lot of "agriculturalists [became] concurrently more hazardous."[20] Early wildlife policies, then, were not simply designed to conserve wildlife from over-hunting, but to control it in terms of numbers, variety, and location.

19. DO Kondoa Irangi, to Provincial Commissioner, Central, May 8, 1934, TNA 13371, Vol. I.
20. Acting PC, Lake, to CS, June 26, 1934; and Assistant District Officer (ADO), Liwale, to PC, Lindi, June 2, 1934, TNA 13371, Vol. I.

Much of the state's focus was on elephants because: (1) ivory was a valuable source of revenue, (2) they were a game species that could command high license fees from European hunters, and (3) in large parts of the territory they were the most destructive agricultural pests. The state, therefore, exclusively reserved for itself the right to shoot elephants for crop protection. Colonial officials devised ambitious and geographically extensive "elephant control schemes" in an attempt to corral elephants into protected areas and exterminate them from areas of human settlement.[21] In the 1920s, Game Preservation Department scouts were killing in excess of eight hundred elephants a year, and by the 1950s that number had risen to 3,000-plus as elephant populations grew.[22] These schemes also served as a part of the strategy to coerce people to "voluntarily" vacate game reserves because the Game Department would neither provide protection within the reserve from wild animals nor allow residents to arm and defend themselves. As an example, a provincial commissioner in 1933, referring to the leader of two hundred families who refused to evacuate the Selous Game Reserve, wrote, "so long as he and his people elect to live in the Game Reserve . . . they can be given no protection as regards their crops from the depredations of elephants and marauding game."[23]

During most of the British colonial occupation, policies were an attempt to balance wildlife conservation with wildlife control, always with an eye toward increasing peasant agricultural production. Tensions arose between the Game Department and colonial administrators who thought restrictions on Africans' use of weapons would expose them to greater hazards and so contradict government development policies. "Hordes of Agricultural Instructors roam the country telling the peasants that they must cultivate," wrote a provincial commissioner in 1943. "Administrative Officers," he continued

are making every effort to attain maximum production of foodstuffs . . . the African must think his overlords extremely illogical when they urge him to cultivate more land but take no steps to relieve him or enable him to relieve himself of the ravages of vermin which it has been estimated destroy annually one third of his crops.[24]

21. Game Ranger (W. O. Harvey) to Acting Game Warden (Teare), January 30, 1935, TNA Accession No. 16, 22/13, Vol. II; and "Elephant Control in Tanganyika Territory." Memorandum by Commander D. E. Blunt, 1933, TNA 21773.

22. "Notes on conversation with Mr. G. Rushby, Acting Game Warden at Arusha at 1430 hours on 12 Dec 1955," Anon. TNA Accession No. 273, MLFW 569; and Tanganyika Game Division (1964).

23. PC, Eastern, to ADO, Kiberege, November 8, 1933, TNA 26899, Vol. I.

24. PC, Eastern, to CS, December 8, 1943, TNA Accession No. 61, 316/1.

Throughout the colonial period, the Game Department spent about 75 percent of its energies arming and supporting European rangers and African scouts in an attempt to control raiders, particularly elephant and hippo.[25] Nevertheless, the government estimated that animals consistently consumed one-quarter to one-third of the territory's food crop production. In addition, peasants living near protected areas were killed by wild animals routinely enough that game rangers joked about it in official reports: "Buffalo have had a good hunting season and, to my knowledge, have killed three local natives and one Game Scout in the Kisaki area" (northern Selous boundary).[26]

This balance between conservation and control has gradually shifted, until, in the early postcolonial years, the interest in promoting a tourism industry outweighed concerns over the vulnerability of peasant agriculture to wild animals. The destruction of food crops by wildlife coming from protected areas thus became a constant threat, for which inadequate protection and no compensation are offered from the government. An example from Arusha National Park demonstrates how tourism came to take precedence over crop protection in bordering communities. Beginning in the 1960s, a local arrangement had been made between the Game Division, which had crop protection responsibilities, and the park authorities. They agreed that Game Division personnel would not shoot at wildlife that were destroying surrounding farms.[27] This policy was based on a fear that the animals would become so frightened of humans that they would "remain deep in the forest where they will be seen by no one" (i.e., out of view of tourists).[28] To illustrate how far policies have shifted from the colonial period, compare the previous attitude to the following report from the Selous boundary in 1935:

The Elephants during the past three years have had such a hot reception every time they have appeared near cultivation that the sound of a shot is sufficient to stampede them for miles. . . . This I submit is quite a satisfactory state of affairs.[29]

25. The basic administrative structure of the Tanganyika Game Department included a game warden at the top, several European game rangers in charge of overseeing a regional division, and dozens of African game scouts under the rangers' supervision.

26. Annual Report of the Game Ranger, Morogoro, December 30, 1953, TNA Accession No. 26, 284/IV.

27. Game Management Officer, Game Division, to Assistant Park Warden, Arusha National Park (ANP), June 30, 1966, Records of the ANP Headquarters.

28. Director, TANAPA, to Game Division, July 11, 1966, Records of the ANP Headquarters.

29. Game Ranger, Eastern Province, Annual Report 1935, January 26, 1936, TNA Accession No. 61, 15/1.

As tourism rose to prominence in the 1960s, the practice of protecting crops by shooting at elephants to drive them deep into the bush, as was the strategy in the 1930s and 1940s, became unthinkable.

Policies against harming wild animals coming from protected areas, no matter how destructive to peasant livelihoods, eventually became commonplace as the Tanzanian government strove to attract foreign tourists. As McCarthy (this volume) points out for the United States, state policies favoring agricultural development and resource extraction gradually gave way in Tanzania to an emphasis on nature preservation to support recreational and tourist uses. By the 1980s, villages surrounding Arusha National Park were getting no aid at all in defending their crops, leading some residents to conclude that government was using wild animals to drive them from their land. As a result, the danger of death or injury from wild animals is ever present, particularly since conservation policies deprive people of most means to defend themselves. In the area surrounding Arusha National Park, buffalo have been a near constant threat to people in their farms or gathering fuel wood in the bush. Deaths are not uncommon. During harvest season, the risk increases because people often sleep in their farms and try to frighten crop raiders away by banging pots or waving torches.

Most recently, in some parts of the country, there is evidence that elephants are becoming increasingly aggressive toward humans and their cultivated crops. A recent radio broadcast reported an elephant killed a man in Tunduru District (southern Selous boundary) practically on his doorstep when he stepped outside to investigate the noise in his millet field.[30] The broadcast said elephants had killed five people in the district in the previous two months.

In many cases, displacements from protected areas have rendered peasant populations more vulnerable to drought. Vulnerability has been increased in a number of ways including the denial of access to water sources, pasture reserves, and wild meat, which had historically been relied on even by nonhunting societies as a way to avoid famine. In the early colonial period, the Game Department aided in this function. The first Director of Game Preservation instructed his scouts to lend a hand in killing for food in famine areas but to "let your Fundis [trained workers] do the necessary shooting."[31] As the newspaper report of contemporary violence in Serengeti cited previously indicates, wildlife still plays an important role in

30. Radio Tanzania, June 10, 1998.
31. Copy of letter of instructions from the Director of Game Preservation (C. F. Swynnerton) to all Cultivation Protectors, Lindi District, September 14, 1927, TNA Accession No. 16, 22/4.

relief from famine. The loss of access to dry season pastures for domestic livestock and water sources for people and livestock, however, have produced the most common form of vulnerability. Seasonal and periodic drought near Arusha National Park, for example, has in the past coincided with increased arrests for livestock trespass.[32] Access to water and dry season pastures also were the main subjects of conflict between Maasai pastoralists and the new Serengeti administration in the 1950s.

Person to Person

By person to person violence, I mean violent actions directly inflicted by one (or more) person(s) on another (or others) that lead to injury or death. This includes rapes, beatings, assaults, and killings. This form of violence is two-way; agents of the state as well as local people are subject to personal harm, unlike the previous two forms of violence. The origins of this type of violence in state-directed conservation are associated with the initial conquest of the territory by the German government. The Maji Maji uprising of 1905, the most extensive African rebellion against colonial rule in Tanzania's history, originated in and around the game reserves, which later became the Selous established by the Germans that same year. German officers later speculated that the rebellion was sparked in part by the severe restrictions imposed by the game laws (Koponen 1995).

From the 1920s through the 1940s, confrontations with the greatest potential for person to person violence involved Africans exercising what they viewed as customary hunting rights in game reserves and game officers trying to stop them. Documentation of confrontations is sketchy in the Game Department's reports, the rhetoric is overblown, and the details often proven to be greatly exaggerated. In Serengeti, for example, a local game ranger warned that "the situation will develop into guerrilla warfare" if the Waikoma continued to attempt to hunt in the reserve.[33] The Morogoro game ranger reported "poaching gangs," numbering 6 to 8, with muzzle loaders and bows and poisoned arrows. He referred to the situation as "an outbreak of war" although there were no reported injuries or killings and only vague references to threats.[34]

There were, however, numerous documented incidents of violent clashes, especially in protected areas, between rangers and people hunting illegally. The Liwale game ranger warned that the "Game Scouts patrolling the [Selous] Game Reserve . . . are likely to be fired on with rifles, muzzle

---

32. Arusha National Park Monthly Report, January 1974, Records of the ANP Headquarters.
33. Game Ranger, Bangai Hill, to PC, Lake Province, July 25, 1938, TNA 13371.
34. Game Ranger, Morogoro, to DC, Morogoro, February 12, 1942, TNA Accession No. 61, 15/IV.

loaders, or poisoned arrows, should they attempt to arrest people found illegally [in the reserve]."[35] In 1942, the Morogoro game ranger reported two incidents over the previous two years where bullets flew: "Game Scout John was fired at by a gang of native hunters. . . . [and] Game Scout Garrus was also fired at by a gang of six, one whose bullets hit the tree alongside which he stood."[36] In these situations, colonial game rangers and scouts were directed to exercise a great deal of restraint and only return fire as a last resort. Nevertheless, game scouts and hunters were killed in the course of confrontations.[37] In the 1940s, the Waikoma, having lost their traditional hunting grounds in the Serengeti, openly boasted to the European game rangers that they would continue to hunt as they pleased and threatened to use poison arrows against anyone trying to stop them.[38] By the 1950s, these confrontations had resulted in a number of killings of hunters by African game scouts. The game warden explained that:

> From time to time Game Scouts have had to shoot and kill poachers in the Serengeti National Park. The cause of these regrettable incidents has been the use of poisoned arrows. The poachers have threatened or actually fired arrows at the Scouts. The Scouts, knowing that they dare not risk getting so much as a scratch from an arrow, have had to fire instantly.[39]

The small arms skirmishes continued sporadically through the 1960s, related in the reports of Tanzania National Parks and the Game Division (e.g., TANAPA 1968; Tanganyika Game Division 1964).

One incident, recently related in an interview with a district game officer, illustrates how encounters in the field between hunters and scouts are charged with potential violence that can erupt with a panicked, split-second decision.

35. Game Ranger, Liwale (Ionides), to PC, Lindi, June 7, 1945, TNA, Accession No. 16, 22/13, Vol. III.

36. Game Ranger, Morogoro, to DC, Morogoro, February 7, 1942, TNA Accession No. 61, 15/IV.

37. Part of an ADO's 1940 report includes an incident of a game scout killed by a poaching gang in Temeke District the previous year. He also reports another case he witnessed in which "the man with the muzzle loader went down on one knee, cocked his muzzle loader and brought it up to aim on the askari," but scouts had him covered and he surrendered. "The killing of game for sale," memo by R. E. Risley, Assistant DO, Rufiji, May 11, 1940, TNA Accession No. 61, 15/A/<1.

38. A game patrol arresting poachers in Serengeti near Musoma had to retreat in the face of Ikoma and Sukuma hunting parties who wanted to attack them. (Report on Game Scout's Patrol in the Serengeti National Park from Game Department, Bangai Hill, Musoma, October 24, 1946, TNA 35773.)

39. GW to MANR, May 10, 1957, TNA Accession No. 273, MLFW 569.

So we start chasing him [the poacher]. Then we had pistols, we shot once, then second, third, fourth. This guy turned to shoot us. Of course he said [to himself] 'Bwana, if this guy is going to catch me then I am going to land there [in prison] for 30 years, so I better kill him and disappear'.

The man eventually surrendered and told the officer how close he had come to shooting him. "Then as we were talking he said 'Bwana, I was ready to shoot but I said okay, as I was turning, bwana you are shooting, I mean you had . . . an automatic weapon and mine is a muzzleloader'."[40]

Other, less dramatic, forms of "everyday" violence usually go undocumented in field reports and court records. For example, villagers near Arusha National Park alleged mistreatment at the hands of the park guards, who, one villager complained, "come only to harass us."[41] In the late 1980s there was a high level of fear and mistrust of the park guards, and a number of villagers made serious accusations of abuse.[42] A villager said that after a park right-of-way was closed (without any legal proceedings), the guards would beat people and rape the women that they caught inside.[43] Others talked about rape if a woman were caught alone collecting fuel wood and complained in general about beatings and threats with guns.[44] One villager claims that he became the victim of harassment because he complained to the local police about park guards bringing a poached buffalo into the village for sale.[45] In a similar incident, two park guards who were arrested for trying to sell buffalo in a nearby village were actually caught by villagers. These particular guards were rumored to be perpetrating a pattern of violence (including rape) directed toward villagers. Finding them bringing poached meat to the village merely gave villagers the opportunity to rid themselves of these "bad apples." One villager sums up the prevalence of violence in encounters between local residents and wildlife and park officials: "The guards are our enemy and to them we are the poachers. If I cross into the park they will shoot me. Are they not my enemy?"[46]

The 1980s saw a significant escalation in violence with the emergence of organized, transnational networks of illegal trade in elephant ivory and

40. Interview with District Game Officer, Morogoro, June 17, 1998.
41. Interview with Isiah Mukuti (pseudonym), July 7, 1990.
42. This is only one aspect of a socially complex and dynamic relationship between park staff and villagers. There are other more cooperative and mutually beneficial aspects that I will discuss later. It also is an accusation that only village men made to me. No women told me of seeing the actual victims, but I would not expect it to be otherwise. Some of the men explained it as simply typical behavior on the part of police and military personnel.
43. Interview with Duluti Kikula (pseudonym), June 12, 1990.
44. Interview with Ngurdoto resident, September 11, 1990.
45. Interview with Duluti Kikula (pseudonym), June 12, 1990.
46. Interview with Martin Karika (pseudonym), July 9, 1990.

rhino horn. In response, the state agencies involved in conservation explicitly developed their paramilitary style of organization. The analogy of warfare, much overused by colonial game officials, became more apt, particularly in 1989 with the Tanzanian government's "Operation Uhai." This operation was implemented after a series of aerial censuses of elephant populations indicated a steep decline resulting from illegal commercial hunting. In announcing the campaign, the Minister of Home Affairs was quoted as saying that poachers were enemies of the nation because their activities "greatly interfere with our efforts to revive the economy" and urged citizens to cooperate in the operation (Tanzania *Sunday News* June 4, 1989: 1). The government's anti-poaching operation, carried out by the combined forces of the Wildlife Department, Tanzania People's Defense Forces, and the police, began sweeping through protected areas and neighboring communities on June 1, 1989. In the course of the operation, which lasted through the end of the year, around 2,500 people were arrested.

A few stories of harassment of villagers by Uhai operatives reached the press (Tanzania *Daily News* October 26, 1989: 3). For the most part, however, the conduct of Operation Uhai remains publicly undocumented. People found inside of game reserves, no matter what their activities, probably were dealt with harshly. The defense of crops was made almost impossible in the crisis atmosphere produced by the elephant censuses, and whatever legal access to protected area resources that remained was curtailed. In the Selous Game Reserve, for example, a long-standing (and once nationally important) practice of bee keeping was halted in the course of Operation Uhai. The operation also greatly reduced the illegal trade in game meat, which was ubiquitous (and also long-standing) in the villages surrounding the reserve.

Patterns and Explanations

A few geographical and temporal patterns are revealed in the previous examples that I want to highlight. First, the level of violence in wildlife conservation, for all the categories I have suggested, is highest in protected areas and diminishes with distance from the boundaries. It is toward protected areas, as the main repositories of wildlife and as the foci of tourism, that most of the state's resources are directed. Second, the geographical displacements of populations for the purposes of wildlife conservation are not limited to the initial establishment of protected areas during the colonial period. Displacements have been ongoing and progressive while undergoing qualitative changes as state conservation laws and policies change. They are progressive because, in and around protected areas, peasants' access to livelihood resources has become increasingly more limited. Third, historical peaks in violence often are associated with a reaction by the state to some threat to its control over revenue generated from wildlife, its domestic political legitimacy, its moral standing in the international sphere, or some combination of these. Editorials in European and North American newspapers, censuses documenting wildlife losses, questions raised in parliaments, and donor pressure have influenced the Tanzanian state's "crackdowns" on illegal hunting. The colonial files contain titles like "Game Poaching and Publicity," which reveal that the government responded to accusations of mismanagement of wildlife with shows of force and more restrictive policies. These peaks in violence often constituted a ratcheting down of state control over land and natural resource access and use. When the crackdowns are over, peasant communities have experienced a permanent, incremental loss of access.

Although I did not set out to demonstrate this, in the course of writing I have found sufficient evidence to conclude that, in the postcolonial period, all categories of violence have increased in frequency and intensity. Admittedly, given the paucity of reliable documentation, it is difficult to quantify this trend. Nevertheless, the postcolonial state has implemented wildlife conservation policies using means that were shunned as politically inexpedient by colonial governors and secretaries of state for the colonies. The poorly planned, forceful, and arbitrary relocations in Ngorongoro in the 1970s and Mkomazi in the 1980s have no parallel in the colonial period. To my knowledge, the colonial government never issued a shoot-on-sight directive for people found inside the protected areas. I have found no historical accounts of bandit gangs, armed with sophisticated weaponry, attacking foreign tourists.

If my conclusion is correct, how are we to explain the trend toward increasing violence? Certainly it is necessary to go beyond the commonplace Malthusian equation of more people equal more violent conflict over resources (Homer-Dixon 1999). Let us begin by looking at the historical population trends of the African elephant, the single species that so influences international and domestic wildlife conservation policies, including crackdowns like Operation Uhai. Elephant numbers in postcolonial Tanzania bottomed out at 50,000 at the end of 1980s. According to Wildlife Department estimates, the population had dropped precipitously from around 365,000 in the 1970s (United Republic of Tanzania [URT] 1994). This is clearly a dramatic and startling decline in numbers. Prior to this decline, however, the country experienced an equally startling increase in elephants. In 1933, the Game Warden gave "a very liberal estimate" of 36,000 to 37,000 elephants in all of Tanganyika.[47] According to government estimates, then, elephant numbers increased ten-fold in the succeed-

---

47. GW to CS, October 21, 1933, TNA 21773.

ing four decades, producing increasing conflict with peasant agriculture. As for human population numbers, let us look at the Selous Game Reserve where elephant numbers dropped an estimated 70 percent between 1976 and 1989 (URT 1995: 17). Most of the adjacent lands include some of the most inaccessible and sparsely populated districts in the country. Liwale District, which shares the southeastern boundary of the reserve has a population of 1.4 people per square kilometer (URT 1990). Village leaders near the boundary complained to me of losing population as people migrate away in search of work. The rise in illegal hunting of elephants and the subsequent decline in numbers can hardly be attributed to human population pressure.

Moving beyond a focus on population pressure opens the analysis to include an inter-linked set of historical and political–economic forces. First, the rise of international conservation organizations has had a powerful influence on Tanzania's wildlife policies. A telling example of this relationship is that the newspaper article that announced Operation Uhai to the (educated, urban) public also included a report on the World Wide Fund for Nature's (WWF) call for a worldwide ban on the ivory trade. Spates of bad international publicity, such as that associated with the decline in elephant numbers, have historically often been followed by government crackdowns.

Another factor influencing policy is the growth of the tourism industry. The government's dependency on tourism as a source of revenue and foreign exchange means that policies are driven by the need to facilitate and expand the flow of foreign visitors to the country's parks. Placed within the current economic and political pressures of structural adjustment, the tensions between peasant agriculture and the tourism industry become even more critical. Apropos of the grim economic conditions, the government has long been financially incapable of mitigating losses of resource access or damage to life and property caused by protected wildlife. Moreover, there is a long history in Tanzania state-led programs (e.g., "villagization," land titling) designed to fundamentally alter society without consultation with, let alone the participation of, the mass of affected people. Set within the context of historical state–peasantry relations, forced evictions from protected areas and other arbitrary uses of violence are not particularly unusual. In fact, they are heartily defended in the name of a greater "public good," specifically "national development."

Some, including many conservation professionals working in the Tanzanian agencies and in international NGOs, would argue that the cases I have used are out-of-date and that there are new conservation policies that involve the people in decision-making and that redistribute the benefits derived from wildlife tourism. The new programs, they might argue, are in place, and if changes on the ground are not evident, it is because they have not had time to take hold. I suggest an alternative: state violence and the new community-oriented initiatives are integrated forms of social control designed to meet the needs and goals of international conservation organizations and the tourism industry. The clearest way to demonstrate this is to turn to an examination of one of the new community-oriented projects, the Selous Conservation Program.

Disciplinary Power in Wildlife Conservation

Around the time that the Tanzanian army and police were rounding up suspected poachers and interlopers in Operation Uhai, state resource agencies, international donors, and conservation NGOs were formulating a new conservation model based on benefit sharing and community participation. Tanzanian resource agencies' embrace of the approach is exemplified by the Tanzania Forestry Action Plan (URT 1989). The plan reviews the existing legal structure of land and resource tenure wherein all the wildlife resources in the country are the property of the state, which is the sole authority for regulating their exploitation and sole recipient of the revenue thereby generated. The plan remarks that illegal hunting, technically the theft of state property, has been the biggest problem in managing this resource. It reports that coercion, including the creation of mobile, paramilitary field forces, has not been an entirely successful management strategy, in part, because "the local population are often antagonistic and not prepared to provide reliable information on the activities of poachers" (14). Violence, in other words, did not effectively bring surrounding communities under the control of government natural resource agencies.

To overcome the limits of state violence and coercion, a new approach is envisaged. The key is village land titling because it would "encourage more sustainable land-use practices as each land owner [most often village councils] would then have an incentive to invest"(16). This is to be combined with the creation of special community wildlife management areas where titled owners would be able to tap material benefits from wildlife resources. This constitutes a partial devolution of property rights from the state to titled property owners. As the report explains, "[i]n this way the Minister [of Lands, Natural Resources, and Tourism] transfers the ownership of game . . . to the landowner(s) on whose property the game exists" (32). Partitioning land through surveying and titling also would help to further rationalize resource management and improve monitoring and surveillance activities. The report directs that "survey teams should establish exact boundar[ies] so that [t]he monitoring of land use would be made easier and enforcement of land-use programmes related to conservation can be made more efficient" (5). These broad policy outlines are reflected in the planning and implementation of the Selous Conservation Program.

The Selous Conservation Programme (SCP) was implemented jointly by the Tanzanian government and the German agency Deutsche Gesellschaft Fur Technische, Zusammenarbeit (GTZ). A 1988 study produced for GTZ recommended that a "buffer zone" be established along the perimeter of the Selous Game Reserve (Lerise and Schuler 1988). Basically, the buffer zone would constitute a strip of land between the reserve boundary and surrounding communities in which wildlife conservation and rural development goals would be combined. In essence, a new type of land designation was identified and demarcated. The SCP initiated its community wildlife management schemes in 1990. In rough outline, the schemes operate as follows. SCP officials initiate contact with neighboring villages with an offer to fund up to 50 percent of the costs for village self-help projects such as school and dispensary buildings and community tree nurseries. Villages also are offered access to the wildlife on their land in return for limiting the extent of cultivation and settlement. As a prerequisite to gaining access to wildlife, the villages must produce village land use plans that designate "wildlife management areas" (i.e., a buffer zone) along with areas for cultivation and forest. Currently between 40–45 villages participate, which equals about half the villages around Selous and 2,000 to 3,000 square kilometers under village wildlife management.

Once the village land use plan and village title application are completed, the Director of Wildlife grants a wildlife utilization quota to the village. This constitutes a partial and temporary devolution of property rights. Under current law, there is no legal basis for transferring the ownership of wildlife, thus each allocation must take the form of a special permit issued by the director. Consequently, the allocation can be revoked at any time at the discretion of the director or SCP officials. The allocation is made to the village council (a legislatively designated corporate body that holds title to village land) and administered through the newly created institution of the village wildlife committee. Each village appoints "village game scouts" (*wahifadhi*) whom the SCP instructs at a training center set up south of the reserve. A syllabus and manual guide the training in order to standardize the performance of duties by all village scouts. The SCP provides uniforms, boots, tents, field gear, and identity cards to the successful trainees. Upon being instructed and equipped, the *wahifadhi* take primary responsibility for monitoring and surveilling village wildlife lands and joint responsibility for securing the game reserve boundary.

What is perhaps most significant about this form of conservation intervention is that the need for overt violence by the state to enforce wildlife laws is seemingly reduced by a new process of self-surveillance at the level of the village. The demarcation of a buffer zone through the rationalization and partitioning of land use is fundamental to this system of self-surveillance and monitoring. People entering the village wildlife management areas now have to account for their presence there. Peasants take control and surveillance duties on themselves after being instructed and trained on standard police procedures and scientific wildlife management. The project thus promotes a further internalization of introduced ideologies of wildlife conservation and shifts the burden of protection further toward villagers (see Sundar this volume). Hence, the success of the plan hinges on the creation of a disciplined peasant society, made possible by the rigid spatial partitioning of land uses, both regionally and within the buffer zone.

A striking aspect of the buffer zone plan and its implementation is its relevance to Foucault's concept of disciplinary power (1979). Disciplinary power, as Foucault conceived it, moves beyond a concept of power as an external restriction forced or coerced upon a population toward a concept of power as internalized and pervasive in the organization of society. Although Foucault developed his ideas of a disciplinary society based on the political and social transformation of Europe in the seventeenth and eighteenth centuries, his work has provided the basis for insights into the process of nineteenth-century colonialism (Mitchell 1988) and twentieth-century rural development programs in Africa (Ferguson 1990).

Mitchell's analysis of the European colonization of Egypt traces how disciplinary "forms of power are based on the re-ordering of space and the surveillance and control of its occupants" (1988). The process of colonizing, according to Mitchell, is a comprehensive alteration of society and space stemming from the introduction of new disciplinary mechanisms. Ferguson (1990) also follows Foucault in his analysis of development projects in Lesotho in southern Africa. His study asks not whether or why development succeeds or fails in its stated goals, but rather what does it do and what are the outcomes? He wrote, "Planned interventions may produce unintended outcomes that end up, all the same, incorporated into anonymous constellations of control" (Ferguson 1990). Among other insights, his work demonstrates how the planning and implementation of development projects, while failing to relieve poverty, effectively expand and extend state mechanisms of control and surveillance into rural societies. From a Foucaultian perspective, then, the buffer zone plan serves as the "discipline-mechanism" to create a different kind of peasant consciousness toward wildlife based on a schema of generalized surveillance (1979: 209).

The SCP and similar projects represent a new type of state initiative to control the populations surrounding protected areas. The first step in this approach to conservation is "to determine the plan" (Mitchell 1988: 33) to transform adjacent rural communities. Control over the populations is achieved not through force and coercion, but primarily through the ordering and partitioning of space. However, as the shoot-on-sight directive issued in Serengeti in 1996 indicates, the ever-present threat of state violence is the subtext for any community conservation scheme. Furthermore, the character of community wildlife management masks the application of power in this process. Villages are not forced to participate in the program and indeed line up to voluntarily join. Every step in the implementation of a village wildlife management area is either conducted by villagers themselves or in close consultation with them. Yet the result is the geographic extension of state control over village lands bordering the game reserve. The "problem" that is resolved by these schemes is not population pressure and poor land use practices but the weaknesses of the state's control over adjacent lands and their inhabitants.

In this analysis of recent wildlife conservation initiatives, I have not attempted to determine whether the community-friendly approach is "better" than more coercive and violent forms. The point is that coercion and violence on the part of the state are not *replaced* by community participation but continue as ever-present threats that influence the behavior and decision-making of local community members. The fact that communities volunteer to participate cannot be straightforwardly read as evidence of a "successful" transition to a new conservation regime. One needs to read community participation against the background of Operation Uhai, the alleged executions in Serengeti, and the national drive to "secure" rural Tanzania for the burgeoning "ecotourism" industry. In volunteering, communities are agreeing to re-inscribe village space with new categories of use and meaning as dictated by the buffer zone plan and to enforce these new uses and meanings themselves, with full knowledge and awareness of the ever-present potential for state violence.

14

Beyond the Bounds? Violence at the Margins of New Legal Geographies

Nandini Sundar

Where the wooded tracts of central India once appeared to colonial officials as places of dark, lurking danger, of malarial madness, and of marksmen whose aim found its way to the heart of the colonial enterprise, they are today areas of denuded scrub whose inhabitants seem engaged in battling each other over the remaining trees. One might argue that with the penetration of sunlight, paradoxically, the potential for violence has increased. Today, in place of the standoff between forest dependent villagers and the state, "intimacy and antagonistic interests come packaged together in the social relations of work and daily life" (Sider 1986: 85).

People have thought about violence in relation to forest environments in various ways, some of which are common to India and other parts of the world. In India, both colonial officials and villagers expressed fears about the unknown and uncontrollable aspects of nature and its potential for vengeance in the form of droughts, floods, forest fires, or attacks by wild animals.[1] For colonial officials, the violence in nature often included the threat of attacks by "savages" whom they associated with nature (in the Indian context see Skaria 1999; Sundar 1995; for colonial anxieties about natives elsewhere see Spurr 1993; Taussig 1987). Colonial foresters looked upon native peasant users of the forest as destructive elements, whose practices caused violence to the environment. In India, scholars like Shiva, Nandy, or Visvanathan have taken an opposite tack, equating the preservation of nature with the activities of the peoples, especially *adivasis* ("tribals"

---

1. McCann points out that for villagers in Gera, Ethiopia, an expansion of forests often represented a retreat of civilization because forests were associated with depopulation. "This view contrasts markedly with a development narrative which equates forest with idealized nature" (McCann 1997: 155; see also Malamoud 1976).

328

or "indigenous peoples") and women, who are dependent on it. In this reading, the blame for destruction of nature is laid on a particular form of Western science (see essays in Nandy 1988).[2]

A somewhat different tradition of scholarship locates environmental violence not in any natural phenomenon, nor just in a particular ideology of scientific domination, although the imposition of this is often an important aspect of violence. Instead, violence is primarily located in the contest between different groups or classes over access to resources, including forests (see Gadgil and Guha 1992; Peluso and Watts, this volume).

Considerable work has been done in India on the structural violence of "scientific forestry," the physical acts of displacement that forest reservation involved, and the everyday infractions and major rebellions that these have engendered among those displaced or denied resources in the colonial period (see Guha and Gadgil 1989; Rangarajan 1996; essays in Arnold and Guha 1995; Grove, Damodaran, and Sangwan 1998). Work in the post-colonial period has highlighted movements like Chipko in North India and Appiko in South India against the felling of local forests by contractors for commercial uses: agitations against the leasing of wastelands to private industries like Harihar Polyfibres in Karnataka; the uprooting of Forest Department eucalyptus plantations in Tumkur, Karnataka, by farmers incensed at the depletion of their water table; tensions between the rules mandating exclusion of people from national parks and sanctuaries and the needs of forest-fringe villages; and everyday confrontations between "headloaders" (firewood collectors) and forest guards. Each of these has made headlines as an example of violent conflict created by the continuation of colonial forestry practices into the post-colonial period (Gadgil and Guha 1995, 1994; Centre for Science and Environment 1985, 1982; Dang 1991; Kothari et al. 1997).

This history of conflict, with its social and ecological consequences, forms the pre-history of Joint Forest Management (JFM), a government policy that aims to redraw the "legal geography" of forest resource rights.[3] Under JFM, instead of keeping villagers out of reserved forests, individual villages are assigned patches of forestland to manage collectively. The policy was first drawn up at the national level in 1990 and subsequently revised in 2000. In 1990, the forestland that villagers were permitted to pro-

2. Much environmental writing in the United States and elsewhere has chronicled the violence that humans have inflicted on nature, with their desire to dominate and shape the elements. See Schama (1995: 13) for a critical discussion on this in the context of a larger argument about the impossibility of finding pristine nature or a landscape that is not a cultural product.

3. See Blomley (1994: 27–58) for a discussion of the concept of "legal geographies." He uses it to describe the manner in which "legal categories are used to construct and differentiate material spaces which, in turn, acquire a legal potency that has a direct bearing on those using and traversing such spaces" (Blomley 1994: 54).

tect was restricted to degraded land (i.e., with less than 40 percent crown density). Under the revised policy (MoEF 2000: paragraph C), the program has been cautiously extended to good forest areas. Apart from usufruct rights, "if they protect successfully" (i.e., succeed in regeneration of trees), they are entitled to a "portion of the proceeds from the sale of trees when they mature" (MoEF 1990: clause v), though the share will vary depending on whether the land protected was initially good forest or degraded (MoEF 2000).

At least one commonly expressed rationale for JFM is the reduction in conflict that it brings about between foresters and villagers. In the versions of at least two forest officials, a Divisional Forest Officer (DFO) and a Range Forest Officer (RFO) in Madhya Pradesh (MP) and Gujarat, respectively, their "change of heart" came after a violent encounter. In MP, villagers protesting against cattle-proof trenches erected by the forest department were fired upon at the DFO's bidding. In Gujarat, the discovery of illegal timber in a villager's house led to an argument that ended with one guard being killed, two others losing their eyes, and serious head and arm injuries to the RFO. In MP, the DFO responsible, and in Gujarat, the RFO who succeeded the injured one, decided that the time had come for reconciliation. They turned to joint forest management. Some nongovernmental organizations (NGOs) and activists portray JFM as a deal they brokered to stop Forest Department (FD) harassment of villagers. In Vankachinta, in Paderu division of Visakapatnam district, villagers were persuaded by the local NGO to stop cultivation on gradient land and work on forest department plantations. In return the FD was persuaded to allow them to retain their encroachment on level forestland (Ravi Pragada, personal communication). The meanings of past violence—who was responsible for destroying the forests in the first place and who provoked conflict—and the responsibility for bringing peace vary depending on the narrator.

But even as it has reduced certain forms of conflict, JFM has generated other tensions. In many cases, collective violence by the dispossessed against the state has been deflected into violence against each other, as the boundaries of access and exclusion have been re-drawn. This chapter is an attempt to chart the manner in which the changing "legal geographies" of forest management have produced new forms of exclusion and entitlement, coercion and collusion; and the repertoire of actions and ideologies (ranging from quiet acceptance to violent engagement) that each involves.

The chapter is divided into two parts. In the first, I discuss some existing theories of environmental violence, focusing on the concept of "territoriality." I argue that it is not territoriality in itself that engenders conflict or aggression, but the particular strategies that are used in the process of territorialization. These often give legal and cultural sanction to violence or extraction in the name of conservation. One such important strategy is the ideology of "scientific forestry." Historically, scientific forestry involved institutionalizing certain sorts of territorial claims on the basis of timber quality and its potential for revenue generation and criminalizing those activities that competed with this goal, like shifting cultivation. Opposition to scientific forestry relied on other sorts of spatial and moral claims (e.g., the claim of "original" residence in an area).

A second theme that runs throughout the chapter is that it is often the incompleteness or indeterminacy of territorial projects, rather than their successful execution, that creates tensions. This (often deliberate) indeterminacy acts in the favor of certain classes over others and leaves room for violence to play a defining role in drawing boundaries (see also Holston 1991). This blurred boundary problem is exemplified in section two.

In the second part, I examine state attempts to fashion new geographies through the promotion of joint or community forest management, and the particular forms of conflict this has introduced. This varies from place to place depending on their earlier histories, but certain problems are intrinsic to the program and common across cases. Both ideologically and structurally, violence is moved out from the venue of state power and dispersed among different constituents in society. Although contemporary forms of intra- or intervillage violence are fueled by gender, caste, or ethnic identifications,[4] what allows these rifts to become violent are the ideologies enforced by the colonial forest department and subsequently internalized by villagers.

Territoriality, Spatial Strategies, and Violence

> Imperialism and the culture associated with it affirm both the primacy of geography and an ideology about control of territory. The geographical sense makes projections—imaginative, cartographic, military, economic, historical, or in a general sense cultural. It also makes possible the construction of various kinds of knowledge, all of them in one way or another dependent upon the perceived character and destiny of a particular geography. (Said 1993: 78)

Sociobiological explanations of aggression, which were especially prominent in the 1960s, often identified it with territoriality (see, for instance, Lorenz 1966; Ardrey 1966; Morris 1967). In this view, aggressiveness is

---

4. These identities too are historically produced and not an essential part of indigenous cultural formations (see Dirks 1989; Cohn 1990; essays in Breckenridge and Van der Veer 1993)

programmed in our genes and is accompanied by an animal instinct of territorial defense. Despite sustained critique (Montague 1976; Sluka 1992: 23–4), this view continues to hold sway in insidious ways. The jury is still out, for instance, on whether territorialization of resource use as a management strategy reduces the possibility of conflict by apportioning resource uses to different groups (Cassimir 1992: 20), or whether something about territory lends itself more easily to emotional identification and subsequently to political manipulation and aggression, even as it permits sharing with others (Smith 1990).

One of the most commonly cited definitions of territoriality is Sack's: "the attempt by an individual or group to affect, influence or control people, phenomena and relationships by delimiting and asserting control over a geographical area" (1986: 19). As Nancy Peluso shows (1995), what needs to be examined is the phenomenon of territorialization itself, or the process of subsuming other kinds of property arrangements (e.g., in trees) to land control, and the development of a new discourse of territorial terms, such as boundaries, spaces, zones, etc. (Peluso, forthcoming).

In order to understand the different forms of violence dealt with in this chapter, we need to understand the new sets of social and spatial relations implicit in changing definitions of property, between different categories of people, and between different categories of resources. Several understandings of environmental scarcity and violence ignore the role and ideology of both local institutions and the state. In Hardin's work on the tragedy of the commons, for instance, there is an assumption that humans instinctively respond to their situation as utility maximizing individuals, unmediated by cultural constraints or any other social arrangement. On the contrary, much work on common property resources (e.g., Bromley 1992; McCay and Acheson 1987) asserts that common property resources are not to be confused with open access resources, and that the former are governed by rules of management in which states and state agencies or actors often play important roles.

Similarly, in Homer-Dixon and colleagues' positing of increased conflict under situations of environmental degradation and scarcity, the causal links implied between environmental scarcity and civil violence assume a particular view of the state as a neutral broker between separate, contending groups. In their view, environmental scarcity puts demands upon the state that it cannot satisfy and thus causes a crisis of legitimacy, increasing the risk of civil violence, including insurgency, ethnic conflicts, riots, and civil war (Homer-Dixon 1994, 1999). The examples they give, such as the conflict between Bangladeshi immigrants and the Assamese over land or the Arab–Israeli conflict over water (Homer-Dixon, Boutwell, and Rothjens 1993), ignore the larger historical and political contexts in which these conflicts occur and overlook the leading roles of both imperial and post-colonial states in creating such a situation (see also Peluso and Watts; Fairhead, this volume).

The raw material for violence, if and when it does occur, is not merely the immediate political/economic context or a desire to control space, but a larger reservoir of cultural imaginings that give meaning to that space (for example, as a homeland or an arena of superior conservation practices). The kinds of exclusions practiced, based on these imaginings, build upon and refashion existing social contradictions. Violence has the capacity to produce boundaries and hierarchies, to change the very language in which people conceptualize themselves, others, and the relations between them. Where boundaries are indeterminate or fluid, violence has the capacity to render them rigid (Mehta and Chatterjee 1995).

A critical concept here is the notion of spatial strategies as elaborated by Satish Deshpande (1998): the ideological and concrete practices whereby an ideal space is actualized into a real physical place "in such a way that these ties also bind people to particular identities, and to the political/practical consequences that they entail" (1998: 4). Connected to the "perceived character and destiny of a particular geography" (Said 1993: 78) are the imputed character and destiny of its inhabitants, their rights, and their obligations. Deshpande uses the concept to understand, for example, the ways in which Hindu revivalism invests the physical town of Ayodhya with the mythical space of Ram Rajya, thereby producing a new sacred geography, or the ways in which the developmental nation state valorizes a certain economic geography by associating certain places/towns with specific kinds of heavy industries (1998: 15).

At the heart of scientific forestry as it has been practiced in colonial and post-colonial India, lies a similar attempt to spatialize management, with peasant users being restricted to certain categories of forest while better forest tracts (in timber terms) were reserved for state extraction. In order to actually work, these rearrangements required the people "in" these spaces to buy into these new identities. In this chapter, I try to bring out the manner in which this process of tying people to new identities is often fraught, contested, and yet often eventually internalized.

Some have debated the degree to which the colonial period marked a radical disjuncture with the nature and extent of pre-colonial controls over the forest, and the compulsions propelling the development of scientific or state managed forestry (see Grove 1995; Gadgil and Guha 1992). Although both colonial and pre-colonial forestry involved restrictions on the cutting of certain species of trees (e.g., teak or sandalwood), on cutting trees above a certain girth, or the setting aside of certain tracts of land for hunting or pasture reserves, colonial forestry was unprecedented in its territorial pretensions (see Rangarajan 1996: 13–14, 39). "Demarcation" or "reserving" certain tracts of land for exclusive use by the forest department was justified with reference to a scientific appraisal of their value to timber production or contribution to climatic control. In the process, the forest department acquired even lands that were not useful for commercial forestry, and today it controls 23 percent of the landmass (Rangarajan 1996: 74, 203).

There were complications, of course. Legal enactments gave differing rights to differing categories of people for different purposes within the same patch of forest.[5] The practice of forestry in particular places inevitably meant that overall policy had to be inflected with specific decisions regarding what sort of trees to manage for and how (e.g., pure stands of *sal* versus a mixed forest, whether to replace fuel- and fodder-bearing mixed coniferous forests in the Himalayas with pine and cedar). Those involved in the creation of colonial forest policy had different views on the extent to which state rights should have preeminence over local access (Gadgil and Guha 1992: 123–134). Eventually, however, decisions were settled in territorial terms, and attempts at accommodating a multiplicity of rights or resources were subordinated to an overarching spatial and territorial classification of forests.

Rights were predominantly mapped onto spaces, producing a new legal politics of space. The Forest Act of 1878 created three classes of forests: reserved forests that were generally completely closed off to the local public, protected forests in which people had "privileges" liable to be changed at state discretion, and, in some provinces, villages, or *nistari*, forests from which people could draw their basic needs, usually on the payment of commutation dues. The post-colonial delineation of national parks, sanctuaries, reserved forests, protected forests, and village forests has continued with this legal/geographical classification on the basis of judgments on the value of the land. If anything, the territorial base has been expanded, with the state takeover of *zamindari* forests (previously owned by large landlords).[6]

The criterion for spatial demarcation has been largely in terms of timber. The classification of existing lands into a hierarchy of value on the basis of timber contained was not in any sense natural or obvious. An alterna-

5. The rights to forest produce of certain categories of people, like agriculturists, were recognized as superior to that of others, such as artisans. Subsistence use was seen as more legitimate than gathering for commerce. Thus, along with a hierarchy of land, there was a hierarchy of users and a negative hierarchy of rights (e.g., collection of non-timber forest product [NTFPs] was allowed in reserve forests, but felling of timber was not. (See Jeffery and Sundar 1995; Tucker 1998: 466.)

6. Sivaramakrishnan points out that while state appropriation of *zamindari* forests in Midnapore, West Bengal, was justified in the name of more scientific management, in fact local people saw this as a period of deforestation. Among other things, state management led to a change in species to monocultural plantations (Sivaramakrishnan 1999).

tive hierarchy created by peasants on the basis of subsistence use may have come up with a different classification of land. Peasants "traditionally" valued mixed forests, which provided a variety of daily needs like leaves for plates, medicinal plants, fruits, and so on. Small timber was preferred to large trees because it was easier to use in making implements, house building, or fencing. Thus, the peasant view of an ideal forest could be markedly different from that of a forest officer (see Savyasachi 1994; Rangarajan 1996: 61). A timber-based classification of forests often meant transforming lands to make them correspond more closely to the official ideal (i.e., replacing mixed forests with pure stands of timber trees). It also meant transforming people to make them worthy of the good forest they inhabited. For instance, tribes with their "wasteful" shifting cultivation were seen as undeserving of good forest.[7] Both swiddening and pastoralism violated a Victorian understanding of the honest toiler: productive permanent cultivators or wage laborers tied to particular pieces of land. (For forest department animus against shifting cultivation and shifting cultivators, see Chakravarty-Kaul 1996: 69; Gadgil and Guha 1992; Rangarajan 1996: 95–137; Sundar 1997: 114–121; Prasad 1994; Skaria 1999; Sivaramakrishnan 1997, 1999; Subhash Chandran 1998.) Both the criterion of classification and the process by which territorialization occurred (demarcation, legal rules, working plans, displacement, and re-education of people) have served as points of violence.

Under the JFM policy too, the forests have been divided on the basis of the timber they contain. While the 2000 JFM policy is a step up from the 1990 policy because it allows villagers the right to protect and harvest good forest land and not just degraded land, it still makes a distinction between the two in terms of benefits offered.

The role of law in legitimizing certain sorts of violence and delegitimizing others is crucial here. Law represents a significant site of contradiction, being both a maker of hegemony and a means of resistance (see Lazarus-Black and Hirsch 1994; Mann and Roberts 1991: 35–6). As one of the major cultural idioms of the British state (see Skillen 1978; Thompson 1975), the "rule of law" was marketed by British colonialism as the great gift of "Empire" to its backward subjects. Law played a significant role in institutionalizing the colonial apparatus as indigenous groups, too, began to make use of colonial legal systems for their own ends. Particular laws, however, expropriating land and resources from groups that formerly controlled them were violent in themselves, and the maintenance of "law and

7. The alleged savagery or wastefulness of natives has been a common excuse for colonial usurpation of land. See Arneil (1996) on the connection between Locke's theory of property as born out of labor and the justification of British colonization of Amerindian land, on the basis of their greater industry.

order" became part of a coercive order rather than any individual law (Burman and Harell-Bond 1979; Sumner 1979).

Forest law was mapped both onto certain territories and onto social classes. In the case of the majority of peasant users, territorial and legal restrictions coincided rather neatly. That this was not the only alternative is evident, not just from the debates that preceded the passing of the forest laws in India, but from alternative trajectories in other British colonies or from the laws framed for different classes of people. For example, nineteenth-century Australian courts were divided on whether aboriginal ownership of land had survived the right of conquest (Hookey 1984) while in India, this right was recognized only for certain classes (e.g., *zamindars*) and not for others, especially those who held resources in common (Singh 1986: 15).

To summarize, forest policy in India has essentially been about demarcating territories on the basis of timber contained. This process has been followed by exclusion of villagers from forest lands thus demarcated, conversion of this land from multiple uses to the single one of timber production for industrial use, and most recently, the handing over of forest land to villages, who in turn exclude other people from it. Exclusion from forest resources has inevitably generated conflict, initially against the state but increasingly directed against other communities and individuals. Rather than assume, however, as some sociobiologists do, that violence or conflict is an inevitable outcome of scarcity and territorial defense the only possible reaction, we need to examine the particular conjunctures that make violence likely and possible. State territorial strategies play an important role in this process, drawing connections between certain categories of people, such as shifting cultivators and the kinds of forests to which they are entitled.[8] Rather than violence being a natural offshoot of human impulses, territorial or otherwise, it is evident that institutions can be designed to configure or prevent violence.

Institutional or legal *indeterminacy*, on the other hand, allows for violence: both territorial classifications and the legal orders that underpin these classifications are subject to very different interpretations from the standpoint of differing interests. In the case of JFM, apart from the forest acts, there are also non-forest laws, repealed laws, and case law that affect practice on the ground and create multiple rights regimes (Lele 1998). In addition to the order passed by the Central Government, twenty-one states have passed their own orders, creating a multiplicity of legal orders that interact with each other, a situation that Santos (quoted in Blomley 1994:

---

8. Little recognition existed of the fact that shifting cultivation may, in fact, have contributed to better forests or to the extension of teak into areas where it may not have grown before. See Guha 1999.

46) describes as *interlegality*. In other words, the JFM order is not the only one that touches upon people's access to forests or their right to manage it.

In addition, there is the question of diverse interpretations of the same order. The same space or forest plot may be subject simultaneously to the very localized understandings of forest guards and villagers themselves; the carrying out of the order by district forest officers based on their personal predilections, the organizational culture of the state forest department, or some understanding of what local ecological conditions require; the Ministry of Environment and Forests with their vision for afforestation; or even the Supreme Court in its adjudications on what is allowed on forest land.[9] Within this, it is important to understand the ways in which new territorial understandings of the forest have come to take shape and how "citizenship" or access rights in forest resources have been redefined. Living in proximity to a degraded forest and working to protect it is seen as conferring certain rights on users, not based on need or class standing. Because forest management can have various goals, however, this "citizenship" continues to be contested even within a village, let alone at other levels.[10]

Violence at the Joints of Joint Forest Management

> The accident of a village being situated close to a forest does not prejudice the right of a country as a whole to receive benefits of a national asset.
>
> Government of India, 1952 Forest Policy

Up to the JFM resolution of 1990, successive forest policies continued to define the "forest question" as one of an opposition between state control and public pressure. Although the village mentioned in this epigraph was assumed to be an "accident," the nation state was naturalized into a unified entity. Historically, the notion of public interest or *eminent domain* was used against small-scale peasants or forest dwelling groups to expropriate them, thus replacing community ownership of resources with individual or state ownership (Singh 1986). Where customary uses were recognized, they were recorded as privileges or concessions rather than tenurial rights.

---

9. Under the forest conservation act, any alienation of forest land to other uses can be done only with central government permission, whether or not that land actually contains trees; the Supreme Court judgment has gone further and completely banned non-forest-related activity on forest land or anything that resembles the popular understanding of forest. This has been challenged by various state forest departments. Supreme Court Orders of 12.12.96, 4.3.97, and 15.1.98 related to the Forest Conservation Act and Environment Protection Act.

10. For instance, a forest can be managed for timber stands or for a variety of products. The taller *sal* (*Shorea robusta*) trees grow and the better they are from a forester's perspective, the harder it gets for women to reach out and pluck leaves to sell.

Given this history of displacement, it is common for NGOs and activists to argue that JFM merely restores control over neighboring forests to those who owned them in the first place—village communities (Dr. Ravindranath, personal communication; Sharma 1995). However, several crucial differences exist. Under the JFM orders, ownership of forest land continues to reside in the state: villagers are merely given usufruct rights and a share of the timber; villages are not necessarily given back their "own" land, but rather, are given whatever land the forest department considers suitable. Finally, ownership and control of lands and forests may have resided in corporate (male) communities of original founding lineages (Kelkar and Nathan 1991). The community that is invoked in joint forest management schemes is quite a different phenomenon from earlier communities because it aims to give forest access and control to the entire village, including women and later settlers. The village itself today is quite a different entity from what it may once have been (see Breman 1997; Chakravarty-Kaul 1996). In short, where the moral claims of local people are being recognized by the state, this is not on the basis of the historical rights of people and the traditional duties of a paternalistic state alone. These ideas are selectively retained and/or transformed into new, limited rights, granted only when villagers have demonstrated their entitlements through their work in reforestation.

Coming after a period of inefficient but exclusive state control over resources, JFM at some level represents a privatization of resources into the hands of local communities. Although previously, legally speaking, all were excluded from reserved forests, now some people have been given the right to exclude others. In practice, of course, in the past those who could afford to bribe the forest guards or politicians (in order to be given timber-felling contracts) were often able to access resources.

Forest management under JFM tends to follow existing patterns of forest management changing merely the enforcers, not the object of policing. In some villages (e.g., Buddhikamari village in Mayurbhanj district of Orissa), protecting villagers even wear the khaki of the Forest Department, drawing on the same mystique of power.[11]

In management terms, I have argued elsewhere that forest departments view the forest-related activities of villagers in three broad categories: FD-tolerated interference, FD-approved involvement and FD-disapproved practices. FD-tolerated interference includes legitimate needs that interfere with the "proper" task of forest management (i.e., timber production) but that nevertheless have to be catered to (such as fuel wood and fodder collection). FD-approved activities are those in which villagers carry out forest department functions (such as wage labor on forest department works and non-timber forest product [NTFP] collection for sale). FD-dis-

11. See Taussig (1993: 62) for mimicry by the colonized.

approved activities include cultivation on forest lands, smuggling, and headloading (Sundar, Jeffery, and Thin, forthcoming). Obviously these categories are not exclusive but they serve as a convenient heuristic device to show how JFM is positioned within the foresters' worldview. In an ideal world according to foresters, villagers would desist from the third category of activities altogether, cut down on activities of the first type (like grazing), and concentrate on the second variety of productive activities like NTFP collection.[12]

Accordingly, several of the formal interventions in JFM programs—rotational closure of grazing areas, "multiple shoot cutting" to ensure a single clean stem, and self-regulation of forest encroachment—represent attempts by the forest department to turn villagers from "unproductive" to "productive" uses, to re-channel their needs into "socially useful" avenues, as defined by foresters. To the extent that JFM is about self-regulation by villagers, it is simply the latest step in a long effort by foresters to convert villagers (engaged in farming, felling, girdling, and grazing in opposition to the forest department) into producing, protecting, pliable supporters of the Forest Department. At the same time, evidence shows that the making over of villagers' forest use practices is far from complete and that in the majority of cases, villagers continue in their old ways, relying on the reserve forests closest to them for fuel wood, grazing, and timber. In those instances where JFM has had an impact, it has largely been on the most vulnerable sections, such as the landless who have encroached government land to cultivate or women who collect headloads of fuel wood for sale. These groups are most vulnerable to "community" pressure and least able to get their needs registered in so-called community decisions.

In the remaining part of the chapter, I attempt to illustrate the ways in which JFM purports to represent a new form of territorialization, with boundaries being drawn between villages (and between types of uses), rather than between villagers and the state. However, even though the parameters of the new territorialization are different, the process continues to be informed by the old ideology of scientific forestry. This enhances conflict, as does the indeterminacy of the process.

Encroachment

Although in most parts of the country, the forest department has been largely successful in restricting swidden agriculture and sendentarizing the population, swidden continues to be practiced in the central Indian forest

---

12. Fuel and fodder are distinguished here from NTFP collection since they do not bring in any revenue or royalty to the Forest Department. Both fuel and fodder are collected either for subsistence or for sale, with the proceeds going directly to the villagers.

belt known as the Dandakaranya region, which stretches from Maharashtra across Madhya Pradesh, Orissa, and Andhra Pradesh. Along with shifting cultivation, more permanent encroachments for settled agriculture into reserved forest areas are described as a major problem by forest officials. The reasoning used is much the same as in the colonial period i.e., that swidden destroys good timber forests. It is routine for forest staff to book cases against villagers, and for the latter to be let off by a judicial magistrate on payment of a fine. The fine papers are carefully stored as evidence of long cultivation in the event of future regularization, the illegality serving as grounds for a future legality.[13]

In many cases, villagers claim that their ancestors had been cultivating land for a long time, but because there was no land settlement in the area, their rights were never recognized. Once the forest department decided to demarcate these areas as reserves, they automatically became encroachers. In other words, many cases of so-called encroachment are really cases where initial title was not recognized or legalized.

In several villages, JFM has been instituted specifically to curb further encroachment, with members of the protection committee, known variously as a Forest Protection Committee (FPC) or Van Suraksha Samiti (VSS), ensuring that it no longer takes place. In some cases, the committee members have themselves refrained from extending cultivation into government lands, but it seems far more common for their policing to be directed against other groups, particularly migrants.

In Paderu, in the hills of Visakapatnam district, Andhra Pradesh, almost all the villagers have some land encroached for swidden agriculture called *podu*. Indeed, the presence of the podu patches on the hills just outside the demarcated area of the protected patch is like a public secret. The Bhagatas and other dominant castes in Paderu are quick to blame the Samanthas or migrants from Orissa for continuing podu. This is partially true. Many of the podu cultivators in the Eastern Ghats, especially in Paderu, are not "shifting cultivators" but "shifted cultivators" displaced by the Machkund and Upper Indravati river valley projects across the border in Orissa (for the phrase, see Dove 1993: 19). Since they have no land, they are forced to encroach into forestland. "However," argue poor Paraja villagers in Kilagada, "under the terms of the VSS which is Bhagata dominated, we are stopped from doing *podu* while the Bhagatas continue to cultivate their *podu* patches." They also feel that since they do not originally come from the area, the Forest Department is uninterested in their problems. Just across the border in Orissa, a newspaper report cites more than two hundred people being injured and hundreds of podu cultivators in five

13. State governments have periodically passed orders to regularize encroachments on forestlands prior to a certain date (e.g., the last MP Government order was passed on January 25, 1995, regularizing encroachments prior to October 24, 1980).

villages of Raighar Block being rendered homeless in organized attacks by a local forest protection committee (VSS). The VSS volunteers from Pendrani village destroyed the paddy crops, razed the houses of the podu cultivators, and also poisoned their wells, tanks, and other water sources (*Indian Express*, August 30, 1996). In the Eastern Ghats, then, large-scale displacement of the traditional *adivasi* (tribal) inhabitants pressures them to encroach on other forest lands for subsistence, and the formation of forest protection committees run by locally dominant castes have all contributed to violence. JFM has territorially empowered some groups against others.

In northwestern Madhya Pradesh similarly, encroachments provide an arena where conflicts over access to forests couched in terms of protection play out through ethnic differences. For instance, the forests of Kheda village in Dewas had been heavily encroached upon by the residents of a neighboring village Dhavadia. Although both are *adivasis*, the Kheda villagers are Bhil Thakurs and consider themselves superior to the Bhils of Dhavadia, who are recent migrants from Jhabua, a neighboring district. In 1996, the Forest Department formed a VSS in Kheda to check further forest loss through encroachment. The Kheda villagers cooperated with the Forest Department by grazing their cattle freely in the standing crop of the Dhavadia encroachers. The Dhavadia villagers retaliated by shooting arrows and nearly killed one girl. Social relations between the two villages have now been severed. Villagers from both sides avoid crossing into each other's territories, leading to a hardening of village identities along territorial lines (Vasavada and Sengupta 1996).

Another significant fissure enabling the eruption of violence, which like encroachments derives from old forest department anxieties, is the arrival of nomadic grazers in a forest. In Mohada, another *adivasi* village in Dewas district that has taken up protection, the earlier close relation between villagers and migrant cattle grazers (Gujjars) who visited their forests during the monsoons has given way to armed conflict. The Gujjars traditionally followed routes that had been recognized by the Forest Department. They would enter into arrangements with villagers along this route. In return for providing manure by folding their sheep in farmers' fields at night, they would be paid by the farmers in cash and kind (see Wade 1994). But in the first year they started protecting their forests through the JFM scheme, there was a pitched battle between the Gujjars and the Mohada villagers, with the Gujjars poised on a hill catapulting rocks down on the villagers. One of the villagers called the Range Forest Officer, who joined them in beating the Gujjars out of the protected patch with sticks. Once the Gujjars realized that the new territorial identifications implied by JFM had little room for them, they stopped visiting the Mohada forests entirely (Vasavada and Sengupta 1996). JFM thus not only privileges territorial identifications along village lines but also privileges settled agriculturists over nomads.

In order to understand these processes better, it might be useful to invoke Daniel's 1996 distinction between real and imagined communities: real communities are made up of people engaged in actual interaction and imagined communities are made of people grouped along some particular form of likeness (1996: 18–19). The power of legal geographies like JFM lies in their ability to arrange real and imagined communities onto the same geographical space, so that belonging to one village with its identification with one plot of forest rules out other forms of interaction across villages or groups. Ethnic or village identities matter less in themselves than they do with the power they acquire when matched with certain legal rights.

Certainly, violence along these fault lines would not be possible were it not for the explicit support of the Forest Department or police. The indeterminacy of enforcement against encroachment—the forest department, for instance, can and often does turn a blind eye to encroachment by the rich who bribe or coerce their way—allows the violence of the rich and the state to coalesce against more vulnerable sections. To take an example closer home to me, in Delhi, the Northern Ridge, which is an important part of the city's forest, has been encroached upon by various powerful elements. The ridge now contains temples, mosques, and churches, and even a golf club. FD proposals to remove these encroachments are strongly resisted, although slum dwellers are routinely bulldozed out.

Boundary Disputes

The drawing of boundaries is critical to any project of territorialization. Invoking boundaries within which villagers protect "their" forests is an essential part of JFM, with its attempt to associate rights with responsibilities. These boundaries, however, are not "naturally" given. Boundaries reflect social classifications, or as Lawrence puts it, "Boundaries are not just created physically but are also ordered by symbolic and juridic parameters, which are transient in kind" (1996: 13). It is the symbolic and juridic parameters or the emotional investment that accompanies boundary drawing that we need to focus on to identify points for conflict, not the fact of boundary drawing itself.

In most states, following the earlier 1990 policy, JFM orders specified that the better forests were to be retained under forest department management and only degraded lands handed over to villagers to afforest and protect.[14] Within this overall limitation, villagers were supposed to be given

14. For example, the Orissa JFM order notes that "(t)he scheme will operate in degraded forestland (Reserved and Protected Forests) with potential for regeneration. Only such forest area will be selected where the villagers of the adjacent village or cluster of villages are willing or can be motivated to offer active co-operation in regeneration and protection of the forest tract; and only such villages shall be involved which are situated adjacent to the

some choice in selecting the actual areas they would protect and acknowledgment was made of the need not to violate existing use rights.[15] Forest departments were expected to assist villagers in their selection through the use of participatory rural appraisal techniques.[16] In practice, decisions about site selection are made through a process of negotiation between competing agendas. In some cases, the choice of the particular plot was left to the villagers (often the more active or visible ones) based on their usage patterns and their knowledge of their immediate environment. In other cases, it was the Forest Department that did the apportioning, based on their mental maps of the forest as degraded or non-degraded.[17] Crown density cover was rarely calculated in practice.

In some areas, particularly the eastern states of Bengal, Bihar, and Orissa, villagers initiated protection on their own to meet the need for fodder, fuel, and timber, in the process pre-empting government orders offering them a share of the harvest. In such cases, land was informally apportioned between hamlets or villages. For instance, the villagers of Kenaloi in Sambhalpur district of Orissa decided to start protecting their forests sometime in the 1980s. Initially there was a village-wide committee, but after a period of flagging protection, villagers decided to overcome the problem by having a subcommittee in each hamlet to look after the protection of the forest patch closest to it. The total forest area was divided into seven parts, and in each hamlet a president and a secretary were made responsible to the original committee (Mishra and Peter 1995–1997). Following the enactment of the state order, the Orissa Forest Department set up a formal forest protection committee in the village with a Village-wide base. This new committee, which was superimposed on the older village-initiated one, no longer functioned at the hamlet level. The Forest Depart-

---

forest area. Sanctuaries and National Parks and forestland allotted for the purpose of commercial or industrial plantation or any other departmental afforestation scheme shall ordinarily be excluded from the ambit of this scheme. A single village committee may be allowed to develop up to a maximum forest area of 200 hectares" (Society for the Promotion of Wastelands Development [SPWD] 1998: 120–121). The Gujarat order states, "(t)he main objective of this scheme is to obtain participation of village communities/village organization in the regeneration, conservation, development and administration of degraded forests" (SPWD 1998: 35).

15. The Government of India (GOI) resolution on JFM states: "Areas to be selected for the programme should be free from the claims (including existing rights, privileges, concessions) of any person who is not a beneficiary under the scheme. Alternatively, for a given site the selection of beneficiaries should be done in such a way that any one who has a claim to any forest produce from the selected site is not left out without being given full opportunity of joining" (MoEF 1990: clause VI).

16. The Andhra Pradesh JFM order lists among functions and responsibilities of the department: "The Forest Department shall be responsible to provide assistance to VSS in selection/demarcation of the Forest area to be put under JFM" (SPWD 1998: 15).

17. An area that appears to foresters as degraded (with less than 40 percent crown density cover) may actually yield a range of intermediate products to villagers, like grasses, tubers, and so on.

ment decided on a patch to be protected by the village as a whole. Once a forest official caught some villagers cutting timber from this protected patch, the villagers decided they wanted to have nothing more to do with the formal government JFM program. In this case, villagers had drawn boundaries for themselves that functioned in an equitable fashion, but the forest department attempts at boundary drawing between areas for legitimate and illegitimate extraction were contested.

Sometimes the Forest Department gives villagers land to protect based on its idea of what is good for a patch of forestland, regardless of which village it "belongs to." In other cases, villagers and foresters subscribe to the same conceptions of custom, such as the idea that forestland within the revenue boundary of a village should be given to it for protection. In still other instances, contemporary notions of village boundaries are determined by settlements made by earlier Forest Departments, and the "customary rights" that villagers fight to retain are the rights conferred by earlier administrations. Thus there is a complex interplay of "customary" boundaries, actual usage, the definition of forest as state property, and new claims as a result of a changed context—all of which may be invoked at different times. Here I give just one example of the fissures that this situation creates for the eruption of boundary disputes.

In 1992, the forester responsible for two neighboring villages in Rajpipla West Division in Gujarat state gave 61 hectares of forestland that fell within the revenue boundaries of Bharada village to Tabda village to protect. The logic behind this was that the Bharada villagers had encroached in the past on state forestland. Tabda was a larger village and therefore also seen as requiring more forests. On this 61 hectares within the Bharada boundary, the Forest Department had planted *khair* (*Acacia catechu*) in 1987 as part of a standard departmental plantation, which would have totally excluded villagers' use. When Tabda received the patch to protect, they started with a five-year plantation. According to the Tabda villagers, the forester told them that since the land belonged to the Forest Department, there was no problem in transferring some of it from Bharada to Tabda. The ranger said, "Whether it is in Bharada or Tabda's revenue boundary, it belongs to the Forest Department and whoever protects the area will be entitled to the timber from it." In contrast, the Bharada villagers feel strongly that the forestland within their revenue boundary is theirs because their ancestors put *veth* (or free labor) into maintaining it in the past. They also say that their "encroachments" represent permanent agriculture of long standing and that they have recently won their case to get title deeds for the land. In fact, there were several hamlets of Bharada in this area and nearby that were depopulated due to cholera, which suggests that the land did not always belong to the Forest Department and was taken over by it only later. Matters are complicated by the practical problems imposed by the type of species planted on the land and by the fresh claims that protection has generated. *Khair*, like teak, takes a long time to mature. The Tabda villagers say that they will return the land with the *khair* plantation to Bharada after the first felling, while the Bharada villagers argue that the Forest Department should give wages for protection for 4 years to Tabda and return the land to Bharada immediately. Bharada also has its own protection committee but is protecting lands that are further off. In short, Bharada has some claim to the *khair* plantation because it is on Bharada land and because the Bharada villagers looked after the plantation for the first five years. Tabda villagers have claim to it because they invested the next 4 years in protecting the trees. Ideally, while some benefit sharing arrangement on the trees could be worked out, the entrenchment of a territorial approach which equates benefits with land under a village's jurisdiction makes this difficult.

The Bharada villagers complain that the Tabda villagers prevent them from bringing their cattle to graze in the plantation and that even those whose fields lie beyond the area find it difficult to pass through. In 1992, there was a major dispute between the villages. According to the Bharada version, a man was going to his field through the forest patch and was stopped and beaten up by the Tabda forest protection patrol. In the Tabda version, which is completely different, the fight occurred when some Tabda cattle were impounded by three drunken Bharada villagers. Some fifty or sixty Tabda men had gone over to Bharada to reclaim their cattle, and on their way back they encountered a man who happened to be the brother of one of the drunken cattle kidnappers. In the ensuing argument, the Bharada man was beaten up. He filed a case against the Tabda villagers that dragged on for a year. Eventually a local NGO brokered an out-of-court settlement, in which elders from both sides, the NGO representative, and a local forester all acknowledged responsibility and pooled money for compensation. Thus, neither side lost face. The plantation problem, however, has not been resolved. (Field notes 1996)

This case shows that apparently unrelated disputes and even drunken brawls may in fact conceal deeper conflicts over resources. Even as they are instantiated in the figures of quarreling individuals, these conflicts are part of a larger process of re-carving spaces, of re-mapping the spatial ordering of power between villages. Ultimately, as has often been pointed out for communal violence (Roy 1996; Das 1990: 14), what makes violence possible is the conjuncture between larger ideological or political configurations (in this case, national and state level JFM resolutions) and very local conflicts (e.g., between neighbors, landlords and tenants, etc.). In the process, both local and regional or national relations between communities are realigned.

Exclusion

Instances exist where boundaries between villages are recognized but have hitherto been ignored. In other words, the boundary between two villages has never been an issue when it comes to resource gathering. With the implementation of JFM schemes, boundaries have come into focus in new ways. The conflicts around access across boundaries come to a head at certain points of the year when particular NTFPs become available. In much the same way, certain events in a ritual calendar can provide the "temporal structure" for generally lived-with antagonisms to surge into violence (Das 1990: 16–20). Again, the victims of intracommunity violence tend to be those who are already alienated within their own communities, especially women, who bear the burden of sexual, domestic, and subsistence-producing labor (see Greenough 1982: 236; Rebel 1989). The fact that women are generally the primary collectors of fuel wood, fodder, and NTFPs means that they are often the first to suffer the coercive policing of new conservation efforts and the first to be turned into "offenders." As Menon and Bhasin argue, in the somewhat parallel context of communal riots, these "diverse, yet linked, kinds of violence (form) part of a continuum of violence. . . . the dramatic episodes of violence against women during communal riots bring to the surface, savagely and explicitly, familiar forms of sexual violence" (1998: 40–41). Two examples from Paderu, Andhra Pradesh, and Mandvi, Gujarat, bring this out.

In Mandvi, the problem centered on a single forest patch surrounded by four villages: Khodamba, Titoi, Regama, and Kalibel. Each has its own protection committee. Hamlets are so spread out, however, that households from one village are sometimes closer to the forest patch of another village than to their own forest patch.

In 1989, the Forest Department guard under whose jurisdiction Kalibel village falls was beaten up by the villagers for arresting some men who were cutting saplings in the Forest Department nursery. But when JFM was started there in approximately 1990, pressure shifted to a dispute over the boundary between the neighboring villages of Regama and Kalibel, with each side attempting to gain more forest area. The villagers went to the Forest Department to settle their dispute. The RFO called the surveyor, and the place was surveyed. The boundary dispute then subsided as both villages agreed to the decision taken in 1992. The elders of both villages were present when the agreement took place.

In 1994, three women from Regama went to the Kalibel protected patch, which is closer to their houses than their own forest is. The women, two of whom come from poor farming families, and one of whom is divorced, say they had gone to get *asitra* leaves in the early evening and were accosted and beaten up by a drunk Kalibel patrol. One of the women had to be hospitalized, and the entire village had to pitch in for her treatment because her family was very poor. The Kalibel villagers claim that the women came at 8:30 P.M., a time when no one would go to collect leaves, and their main intention was to steal grass. Grass is a more valuable resource and one that is generated through the protection efforts of the Kalibel villagers. The Regama villagers filed a case against the Kalibel patrol for assault. The chairperson of the Kalibel committee had to make several trips to the courts, but the Regama appellants did not bother to show up. Eventually elders in Kalibel and Regama negotiated a settlement with the Kalibel forest protection committee paying the affected women Rs. 1500 as compensation. (Field notes 1995, 1999)

This example reveals, first, the shift in conflict between the Forest Department and a village to conflict between two neighboring villages; second, the multiplicity of interpretations that are involved with both villages telling a different version; third, the fact that women are especially vulnerable to this kind of policing. Fourth, in the absence of external efforts to arbitrate, there is no incentive to settle a case. Court cases drag on because the offended party is not bound to attend court hearings.[18] Fifth, because many of these boundary disputes originate only when the Forest Department assigns one village land to protect and gives it the backing to exclude others, it shows the need for the Forest Department to consult all sections in neighboring villages before demarcating areas for protection. Finally, it carries hope for the future because the conflict was resolved by the villages concerned. In both Gujarat and Orissa, villages have formed themselves into federations that deal with such disputes between villages. They may suggest joint policing by neighboring villages if a patch of land is shared or some other arrangement to avoid disputes.

Similar issues are at stake in the other example from Andhra Pradesh. April and May are the two months when villagers around Paderu collect *adda* leaves (*Bauhinia vahlii*) and sell them to manufacturers of leaf plates. This is an agriculturally slack season, and families as a whole go to the forest and collect leaves. Approximately five hundred leaves sell at Rs. 20 to 25 (approximately 50 cents). Per day a family can make Rs. 150 to 200, or $3–5. In one incident that occurred in 1996, women from Kunchapally entered the protected forest of Kothauru village (VSS started in 1995) where they had an encounter with the Kothauru patrol. The Kunchapally

---

18. If both parties to a dispute do not appear in court, the hearing is simply postponed for another day. The accused is bound to be present, although there is no similar burden for the person who has filed the complaint.

women said they were threatened with rape, and one of the women lost a gold ring in the melee.

At a conflict resolution meeting held in a neutral village and attended by the Forest Department, the "grievance party" said: "We have been collecting leaves and firewood from the forest (Kothauru) since time immemorial. Currently around seven to eight villages depend on this forest. So what if we collect some leaves? We are not destroying the forest. Just because the Forest Department has given the Kothauru VSS the right to protect the forest, they cannot misbehave with our women. Is it proper to use words like 'rape' with women? Our women have been harassed so much that one woman has lost her gold ring has been injured. It is our customary right to collect forest produce. If you stop us, where shall we go?" At this point three or four people from the "accused party" shouted back asking for proof and witnesses that they misbehaved with the women. Accusations and counter-accusations flew back and forth. One of the Kunchapally women shouted at a Kothauru women, "Yes, Yes, DFO has given a very big letter authorizing you. Maybe you are sleeping with him, so he is so pleased to give the hill."

When the range officer tried to convince the Kothauru villagers to let the Kunchapally women in, even if only for the two months of the *adda* season, they refused. The Kothauru VSS chairperson reiterated that "They (Kunchapally) should not enter our protected patch; we are authorized to protect it, and we are doing so. This is a warning to all that nobody should enter here. Of course, we are aware of the problems of neighboring villages. But they have to ask us before collecting leaves or firewood." Another old man added, "If we allow them, they will not only collect NTFPs but will cut wood and take it home. If you ask us to allow others in, what's the point of protection? We work day and night to protect our forests. We don't want someone else to come and benefit from this and destroy our forest in the process." Following him, some four or five people from Kothauru chimed together. "If this is the case, then we do not want the VSS." Saying this, they went out of the room. Eventually the range officer went out and announced that officially the Kunchapally villagers were not permitted into the Kothauru patch. But if the VSS members wanted, then they could allow other villagers to collect NTFPs and firewood in the protected patch. He added that this matter would be discussed in the DFO's office and very soon the problem would be solved. After closing the meeting, he went back to warn both groups not to enter into any such conflict again. The range officer's policy was eventually to let the affair tide over with the hope that once the *adda* leaf season ended, both sides would forget it. (Gorada 1996)

Both the Kunchapally-Kothauru case in Andhra Pradesh and the Kalibel-Regama case in Gujarat bring out the sexual threats that lurk like shadows over and beyond the actual dispute. People are quick to lay these charges on each other precisely because the threat of rape is part of every-day mechanisms of control (Scheper-Hughes 1992: 229–230). The sexual politics involved, however, are never simple. Allegations about sexual conduct can be a language not only of violence but also of negotiation. Talking to a group of women in Makhenjar village, Mandvi, we learnt that they find it easier to get fuel wood from the forests than the men do because the guards know they are unlikely to be cutting big timber. Unlike men, they simply cannot cut and carry large logs home. "Moreover," they said, "the guard knows that if he prevents us, and says or does anything wrong, we can go to the police station and report him." Skeptics might well point out that their view of the police is not likely to prove so rosy in practice, with the police more inclined to take the guards' side than theirs. But what is interesting in the telling is the manner in which they play upon their own position as victims, using it in practice as a strength that enables them to cut wood from the forest. At the same time, the idea that women should act as the vanguard for a raiding party (metaphorically speaking) into a reserved forest or into some other village's protected patch also enables the division of labor to be perpetuated. Women are forced to retain the tasks of fuel wood collection simply because it is "easier" for them not to get caught, as compared to men.

On the other hand, this notion of women as victims of assault also is used by men of their own village to get even with men of another village, for instance, by accusing the opposite patrol of molesting their women. The latter, of course, deny such charges and claim they were only exercising their right of protection. This is strongly reminiscent of the argument that women are merely used as pawns in a game of "honor" that men play with each other, the repositories of one party's pride against another (Menon and Bhasin 1998: 45). Women's bodies, too, have been likened to territories, to be "conquered, claimed or marked by the assailant" as a stand-in for a whole community (Menon and Bhasin 1998: 43–44; Mehta and Chatterjee 1995: 19).

Even as women's honor becomes an issue in some intervillage disputes, within a village itself, women, especially poor and heavily forest-dependent ones, can be subject to strict policing by their own village patrols. As one desperate women in Gujarat asked her village forest protection committee, which had just arrested her for taking wood from the protected patch, "Do you expect me to cut off my hands to feed the hearth?" (Sarin 1998).

Furthermore, women are increasingly being used to exclude other women. Madhu Sarin, who has worked extensively on the gender differentiated effects of JFM, quotes a male tribal leader on this practice: "On seeing the women (of a lower status tribal community) cutting firewood from our protected forest, we sent some children to tell them to stop. Instead of agreeing, the women threatened the children, who ran back in fright. We then went ourselves, caught the women, locked them up, and went to bring the men from their households in their village. Then we got our women to beat the apprehended women in front of their men. We had instructed our women to confine the beating to below the neck (Sarin 1998: 18). Women become simultaneously victims and perpetrators.

Finally, even in their role as disputants and oppressors of others, women are allowed to express themselves only as long as it is convenient for the men to let them do so. One reason given by a forest officer in Paderu for not involving women in the management committees was that they were too vocal in their complaints. The sexual allegations leveled by women against each other in the Kothauru-Kunchapally case (such as accusing women from the other village of sleeping with the DFO) were treated with embarrassment by the men. This, in turn, is linked to hierarchies of speech, where women's directness is said to be an impediment to skillful negotiation (Gal 1991: 179).

With all this, however, women do benefit when their forests regenerate. All-women patrolling squads are not just about catching other women; they are also about solidarity within. When we spoke to women who regularly patrolled their forests in parts of Gujarat and Orissa, they talked about the sense of change from their daily work and the power they gained through collective action. The area under forests has increased as a result of JFM, according to figures released by the Forest Survey of 1997, and there is at least some theoretical awareness being generated among foresters and NGO staff that women must be consulted, whether or not they do so in practice.

In the new legal geography that JFM represents, disputes over where to draw boundaries and what those boundaries are meant to signify (exclusion from access to resources) play an important role. Villagers are mobilized to maintain these boundaries, which in turn are contested by residents of other neighboring villages. In some cases, the Forest Department staff has a stake in keeping these boundaries indeterminate so that their own role as arbitrators is secured. Individual foresters, who might wish to resolve disputes conclusively, are sometimes hampered by the framework of the JFM orders, which are vague in many respects, although the ability to distribute good forest land for protection that the new order envisages will reduce much of this conflict. Most disputes over resources under JFM involve poor women and small farmers who are heavily dependent on forest resources but require elders and village leaders to resolve them once it becomes a question of "village" territory.

Conclusion

I have attempted here to bring out the manner in which the institutionalization of changing legal geographies is associated with different forms of violence. These changing legal geographies include, for example: the spatial distributions of power implied by appropriation of resources away from villages; the centralization of management in a Forest Department with a single ideology and mode of operation; and the subsequent de-centralization of forest management under schemes like community or joint forest management.[19]

The focus here has been partly on territorialization—the association of certain tracts of territory with certain material and ideological claims to resources and the power to exclude others—as well as the kinds of strategies that are used to achieve this identification. Territorialization has contributed to violence, both by the state against villagers and by villagers against each other, but a large part of this power to engender violence derives from the ideology of scientific forestry. It is to the history of "scientific forestry" and state repression against errant users of the forest that we must look to understand the contemporary tensions around Joint Forest Management, rather than to the politics of scarcity or some instinct of territorial defense. The objects of villagers' wrath follow the familiar lines of colonial foresters' aversions (e.g., to particular forms of resource use such as shifting cultivation). In this ideology, pure timber stands are valued over mixed forests, and the users of this timber (industry, military, etc.) valued over the users of mixed forests (peasants). As Said says, various kinds of knowledge are constructed that create and perpetuate the idea of a given "character and destiny" for a given geography.

Although territorialization based on scientific forestry has been an important source of violence, the incompleteness of the territorialization project has further enhanced the possibility of conflict. Several disputes over "encroachment" or over boundaries between villages occur because demarcation was not fully carried out and villagers claims were not settled with title deeds or were turned out of their homes on legal grounds that were at variance with local concepts of belonging. Significant work still needs to be done on re-framing "local rights" on theoretical and legal grounds, which may or may not be territorially based. A suitable balance needs to be drawn between a principle of rights in exchange for labor invested, starting from a cut-off date in the present and some redress of historical wrongs that avoids chauvinism. While villagers who are willing to invest effort into protection and management of their forests deserve rights to harvest them under JFM or some other arrangement, a serious problem is introduced by the history of land alienation and displacement in tribal areas.

19. No doubt this dichotomy between a centralized forestry service and decentralized community management is not as clear as I have made out here, and in practice much of the work of the Forest Department grew out of very localized conditions (see Sivaramakrishnan 1997). But sometimes it is necessary to paint the larger picture, albeit with cruder brushstrokes.

Finally, while territorialization based on an ideology of scientific forestry has led to displacement, exclusion, and violence, it is important to remember the real issue. This is a form of territorialization that benefits certain classes in society (capitalists, rich immigrants in *adivasi* or tribal areas, dominant castes in a village, politically powerful and economically prosperous villages) at the expense of others (peasant forest users, displaced *adivasis*, smaller villages, etc.).

In this chapter, I have attempted to bring out the manner in which state disapproval about "inappropriate" village uses of the forest (such as for swidden or pastoralism) has now been routinized and even internalized by villagers. This chapter, like Neumann's in this volume, makes the point that rather than representing a shift away from state control, community involvement in conservation and management often represents merely a shift to more micro-disciplinary forms of power. In programs like Joint Forest Management that shift the burden of protection onto villagers, the power of villagers to enforce exclusive claims to resources is really an extension of the power of the state. More accurately, there is a process of mirroring along different nodes of power. In some cases, state power coalesces with indigenous cultural inequities to produce dual victimization. Because they are marginalized within the domestic unit, women, especially laboring women, tend to be the first to bear the brunt of degradation, are the first to get involved in conflicts, are silenced when they voice their opinions, and are allowed voices only as the outraged emblems of male honor.

The power of innovations like JFM lies in the fact that they can be and are justified in terms of a larger public interest: the regeneration of forest cover; the provision of fuel wood, fodder, and employment to villages; and the lessening of conflict between villagers and the government. In the process, a new image of the state is developed, of the state as impartial arbitrator of conflicts, and of a developmental state keen to combine conservation with service to its citizens. Thus, not only is community conservation successful at moving power outwards and downwards, it is also successful in shoring up power at the center through its harnessing of legitimacy.

At the same time, the disciplining of peasants is not complete—the growth of federations between villages, the attempts by villagers to negotiate with foresters over which land to protect, the recognition that women must be involved in deciding on forest management—all point to the fact that there are resurgent spaces in society that can help to minimize violence.[20] Joint forest management may in fact be the first step in actually making state legitimacy work. The state may have to perform for the

---

20. For greater details on conflict resolution mechanisms, see Sundar 1996.

people against its other interests, as witnessed by the fact that it has had to take into account several concerns voiced by NGOs in framing a revised order. Although villagers may appear, therefore, to be engaged in battling each other due to scarcity, this is a temporary phase before more rational forms of management assert themselves.

15

Written on the Body, Written on the Land: Violence and Environmental Struggles in Central India

Amita Baviskar

The inherently violent effects of capitalist state practice are writ large on Southern peoples and landscapes (Alvares 1992). Small peasants, tribal groups, poor women, and the lands and forests they live and work with, are the reluctant subjects of development, a process that employs new technologies and ideologies to exploit vulnerable social groups and the natural base that sustains them, even as it claims to improve both. New and accelerated modes of extraction, which seek to control nature through river valley projects or forestry schemes, are justified in terms of causes such as the national interest and biodiversity conservation. These causes are so transcendental that only the omniscient state claims the authority to safeguard them.[1] The union of politics and violence is thus informed by the myth of the state. This myth is created through a constitutive split between the "profane" dimensions of the state, its incoherence, the brutality and the banality of governance, and the "sublime" qualities attributed to the state, the illusion that it serves higher forms of rationality.[2] Social groups within the nation-state who challenge the state's monopoly over the determination of national interest and conservation have to struggle to establish alternative bases for their legitimacy.

Such legitimacy may be derived from the discourse of development itself. In the words of James Scott, "a hegemonic ideology must, by definition, represent an idealization, which therefore inevitably creates the contradictions that permit it to be criticized *in its own terms*" (Scott 1985: 315;

1. The state's claims of being the sole authority are also contested through international discourses around development and the environment (see Ferguson 1994).
2. I am grateful to Deepak Mehta for suggesting this formulation.

354

italics in original). Development also is ostensibly about increasing human welfare, empowerment and the exercise of democratic freedoms, and about establishing sustainable and just ways of using the physical and biological environment. This idealization, coupled with the experience of exploitation, creates the possibility of a politics of resistance that combines conflict with collaboration, criticizing the state even while engaging in dialogue and negotiating with it. That is, the "sublime" dimension of the state makes it possible for ordinary people to interpret dispersed experiences of being governed as meaningful signs of a larger, ordered system. Strategies of resistance are typified by what Levi-Strauss, speaking of myth making, calls *bricolage*—the use of a heterogeneous repertoire of resources (1966: 17). Increasingly, we see a tendency for such a repertoire to draw upon globally circulated knowledge, modes of organization, and institutions (Brosius 1999).

The myth of a "sublime" state, an idealization that creates its own dissonance, is continually contested. More difficult questions, however, arise from the fact that "every established order tends to produce . . . the naturalization of its own arbitrariness" (Bourdieu 1977: 164). State violence is routinized by the constitution of social categories—those who can legitimately use violence; those against whom violence can be legitimately used. The state also leads in defining the context where violence is justified; the definition of a conflict as a "law and order problem" becomes a step toward its suppression. By shaping definitions and assumptions, the state seeps into cultural codes, making it difficult to ask certain questions or think certain thoughts. Those who seek to shatter this consensus mobilized by the state, endeavor to make visible violence that is implicit.

This new visibility challenges three aspects of state power that were earlier taken for granted and accepted as manifestations of authority. First, it exposes the violence embedded in categorizations of tribe, caste, and gender, and the attribution of "natural" qualities to these groups (the "wildness" of tribes or the "promiscuity" of tribal women, for instance). Second, it highlights the violence inherent in processes, such as the colonial classification of lands and forests, and the displacement that accompanies development. Third, it criticizes the selective abuse of the punitive power of the state against peaceful demonstrators, in "encounter" killings, custodial torture, and more insidious acts of surveillance and defamation.

The attempt by social movements to shift perceptions from violence-as-normal to violence-as-pathological and to move from the banal routine of development-as-domination to a collective resistance against state violence, invites further violence in the form of state repression. If the new strategies of resistance are effective in challenging established modes of state discipline, they are answered by fresh violence. Yet there are variations in the response of the state to collective resistance. This chapter describes two contemporary social movements around issues of the environment and development in central India. These movements have simultaneously challenged the state but have met with strikingly different responses from it. What has enabled one movement, the Maheshwar anti-dam struggle, to negotiate state violence more effectively than the other movement, the Adivasi Mukti Sangathan (Organization for Tribal Liberation)?

This chapter argues that the "arts of resistance" seem to be more successful if a struggle manages to represent itself as an environmental movement within a framework recognized by certain global audiences. Claims to environmentalism are more likely to be accepted if they fit into a preexisting template of "green politics" as developed in the North over the last three decades. Southern movements, however, have enlarged this template and expanded the "green agenda" by demonstrating the convergence between subsistence livelihood practices and environmental sustainability (Guha and Martinez-Alier 1998: 3–21). Where Southern movements have not been able to prove beyond doubt that their practices are ecologically sustainable, they have at least shown that their use of natural resources is less degrading than that of anyone else, especially the state's. That is, minimally, Southern movements claim to be "environmentalists by default" (Baviskar 1995: 239).

Strategically, besides invoking one's own ecological superiority, a claim to environmentalism is more likely to succeed if it also creates ecological genealogies. That is, a social movement must be able to represent its subjects as "natural" communities with virtuous ancestries. It must convert fluid identities into primordial and unitary categories; tribes, women, or peasants, all must appear to be internally undifferentiated and uniformly opposed to the state. Where such unified representations cannot be created, resistance is more vulnerable to challenge and violent repression by the state.

Through an account of two "environmental" struggles in Madhya Pradesh (MP), a state in central India, this chapter discusses: (1) how social movements move violence from the realm of the "normal" to the "pathological"; (2) how the state seeks to absorb, explain, and otherwise neutralize accounts of its own pathology; and (3) how the process of challenging state hegemony entails entering into the dual modes of conflict and collaboration. The chapter compares the different responses meted out to the two movements by the state. It argues that in the case of the Adivasi Mukti Sangathan, the failure to prove ecological superiority and to mobilize unitary communities severely compromised the movement, enabling the state to unleash brutal violence against it. On the other hand, the Maheshwar anti-dam movement was able to tap a global discourse on dams and the environment that gave it the legitimacy necessary to deflect state violence.

As used here, "the state" specifically refers to the government of Madhya Pradesh. This complex entity nests within the federal system of Indian states (provinces) under the rubric of the central Union government. It consists of elected representatives to the legislature as well as permanently appointed members of the bureaucracy. Historically, except for brief periods when the rightist Bharatiya Janata Party came to power, Madhya Pradesh has been ruled by the centrist Congress Party. The elected representatives and the bureaucracy together form an institution that has tremendous inertia, an ability to endure while changing only slightly.

The state works at multiple levels by engaging with different actors. The structure of rural polity makes local elites in villages a natural ally of the state. Within Madhya Pradesh, the support of local capitalists (traders, contractors, and large farmers) has always shaped state practice, even as populist schemes have been aimed at the largely tribal voting masses. The state also expands outwards beyond the geographical limits of Madhya Pradesh through its links with the Union government, national political parties, the national civil service, and, increasingly, with international capital. Besides bilateral aid, the World Bank funds several large projects in the state, including the forestry and education sectors. With the liberalization of the Indian economy, several multinational corporations and other foreign firms have been invited to set up extractive industries and to execute public utility projects in Madhya Pradesh. Kickbacks and commissions are a sine qua non in such deals, and the state acts in close complicity with capital at different levels.

The outcomes of state processes, however, are not always foregone conclusions. Competing factions within the state and the necessity of maintaining legitimacy at different levels create opportunities for playing one set of actors against another. These fault lines within the state and the tensions inherent in them, together with the pressure of opposing forces, enable political changes that go against the interests of the state. Social movements that engage with the state at different levels try to choose an arena for action that suits their ideology and capacity, even as the state attempts to preempt that choice.

This chapter examines these political processes from a perspective that differs from that of the main actors themselves. I write this chapter as a student of these movements but also from the vantage point of a Delhi-based civil liberties activist, involved in supporting such movements to withstand moments of crisis. By now there are well-established lines of action by which metropolitan human rights organizations deal with such violence, and the chapter will discuss the routinization of such responses—working the media, sending a human rights investigative team, publicizing its report, approaching the Supreme Court and the National Human Rights Commission. This discussion is fore-grounded so that the complexities of dealing with the state—the object of our deepest terrors as well as our highest hopes—are brought out from personal experience. This rendering should not give the misleading impression that the perspectives of actors more directly involved in the struggle are less important or that these actors in Madhya Pradesh participate in events only as victims. I do not have the resources to write on behalf of critically important others, such as the tribal members of the Adivasi Mukti Sangathan, the peasants of the Narmada Bachao Andolan, or the activists who work with them. This narrative does not try to be a totalizing one. I hope that by sharing this very partial account with different groups, it will bring forth other voices and other stories, most importantly of those men and women who are engaged in fighting for their lives, bodies, and land. In the process, it also may explore the potential for more effective struggles for social and environmental justice.

The chapter begins with a quick look at the Narmada Bachao Andolan's recent struggle against the Maheshwar dam, the response of the state through the twin modes of *saam* (equal, respectful treatment) and *danda* (punitive action).[3] This part of the chapter argues that the Andolan is able to deflect state violence and even turn it to advantage because the movement fits into certain preexisting notions of environmentalism in the minds of the intelligentsia. This section also suggests that the anti-dam movement's environmental politics enable it to short-circuit local structures of power and successfully negotiate with a state that is dispersed across several locales nationally and internationally. The next part has a fuller discussion of another movement from the same district in central India, the Adivasi Mukti Sangathan (AMS). The AMS's mobilization of tribal people against their immediate oppressors has elicited extremely violent state action. The lines of conflict are blurred, however, because of the complicity of some tribal people in the structures of domination. This complicity allows the state to use the weapons of *daama* (buying out) and *bhed* (inciting differences) along with *danda* (punitive action) so that violence appears to be internal and natural to the tribal condition.

The chapter argues that violence is structured through both state and civil society, and it would be erroneous to attribute it only to state processes and instruments of domination. Violence also emanates from the institutions of caste and patriarchy. While some types of violence, however, such as that which occurs within a feud or factional dispute, may have their roots in civil society, the new strategies of domination and resistance reconfigure the feud so that it gets embedded in the asymmetrical struc-

3. Kautilya, the great political scientist of the Mauryan period, in his masterpiece *Arthashastra* (c. 250 A.D.) describes four weapons wielded by a ruler to subdue his opponents— *saama, daama, danda, bhed.* Only one of these, *danda*, refers to outright repression. *Bhed* suggests instigating differences among your enemies; *daama* that you buy them over, and, the subtlest of all; *saama*, that you co-opt opponents by involving them in dialogue.

tures of power nurtured by the state. The final part of this chapter dwells on the role of metropolitan human rights networks in supporting grassroots organizations battling against state repression. It discusses some of the dilemmas of dealing with "the myth of the state"—our belief that, to maintain its legitimacy, the state must make itself partially accountable to those whom it oppresses.

Maheshwar: Green Politics and the Soft State

The Maheshwar dam is a hydroelectric project being built on the river Narmada in district Khargone, Madhya Pradesh in central India. It is a part of the much larger Narmada Valley Project, which envisages the construction of 30 large dams, 135 medium dams, and 3000 small dams.[4] With the contract for this 400-megawatt project being awarded to a consortium of Indian and German capitalists, led by the firm of S. Kumars, this will be India's first private hydroelectric project. The controversy around the dam touches upon issues that are now well known, thanks in large measure to the indefatigable work of the Narmada Bachao Andolan (NBA [Campaign to Save the Narmada]) against the Sardar Sarovar Project and against large dams in general. Maheshwar is an important temple town, a center of pilgrimage with many historic monuments, and a thriving center of handloom weaving. Earlier, the project would have submerged parts of Maheshwar town, but the uproar forced the state to redesign the project so that the town was left out. Now the project will submerge around 5,000 hectares of rich agricultural land in sixty-one villages of the Nimar plains, displacing about 2,200 resident households and destroying the livelihoods of thousands of migrant workers. These are mixed-caste villages dominated by landowners of the Patidar Caste, with other groups (including the Scheduled Castes, Scheduled Tribes, and Muslims) also represented.[5] As

---

4. Of the large dams, Tawa, Bargi, Barna and Sukta have already been built. Work continues on the Sardar Sarovar Project, which is now recognized internationally as an icon of the struggle against large dams, and on the Narmada Sagar. The Narmada Bachao Andolan started with Sardar Sarovar and went on to also mobilize those displaced by the Bargi dam and those threatened by Narmada Sagar.

5. A mixed-caste village in India consists of several Hindu and Muslim castes, ranked hierarchically in terms of purity and pollution and separated by rules about marriage and food sharing. Except at the very top (Brahmins), ritual ranking generally coincides with economic and political power. As a numerically significant, landowning group that is also fairly high in the caste hierarchy, Patidars form the dominant caste within these villages. The Scheduled Castes comprise the former "untouchables," castes considered to be so impure that they lay outside the caste system. The Scheduled Tribes (or *adivasis* [original dwellers] as they refer to themselves) consist of disparate social groups that were first classified as "tribal" by the colonial state (Beteille 1998). Both Scheduled Castes and Tribes comprise the poorest and most exploited sections of Indian society.

with all displacement, the loss will not only involve material impoverishment but deeper cultural and emotional dislocation.[6]

Since 1996, the NBA has mobilized villagers in the submergence zone of the dam around the critical issues of human displacement and socioeconomic rehabilitation. Although the state government proposes to compulsorily acquire their land, no alternative land has been provided for resettlement. Instead, only meager sums of money, much below the market price for land, have been paid out. Although this government procedure conforms to the provisions of the Land Acquisition Act of 1894, the NBA has forcefully argued that legal sanction, especially that derived from an outdated colonial law, is an inadequate basis for state action. Justice demands actions that may have to *transform* law; therefore, the NBA has led a struggle to amend the Land Acquisition Act at the national level (see Asif 1999).

Closely related to the issue of displacement is that of environmental impact. All proposed large dams need clearance by the Ministry of Environment and Forests. Maheshwar was given "conditional clearance" in 1994, subject to resettlement being completed by 1997–1998 and subject to studies on environmental impact being carried out. "Conditional clearance" is a slippery slope because, even if permission is later revoked because of conditions not being met or because the studies show major problems with the project, the fait accompli of construction means that it is too late to stop the project. In the case of Maheshwar, successful mobilization by the NBA on the issues of displacement and environmental impact compelled the Madhya Pradesh (MP) government to announce in January 1998 that it would suspend all work on the dam, power house, and land acquisitions pending a comprehensive review of costs, benefits, and alternatives. This review would be conducted by a joint Task Force that would include representatives of the NBA.

The relatively prompt capitulation of the MP government to the NBA's demands is unusual and requires explanation. The history to this relationship goes back to the NBA's twelve-year-old struggle against the Sardar Sarovar Project (SSP). In the case of the SSP, while much of the submergence lies in Madhya Pradesh, almost all the benefits go to the neighboring state of Gujarat. The present MP State Government has argued that the SSP hurts the interests of the state. In March 1998, the government even asked for a reassessment of the decision of the Narmada Water Disputes Tribunal on the sharing of water between riparian states in the light of the new problems that emerged after the Tribunal's decision.[7] Since this stand,

6. The literature on the social impact of displacement is vast. For Sardar Sarovar alone, see Dreze, Samson, and Singh (1997); Fisher (1995); Baviskar (1995); and Morse and Berger (1992).

7. Data collected after the Tribunal's decision in 1978 showed that the Narmada River had significantly less water than planned for and that the scale of displacement was much larger

adopted to show concern for safeguarding the interests of the people of Madhya Pradesh, happens to support the position of the NBA, relations between the MP State Government (especially the Chief Minister Digvijay Singh) and the anti-dam movement have become relatively cordial.

Another important factor is the substantial international clout of the Andolan. The campaign against Sardar Sarovar was an extraordinarily successful example of organized mobilization. Besides the affected people, the campaign brought together national and international media, international nongovernmental organizations (NGOs) (Environment Defense Fund, Survival International, Friends of the Earth, International Rivers Network), lobbyists, and ordinary environmentalists attracted by, among other factors, the potent iconography of the movement. The NBA has maintained this network with the aid of new technologies such as the Internet. Events in Maheshwar unleashed a barrage of reportage in the national and international media, the attention of several monitoring bodies, and a spate of protest letters to the Indian and MP government. The present MP Chief Minister strives hard to project an image of being development-oriented;[8] this is a prerequisite for getting loans from the World Bank, Asian Development Bank, and so on. The state also must appear to be "environmentally correct" and, in fact, the Chief Minister has been recently rated as the second most "green" politician by the Centre for Science and Environment, a Delhi-based NGO. So being on good terms with a celebrity social movement is important. Thus, in the case of Maheshwar, the Chief Minister personally spoke to the Andolan leadership and suspended construction of the dam.

The joint Task Force met in February 1998 in a "cordial atmosphere," and the MP government made data available to the NBA.[9] The state government agreed to prepare a detailed note justifying various aspects of the project, while the NBA agreed to prepare its own document on project costs, benefits, and alternatives by April. While this dialogue was on, however, the contractors of the project placed large advertisements in local newspapers proclaiming the project's "massive benefits" and "minimal displacement." In March, the contractors asked the government for permission to build a wall for "safety purposes" to prevent damage during the monsoons to existing excavations. The Chief Minister granted permission. Then the NBA discovered that the wall would be a permanent structure and an integral part of the dam. A series of demonstrations at the state

---

than estimated. Changes in these two critical factors would drastically alter the distribution of the project's benefits and costs.

8. MP is the only state to publish a Human Development Report along the lines of the United Nations Development Program's annual offering. It also has several Technology Missions—for Primary Education, Watershed Development, Immunization, and so on.

9. NBA News Alert and Update on Maheshwar in the *India Environment Digest*, April 8, 1998 (Vol.1: No.25), IndiaLink-Environment.

capital Bhopal and at the dam site ensued to protest against the state's reneging on its agreement with the NBA. On April 22, hundreds of villagers, mobilized by the NBA, converged at the dam site to stop construction only to be surrounded by policemen, some of them on horseback. As protesters surged forward to break through the cordon, they were beaten with *lathis* (batons), kicked, dragged to waiting police vans, and arrested. The villagers reassembled the next day and again tried to force construction to a standstill only to be brutally beaten and arrested. There were large numbers of women among the demonstrators; their clothes were torn, they were verbally abused and threatened with sexual assault.

Mobilization against this outrage was swift. Extensive coverage in the media ensued. The National Commission for Women and the National Commission for Human Rights (independent quasi-judicial commissions of the government of India) sent investigating teams. Hundreds of activists and social workers belonging to the National Alliance of People's Movements and organizations all over Madhya Pradesh, as well as prominent persons (such as Justice Krishna Iyer and Swami Agnivesh), visited Maheshwar or issued statements in solidarity with the NBA.[10] In response to a call from the NBA, human rights organizations in Delhi also sent a team to investigate. Generally, assembling a team is exhausting work but for the NBA, more volunteers were there than were needed. On its return, the team's report received fairly wide coverage by the media. Because the immediate crisis of state repression seemed rather mild (when compared to the horrors that happen all over the country every day), the report judiciously chose to focus on the larger issue of the project and the injustice of displacement. The bruised and battered bodies of the demonstrators and their torn clothes testified to the violence of the state, a violence that fleshed out the equally savage yet imperceptible process of forced displacement. The blockade at the dam site, with its massed bodies, dramatized the broader struggle against the state's power to evict people at will. The human rights teams thus focused not only on the immediate incidents of violence but also on the context of forced displacement within which they occurred.

The well-oiled response that the NBA was able to elicit in a case of relatively mild human rights violation comes from its present preeminent position as a social movement par excellence. This position has been achieved over time by carving out a distinctive ideological territory as a nonviolent movement of small peasants and tribal people led by Medha Patkar, a charismatic woman. The Narmada Bachao Andolan's respectability in the eyes of the media and other "reference publics" also derives from its use of

10. A full description of the mobilization may be found in Narmada Samachar (NBA Update: June–July 1998).

Gandhian idioms of protest, the palpable probity of its leaders and members, and its transparent functioning. The Andolan has defined its struggle against the Sardar Sarovar Project as the fight against "destructive development," a process that does violence to nature and to people. Although NBA politics point towards a rich understanding of the environment–development connection, with ecological Marxist underpinnings, this ideology is little known and rarely accepted by people other than committed supporters of the cause.[11] Despite the Andolan's frequent assertion that it is not an environmental movement in the popular sense of protecting "nature," but that it has a much more far-reaching critique of the present connections between development and environment from the point of view of social justice as well as ecological sustainability, this political critique has not found a wide audience. The Andolan is commonly perceived to be an environmental movement because it is identified as opposed to the submergence of forests and the displacement of forest-dwelling communities. Its broader critique of development as a global process that constantly extracts and destroys resources, skews technological choices, and worsens social inequality has few takers. In the popular imagination, dams appear to be isolated monuments jutting out of a misty political-economic landscape.

Even though the Andolan's critique of development as a general process has not won many followers, the movement *has* achieved the goal of eroding the credibility of big dams in India. Building on the growing international campaign against dams (Goldsmith and Hildyard 1984; McCully 1996) and the burgeoning environmentalism among sections of the intelligentsia since the 1970s, the NBA has succeeded in knitting together an impressive coalition ranging from a grassroots movement of the displaced population to urban middle-class supporters all over the country and abroad.

This innovative mix of "people power," along with advocacy, lobbying, media and event management, parallels some of the campaigns of the Indian freedom struggle in the 1940s.[12] The Andolan created the political space where the rights of *adivasis* (tribal groups) received special attention; its discussion of displacement brought to center-stage issues of control over the ownership of land, forests, and water. In the process, it also defined forbidden zones of violation—acts and attitudes that were no longer acceptable—for instance, displacing people against their will in the name of national interest and not consulting people about their impending fate. Yet these enormous political gains do not appear to have spread.

---

11. Lack of space prevents a fuller discussion of the Andolan's ideology. A more detailed account may be found in Baviskar (1995). For the Andolan's statement about its politics, see NBA (1991, 1994).

12. I am grateful to Paul Greenough for pointing this out.

In the same district of Khargone, where the MP government has been compelled over time to treat the Andolan with circumspection, the Adivasi Mukti Sangathan experienced a totally different face of the state.

Adivasi Mukti Sangathan: The State and Contested Communities

The images that the state of Madhya Pradesh evokes most often are of forests, *adivasis* (tribal people), poverty, and "backwardness." About a third of its area, 133,000 square kilometers, is covered by forests. Every fourth person in the state belongs to a Scheduled Tribe. Of the state's rural population, 60 percent live below the poverty line. Average life expectancy for men and women is 54 years. The infant mortality rate (IMR) is 111 per thousand live births (for India as a whole, the IMR is 80/1000). Only 58 percent of the men and 29 percent of the women are literate. Only 5.6 percent of villages have medical facilities. Only half the rural households have access to safe drinking water.[13]

Explanations for the convergence of these factors—forests, adivasis, poverty, and "backwardness"—vary. Non-adivasis blame adivasis for being lazy and shiftless, prone to drunkenness and violence. The state administration, which is overwhelmingly manned by non-adivasis, appends remoteness as another reason for the absence of development inputs such as education and health services.

On the other side are the explanations of organizations such as the Adivasi Mukti Sangathan ([AMS] Organization for Tribal Liberation), that has been working in the Nimar plains (Khargone and Khandwa districts, southwest Madhya Pradesh) since 1992. According to the AMS, adivasis are poor because they do not control their basic means of subsistence—*jal, jangal, zameen* (water, forests, and land). Adivasi agricultural lands have been gradually alienated by non-adivasi moneylenders, exploiting the opportunities afforded by chronic adivasi indebtedness. Small loans taken by *adivasis* to tide over seasons of scarcity or moments of crisis are tied to extortionate interest rates (up to 240 percent per annum) and fraud so that the debtor often ends up losing his land. In the case of the Nimar plains, the alienation of adivasi lands by non-adivasis has a history that goes back at least two centuries; it includes several waves of migrants who were encouraged to settle here by erstwhile governments because they belonged to "industrious" peasant castes such as the Patidars (GoMP 1970). Antagonisms with Patidars and worsening conditions of subsistence brought

13. All data from Dreze and Sen (1996), except data on forests (Buch 1991) and tribes (GoMP 1995).

about by the alienation of the commons contributed to the escalation of crime in the form of armed robberies by tribal groups.[14]

Over time, the Patidars acquired the best alluvial lands in the plains next to the river Narmada, while the low hills with prospects only of dry land farming were left to the adivasis. The expanding population cut into the forests which, since Independence, have come to be fully under state control. Adivasis who cleared areas under the control of the Forest Department for cultivation now face the charge of being encroachers and destroyers of forests. Without secure access to land, adivasis are constantly harassed by the Forest Department and forced to pay bribes to avoid trouble with the authorities.

Control over land, especially forestland, is highly contested, and the increasing presence of the AMS has changed the situation significantly, as the following incident reveals. According to a public statement made by the Divisional Forest Officer of Burhanpur (Khandwa district) on August 28, 1997, he received information that many trees had been felled in Mandwa village. Villagers had encroached on forestland and planted crops. The Forest Officer went with a party of four hundred Forest Department personnel, several armed Special Action Force men, and about twenty regular policemen. They recovered felled teakwood from the spot. As they were leaving, they were surrounded by two hundred adivasis who attacked them with stones launched from catapults. The Special Armed Force fired in self-defense, first into the air and then aiming at people. Two villagers were killed and six others were seriously injured.

The Forest Officer's statement conflicts with villagers' account of events. According to the villagers in Mandwa, about twenty of them were working in their fields, which had an almost mature crop of sorghum. They had been cultivating these fields for several years, and the Forest Department knew all about it because they were regularly bribed to look the other way. No trees had stood in these fields for twenty years. In the last elections, the MLA (Member of the State Legislative Assembly) had promised that adivasis would be given leases on forestland which they had been cultivating, but so far no leases had been granted.[15] Since they joined the AMS a year

14. Although it is tempting to reinterpret colonial accounts of tribal crime from a subaltern perspective, it would be simplistic to invert crime in retrospect as resistance. If these are the first footprints of rebellion, they bear the hallmark of a complex relationship with the state. Such a relationship was enmeshed in patron–client networks with shared notions of honor and fair play. "Crime"/"Resistance" was often the outcome of a moral economy betrayed (for an account of the relationship between Khajya Naik, a celebrated tribal rebel of Khargone, and the Holkar princely state, see Baviskar 1992: Appendix 1).

15. Encroachments on forestland can be regularized if they occurred before October 1980, if the encroacher's legal holdings do not exceed two hectares, and if the gradient of the encroached field is less than 30 degrees. However, few adivasis have documentary proof

ago, the villagers had stopped paying bribes to forest officials. This had brought down the Forest Department's wrath on their heads. On August 27, police and forest personnel came to their fields and began uprooting the standing crop.[16] Villagers threw stones to stop them, and the officers opened fire. The two people who were shot were taken away by the police who cremated their bodies, denying their families' pleading for a proper funeral. The other six injured farmers were left to fend for themselves. Nine farmers' crops were completely uprooted, destroying their only source of food for the whole year.

An investigation by the People's Union for Civil Liberties (PUCL) found that the First Information Report filed with the police by the Sub-divisional Forest Officer immediately after the incident makes no mention of tree-felling or teak wood recovery from villagers. This version seems to have been concocted later to justify the extreme use of force by the police. Also, no wood was reported to have been recovered from the village. The circumstances, especially the presence of such a large armed party, suggest that the Forest Department went with the intention of forcibly removing encroachments, without trying any legal or other measures first. No preventive steps were taken to avoid a confrontation, nor were less brutal techniques of control (tear gas, *lathi* charge) attempted. The deaths and the injuries were caused by the excessive use of force by the Forest Department and the police.

How was this extraordinary violence justified? Why were less lethal techniques of crowd control not used? The answer lies in the status of adivasis, whose economic oppression is tethered to social discrimination. Adivasis, especially those who follow their traditional lifestyle, are generally treated by non-adivasis as subhuman, as objects of contempt and ridicule mingled with an underlying current of fear. Even today, the everyday caste pollution rules prohibit both Scheduled Caste and Scheduled Tribe members from sharing food, water, and space with caste Hindus and punish transgressions with fines and physical violence. Adivasi women are harassed routinely by non-adivasi men. Also, more extreme instances of bullying and even sadism are used to keep the adivasis in their place. In 1996, three adivasi men were stripped and beaten and then tied to the back of a Forest

---

of occupation before 1980 because most of them paid bribes that disappeared into the pockets of forest officials. (For a fuller discussion of the problems around forest encroachments, see Baviskar 1994.)

16. Eight years ago I met a policeman who had been involved in a similar operation in the Taloda forest in Maharashtra. In Taloda, *adivasi* encroachers were forcibly evicted in order to settle other *adivasis* displaced from the Sardar Sarovar dam. The policeman spoke of his anguish in having to destroy a standing crop, "I come from a farming family myself. I felt like I was cutting off my hand." State violence victimizes people on both sides; the agents of the state may also be crushed by its brutality.

Department jeep and made to run behind it for several kilometers to the Forest Range office, where their heads were shaved and their faces tarred. Their homes also were burnt. All this because they could not immediately pay a bribe of RS 20,000[17] to forest officials for overlooking their encroachment on forestland.

The adivasi body is the site for proclaiming one's power; through torture and humiliation, the social fact of adivasi wretchedness is branded on the physical self and on the psyche. In April 1997, a local trader murdered an adivasi servant who had been working for him for six years and threw away his body in a nearby stream because he had absented himself from work for one day. Although the police registered a case, no further action was taken. In May 1997, officers of a cooperative bank arrested an adivasi youth and killed him. His offense? His father owed the bank RS 3,500. In June 1997, an adivasi boy was beaten and forced to drink his own urine because he took water from a public well. Such depressingly familiar stories occur routinely not only in Khargone, but all over western Madhya Pradesh. To be an adivasi is to be a legitimate target for non-adivasi violence; to be an adivasi who talks back is to ask for trouble.

The AMS squarely attributes adivasi oppression to their powerlessness before the state and in the market. Corrupt revenue officials, brutal policemen and foresters, missing schoolteachers, and moonlighting doctors make up a system that militates against adivasi empowerment. The developmental state is conspicuously absent in the markets where adivasis who come to sell their produce face a cartel of cheating traders. Adivasis are denied the basic human right to live with dignity by upper-caste Hindus. Yet this divide of exploiter and exploited, dominant and subordinate, is not an unambiguous social cleavage between non-adivasis and adivasis. The fault line of social conflict is held together by the glue of *dalals* (middlemen), the adivasis who are go-betweens and agents serving non-adivasi bosses.

Many dalals are village headmen who trade in the currency of patronage in the powerful economy of votes, fixing elections, getting government work done, offering protection for a price. Young men from relatively wealthy families who have access to state education gradually become dalals as they hang out with Hindi-speaking non-adivasi shopkeepers and government employees.[18] Some dalals go on to become members of the State Legislature. The AMS blames this local elite and its nexus with the local timber and liquor mafia that is politically backed by the Congress Party (the ruling party in Madhya Pradesh) for the oppression of adivasis.

---

17. Rs 43 = $1.

18. An economic nexus is buttressed by the cultural codes embedded in formal education. By learning to look down on *adivasi* dialect, dress, and other markers of tribal identity, educated tribal youth seek to emulate the habits of caste Hindus.

In the last three years, the AMS's political activities have brought it into direct confrontation with this power elite. Through massive demonstrations and other displays of strength outside the district administration offices, in the nearby city of Indore and at the state capital, the AMS has successfully compelled the government to retrieve adivasi lands and other property that had been taken over by moneylenders. The AMS's campaigns forced the government to suspend several corrupt revenue officers, policemen, and forest officers. Forest guards, rangers, and police inspectors have had to return money that they earlier extorted. Mobilization in the local markets resulted in the installation of electronic weighing machines and fairer prices. Atrocities against adivasis, which would earlier have gone unremarked, are now reported to the administration and the press, and the victims' demand for justice has led to punitive transfers and suspensions of guilty officers. Besides local issues, the AMS made a bid to mobilize adivasis across the country by holding an impressive rally calling for adivasi self-rule in areas where they are numerically dominant.[19] Not only did such activism hurt the economic interests of the dominant non-adivasis but also such visible flexing of organizational muscle obviously threatened the power base of the adivasi leaders affiliated with the ruling Congress Party. The bribes and commissions from non-adivasi traders and from illicit trafficking were jeopardized, as were the votes from adivasis who had begun to ask uncomfortable questions about corruption.

To counter the AMS, Subhash Yadav (a non-adivasi), the deputy chief minister of Madhya Pradesh, whose economic and political hold over his constituency in Khargone district was being undermined by the AMS, organized the Adivasi Samaj Sudhar Shanti Sena ([ASSSS] Tribal Social Reform Peace Army) in 1997. This has further reinforced the complexity of the AMS's battles with the oppressors of adivasis. Instead of non-adivasi officials and traders, they are mainly confronted by adivasi groups mobilized by adivasi dalals affiliated with Subhash Yadav and the ruling Congress Party. Pitting adivasis against adivasis gives the state much more leeway to explain violence as a "normal" aspect of tribal culture and to disguise its own culpability in violent encounters.

A key confrontation that gives insight into the sort of trouble that the AMS's work stirred up is the incident at Kabri village in early 1996. The AMS's anti-liquor campaign resulted in the closure of legal and illegal liquor vends in around 250 villages and considerable losses to both ven-

19. The cause of tribal self-government received legislative recognition with the central government's enactment of the Provisions of the Panchayats (Extension to the Scheduled Areas) Act of 1996. This act gives significant powers to the *gram sabha* (village assembly) over the natural resources of the village and over the development funds received from the state government. However, the enactment has not been followed by the necessary step of notification, which would move the act from paper to practice.

dors and their protectors—the police and local dalals. One such "injured party" was Jhagdia patel, the hereditary adivasi headman of Kabri and the block Congress committee president. The AMS took the battle to Jhagdia's own door when its members in Kabri declared that no liquor would be sold in the village during Indal, the most important adivasi festival.[20] Jhagdia and his men retaliated by abducting one of the anti-liquor activists off a bus, breaking his leg and arm and, when he asked for water, urinating into his mouth. When villagers went to complain, the local police refused to register a case against Jhagdia because they were in league with him and because the AMS had earlier earned the hatred of the police inspector by making him return RS 1,000, which he had extorted from a villager.

After a few days, the police inspector called Rem Singh, the *sarpanch* (elected village head) and leader of the anti-liquor campaign, to the police station, ostensibly to effect a compromise between his faction and Jhagdia patel's. It is customary for the police to arbitrate in village-level disputes. Rem Singh went warily, with two companions armed with bows and arrows. Their motorcycle was ambushed by Jhagdia's group, which was accompanied by the police. In trying to escape, one of Rem Singh's men shot dead one of Jhagdia's men. The next day, the police came to Kabri to "investigate" and beat up the only people they found—all women. The day after, Jhagdia patel and his men, with the police standing by, went on a spree looting, vandalizing, and burning the homes of Rem Singh and the anti-liquor group affiliated with the AMS. AMS activists responded by complaining to senior police officers at the district and division headquarters, the Chief Secretary and Home Secretary of the state and the State Tribal Welfare Minister. Senior officials visited Kabri at the AMS's behest, but no further action was taken.

The Kabri incident is explained by the AMS as a struggle against a liquor mafia that enjoys police protection. Yet this story is written over another, which had not been erased—the long-standing tussle between Jhagdia and Rem Singh for control over the village. The rise of the AMS in the region offered Rem Singh an opportunity to ally with an alternate power center that could challenge Jhagdia's supremacy. This element of rivalry between the two factions enabled the police to pose as mediators, neutral agents resolving a dispute between feuding tribal factions in a time-hon-

---

20. Indal is traditionally celebrated with vast amounts of home-brewed alcohol made from *mahua* (*Madhuca indica*), which is first ritually offered to the gods and the ancestors and then drunk by all. This drinking was circumscribed both socially (by being confined to specific occasions) and naturally (by the amount of *mahua* available). With the MP government's liberalized policy of licensing liquor vends in the state, cheap factory-manufactured alcohol in polyethylene packets is available on hand throughout the year. The dynamics of drinking have changed to encourage excessive drinking with all its attendant problems of alcoholism, domestic violence, and financial ruin (see Hardiman 1987: Chapter 7).

ored fashion. The killing (in self-defense) of one of Jhagdia's men allowed the police to terrorize AMS supporters and then tacitly support the loot and arson of their homes. In the local press, the sequence of events in Kabri mainly was recorded as a murderous feud between two tribal groups, without going into the wider politics of the issue. However, Jhagdia patel's group and others in the Congress Party identified the AMS as a major threat to their interests. The Kabri incidents highlight the fusion of factional rivalry with an ideological agenda created by the AMS. As the state changed the social context of drinking alcohol, the anti-liquor campaign of the AMS, besides other effects, transformed political resources that some villagers attempted to seize. The result was a potent brew of liquor-laced factional politics. The police, on their part, attempted to contain this dynamism and complexity by framing it within the familiar matrix of the feud.

State Violence and Human Rights Activism: Unfolding Events and My Annotations

Late August 1997. A small news item on the "states" page of Delhi newspapers states: "Block Congress president killed by militant group in MP." It mentions that Jhagdia patel was killed by a mob led by AMS activists. The report is datelined Khargone, so I read it with attention. I have known the AMS from the time when I worked in a similar organization, the Khedut Mazdoor Chetna Sangath (KMCS), in the neighboring district of Jhabua. The AMS and KMCS would often coordinate their campaigns and so we had friends among the activists there. I know that the AMS has had a number of skirmishes with the Congress Party in the past, but this report of a violent death is worrying. A couple of days later, another news item datelined Khandwa reports "Two killed in police firing in MP."

September 4. I get a call from Bijoy, an AMS activist.[21] He is in Delhi, trying to muster support for the AMS, which is reeling under a wave of state repression. The police have registered cases falsely accusing hundreds of AMS members and activists of murder, violent attacks on the police and forest guards, and a slew of other charges. AMS workers are being picked up and arrested. A simultaneous smear campaign against the organization is being conducted in the Madhya Pradesh press, calling them Naxalites.[22] There are

21. AMS conforms to the pattern of struggle-oriented mass organizations initiated by people from urban, middle-class backgrounds, which is common in tribal areas. Bijoy and Nikunja, two young men from Orissa, started the AMS in 1992. Bijoy used to work with Oxfam earlier. Two years ago, they were joined by Madhuri, a historian by training who had worked with the voluntary organization Ekta Parishad in central MP. These three "outside" activists have been joined by several full-time, local activists.

reports that the AMS may be banned. I call up various rights organizations in Delhi on behalf of my own organization, the People's Union for Civil Liberties (PUCL). We meet at the Gandhi Peace Foundation on September 5. Bijoy explains the situation and passes around cuttings from MP newspapers. They are scary; if you believe them, you'd think that the AMS is a dangerous gang of criminals, inciting adivasis to violence and instigating fights between them. There are authoritative statements from senior police officers saying that AMS harbors "history-sheeters," people who are recorded as notorious bad characters in police files. High-ranking forest officers say that the entire forest administration is terrorized by the AMS, which encourages adivasis to encroach on forests and cut trees illegally. Subhash Yadav, the deputy Chief Minister, asserts that if he were Home Minister, the AMS would be extirpated from not just MP, but out of India. He goes on to say that the organization does its best to sabotage development work because development would bring the adivasis closer to the government.[23] The AMS has a vested interest in keeping adivasis poor and powerless. Each newspaper report is damning; the cumulative burden of lies frightening. (Author's field notes)

Why do I assume so readily that the reports against the AMS are untrue? I disbelieve them because in 1993, the Khedut Mazdoor Chetna Sangath lived through a crisis such as this. Every day the papers would publish lies that sounded completely plausible. There were police cases against us about incidents that were totally fabricated, and we were arrested, charged, and put on trial. Later, because of the intervention of the Supreme Court, I had an opportunity to examine the police diaries (which record offenses and their investigation) for these cases. The case diaries were a Kafkaesque genre of fiction. I read about myself and my friends at-

22. Naxalites are Maoist groups who believe in armed struggle for land reform and other causes of the oppressed. In Madhya Pradesh, they are active in forested regions in the east where their guerrilla tactics keep the state administration and non-*adivasi* exploiters on edge. Calling an organization "naxalite" is an easy first step in justifying the use of state violence against it.

23. This statement is made at a public meeting organized by the Forest Department to inaugurate an ecodevelopment center where villagers would be trained in forest conservation and techniques of improved management (Chautha Sansar newspaper, June 23, 1997). This is the approved model of conservation of the Joint Forest Management (JFM) as funded through the World Bank's MP Forestry Project, where "reputed NGOs" join hands with the government to teach villagers how to participate in forest protection. The agenda is preset; areas, tasks, and species are chosen by the state. Basic issues, such as conflict over encroachments, are either sidelined or unilaterally resolved. There is money for small handouts (loans for women, self-employment for young men) and for large accretions to the Forest Department. Although there are considerable variations in JFM practices across the country, in Madhya Pradesh the reluctance of the Forest Department to alter its stateist orientation has made JFM largely ineffective.

tacking government officials with bows and arrows, using abusive language that "hurt the ears of the police," threatening to kill adivasis—all this backed up by the statements of witnesses, confessions, weapons seizure memos, and many other authoritative documents. The totality of untruths was so seamless that I could not find the tiniest flaw to pierce through this virtual universe of crime where we figured as the villains. This did not happen, I told myself, and it sounded weak to my own ears.

To counter this onslaught, the AMS needs to get out an alternative version of events in the media. It also needs to muster support to make the MP government stop its terror tactics.

> In Delhi, we decide to contact friendly journalists in the press and in TV to cover Bijoy's story and to travel to MP. On behalf of the People's Union for Civil Liberties, I volunteer to organize an investigation team to probe the incidents. An activist from the Delhi Forum agrees to circulate a protest letter for a signature campaign. Another activist from the National Alliance of People's Movements offers to set up interviews with the Home Minister, sympathetic members of parliament, and so on. We have limited time and even more limited resources. What is the most effective strategy to help the AMS? All of September 6 goes into making hundreds of phone calls to set up the fact-finding team. (Field notes)

Such a team is now an essential response to a crisis involving state repression. It provides some support to the beleaguered organization for it reminds the state to be more circumspect because a third party is monitoring it. The victims of repression often find such visits cathartic because they can talk out the horrors that they have experienced. And there is some reassurance that you are not alone. The investigation team's report is publicized through a press conference and sent to various state human rights bodies or to the courts, where it is often an important instrument for lending credibility to the organization's side of the story. Yet the investigations by human rights groups always walk a tightrope between being independent and being partisan, between being judicial and being activist. We choose from within a circle of people who are already committed to the cause and who we know will submit a report that will support the organization. We look for people who can read between the lines of hostile news reports, who will automatically suspect every statement made by a police officer and forester, who can see through the power of the state's imagination. And yet these must be people whose names carry weight with the establishment they try to challenge.

Phone calls, protocol. Who should be asked to call whom for maximum effect? Many refuse because they are already tied up with other crises, equally important tasks. Others can't travel at such short notice. Also, the AMS is not a very well-known organization in Delhi; their social capital is too scarce to summon anything more than statements of concern from most people on this circuit. Eventually we have a team headed by a retired High Court judge with three other seasoned human rights activists. We meet to decide on their terms of reference. PUCL coordinates the logistics of their schedule, transport, press conferences in Indore and Delhi with MP-based activists. Even as all these arrangements take place, we learn that Jhagdia patel's killer, an AMS activist named Kalia who surrendered to the police, was hacked to death in police custody.

Findings from the Report of the Independent Investigation Team[24]

Kalia, an AMS activist, was among the *panchayat* mediators in a property dispute between two brothers in his village Julwania.[25] When the collective decision went against one of the brothers, he held Kalia responsible for his defeat. Jhagdia patel, the Congress leader from Kabri who had battled the AMS during the anti-liquor campaign, saw this as his chance to hit out at the AMS, which was eroding his hegemony in the villages. He stoked the ire against Kalia by holding a meeting in Kabri and exhorting people to "teach Kalia a lesson." Apprehending trouble, AMS activists met the District Superintendent of Police thrice in August, but he did not take any action to defuse the situation. On August 24, Jhagdia patel met the Superintendent to demand police protection, which he was given. On August 25, Jhagdia patel and about thirty-five other men, accompanied by the police, went to Kalia's house in Julwania. He wasn't home, so they stripped and gang-raped his wife Namlibai. They then proceeded to rape at least five other women in the adjoining houses. Before they were raped, 19-year-old Batlabai's two-month-old baby and Munnibai's three-month-old infant were snatched from their arms by the Shanti Sena men and police, who prodded them with rifles. Both the infants were dashed into a nearby stream. Their bodies were not found. Later, the women fled from their homes, which were being looted by their rapists, and took refuge in the forest where they stayed in hiding for 2–3 weeks. Other villagers, fearing further violence, left their homes and went away. The police did not register a case against Jhagdia and others.

24. The People's Union of Civil Liberties team consisted of Ram Bhushan Mehrotra (former High Court judge), Dr. R. M. Pal (editor, *PUCL Bulletin*), Lakshmi Murthy (Saheli Women's Resource Centre), and Govindan Kutty (All-India People's Resistance Forum).
25. A group of elders may be constituted as an *adivasi panchayat* to settle disputes within the community. The parties to the dispute voluntarily agree to be bound by the decision of the *panchayat*.

On August 26, when Jhagdia patel and his protective police escort had stopped to cross a swollen stream, they were surrounded by Kalia and about 150 other men. Jhagdia and his party rushed into a nearby house and barricaded themselves. Kalia and his men gathered outside the door, asking the police to hand over Jhagdia. The police then pushed Jhagdia out, where he was killed with an arrow and then his body stoned. Later, Jhagdia's body was recovered by his relatives who vowed at his funeral to avenge his death in the same manner. The police were present at the funeral. On August 27, cases were registered for the murder of Jhagdia. The police announced a reward of RS 10,000 for Kalia's arrest and RS 1,000 for Rem Singh of Kabri (Jhagdia's old rival). On August 31, a ministerial team led by Deputy Chief Minister Subhash Yadav arrived in the area. The administration announced that Jhagdia's family would be given RS 100,000 as compensation.

On September 14, Kalia and sixteen other accused surrendered before the Deputy Inspector General of Police on the advice of AMS leaders. They were remanded to police custody by the court for two days on September 15. On September 17, Kalia was taken with an armed escort of fifteen policemen in two jeeps "to recover a firearm used in Jhagdia's murder" (Jhagdia had been killed with an arrow and stones). On the way back, the vehicles passed through Jhagdia's hamlet. The jeeps were "suddenly" surrounded by two hundred men. The police handed Kalia over to them, and he was killed with an axe.

The PUCL investigation found evidence that Kalia's death was probably set up by the police in collaboration with the Congress. The Congress-backed Shanti Sena workers were touring the area with the police after Jhagdia's death. There was no good reason to take Kalia for recovering a firearm because Jhagdia had been murdered with an arrow and stones; nor was there a need to use a route that passed through Jhagdia's village. Then there were the statements of support from the Deputy Chief Minister. The PUCL concluded that: "Taking all circumstances into consideration, the team [was] of the *prima facie* view that there [was] complicity of the police in the custodial death of Kalia."

Violence and the Environment

What is the connection between these violent incidents and the environment? Perhaps it is this apparent *lack* of connection that is precisely the problem. In the mind of a wider urban public, the AMS's credibility is low. It is represented and perceived as a lawless organization, urging adivasis to destroy the forest, inciting them to take arms against the state, sheltering murderers. The odds are stacked against it—the administration, the political party in power, the press—all the elements conspire to represent the organization in an unfavorable light. Much of the mud sticks. How can the AMS defend itself? It can argue that the fate of the forest is inseparable from the issue of tribal rights to the forest and also from the related issue of rights to agricultural land, water, and credit. It can assert that access to these, in turn, hinges upon adivasis being accepted as equal citizens who are preeminently entitled to government resources and protection. It can attest that for years the administration and the Congress Party have kept adivasis subservient and that it is this oppression that must be resisted. It can argue that as long as lands remain under the control of a Forest Department with the power to decide whether they will bear trees or crops or whether forests will be sold on the sly to the timber mafia, adivasis will continue to be blamed for destroying forests. It also can argue that adivasis are fighting to shed their present status as subhuman creatures and savages and to be recognized as a class that, with the greatest stake in the conservation of forest, must at least participate in decision making. But this answer to the environment question is too complex to be readily understood by possible sympathizers in the intelligentsia.

But what of the tragedy of murder, revenge, rape, and more murder? The structural framework of radical politics, the mass-based AMS versus the local state, is not sufficient explanation for this cycle of violence. Murder and rape, especially in retaliation for similar acts, are elements in a traditional feud of honor that acquire entirely new dimensions because of the larger politics in which they are now embedded. Yet in its explanations, the state chooses to ignore both the wider political context and the complicity of some of its agents in these crimes. It presents violence as a normal event within tribal society. The PUCL team repeatedly was told by senior state officials that "among tribals, it is natural to avenge murder with murder. We couldn't have stopped it." Yet political affiliation decides how the murderer and the victims' families are treated. While Jhagdia's family gets state compensation, Kalia's killers are still loose. Though Kalia died in police custody, there is no state compensation for his widow who is still traumatized by rape, the destruction of her home, and the fear of further reprisals. A police officer confidently asserted to the press that, "rape is very common in tribal society. After all, adivasi girls are promiscuous. They run off and get married; they have divorce, too. The women of Julwania have not filed a complaint because it is a trivial matter for them." The freedom to select a husband and to divorce, a part of tribal culture, is interpreted by caste Hindus as a sign of loose morals that deny an adivasi woman the right to her own body. Her "promiscuity" makes rape inconsequential. Tribal culture, and the status of women within it, becomes a convenient device to fix and explain violence, to routinize it. But scarred bodies and the scarred land tell a different story.

Human Rights and the State

The PUCL report is released in press conferences in Indore (MP) and Delhi. The coverage in the Indore papers is extensive; this is a local issue, and a team from the national capital carries weight. In Delhi, the press is busy covering the Assam government's appeal for more armed forces to fight militancy in the state, so the MP report release is a tiny event. We have an appointment with the Home Minister to ask for an inquiry by the Central Bureau of Investigation, but he cancels it after making us wait for two hours. We meet the National Human Rights Commission with the report. They make concerned noises, promise to send their own team to MP, and ultimately do nothing beyond advising that the AMS petition the Supreme Court. We approach the Madhya Pradesh State Human Rights Commission, which visits the area six weeks later. By this time the police and the Congress have fabricated an entirely new story complete with witnesses, evidence, and documents. Their report recommends that adivasis must not fight amongst themselves. The National Commission for Women sent a team with commendable promptness to investigate the rapes, but it could not trace many of the women who were still hiding. In October and November, solidarity rallies were held by supporting organizations in Indore, Sendhwa (Khargone district), and Delhi. However, the state sought to curb the MP rallies by prohibiting public meetings and detaining people who were going to participate. A talk show on television offered the AMS a chance to appear along with the Chief Minister of Madhya Pradesh and to grill him on the ongoing repression. The AMS was quite satisfied with the way the program had been recorded, with the Chief Minister clearly indicted for his government's excesses. However, when the program was broadcast, it was edited out of all recognition. The AMS's charges were totally garbled, and the Chief Minister had the last word every time. The AMS sounded confused and their grievances boringly dreary while the Chief Minister, seated at a height, gave bland assurances and exuded a general air of complacence. (Field notes)

There is a certain inevitability to all this. Do we seriously expect the Human Rights Commissions to take our side? Even if they do corroborate our version, they are toothless bodies that can only recommend government action, not order it. All the effort that we put into producing reports, pursuing things with the authorities, isn't it a complete waste of time? The Supreme Court may give us a tiny reprieve, a hint of justice, and our flickering hopes leap up afresh; but cases drag on, evidence is impossible to collect, and even if the investigating agency is the Central Bureau of Investigation, half of its officers are policemen on deputation. The learned judges of the court rarely take to organizations like the AMS, low-key and unglamorous as they are. Once again, the politics of what the AMS does is much too complex and threatening to be easily intelligible.

Yet we persevere, engaging with the same sets of actors and institutions of the state, using our middle-class skills of report writing and working the press and the judiciary. Are we challenging the state to live up to its own rhetoric of human rights or are we just getting co-opted into further buttressing the state's legitimacy? This collaboration is a double-edged sword; even as the state displays its reasonable, judicial credentials and swallows up dissent in a maw of discussion, we push for real and not cosmetic concessions. By keeping up the clamor for justice, we are trying to keep the crisis going so that "normalization" is postponed. Before it is back to business as usual, we hope to push aside a little more the unyielding weight of public opinion that makes criminals out of adivasis and Naxalites out of the AMS. At the end of the day, what has been achieved? The transfer of three district police and civil administration heads who supervised the action against the AMS and who are known for their proximity to the deputy Chief Minister. More important, the AMS has survived state repression. Many local people and the members of this mass organization have suffered intensely but, by and large, after a period underground, they continue to be publicly involved in its campaigns. This ability to endure, to keep fighting, is perhaps the most notable success of the organization.

Conclusion

The violence intrinsic to domination is embedded in the everyday practices of caste, capitalism, and patriarchy. Its ubiquity is matched by its intangibility; it is everywhere experienced yet it is so difficult to capture in analysis. Violence leaves its imprint. It is written on the bodies of tribal women and men. It is written on the land that once bore a sorghum crop and now supports straggly teak or lies under water. The scars on the bodies of adivasis and on the face of the land are only one reminder of the sedimented histories of exploitation and struggle, of efforts to resculpt social relations. These scars brand particular bodies more than others—the adivasi rather than the non-adivasi, women more than men. The power of the state is always unequally exercised.

Both of the struggles that we have examined in this chapter, the Narmada Bachao Andolan and the Adivasi Mukti Sangathan, make violence visible. Both try to problematize categories and concepts such as tribe, forest, development, and environment. Both show how violence is embedded in the categories themselves, produced by those in power. Some categories, such as gender and tribe, may have their roots in civil society, while those designating land use or development are primarily created by the state. Once created, however, the forms as well as the contents of these categories are contested through everyday practice and through extraordinary events. Violence, once considered to be either normal or even invisible, is made pathological.

While both these struggles challenge established lines of repression, they meet with very different responses from the state. In both cases, the state seeks to control popular resistance to violence-made-pathological through its apparatuses of repression and an escalation into more violence-made-pathological, but the state's ability to explain, absorb and neutralize pathology varies. Is the Narmada Bachao Andolan able to act more effectively because it has greater legitimacy as an "environmental" movement? The Andolan's public image is unambiguous; all complexity and nuance have been smoothed out to construct clear-cut identities—of nonviolent peasants against the state. Also, within global environmentalism, the large dam is perceived to be unquestionably evil. Violence against the Andolan appears more pathological because it is directed against a movement that is widely supported by the intelligentsia. The Andolan is able to use its social capital like a shield that deflects violence, even causing it to boomerang on the state. Victimhood itself becomes a mode of resistance.

The Adivasi Mukti Sangathan, on the other hand, has no strong public image. The only impression that the press has given is of a somewhat disreputable set of adivasis, fighting among themselves, who may have Naxalite tendencies. The AMS has not been able to shrug off this stigma because it cannot construct neat heroes or a clear demonology. Its struggles against the state are either placed within the discourse of the feud, enabling the disciplining state to step in as arbiter and law-giver, or are tarred with the illegitimacy of Naxalite armed revolution, enabling the punitive state to unleash its full violent potential. The inability to make a case for the superiority of its ecological practices and the failure to construct a unitary tribal identity for its members, undermine the AMS's claims to environmentalism.

Can the varied state responses to the Narmada Bachao Andolan and the Adivasi Mukti Sangathan be explained in terms of the class character of their membership? Both campaigns mobilize groups that are socially vulnerable. Both rely on middle-class activists to forge links with supporters outside the area. Yet, the Andolan succeeds where the Sangathan does not.

One factor that could shed light on the difference between the Andolan and the AMS is the nature of the state and capital that they address. The NBA does not embroil itself in local politics at the state level. How can it choose to remain aloof from the hurly-burly of local politics when it has a significant grassroots base? Perhaps the contrast lies in the fact that the AMS poses a threat to relatively immobile political and economic capital. A powerful AMS undermines vested interests in the area and they have nowhere to go, whereas the NBA targets a specific project with investment from a group of Indian and international companies. They can cut their losses and leave; that is a cheaper solution than the hostile publicity of fighting a world-renowned social movement. So the Narmada Bachao Andolan gets the soft responses from the state—dialogue, negotiation, and mild repression, while the Adivasi Mukti Sangathan bears the brunt of naked aggression. The environmentalism of the Andolan wins the day. The Sangathan's aim of tribal liberation must struggle against worse odds.

Despite these differences, both the Narmada Bachao Andolan and the Adivasi Mukti Sangathan take recourse to the same strategies of combining conflict with collaboration, petitioning the "good" state while fighting the "bad." This Janus-faced state is made to surrender some of its power—over bodies and lands, social and natural, in order to survive.

16

Toward a Metaphysic of Environmental Violence: The Case of the Bhopal Gas Disaster

S. Ravi Rajan

Within a few fateful hours on a cold December night in 1984, an industrial accident involving the U.S. multinational company, Union Carbide, killed two thousand and permanently maimed more than half a million in Bhopal, India.[1] On the face of it, environmental and societal violence of such extreme dimensions defies explanation. Like wars and the nuclear bomb, they are, at a basic human level, incomprehensible, even irrational. Yet, they are far from being freak incidents, results of a stochastic roll of the dice of history. On the contrary, disasters are often explicable in clearly discernible terms. Indeed, as a vast body of research has shown, they are but extreme manifestations of embedded structures of environmental and societal violence. For this reason, they are "a natural laboratory or a *crise révelatrice*, as the fundamental features of society and culture are laid bare in stark relief" (Smith and Hoffman 1996: 304). Studies of sites of extreme violence, such as the Bhopal gas disaster have potential, therefore, to shed light not only on those specific events but also more widely on the nature of environmental violence in the societies in which they occur.

The purpose of this chapter is to examine the Bhopal gas disaster with the view of understanding environmental violence as a societal phenomenon. To this end, the chapter differentiates between and discusses the characteristics of five distinct attributes that apply to Bhopal as a site of violent environments. They are, respectively, technological violence, corpo-

---

1. Throughout this paper, "Union Carbide Corporation" refers both to the United States–based company and its Indian subsidiary Union Carbide India Limited. For an account of the death toll in the immediate aftermath of the accident, see Centre for Science and Environment (CSE) 1985: 210.

rate violence, distributive violence, bureaucratic violence, and discursive violence. The five sections that follow describe each of these different types of violence with particular reference to the Bhopal case. In conclusion, the chapter will grapple with the lessons that Bhopal offers to the brave new world that has emerged in its aftermath.

Technological Violence, or the Violence of the "Normal Accident"

In an important and influential book published following the Three Mile Island nuclear accident, sociologist Charles Perrow coined what at first sounds like an analytically contrary term (Perrow 1984). The phrase "normal accident" was borne of his analysis of the organizational and institutional factors underlying certain categories of industrial accidents. Perrow begins by defining two characteristics of large technological systems such as chemical or nuclear plants. The first of these, "interactive complexity," refers to "a systemic characteristic in a technological system with a lot of components (parts, procedures, and operators), wherein two or more failures among components interact in some unexpected way. For example, when X fails, Y would also be out of order and the two failures would interact so as to start a fire and put out the fire alarm." Perrow's second term, "tight coupling," refers to "another systemic characteristic in a technological system wherein one event or process affects another event or process directly and quickly, thus making human intervention difficult when something goes wrong." Perrow argues that when interactive complexity and tight coupling, which are *characteristics* of the technological system, inevitably combine to produce an accident, such an accident is not "accidental" (Perrow 1984: Chapter 1). In the conventional sense of the term, an accident connotes "anything that happens without foresight or expectation; an unusual event, which proceeds from some unknown cause, or is an unusual effect of a known cause; a casualty, a contingency" (Oxford English Dictionary 1989). When an accident is a consequence of characteristics of the system, Perrow argues, it is anything but unpredictable, unusual, or a result of an unknown cause. It is, in a clearly comprehensible sense, "normal."

In Bhopal, the immediate accident was a result of an exothermic reaction that occurred when water that was being used to flush and clean pipes leading up to tanks that stored liquid methyl isocyanate (MIC) leaked into the tanks. Within minutes, a worker noticed that the temperature gauge on the tank had reached the peak of its scale and that the pressure was rapidly moving toward the point at which the emergency relief valve opens. He rushed to the storage tanks, to hear "a tremendous sound, a messy boiling sound underneath the slab, like a cauldron." About that time, he also began to notice that a concrete slab 60 feet long and 6 inches thick was cracking. Soon, there was tremendous heat, and he heard a loud hissing sound and saw gas shoot out of a stack attached to the tank and form a white cloud that drifted toward the immediate surroundings (CSE 1985: 207–208).

An important reason for the Bhopal accident was a crucial design decision—to opt for the storage of MIC in underground tanks, as opposed to a process that would have involved producing and consuming the chemical as and when needed to synthesize the factory's primary products. At the time the plant was conceived, many in the Indian subsidiary of Union Carbide had argued for a design that involved nominal storage of MIC, as determined by downstream requirements (Dembo, Morehouse, and Wykle 1990: 87). Indeed, other companies that used MIC at that time, such as Bayer in Germany, DuPont in Texas and Mitsubishi Chemicals in Japan, did so without any storage at all, on grounds that "the material is too dangerous to store in a tank" (CSE 1985: 216; Dembo, Morehouse, and Wykle 1990: 87). Union Carbide's design engineers in the United States, to whom (according to a video testimony by Edwardo Munoz, a senior executive of Union Carbide) the company's executives usually delegated decisions about technological design, however, decided to opt for a process that involved substantial storage (Karliner 1996). In selecting such a design, the engineers had thus inadvertently added to the plant's potential to engender societal and environmental harm.

The company complemented the high-risk design by neglecting to put in place many of the safety features that were present in its similar facility in West Virginia. It did not, for example, have a computerized early-warning system. Key safety devices, such as the scrubber and the flare tower, were underdesigned. Moreover, there was no emergency evacuation procedure. The community living near the plant had not even been educated about the alarm system. The danger alarm resembled a nearby factory's shift change hooter, and on a number of occasions when the alarm went off accidentally, many workers had actually rushed toward that factory (CSE 1985: 207–208, 215–216; Chouhan et al. 1994: 43–60; Morehouse and Subramanian 1986: 1–22).

On the night of the disaster, workers noticed that the pressure in tank 610—the tank from which the MIC gas leaked—had suddenly risen from 2 to 10 psi (pounds per square inch). This sudden rise in pressure was, however, dismissed initially on grounds that "instruments often didn't work . . . they got corroded. . . . Crystals would form on them" (CSE 1985: 207–208; Chouhan et al. 1994: 43–60). When Shakil Qureshi, the supervisor on duty, realized the potential enormity of the gas leak, he attempted a number of remedial actions. He ordered water sprayed on the leak. The water jet, however, failed to reach the top of the 120-foot stack from which the gas was escaping. The vent gas scrubber, which was meant to help neutralize escaping gas, was, at that time, under maintenance. As the final straw, the flare tower, which was meant to burn off escaping gas, was also not working that fateful night (CSE 1985: 207–208; Chouhan et al. 1994: 43–60). The Bhopal accident was thus a product of interactive complexity involving machines, instruments, and human operators. Moreover, once the gas leak started, the accident mutated rapidly into a tightly coupled process, over which the plant workers had very little control. Bhopal was thus a classic example of a normal accident.

Writing about risk and society, sociologist Niklas Luhmann observes that preventing normal accidents necessitates what he calls "error-friendly" design. An important characteristic of such design, he argues, ought to be that the structural couplings between societal systems and technical realizations are such that the technology functions *resiliently* in a contingent environment (Luhmann 1993). Producing such design is, however, not a simple task. A case in point is described in a meticulously researched book on the causes of the fatal crash of the *Challenger* space shuttle on January 28, 1986 (Vaughan 1996). In that book, Diane Vaughan argues that the decision to launch the spacecraft was taken by the engineers and managers involved, based on engineering data and their past safety procedures. Although it is possible, in hindsight, to point to the errors made by the engineers involved with making the decision to launch the spacecraft, Vaughan argues, it is hard to claim that their judgment was unreasonable in light of the available technical expertise and information.

If there is a lesson to be learned from Vaughan's analysis of the *Challenger* crash, it is that technological design, especially of large and complex engineering systems, is by its nature fraught with uncertainty and potential risk. Even the best designs have unknown elements that, under certain critical circumstances, can pronounce disaster. In such a scenario, it is crucial to be scrupulously meticulous when it comes to designing safety systems. Further, it is equally important to acknowledge lurking uncertainties and potential risks and to educate the workforce and the public about them.[2] As Collins and Pinch note in their excellent summary of Vaughan's book, "historically, it (NASA) has chosen to shroud its space vehicle in a blanket of certainty. Why not reveal some of the spots and pimples, scars and wrinkles of untidy golem engineering? Maybe the public would come to value the shuttle as an extraordinary human achievement and also learn

---

2. A large literature on risk and uncertainty exists. In addition to the research on workplace hazards and accidents, the literature raises a host of wider issues, such as the burden of proof (Caldwell 1996; Schrader-Frechette 1996); the problems of risk assessment (Russell and Gruber 1987; Ruckelshaus 1985; Slovic 1991; Funtowicz and Ravetz 1992; Silbergeld 1991; Mayo and Hollander 1991); and the problems of credibility (Epstein 1995; Jasanoff 1985).

something about the inherent riskiness of all such ventures" (Collins and Pinch 1998: 55–56).

It is also important that there be some manner of societal consensus about the risks involved, some process whereby those who make decisions about risk and safety reflect public opinion or be in some sense publicly accountable.[3] In Bhopal, the design engineers chose to adopt a technology that was, on the account of one of their own executives, not the safest among its alternatives. In doing so, they risked exposing their workers and the people near the plant to a normal accident such as that which occurred in December 1984. Further, they failed to communicate the potential risks associated with the plant to the workforce, the community, or the local government. Moreover, nowhere during the process of the choice over the design was the community living near the plant or the public at large consulted.

Technological violence occurs whenever engineering design is less than meticulous. It is perpetrated when conditions for the occurrence of a normal accident are produced and maintained, when there is inadequate public debate, and where there is little or no risk communication, societal consensus, or public accountability.

Corporate Violence, or the Violence of Irresponsible Capital

Technological violence is often, though not always, accompanied by some of the other facets of violence discussed in this chapter. One of the most important of these is corporate violence. A sense of what is entailed in this type of violence is provided by the public relations company Burston-Marsteller (B-M), which was hired by Union Carbide Corporation in the aftermath of the Bhopal accident to manage the public image of the company. Founded by Harold Burston and Bill Marsteller more than 40 years ago, B-M had previously been hired by Babcock and Wilcox in the aftermath of the Three Mile Island nuclear accident and by A. H. Robins during its problems with the Dalkon Shield contraceptive device. B-M had also advised Eli Lilly over the Prozac controversy and Exxon following the oil spill.

According to B-M's corporate brochure, "Often corporations face long-term issue challenges which arise from activist concerns (e.g., South Africa,

3. Perhaps the most sustained work on democracy and technology has been done by the nonprofit organization Loka Institute. See its webpage for an excellent set of resources and documents (www.loka.org). For an excellent book on democracy in the context of environmental disputes, see Williams and Matheny (1995).

infant formula) or controversies regarding product hazards. . . . B-M issue specialists have years of experience helping clients to manage such issues. They have gained insight into the key activist groups (religious, consumer, ethnic, environmental) and the tactics and strategies of those who tend to generate and sustain issues. Our counselors around the world have helped clients counteract activist-generated . . . concerns" (Greenpeace 1992). To deal specifically with environmental issues, B-M has established a World-wide Environmental Practice Group (EPG)—an international network of professionals who "specialize in various aspects of environmental communications" (B-M Internet website, http://www.bm.com).

B-M's outlook on such communications has been laid down clearly in a paper by Harold Burston, Chairman of Burston-Marsteller, in which he argues that "being the professional corporate conscience is not part of the job description of other executives. It is part of the job description of the Chief Public Relations Officer" (Burston n.d.). Burston goes on to add that: "A corporation cannot compensate for its inadequacies with good deeds. Its first responsibility is to manage its own affairs profitably" and, "We should no more expect a corporation to adopt a leadership role in changing the direction of society than we should expect an automobile to fly. The corporation was simply not designed for that role" (Burston n.d.).

Herein lies the nub of the second type of environmental violence—the violence that arises when corporations put profit over safety. The case of Union Carbide was one in which the company did just this throughout its operational history in just about every country in which it operated. The Bhopal accident was therefore not an exception, but the rule.[4]

Union Carbide's Bhopal plant was established in 1969 to synthesize a range of pesticides and herbicides. However, from its inception to the December 1984 gas leak, the plant was plagued with accidents. On November 24, 1978, for example, the Alpha-Naphtol storage area had a huge fire that took 10 hours to control. Again, on December 26, 1981, Mohammad Ashraf, the plant operator, was killed as a result of a phosgene gas leak. In January 1982, another phosgene leak caused severe injuries to twenty-eight people. On April 22, 1982, three electrical operators were severely burned while working on a control system panel, and on October 5 of the same year, MIC escaped from a broken valve and seriously affected four workers besides causing irritation to several residents nearby. Two similar incidents were reported in 1983 (Chouhan et al. 1994: 17—61).

In light of this history, what happened on December 3, 1984, was clearly not accidental in the sense of a chance, random, unpredictable event. To

4. For an excellent account of Union Carbide's safety record in the United States and abroad, see Dembo, Morehouse, and Wykle 1990: 46–68. See also CSE 1985: 213–214.

begin with, the company was not unaware of the consequences of its choices on issues such as risk and safety. In addition to the protesting workers and the litany of accidents that had plagued the plant, an internal investigation in May 1982 by a team of three Union Carbide experts had raised a number of important safety concerns. It had found, among other things, that the tank relief valve could not contain a runaway reaction, that many pressure gauges were defective, that valve leakages were endemic, and that there was no water spray system for fire protection or vapor dispersal in the MIC operating or storage area. Moreover, a number of articles in the local press had carried predictions of an impending disaster (CSE 1985: 216).

Given these unsafe working conditions, between one-half and two-thirds of the engineers who had been hired when the plant was commissioned had quit by December 1984. The result was a great reduction in operator strength. In the MIC plant, for example, the number of operators had been reduced to six from the original eleven. In its control room, normally staffed by two people, there was only one operator at the time of the accident, with the virtually impossible job of checking the seventy-odd panels, indicators, and controllers (CSE 1985: 216; Chouhan et al. 1994: 23–38, 55–60). The resignation of qualified engineers had also resulted in the company forcing underqualified and underpaid workers to operate highly complicated and potentially risky technological systems. An example is the case of T. R. Chouhan, an operator who was transferred to the MIC plant in 1982. At the time of his appointment, Chouhan did not have the necessary background to operate the plant. (He had neither a degree in science nor a diploma in engineering, the company's prerequisites for the position.) To compensate for this, he was promised six months of training before being put on the job. After a week of classroom training and a month on the job, however, Chouhan was ordered to take charge as a full-fledged plant operator at the MIC plant. When he refused, he was treated as a recalcitrant worker and reported to superior authorities (Chouhan et al. 1994: 31–32). Chouhan was not alone in seeking adequate training and working conditions. The labor force protested on a number of occasions with similar demands. Their protests also drew attention to the abysmal safety record of the plant. The company's response to the protests, however, was to deploy force to dispel what it saw as labor unrest (Chouhan et al. 1994: 35).

One more facet of Union Carbide's corporate violence in Bhopal had to do with its response in the aftermath of the accident. In an earlier case involving pollution in New York State, the company had, according to one account, deployed a five-pronged strategy to deal with the situation. First, it had attempted to deny the problem. An example of denials included

[margin annotation: reduced qualified staff]

statements such as: "Minute traces of . . . TEMIK aldicarb have been recently detected in wells in the vicinity . . . in amounts measurable only by ultra modern technology." Second, the company attempted to put the problem "in perspective" by arguing: "It is well known that much larger residues of other agricultural chemicals . . . have been found in the same water for many years." Third, the company attempted to redirect the focus of the problem by blaming "a hysterical public" with statements such as: "Some people have an unarticulated worry over the possibility of unspecified future health impairment . . . however unjustified." In the same breath, the company also overtly blamed the victim: "Victims mislead in claiming that TEMIK is a poison although it is they who have refused to take prophylactic measures to protect themselves." Fourth, Union Carbide attempted to divide and conquer the plaintiffs in the lawsuit against it by telling farmers and developers that they had conflicting interests and would do better by settling with Union Carbide. Finally, it attempted to settle with the government when it became less expensive to do so (Dembo, Morehouse, and Wykle 1990: 46–52).

In Bhopal, Union Carbide began by similarly denying any responsibility for the accident. Its works manager in Bhopal, J. Mukund, for example, told the additional district magistrate on the night of the accident that "The gas leak can't be from my plant. The plant is shut down. Our technology just can't go wrong. We can't have such leaks" (CSE 1985: 206). This initial denial soon evolved into a strategy, of which the most blatant manifestation was the claim of employee sabotage, a claim so vacuous that it was abandoned by the UCIL's chief lawyer, Rajendra Singh, in the Bhopal court that heard the criminal charges of culpable homicide against the company (Chouhan et al. 1994: 61–70). Despite this, to date the company continues to invoke the sabotage theory as the explanation of the accident in its dealings with the media and the public in the United States and elsewhere.

Union Carbide also attempted in Bhopal to put the accident "in perspective" and to blame the victim. As victims poured in to the Hamidia hospital, L. D. Loya, the company's medical officer told frantic doctors that "The gas is non-poisonous. There is nothing to do except ask the patients to put a wet towel over their eyes" (CSE 1985: 206). Again, the works manager, J. Mukund, told the media barely 15 days after the accident that "MIC is only an irritant, it is not fatal. It depends on how one looks at it. In its effects, it is like tear gas, your eyes start watering. You apply water and you get relief. What I say about fatalities is that we don't know of any fatalities either in our plant or in other Carbide plants due to MIC" (CSE 1985: 206). The company claimed subsequently that the large mortality was due to a combination of undernourishment and a lack of education among the people affected. It also claimed that the persistent morbidity had to do with baseline diseases such as tuberculosis in the gas-affected areas and that the victims were responsible for their own plights by maintaining poor standards of public hygiene. Union Carbide subsequently began to downplay the potency of the gas in the media and in courts. Moreover, in Bhopal following the disaster, it sponsored research and data gathering on the toxicological impact of the gas on the physiology of the Bhopal survivors, to counter the data of state hospitals and other nongovernmental organization (NGO) clinics.[5]

Union Carbide employed a "divide and conquer" strategy in Bhopal by adopting political campaigning and hiring several prominent persons, including a former British member of parliament, for this purpose. Consequently, the lingering criminal and civil cases and the continued support these cases were getting from environmental, labor, and consumer movements internationally were portrayed to Western governments as a dangerous consolidation of anti-Western and anticapitalist forces. As a result of sustained lobbying, the U.S. administration at that time brought enormous pressure to bear on the Rajiv Gandhi administration, which was then desperately interested in attracting global capital.[6] Ultimately, the Indian government succumbed to the pressure. Without any consultation with victims or their representatives, in the spring of 1988 the government of India offered a settlement package to Union Carbide in the chambers of the Chief Justice of the Supreme Court of India R. S. Pathak (Chouhan et al. 1994: 124–125).

The upshot of Union Carbide's postdisaster strategy is palpably visible in the settlement ledger. In the aftermath of the accident, victims' organizations in Bhopal staked a claim of $10 billion, based on standards in the United States. The Indian government, meanwhile, claimed $3.3 billion. Union Carbide's initial offer was $300—$350 million, and the final settlement was worth $470 million. The cost to Union Carbide was a mere 43 cents a share. In its annual report following the settlement, Union Carbide boasted, "The year 1988 was the best in the 71-year history of Union Carbide, with a record $4.88 earnings per share which included the year-end charge of 43 cents a share related to the resolution of the Bhopal litigation" (Union Carbide Annual Report 1988). The parent company then proceeded to sell its entire 50.9 percent shares in UCIL to the Calcutta-based McLeod Russell India Ltd., clearing the way for Union Carbide to

---

5. See several issues of *Bhopal*, the bulletin of the Bhopal Group for Information and Action in 1986.
6. Conversation with an officer in the Indian commerce ministry who wanted to remain anonymous.

exit India without any further involvement with Bhopal (Chouhan et al. 1994: 174).

Distributive Violence, or the Violence of Environmental Justice

Corporate violence, such as the case of the Bhopal disaster, is often caused by the existence of vertical power gradients wherein corporate entities are vastly more powerful than communities of citizens and, in many cases, than local and national governments. Such violence, however, is often accompanied by what is perhaps best described as "distributive violence," or the violence of environmental injustice.

The idea of environmental justice is derived from the terms *environmental racism* and *environmental equity*. Bunyan Bryant, an American environmental justice advocate, defines *environmental racism* as follows: "It is an extension of racism. It refers to those institutional rules, regulations, and policies or government or corporate decisions that deliberately target certain communities for least desirable land uses, resulting in the disproportionate exposure of toxic and hazardous waste on communities based upon certain prescribed biological characteristics. Environmental racism is the unequal protection against toxic and hazardous waste exposure and the systematic exclusion of people of color from environmental decisions affecting their communities" (Bryant 1995: 5). *Environmental equity*, in turn, refers to: "The equal protection of environmental laws. For example, under the Superfund clean-up program it has been shown that abandoned hazardous waste sites in minority areas take 20 percent longer to be placed on the national priority action list than those in white areas. It has also been shown that the government's fines are six times greater for companies in violation of RCRA in white than in black communities. This is unequal protection" (Bryant 1995: 5–6). Where either environmental racism or environmental inequity prevails, it is thus argued, environmental injustice occurs.

In a global context, often a direct correlation exists between economic class and vulnerability to risk, both within regional contexts in developed and the developing worlds and across the economic divide that separates nation-states within the world system (Blaikie et al. 1994). On one hand, industries that pose environmental and occupational risks have increasingly moved during the past two decades from the developed to the developing parts of the world. On the other, a part of the reason they have moved is that developing countries, for a variety of reasons ranging from developmental priorities to a lack of an adequate environmental institutional infrastructure, often are unable to enforce adequate regulatory protection. Further, within developing countries, hazardous industries are often located in sites closest to liminal or marginal populations (Weir 1986; CSE 1985).

In Bhopal, the people most exposed to the gas leak were those who were economically and politically marginal. At the outset, those who lived near the Union Carbide plant did so because it was the only place they could afford. Being in an industrial location, with the associated problems of noise, air, and water pollution, meant that the land around the Union Carbide plant was the least desirable and, consequently, the least expensive. Moreover, the people who were most exposed to the gas were those who lived in semipermanent dwellings. These were shanty houses whose windows and doors, where they existed, did not seal tightly enough to keep the gas out in any effective manner. The upshot of these factors was that the economic status of those who became gas victims forced them to live in an explicitly violent environment.

Another facet of the environmental justice issues in Bhopal centered on the political marginality of those who were affected by the gas leak. When Union Carbide built its MIC plant in 1979, it did so within its existing facility, which was located next to a densely populated neighborhood and a heavily used railway station. In doing so, it violated the 1975 Bhopal Development Plan, which had stipulated that hazardous industries such as the MIC plant ought to have been located in the northeast end of the city away from and downwind of the heavily congested areas. According to M. N. Buch, one of the authors of the plan, UCIL's initial application for a municipal permit for the MIC plant was rejected. The company, however, managed to procure the received approval from the central governmental authorities and went ahead and built the MIC unit in the midst of a dense urban settlement (CSE 1985: 216).

The political economy that defined the relations between the company and the decision-making elites within the state was an important reason for the power of the corporation relative to that of the community. To begin with, relatives of a number of powerful politicians and bureaucrats were either employed by the company or had received illegal favors from it. The company's legal adviser at the time of the gas leak, for example, was an important leader of the ruling Congress (I) party, and its public relations officer was a nephew of a former education minister of the state. The chief minister himself was facing a court case over claims that he had personally received favors from the company. Besides, his wife had received the company's hospitality during visits to the United States in 1983 and 1984. Moreover, the company's plush guesthouse was regularly used by the chief minister and had been placed at the disposal of the Congress party for its 1983 convention (CSE 1985: 216). All this meant, among other things, that the state government often looked the other way when Union Carbide violated environmental regulations or cracked down on the worker protests.

Underlying the correlation between environmental injustice and economic and political status in Bhopal, thus, was a political economy that manufactured both a physical and a moral metaphysic of environmental violence. This metaphysic, as the foregoing account has shown, had structurally built-in potentialities for serious risk to the workers and the community. When not physically actualized, the agents responsible for creating the metaphysic were morally lucky.[7] However, when the potentiality was actualized, as happened in December 1984, the moral metaphysic underlying the environmental injustice in Bhopal produced a catastrophic disaster.[8] Because this moral metaphysic was based on distributive inequity, the type of violence it engenders is perhaps best described as distributive violence, or the violence of environmental justice.

Bureaucratic Violence

Distributive violence in Bhopal was exacerbated by yet another, everyday form of violence that was perpetrated by the bureaucrats and technocrats assigned by the state machinery to help put together a rehabilitation program for the victims in the aftermath of the gas leak. To begin with, there was what is perhaps best described as the "violence of absence." At the outset, effective regulation was, for the reasons associated with distributive violence, almost nonexistent. Besides, there was no preemptive program to prepare the community near the plant to respond adequately in the event of an accident. Nor was there any coordinated or systematic contingency plan drawn up, let alone rehearsed, whereby some designated agency of the state could respond effectively in emergencies (CSE 1985: 216). The violence of the technological design, and of environmental injustice and corporate indifference, was thereby complemented by the violence of bureaucratic absence. Indeed, the lack of what has been described in this book as "green governmentality" was, in itself, a potent source of violence. The consequence of this absence was not just the accident itself but the ad hoc nature of the governmental response on the night of the disaster—ineffective warnings, the failure of the mass media to provide proper instruc-

absence

---

7. Moral luck refers to cases in which luck makes a moral difference. The idea of moral luck poses a philosophical problem in that it sets up a clash between the apparently widely held intuition that cases of moral luck should not occur and the fact that it is arguably impossible to prevent such cases from arising. For an introduction to this concept, see Williams (1981, 1993a and b) and Nagel (1993).

8. The terms *potentiality* and *actuality* have been adopted from Aristotle's discussion of motion (Barnes 1983). See, especially, Aristotle's *Physics*.

tion on how to cope, and little or no evacuation. Moreover, the violence of absence was compounded in the days after the immediate accident when the state bureaucracy failed to adequately cope with tasks as basic as removing carcasses from the streets. Perhaps the most palpable illustration of this violence lay in the fact that it took 40 hours for the secretaries and heads of departments to set up the first coordination meeting to take stock of the relief process (CSE 1985: 206–211).

A second facet of bureaucratic violence concerned the rituals of everyday governance. The form and the certificate became, for the bureaucrats, the primary criteria for accepting the authenticity of the claims of victims. Obvious expressions of pain and suffering were inadequate—required were official certificates issued by governmentally sanctioned doctors and officials. Moreover, the process of applying for such certificates meant negotiating with complex forms and a Byzantine administrative process. In the context of prevailing illiteracy and desperation, the upshot was the mushrooming of touts who knew both how to fill in the forms and how to get them successfully through the governmental process. Although the existence of the touts ensured that the victim claimants got at least some relief, it also meant that they did not receive the entirety to which they were entitled (Rajan 1988).

A third manifestation of bureaucratic violence was the violence of the routine. In the aftermath of an enormous disaster, all the bureaucracy could muster by way of rehabilitation programs were dusted-off schemes from the shelves of the secretariat. Initially, during the first 6 months after the disaster, this meant implementing the standard models of disaster relief used in floods and cyclones—ex gratia payments and the distribution of rations. Later, as it became clear that there would be a chronic disaster needing a long-term rehabilitation strategy, the bureaucracy's response was to bring to Bhopal a standard poverty alleviation program that involved providing small loans that would help victims set up businesses in either the retail or service sectors. In essence, the bureaucracy failed to muster anything other than the routine in the context of a disaster that was, if anything, extraordinarily beyond the routine. It also failed to institutionalize a monitoring process to assess the effectiveness of the programs that it had initiated. As a consequence, its programs collapsed for reasons ranging from economic unviability to ergonomic inefficacy to plain graft. Moreover, when the programs began to fail, the bureaucracy did very little to put things right, being content to let the rehabilitation program lapse into another routine administrative entity beyond the pale of public accountability (Rajan 1999).

Bureaucratic violence also involved a sort of concealment and lack of transparency that began long before the December 1984 accident. Far from ensuring public debate and consensus about the risks involved in siting a highly hazardous facility within a dense urban settlement, the communities involved were provided with little or no information about the plant and the threats it potentially posed. During the accident, as pointed out earlier, the affected community was not given basic information about how to respond to the gas. In the immediate aftermath of the accident, when a major decision regarding detoxifying the plant was made, the public was once again not made privy to the details of the process or the risks involved. As a result, "Operation Faith," as the program was called, succeeded in spreading panic and, eventually, a mass migration of more than 100,000 people and their animals from the city on December 13 (CSE 1985: 212–217). Next, there was no transparency in the medical research process and little, if any, dissemination to the affected community of the results of the countless studies that were conducted on the surviving population. Indeed, members of a commission appointed by the Supreme Court of India to examine the medical rehabilitation process were not provided with documents concerning the results of the ongoing medical research.[9] The official report on the cause of the December 1984 accident has yet to be released, more than 15 years after the accident. In short, vital information about almost every facet of the disaster was and has been concealed from the affected community, the public at large, and some concerned professionals. Far from a climate of transparency, what happened in Bhopal was the classification of everything from meteorological data to medical and engineering analysis as official secrets. On the few occasions when activists attempted to gain access to what should have been freely available information, they were arrested under the draconian Official Secrts Act.[10]

Bureaucratic violence also concerned what might best be described as the violence of scientism.[11] One illustration of this type of violence was the language used by the doctors to describe the claims of the gas victims. The origins of women's medical problems, for example, were attributed to a variety of factors including "faking; psychological; or due to poverty and poor hygiene." Men, in turn, were accused of "compensation neurosis" (Sathyamala 1988: 50). In essence, as in the case of the certificate and the form, the only method of accepting the authenticity of the pain of the victim was some "objective" measure of truth. For the doctors, nothing but "objective" physical measurements could count. The obsession with "objec-

9. Conversations with Dr. Anil Sadgopal, member of the Supreme Court Committee, 1986.
10. One such arrest involved members of the Bhopal Group for Information and Action in 1986.
11. *Scientism* refers to "a belief in the omnipotence of scientific knowledge and techniques; also to the view that the methods of study appropriate to physical science can replace those used in other fields such as philosophy and, esp., human behaviour and the social sciences" (OED On-line edition).

tive" evidence and the simultaneous rejection of subjective testimonies by suffering victims of their pain was widely prevalent within the medical research establishment. An example is some of the work conducted by the Indian Council of Medical Research (ICMR), which focused on assessing chromosomal aberrations and the mutagenic effects of the chemicals that entered the body by using sentinel phenotypes, protein markers, and cytogenic studies. In addition to the various Duhemian problems posed by these studies (such as that numerous factors other than chemical mutagens [e.g., viral infections, specimen handling procedures] can cause somatic chromosome breakage or rearrangement), these methods were tremendously time-consuming and expensive and required enormously large samples of data. An alternative and less expensive way of assessing mutagenic effects, however, was examining the incidence of spontaneous abortion rates, which in Bhopal, had, by the admission of the ICMR doctors themselves, clearly increased. This method, however, relied on interviews with affected women. In September 1985, the Medico Friends Circle, a medical NGO, conducted a study that showed a significantly high increase in spontaneous abortion rates. When this study was presented to the medical rofession, its response was: "The study is quite useless because . . . memory recall can never be relied upon in a disaster situation. . . . the population would definitely exaggerate its symptoms" (Sathyamala 1988: 49).

Yet another facet of the violence of scientism was the prevalent culture of resolving scientific controversies. Perhaps nothing is more illustrative of this culture than the infamous "Thyiocyanate Controversy." It arose around the question of what to make of the observations during the autopsies of hundreds of bodies in the aftermath of the gas leak. For some professionals, including forensic pathologists and the ICMR, the autopsies showed unmistakable signs of cyanide poisoning. These professionals propounded a scientific theory, known as the "enlarged cyanogen-pool theory," to explain the effects of gas-exposure (Medico Friends Circle [MFC] 1985: 6–10) The theory postulated that the effect of gas exposure was that of chronic cyanide poisoning and proposed a policy prescription of detoxification through the administration of a known antidote for cyanide. Another group of medical professionals, however, disagreed with such a diagnosis; they argued that physical examinations of gas victims indicated that the gas had affected only the lungs. While postulating their alternative hypotheses, the "pulmonary pathology theory" or the "lung fibrosis theory," they argued further that there was no evidence in the medical literature of the phenomenon of "chronic cyanide poisoning" (MFC 1985: 6; Sathyamala 1988: 41–43). The controversy spiraled without any apparent conclusion and degenerated into a petty conflict between certain personalities (Rajan 2000).

Each of these five types of violence associated with the administrative and medical bureaucracy was embedded within the social stratification endemic to the society at large in Bhopal. The interactions between the bureaucracy and the gas-affected community were thus almost always mediated through wider societal prisms including class, caste, gender, and religion. At the same time, these interactions were informed by what Kleinman, Das, and Lock call the "rationalized bureaucratic apparatus of the modern state" (1997: xix) and, especially, the obsessive demand for objectively certifiable authenticity as opposed to the acknowledgment of subjective pain and suffering. These two factors, combined with the nature of the local political and moral economy, produced a mosaic of violence described here as "bureaucratic."

Discursive Violence: The Violence of the Symbolic Appropriation of Social Suffering[12]

Finally, Bhopal was also a site of a more abstract type of violence that nevertheless had important material manifestations. This category of violence, which is perhaps best described as "discursive," had at least three expressions. The first of these was the violence of "development" as a geopolitical project.[13] Perhaps the best illustration of the nature of this violence in Bhopal can be found in a statement by a state labor minister, Tara Singh Viyogi. In a context in which workers in the Union Carbide factory had been protesting and petitioning for better safety in the operation of the plant, Viyogi argued that the factory was "not a stone which I could lift and place elsewhere. The factory has its ties with the entire country. And it is not a fact that the plant is posing a major danger to Bhopal or that there is any such possibility" (CSE 1985: 216). Implicit in such a statement was a primordial commitment to a risk assessment strategy that put "economic advancement" above all else.

A second facet of discursive violence in Bhopal concerned the appropriative violence of some of the nonprofit organizations that worked there in the aftermath. Bhopal provided an opportunity for a number of these groups to highlight their central outlooks and ideologies. These ranged from a concern with the negative consequences of the spread of multinational organizations and the world capitalist system to a deep-rooted skepticism of technologies such as the "green revolution." Their approach to political mobilization, therefore, was to use an immense human tragedy to

12. The term *discourse* refers to "a particular area of language use related to a certain set of institutions and expressing a particular standpoint" (Peet and Watts 1993: 228).
13. For a critical discussion of the genealogy of development as a geopolitical project, see Esteva 1997 and Norgaard 1994. The idea of development in the context of economic progress, however, has a long and complex history. See, for example, Cowen and Shenton (1996).

bring to public consciousness the issues that concerned them. In doing so, they often described themselves as "victims' organizations" and spoke on behalf of those affected by the gas disaster. However, they failed to focus their attention on the day-to-day needs of the victims such as, for example, the need for effective rehabilitation. Although their rhetoric accused the state and the company of not doing enough in this regard and of being part of an "anti-people" conspiracy, it never managed to provide any details or to mobilize any expertise that would help shed light on how viable relief could be provided. The result was the appropriation of the pain and the voice of the victims with no tangible benefits to them.[14]

Finally, Bhopal witnessed the violence of discursive absence. At the time the government first attempted to create a rehabilitation program, it appealed to various Indian universities and institutions of higher learning to help them in this process. This call was met with an extraordinary amount of silence.[15] Although anthropologists and political scientists decried the discourse of development, the nature of the world capitalist system, and the "econometrics of suffering" produced during the course of the state rehabilitation process (e.g., Das 1995; Visvanathan 1988), they did very little tangibly to help address and solve the complex problems associated with rehabilitation. No social scientist, for example, committed to conduct long-term research toward this end. Even those institutions that did respond, such as the Tata Institute of Social Sciences, which the government commissioned to conduct a socioeconomic survey, could not adequately deliver. These material absences are symptoms of a wider phenomenon, described elsewhere as the politics of missing expertise (Rajan 2001). No middle ground existed between the heady discourse of technocratic optimism, on the one hand, and the equally vehement antidevelopmental pessimism and social scientific discourse obsessed with describing power gradients and discourses of governmentality, on the other. Crucially, no prevalent culture of material practice in the social sciences existed that could tangibly intervene in the thicket of pragmatic detail that putting together a rehabilitation program demands.[16]

Conclusion

As a site of violent environments, Bhopal was clearly an extreme case. However, the various phenomena of environmental violence witnessed there exist in several other contexts. Technological violence, for example, is not

14. For an introspective and reflexive discussion of the issues underlying "appropriative violence" see Rajan (1999; 2000).
15. Conversations with Dr. Ishwar Das, then Commissioner of Gas Relief, 1996.
16. For a more comprehensive discussion of this issue, see Rajan (2000).

restricted to accidents such as Bhopal. On the contrary, a poorly designed plant, inadequate command and control systems, the use of chemical pesticides, or the release of genetically modified organisms without meticulous attention to safety or insufficient public debate and consensus about risk are all examples of technological violence in one form or another. Corporate violence also is rampant, as case studies in this book as well as the wider literature on the impact of economic globalization show (Korten 1998; Goldsmith and Mander 1996; Wallach and Sforza 1999; Anderson, Cavanagh, and Lee 2000). Moreover, environmental injustice is widespread within both the developing and the developed worlds, as well as between the nations of the North and the South (Szasz 1994; Bryant 1995; Faber 1998; CSE 1992). Equally widespread is bureaucratic and discursive violence. Bhopal was thus but a potent microcosm of a more general global trend of environmental violence.

What, then, is the moral of the Bhopal story? At one level, all that the earlier discussion provides is a pointer toward a series of absences, ranging from the technological to the discursive. Yet, an awareness of what is missing can be used to determine what can be actively done, both in the realms of research and in policy and advocacy.

Perhaps a good place to start is with the need to cultivate material skills that can help mitigate environmental violence. The basic intuition in this regard is already prevalent in the many calls for good governance and, specifically, in the demands for accountability and democracy (CSE 1992). They also are visible in the numerous attempts toward this goal, especially in the realm of the management of various local resource commons (e.g., Poffenberger and McGean 1996; Jeffery and Sundar 1999; Saxena 1997). A great deal in the rich body of experience concerning bureaucratic reform potentially informs the question of how to cope with the phenomena related to bureaucratic violence.

The cataclysmic nature of the Bhopal event, however, also forces us to reexamine our very measures of the quality of life. How, for example, do we philosophically articulate a relatively self-evident intuition that, other things being equal, people are better off when they live in less violent environments? Next, how do we translate such a philosophical framework into a theory of economic progress or of risk measurement? Answers to such questions are crucial to tackling facets of technological, distributive, and discursive violence. Some preliminary tools to address such questions exist in discussions of the idea of entitlements and the quality of life (e.g., Sen 1999a; Sen 1999b; Nussbaum and Sen 1999; Sen 1999c; Ahmed et al. 1991; Winfield 1990), and in the use of Rawlsian approaches to risk assessment (e.g., Schrader-Frechette 1991). Equally important are the vigorous debates about institutionalizing the precautionary principle and developing a theory of alternatives assessment (e.g., Raffenseperger and Tickner 1999; Freestone and Hay 1996; O'Brien 2000) and a potentially fruitful body of research and action on science, technology, and public accountability (e.g., Sclove 1995). What Bhopal demands is that these important, but disparate efforts be synthesized in some meaningful manner that enriches our idea of the quality of life and helps build a powerful theory of environmental entitlements. Such a theory is crucial to counter the structural dynamic that underlies technological violence. It also is crucial to address those aspects of discursive and distributive violence that deal with societal goals, such as those concerning the idea and meaning of development.

Finally, the problem of corporate violence and aspects of distributive violence force us to reexamine our very notion of human rights. In 1948, in the aftermath of World War II, the United Nations General Assembly adopted the Universal Declaration of Human Rights, which spelled out not only civil and political rights but also economic, social, and cultural rights. This declaration, though not legally binding, gave rise to many covenants and conventions that laid out clear obligations for nation-states. These included the International Covenant for Civil and Political Rights; the International Covenant for Economic, Social and Cultural Rights; the Convention on the Rights of the Child; and the Convention on the Elimination of Discrimination against Women. Recently, in the tumultuous aftermath of the end of the Cold War and the beginning of the brave new world of globalization, citizen groups and civic organizations across the world have begun to articulate a more specific form of human rights. These refer particularly to the rights of people to live with economic dignity and to demand access to food and living wages and, in doing so, to broaden the idea of human rights far beyond the civil and the political.[17] Bhopal, as a site of extreme violence, demands an even further extension of our idea of rights to include the right to live in nonviolent environments. Such an extension is extremely important if the issues of corporate and distributive violence are to be meaningfully addressed.[18]

Bhopal, as a symptom and an extreme manifestation of environmental violence, demands three simultaneous responses. It *requires* a radical reworking of the institutions of governance and accountability. It *asks* for a systematic articulation of a "green" social and political philosophy. Last, but by no means the least, it makes a strong case for a major international political movement for an expanded set of human rights that includes both the economic and environmental. Anything less will invite a repeat of history.

17. For a sustained discussion on economic human rights, see the website of the Institute of Food and Development Policy (Food First: www.foodfirst.org). See also Mittal and Rosset (1999).
18. For a discussion of rights of corporations relative to individuals, see Grossman et al. (1993).

References

Abdullah, I. 1997. "Bush Path of Destruction: The Origin and Character of the Revolutionary United Front." *Africa and Development* 22.

Abdullah, I., and P. K. Muana. 1998. "The Revolutionary United Front of Sierra Leone (RUF/SL)." In *African Guerrillas*, edited by C. Clapham. Oxford: James Currey.

Agarwal, Anil, and Sunita Narain. 1992. *Towards a Green World: Should Global Environmental Management Be Built on Legal Conventions or Human Rights?* New Delhi: Center for Science and Environment.

Agarwal, Bina. 1997. "Re-sounding the Alert—Gender, Resources and Community Action." *World Development* 25:1373–1380.

Ahmed, Ehtisham, Jean Dreze, John Hill, and Amartya Sen. 1991. *Social Security in Developing Countries.* New York: Oxford University Press.

Ahmed, Faris. 1998. *In Defense of Land and Livelihood: Coastal Communities and the Shrimp Industry in Asia.* CUSO, Consumers Association of Penang, Inter Pares, Sierra Club of Canada.

Albert, K., W. Hull, and D. Sprague. 1989. "The Dynamic West: A Region in Transition." Report, Council of State Governments.

Alexander, Jeffrey C. 1995. *Fin de Siécle Social Theory: Relativism, Reduction, and the Problem of Reason.* London: Verso.

Alvares, Claude. 1992. *Science, Development and Violence: The Revolt against Modernity.* Delhi: Oxford University Press.

Amnesty International. 1992. *The Extra Judicial Execution of Suspected Rebels and Collaborators.* London: International Secretariat of Amnesty International, Index AFR 51/02/92.

Anderson, Benedict. 1983. *Imagined Communities: Reflections on the Origin and Spread of Nationalism.* London: Verso.

Anderson, Perry. 1980. *Arguments within English Marxism.* London: Verso.

Anderson, Sarah, John Cavanagh, and Thea Lee. 2000. *Field Guide to the Global Economy.* New York: New Press.

André, C., and J. P. Platteau. 1995. "Land Tenure under Unendurable Stress: Rwanda Caught in the Malthusian Trap." Working Paper, Centre de Recherche en Economie du Développement, University of Namur, Belgium.

Arad, R. W., and U. B. Arad. 1979. "Scarce Natural Resources and Potential Conflict." Pp. 23–104. In *Sharing Global Resources*, edited by R. W. Arad et al. New York: McGraw-Hill.

Arbatov, A. 1986. "Oil as a Factor in Strategic Policy and Action: Past and Present." Pp. 21–37. In *Global Resources and International Conflict: Environmental factors in Strategic Policy and Action*, edited by A. Westing. Oxford: Oxford University Press.

Archivo General Agrario (AGA). "Secretariat of Agrarian Reform Documents Related to the Formation of Ejidos in Chilón, Yajalón, Sitalá, and Salto de Agua." Mexico D.F.

Ardrey, Robert. 1966. *The Territorial Imperative.* New York: Atheneum.

Aristotle. 1983. "Physics." In *The Complete Works of Aristotle*, edited by Jonathan Barnes. The Revised Oxford Translation (Bollingen Series, 71:2).

Arneil, Barbara. 1996. "The Wild Indian's Venison: Locke's Theory of Property and English Colonialism in America." *Political Studies* 44:60–74.

Arnold, David, and Ramachandra Guha (eds.). 1995. *Nature, Culture, Imperialism: Essays on the Environmental History of South Asia.* Delhi: Oxford University Press.

Arnold, R. 1997. *Eco-Terror: The Violent Agenda to Save Nature.* Bellevue, Wash.: Free Enterprise.

Asia Yearbook. 1998. *Far Eastern Economic Review.*

Asian Development Bank. 1998. "Statistical Data of DMCs." Available on the Internet at http://www.internotes.asiandevbank.org.

Asif, Mohammed. 1999. "Land Acquisition Act: Need for an Alternative Paradigm." *Economic and Political Weekly* 34:1564–1566.

Associated Press. 1995. "Postcard Threatens Catron Company Manager and Ten Others." Wire Services.

Aubry, Andrés. 1997. "¿Quiénes son los 'paramilitares'?" *La Jornada*, 23 December, electronic edition.

Aviation Week & Space Technology. 1994. Vol.140, No. 24 (13 June).

Baechler, Gunther. 1998. "Why Environmental Transformation Causes Violence: A Synthesis." *Environmental Change and Security Project Report* Spring (4).

Baechler, Gunther, and Kurt R. Spillman. 1996. "Environmental Degradation as a Cause of War." Vol. 2 & 3, *Research and Country Studies of Research Fellows.* Zurich: Verlag Ruegger.

Bailey, C., and M. Skladany. 1991. "Aquacultural Development in Tropical Asia: A Re-Evaluation." *Natural Resources Forum* 15:66–73.

Bailey, C., S. Jentoft, and P. Sinclair (eds.). 1996. *Aquacultural Development: Social Dimensions of an Emerging Industry.* Boulder: Westview.

Bailey, Conner. 1988. "The Social Consequences of Tropical Shrimp Mariculture Development." *Ocean & Shoreline Management* 11:31–44.

Bailey, Conner. 1997. "Aquaculture and Basic Human Needs." *World Aquaculture* 28:28–31.

BANAMEX. 1998. *Datos Básicos de Mexico.* Mexico D.F.: División de Estudios Económicos y Sociales, Banamex. Web edition.

Barbier, Edward, and Thomas Homer-Dixon. 1996. "Resource Scarcity, Institutional Adaptation, and Technical Innovation: Can Poor Countries Attain Endogenous Growth?" Washington, D.C.: Project on Environment, Population and Security of the American Association for the Advancement of Science and the University of Toronto.

Bardach, John E. (ed.). 1997. *Sustainable Aquaculture.* New York: Wiley.

Bari, J. 1994. *Timber Wars.* Monroe, Maine: Common Courage.

Barraclough, Solon, and Krishna Ghimire. 1990. "The Social Dynamics of Deforestation in Developing Countries: Principal Issues and Research Priorities." Discussion Paper 16. Geneva: United Nations Research Institute for Social Development.

Barraclough, Solon, and Andrea Finger Stich. 1996. "Some Ecological and Social Implications of Commercial Shrimp Farming in Asia." Geneva, Switzerland: United Nations Research Institute for Social Development in Collaboration with the World-Wide Fund for Nature International.

Barry, Tom. 1995. *Zapata's Revenge: Free Trade and the Farm Crisis in Mexico.* Boston: South End.

Bartra, Armando. 1996. "A Persistent Rural Leviathan." In *Reforming Mexico's Agrarian Reform,* edited by Laura Randall. New York: M. E. Sharpe.

Baviskar, Amita. 1992. "Development, Nature and Resistance: The Case of Bhilala Tribals in the Narmada Valley." Ph.D. diss., Cornell University.

Baviskar, Amita. 1994. "The Fate of the Forest: Conservation and Tribal Rights." *Economic and Political Weekly* 29:2493–2501.

Baviskar, Amita. 1995. *In the Belly of the River: Tribal Conflicts over Development in the Narmada Valley.* Delhi: Oxford University Press.

Bayart, F., D. Ellis, and B. Hibou (eds.). 1997. *La Criminalisation de l'Etat en Afrique.* Bruxelles: Editions Complexe.

Beck, Ulrich, Anthony Giddens, and John Lash. 1994. *Reflexive Modernization.* London: Polity.

Beinart, W. 1996. "Soil Erosion, Animals and Pasture over the Longer Term." Pp. 54–72. In *The Lie of the Land: Challenging Received Wisdom on the African Environment,* edited by M. Leach and R. Mearns. Oxford: James Currey.

Benjamin, Thomas. 1996. *A Rich Land, a Poor People: Politics and Society in Modern Chiapas.* Albuquerque: University of New Mexico Press.

Benjamin, W. 1969. *Illuminations.* New York: Vintage.

Benka-Cocker, M., and J. Ekundayo. 1995. "Effects of an Oil Spill on Soil Physico-Chemical Properties of a Spill Site in the Niger Delta." *Environmental Monitoring and Assessment* 30:93–104.

Bennet-Ross, Jane. 1971. "Aggression as Adaptation: The Yanomamo Case." Department of Anthropology, Columbia University.

Bennett, O. (ed.). 1991. *Greenwar: Environment and Conflict.* London: Panos.

Benton, Ted. 1993. *Natural Relations: Ecology, Animal Rights, and Social Justice.* London: Verso.

Berdal, M., and D. Keen. 1997. "Violence and Economic Agendas in Civil Wars: Some Policy Implications." *Millennium: Journal of International Studies* 26(3):795–818.

Berlant, L. 1991. *The Anatomy of National Fantasy: Hawthorne, Utopia and Everyday Life.* Chicago: University of Chicago Press.

Beteille, Andre. 1998. "The Idea of Indigenous People." *Current Anthropology* 19:187–191.

Beyers, W.B. 1996. "Explaining the New Service Economies of the Rural West." Paper presented at the Association of American Geographers Annual Meeting, Charlotte, N.C., April 9–13.

BGIA. 1986. *The Newsletter of the Bhopal Group for Information and Action* (BGIA).

Biarnes, P. 1980. *L'Afrique aux africaines.* Paris: Colin.

Biot, Y. 1992. "What's the Problem? An Essay on Land Degradation, Science and Development in Sub-Saharan Africa." Discussion Paper, UEA/SDS.

Blaikie, P., and H. Brookfield. 1987. *Land Degradation and Society.* London: Methuen.

Blaikie, Piers. 1985. *The Political Economy of Soil Erosion in Developing Countries.* London: Longman.

Blaikie, Piers, Terry Cannon, Ian Davis, and Ben Wisner. 1994. *At Risk: Natural Disasters, People's Vulnerability, and Disasters.* New York: Routledge.

Blomley, Nicholas K. 1994. *Law, Space and the Geographies of Power.* New York: Guilford.

Boal, Ian. 1998. "The New Enclosures." Talk presented at Berkeley Workshop in Environmental Politics, Berkeley, Calif.

Bonanno, A. (ed.). 1994. *From Columbus to ConAgra: The Globalization of Agriculture and Food.* Lawrence: University of Kansas Press.

Bonners Ferry Herald. 1992. Boundary County, Idaho. February 12.

Boonchoo, Punjapol. N.d. "The Biological, Physical, Socio-Economic, and Environmental Impacts of Shrimp Culture on a Rice Growing Hamlet in Pak Phanang Basin in Southern Thailand." Unpublished paper, Prince of Songkla University, Faculty of Natural Resources, Hat Yai, Thailand.

Bourdieu, Pierre. 1977. *Outline of a Theory of Practice.* Cambridge: Cambridge University Press.

Boyce, James K. 1993. *The Philippines: The Political Economy of Growth and Impoverishment in the Marcos Era.* London: MacMillan.

Boyce, James K. 1997. "NAFTA, the Environment and Security: The Maize Connection." *Political Environments* 5:S22–S25.

Bradbury, M. 1995. "Rebels without a Cause: An Exploratory Report for CARE-Britain on the Conflict in Sierra Leone." Unpublished paper.

Breckenridge, Carol, and Peter Van der Veer. 1993. *Orientalism and the Postcolonial Predicament.* Philadelphia: University of Pennsylvania Press.

Breman, Jan. 1997. "Introduction." In *The Village in Asia Revisited,* edited by J. Breman, P. Kloos, and A. Saith. Delhi: Oxford University Press.

Brock, L. 1991. "Peace through Parks: The Environment on the Peace Resource Agenda." *Journal of Peace Research* 28:407–422.

Bromley, D. 1998. "Rousseau's Revenge: The Demise of the Freehold Estate." In *Who Owns America,* edited by M. Jacobs. Madison: University of Wisconsin Press.

Bromley, Daniel W. (ed.). 1992. *Making the Commons Work.* San Francisco: Institute for Contemporary Studies Press.

Brooke, J. 1998. "It's Cowboys vs. Radical Environmentalists in the New Wild West." *New York Times,* September 20.

Brosius, J. Peter. 1997. "Prior Transcripts, Divergent Paths: Resistance and Acquiescence to Logging in Sarawak, East Malaysia." *Comparative Studies in Society and History.*

Brosius, Peter. 1999. "Analyses and Interventions: Anthropological Engagements with Environmentalism." *Current Anthropology* 40(3).

Bryant, Bunyan. 1995. *Environmental Justice: Issues, Policies and Solutions.* Washington, D.C.: Island.

Bryant, Raymond L., and Sinead Bailey. 1997. *Third World Political Ecology.* London: Routledge.

Buch, M. N. 1991. *The Forests of Madhya Pradesh.* Bhopal: Madhya Pradesh Madhyam.

Buck-Morse, S. 1989. *The Dialectics of Seeing.* Boston: MIT Press.

Burman, Sandra, and Barbara Harell-Bond (eds.). 1979. *The Imposition of Law.* New York: Academic.

Burston, Harond. "The Role of the Public Relations Professional," http://www.bm.com/files/per/PER-R07a.html.

Buttel, F. 1992. "Environmentalization: Origins, Processes, and Implications for Rural Social Change." *Rural Sociology* 57(1).

Butts, Ken. 1994. "Why the Military is Good for the Environment." Pp. 83–109. In *Green Security or Militarized Environment?*, edited by Jyrki Kakonen. Aldershot: Dartmouth.

Caldwell, Lynton. 1996. "Science Assumptions and Misplaced Certainty." Pp. 394–442. In *Natural Resources,* edited by John Lemons. Cambridge, Mass.: Blackwell.

Cassimir, Michael J. 1992. "The Dimensions of Territoriality." In *Mobility and Territoriality: Social and Spatial Strategies Among Foragers, Fishers, Pastoralists and Peripatetics,* edited by Michael Cassimir and Aparna Rao. Providence: Berg.

Catron, J. 1995a. "Reconstruction." Hatch, NM *Courier,* March 2.

Catron, J. 1995b. "Keltoi." Hatch, NM *Courier,* July 20.

Catron, J. 1995c. "Deeds, Not Words." Hatch, NM *Courier,* July 27.

Catron, J. 1995d. "Savage." Hatch, NM *Courier,* September 14.

Catron, J. 1995e. "Demons." Hatch, NM *Courier,* November 2.

Centre for Science and Environment. 1982. *"The State of India's Environment, 1981–1982: A Citizens Report."* New Delhi.

Centre for Science and Environment. 1985. *"The State of India's Environment, 1984–1985: The Second Citizen's Report."* New Delhi.

Centro de Derechos Humanos Fray Bartolomé de las Casas y Centros de Derechos Indígenas, A.C. (CDHFBC and CEDIAC). 1996. "Reporte sobre el contexto social e histórico del conflicto en San Gerónimo de Bachajón." May 9.

Cervenka, Z. 1971. *Nigerian War 1967–70: History of the War, Selected Bibliography and Documents.* Frankfurt am Main: Bernard & Graefe Verlag fur Wehrwesen.

CESMECA. 1998. Compilation of unpublished Secretaria de Reforma Agraria and Secretaria de Desarrollo Agrario data on deposit at CESMECA, San Cristobal de las Casas, Chiapas.

Chabal, P., and J. P. Daloz. 1999. *Africa Works: Disorder as Political Instrument.* Oxford: James Currey.

Chagnon, Napolean. 1974. *Studying the Yanomamo.* New York: Holt, Rinehart, and Winston.

Chagnon, Napolean. 1977. *Yanomamö: The Fierce People.* 2d ed. New York: Holt, Rinehart, and Winston.

Chagnon, Napolean. 1983. *Yanomamö: The Fierce People.* 3d ed. New York: Holt, Rinehart, and Winston.

Chairman of the Joint Chiefs of Staff. 1993. "Report on the Roles, Missions, and Armed Forces of the United States." Washington, D.C.

Chakravarty-Kaul, Minoti. 1996. *Common Lands and Customary Law: Institutional Change in North India over the Past Two Centuries.* Delhi: Oxford University Press.

Chauvet, Michelle. 1996. "La Crisis de la Ganadería Bovina de Engorda."

In *La Inserción de la Agricultura Mexicana en la Economía Mundial,* edited by S. M. L. Flores and M. Chauvet. Mexico D.F: Plaza y Valdés.

Chauvet, Michelle. 1997. "La Ganadería Mexicana Frente al Fin del Siglo." Paper read at LASA 1997, April 17–19.

Cherniack, Martin. 1986. *The Hawk's Nest Incident: America's Worst Industrial Disaster.* New Haven: Yale University Press.

Chew, Daniel. 1990. *Chinese Pioneers on the Sarawak Frontier.* Singapore: Oxford University Press.

China Lake Naval Weapons Center. 1968. "1968 Naval Weapons Center Silver Anniversary." China Lake, Calif.: Technical Information Department Publishing Division.

Chouhan, T. R., et al. 1994. *Bhopal: The Inside Story. Carbide Workers Speak Out on the World's Worst Industrial Disaster.* New York: Apex.

Christopher, Warren. 1996. "American Diplomacy and the Global Environmental Challenges of the 21st Century." Speech presented at Stanford University, Palo Alto, CA., April 9. Reprint, Woodrow Wilson Center, *Environmental Change and Security Project Report* (1996):81–85.

Clay, D. D., and Laurence A. Lewis. 1990. "Land Use, Soil Loss and Sustainable Agriculture in Rwanda." *Human Ecology* 18(2).

Clear View. 1999. Electronic newsletter 6(3). Washington, D.C.: Clearinghouse on Environmental Advocacy and Research.

Cleary, Mark, and Peter Eaton. 1992. *Borneo Change and Development.* Oxford: Oxford University Press.

Cliffe, L., et al. 1997. "Environmental, Military and Food Security in the Horn of Africa and Southern Africa." Unpublished paper.

Clinton, William J. 1994. "Remarks by the President to the National Academy of Sciences." U.S. Department of State, June 29, 1994. Washington, D.C.: White House, Office of the Press Secretary.

Cochran, Thomas B., Robert Norris Standish, and Kristen L. Suokko. 1993. "Radioactive Contamination at Chelyabinsk-65, Russia." *Annual Review of Energy Environment* 18.

Cockburn, A. 1995. "Who's left? Who's right?" *The Nation.* June 12.

Cockburn, A., and J. St. Clair. 1996. "Earth First! The Press and the Unabomber." *The Nation.* May 6.

Coggins, G., and C. Wilkinson (eds.). 1987. *Federal Public Land and Resources Law.* Mineola, N.Y.: Foundation.

Cohn, Bernard. 1990. *An Anthropologist among the Historians and Other Essays.* Delhi: Oxford University Press.

Colinvaux, P. 1980. *Fates of Nations: A Biological Theory of History.* New York: Simon and Schuster.

Collier, George Allen, and Elizabeth Lowery Quaratiello. 1994. *Basta!: Land and the Zapatista Rebellion in Chiapas.* Oakland, Calif.: Food First Books, The Institute for Food and Development Policy.

Collier, Paul. 1999. "Doing Well Out of War." Paper prepared for the Conference on Economic Agendas in Civil Wars, London, April 26–27.

Collins, Harry M. 1985. *Changing Order: Replication and Induction in Scientific Practice.* London: Sage.

Collins, Harry, and Trevor Pinch. 1998. "The Challenger Launch Decision." Pp.30–56. In *Golem at Large: What You Should Know about Technology*, edited by H. Collins and T. Pinch. Cambridge: Cambridge University Press.

Conpaz. 1996. *Militarización y Violencia en Chiapas.* Mexico D.F.: Impretei.

Coppel, Charles. 1983. *Indonesian Chinese in Crisis.* Kuala Lumpur: Oxford University Press.

Coronil, F. 1996. "Beyond Occidentalism: Toward Nonimperial Geohistorical Categories." *Cultural Anthropology* 11: 51–87.

Coronil, F. 1997. *The Magical State.* Chicago: University of Chicago Press.

Court, B. 1998. Fish Info Service.

Cowen, M. P., and R. W. Shenton. 1996. *Doctrines of Development.* New York: Routledge.

Crenson, Matthew A. 1971. *The Un-politics of Air Pollution: A Study of Non-Decision Making in the Cities.* Baltimore: Johns Hopkins Press.

Cronon, W. 1996. "The Trouble with Wilderness." In *Uncommon Ground*, edited by W. Cronon. New York: Norton.

Cruz-Torres, Maria L. 1992. "Evaluation of the Impact of Shrimp Mariculture Development upon Rural Communities in Mexico." Pp. 54–72. In *Coastal Aquaculture in Developing Countries: Problems and Perspectives*, edited by R.B. Pollnac and P. Weeks. Kingston: International Center for Marine Research Development, The University of Rhode Island.

Cruz-Torres, Maria L. 1996. "Shrimp Mariculture Development in Two Rural Mexican Communities." Pp. 171–192. In *Aquacultural Development: Social Dimensions of an Emerging Industry*, edited by C. Bailey, S. Jentoft, and P. Sinclair. Boulder: Westview.

Dalby, Simon. 1996. "The Environment as Geopolitical Threat," *Ecumene* 3/4:472–496.

Dalby, Simon. 1998. "Human Security: Environmental Dimensions of a Contested Concept." Paper read at Government of Canada, Department of Foreign Affairs and Trade Workshop, "Taking Human Security Seriously," Quebec, Canada.

Dalby, Simon. 1999a. "Globalization and the Natural Environment: Geopolitics, Culture and Resistance." Paper read at International Roundtable on the Challenges of Globalization, at University of Munich, Germany.

Dalby, Simon. 1999b. "Threats from the South? Geopolitics, Equity, Environmental Security." In *Contested Grounds: Security and Conflict in the New*

Environmental Politics, edited by D. Deudney and R. Matthew. Albany: State University of New York Press.

Dalby, Simon. N.d. "Ecological Metaphors of Security: World Politics in the Biosphere."

Dalton, Russell J., Paula Garb, Nicholas P. Lovrich, John C. Pierce, and John M. Whiteley. 1999. *Critical Masses: Nuclear Weapons Production, and Environmental Destruction in the United States and Russia.* Boston: MIT Press.

Dang, Himraj. 1991. *Human Conflict in Conservation. Protected Areas: the Indian Experience.* Delhi: Vikas Publishing House.

Daniel, E. Valentine. 1996. *Charred Lullabies: Chapters in an Anthropography of Violence.* Princeton: Princeton University Press.

Das, Veena. 1990. "An Introduction: Communities, Riots, Survivors—The South Asian Experience." Pp. 1–36. In *Communities, Riots and Survivors in South Asia,* edited by V. Das. Delhi: Oxford University Press.

Das, Veena. 1995. *Critical Events. An Anthropological Perspective on Contemporary India.* Delhi: Oxford University Press.

Davidson, Jamie. 1998. "State Instigated Violence in the Outer Islands of Indonesia: West Kalimantan." *Journal of Select Asian Studies Papers* 1:1.

Davies, G. 1987. *The Gola Forest Reserves, Sierra Leone: Wildlife Conservation and Forest Management.* Cambridge: International Union for Conservation of Nature and Natural Resources.

Davis, C. (ed.). 1997. *Western Public Lands and Environmental Politics.* Boulder: Westview.

Dean, M. *Governmentality.* 1999. Thousand Oaks, Calif.: Sage.

Debord, G. 1978. *Society of the Spectacle.* Detroit: Black and Red Books.

Decraene, P. 1982. *Vielle Afrique. Jeunes Nations.* Paris: PUF.

de Janvry, Alain, Elisabeth Sadoulet, Benjamin Davis, and Gustavo Gordillo. 1996. "Ejido Sector Reforms: From Land Reform to Rural Development." In *Reforming Mexico's Agrarian Reform,* edited by Laura Randall. New York: M. E. Sharpe.

de la Fuente, Juan, Arturo Garmendia, Margarita Gonzalez, and Maria Luisa Jimenez. 1989. *Bonanza y Crisis de la Ganadaría Nacional.* Chapingo: Universidad Autónoma de Chapingo.

Dembo, David, Ward Morehouse, and Lucinda Wykle. 1990. *Abuse of Power, Social Performance of Multinational Corporations: The Case of Union Carbide.* New York: New Horizons.

Dennis, Peter, and Jeffrey Grey. 1996. *Emergency and Confrontation: Australian Military Operations in Malaya & Borneo 1950–1966.* St. Leonards, Australia: Allen & Unwin in association with the Australian War Memorial.

Deshpande, Satish. 1998. "Hegemonic Spatial Strategies: The Nation-

Space and Hindu Communalism in Twentieth Century India." *Public Culture* 10:249–283.

de Soysa, Indra. 2000. "Natural Resources and Civil War: Shrinking Pie or Honey Pot?" Paper presented at the 41st Annual Convention of the International Studies Association, Los, Angeles, Calif., March 14–18.

Deudney, D., and Richard Matthew (eds.). 1999. *Contested Grounds: Security and Conflict in the New Environmental Politics.* Albany: SUNY Press.

Devereaux, Steven. 1993. *Theories of Famine.* London: Harvester Wheatsheaf.

de Vos, Jan. 1995. El Lancandon: Una Introducción Histórica. In *Chiapas: Los Rumbos a otra Historia,* edited by J. P. Viquiera and M. H. Ruz. Mexico D.F.: Universidad Nacional Autonoma de Mexico.

de Waal, A. 1989. *Famine that Kills:* Oxford: Oxford University Press.

de Waal, A. 1996. "Contemporary Warfare in Africa: Changing Context, Changing Strategies." *IDS Bulletin* 27: 6–16.

Dirks, Nicholas. 1989. "The Original Caste: Power, History and Hierarchy in South Asia." *Contributions to Indian Sociology* 23(1).

Divale, William, and Marvin Harris. 1976. "Population, Warfare, and the Male Supremacist Complex." *American Anthropologist* 78:521–538.

Djuweng, Stephanus. 1997. "Development is an Extension of Colonialism." *Inside Indonesia* July–September:13.

Douglas, M. 1993. *In the Wilderness: The Doctrine of Defilement in the Book of Numbers.* Sheffield: JSOT.

Douglas, M., and S. Ney. 1998. *Missing Persons.* Berkeley: University of California Press.

Dove, Michael. 1985. "The Kantu System of Land Tenure: The Evolution of Tribal Land Rights in Borneo." *Studies in Third World Societies* 33:159–182.

Dove, Michael. 1993. "A Revisionist View of Tropical Deforestation and Development." *Environmental Conservation* 20:17–24,56.

Dove, Michael. 1997. *Inside Indonesia,* July-September.

Dowie, M. 1995. "With Liberty and Firepower for All." *Outside,* November.

Dreze, J., and A. K. Sen. 1996. *India: Economic Development and Social Opportunity.* Delhi: Oxford University Press.

Dreze, J., M. Samson and S. Singh (eds.). 1997. *The Dam and the Nation: Displacement and Resettlement in the Narmada Valley.* Delhi: Oxford University Press.

Duffield, M. 1998. "Aid Policy and Post-Modern Conflict: A Critical Review." Unpublished paper, School of Public Policy, International Development Department, University of Birmingham.

Dumont, Jean-Paul. 1992. "Ideas on Philippine Violence: Assertions, Negations, and Narrations." In *The Paths to Domination, Resistance, and Terror,* edited by C. Nordstrom and J. Martin. Berkeley: University of California Press.

Dumont, Jean-Paul. 1995. "Ideas on Philippine Violence." In *Discrepant Histories*, edited by V. Raphael. Philadelphia: Temple University Press.

Durham, William H. 1979. *Scarcity and Survival in Central America: Ecological Origins of the Soccer War*. Stanford: Stanford University Press.

Dymond, David. 1990. "A Lost Social Institution: The Camping Close." *Rural History* 1:165–92.

Edelman, Marc. 1992. *The Logic of Latifundio: The Large Estates of Northwestern Costa Rica since the Late Nineteenth Century*. Stanford: Stanford University Press.

Eder, James F. 1987. *On the Road to Tribal Extinction: Depopulation, Deculturation, and Adaptive Well-Being among the Batak of the Philippines*. Berkeley: University of California Press.

Edwards, Rob. 1998. "End of the Germ Line." *New Scientist* 157:22.

Egan, T. 1990. *The Good Rain*. New York: Vintage.

Egelko, B. 1998. " 'Liberty' Issue in Pepper Spray Case." *San Francisco Examiner*, August 22.

Ellen, Roy. 1999. "Forest Knowledge, Forest Transformation: Political Contingency, Historical Ecology and the Renegotiation of Nature in Central Seram." In *Transforming the Indonesian Uplands*, edited by T. M. Li. Singapore: Harwood Academic Publishers.

Ellis, S. 1999. *The Mask of Anarchy: The Destruction of Liberia and the Religious Roots of an African Civil War*. New York: New York University Press.

Environmental Conflict and Security Project Report (ECSR). 1995. Vol. 1.

Epstein, Steven. 1995. "The Construction of Lay Expertise: AIDS Activism and the Forging of Credibility in the Reform of Clinical Trials." *Science, Technology, & Human Values* 20:408–437.

Erikson, Kai T. 1972. *Everything in its Path: Destruction of Community in the Buffalo Creek Flood*. New York: Simon and Schuster.

Erikson, Kai T. 1991. "Radiation's Lingering Dread." *Bulletin of the Atomic Scientists* 47:34–39.

Escobar, Arturo. 1999. "Steps to an Antiessentialist Political Ecology." *Current Anthropology* 40:1.

Esty, Daniel C., Jack A. Goldstone, Ted R. Gurr, Barbara Harff, Marc Levy, Geoffrey D. Dabelko, Pamela T. Surko, and Alan N. Unger. 1999. "State Failure Task Force Report: Phase II Findings." Pp. 49–72. In *Environmental Change and Security Project Report*. Washington, D.C.: Woodrow Wilson Center.

Evans, Kate. 1998. *Copse*. Wiltshire: Orange Dog.

Faber, Daniel (ed.). 1998. *The Struggle for Ecological Democracy: Environmental Justice Movements in the United States*. New York: Guilford.

Fairfax, S., L. Fortmann, A. Hawkins, L. Huntsinger, N. Peluso, and S. Wolf. 1999. "The Federal Forests Are Not What They Seem: Formal and Informal Claims to Federal Lands." *Ecology Law Quarterly* 25(4).

Fairhead, J. 1990a. "Fields of Struggle: Towards a Social History of Farming Knowledge and Practice in a Bwisha Community." Ph.D. thesis, School of Oriental and African Studies, University of London.

Fairhead, J. 1990b. "Food Security in North and South Kivu, Zaire 1989." Report for OXFAM.

Fairhead, J. 1997. "Conflicts over Natural Resources: Complex Emergencies, Environment and a Critique of 'Greenwar' in Africa." Paper presented to the UNU/WIDER and QEH Meeting of the Project on The Political Economy of Humanitarian Emergencies, Queen Elizabeth House, Oxford, July 3–5.

Fairhead, J., and M. Leach. 1995. "False Forest History, Complicit Social Analysis: Rethinking Some West African Environmental Narratives." *World Development* 23:1023–1036.

Fairhead, J., and M. Leach. 1996a. "Rethinking the Forest-Savanna Mosaic: Colonial Science and its Relics in West Africa." In *The Lie of the Land: Challenging Received Wisdom on the African Environment*, edited by Melissa Leach and Robin Mearns. Oxford: International African Institute with James Currey and Heinemann.

Fairhead, J., and M. Leach. 1996b. *Misreading the African Landscape: Society and Ecology in a Forest-Savanna Mosaic.* Cambridge: Cambridge University Press.

Fairhead, J., and M. Leach. 1997. "Deforestation in Question: Dialogue and Dissonance in Ecological, Social and Historical Knowledge of West Africa—Cases from Liberia and Sierra Leone." *Paideuma* 43.

FBI (Federal Bureau of Investigation). 1995. "Terrorism in the United States: 1994." Washington, D.C.: United States Department of Justice.

Feith, Herbert. 1968. "Dayak Legacy." *Far Eastern Economic Review*, January 21.

Feldman, Allen. 1991. *Formations of Violence: The Narrative of the Body and Political Terror in Northern Ireland.* Chicago: University of Chicago Press.

Feldman, Allen. 1995. "Ethnographic States of Emergency." In *Fieldwork Under Fire: Contemporary Studies of Violence and Survival*, edited by A. C. G. M. Robben and C. Nordstrom. Berkeley: University of California Press.

Ferguson, J. 1990. *The Anti-Politics Machine: Development, Depoliticization, and Bureaucratic Power in Lesotho.* Cambridge: Cambridge University Press.

Ferguson, James. 1994. *The Anti-politics Machine: Development, Depoliticization and Bureaucratic power in Lesotho.* Minneapolis: University of Minnesota Press.

Ferguson, R. B. 1984. "Studying War." In *Warfare, Culture, and Environment*, edited by R. B. Ferguson. New York: Academic.

Fernandez Ortiz, Luis M., and Maria Tarrio Garcia. 1983. *Ganadería y Estructura Agraria en Chiapas.* Mexico, D.F.: Universidad Autonoma Metropolitana, Unidad Xochimilco.

Feshbach, M., and A. Friendly, Jr. 1992. *Ecocide in the USSR: Health and Nature Under Siege.* New York: Basic.

Findley, S. 1994. "Does Drought Increase Migration?" *International Migration Review* 28:539–53.

Fine, B. 1994. "Coal, Diamonds and Oil." *Review of Political Economy* 6(3):279–302.

Firth, Stewart (ed.). 1997. "A Nuclear Pacific." In *The Cambridge History of the Pacific Islanders,* edited by Donald Denoon with Stewart Firth et. al. Cambridge: Cambridge University Press.

Fischer, D. 1989. *Albion's Seed: Four British Folkways in America.* Oxford: Oxford University Press.

Fisher, William. 1995. *Toward Sustainable Development: Struggling over India's Narmada River.* New York: M. E. Sharpe.

Fithen, C. 1999. "Diamonds and War in Sierra Leone: Cultural Strategies for Commercial Adaptation to Endemic Low-intensity Conflict." Ph.D. thesis, Department of Anthropology, University College London.

Flaherty, Mark, and Choomjet Karnjanakesorn. 1995. "Marine Shrimp Aquaculture and Natural Resource Degradation in Thailand." *Environmental Management* 19:27–37.

Flaherty, Mark, and V. Filipacchi. 1993. "Forest Management in Northern Thailand." *Geoffrey* 24:263–275.

Flaherty, Mark, P. Vandergeest, and Paul Miller. 1999. "Rice Paddy or Shrimp Pond?: Tough Decisions in Rural Thailand." *World Development* 27(12):2045–2060.

Flora, C. 1990. "Presidential Address—Rural Peoples in a Global Economy." *Rural Sociology* 55:157–177.

Ford, Robert E. 1995. "The Population-Environment Nexus and Vulnerability Assessment in Africa." *Geojournal* 35: 207–216.

Foreman, D., and B. Haywood (eds.). 1985. *Ecodefense: A Field Guide to Monkeywrenching.* Tucson, Ariz.: Ned Ludd Books.

Fortey, Richard. 1993. *The Hidden Landscape: A Journey into the Geological Past.* London: J. Cape.

Fosbrooke, Henry. 1990. "Pastorals and Land Tenure." Paper presented at the Workshop on Pastoralism and the Environment, Arusha, Tanzania, April.

Foucault, Michel. 1979. *Discipline and Punish: The Birth of the Prison.* Translated by Alan Sheridan. New York: Vintage.

Foucault, Michel. 1982. "The Subject and Power." In *Beyond Structuralism and Hermeneutics,* edited by H. Dreyfus. Chicago: University of Chicago Press.

Foucault, Michel. 1984. *The Foucault Reader,* edited by Paul Rabinow. New York: Pantheon Books.

Fox, Jonathan, and Gustavo Gordillo. 1989. "Between State and Market:

The Campesino's Quest for Autonomy." In *Mexico's Alternative Political Futures*, edited by Wayne J. Cornelius and P. Smith. San Diego: Center for U.S.-Mexican Studies.

Fox, Jonathan. 1993. *The Politics of Food in Mexico: State Power and Social Mobilization*. Ithaca: Cornell University Press.

Fox, Jonathan. 1994. "The Roots of Chiapas." *Dollars and Sense* 194:30–34.

Fraser, N. 1996. *Justice Interruptus*. London: Routledge.

Freeman, J. D. 1955. "Iban Agriculture: A Report on the Shifting Cultivation of Hill Rice by the Iban of Sarawak." London: HMSO.

Freestone, David, and Ellen Hay. 1996. *The Precautionary Principle and International Law: The Challenge of Implementation*. Boston: Kluwer Academic Publishers Group.

Funtowicz, Silvio, and Jerome Ravetz. 1992. "Three Types of Risk Assessment and the Emergence of Post-Normal Science." Pp. 251—274. In *Social Theories of Risk*, edited by Sheldon Krimsky and Dominic Golding. Westport, Conn.: Praeger.

Furro, T. 1992. "Federalism and the Politics of Revenue Allocation in Nigeria." Ph.D. diss., Clark Atlanta University.

Gadgil, Madhav, and Ramachandra Guha. 1992. *This Fissured Land: An Ecological History of India*. Delhi: Oxford University Press.

Gadgil, Madhav, and Ramachandra Guha. 1994. "Ecological Conflicts and the Environmental Movement in India." *Development and Change* 25:101–136.

Gadgil, Madhav, and Ramachandra Guha. 1995. *Ecology and Equity: the Use and Abuse of Nature in Contemporary India*. New Delhi: Penguin.

Gain, P. 1995. "Bangladesh: Attack of the Shrimps." *Third World Resurgence* 58:18–19.

Gal, Susan. 1991. "Between Speech and Silence: The Problematics of Research on Language and Gender." In *Gender at the Crossroads of Knowledge: Feminist Anthropology in the Postmodern Era*, edited by Micaela de Leonardo. Berkeley: University of California Press.

Gallagher, Carole. 1993. *America Ground Zero: The Secret Nuclear War*. New York: Random House.

Garcia-Barrios, R., and L. Garcia-Barrios. 1990. "Environmental and Technological Degradation in Peasant Agriculture: A Consequence of Development in Mexico." *World Development* 18:1569–85.

García de León, Antonio. 1998. *Resistencia y utopia: memorial de agravios y crónica de revultas y Profecias Acaecidas en la provincia de Chipas durante los ultimos quinientos años de su historia*. Mexico, D.F.: ERA.

Geddes, W. R. 1954. *Report on the Land Dayaks of the First Division*. Kuching: Colonial Printing Office.

Genetic Engineering Network. 1998. Website at http://www.dmac.co.uk/gen.html.

Gibbs, Geoffrey. 1998. "Devon Farmer Fights Monsanto." *Guardian*, August 5.

Gila Watch. 1996. Newsletter: *Barbed Wire*, No. 7. Silver City, New Mexico.

Gilsenan, Michael. 1996. "Violence and the Public Sphere." Unpublished paper, Department of Anthropology, New York University.

Gladyshev, Mikhail. 1990. "Memoirs." Recorded by Pyotr Tryakin. Unpublished manuscript.

Glasmeier, A., et al. 1997. "Global and Local Challenges to Theory, Practice, and Teaching in Economic Geography." Final report of the 1997 National Science Foundation Workshop on the Future of Economic Geography. State College, Institute for Policy Research and Evaluation, Pennsylvania State University, University Park.

Gledittch, Nils Petter (ed.). 1997. *Conflict and the Environment*. Dordecht: Kluwer.

Gleick, P. H. 1990. "Environment, Resources, and International Security and Politics." Pp. 501–533. In *Science and International Security: Responding to a Changing World*, edited by E. H. Arnett. Washington, D.C.: American Association for the Advancement of Science.

Godwin, Sir Harry. 1960. Preface to Joyce M. Lambert (and others). *The Making of the Broads: A Reconsideration of Their Origins in the Light of New Evidence*. Murray: London Geographical Society.

Goldsmith, Edward, and Nicholas Hildyard. 1984. *The Social and Environmental Effects of Large Dams*. San Francisco: Sierra Club Books.

González Esponda, Juan, and Elizabeth Pólito B. 1995. "Notas para comprender el origen de la rebelión Zapatista." *Chiapas* 1:101–23.

Goodman, Sherri W. 1997. Deputy Undersecretary of Defense (E.S) Speech to Army War College, February 10.

Gorada, Prafulla. 1995–97. Field Notes on JFM in Paderu Divsiion, Andhra Pradesh for the Edinburgh University Project on Joint Forest Management.

Gordon, Colin (ed.). 1980. *Michel Foucault: Power/Knowledge*. London: Harvester.

Gottlieb, A. (ed.). 1989. *The Wise Use Agenda*. Bellevue, Wash.: Free Enterprise.

Gottlieb, R. 1993. *Forcing the Spring*. Washington, D.C.: Island.

Gottlieb, R. 1998. "The Meaning of Place: Reimagining Community in a Changing West." In *Reopening the American West*, edited by H. Rothman. Tucson: University of Arizona Press.

Goulding, M. 1999. "The United Nations and Conflict in Africa Since the Cold War." *African Affairs* 98: 155–66.

Government of Honduras. *Economic Profile of Honduras*.

Government of Madhya Pradesh (GoMP). 1995. The Madhya Pradesh Human Development Report. Bhopal.

Gramsci, Antonio. 1971. *Selections from the Prison Notebooks*. New York: International.

Gray, Andrew. 1995. "The Indigenous Movement in Asia." In *Indigenous Peoples of Asia*, edited by R. H. Barnes, Andrew Gray, and Benedict Kingsbury. Ann Arbor: Asian Studies Association with the University of Michigan.

Greenough, Paul. 1982. *Prosperity and Misery in Modern Bengal: The Famine of 1943–1944*. Delhi: Oxford University Press.

Greenpeace. 1992. *The Greenpeace Book of Greenwash*. Greenpeace International. Available on the Internet at http://www.greenpeace.org.

Greenpeace. 1994. *Shell Shocked*. Amsterdam: Greenpeace International.

Grove, Richard. 1995. *Green Imperialism: Colonial Expansionism, Tropical Edens and the Origins of Environmentalism*. Delhi: Oxford University Press.

Grove, Richard, Vinita Damodaran, and Satpal Sangwan, (eds.). 1998. *Nature and the Orient: The Environmental History of South and South East Asia*. Delhi: Oxford University Press.

Guha, Ramachandra, and Madhav Gadgil. 1989. "State Forestry and Social Conflict in British India." *Past and Present*, no. 123:141–177.

Guha, Ramachandra, and Juan Martinez-Alier. 1998. *Varieties of Environmentalism: Essays North and South*. Delhi: Oxford University Press.

Guha, Sumit. 1999. *Environment and Ethnicity*. Cambridge: Cambridge University Press.

Gusterson, Hugh. 1998. "The New Face of Russian Environmentalism." Unpublished manuscript.

Hajer, Maarten A. 1995. *The Politics of Environmental Discourse: Ecological Modernization and the Policy Process*. New York: Oxford University Press.

Hall, Stuart. 1996. "On Postmodernism and Articulation." In *Stuart Hall: Dialogues in Cultural Studies*, edited by David Morley and Kuan-Hsing Chen. London: Routledge.

Hamilton, Nora. 1982. *The Limits of State Autonomy: Post-Revolutionary Mexico*. Princeton: Princeton University Press.

Hammer, J. 1996. "Nigerian Crude." *Harpers Magazine* 58–68.

Hardiman, David. 1987. *The Coming of the Devi: Adivasi Assertion in Western India*. Delhi: Oxford University Press.

Harre, Rom. 1998. *The Singular Self: An Introduction to the Psychology of Personhood*. London: Sage.

Harre, Rom, Jens Brockmeier, and Peter Mulhausler. 1999. *Greenspeak: A Study of Environmental Discourse*. Thousand Oaks, Calif.: Sage.

Harris, Marvin. 1977. *Cannibals and Kings: The Origins of Cultures*. New York: Random House.

Hartmann, Betsy. 1995. *Reproductive Rights and Wrongs: The Global Politics of Population Control*. Boston: South End.

Hartmann, Betsy, and James K. Boyce. 1983. *A Quiet Violence: View From a Bangladesh Village*. London: Zed.

Harvey, David. 1993."From Space to Place and Back Again: Reflections on the Condition of Postmodernity." In *Mapping the Futures: Local Cultures, Global Change*, edited by B. C. Jon Bird, Tim Putnam, George Robertson, and Lisa Tickner. London: Routledge.

Harvey, David. 1996. *Justice, Nature and the Geography of Difference*. Cambridge: Blackwell.

Harvey, Neil. 1990. "Peasant Strategies and Corporatism in Chiapas". In *Popular Movements and Political Change in Mexico*, edited by J. Foweraker and A. L. Craig. Boulder: Lynne Rienner.

Harvey, Neil. 1994. "Rebellion in Chiapas: Rural Reforms, Campesino Radicalism, and the Limits to Salinismo." In *Rebellion in Chiapas: Rural Reforms, Campesino Radicalism, and the Limits to Salinismo*, edited by N. Harvey. San Diego: Center for U.S.-Mexican Studies, UCSD.

Harvey, Neil. 1996. "Rural Reforms and the Zapatista Rebellion: Chiapas 1988–1995." In *Neo-liberalism Revisited: Economic Restructuring and Mexico's Political Future*, edited by G. Otero. Boulder: Westview.

Harvey, Neil. 1998. *The Chiapas Rebellion: The Struggle for Land and Democracy*. Durham: Duke University Press.

Harwell, Emily. 1997. "Law and Culture in Resource Management: An Analysis of Local Systems for Resource Management in the Danau Sentarum Wildlife Reserve." Indonesia-UK Tropical Forest Management Programme, Project 5 Conservation.

Harwell, Emily. 2000. "The Un-natural History of Culture: Ethnicity, Tradition and Territorial Conflicts in West Kalimantan, Indonesia, 1800–1997." Ph.D. diss., Yale University.

Hauge, Wenche, and Tanja Ellingsen. 1998. "Beyond Environmental Scarcity: Causal Pathways to Conflict." *Journal of Peace Research* 35(3):298–317.

Hausman, R. 1981. "State Landed Property." Ph.D. diss., Cornell University.

Hays, Samuel. 1987. *Beauty, Health, and Permanence*. Cambridge: Cambridge University Press.

Hecht, Susana. 1985. "Environment, Development, and Politics: Capital Accumulation and the Livestock Sector in Eastern Amazonia." In *Development Studies, A Reader*, edited by Stuart Corbridge. New York: Arnold.

Hellden, U. 1991. "Desertification: Time for an Assessment?" *Ambio* 20:372–383.

Helvarg, D. 1994. "Anti-Enviros Are Getting Uglier." *The Nation*, November 28.

Helvarg, D. 1995. "Property Rights and Militias: The Anti-Enviro Connection." *The Nation*, May 22.

Helvarg, D. 1996. "The Bombthrowers." *Terrain*, December. Berkeley, Calif.: Ecology Center.

Helvarg, D. 1997. *The War Against the Greens.* San Francisco: Sierra Club Books.

Hernandez Navarro, Luis. 1994. "The Chiapas Uprising." In *Rebellion in Chiapas: Rural Reforms, Campesino Radicalism, and the Limits to Salinismo,* edited by N. Harvey. San Diego: Center for U.S.-Mexican Studies, UCSD.

Hernandez, Luis, and Fernando Célis. 1994. "Solidarity and the New Campesino Movments: The Case of Coffee Production." In *Transforming State-Society Relations in Mexico: The National Solidarity Strategy,* edited by Wayne Cornelius, Ann Craig, and Jonathan Fox. San Diego: Center for U.S.-Mexican Studies.

Hess, K. 1992. *Visions Upon the Land: Man and Nature on the Western Range.* Washington, D.C.: Island.

Hirt, P. 1994. *A Conspiracy of Optimism: Management of the National Forests Since World War Two.* Lincoln, Nebr.: University of Nebraska Press.

Hiti Tau (Tahitian NGO) and the Christian World Service. Video: "Hiti Tau: Building a New Nation."

Hoberg, G. 1997. "From Localism to Legalism: The Transformation of Federal Forest Policy." In *Western Public Lands and Environmental Politics,* edited by C. Davis. Boulder: Westview.

Hobsbawm, E. J. 1994. *Age of Extremes: The Short Twentieth Century, 1914–1991.* New York: Viking Penguin.

Holston, James. 1991. "The Misrule of Law: Land and Usurpation in Brazil." *Comparative Studies in Society and History* 33:695–725.

Homer-Dixon, Thomas. 1991. "On the Threshold: Environmental Changes as Causes of Acute Conflict." *International Security* 16:76–116.

Homer-Dixon, Thomas. 1994. "Environmental Scarcities and Violent Conflict: Evidence from Cases." *International Security* 19:5–40.

Homer-Dixon, Thomas. 1995a. "The Ingenuity Gap: Can Poor Countries Adapt to Resource Scarcity?" *Population and Development Review* 21:587–612.

Homer-Dixon, Thomas. 1995b. "Strategies for Studying Causation in Complex Ecological Political Systems." Washington, D.C.: The Project on Environment, Population and Security of the American Association for the Advancement of Science and the University of Toronto.

Homer-Dixon, Thomas. 1996. "The Project on Environment, Population and Security: Key Findings of Research." Environmental Change and Security Project Report. Washington, D.C.: Woodrow Wilson Center.

Homer-Dixon, Thomas. 1999. *Environment, Scarcity and Violence.* Princeton: Princeton University Press.

Homer-Dixon, Thomas F., and Jessica Blitt (eds.). 1998. *Ecoviolence: Links among Environment, Population and Security.* Lanham MD: Rowman and Littlefield.

Homer-Dixon, Thomas F., Jeffrey H. Boutwell, and George W. Rathjens.

1993. "Environmental Change and Violent Conflict." *Scientific American* 268:38–45.

Homer-Dixon, Thomas, Marc Levy, Gareth Porter, and Jack Goldstone. 1996. "Environmental Scarcity and Violent Conflict: A Debate." Pp. 49–71. In Environmental Change and Security Project Report. Washington, D.C.: Woodrow Wilson Center.

Homer-Dixon, Thomas, and Valerie Percival. 1996. *Environmental Scarcity and Violent Conflict: Briefing Book.* University of Toronto: American Association for the Advancement of Science.

Hookey, John. 1984. "Settlement and Sovereignty." In *Aborigines and the Law,* edited by Peter Hanks and Bryan Keon-Cohen. Sydney: George Allen and Unwin.

Howard, Philip. 1998. "The History of Ecological Marginalization in Chiapas." *Environmental History* 3: 357–377.

Howard, Phillip, and Thomas Homer-Dixon. 1995. "Environmental Scarcity and Violent Conflict: The Case of Chiapas, Mexico." Toronto: University of Toronto, Project in Environment, Population, and Security.

Howard, Philip, and Thomas Homer-Dixon. 1998. "The Case of Chiapas, Mexico." In *Ecoviolence: Links among Environment, Population and Security,* edited by Homer Dixon and Jessica Blitt. Lanham MD: Rowman and Littlefield.

Howe, H. 1998. "Global Order and Security Privatization." Strategic Paper 140, National Defense University, Institute for National Strategic Studies. Available on the Internet at http://www.ndu.edu/inss/strforum/forum.

Human Development Report. 1998. *Croatia.* Zagreb: United Nations Development Program.

Human Rights Watch. 1995. *The Ogoni Crisis.* Report #7/5. New York: Human Rights Watch.

Human Rights Watch. 2000. "Update on Human Rights Violations in the Niger Delta. New York: Human Rights Watch. Available on the Internet at http://www.hrw.org/backgrounder/africa/nigeriabkg1214.htm.

Human Rights Watch, Asia. 1997a. "Java Migrants Started Riots in Kalimantan, Says Army Chief." http://straitstimes.asia1.com/pages/stsea5.html.

Human Rights Watch, Asia. 1997b. "Indonesia: Communal Violence in West Kalimantan," in *Human Rights Watch/Asia Report.*

Human Rights Watch, Asia. 1997c. "Communal War in West Kalimantan." *Inside Indonesia.*

Huntington, Samuel P. 1996. *The Clash of Civilizations and the Remaking of World Order.* New York: Simon and Schuster.

Hvalkof, S. Forthcoming. "Outrage in Rubber and Oil." *People, Plants and Justice,* edited by C. Zerner. New York: Columbia University Press.

IDRD. 1998. "The Role of Adat in the Dayak and Madurese War." Unpublished manuscript. Pontianak.

Ikein, A. 1990. *The Impact of Oil on a Developing Country*. New York: Praeger.

Ikporukpo, C. 1993. "Oil Companies and Village Development in Nigeria." *OPEC Review*, 83–97.

Ikporukpo, C. 1996. "Federalism, Political Power and the Economic Power Game: Control Over Access to Petroleum Resources in Nigeria." *Environment and Planning* C 14: 159–177.

Iliffe, J. 1979. *A Modern History of Tanganyika*. Cambridge: Cambridge University Press.

Institut Studi Arus Informasi, and Institute Dayakology Research and Development (ISAI and IDRD). 1999. *Sisi Gelap Kalimantan Barat*. Pontianak: PT Midas Surya Grafindo.

Instituto Nacional de Estadística Geografía e Información. (INEGI). 1990. *Anuario Estadístico del Estado de Chiapas*. Aguascalientes: INEGI.

Instituto Nacional de Estadística Geografía e Información. (INEGI). 1994. "Chiapas, Resultados Definitivos, VII Censo Agricola-Ganadero, 1990." Aguascalientes: INEGI.

Irwin, Graham. 1955. *Nineteenth Century Borneo: A Study in Diplomatic Rivalry*. Singapore: Donald Moore Books.

Jackson, James C. 1970. Chinese in the West Borneo Goldfields: A Study in Cultural Geography." Occasional Papers in Geography no. 15, University of Hull, United Kingdom.

Jackson, R.H. 1994. "Geography and Settlement in the Intermountain West—Creating an American Mecca." *Journal of the West*, 33(3):22–34.

Jasanoff, Sheila. 1992. "Science, Politics, and the Renegotiation of Expertise at EPA," *Osiris*, 2d Series, 7:195–217.

Jeffery, Roger, and Nandini Sundar. 1995. "A Move from Major to Minor: Competing Discourses of Non-Timber Forest Products in India." Paper presented at SSRC Conference on Environmental Discourses in South and Southeast Asia, Hawaii, December 28–30.

Jeffery, Roger, and Nandini Sundar. Forthcoming. *Branching Out: A Comparative Study of Joint Forest Management in Four Indian States*. Delhi: Oxford University Press.

Jeffery, Roger, and Nandini Sundar (eds.). 1999. *A New Moral Economy for India's Forests? Discourses of Community and Participation*. New Delhi: Sage.

Johnston, R. J., Peter J. Taylor, and Michael Watts, (eds.). 1995. *Geographies of Global Change: Remapping the World in the Late Twentieth Century*. Cambridge, Mass.: Blackwell.

Jones, Gregg. 1986. "Marcos Profited from Smuggling $1b in Timber, Officials Say." *Boston Globe*, May 22.

Jones, Jonathan. 1998. "Why I'm Happy to 'Play God' with Your Food." *Independent* (London), June 9, p. 4.

Kane, J. 1996. *Savages*. New York: Vintage.

Kaplan, R. D. 1994. "The Coming Anarchy: How Scarcity, Crime, Overpopulation, and Disease are Rapidly Destroying the Social Fabric of Our Planet." *Atlantic Monthly*, February, 44–76.

Kaplan, R. D. 1996. *The Ends of the Earth: A Journey at the Dawn of the 21st Century*. New York: Random House.

Kaplan, Robert D. 1999. "In the Balkans, No Wars are Local." *New York Times*, April 7.

Kapuscinski, R. 1982. *Shah of Shahs*. New York: Harcourt.

Karl, T. 1997. *The Paradox of Plenty*. Berkeley: University of California Press.

Karliner, Joshua. 1996. "Bhopal: Setting the Record Straight -A Conversation with Edward A. Munoz, former Managing Director of Union Carbide India, Limited." Available on the Internet at http://www.igc.org/trac/bhopal/munoz.html.

Keane, John. 1996. *Reflections on Violence*. New York: Verso.

Keen, David. 1994. *The Benefits of Famine*. Princeton: Princeton University Press.

Keen, David. 1997. "Conflict and Rationality in Sudan." Paper presented at Queen Elizabeth House Workshop on Economies During Conflict, June.

Keen, David. 1998. "The Economic Functions of Violence in Civil Wars." Adelphi Paper 320, International Institute for Strategic Studies. New York: Oxford University Press.

Kelkar, Govind, and Dev Nathan. 1991. *Gender and Tribe*. New Delhi: Kali for Women.

Kellogg, Sanoma Lee, and Elizabeth J. Kirk (eds.). 1997. *Assessing Health and Environmental Risks from Long-Term Radiation Contamination in Chelyabinsk, Russia: Proceedings from the 1996 AAAS Annual Meeting Symposium*, Washington, D.C.: American Association for the Advancement of Science.

Kennedy, Donald. 1998. "Environmental Quality and Regional Conflict." *A Report to the Carnegie Commission on Preventing Deadly Conflict*. New York: Carnegie Corporation of New York.

Khan, S. A. 1994. *Nigeria: The Political Economy of Oil*. London: Oxford University Press.

Kharoufi, H. 1994. "Forced Migration in the Senegalese-Maruitanian Conflict: Consequences for the Senegal River Valley." In *Population Displacement and Resettlement: Development and Conflict in the Middle East*, edited by S. Shami. New York: Centre for Migration Studies.

Kimerling, J. 1996. "Oil, Lawlessness and Indigenous Struggles in Ecuador's Oriente." In *Green Guerillas*. edited by H. Collinson. New York: Monthly Review.

King, P. 1986. *An African Winter*. Harmondsworth: Penguin.

King, Victor. 1993. *The Peoples of Borneo*. Oxford: Blackwell.

Kingsbury, Benedict (ed.). 1995. *Indigenous Peoples of Asia*, edited by R. H. Barnes, Andrew Gray, and Benedict Kingsbury. Ann Arbor: The Association for Asian Studies.

KIPOC. 1992. "The Foundation Program: Program Profile and Rationale." Principal Document No. 4, Korongoro Integrated Peoples Oriented to Conservation, Loliondo, Tanzania.

Kjekshus, H. 1977. *Ecology Control and Economic Development in East African History: The Case of Tanganyika 1850–1950*. Berkeley: University of California Press.

Kleinman, Arthur, Veena Das, and Margaret Lock (eds.). 1997. *Social Suffering*. Berkeley: University of California Press.

Klyza, C. 1996. *Who Controls Public Lands?* Chapel Hill, N.C.: The University of North Carolina Press.

Koponen, Juhani. 1995. *Development for Exploitation: German Colonial Policies in Mainland Tanzania, 1884–1914*. Helsinki: Tiedekirja.

Korten, David. 1998. *When Corporations Rule the World*. West Hartford, Conn.: Kumarian.

Kossenko, Mira M. 1997. "Health Effects Resulting from Radiation Contamination in the Chelyabinsk Region: Results of a Thirty-Year Continuing Research Project." In *Assessing Health and Environmental Risks from Long-Term Radiation Contamination in Chelyabinsk, Russia: Proceedings from the 1996 AAAS Annual Meeting Symposium*, edited by Sanoma Lee Kellogg and Elizabeth J. Kirk. Washington, D.C.: American Association for the Advancement of Science.

Kothari, Ashish, Farhad Vania, Priya Das, K. Christopher, and Suniti Jha. 1997. *Building Bridges for Conservation*. Delhi: Indian Institute of Public Administration.

Kuletz, Valerie. 1998. *The Tainted Desert: Environmental and Social Ruin in the American West*. New York: Routledge.

Kummer, David M. 1992. *Deforestation in the Post-War Philippines*. Chicago: University of Chicago Press.

Kunstadter, P., C. F. Bird, and S. Sabhasri (eds.). 1986. *Man in the Mangroves: The Socio-economic Situation of Human Settlements in Mangrove Forests*. Tokyo: United Nations University.

Last, D. 1998. "Private Property Rights with Responsibilities." In *Who Owns America?*, edited by H. Jacobs. Madison: University of Wisconsin Press.

Lathrap, Donald. 1968."The Hunting Economics of the Tropical Forest Zone of South America: An Attempt at Historical Perspective." In *Man the Hunter*, edited by R. Lee and I. DeVore. Chicago: Aldine.

Lawrence, Roderick J. 1996. "The Multidimensional Nature of Boundaries: An Integrative Historical Perspective." In *Setting Boundaries: The Anthropology of Spatial and Social Organisation*, edited by Deborah Pellow. Westport, Conn.: Bergin and Garvey.

Lazarus-Black, M., and S. Hirsch. 1994. *Contested States: Law, Hegemony and Resistance*. New York: Routledge.

Leach, Melissa, and Robin Mearns (eds.). 1996. *The Lie of the Land: Challenging Received Wisdom on the African Environment*. Oxford: International African Institute with James Currey and Heinemann.

Leach, Melissa, Robin Mearns, and Ian Scoones. 1997. "Environmental Entitlements: A Framework for Understanding the Institutional Dynamics of Environmental Change." IDS Discussion Paper 359, University of Sussex Institute of Development Studies, Brighton, United Kingdom.

Lefebvre, Henri. 1974. *The Production of Space*. Translated by Donald Nicholson-Smith. Cambridge: Blackwell.

Lele, Sharachchandra. 1998. "Indian Forest Policy, Forest Law and Forest Rights Settlement: A Serious Mismatch." Paper presented at the International Workshop on Capacity Building in Environmental Governance for Sustainable Development at the Indira Gandhi Institute for Development Research, Mumbai, December 8–10.

Leobardo, José Luis, and Arellano Monterrosas. 1994. "La degradación del suelo por erosión hídrica en Chiapas: evaluación y principios tecnologicos para su control." Professional thesis, Department of Irrigation, Universaidad Autónoma Chapingo.

Lerise, F., and U. Schuler. 1988. *Conflicts Between Wildlife and People*. Dar es Salaam: Selous Conservation Programme.

Levi-Strauss, Claude. 1966. *The Savage Mind*. Chicago: University of Chicago Press.

Levy, Marc A. 1995. "Is the Environment a National Security Issue?" *International Security* 20:35–62.

Lewis, M. 1992. *Green Delusions*. Durham: Duke University Press.

Lewis, P. 1996. "From Prebendalism to Predation: The Political Economy of Decline in Nigeria." *Journal of Modern African Studies* 24:79–104.

Lewontin, Richard. 1998. "The Maturing of Capitalist Agriculture." *Monthly Review* 50:3.

Leyva Solano, Xochil, and Gabriel Ascencio Franco. 1996. *Lacandonia al filo del agua*. Mexico D.F.: CIESAS.

Li, Tania Murray. 1996. "Images of Community: Discourse and Strategy in Property Relations." *Development and Change* 27:501–527.

Li, Tania Murray. 1997. "Constituting Tribal Space." Paper presented to the Environmental Politics Workshop, University of California, Berkeley, October 17.

Li, Tania Murray. 1998. "Compromising Power: Development, Culture, and Rule in Indonesia." Unpublished paper.

Lietzmann, Kurt M., and Gary D. Vest. 1999. *Environment and Security in an International Context. Final Report*. Germany: NATO Committee on the Challenges of Modern Society.

Limerick, P. 1987. *The Legacy of Conquest.* New York: Norton.

Lindblane, K., G. Carswell, and J. K. Tumuhairwe. 1997. "The Mediating Effects of Land Use and Land Management on the Relationship Between Population Growth and Land Degradation in Southwestern Uganda." Ambio.

Lissu, Tundu A. 1999. Personal Communication, June 9 and 18.

Locke, J. 1978. "Of Property." Reprinted in *Property,* edited by C. B Macpherson. Toronto: University of Toronto Press.

London, J. 1998. "Common Roots and Entangled Limbs: Earth First! And the Growth of Post-Wilderness Environmentalism on California's North Coast." *Antipode* 30:2.

Lonergan, Steve. 1999. "Global Environmental Change and Human Security Science Plan." International Human Dimensions Program (IHDP) Report No. 11. Bonn, Germany: IHDP.

Loolo, G. 1981. *A History of the Ogoni.* Port Harcourt: Saros.

Loomis, David. 1994. *Combat Zoning: Military Land-Use Planning in Nevada.* Reno: University of Nevada Press.

Lorenz, Konrad. 1966. *On Aggression.* New York: Harcourt, Brace and World.

Luhmann, Niklas. 1993. *Risk: A Sociological Theory.* Translated by Rhodes Barrett. New York: A. de Gruyter.

Lutz, Catherine, and Don Nonini. 1999. "The Economies of Violence and the Violence of Economies." Pp. 73–113. In *Anthropological Theory Today,* edited by Henrietta Moore. London: Polity.

Lynch, O., and K. Talbott. 1995. *Balancing Acts: Community-Based Forest Management and National Law in Asia and the Pacific.* Washington, D.C: World Resources Institute.

MacKenzie, J.M. 1988. *The Empire of Nature: Hunting, Conservation, and British Imperialism.* Manchester: Manchester University Press.

Mackie, J. A. C. 1974. *Konfrontasi: The Indonesia-Malaysia Dispute 1963–1966.* Kuala Lumpur: Oxford University Press.

Macnaughten, Phil, and John Urry. 1998. *Contested Natures.* London: Sage.

Macrae, J., and A. Zwi (eds.). 1994. *War and Hunger: Rethinking International Responses to Complex Emergencies.* London: Zed.

Magilligan, F., and P. McDowell. 1997. "Stream Channel Adjustments Following Elimination of Cattle Grazing." *Journal of the American Water Resources Association* 33:4.

Makhijani, Arjun, and Scott Salesks. 1992. *High Level Dollars, Low Level Sense: A Critique of Present Policy for the Management of Long-Lived Radioactive Wastes and Discussion of an Alternative Approach.* Takoma Park, Md.: Institute for Energy and Environmental Research.

Malamoud, C. 1976. "Village et Forêt dans l'Idéologie de l'Inde Brahmanique." *Archives Européennes de Sociologie* 17:3–20

Mamdani, M. 1996. *Citizen and Subject*. Princeton: Princeton University Press.

Mander, Jerry, and Edward Goldsmith (eds.). 1996. *The Case Against the Global Economy: and for a Turn Toward the Local*. San Francisco: Sierra Club Books.

Mann, Kirsten, and Richard Roberts (eds.). 1991. *Law in Colonial Africa*. London: Heinemann Educational Books.

Marsden, T., et al. 1993. *Constructing the Countryside*. Boulder: Westview.

Marx, K. 1967. *Capital*, Volume 1. New York: International.

Maughan, R., and D. Nilson. 1995. "What's Old and What's New about the Wise Use Movement." *Green Disk* 3(3).

Maxwell, Alan. 1996. "Headhunting in Northern Borneo." In *Headhunting and the Social Imagination in Southeast Asia*, edited by J. Hoskins. Stanford: Stanford University Press.

Mayo, Deborah, and Rachelle Hollander. 1991. *Acceptable Evidence: Science and Values in Risk Management*. New York: Oxford University Press.

McCann, James C. 1997. "The Plow and the Forest: Narratives of Deforestation in Ethiopia, 1840–1992." *Environmental History* 2:138–159.

McCarthy, J. 1998. "Environmentalism, Wise Use, and the Nature of Accumulation in the Rural West." In *Remaking Reality: Nature at the Millenium*, edited by B. Braun and N. Castree. London: Routledge.

McCarthy, J. 1999. "The Political and Moral Economies of Wise Use." Ph.D. diss., University of California, Berkeley.

McCay, Bonnie J., and James M. Acheson (eds.). 1987. *The Question of the Commons*. Tucson: University of Arizona Press.

McCoy, C. 1995. "Catron County, N.M., Leads a Nasty Revolt Over Eco-protection." *Wall Street Journal*, January 3.

McCully, Patrick. 1996. *Silenced Rivers: The Ecology and Politics of Large Dams*. Delhi: Orient Longman.

McKeen, H. 1993. Interview with *Albuquerque Tribune*. December.

Medico Friends Circle (MFC). 1985. *The Bhopal Disaster Aftermath: An Epidemiological and Socio-Medical Survey*. Bhopal: Medico Friends Circle.

Mehta, Deepak, and Roma Chatterjee. 1995. "A Case Study of a 'Communal Riot' in Dharavi, Bombay." *Religion and Society* 42:5–60.

Mello, Fatima. 1997. "Security, Livelihood and the Politics of Space in Brazil: An Interview with Jean Pierre Leroy." *Political Environments* 5:S18–S21.

Menon, Ritu, and Kamla Bhasin. 1998. *Borders and Boundaries: Women in India's Partition*. New Delhi: Kali for Women.

Ministry of Information. 1996. "Ogoni Crisis." Lagos, Ministry of Information, Nigerian Federal Government.

Mishra, Abha, and Peter Neeraj. 1995–97. Field Notes on JFM in Sambhalpur Division, Orissa for the Edinburgh University Project on Joint Forest Management.

Mitchell, T. 1988. *Colonizing Egypt.* Berkeley: University of California Press.

Mittal, Anuradha, and Peter Rosset. 1999. *America Needs Human Rights.* Oakland, Calif: Food First Books.

MoEF. 1990. "Circular on Involvement of Village Communities and Voluntary Agencies for Regeneration of Degraded Forest Lands." Ministry of Environment and Forests No.6–21/89–F.P.

MoEF. 2000. *Guidelines for Strengthening of Joint Forest Management Programme.* No. 22–8/2000–JFM (FPD).

Molvaer, R. 1991. "Environmentally Induced Conflicts? A Discussion Based on Studies from the Horn of Africa." *Bulletin of Peace Proposals* 22(2):135–142.

Moniaga, S. 1993. "Toward Community-Based Forestry and Recognition of Adat Property Rights in the Outer Islands of Indonesian." In *Legal Frameworks for Forest Management in Asia: Case Studies of Community/State Relations,* edited by J. Fox. Honolulu: East-West Center Occasional Papers of the Program on Environment.

Montague, Ashley. 1976. *The Nature of Human Aggression.* New York: Oxford University Press.

Moore, Barrington. 1966. *Social Origins of Dictatorship and Democracy: Lord and Peasant in the Making of the Modern World.* Boston: Beacon.

Morehouse, Ward, and M. Arun Subramanian. 1986. *The Bhopal Tragedy: What Really Happened and What it Means for American Workers and Communities at Risk.* New York: Council on International and Public Affairs.

Morris, Desmond. 1967. *The Naked Ape.* New York: McGraw-Hill.

Morse, Bradford, and Thomas Berger. 1992. *Sardar Sarovar: The Report of the Independent Review.* Ottawa: Resource Futures International.

Mozgovaya, Alla V. 1993. "Social Consequences of the Chernobyl Catastrophe: Some Results of Sociological Research." Preliminary Paper 198, University of Delaware Disaster Research Center, Newark.

Muana, P. K. 1997. "The Kamajoi Militia: Civil War, Internal Displacement and the Politics of Counter-Insurgency." *Africa Development* 22(3/4): 77–100.

Murton, J. 1997. "Coping With More People." Ph.D. diss., University of Cambridge, Department of Geography.

Mustafa, K. 1993. "Eviction of Pastoralists from Mkomazi Game Reserve in Tanzania: A Statement". Unpublished manuscript, International Institute for Environment and Development.

Myers, N. 1985. "Critical Link Between the Environment, Natural Resources, and War." Pp. 47–53. In *Second Biennial Conference on the Fate of the Earth,* edited by A. S Kelly. San Francisco: Earth Island Institute.

Myers, Norman. 1993a. "Environmental Refugees in a Globally Warmed World." *Bioscience* 43:752–761.

Myers, Norman. 1993b. *Ultimate Security: The Environmental Basis of Political Stability.* New York: Norton.

Myers, Norman. 1996. *Ultimate Security: The Environmental Basis of Political Stability.* New York: Norton.

Myhre, David. 1998. "The Achilles' Heel of the Reforms: The Rural Finance System." In *The Transformation of Rural Mexico: Reforming the Ejido Sector,* edited by Wayne Cornelius and David Myhre. San Diego: Center for U.S.-Mexican Studies.

Naanen, B. 1995. "Oil Producing Minorities and the Restructuring of Nigerian Federalism." *Journal of Commonwealth and Comparative Politics* 33:46–58.

Nafziger, W. 1976. "The Political Economy of Secessionist Conflict." *Journal of Peace Research* 13(2):91–109.

Nafziger, W. 1983. *The Economics of Political Instability: The Nigerian-Biafran War.* Boulder: Westview.

Nagel, Thomas. 1993. "Moral Luck." Pp. 57–71. In *Moral Luck,* edited by Daniel Statman. Albany: State University of New York Press.

Nandy, Ashis (ed.). 1988. *Science, Hegemony and Violence.* Delhi: Oxford University Press.

Narmada Bachao Andolan (NBA). 1991. "Towards Sustainable and Just Development: The Peoples' Struggle in the Narmada Valley." Mimeograph.

Narmada Bachao Andolan (NBA). 1994. Hum Ladenge Saathi: Narmada Ghaati ka Jan Sangharsh. [We Will Fight, Comrade: People's Struggle in the Narmada Valley]. Narmada Bachao Andolan, Hoshangabad and Pune Units.

Nash, R. 1990. *American Environmentalism.* New York: McGraw-Hill, Inc.

National Cancer Institute. 1997. "Executive Summary: National Cancer Institute Study Estimating Thyroid Doses of I-131 Received by Americans from Atmospheric Nuclear Bomb Tests." Washington, D.C., July.

National Cattlemen's Beef Association. 1997. "Cattle and Beef Industry Statistics." Chicago.

National Inholders Association. 1997. "Eco-Terror Suspected in Fires." *Land Rights Advocate,* January.

Nelson, R. 1997. "Is 'Libertarian Environmentalism' an Oxymoron?" In *The Next West: Public Lands, Community, and Economy in the American West,* edited by J. Baden and D. Snow. Washington, D.C.: Island.

Netting, Robert. 1973. "Fighting, Forest and the Fly." *Journal of Anthropological Research* 29:164–179.

Neumann, R., and R. Schroeder. 1995. "Manifest Ecological Destinies: Local Rights and Global Environmental Agendas." *Antipode* 27:4.

Neumann, R. P. 1998. *Imposing Wilderness: Struggles Over Livelihood and Nature Preservation in Africa.* Berkeley: University of California Press.

Neumann, R. P. 1999. "Disease, Development, and Conservation: Changing Images of People and Place in Colonial Tanzania". Paper presented at the Conference on African Environments: Past and Present, St. Antony's College, Oxford, July 5–7.

Nietschmann, Bernard. 1980. "The Limits to Protein." In *Studies in Hunting and Fishing in the Neotropics,* edited by R. Hames. Bennington: Bennington College.

Nigerian Environmental Study Action Team (NEST). 1991. *Nigeria's Threatened Environment.* Ibadan, Nigerian Environmental Study Action Team.

Nordstrom, Carolyn. 1997. *A Different Kind of War Story.* Philadelphia: University of Pennsylvania Press.

Norgaard, Richard. 1994. *Development Betrayed: The End of Progress and a Coevolutionary Revisioning of the Future.* New York: Routledge.

North, Lisa, and David Raby. 1977. "The Dynamic of Revolution and Counter-Revolution: Mexico Under Cardenas, 1934–1940." *LARU Studies* 2(1):25–53.

Nuclear Free Indian Lands Project/National Environmental Coalition of Native Americans. Video: *Wasteland.*

Nuclear Regulatory Commission. 1999. "Repository Licensing Rule." June.

Nugent, Stephen. 1981. "Amazonia: Ecosystem and Social System." *Man* 16:62–74.

Nussbaum, Martha, and Amartya Sen. 1999. *The Quality of Life.* Oxford India Paperbacks.

O'Brien, Karen L. 1995. "Deforestation and Climate Change in the Selva Lacandona of Chiapas, Mexico." Ph.D. thesis, Pennsylvania State University.

O'Brien, Mary. 2000. *Making Better Environmental Decisions: An Alternative to Risk, Assessment.* Cambridge, Mass.: MIT Press

O'Connor, James R. 1998. *Natural Causes: Essays in Ecological Marxism.* New York: Guilford.

Okilo, M. 1980. *Derivation: A Criterion of Revenue Allocation.* Port Harcourt: Rivers State Newspaper Corporation.

Okpu, U. 1977. *Ethnic Minority Problems in Nigerian Politics.* Stockholm: Wiksell.

Oliver-Smith, Anthony. 1996. "Anthropological Research on Hazards and Disasters." *Annual Review of Anthropology* 25:303–28.

Olson, Jennifer. 1995. "Behind the Recent Tragedy in Rwanda." *Geojournal* 35:2.

Orlove, Benjamin S. 1994. "The Dead Policemen Speak: Power, Fear, and Narrative in the 1931 Molloccahua Killings." In *Unruly Order: Violence,*

Power, and Cultural Identity in the Highland Provinces of Southern Peru, edited by D. Poole. Boulder: Westview.

Orlove, Benjamin S., and Glynn Custred. 1980. *Land and power in Latin America: Agrarian Economies and Social Processes in the Andes.* New York: Holmes and Meier.

Osaghae, E. 1995. The Ogoni Uprising. *African Affairs* 94:325–344.

O Tuathail, Gearoid. 1996. *Critical Geographies: The Politics of Writing Global Space.* Minneapolis: University of Minnesota Press.

O Tuathail, Gearoid, Simon Dalby, and Paul Routledge (eds.). 1998. *The Geopolitics Reader.* London: Routledge.

Oxford English Dictionary (OED). Online edition at http://dictionary. oed.com/entrance.dtl.

Padoch, Christine. 1983. *Migration and its Alternatives Among the Iban of Sarawak.* The Hague: Martinus Nijhoff.

Paige, Jeffery. 1975. *Agrarian Revolution: Social Movements and Export Agriculture in the Underdeveloped World.* London: The Free Press.

Paige, Jeffery. 1997. *Coffee and Power: Revolution and the Rise of Democracy in Central America.* Cambridge: Harvard University Press.

Parry, Richard Lloyd. 1998. "What Young Men Do." *Granta* 62 (Summer).

Patmasirwat, Direk. 1997. "Environmentally Sensitive Sector: A Case Study of Shrimp Aquaculture in Thailand Based on Farm Survey." Institute draft paper, Thailand Development Research, Bangkok.

Pavanello, M. 1995. "The Work of the Ancestors and the Profit of the Living: Some Nzema Economic Ideas." *Africa* 65:36–57.

Payne, W. J. A. 1990. *An Introduction to Animal Husbandry in the Tropics.* New York: Longman Scientific.

Peet, Richard, and Michael Watts. 1993. "Introduction: Development Theory and Environment in an Age of Market Triumphalism," *Economic Geography* 69(3):227–253.

Peet, Richard, and Michael Watts. 1996. *Liberation Ecologies: Environment, Development, Social Movements.* London: Routledge.

Peluso, Nancy L. 1992. *Rich forests, Poor People: Forest Access and Control in Java.* Berkeley: University of California Press.

Peluso, Nancy Lee. 1993. "Coercing Conservation? The Politics of State Resource Control." *Global Environmental Change* 3(2):199–218.

Peluso, Nancy L. 1996a. " 'Reserving Value': Conservation Ideology and State Protection of Resources." In *Creating the Countryside: The Politics of Rural and Environmental Discourse.* Philadelphia: Temple University Press.

Peluso, Nancy. 1996b. "Fruit Trees and Family Trees in an Anthropogenic Forest: Ethics of Access, Property Zones, and Environmental Change in Indonesia." *Comparative Studies in Society and History: An International Quarterly* 38(3):510–548.

Peluso, Nancy. N.d. "Weapons of the Wild: Strategic Deployment of Violence and Wilderness in Western Borneo." In *In Search of the Rainforest*, edited by Candace Slater.

Peluso, Nancy. Forthcoming. "Territorializing Local Struggles for Resource Control: A Look at Environmental Discourses and Politics in Indonesia." In *Environmental Discourses in South and Southeast Asia*, edited by Paul Greenough and Anna Tsing. Raleigh: Duke University Press.

Peluso, Nancy Lee, and Peter Vandergeest. Forthcoming. "Genealogies of Forest Law and Customary Rights in Indonesia, Malaysia, and Thailand." *Journal of Asian Studies*.

Pemberton, John. 1994. *On the Subject of Java*. Ithaca: Cornell University Press.

Percival, Valerie, and Thomas Homer-Dixon. 1998a. "The Case of South Africa." In *Ecoviolence: Links among Environment, Population and Security*, edited by Thomas Homer-Dixon and Jessica Blitt. Lanham, Md.: Rowman and Littlefield.

Percival, Valerie, and Thomas Homer-Dixon. 1998b. "The Case of Rwanda." In *Ecoviolence: Links among Environment, Population and Security*, edited by Thomas Homer-Dixon and Jessica Blitt. Lanham, Md.: Rowman and Littlefield.

Perrow, Charles. 1984. *Normal Accidents: Living with High-Risk Technologies*. New York: Basic.

Peters, K., and P. Richards. 1998. "Why We Fight: Voices of Youth Ex-combatants in Sierra Leone." *Africa* 68(1):183–210.

Pinchot, G. 1910. *The Fight for Conservation*. Seattle: University of Washington Press.

Pincus, Walter. 1998. "U.S. Has Spent $5.8 Trillion on Nuclear Arms Since 1940, Study Says." *The Washington Post*, July, 1:A2.

Pirages, D. C. 1991. "The Greening of Peace Research." *Journal of Peace Research* 28(2):129–133.

Place, F., and P. Hazell. 1993. "Productivity Effects of Indigenous Land Tenure Systems in Sub-Saharan Africa." *American Journal of Agricultural Economics* 75:10–19.

Platteau, J. P. 1995. "The Food Crisis in Africa: A Comparative Structural Analysis." Pp. 445–553. In *The Political Economy of Hunger—selected essays*, edited by J. Dreze, A. Sen, and A. Hussain. Oxford: Clarendon.

Poffenberger, Mark, and Betsy McGean. 1996. *Village Voices, Forest Choices: Joint Forest Management in India*. Delhi: Oxford India Paperbacks.

Potter, Lesley. 1996. "Forest Degradation, Deforestation, and Reforestation in Kalimantan: Towards a Sustainable Land Use?" In *Borneo in Transition: People Forests, Conservation, and Development*, edited by Christine Padoch and Nancy Lee Peluso. Kuala Lumpur: Oxford University Press.

Pottier, J., and J. Fairhead. 1991. "Post-famine Recovery in Highland Bwisha, Zaire: 1984 in its Context." *Africa* 61(4):437–470.

Poulantzas, N. 1978. *State, Power, Socialism.* London: New Left Books.

Power, T. M. 1996. *Lost Landscapes and Failed Economies: The Search for a Value of Place.* Washington, D.C.: Island.

Prasad, Archana. 1994. "Forests and Subsistence in Colonial India: A Study of the Central Provinces, 1830–1945." Ph.D. thesis, Jawaharlal Nehru University.

Primavera, J. Honculada. 1991. "Intensive Prawn Farming in the Philippines: Ecological, Social, and Economic Implications." *Ambio* 20(1):28–33.

Primavera, J. Honculada. 1993. "A Critical Review of Shrimp Pond Culture in the Philippines." *Reviews in Fisheries Science* 1(2):151–201.

Primavera, J. Honculada. 1996. "Socioeconomic Impacts of Shrimp Culture." Workshop on Aquaculture Research and Sustainable Development in Inland and Coastal Regions in South-East Asia, Can Tho, Viet Nam, University of Can Tho.

Pryne, E. 1994. "Park Plan Called Twisted Global Plot to Destroy Nation." *Idaho Spokesman-Review,* October, 23.

Raffensperger, Carolyn, and Joel Tickner. 1999. *Protecting Public Health and the Environment: Interpreting the Precautionary Principle.* Washington, D.C.: Island.

Rainforest Action Network. 1997. "Human Rights and Environmental Operations Information on the Royal Dutch/Shell Group of Companies." London.

Rajan, S. Ravi. 1988. "Rehabilitation and Volunteerism in Bhopal." *Lokayan Bulletin* 6:3–32.

Rajan, S. Ravi. 1999. "Bhopal: Vulnerability, Routinization and the Chronic Disaster." In *The Angry Earth: Disaster in Anthropological Perspective,* edited by Anthony Oliver-Smith and Susanna Hoffman. New York: Routledge.

Rajan, S. Ravi. 2000. "The World Risk Society and the Problem of Missing Expertise: Lessons from the Bhopal Gas Disaster." Forthcoming. In *Catastrophe and Culture,* edited by Susanna Hoffman and Anthony Oliver-Smith. SAR Press.

Rangarajan, Mahesh. 1996. *Fencing the Forest: Conservation and Ecological Change in India's Central Provinces.* Delhi: Oxford University Press.

Rappaport, Roy. 1967. "Ritual Regulation of Environmental Relations among a New Guinea People." *Ethnology* 6:17–30.

Rappaport, Roy. 1968. *Pigs for the Ancestors: Ritual in the Ecology of a New Guinea People.* New Haven: Yale University Press.

Rasker, R., et al. 1992. "The Wealth of Nature: New Economic Realities in the Yellowstone Region." Washington, D.C.: Wilderness Society.

Ratafia, Manny. 1995. "Aquaculture Today: A Worldwide Status Report." *World Aquaculture,* 26(2):18–24.

Rebel, H. 1983. *Peasant Classes: The Bureaucratization of Property and Family Relations under Early Habsburg Absolutism, 1511–1636.* Princeton, N.J.: Princeton University Press.

Rebel, Hermann. 1989. "Cultural Hegemony and Class Experience: A Critical Reading of Recent Ethno-Historical Approaches (parts 1 & 2)." *American Ethnologist* 16:1–2.

Reid, Anthony. 1988. *The Land Beneath the Winds.* Vol. 1. New Haven: Yale University Press.

Renner, Michael, M. Pianta, and C. Franchi. 1991. "International Conflict and Environmental Degradation." Pp. 108–128. In *New Directions in Conflict Theory, Conflict Resolution and Conflict Transformation,* edited by Raimo Väyrynen. London: Sage.

Renner, Michael. 1996. *Fighting for Survival: Environmental Decline, Social Conflict, and the New Age of Insecurity.* New York: Norton.

Reno, William. 1995. *Corruption and State politics Is Sierra Leone.* Cambridge: Cambridge University Press.

Reno, William. 1997. "African Weak States and Commercial Alliances." *African Affairs* 96(383):165–186.

Reno, William. 1998. *Warlord Politics and African States.* Boulder: Lynne Reinner.

Reyes Ramos, Maria Eugenia. 1992. *El Reparto de Tierras y la Política Agraria en Chiapas 1914–1988.* Mexico D.F.: Universidad Nacional Autonoma de Mexico.

Reyes Ramos, Maria Eugenia. 1998a. "Las Fuentes Del Conflicto Agrario En Chiapas: Viejos Problemas, Nuevos Actores." Paper read at Congresos Nacional "Politicas De Ajuste Estructural En El Campo Mexicano, Effectos y Respuestas," Queretero, March 1–4.

Reyes Ramos, Maria Eugenia. 1998b. "Los Acuerdos Agrarios en Chiapas: ¿una política de conexión social?" In *Transformaciones Rurales En Chiapas,* edited by Ramos Reyes, Maria Eugenia, Reyna Moguel Viveros, and Gemma van der Haar. Mexico D.F.: UAM.

Reyes Ramos, Maria Eugenia. 2000. "El Movimiento Zapatista y la Redefinación de la Política Agraria En Chiapas." Paper presented at Latin American Studies Association, Miami.

Richards, P., and C. Fithen. Forthcoming. "Making War, Crafting Peace: Militia Solidarities and Demobilization Opportunities in Sierra Leone." In *No Peace, No War: Learning to Live Beyond Violent Conflict,* edited by B. Helander and P. Richards.

Richards, Paul. 1996. *Fighting for the Rainforest: War, Youth and Resources in Sierra Leone.* Oxford: International African Institute in Association with James Currey and Heinemann.

Richards, Paul. 1998. "La Nouvelle Violence Politique en Afrique Noire: Sectarisme Seculaire au Sierra Leone." *Politique Africaine* 70:85–104.

Richards, Paul. 1999a. "New Political Violence in Africa: Secular Sectarianism in Sierra Leone." *GeoJournal* 47:433–444. Expanded English version.

Richards, Paul. 1999b. "Post-modern Warfare in Sierra Leone? Re-asserting the Social in Global-Local Constructions of Violence." Forthcoming. In *Transboundary Formations: Global-Local Constructions of Authority in Africa,* edited by Thomas Callaghy, Ronald Kassimir and Robert Latham.

Riebsame, W., and R. Woodmansee. 1995. "Mapping Common Ground on the Public Rangelands." In *Let the People Judge: Wise Use and the Property Rights Movement,* edited by J. Echeverria and R. Eby. Washington, D.C.: Island.

Robben, Antonius C. G. M., and Carolyn Nordstrom (eds.). 1995. *Fieldwork Under Fire: Contemporary Studies in Violence and Survival.* Berkeley: University of California Press.

Robins, N., and C. Pye-Smith. 1997. "The Ecology of Violence." *New Scientist* March:12–13.

Rocheleau, Dianne E., Philip E. Steinberg, and Patricia A. Benjamin. 1995. "Environment, Development, Crisis, and Crusade: Ukambani, Kenya, 1890–1990." *World Development* 23:1037–1051.

Rodwin, L., and H. Sazanami (eds.). 1989. *Deindustrialization in the Unites States: Lessons for Japan.* Boston: Unwin Hymin.

Roe, Emery M. 1995. "Except Africa: Postscript to a Special Section on Development Narratives." *World Development* 23:1065–1069.

Romo, R. 1998. "Ranchers Dispute Link to Radicals." *Albuquerque Journal,* July 11.

Rosenberry, Bob. 1998. "World Shrimp Farming 1998." *Shrimp News International.*

Ross, Michael. 1997. "The Political Economy of Boom and Bust Logging in Indonesia, The Philippines, and East Malaysia, 1950–1994." Ph.D. diss., Princeton University.

Rossi, G. 1991. Croissance de la Population, Mise en Valeur et Equilibre des Versants: Quel Avenir Pour le Rwanda? *Cahiers d'Outre Mer* 44 (173):29–45.

Roth, Henry Ling. 1896. *The Natives of Sarawak and British North Borneo.* London: Truslove and Hanson; reprint, Kuala Lumpur: University of Malaya Press, 1912.

Rousseau, Jerome. 1990. *Central Borneo: Ethnical Identity and Social Life in a Stratified Society.* New York: Oxford University Press.

Rowell, A. 1996. *Green Backlash.* London: Routledge.

Roy, Beth. 1996. *Some Trouble with Cows: Making Sense of Social Conflict.* New Delhi: Sage.

Ruckelshaus, W. 1985. "Risk, Science and Democracy." *Issues in Science and Technology* 1:19–38.

RUF/SL. 1995. "Footpaths to Democracy: Toward a New Sierra Leone." Unpublished manuscript, Revolutionary United Front of Sierra Leone.

RUF/SL. 1999. "Lasting peace in Sierra Leone: The Revolutionary United Front (RUF/SL) Perspective and Vision." Unpublished manuscript, Revolutionary United Front of Sierra Leone.

Rus, Jan. "The 'Comunidad Revolucionaria Institucional': The Subversion of Native Government in Highland Chiapas, 1936–1968." In *Everyday Forms of State Formation: Revoltion and the Negotiation of Rule in Modern Mexico*, edited by Gilbert Joseph and Daniel Nugent. Durham: Duke University Press.

Russell, Milton, and Michael Gruber. 1987. "Risk Assessment in Environmental Policy-Making." *Science* 236:286–290.

Sachs, Wolfgang (ed.). 1997. *The Development Dictionary*. London: Longmann.

Sack, Robert David. 1986. *Human Territoriality: Its Theory and History*. Cambridge: Cambridge University Press.

Said, Edward. 1993. *Culture and Imperialism.* New York: Knopf.

Salih, M. 1997. "Politics of Poverty Management and Environment: Displacement by Conservation." Paper presented at Workshop on Politics of Poverty and Environmental Interventions. Nordic Africa Institute, Salih, Institute of Social Studies, The Hague, Netherlands, May.

Sanderson, Steve E. 1986. *The Transformation of Mexican Agriculture: International Structure and the Politics of Rural Change*. Princeton: Princeton University Press.

Sanderson, Steven E. 1981. *Agrarian Populism and the Mexican State: The Struggle for Land in Sonora*. Berkeley: University of California Press.

Sarin, Madhu. 1998. *Who is Gaining? Who is Losing? Gender and Equity Concerns in Joint Forest Management*. New Delhi: Society for the Promotion of Wastelands Development.

Saro-Wiwa, K. 1989. *On A Darkling Plain*. Port Harcourt: Saros.

Saro-Wiwa, K. 1990. *Similia: Essays on Anomic Nigeria*. Port Harcourt: Saros.

Saro-Wiwa, K. 1992. *Genocide in Nigeria*. Port Harcourt: Saros.

Saro-Wiwa, K. 1995. *A Month and a Day*. London: Penguin.

Sather, Clifford. 1990. "Trees and Tree Tenure in Paku Iban Society: The Management of Secondary Forest Resources in a Long-Established Iban Community." *Borneo Review* 1:16–40.

Sathyamala. 1988. "The Medical Profession and the Bhopal Tragedy." *Lokayan Bulletin* 6:33–56.

Savyasaachi. 1994. "The Tiger and the Honey-bee." *Seminar* 423.

Sawyer, S. 1996. "The Politics of Petroleum." Unpublished manuscript.

Sawyer, S. Forthcoming. "Fictions of Sovereignty." *Journal for Latin American Anthropology.*

Saxena, N.C. 1997. *The Saga of Participatory Forest Management in India.* Jakarta: Center for International Research on Forestry (CIFOR).

Sayer, Andrew. 1980. *Theory and Method in Social Science.* London: Methuen.

Scarborough, Rowan. 1998. " 'Peace Dividend' Apparently Paying Off," *Washington Times,* March 9.

Scasz, Andrew. 1995. *Ecopopulism: Toxic Waste and the Movement for Environmental Justice.* Minneapolis: University of Minnesota Press.

Schama, Simon. 1995. *Landscape and Memory.* London: Harper Collins.

Schatzberg, M. 1988. *The Dialectics of Oppression in Zaire.* Bloomington: Indiana University Press.

Scheper-Hughes, Nancy. 1992. *Death Without Weeping: The Violence of Everyday Life in Brazil.* Berkeley: University of California Press.

Schrader-Frechette, Kristin. 1991. *Risk and Rationality: Philosophical Foundations for Populist Reforms.* Berkeley: University of California Press.

Schrader-Frechette, Kristin. 1996. "Methodological Rules for Four Classes of Scientific Uncertainty." In *Scientific Uncertainty and Environmental Problem Solving,* edited by John Lemons. New York: Blackwell.

Schroeder, Richard. 1995. "Resource Stabilization." Antipode.

Schroeder, Richard. Forthcoming. *Shady Practices.* Berkeley: University of California Press.

Schryer, Frans. 1990. *Ethnicity and Class Conflict in Rural Mexico.* Princeton: Princeton University Press

Sclove, Richard. 1995. *Democracy and Technology.* New York: Guilford.Scott, David Clark. 1994a. "Chiapas Ranchers Reclaim Land they Say was Stolen by Peasants." *Christian Science Monitor,* March 3, electronic edition.

Scott, David Clark. 1994b. "Chiapas Ranchers Vow to Take Law into their Own Hands." *Christian Science Monitor,* April 14, electronic edition.

Scott, James C. 1985. *Weapons of the Weak: Everyday Forms of Peasant Resistance.* New Haven: Yale University Press.

Scott, James C. 1998. *Seeing Like a State: How Certain Schemes to Improve the Human Condition Have Failed.* New Haven: Yale University Press.

Seager, Joni. 1993. *Earth Follies: Coming to Feminist Terms with the Global Environmental Crisis.* New York: Routledge.

Secretaria de Agricultura y Ganaderia. (SAGAR). 1997. "Datos Sobre la Ganaderia: Centro de Estadisticas Agricolas, Banco de Mexico." Mexico D.F.: SAGAR.

Secretaria de Agricultura y Recursos Hidraulicos. (SARH). 1992. "Articulo 27 Constitucional Ley Agraria." Mexico D.F.: SARH.

Secretaría de Economía. 1930. *Censo Agrícola-Ganadero de 1930.* Mexico D.F.: Secretaría de Economía.

Secretaría de Economía. 1951. *Segundo Censo Agrícola-Ganadero de los Estados Unidos Mexicanos.* Mexico: Secretaría de Economía.

Secretaría de Industria y Comercio. 1965. "IV Censo Agricola-Ganadero, 1960." Mexico D.F.: Secretaria de Industria y Comercio.

Sen, Amartya. 1999a. *On Ethics and Economics.* Delhi: Oxford India Paperbacks.

Sen, Amartya. 1999b. *On Economic Inequality.* Delhi: Oxford India Paperbacks.

Sen, Amartya. 1999c. *Inequality Reexamined.* Delhi: Oxford India Paperbacks.

Sen, Amartya. 2000. *Development As Freedom.* Garden City, N.Y.: Anchor.

Servicios Informativos Procesados A.C. 1994. "Los Hombres Sin Rostros." Mexico D.F.: Impretei.

Sharma, B. D. 1995. *Whither Tribal Areas? Constitutional Amendments and After.* New Delhi: Sahyog Pustak Kutir.

Shearer, D. 1997. "Exploring the Limits of Consent: Conflict Resolution in Sierra Leone." *Millennium: Journal of International Studies* 26(3):845–860.

Shiva, Vandana. 1995. "The Damaging Social and Environmental Effects of Aquaculture." *Third World Resurgence* (59).

Shrader-Frachette, K.S. 1993. *Burying Uncertainty: Risk and the Case Against Geological Disposal of Nuclear Waste.* Berkeley: University of California Press.

Sider, Gerald M. 1986. *Culture and Class in Anthropology and History: A Newfoundland Illustration.* Cambridge: Cambridge University Press.

Silbergeld, Ellen. 1991. "Risk Assessment and Risk Management: An Uneasy Divorce." Pp. 99–114. In *Acceptable Evidence: Science and Values in Risk Management,* edited by D.G. Mayo and R. Hollander. New York: Oxford University Press.

Simmons, Dabelko. 1997. "Environment and Security." *SAIS Review* Winter:127–146.

Sims, B. 1993. "Private Rights in Public Lands?" Southwest Research and Information Center (Albuquerque) *Workbook Summer* 18(2).

Singh, Chhatrapati. 1986. *Common Property and Common Poverty.* Delhi: Oxford University Press.

Siskind, Janet. 1973. "Tropical Forest Hunters and the Economy of Sex." In *Peoples and Cultures of Native South Amercia,* edited by D. Gross. New York: Natural History Press.

Sivan, E. 1995. "The Enclave Culture." In *Fundamentalisms Comprehended,* edited by M. Marty. Chicago: Chicago University Press.

Sivaramakrishnan, K. 1997. "A Limited Forest Conservancy in Southwest Bengal, 1864–1912." *The Journal of Asian Studies* 56(1):75–112.

Sivaramakrishnan, K. 1999. "Landlords, Regional Development, and National Forestry Projects: Midnapore (West Bengal), India, 1930s–1960s." In *A New Moral Economy for India's Forests: Discourses of Community and Participation,* edited by R. Jeffery and N. Sundar. Delhi: Sage.

Skaria, Ajay. 1999. *Hybrid Histories: Forests, Frontiers and Wildness in Central India.* Delhi: Oxford University Press.

Skillen, Anthony. 1978. *Ruling Illusions.* Atlantic Highlands, N.J.: Humanities.

Skinner, Michael. 1994. *Red Flag.* Novato, Calif.: Presidio.

Slovic, Paul. 1991. "Beyond Numbers: A Broader Perspective on Risk Perception and Communication." Pp. 48—65. In *Acceptable Evidence: Science and Values in Risk Management,* edited by D.G. Mayo and R. Hollander. New York: Oxford University Press.

Sluka, Jeffrey A. 1992. "The Anthropology of Conflict." In *The Paths to Domination, Resistance and Terror,* edited by Carolyn Nordstrom and John Martin. Berkeley: University of California Press.

Smith, David M. 1990. "Introduction: The Sharing and Dividing of Geographical Space." In *Shared Space: Divided Space,* edited by Michael Chisholm and David M. Smith. London: Unwin Hyman, Ltd.

Smith, Glen. 1996. "Carok Violence in Madura." Paper read at American Anthropological Association, San Francisco, California.

Snow, D. 1994. "Wise Use and the Public Lands in the West." In *Northern Lights.* Missoula, Mont.: Northern Lights Research and Education Institute.

Society for Promotion of Wastelands Development (SPWD). 1998. Joint Forest Management Update. New Delhi: SPWD.

Solovyova, Nina. 1994. "After the Cold War: Disarmament, Conversion and Security." Paper presented at The Second International Radiological Conference, Krasnoyarsk-Tomsk, Russia, September 12–18.

Soper, Kate. 1995. *What is Nature?* Oxford: Blackwell.

Spicer, T. 1998. "Why We Can Help Where Governments Fear to Tread." *Times* (London), Sunday, May 24.

Spurr, David. 1993. *The Rhetoric of Empire.* Durham: Duke University Press.

Starrs, P., and J. Wright. 1995. "Great Basin Growth and the Withering of California's Pacific Idyll." *The Geographical Review* 85(4):417–435.

Steen, H. (ed.). 1992. *The Origins of the National Forests.* Durham, N.C.: Forest History Society.

Stephen, Lynn. 1997a. "Redefined Nationalism in Building a Movement for Indigenous Autonomy in Southern Mexico." *Journal of Latin American Anthropology* 3:72–101.

Stephen, Lynn. 1997b. "The Zapatista Opening: The Movement for Indigenous Autonomy and State Discourses on Indigenous Rights in Mexico, 1970–1996." *Journal of Latin American Anthropology* 2:2–41.

Stocking, Michael. 1996. "Soil Erosion: Breaking New Ground." In *The Lie of the Land: Challenging Received Wisdom on the African Environment,* edited by Melissa Leach and Robin Mearns. Oxford: International African Institute with James Currey and Heinemann.

Stockton, N. 1997. "Rwanda: Rights and Racism." Paper presented at the Conference: Towards Understanding the Crisis in the Great Lakes Region, February 1. Nissan Centre and Queen Elizabeth House, Oxford.

Stonich, Susan C. 1991. "The Promotion of Nontraditional Exports in Honduras: Issues of Equity, Environment, and Natural Resources Management." *Development and Change* 22(4):725–755.

Stonich, Susan C. 1995. "The Environmental Quality and Social Justice Implications of Shrimp Mariculture in Honduras." *Human Ecology* 23(2): 143–168.

Stonich, Susan C. 1996. "Reclaiming the Commons: Grassroots Resistance and Retaliation in Honduras." *Cultural Survival Quarterly* 20(1):31–35.

Stonich, Susan C., J. Bort, and L. Ovares. 1997. "Globalization of Shrimp Mariculture: The Impact on Social Justice and Environmental Quality in Central America." *Society and Natural Resources* 10(2):161–179.

Sturgeon, Janet. 2000. "Practices on the Periphery: Marginality, Border Powers, and Land Use in China and Thailand." Ph.D. diss., Yale University.

Subhash Chandran, M. D. 1998. "Shifting Cultivation, Sacred Groves and Conflicts in Colonial Forest Policy in the Western Ghats." In *Nature and The Orient*, edited by Richard Grove, Vinita Damodaran, and Satpal Sangwan. Delhi: Oxford University Press.

Suliman, M. (ed.). 1999 *Ecology, Politics and Violent Conflict.* London: Zed.

Sumner, Colin (ed.). 1982. *Crime, Justice and Underdevelopment.* London: Heinemann.

Sundar, Nandini. 1995. "The Dreaded Danteswari: Annals of Alleged Sacrifice." *Indian Economic and Social History Review* 32(3):345–374.

Sundar, Nandini. 1996. "Conflict and Conflict Resolution Mechanisms in JFM." Paper presented at a National Network Meeting on JFM, Delhi.

Sundar, Nandini. 1997. *Subalterns and Sovereigns: An Anthropological History of Bastar, 1854–1996.* Delhi: Oxford University Press.

Sundar, Nandini, Roger Jeffery, and Neil Thin. Forthcoming. *Branching Out: A Comparative Study of Joint Forest Management in Four Indian States.* Delhi: Oxford University Press.

Suparlan, Parsudi. 2000. "A Report on the Madurese-Dayak Violence of 1999 in Sambas, West Kalimantan." In *Proceedings of the Annual Borneo Research Council Meetings*, edited by Michael Leigh, Kuching, Sarawak, August.

Suttles, Wayne. 1961. "Subhuman and Human Fighting." *Anthropologica* 3:148–163.

Sweet, Louise. 1970."Camel Raiding of North Arabian Bedouin: A Mechanism of Ecological Adaptation." In *Peoples and Cultures of the Middle East*, edited by L. Sweet. New York: Natural History Press.

Swift, Jeremy. 1996. "Desertification: Narratives, Winners, and Losers." In *The Lie of the Land: Challenging Received Wisdom on the African Environment*, edited by Melissa Leach and Robin Mearns. Oxford: International African Institute with James Currey and Heinemann.

Tabor, Peter. 1996. "More than Meats the Eye." *Business Mexico*, May 12–14.

Taliman, Valerie. 1994. "Nuclear Guinea Pigs: Native People Were on Front Lines of Exploitation" *Native American Smoke Signals*, January.

Tanganyika Game Division. 1964. *Annual Report of the Game Division, 1963*. Dar Es Salaam: Government.

Tanganyika National Parks. 1964. *Report and Accounts of the Board of Trustees for the Period 1st July, 1963 to 30 June, 1964*. Arusha, Tanzania: East African Printers Tanganyika.

Tanzania National Parks (TANAPA). 1968. *Report and Accounts of the Board of Trustees for the Period 1st July, 1967 to 30 June, 1968*. Arusha, Tanzania: East African Printers Tanganyika.

Taussig, M. 1984. "Culture of Terror—Space of Death. Roger Casement's Putumayo Report and the Explanation of Torture." *Comparative Studies in Society and History* 26(3):467–497.

Taussig, Michael. 1987. *Shamanism, Colonialism, and the Wild Man: A Study in Terror and Healing*. Chicago: University of Chicago Press.

Taussig, Michael. 1993. *Mimesis and Alterity: A Particular History of the Senses*. New York: Routledge.

Thamina, Q. 1995. "Profit by Destruction: International Workshop on Ecology, Politics, and Violence of Shrimp Cultivation for Export." Bangladesh.

Thiam, I. D., and J. Mulera. 1993. "Africa and the Socialist Countries." Pp. 798–828. In *General History of Africa*, vol. 8, edited by A. Mazrui. Berkeley: UNESCO/Heinemann.

Thompson, E. P. 1975. *Whigs and Hunters: The Origins of the Black Act*. New York: Pantheon.

Thompson, E. P. 1991. *Customs in Common*. New York: Norton.

Thompson, E. P. 1996. *The Making of the English Working Class*. New York: Vintage.

Tiffen, Mary, Michael Mortimore, and Frances Gachuki. 1993. *More People: Less Erosion*. London: Wiley.

Tiffen, Mary, Michael Mortimore, and Frances Gichuki. 1994. *More People, Less Erosion: Environmental Recovery in Kenya*. London: Overseas Development Institute and J. W. Wiley.

Timberlake, L. 1985. "Conflict, Refugees and the Environment." Pp. 185–198. In *Africa in Crisis: The Causes, the Cures of Environmental Bankruptcy*, edited by L. Timberlake and J. Tinker. London: Earthscan.

Timberlake, L., and J. Tinker. 1984. "Environment and Conflict." Earth-scan Briefing Document 40, London: IIED.

Trouillot, Michel-Rolph. 1991. "Anthropology and the Savage Slot: The Poetics and Politics of Otherness." In *Recapturing Anthropology: Working in the Present*, edited by R. Fox. Santa Fe: School of American Research.

Tsing, Anna L. 1995. "Environment, Development and Equity in Indonesia." Paper presented to the Peace and World Security Studies Program Winter Workshop, Amherst College, January 18–20.

Tsing, Anna L. 1996. "Telling Violence in the Meratus Mountains." In *Headhunting and the Social Imagination in Southeast Asia*, edited by J. Hoskins. Stanford: Stanford University Press.

Tucker, Richard. 1998. "Non-Timber Forest Products Policy in the Western Himalyas Under British Rule." In *Nature and The Orient*, edited by Richard Grove, Vinita Damodaran, and Satpal Sangwan. Delhi: Oxford University Press.

Turner, B. L. II, Goran Hyden, and Robert W. Kates (eds.). 1993. *Population Growth and Agricultural Change in Africa*. Gainesville: University Press of Florida.

Turton, 1996. "War and Ethnicity: Global Connections and Local Violence in North East Africa and Former Yugoslavia." *Oxford Development Studies* 25:77–94.

Twose, N. 1991. "Introduction: What is Greenwar?" Pp.1–8. In *Greenwar: Environment and Conflict*, edited by O. Bennett. London: Panos.

U.S. Patent no. 5723765; Detailed Description, Column 6.

Union Carbide. 1988. Union Carbide Annual Report.

United Nations Development Program (UNDP). 1993. *Human Development Report 1993*. New York: Oxford University Press.

United Nations Development Program (UNDP). 1998. *Human Development Report 1998*. New York: Oxford University Press.

United Nations. 1996. *Report of the Fact-Finding Mission of the Secretary-General to Nigeria: Summary of Information and Views Received*. New York: United Nations.

Unrepresented Nations and Peoples Organization (UNPO). 1995. "Ogoni: Report of the UNPO Mission to Investigate the Situation of the Ogoni." The Hague: UNPO.

URT. 1989. *Tanzania Forestry Action Plan, 1990/91–2007/08*. Vol 2, *Technical Annexes*. Dar es Salaam: United Republic of Tanzania, Ministry of Lands, Natural Resources and Tourism.

URT. 1990. *1988 Population Census*. Dar es Salaam: United Republic of Tanzania.

URT. 1994. *Policy for Wildlife Conservation and Utilization*. Dar es Salaam: United Republic of Tanzania, Ministry of Tourism, Natural Resources and Environment.

URT. 1995. *Selous Game Reserve General Management Plan.* Dar es Salaam: Selous Conservation Programme.

Vail, Leroy. 1989. "Introduction: Ethnicity in Southern African History." In *The Creation of Tribalism in Southern Africa,* edited by L. Vail. London: James Curry.

Vandergeest, Peter. 1996. "Property Rights in Protected Areas: Obstacles to Community Involvement as a Solution in Thailand." *Environmental Conservation* 23:259–268.

Vandergeest, Peter, and Nancy Lee Peluso. 1995. Territorialization and State Power in Thailand. *Theory and Society: Renewal and Critique in Social Theory* 24 (3):385–426.

Vandergeest, Peter, Chintana Platong, Mark Flaherty, and Paul Miller. 1999a. "Shrimp Aquaculture and the Politics of Zoning in Thailand." Paper presented at the 7th International Conference on Thai Studies, Amsterdam, July 4–8.

Vandergeest, Peter, Mark Flaherty, and Paul Miller. 1999b. "A Political Ecology of Shrimp Aquaculture in Thailand." *Rural Sociology* 64(4):573–596.

Vasavada, Shilpa, and Nabarun Sengupta. 1996–1997. Field Notes on JFM in Dewas Division, Madhya Pradesh, for the Edinburgh University Research Project on Joint Forest Management.

Vaughan, Diane. 1996. *The Challenger Launch Decision: Risky Technology, Culture, and Deviance at NASA.* Chicago: University of Chicago Press.

Vayda, Andrew P. 1961. "Expansion and Warfare Among Swidden Agriculturalists." *American Anthropologist* 63: 346–358.

Vayda, Andrew P. 1969. "The Study of the Causes of War, With Special Reference to Headhunting Raids in Borneo." *Ethnohistory* 16:211–224.

Vayda, Andrew P. 1976. *War in Ecological Perspective: Persistence, Change and Adaptive Processes in Three Oceanian Societies.* New York: Plenum.

Vayda, Andrew P. 1999. "Against Political Ecology." *Human Ecology* 27(1).

Väyrynen, R. 1997. "Political Causes of Humanitarian Emergencies: State Failures and Protracted Crises." Paper presented to UNU/WIDER-Queen Elizabeth House, Oxford meeting on the Political Economy of the Prevention of Humanitarian Emergencies, Oxford, July 3–5.

Vazquez, Jorge. 1997. *Ganadería Tropical Mexicana: Retos, Fortaleza Y Debilidad.* Tuxtla Gutierrez: Universidad Autónoma de Chiapas.

Vickers, Adrian. 1998. "Reopening Old Wounds: Bali and the Indonesian Killings—A Review Article." *Journal of Asian Studies* 57(3):774–785.

Vidal, John. 1999. "Trashing the Crops." *Guardian,* July 31:16.

Villafuerte Solís, Daniel, and José Luis Pontigo Sanchez. 1990. "Las Contradicciones de la Expansión Ganadera en las Fronteras Norte y Sur de Mexico." *Estudios Fronterizos* 1:113–135.

Villafuerte Solis, Daniel, Salvador Meza Diaz, Gabriel Ascencio Franco,

Maria del Carmen Garcia Aguilar, Carolina Rivera Farfan, Miguel Lisbona Guillen, and Jesus Morales Bermudez. 1999. *La Tierra en Chiapas: Viejos problemas nuevos*. Mexico D.F.: Plaza y Valdes.

Villafuerte, Daniel, Maria del Carmen Garcia, and Salvador Meza. 1997. *La Cuestión Ganadera y la Deforestación: Viejos y Nuevos Problemas En el Tropico y Chiapas*. Tuxtla Gutierrez: Universidad de Ciencias y Artes del Estado de Chiapas.

Visvanathan, Shiv. 1988. "Reflections on the Transfer of Technology: Notes on the New Panopticon." *Lokayan Bulletin* 6(1/2):147–160.

Voight, R. 1996. "Eye of the Nation Watching Fight Over Maine's Forest." Lewiston, Maine *Sun-Journal*, July 3.

Vyner, Henry M. 1988. *Invisible Trauma: The Psychological Effects of Invisible Environmental Contaminants*. Lexington, Mass.: Lexington Books.

Wade, Robert. 1994. *Village Republics: Economic Conditions for Collective Action in South India*. San Francisco: Institute for Contemporary Studies.

Wallach, Lori, and Michelle Sforza. 1999. Whose Trade Organization? Corporate Globalization and the Erosion of Democracy. Public Citizen.

Walraven, K. V. 1999. *Containing Conflict in the Economic Community of West African States: Lessons form the Intervention in Liberia, 1990–1997*. Den Haag: Netherlands Institute of International Relations "Clingendael."

Watts, Michael. 1983. *Silent Violence: Food, Famine & Peasantry in Northern Nigeria*. Berkeley: University of California Press.

Watts, Michael. 1985. "Social Theory and Environmental Degradation." In *Desert Development*, edited by Y. Gradus. Dordrecht: D. Reidel.

Watts, Michael. 1990. "Is There Politics in Regional Political Ecology." *Capitalism, Nature, Socialism* (4): 123–131.

Watts, Michael. 1994. "The Devil's Excrement." Pp.406–445. In *Money, Power and Space*, edited by S. Corbridge, R. Martin, and N. Thrift. Oxford: Blackwell.

Watts, Michael. 1995. "Sustainability and Struggles Over Nature: Political Ecology or Ecological Marxism?" In *Investigating the Local: Structure, Place, Agency* Geografi Bergen, Serie B (Monografier fra Institutt for Geografi):175–196.

Watts, Michael. 1996. "Mapping Identity." In *The Geography of Identity*, edited by P. Yaeger. Ann Arbor: University of Michigan Press.

Watts, Michael. 1997. "Black Gold, White Heat." Pp.33–67. In *Geographies of Resistance*, edited by S. Pile and M. Keith. London: Routledge.

Watts, Michael. 1999. "Collective Wish Images." In *Human Geography Today*, edited by J. Allen and D. Massey. Cambridge: Polity.

Watts, Michael. 2000. *Struggles Over Geography: Violence, Freedom, and Development at the Millennium*. Heidleberg: Department of Geography, University of Heidleberg, Germany.

Weir, David. 1986. "The Bhopal Syndrome: Pesticides Manufacturing and the Third World." International Organization of Consumer Unions.

Welch, C. 1995. "The Ogoni and Self Determination." *Journal of Modern Africa Studies* 33(4):635–650.

West, Patrick. 1982. *Natural Resource Bureaucracy and Rural Poverty.* School of Natural Resources, Monograph no. 2. Ann Arbor: University of Michigan.

West Nimar Gazetteer (WNG). 1970. *Gazetteer of India: Madhya Pradesh: West Nimar.* District Gazetteers Department. Bhopal: Madhya Pradesh.

Westing, Arthur. 1986. "Environmental Factors in Strategic Policy and Action: An Overview." Pp.3–20. In *Global Resources and International Conflict: Environmental Factors in Strategic Policy and Action.* Edited by Arthur Westing. Oxford: Oxford University Press.

Whelch, C. 1995. "The Ogoni and Self Determination." *Journal of Modern African Studies* 33(4):635–650.

White, Leslie. 1969. *The Science of Culture: A Study of Man and Civilization.* 2d ed. New York: Farrar, Straus, Giroux.

White, R. 1991. *It's Your Misfortune and None of My Own: A New History of the American West.* Norman: University of Oklahoma Press.

White, Richard. 1995. "Are You an Environmentalist, Or Do You Work For a Living?" In *Uncommon Ground,* edited by W. Cronon. New York: Norton.

Whiteley, John M. 1999. "The Compelling Realities of Mayak." In *Critical Masses: Nuclear Weapons Production, and Environmental Destruction in the United States and Russia,* edited by Russell J. Dalton, Paula Garb, Nicholas P. Lovrich, John C. Pierce, and John M. Whiteley. Boston: MIT Press.

Wilkinson, C. 1992. *Crossing the Next Meridian: Land, Water and the Future of the West.* Covelo: Island.

Williams, Bernard Arthur Owen (ed.). 1981. *Moral Luck: Philosophical Papers.* New York: Cambridge University Press.

Williams, Bernard Arthur Owen. 1993a. "Moral Luck." Pp. 35–55. In *Moral Luck,* edited by Bernard Arthur Owen Williams. Albany: State University of New York Press.

Williams, Bernard Arthur Owen. 1993b. "Postscript." Pp. 251–258. In *Moral Luck,* edited by Bernard Arthur Owen Williams. Albany: State University of New York Press.

Williams, Bruce, and Albert Matheny. 1995. *Democracy, Dialogue and Environmental Disputes.* New Haven: Yale University Press.

Williams, T. 1995. "Conservation." *Fly Rod & Reel,* March.

Winfield, Richard. 1990. *The Just Economy.* New York: Routledge.

Winichakul, Thongchai. 1994. *Siam Mapped: A History of the Geo-Body of a Nation.* Honolulu: University of Hawaii Press.

Wirth, Timothy. 1994. "Sustainable Development Vital to New U.S. Foreign Policy." Speech presented to the National Press Club, Washington, D.C., July 12.

Woodrow Wilson Center. 1998. "Report: Environmental Change and Security Project." Washington, D.C.

World Bank. 1999. *World Development Report 1998/99.* Washington, D.C.: The World Bank.

World Commission on Environment and Development. 1987.

Wyckoff, W. 1995. "Postindustrial Butte." *The Geographical Review* 85:478–496.

Zack-Williams, A. B. 1995. *Tributors, Supporters and Merchant Capital: Mining and Under-development in Sierra Leone.* Aldershot: Avebury Press.

Zerner, Charles. 1994. "Through a Green Lens: The Construction of Customary Environmental Law and Community in Indonesia's Maluku Islands." *Law & Society Review* 28(5).

Zimmerer, Karl S. 1996. *Changing Forests: Biodiversity and Peasant Livelihood in the Peruvian Andes.* Los Angeles: University of California Press.

About the Authors

Amita Baviskar teaches sociology at the University of Delhi, India, and was a Fellow in Environmental Politics at the University of California, Berkeley, for the 1999–2000 academic year. She is author of *In the Belly of the River: Tribal Conflicts over Development in the Narmada Valley* (Delhi 1995). Her research interests include environmental sociology, the sociology of development, social movements, human rights issues, and the sociology of Indian tribal communities.

Iain A. Boal is attached to the Department of Geography at the University of California, Berkeley, but has also taught at Stanford University and New College, San Francisco. Trained at Cambridge University, he is currently working on projects that encompass the work of Henry Moore and the atomic age and resistance to the new agricultural biotechnologies in the United Kingdom and elsewhere.

Aaron Bobrow-Strain is a doctoral candidate in the Department of Geography at the University of California, Berkeley. He is currently completing a doctoral dissertation project based in Chiapas, Mexico, on the history of violence and the ranching economy.

James Fairhead is a reader in social anthropology at the School of Oriental and African Studies, University of London. His fieldwork in the Democratic Republic of Congo and the Republic of Guinea has focused on issues of fertility, productivity and health in crops and soils, and on environmental management and policy. His books include *Misreading the African Landscape* (Cambridge 1996) and *Reframing Deforestation* (London 1998), coauthored with Melissa Leach.

Paula Garb is adjunct associate professor in the School of Social Ecology and associate director of Global Peace and Conflict Studies at the University of California, Irvine. She is coauthor of *Critical Masses: Citizens, Nuclear Weapons Production, and Environmental Destruction in the United States and*

Russia (Cambridge, Mass. 1999) and the author of two other books and numerous articles on environmental and ethnic issues in Russia and other territories of post-Soviet Eurasia.

Betsy Hartmann is director of the Population and Development Program at Hampshire College and a co-coordinator of the Committee on Women, Population, and the Environment. She is the author of *Reproductive Rights and Wrongs: The Global Politics of Population Control* (Boston 1995) and coauthor of *A Quiet Violence: View from a Bangladesh Village* (London 1983). She is currently working on a book about the evolution and impact of the environmental security field.

Emily Harwell finished her Ph.D. dissertation on ethnicity, territory, and resource conflicts in West Kalimantan at the Yale School of Forestry and Environmental Studies in December 2000. She is currently a Research Associate at the Yale School of Forestry and Environmental Studies and is consulting for the Center for International Environmental Law in Washington, D.C., and the Institute for Community Research and Advocacy (ELSAM) in Jakarta, Indonesia.

Galina Komarova is a senior researcher in the Department of Interethnic Relations Studies at the Institute of Ethnology and Anthropology in Moscow. She is the author of several books, including *A Chronicle of Interethnic Conflicts in Russia*, vols. 1–3, the coauthor of *Ethnic-Cultural Processes in the Urals-Volga Region*, and the author of numerous articles on ethnic and gender issues in Russia and other countries of the former Soviet Union.

Valerie Kuletz is lecturer in American studies at the University of Canterbury, New Zealand. Her teaching and research concerns issue of environment, culture, and politics. Her book *The Tainted Desert* (New York 1998) received the American Sociological Association's Award for Technology and Humanism. She is currently engaged in field work on postcolonialism and postnuclear economies in Micronesia and Polynesia.

James McCarthy is assistant professor of geography at Pennsylvania State University. His research focuses on environmental politics and social movements, nature-society theory, and regional political economy. His research on the Wise Use movement brings approaches from political ecology and agrarian studies to bear on environmental conflicts in the United States.

Roderick P. Neumann is associate professor of geography in the Department of International Relations at Florida International University. He has conducted research in Africa for the past twelve years on the politics and culture of conservation and on the relationship between peasant communities and protected areas. From this research came his *Imposing Wilderness* (Berkeley 1998).

Nancy Lee Peluso is associate professor of political ecology in the Department of Environmental Science, Policy, and Management, University of California, Berkeley, and chair of the Berkeley Workshop on Environmental Politics. She is the author of *Rich Forests, Poor People: Resource Control and Resistance in Java* (Berkeley 1994) and coeditor (with Christine Padoch) of *Borneo in Transition: People, Forests, Conservation and Development* (Oxford 1996).

S. Ravi Rajan teaches environmental studies at the University of California, Santa Cruz. He received his Ph.D. from Oxford University and subsequently held a Wantrup Postdoctoral Fellowship at the University of California, Berkeley. He has just completed a book project on the history of Indian forestry and has initiated a new research agenda on environmental risk.

Paul Richards is professor at Wageningen University and Research Centre in The Netherlands and chair of the Research Group on Technology and Agrarian Development. He is also professor of anthropology at University College, London. Over thirty years he has worked mainly in Nigeria and Sierra Leone, studying resource conflict issues. He wrote a book on the civil war in Sierra Leone, *Fighting for the Rain Forest: War, Youth and Resources in Sierra Leone* (London 1996). He is currently researching issues of social conflict surrounding biotechnology.

Susan C. Stonich is professor of anthropology at the University of California, Santa Barbara. Her work examines the human and environmental consequences of economic development within the recent wave of the globalization of capital. She is author of *I Am Destroying the Land: The Political Ecology of Poverty and Environmental Destruction in Honduras* (Boulder, Colo. 1993). In 1997 she was appointed to the National Academy of Science/National Research Council, Committee on the Human Dimensions of Global Change.

Nandini Sundar is associate professor of sociology at the Institute of Economic Growth, Delhi. Her publications include *Subalterns and Sovereigns: An Anthropological History of Bastar, 1854–1996* (Delhi 1997); a work coedited with Roger Jeffrey, *A New Moral Economy for India's Forests? Discourses of Community and Participation* (Delhi 1999); and *Branching Out: A Comparative Study of Joint Forest Management in Four Indian States,* with Roger Jeffery and Neil Thin (Delhi forthcoming).

Peter Vandergeest is associate professor of sociology at York University, Toronto. His main area of research concerns the cultural politics of environment and development in Southeast Asia. Current projects include a book with Nancy Peluso on the genealogy of forestry practice in Thailand,

Malaysia, and Indonesia, and research on the political economy of shrimp aquaculture in Thailand and India.

Michael Watts is director of the Institute of International Studies and Chancellor's professor of geography and development studies at the University of California, Berkeley, where he has taught for twenty years. He is currently working on a comparative study of oil politics.

Index